NEW ENGLAND HIKING

JACQUELINE TOURVILLE

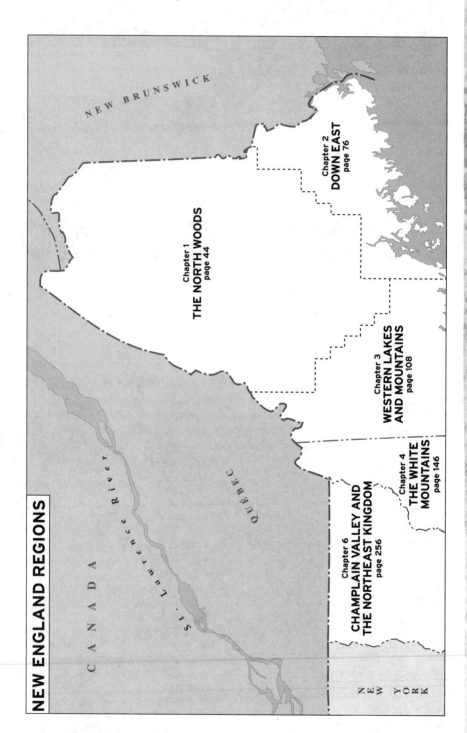

NEW ENGLAND REGIONS

NEW BRUNSWICK

Chapter 2
DOWN EAST
page 76

Chapter 1
THE NORTH WOODS
page 44

Chapter 3
WESTERN LAKES
AND MOUNTAINS
page 108

Chapter 4
THE WHITE
MOUNTAINS
page 146

Chapter 6
CHAMPLAIN VALLEY AND
THE NORTHEAST KINGDOM
page 256

CANADA

QUÉBEC

St. Lawrence River

NEW YORK

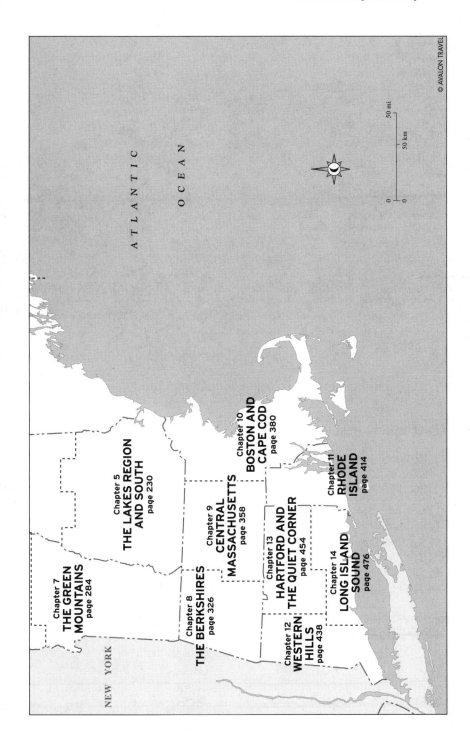

© AVALON TRAVEL

ATLANTIC

OCEAN

50 mi

50 km

0

0

Chapter 5
**THE LAKES REGION
AND SOUTH**
page 230

Chapter 10
**BOSTON AND
CAPE COD**
page 380

Chapter 9
**CENTRAL
MASSACHUSETTS**
page 358

Chapter 11
**RHODE
ISLAND**
page 414

Chapter 7
**THE GREEN
MOUNTAINS**
page 284

Chapter 8
THE BERKSHIRES
page 326

Chapter 13
**HARTFORD AND
THE QUIET CORNER**
page 454

Chapter 14
**LONG ISLAND
SOUND**
page 476

Chapter 12
**WESTERN
HILLS**
page 438

NEW YORK

Contents

《 Best Backpacking Hikes
《 Best for Bird-Watching
《 Best Coastal or Island Hikes
《 Best for Fall Foliage
《 Best for Kids
《 Best for Lakes and Swimming Holes

《 Best Summit Hikes
《 Best for Sunrises
《 Best for Sunsets
《 Best for Waterfalls
《 Best for Wheelchair Access

Maine
New Hampshire
Vermont

Massachusetts
Rhode Island
Connecticut

Vermont
Chapter 6
Champlain Valley and the Northeast Kingdom

Chapter 7

Massachusetts
Chapter 8

Chapter 9

Chapter 10

How to Use This Book

ABOUT THE TRAIL PROFILES

Each hike in this book is listed in a consistent, easy-to-read format to help you choose the ideal hike. From a general overview of the setting to detailed driving directions, the profile will provide all the information you need. Here is a sample profile:

Map number and hike number →

Round-trip mileage → (unless otherwise noted) and the approximate amount of time needed to complete the hike (actual times can vary widely, especially on longer hikes)

1 SOMEWHERE USA HIKE

9.0 mi/5.0 hrs

👟 3 ⛰ 8 ← Difficulty and quality ratings

at the mouth of the Somewhere River ← General location of the trail, named by its proximity to the nearest major town or landmark

BEST (

Each hike in this book begins with a brief overview of its setting. The description typically covers what kind of terrain to expect, what might be seen, and any conditions that may make the hike difficult to navigate. Side trips, such as to waterfalls or panoramic vistas, in addition to ways to combine the trail with others nearby for a longer outing, are also noted here. In many cases, mile-by-mile trail directions are included.

Symbol indicating that the hike is listed among the author's top picks

User Groups: This section notes the types of users that are permitted on the trail, including hikers, mountain bikers, horseback riders, and dogs. Wheelchair access is also noted here.

Permits: This section notes whether a permit is required for hiking, or, if the hike spans more than one day, whether one is required for camping. Any fees, such as for parking, day use, or entrance, are also noted here.

Maps: This section provides information on how to obtain detailed trail maps of the hike and its environs. Whenever applicable, names of U.S. Geologic Survey (USGS) topographic maps and national forest maps are also included; contact information for these and other map sources are noted in the Resources section at the back of this book.

Directions: This section provides mile-by-mile driving directions to the trailhead from the nearest major town.

Contact: This section provides an address and phone number for each hike. The contact is usually the agency maintaining the trail but may also be a trail club or other organization.

ABOUT THE ICONS

The icons in this book are designed to provide at-a-glance information on the difficulty and quality of each hike.

The **difficulty rating** (rated **1–5** with **1** being the lowest and **5** the highest) is based on the steepness of the trail and how difficult it is to traverse.

The **quality rating** (rated **1–10** with **1** being the lowest and **10** the highest) is based largely on scenic beauty, but also takes into account how crowded the trail is and whether noise of nearby civilization is audible.

ABOUT THE DIFFICULTY RATINGS

Trails rated 1 are very easy and suitable for hikers of all abilities, including young children.

Trails rated 2 are easy-to-moderate and suitable for most hikers, including families with active children 6 and older.

Trails rated 3 are moderately challenging and suitable for reasonably fit adults and older children who are very active.

Trails rated 4 are very challenging and suitable for physically fit hikers who are seeking a workout.

Trails rated 5 are extremely challenging and suitable only for experienced hikers who are in top physical condition.

MAP SYMBOLS

Expressway	(80) Interstate Freeway	Airfield
Primary Road	(101) U.S. Highway	Airport
Secondary Road	(21) State Highway	○ City/Town
Unpaved Road	(66) County Highway	▲ Mountain
Ferry	Lake	Park
National Border	Dry Lake	Pass
State Border	Seasonal Lake	◉ State Capital

INTRODUCTION

Author's Note

What keeps me calm when my commute comes to a grinding halt in Boston's nightmarish traffic? Thinking about my hiking gear stored neatly in the trunk, ready for another weekend away from the urban hustle and bustle. From beginner-friendly, low terrain treks to alpine adventures in New England's higher elevations, my Saturday escapes give me the chance to explore just about every peak and valley in nearby Maine, New Hampshire, Massachusetts, Vermont, Connecticut, and Rhode Island (yes, even tiny "Rhody" offers some excellent lower elevation hikes).

My first blisters from my first pair of hiking boots were the result of my first "real" New England hike, climbing Mount Monadnock in New Hampshire. I write about outdoor activities from the perspective of someone whose heels still wear a few scars from that day—sympathetic to beginners, but also with an eye on what experts want to know. If, after shredding my feet on that first climb, I had not read about all the magical advanced hikes I could take once I improved my skills, I doubt I would have had the motivation to lace up my boots a few weeks later and try again. It's this dual perspective that I hope to bring to *Moon New England Hiking*.

Rambling about the New England countryside for more than ten years since moving here from my native New York State, I find the first few words from that famous line in Henry David Thoreau's *Walden* a constant echo in my thoughts, "I went to the woods because I wished to live deliberately, to front only the essential facts of life, and see if I could not learn what it had to teach . . . " Whether in the woods, along the coast, or high up on a rocky summit, the landscape of New England still beckons as a place of wilderness escape, an irresistible chance to drink in the geology, history, and sheer beauty of this unique corner of the United States.

Best Hikes

Can't decide where to hike this weekend? Here are my picks for the best hikes in New England in several categories:

◖ Best Backpacking Hikes

Russell Pond/Davis Pond Loop, The North Woods, Maine, page 48.

100-Mile Wilderness, The North Woods, Maine, page 63.

Half a 100-Mile Wilderness, The North Woods, Maine, page 67.

Bigelow Range, Western Lakes and Mountains, Maine, page 109.

Saddleback Range, Western Lakes and Mountains, Maine, page 115.

The Mahoosuc Range, Western Lakes and Mountains, Maine, page 126.

Kilkenny Loop, The White Mountains, New Hampshire, page 151.

Mahoosuc Range: Gentian Pond, The White Mountains, New Hampshire, page 154.

Presidential Range Traverse, The White Mountains, New Hampshire, page 162.

The Carter-Moriah Range, The White Mountains, New Hampshire, page 164.

Pemigewasset Wilderness Traverse, The White Mountains, New Hampshire, page 203.

nearing the summit of Saddleback Mountain, Maine

© KD TALBOT/WWW.GHOSTFLOWERS.COM

The Long Trail: Appalachian Gap to the Winooski River, Champlain Valley and the Northeast Kingdom, Vermont, page 276.

The Monroe Skyline, Champlain Valley and the Northeast Kingdom, Vermont, page 278.

The Long Trail: Route 103 to U.S. 4, The Green Mountains, Vermont, page 302.

Glastenbury Mountain, The Green Mountains, Vermont, page 316.

The Long Trail: Massachusetts Line to Route 9, The Green Mountains, Vermont, page 317.

The Riga Plateau, The Berkshires, Massachusetts, page 349.

◖ Best for Bird-Watching

Great Wass Island, Down East, Maine, page 101.

Mount Agamenticus, Western Lakes and Mountains, Maine, page 137.

Great Bay National Estuarine Research Reserve, The Lakes Region and South, New Hampshire, page 241.

Spruce Hill, The Berkshires, Massachusetts, page 334.

© J. D. BROWN

Button Bay on Lake Champlain, Vermont

◖ Best for Kids

Kidney Pond Loop, The North Woods, Maine, page 61.

Sabbaday Falls, The White Mountains, New Hampshire, page 216.

Burton Island, Champlain Valley and the Northeast Kingdom, Vermont, page 257.

Stowe Pinnacle, Champlain Valley and the Northeast Kingdom, Vermont, page 267.

Mohawk Trail, The Berkshires, Massachusetts, page 335.

Minute Man National Historical Park, Boston and Cape Cod, Massachusetts, page 391.

Block Island: Clay Head Trail and the Maze, Rhode Island, page 427.

Mount Tom State Park Tower, Western Hills, Connecticut, page 447.

Soapstone Mountain, Hartford and the Quiet Corner, Connecticut, page 458.

Castle Crag and West Peak, Hartford and the Quiet Corner, Connecticut, page 468.

◖ Best for Lakes and Swimming Holes

Sandy Stream Pond/Whidden Ponds Loop, The North Woods, Maine, page 50.

Gulf Hagas, The North Woods, Maine, page 69.

Jordan Pond Loop, Down East, Maine, page 98.

Emerald Pool, The White Mountains, New Hampshire, page 191.

Burton Island, Champlain Valley and the Northeast Kingdom, Vermont, page 257.

Button Bay State Park, Champlain Valley and the Northeast Kingdom, Vermont, page 275.

Skylight Pond, The Green Mountains, Vermont, page 289.

Benedict Pond and The Ledges, The Berkshires, Massachusetts, page 344.

Long Pond, Rhode Island, page 424.

Breakneck Pond, Hartford and the Quiet Corner, Connecticut, page 459.

the lighthouse and cliffs at Aquinnah, Martha's Vineyard, Massachusetts

◖ Best Summit Hikes

North Traveler Mountain, The North Woods, Maine, page 45.

Saddleback Mountain and The Horn, Western Lakes and Mountains, Maine, page 117.

North Percy Peak, The White Mountains, New Hampshire, page 149.

Mount Adams: King Ravine, The White Mountains, New Hampshire, page 157.

Mount Madison: Madison Gulf and Webster Trails, The White Mountains, New Hampshire, page 159.

Mount Jefferson: The Castellated Ridge, The White Mountains, New Hampshire, page 160.

Mount Washington: Huntington Ravine and the Alpine Garden, The White Mountains, New Hampshire, page 166.

Mount Washington: Tuckerman Ravine, The White Mountains, New Hampshire, page 168.

The Baldies Loop, The White Mountains, New Hampshire, page 190.

Mount Cardigan: West Side Loop, The Lakes Region and South, New Hampshire, page 235.

Mount Abraham, The Green Mountains, Vermont, page 285.

Bear Mountain, Western Hills, Connecticut, page 439.

◖ Best for Sunrises

Cadillac Mountain: South Ridge Trail, Down East, Maine, page 99.

Skylight Pond, The Green Mountains, Vermont, page 289.

Mount Everett, The Berkshires, Massachusetts, page 347.

Bar Head Drumlin/Plum Island, Boston and Cape Cod, Massachusetts, page 383.

Bear Mountain, Western Hills, Connecticut, page 439.

Mount Tom State Park Tower, Western Hills, Connecticut, page 447.

◖ Best for Sunsets

Isle au Haut: Eben's Head, Down East, Maine, page 79.
Presidential Range Traverse, The White Mountains, New Hampshire, page 162.
The Carter-Moriah Range, The White Mountains, New Hampshire, page 164.
Burlington Waterfront Bike Path, Champlain Valley and the Northeast Kingdom, Vermont, page 261.
Mount Mansfield: Sunset Ridge and Laura Cowles Trails, Champlain Valley and the Northeast Kingdom, Vermont, page 263.
Mount Philo, Champlain Valley and the Northeast Kingdom, Vermont, page 270.
Button Bay State Park, Champlain Valley and the Northeast Kingdom, Vermont, page 275.
Falls of Lana and Rattlesnake Cliffs, The Green Mountains, Vermont, page 292.
Great Island Trail, Boston and Cape Cod, Massachusetts, page 403.
Aquinnah, Boston and Cape Cod, Massachusetts, page 407.
Peak Mountain, Hartford and the Quiet Corner, Connecticut, page 458.
Ragged Mountain Preserve Trail Loop, Hartford and the Quiet Corner, Connecticut, page 466.

◖ Best for Waterfalls

Screw Auger Falls, Western Lakes and Mountains, Maine, page 122.
Step Falls Preserve, Western Lakes and Mountains, Maine, page 123.
Glen Ellis Falls, The White Mountains, New Hampshire, page 177.
Ethan Pond/Thoreau Falls, The White Mountains, New Hampshire, page 185.
Mounts Lincoln and Lafayette, The White Mountains, New Hampshire, page 198.
Bash Bish Falls, The Berkshires, Massachusetts, page 350.
Wadsworth Falls State Park, Hartford and the Quiet Corner, Connecticut, page 470.

◖ Best for Wheelchair Access

Portland: Back Cove Trail and Eastern Promenade, Western Lakes and Mountains, Maine, page 136.
Diana's Bath, The White Mountains, New Hampshire, page 214.
Burlington Waterfront Bike Path, Champlain Valley and the Northeast Kingdom, Vermont, page 261.
Pittsfield State Forest: Tranquility Trail, The Berkshires, Massachusetts, page 340.
East Bay Bike Path, Rhode Island, page 417.
McIntosh Wildlife Refuge and Boardwalk, Rhode Island, page 418.
Braille Trail, Hartford and the Quiet Corner, Connecticut, page 455.

New England Overview

From the summit of Mount Monadnock in New Hampshire, on a clear, sunny day, the view goes on forever. Vast and serene, the whole of New England radiates out from this central spot, providing a panoramic glimpse of what makes hiking in this six-state region so varied and inviting.

From Monadnock's north-facing precipice, the White Mountains rise suddenly in the distance, their rugged, alpine peaks dominating the far-off landscape. Just beyond, it's possible to make out Maine's isolated western summits, brooding against the skyline's edge, deep purple and mysterious. And to the west, the Green Mountains stay true to their name as the verdant uplands of Vermont beckon brightly from the other side of the Connecticut River Valley.

Turning around to face south, the views are no less stunning. Massachusetts and its Berkshire Mountains, Rhode Island, and Connecticut join together here to form New England's gentler face. Towns and cities you know are there seem to disappear within the folds of the area's rolling hills and pastoral valleys. Glimmering at the fringes of this vista is the Atlantic Ocean, a reminder of New England's many miles of scenic coastal shoreline.

From the rugged terrain of Acadia National Park in Maine to a quiet stroll around a forgotten bog in Connecticut's Quiet Corner, there is plenty to explore throughout New England. The rich mix of trails here unlocks the region's natural resources in a way that readily accommodates the young and old, the physically challenged, the most expert of hikers, and the novice. Reflecting the Yankee spirit of rugged individualism, each New England state possesses a unique blend of geographical features and homegrown hiking opportunities. Find out how to walk the spine of the Green Mountains all the way to the Canadian border or make plans to triumphantly reach the Appalachian Trail's final U.S. summit (Maine's Mount Katahdin). Think about taking your family on a sandy trek on Cape Cod or find that perfect trail for taking in the bright hues of fall foliage season. Craggy summits, ethereal forests, glacier-carved lakes, walking paths, waterfalls, and true wilderness adventures await you. Pick a hike and pack your gear!

Maine

There's plenty of room to roam in this sprawling state of more than 33,000 square miles—roughly the area of the other five New England states combined. Maine's mountains are the place to go if you crave solitude; on many trails, you are more likely to come across a moose than you are another human. The state's most prominent mountains comprise the northernmost reaches of the Appalachian chain, stretching from the White Mountain National Forest in western Maine to Baxter State Park and Katahdin in the far north. The Appalachian Trail, extending 281 miles through Maine alone, forms the backbone of the area's trail networks, blazing through a vast wilderness of thick forest, forgotten rivers, and rugged peaks. Beyond the mountains, there's the crown jewel of Maine's seacoast, Acadia National Park. On Mount Desert Island in the heart of Down East, Acadia offers world-famous coastal hiking on rocky mountains so close to the water's edge they seem to stand up from the Atlantic's salty, roiling surf. No surprise for those who have witnessed the majesty of Mount Desert Island firsthand, Acadia is one of the most popular National Parks in the country.

Odiorne Point State Park, New Hampshire

New Hampshire

The Granite State is home to probably the most popular destination in New England among serious hikers: the White Mountain National Forest. It covers nearly 800,000 acres and pushes numerous summits and ridges far above the tree line, with 48 summits higher than 4,000 feet, including Mount Washington (6,288 ft.), the rooftop of New England and the tallest peak in the entire Northeast. The Appalachian Trail extends for 161 miles through New Hampshire, from the Connecticut River in Hanover to the Mahoosuc Range on the Maine border. The state also manages 206 state parks and forests from the coast to the remote and wild North Country. And beyond the tall peaks to the north, Mount Monadnock and the smaller mountains and hills scattered throughout the lower portion of the state reward hikers with sweeping views and interesting sights. Two long-distance trails in southern New Hampshire—the 21-mile Wapack Trail and the 50-mile Monadnock-Sunapee Greenway—offer truly scenic hiking over hills that offer a deep sense of solitude and remoteness, though you are never too far from civilization.

Vermont

Like no other state in New England, Vermont is defined by its mountains. The Green Mountains run the length of the state, rolling up from round, forested hills in the south to the taller, sometimes craggy peaks in the state's midsection, and on to the rambling hills and peaks of the north country. The Green Mountains are the locus of much of the state's hiking—the 350,000-acre Green Mountain National Forest has 500 miles of hiking trails; many of Vermont's best hikes take place on the same mountains that come to life in winter as world class ski resorts. And many of these hikes take place on the Long Trail (LT), the nation's first long-distance hiking trail, running for about 270 miles along the Green Mountains' spine, from the edge of Massachusetts to the Canadian border. Although an estimated 60 to 80 people through-hike the Long Trail every year, countless hikers access parts of the trail for day hikes or weekend backpacking treks. Beyond the Long Trail, other hiking locales in Vermont take you to such scenic spots as the shores of Lake Champlain and Quechee Gorge in Woodstock.

Massachusetts

From the rolling green hills of the Berkshires to the Cape Cod National Seashore's sandy dunes, what the Bay State lacks in soaring heights, it more than makes up for in sheer variety of quality, easy-access hikes. The highest summit in Massachusetts, Mount Greylock (3,491 ft.), is a natural magnet for hikers. But the state also boasts one of the largest state park and forest systems in the country, with nearly 100 properties covering more than 270,000 acres—most of them crisscrossed by trails and old woods roads— and three long-distance trails bisecting the state north to south: 89 miles of the Appalachian Trail, the 117-mile Metacomet-Monadnock Trail, and the 92-mile Midstate Trail. In addition to this vast repertoire of outdoor destinations, hikers will also find an abundance of bird and wildlife preserves, recreational paths, and quiet woodland trails, with many of these locales only minutes from Boston.

Rhode Island

Don't let its small size fool you. Rhode Island is home to nothing short of a stellar number of quality, lower elevation hiking trails and walking paths, many of them tucked away in surprisingly large wildlife and nature preserves. In Newport, the famous Cliff Walk, a seaside hike in the shadow of sprawling Gilded Age mansions, has no equal in New England. Elsewhere in the Ocean State, opportunity abounds for bird-watching, coastal walks, and long rambles through quiet patches of woods. From Providence, the long-distance East Bay Bike Path hugs the shore of Narragansett Bay, leading to, among other stops, the beautiful salt marsh shore of the Rhode Island Audubon Society's Environmental Education Center. And just 13 miles off the mainland coast is Block Island, named by the Nature Conservancy as one of "The Last Great Places" in the Western Hemisphere. Though it's one of Rhode Island's most popular summer tourist destinations, roughly 20 percent of the island has been set aside for conservation, preserving Block's wild, lonesome feel.

Connecticut

While the bigger peaks of northern New England steal the show for spectacle and remoteness, don't overlook the extensive trail system in Connecticut. The so-called Blue Trails network comprises more than 700 miles of trails across the state, much of that on private land and maintained by volunteer members of the nonprofit Connecticut Forest and Park Association. The Appalachian Trail jogs for 52 miles through northwestern Connecticut's hills. Numerous private preserves have trails open to the public. And from Macedonia Brook State Park and People's State Forest in the west to Mashamoquet Brook State Park and Pachaug State Forest in the east, Connecticut is peppered with dozens of state lands ideal for activities from hiking and mountain biking to snowshoeing and cross-country skiing. The trails here are more civilized than elsewhere in New England; most are short hikes with little elevation gain and loss, and many offer bucolic views of a well-settled, pastoral landscape.

Hiking Tips

HIKING ESSENTIALS

It doesn't require much more than a little wilderness knowledge and a backpack's worth of key items to ensure your day hike in New England is a safe and fun adventure. Here's a list of outdoor essentials.

Water and Food

Like any physical activity, hiking increases your body's fluid needs by a factor of two or more. A good rule of thumb for an all-day hike is two liters of water per person, but even that could leave you mildly dehydrated, so carry a third liter if you can. Dehydration can lead to other—more serious—problems, like heat exhaustion, hypothermia, frostbite, and injury. If you're well hydrated, you will urinate frequently and your urine will be clear. The darker your urine, the greater your level of dehydration. If you feel thirsty, dehydration has already commenced. In short: Drink a lot.

Streams and brooks run everywhere in New England. If you're out for more than a day in the backcountry, finding water is rarely a problem (except on ridge tops and summits). But microscopic organisms *Giardia lamblia* and *Cryptosporidium* are common in backcountry water sources and can cause a litany of terrible gastrointestinal problems in humans. Assume you should always treat water from backcountry sources, whether by using a filter or iodine tablets, boiling, or another proven method to eliminate giardiasis and other harmful bacteria. Day-hikers will usually find it more convenient to simply carry enough water from home for the hike.

Similarly, your body consumes a phenomenal amount of calories walking up and down a mountain. Feed it frequently. Carbohydrate-rich foods such as bread, chocolate, dried fruit, fig bars, snack bars, fresh vegetables, and energy bars are all good sources for a quick burst of energy. Fats contain about twice the calories per pound than carbs or protein, and provide the slow-burning fuel that keeps you going all day and keeps you warm through the night if you're sleeping outside; sate your need for fats by eating cheese, chocolate, canned meats or fish, pepperoni, sausage, or nuts.

On hot days, "refrigerate" your water and perishables such as cheese and chocolate: Fill a water bottle (the collapsible kind works best) with very cold water, and ice cubes if possible. Wrap it and your perishables in a thick, insulating fleece and bury it inside your pack. Or the night before, fill a water bottle halfway and freeze it, then fill the remainder with water in the morning before you leave for the hike.

Trail Maps

A map of the park, preserve, or public land you are visiting is essential. Even if you have hiked a trail a hundred times, carry a map. Unexpected trail closures, an injury requiring a shorter route, bad weather, or an animal encounter can all result in a sudden change of plans that require map assistance. Some may believe a GPS device takes the place of a map, but this isn't always true. If you get lost, a detailed trail map showing lakes, rivers, ridge lines, trail junctions, and other landmarks is still the most reliable way to get back on trail.

Many land agencies provide free paper maps at the trailhead, though be aware that some state parks and land agencies are much more vigilant about restocking than others.

GLOBAL POSITIONING SYSTEM (GPS) DEVICES

Working with a system of orbiting satellites, GPS receivers are able to accurately pinpoint your position, elevation, and time anywhere on the face of the earth. Out on the trail, GPS devices can help you navigate from point to point, indicating bearings and the distance remaining to reach your destination. It can also help should you become lost.

Despite these advances, GPS technology is not a replacement for the old standby of a compass and paper topographical map. GPS units are not yet able to provide an adequately detailed view of the surrounding landscape, batteries typically wear out in less than a day, and some landscape conditions can interfere with signal strength. Still, when used in concert with topographical maps, GPS is an extremely useful addition to your navigational toolbox.

Every hike in this book lists GPS coordinates for the hike's trailhead. Use these for better road navigation on the drive to your destination. Inputting the trailhead GPS coordinates before leaving on your hike will also help you retrace your steps if you become lost.

Check the agency's website to see if maps can be printed out beforehand or call to request a map be sent to you. For hikers along the Appalachian Trail, numerous trail maps are available. The best—and most complete—maps are published by the Appalachian Mountain Club and the Appalachian Trail Conservancy.

BLAZES AND CAIRNS

New England's forests abound with blazes—slashes of paint on trees used to mark trails. Sometimes the color of blazes seems random and unrelated to other trails in the same area, but most major trails and trail systems are blazed consistently. The Appalachian Trail (AT) bears white blazes for its entire length, including its 734 miles through five New England states. Most side trails connecting to the AT are blue-blazed. Vermont's 270-mile Long Trail, which coincides with the AT for more than 100 miles, is also blazed in white. Connecticut's Blue Trails system of hiking paths scattered across the state is, as the name suggests, marked entirely with blue blazes.

Although not all trails are well blazed, popular and well-maintained trails usually are—you'll see a colored slash of paint at frequent intervals at about eye level on tree trunks. Double slashes are sometimes used to indicate a sharp turn in the trail. Trails are blazed in both directions, so whenever you suspect you may have lost the trail, turn around to see whether you can find a blaze facing in the opposite direction; if so, you'll know you're still on the trail.

Above tree line, trails may be marked either with blazes painted on rock or with cairns, which are piles of stones constructed at regular intervals. In the rocky terrain on the upper slopes of New England's highest peaks, care may be needed to discern artificially constructed cairns from the landscape surrounding them, but the cairns in rocky areas are usually built higher and are obviously constructed by people.

Extra Clothing

At lower elevations amid the protection of trees or on a warm day, you may elect to bring no extra clothing for an hour-long outing, or no more than a light jacket for a few hours or more. The exception to this is in the Seacoast region, where hikes are more exposed to cool wind. But higher elevations, especially above tree line, get much colder than the valleys—about three degrees Fahrenheit per thousand feet—and winds can grow much stronger. Many a White Mountains hiker has departed from a valley basking in summerlike weather and reached a summit wracked by wintry winds and lying under a carpet of fresh snow, even during the summer months.

Insulating layers, a jacket that protects against wind and precipitation, a warm hat, gloves, a rain poncho, and extra socks are always a good idea to bring along when out on a long hike, especially when scaling New England's highest peaks. Look for wool blends or the new breed of high tech synthetics, fabrics that wick moisture from your skin and keep you dry. Even on a shorter trek, stowing a jacket, hat, and extra pair of socks in your backpack is always a good idea.

Flashlight

Carrying a flashlight in your pack is a must, even when your hike is planned to end well before dusk. Emergencies happen, and being stuck on the trail after dark without a flashlight only compounds the situation. Plus, if you have ever been in New England right before a thunderstorm, you know fast moving cloud cover can turn the landscape pitch dark in seconds. Micro flashlights with alloy skins, xenon bulbs, and a battery life of eight hours on two AA batteries provide ample illumination and won't add much weight to your pack. Throw in some spare batteries and an extra light—or just pack two flashlights to always be covered. A reliable, compact, and waterproof micro flashlight can typically be purchased for under $20.

Sunscreen and Sunglasses

As you climb to higher elevations, the strength of the sun's ultraviolet rays increases. Applying sunscreen or sunblock to exposed skin and wearing a baseball cap or wide-brimmed hat can easily prevent overexposure to sun. SPF strengths vary, but applying sunscreen at least a half-hour before heading out gives the lotion or spray enough time to take effect. When deciding which sunscreen to buy, look for a fragrance-free formula; strongly scented lotions and sprays may attract mosquitoes. And don't forget your sunglasses. Squinting into the sun for hours on end is not only bad for the delicate skin around your eyes, it's almost a certain way to develop a bad case of eye strain. Look for sunglasses with lenses that provide 100 percent UVA and UVB protection.

First-Aid Kit

It's wise to carry a compact and lightweight first-aid kit for emergencies in the backcountry, where an ambulance and hospital are often hours, rather than minutes, away. Prepare any first-aid kit with attention to the type of trip, the destination, and the needs of people hiking (for example, children or persons with medical conditions).

A basic first-aid kit consists of:

- aspirin or an anti-inflammatory
- 4 four-inch-by-four-inch gauze pads
- knife or scissors
- moleskin or Spenco Second Skin (for blisters)
- 1 roll of one-inch athletic tape
- 1 six-inch Ace bandage

- paper and pencil
- safety pins
- SAM splint (a versatile and lightweight splinting device available at many drug stores)
- several alcohol wipes
- several one-inch adhesive bandages
- tube of povidone iodine ointment (for wound care)
- 2 large handkerchiefs
- 2 large gauze pads

Pack everything into a thick, clear plastic resealable bag. And remember, merely carrying a first-aid kit does not make you safe; knowing how to use what's in it does.

HIKING GEAR

Much could be written about how to outfit oneself for hiking in a region like New England, with its significant range of elevations and latitudes, alpine zones, huge seasonal temperature swings, and fairly wet climate.

Don't leave your clothing, gear, and other equipment choices to chance. New England is packed with plenty of friendly, locally owned stores that offer quality, outdoor clothing and footwear options (and knowledgeable staff to help you). Or, take part in the venerable Yankee tradition of the swap meet. Many of New England's mountain clubs hold semi-annual or seasonal meets, giving hikers the irresistible chance to scoop up quality used gear at a very frugal price. Swap meets are also a fun and easy way to meet others in the hiking community.

Clothing

Clothes protect you against the elements and also help to regulate body temperature. What you wear when you go hiking should keep you dry and comfortable, no matter what the weather and season. From underwear to outerwear, pick garments that offer good "breathability." Wool blends and the new breed of synthetic microfibers do a good job at wicking moisture away from the skin. Shirts and pants made from microfiber polyesters are also extra-light and stretchy, allowing for maximum range of movement.

You will also want to dress in layers: underwear, one or more intermediate layers, and, finally, an outer layer. Wearing multiple layers of clothing offers you lots of flexibility for regulating body temperature and exposure. Test your clothing at different temperatures and levels of activity to find out what works best for you.

Rain Gear

Coastal currents smashing up against weather fronts dropping south from Canada give New England its famously fickle weather. Especially in summer, a sunny late morning start to your hike could mean a return trip in a raging rainstorm, often with very little warning time. No matter where you go or how long you expect to be out on the trail, bring along rain gear. It doesn't need to be elaborate: a vinyl foul weather poncho left in its packaging until needed is a compact addition to your pack.

If you do end up getting caught in a thunderstorm or sudden downpour, move away from high ground and tall trees immediately. Take shelter in a low spot, ravine, or thin place in the woods, cover up with your poncho, and wait for the storm to pass. Also,

HIKING GEAR CHECKLIST

Long-distance backpackers need to worry about hauling along camping and cooking equipment, but besides good boots, comfortable clothes, water, food, and a trusty map, it doesn't take much to have all the gear you need for a day hike. Here are some must-haves for your next outing.

IN CASE OF EMERGENCY

Altimeter

Compass

Extra clothes

First-aid kit

Lightweight (or mylar) blanket

Pen/pencil and paper

Swiss army-style knife

Waterproof matches

CREATURE COMFORTS

Binoculars

Bird, wildlife, and tree/flower identification guides

Bug spray/sunscreen

Camera

Face cloths

Fishing pole and fishing license

Picnic supplies

Trekking pole

And, of course, bring along your hiking guide!

---

look carefully at your surroundings, making sure you are not standing in a dry riverbed or wash while waiting, in case of flash floods.

Being out in rainy weather is also a concern for your feet and legs. Brushing up against wet ferns or low-lying plants can make for uncomfortably damp pant legs and soaked socks and boots. In case you do get stuck in the rain, another good piece of equipment to have on hand is a pair of gaiters, leggings made of Gore-Tex or other water-repellant materials. Gaiters are held in place under each boot with a stirrup and extend over your pants to just below the knee.

Shoes and Socks

The most important piece of gear may be well-fitting, comfortable, supportive shoes or boots. Finding the right footwear requires trying on various models and walking around in them in the store before deciding. Everyone's feet are different, and shoes or boots that feel great on your friend won't necessarily fit you well. Deciding how heavy your footwear should be depends on variables like how often you hike, whether you easily injure feet or ankles, and how much weight you'll carry. My general recommendation is to hike in the most lightweight footwear that you find comfortable and adequately supportive.

There are three basic types of hiking boots. Sneaker-like trail shoes are adequate when you are hiking in a dry climate and on well-established paths. Traditional hiking boots, sometimes called trail hikers or trail boots, are constructed with a higher cut and slightly stiffer sole to provide support on steep inclines and muddy paths. Mountaineering boots are for those who might need to attach crampons for a better grip on glaciers or hard-packed snow on mountain hikes and rock or ice climbing. Mountaineering boots are built with a very stiff sole to give your feet and ankles support and protection as you climb more challenging terrain.

The hiking boot experts at L.L.Bean, New England's premier shopping destination for outdoor gear and equipment, recommend hikers consider the various advantages of fabric-and-leather boots and all-leather boots. Fabric-and-leather boots are lighter and easier to break in, but all-leather boots offer added protection and durability in rigorous terrain, as well as being water resistant and breathable. Quality boots can be found in either style.

HIKING BOOTS

Try boots on at the end of the day when your feet are more swollen and wear the socks you plan to wear on the trail. Boots should feel snug but comfortable, so you can still wiggle your toes. Most hiking boots won't feel as instantly comfortable as sneakers, but they shouldn't pinch, cause hot spots, or constrict circulation. They should fit securely around your ankle and instep. Try walking down an incline at the store. Your feet should not slide forward, nor should your toenails scrape against the front of your boot. If your foot slides forward, the boot could be too wide. If the back of your heel moves around, your boots might not be laced up tight enough.

Once you purchase a pair of boots, break them in slowly with short hikes. Leather boots in particular take a while to break in, so take a couple of two- or three-hour hikes before your big trip or wear them around the house. If you find any sharp pressure points, use leather conditioner to soften the leather.

SOCKS

With exertion, one foot can sweat up to two pints of vapor/fluid per day. That's why wicking technology in hiking socks is so important. Without it, bacteria and fungus can become a problem. The best hiking socks are made from 100 percent wool or a wool blend of at least 50 percent wool. Unlike most synthetic fibers, which have to wait for moisture to condense into a liquid before wicking it away from your skin, wool socks absorb and transfer moisture in its vapor state, before it condenses. When it's hot, this creates a mini air-conditioning unit next to your feet, releasing heat through your socks and boots. And when it's cold, wicking keeps bone-chilling moisture at bay.

Some newer synthetics and synthetic blends are engineered to wick moisture; read the package label carefully and ask the store clerk for recommendations. The one fiber to stay away from is cotton, which absorbs water and perspiration and holds it next to your skin. If you are hiking with wet feet and the temperature drops below freezing, you risk getting frostbite. A good sock system and hiking boots reduce that possibility.

For comfort and good circulation, look for socks that won't bind your feet and avoid those made with excessive stitching or a scratchy knit that could lead to chafing. Terry woven socks are a good pick to distribute pressure and support your natural posture. And thicker isn't always better. Depending on the fit of your boots and the climate you'll be hiking in, a medium-weight wool sock that fits to mid-calf is often your best bet.

FOOTCARE

At an Appalachian Mountain Club hiking seminar, one instructor wisely noted that, besides the brain, "Your feet are the most important part of your body." Hurt any other

THE APPALACHIAN TRAIL

Perhaps the most famous hiking trail in the world, the Appalachian Trail (AT) runs 2,174 miles from Springer Mountain in Georgia to Mount Katahdin in Maine, along the spine of the Appalachian Mountains in 14 states. About 734 miles − or more than one-third − of the AT's length passes through five New England states: Connecticut (52 miles), Massachusetts (90 miles), Vermont (150 miles), New Hampshire (161 miles), and Maine (281 miles). New England boasts some of the AT's most spectacular, best-known, and rugged stretches, including the White Mountains, the southern Green Mountains, the Riga Plateau of Massachusetts and Connecticut, and Maine's Mahoosuc, Saddleback, and Bigelow ranges, 100-mile Wilderness, and Katahdin. A few hundred people hike the entire trail end to end every year, but thousands more take shorter backpacking trips and day hikes somewhere along the AT.

Maintained by hiking clubs that assume responsibility for different sections of the AT, the trail is well marked with signs and white blazes on trees and rocks above tree line. Shelters and campsites are spaced out along the AT so that backpackers have choices of where to spend each night. But those shelters can fill up during the busy season of summer and early fall, especially on weekends. The prime hiking season for the AT in New England depends on elevation and latitude, but generally, that season runs May–October in southern New England and mid-June–early October at higher elevations in northern New England.

body part and we might conceivably still make it home under our own power. Hurt our feet, and we're in trouble.

Take care of your feet. Wear clean socks that wick moisture from your skin while staying dry. Make sure your shoes or boots fit properly, are laced properly, and are broken in if they require it. Wear the appropriate footwear for the type of hiking you plan to do. If you anticipate your socks getting wet from perspiration or water, bring extra socks; on a multiday trip, have dry socks for each day, or at least change socks every other day. On hot days, roll your socks down over your boot tops to create what shoe manufacturers call "the chimney effect," cooling your feet by forcing air into your boots as you walk.

On longer treks, whenever you stop for a short rest on the trail—even if only for 5 or 10 minutes—sit down, pull off your boots and socks, and let them and your feet dry out. When backpacking, wash your feet at the end of the day. If you feel any hot spots developing, intervene before they progress into blisters. A slightly red or tender hot spot can be protected from developing into a blister with an adhesive bandage, tape, or a square of moleskin.

If a blister has formed, clean the area around it thoroughly to avoid infection. Sterilize a needle or knife in a flame, then pop and drain the blister to promote faster healing. Put an antiseptic ointment on the blister. Cut a piece of moleskin or Second Skin (both of which have a soft side and a sticky side with a peel-off backing) large enough to overlap the blistered area. Cut a hole as large as the blister out of the center of the moleskin, then place the moleskin over the blister so that the blister is visible through the hole. If done properly, you should be able to walk without aggravating the blister.

Backpack

When just out for the day, a roomy backpack will do to hold your belongings; toting an over-sized metal frame pack is not necessary unless you plan on camping overnight and need to bring along camp stove, bed roll, tent, and other extra gear. Shoulder straps should be foam padded for comfort. Look for backpacks made of water-resistant nylon. And just like clothes or shoes, try the pack on to make sure it has the fit you want.

Trekking Poles

For hikers who need a little extra physical support, trekking poles or walking sticks relieve feet and legs of tens of thousands of pounds of pressure over the course of an all-day hike. They are particularly useful in helping prevent knee and back pain from rigorous hiking. If you find a good walking stick along your journey, before heading back to your car, leave the stick in an obvious spot for another weary hiker to stumble upon. It warmed the bottom of my heart one day to find at least a dozen walking sticks leaning against a trailhead signpost in Massachusetts, free for anyone to use.

CLIMATE

With New England's biggest peaks in the northern states and its smaller hills and flatlands in the southern states, as well as an ocean moderating the Seacoast climate, this region's fair-weather hikers can find a trail to explore virtually year-round. But the wildly varied character of hiking opportunities here also demands some basic knowledge of and preparation for hitting the trails.

The ocean generally keeps coastal areas a little warmer in winter and cooler in summer than inland areas. Otherwise, any time of year, average temperatures typically grow cooler as you gain elevation or move northward.

New England's prime hiking season stretches for several months from spring through fall, with the season's length depending on the region. In general, summer high temperatures range 60°F–90°F with lows from 50°F to around freezing at higher elevations. Days are often humid in the forests and lower elevations and windy on the mountaintops. July and August see occasional thunderstorms, but July through September is the driest period. August is usually the best month for finding ripe wild blueberries along many trails, especially in northern New England.

September is often the best month for hiking, with dry, comfortable days, cool nights, and few bugs. Fall foliage colors peak anywhere from mid-September or early October in northern New England to early or mid-October in the south; by choosing your destinations well and moving north to south, you can hike through vibrant foliage for three or four successive weekends. The period from mid-October into November offers cool days, cold nights, no bugs, few people, and often little snow.

In the higher peaks of Vermont's Green Mountains, New Hampshire's White Mountains, Maine's northern Appalachians, and along the Appalachian Trail in parts of western Massachusetts and Connecticut, high-elevation snow disappears and alpine wildflowers bloom in late spring; by late October, wintry winds start blowing and snow starts flying (though it can snow above 4,000 feet in any month of the year). Spring trails are muddy at low elevations—some are closed to hiking during the April/May "mud season"—and buried under deep, slushy snow up high, requiring snowshoes. Winter conditions set in by mid-November and can become very severe, even life threatening.

CROSS-COUNTRY SKIING AND SNOWSHOEING

Many hikes in this book are great for cross-country skiing or snowshoeing in winter. But added precaution is needed. Days are short and the temperature may start to plummet by mid-afternoon, so carry the right clothing and don't overestimate how far you can travel in winter. Depending on snow conditions and your own fitness level and experience with either snowshoes or skis, a winter outing can take much longer than anticipated – and certainly much longer than a trip of similar distance on groomed trails at a cross-country ski resort. Breaking your own trail through fresh snow can also be very exhausting – take turns leading and conserve energy by following the leader's tracks, which also serve as a good return trail.

The proper clothing becomes essential in winter, especially the farther you wander from roads. Wear a base layer that wicks moisture from your skin and dries quickly, middle layers that insulate and do not retain moisture, and a windproof shell that breathes well and is waterproof or water-resistant (the latter type of garment usually breathes much better than something that's completely waterproof). Size boots to fit over a thin, synthetic liner sock and a thicker, heavyweight synthetic-blend sock. For your hands, often the most versatile system consists of gloves and/or mittens that also can be layered, with an outer layer that's waterproof and windproof and preferably also breathable.

Most importantly, don't overdress: Remove layers if you're getting too hot. Avoid becoming wet with perspiration, which can lead to too much cooling. Drink plenty of fluids and eat snacks frequently to maintain your energy level; feeling tired or cold on a winter outing may be an indication of dehydration or hunger.

As long as you're safe, cautious, and aware, winter is a great time to explore New England's trails. Have fun out there.

Going above the tree line in winter is considered a mountaineering experience by many (though these mountains lack glacier travel and high altitude), so be prepared for harsh cold and strong winds.

The second strongest wind gust ever recorded on Earth was measured on April 12, 1934, at the weather observatory on the summit of New Hampshire's Mount Washington. The gust was clocked at 231 mph. The summit of Mount Washington remains in clouds 60 percent of the time. Its average temperature year-round is 26.5°F; winds average 35 mph and exceed hurricane force (75 mph) on average 104 days a year. Be aware that in the higher peaks of the Whites as well as alpine peaks in Vermont and Maine, weather conditions change rapidly. It is not uncommon to set off from the trailhead in hot, sunny weather only to hit driving rain and hail on the summit.

In the smaller hills and flatlands of central and southern New England, the snow-free hiking season often begins by early spring and lasts into late autumn. Some of these trails are even occasionally free of snow during the winter, or offer opportunities for snowshoeing or cross-country skiing in woods protected from strong winds, with warmer temperatures than you'll find on the bigger peaks up north. Many Seacoast trails, even in Maine, rarely stay snow-covered all winter, though they can get occasional heavy snowfall and be very icy in cold weather. For more information about weather-related trail conditions, refer to the individual hike listings.

SAFETY AND FIRST AID

Few of us would consider hiking a high-risk activity. But like any physical activity, it does pose certain risks, and it's up to us to minimize them. For starters, make sure your physical condition is adequate for your objective—the quickest route to injury is over-extending either your skills or your physical abilities. You wouldn't presume that you could rock climb a 1,000-foot cliff if you've never climbed before; don't assume you're ready for one of New England's hardest hikes if you've never—or not very recently—done anything nearly as difficult.

Build up your fitness level by gradually increasing your workouts and the length of your hikes. Beyond strengthening muscles, you must strengthen the soft connective tissue in joints like knees and ankles that are too easily strained and take weeks or months to heal from injury. Staying active in a variety of activities—hiking, running, bicycling, Nordic skiing—helps develop good overall fitness and decreases the likelihood of an overuse injury. Most importantly, stretch muscles before and after a workout to reduce the chance of injury.

New England's most rugged trails—and even parts of its more moderate paths—can be very rocky and steep. Uneven terrain is often a major contributor to falls resulting in serious, acute injury. Most of us have a fairly reliable self-preservation instinct—and you should trust it. If something strikes you as dangerous or beyond your abilities, don't try it, or simply wait until you think you're ready for it.

An injury far from a road also means it may be hours before the victim reaches a hospital. Basic training in wilderness first aid is beneficial to anyone who frequents the mountains, even recreational hikers. New England happens to have two highly respected sources for such training, and the basic course requires just one weekend. Contact SOLO (Conway, NH, 603/447-6711, www.soloschools.com) or Wilderness Medical Associates (Scarborough, ME, 207/730-7331, www.wildmed.com) for information.

Plants

From fern-choked forest floors to fields filled with wild blueberries, plant life in New England is varied and diverse. And luckily, there are only a few poisonous plant species to be wary of: poison ivy, poison oak, and poison sumac. The three plants contain urushiol, an oil that causes an allergic reaction and rash in humans. According to the American Academy of Dermatology, humans typically come in contact with urushiol by brushing up against or touching the plants, touching an object or animal that has come in contact with the oil, or breathing in urushiol particles if a poison plant is burned in a campfire.

Urushiol penetrates the skin in minutes, but the rash usually takes anywhere from 12 to 72 hours to appear, followed quickly by severe itching, redness, swelling, and even blisters. When the rash develops, streaks or lines often reveal where the plant brushed against the skin. A rash triggered by urushiol does not spread and is not contagious.

RECOGNIZING POISONOUS PLANTS

Hikers best protection against the itchy rash caused by urushiol is learning how to identify the plants that contain the oil.

Poison Ivy: Leaves of three, let them be... Poison ivy grows as vines or low shrubs almost everywhere in New England and true to that famous phrase from summer camp, the plant consists of three pointed leaflets; the middle leaflet has a much longer stalk than the two side ones. Leaflets are reddish when they bud in spring, turn green during the summer, and then become various shades of yellow, orange, or red in the autumn. Small greenish flowers grow in bunches attached to the main stem close to where each leaf joins it. Later in the season, clusters of poisonous berries form. They are whitish, with a waxy look.

Poison Oak: There are two main species of poison oak, but the species commonly found in New England is the Atlantic Poison Oak a vine plant or bush. Poison oak leaves grow in clusters of three leaves; the lobbed appearance of each leaf resembles the white oak. Plants put out berries in spring that are white or yellowish-green in color and leaflets change color with the seasons. Poison oak tends to grow in sandy soils.

Poison Sumac: Though it is one of New England's native tree species, poison sumac is the rarest of the urushiol-containing plants.

Avoiding Poison Oak: Remember the old Boy Scout saying: "Leaves of three, let them be."

Sumac can be identified by its row of paired leaflets that contains an additional leaflet at the end. Often the leaves have spots that resemble blotches of black enamel paint. These spots are actually urushiol, which when exposed to air turn brownish-black. Poison sumac tends to grow near wet areas and bogs.

TREATING POISON IVY, POISON OAK, AND POISON SUMAC

When an allergic reaction develops, the skin should be washed well with lukewarm water and soap. All clothing should be laundered, and everything else that may be contaminated with urushiol should be washed thoroughly. Urushiol can remain active for a long time. For mild cases, cool showers and an over-the-counter product that eases itching can be effective. Oatmeal baths and baking-soda mixtures also can soothe the discomfort. When a severe reaction develops contact a dermatologist immediately, or go to an emergency room. Prescription medication may be needed to reduce the swelling and itch.

Insects

Black flies, or mayflies, emerge by late April or early May and pester hikers until late June or early July, while mosquitoes come out in late spring and dissipate (but do not disappear) by midsummer. No-see-ums (tiny biting flies that live up to their name) plague some wooded areas in summer. Of particular concern in recent years has been the small, but growing number of cases of eastern equine encephalitis (EEE) in humans, spread by EEE-infected mosquitoes. It's still very rare, but cases of EEE tend to emerge each year at the end of summer and early fall. Mosquitoes acquire EEE through contact with diseased birds.

LYME DISEASE

Deer ticks are often carriers of the bacteria that causes Lyme disease. Hundreds of cases of the disease – most mild and treatable with antibiotics – are diagnosed in New England each year. The easiest way to avoid tick bites is to wear socks, long pants, and a long-sleeve shirt whenever you hike, and especially when you hike in areas with tall grass and/or large deer populations. Tucking your pant legs into your socks prevents the best protection against the tiny ticks, but never fail to check your skin thoroughly at the end of a hike. Most tick bites cause a sharp sting, but some may go unnoticed.

If you do find a tick, don't panic. Take a pair of tweezers and place them around the tick as close to your skin as possible. Gently pull the tick straight out to avoid parts of it breaking off still attached to the skin. The majority of tick bites are no more of a nuisance than a mosquito or black fly bite. If you do notice a rash spreading out from around the bite within a week of finding the tick, it may be an early sign of Lyme disease. Other symptoms are similar to the flu – headache, fever, muscle soreness, neck stiffness, or nausea – and may appear anywhere from a few days to a week or so after being bitten. If you do notice any symptoms, seek medical help immediately. When caught in its early stages, Lyme disease is easily treated with antibiotics; left untreated, the disease can be debilitating.

You will want to have some kind of bug repellant with you no matter where your hike takes you. (Even the windswept coast isn't free of insects; New England's swarms of black flies first appear on the coast and then move inland.) There is much debate about the health effects of wearing sprays containing the chemical DEET; some may prefer ointments made with essential oils and herbs believed to deter bugs. Or skip the sprays and salves and wear a lightweight jacket made of head-to-waist (or head-to-toe) mosquito netting. These unusual creations are made by Bug Baffler, a New Hampshire-based company, and sold on the web (www.bugbaffler.com).

Wildlife

The remarkable recovery of New England's mountains and forests during the past century from the abuses of the logging industry has spawned a boom in the populations of many wild animals, from increased numbers of black bears and moose to the triumphant return of the bald eagle and peregrine falcon. For the most part, you don't have to worry about your safety in the backcountry when it comes to wildlife encounters. It's typical for hikers to see lots of scat and a traffic jam of prints on the trail without ever actually spotting the animals that left this evidence behind.

Still, a few sensible precautions are in order. If you're camping in the backcountry, know how to hang or store your food properly to keep it from bears and smaller animals like mice, which are more likely to be a problem. You certainly should never approach the region's two largest mammals: moose, which you may see in northern New England, or bear, which you may never see. These creatures are wild and unpredictable, and a moose can weigh several hundred pounds and put the hurt on a much smaller human. The greatest danger posed by moose is that of hitting one while driving on dark back roads at night; hundreds of collisions occur in Maine and New Hampshire every year, often wrecking vehicles and injuring people. At night, drive more slowly than you would during daylight. As one forest ranger warns, "the most dangerous part of hiking in the mountains is the drive to the trailhead."

First Aid

Hypothermia

In humans and other warm-blooded animals, core body temperature is maintained near a constant level through internal temperature regulation. When the body is over-exposed to cold, however, internal mechanisms may be unable to replenish excessive heat loss. Hypothermia is defined as any body temperature below 95°F (35 °C). Despite its association with winter, hypothermia can occur even when the air temperature is in the 50s. Often the victim has gotten wet or over-exerted himself or herself on the trail. Hypothermia is a leading cause of death in the outdoors.

Symptoms of hypothermia include uncontrollable shivering, weakness, loss of coordination, confusion, cold skin, drowsiness, frost bite, and slowed breathing or heart rate. If a member of your hiking party demonstrates one or more of these symptoms, send a call out for help and take action immediately. Get out of the wind and cold and seek shelter in a warm, dry environment. Help the victim change into windproof, waterproof clothes and wrap up in a blanket, if one is available; start a fire to add extra warmth. Encourage the victim to eat candy, energy bars, and other high-sugar foods to boost energy. Do not offer alcohol, it only makes heat loss worse.

Victims of mild to moderate hypothermia may be suffering from impaired judgment and not be making rational decisions. They might try to resist help; be persistent.

Heat Stroke

Our bodies produce a tremendous amount of internal heat. Under normal conditions, we cool ourselves by sweating and radiating heat through the skin. However, in certain circumstances, such as extreme heat, high humidity, or vigorous activity in the hot sun, this cooling system may begin to fail, allowing heat to build up to dangerous levels.

If a person becomes dehydrated and cannot sweat enough to cool their body, their internal temperature may rise to dangerously high levels, causing heat stroke. Symptoms include headache, mental confusion, and cramps throughout the entire body. If you have these symptoms, or notice them in a member of your hiking party, take immediate action to lower the body's core temperature. Get out of the sun and move to a shadier location. Pour water over the victim and fan the skin to stimulate sweating; sit in a nearby stream, if possible. Encourage the victim to drink liquids and rest. If symptoms are severe or don't improve within a few minutes of starting first aid, do not hesitate to call for help.

Probably the most effective way to cut risk for heat stroke is to stay adequately hydrated. When the temperatures soar on a New England summer day, stop frequently on the trail for water and rest breaks.

Sprains and Breaks

For any sprain or strain, remember RICE: rest, ice, compression, elevation. First, have the patient rest by lying down on the ground or nearest flat surface. Next, reduce swelling by gently placing a plastic freezer bag filled with cold water on the injury. To compress the ankle, snugly wrap the injury in an ACE bandage. (First-aid tape will also work.)

The wrap should cover the entire foot except for the heel and end several inches above the ankle. Most compression wraps are self-fastening or come with clip fasteners—or use tape to secure the end. If toes become purplish or blue, cool to the touch, or feel numb or tingly according to the patient, the wrap is too tight and should be loosened.

Keep the leg elevated until swelling is visibly reduced. When you or someone you are with suffers a sprained ankle or other minor injury on the trail, keep an open mind about finishing the hike. Because it's always more enjoyable when everyone can fully participate, it might be best to cut your losses and come back another time.

Navigational Tools

At some point, almost every hiker becomes lost. Torn down trail signs, trail detours, faded blazes, and snow, fog, and other conditions can make staying the course very rough going. First, take every step to prevent becoming lost. Before you hike, study a map of the area to become familiar with the trails, nearby roads, streams, mountains and other features. Leave a trip plan with family or friends and sign in at the trailhead register or nearby ranger cabin, if a hiker registry is available.

Always hike with a map and compass. And as you ramble along the trail, observe the topography around you (ridges, recognizable summits, rivers, etc.). They serve as good reference points, particularly when you are above the tree line. Some hikers leave small piles of rocks spaced at regular intervals to help them navigate treeless, alpine areas. Should you become disoriented, stop, pull out your map and look at the countryside for familiar landmarks.

Few people remain truly lost after consulting a map and calmly studying the terrain for five minutes. If you still need help orienting yourself, you may want to head to a ridge or high ground so you can identify hills or streams that are marked on your topographical map. Lay your map on the ground and put your compass on top to orient north. Another helpful gadget is an altimeter, which can tell you your approximate elevation; you can then pinpoint this elevation on a topographic map. Until you have your bearings, don't wander too far from your original route. If you told family members or fellow hikers where you plan to hike, that area is where rescuers will start searching for you.

Should you continue to be lost, S.T.O.P. (stop, think, observe, and plan). And don't panic. Not only does it cloud your judgment, you will be using up energy that you may need later on. Stay put and, if you carry a whistle, blow it at timed intervals to signal rescuers or other hikers (yelling also works).

HIKING ETHICS

Trail Etiquette

One of the great things about hiking is the quality of the people you meet on the trail. Hikers generally do not need an explanation of the value of courtesy, and one hopes this will always ring true. Still, with the popularity of hiking on the increase, and thousands of new hikers taking to the trails of New England every year, it's a good idea to brush up on some etiquette basics.

As a general rule and a friendly favor to other hikers, yield the trail to others whether you're going uphill or down. All trail users should yield to horses by stepping aside for the safety of everyone present. Likewise, horseback riders should, whenever possible, avoid situations where their animals are forced to push past hikers on very narrow trails.

Mountain bikers should yield to hikers, announce their approach, and pass nonbikers slowly. During hunting season, nonhunters should wear blaze orange, or an equally bright, conspicuous color. The hunters you may come across on the trail are usually responsible and friendly and deserve like treatment.

Many of us enjoy the woods and mountains for the quiet, and we should keep that in mind on the trail, at summits, or backcountry campsites. Many of us share the belief that things like cell phones, radios, and CD players do not belong in the mountains. High tech devices may also pose serious safety risks when used on the trail. Texting while hiking? Not a good idea when you should be watching out for exposed tree roots and rocky footing. Likewise, listening to a MP3 player could prevent you from hearing another hiker alerting you to dangers ahead.

New England has seen some conflict between hikers and mountain bikers, but it's important to remember that solutions to those issues are never reached through hostility and rudeness. Much more is accomplished when we begin from a foundation of mutual respect and courtesy. After all, we're all interested in preserving and enjoying our trails.

Large groups have a disproportionate impact on backcountry campsites and on the experience of other people. Be aware of and respect any restrictions on group size. Even where no regulation exists, keep your group size to no more than 10 people.

TIPS FOR AVOIDING CROWDS

Even on New England's most popular peaks, it is still possible to beat the crowds and have the trail all—or mostly—to yourself. Timing is everything. For hikes of less than six or seven miles round-trip, try to arrive at the trailhead early in the morning. Depending on the elevation gain, a seven-mile round-tripper will take the average hiker somewhere around three hours to complete—the perfect length for a late morning or early afternoon trek. Start your hike by 7 A.M. on a sunny Saturday morning and you will probably be returning to your car just as the weekend crush is arriving. For very short hikes, waiting until late afternoon or early evening before hitting the trail almost always ensures low boot traffic. But keep these late day hikes short and to destinations with easy footing just in case you're still out on the trail when night falls.

For very long hikes of nine miles round-trip or more, this early-bird strategy will not work, since early morning is the normal start time for most longer hikes. To still salvage a little solitude on your journey, you might want to consider breaking high mileage hikes into a two-day trek with an overnight stay at a shelter or backcountry campground. Start out on the trail later in the day and aim to camp at least halfway to the summit (within a mile of the summit is ideal). As early as you can the next day, finish the climb and enjoy the peaceful stillness.

Another way to avoid the crowds is to hike during the work week, when even the busiest of New England's trailheads are almost empty. If it felt as though you were part of a conga line climbing to the top of Mount Washington on a warm, sunny Sunday afternoon, come back on Wednesday and find almost no one around. Similarly, time your hikes according to the seasons. With the exception of a few places in northern New England that tend to stay muddy and even icy well into late spring, June is often the best month for encountering light boot traffic. Birds chirp, the air is fresh, wildflowers bloom in the meadows, and the throngs of summer tourists—and swarms of mosquitoes—have yet to arrive. Similarly, the week after Labor Day weekend is often quiet on the trail, with family vacationers gone back to school and the fall foliage season not yet underway.

Hiking with Children

Exploring the great outdoors with kids is one of life's great rewards. Starting from a very young age, a baby can be placed in a front carrier and taken out on almost any trail where the walking is flat and the environment serene; the rhythmic pace of hiking tends to lull even the fussiest of infants right to sleep. Backpack carriers are a good way to tote toddlers on-trail and, depending on the model, can accommodate a child of up to 35 pounds. When hiking with a child-carrier pack, keep a small mirror in your pocket so you can frequently check on your passenger without having to stop and remove the pack.

Around age three, kids are ready to hit the trail along with the rest of the family. But, little legs don't travel very far. Make your family outings kid-centric by picking short hikes that lead to such exciting features as waterfalls, duck-filled ponds, giant glacial erratics, huge gnarled tree trunks, beaver dams, and small hills with big views. Even if the hike is under a half mile in total length, plan extra time for rest stops and lots of unfettered exploration. Most children love the grown-up feel of having their own lightweight backpack; fill the pack with a water bottle and snack treats.

When a child reaches school age, physical ability rises dramatically. And so does his or her responsibility as a hiker. Teach your children how to read maps, how to use a compass, and what to do if lost. Show by example how to be courteous to the other hikers you encounter on the trail. Your efforts will be appreciated.

Hiking with Pets

Dogs are great trail companions and generally love the adventure of hiking every bit as much as their owners do. But dogs can create unnecessary friction in the backcountry. Dog owners should respect any regulations and not presume that strangers are eager to meet their pet. Keep your pet under physical control whenever other people are approaching. And for your dog's protection, always bring a leash along, even if regulations don't call for one.

Due to its large wildlife population, Baxter State Park in Maine is one notable destination that does not permit pets of any kind inside its borders. If you do have your dog along, check in with the campsites lining the access roads to Baxter. Many offer day boarding for dogs. Several bird refuges and Audubon sanctuaries also prohibit dogs. Call ahead to these and other destinations to find out trail regulations for pets.

Leave No Trace

Many of New England's trails receive heavy use, making it imperative that we all understand how to minimize our physical impact on the land. The nonprofit organization Leave No Trace (LNT) advocates a set of principles for low-impact backcountry use that are summarized in these basic guidelines:

- Be considerate of other visitors.
- Dispose of waste properly.
- Leave what you find.
- Minimize campfire impact.
- Plan ahead and prepare.

• Respect wildlife.

• Travel and camp on durable surfaces.

LNT offers more in-depth guidelines for low-impact camping and hiking on its website: www.lnt.org. You can also contact them by mail or phone: Leave No Trace Inc., P.O. Box 997, Boulder, CO 80306; 303/442-8222 or 800/332-4100.

Camping

The following are more recommendations that apply to many backcountry areas in New England:

• Avoid building campfires; cook with a backpacking stove. If you do build a campfire, use only wood found locally as a way to prevent the spread of destructive forest pests introduced from areas outside New England. In all six states, campers are encouraged not to move firewood more than 50 miles from its original source. Store-bought, packaged firewood is usually okay, as long as it is labeled "kiln dried" or "USDA Certified." Wood that is kiln dried is generally free of pests, although if the wood is not heated to a certain temperature, insects can survive.

• Avoid trails that are very muddy in spring; that's when they are most susceptible to erosion.

• Bury human waste beneath six inches of soil at least 200 feet from any water source.

• Burn and bury, or carry out, used toilet paper.

• Carry out everything you carry in.

• Choose a campsite at least 200 feet from trails and water sources, unless you're using a designated site. Make sure your site bears no evidence of your stay when you leave.

• Do not leave any food behind, even buried, as animals will dig it up. Learn how to hang food appropriately to keep it from bears. Black bears have spread their range over much of New England in recent years, and problems have arisen in isolated backcountry areas where human use is heavy.

• Even biodegradable soap is harmful to the environment, so simply wash your cooking gear with water away from any streams or ponds.

• Last but not least, know and follow any regulations for the area you will be visiting.

Maine

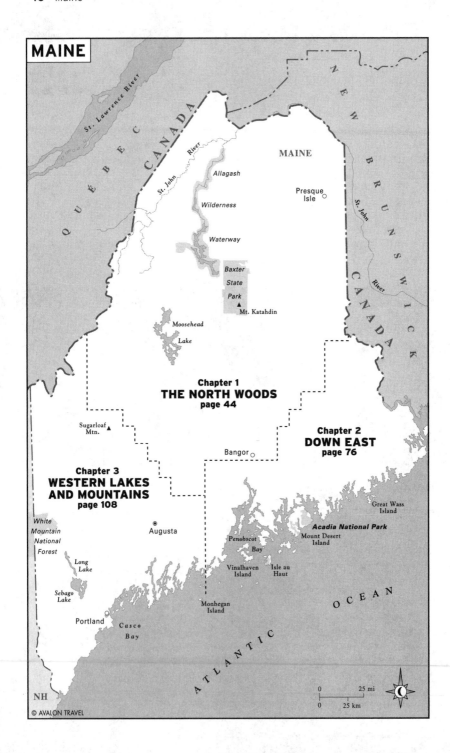

MAINE

QUEBEC

St. Lawrence River

CANADA

St. John River

Allagash
Wilderness
Waterway

MAINE

Presque Isle ○

NEW BRUNSWICK

St. John River

CANADA

Baxter State Park
▲ Mt. Katahdin

Moosehead Lake

Chapter 1
THE NORTH WOODS
page 44

Sugarloaf ▲
Mtn.

Chapter 2
DOWN EAST
page 76

Bangor ○

Chapter 3
WESTERN LAKES
AND MOUNTAINS
page 108

White Mountain National Forest

Augusta ◉

Great Wass Island

Acadia National Park
Mount Desert Island

Penobscot Bay

Long Lake

Vinalhaven Island   Isle au Haut

Sebago Lake

Portland

Monhegan Island

Casco Bay

ATLANTIC OCEAN

NH

© AVALON TRAVEL

0   25 mi
0   25 km

THE
NORTH WOODS

© JOHN "TJ AKA TEEJ" GORDON

BEST HIKES

If hiking in New England conjures images of

scaling mountains in the shadow of ski lifts or topping small hills with expansive views of rolling farmland, the trails found in Maine's North Woods stand out in sharp contrast. Here in this northernmost section of the state (east of U.S. 201 and north of Routes 2 and 9), the landscape is dominated by dense forest, wild lakes, roaming moose and bear, and mountain terrain that may seem more at home in rugged Alaska than genteel New England. Penetrating the very heart of this isolated region, the 26 hikes described in this chapter lie on public land and fall within two of Maine's greatest hiking areas: Baxter State Park and the 100-Mile Wilderness stretch of the Appalachian Trail.

With 204,733 acres remaining as close to true wilderness as managed lands come, Baxter is Maine's flagship state park. It provides a hiking experience that's rare in New England: remote and untamed. Maine's highest peak, 5,267-foot Mount Katahdin, dominates the park's south end and attracts the bulk of hiker traffic. It's legendary as the northern terminus of the Appalachian Trail and the home of the Knife Edge, the fin-like glacial ridge often dubbed, "the longest mile in Maine." Baxter State Park boasts more than 47 other peaks, including standouts Mount Coe, Doubletop, the Owl, the Brothers, and the Traveler, a massive ancient volcano along the park's northeastern boundary. Away from the summits, Baxter's many trails take visitors to waterfalls, ponds, and deep into the woods where the potential is high for a close encounter with moose, bears, beavers, foxes, and countless other forms of northern wildlife.

At busy times in the summer, some parking lots at popular trailheads – usually Katahdin trails – fill up, and the park will not allow any more vehicles in those lots on that day, effectively forcing visitors who come later to choose other trailheads and hikes. There are no overflow parking areas, but trailhead parking north of Katahdin rarely fills, so you can always find someplace to hike. The park's Tote Road is not open to vehicles in winter and access by ski or snowshoe is required. Millinocket Road is maintained in winter as far as Abol Bridge Campground; the road to the park's Matagamon Gate entrance is maintained only as far as a private campground about four miles east of the gate.

The 100-Mile Wilderness stretch of the Appalachian Trail is neither officially designated federal wilderness nor true wilderness as found in the American West or Alaska – you may hear the distant thrum of logging machinery while hiking here. But the Wilderness does offer some of the most remote hiking in all New England, and the big lakes here are home to loons and many other birds and are a favorite haunt of moose. The 100-Mile Wilderness stretch is also the longest hike you can do on trail in the region without crossing a paved or public road (it does, however, cross several logging roads). The busiest months in the Wilderness are August and September, when you're likely to encounter lots of other backpackers, though still not as many as on popular White Mountains trails.

The hiking season begins with the disappearance of snow in late spring – though the black flies, no-see-ums, and mosquitoes also emerge – and extends into October, when the first snow may start flying. There are no public water sources in Baxter State Park or along the 100-Mile Wilderness; treat your water or bring an adequate supply with you. Advance reservations for Baxter State Park campground sites and backcountry campsites are essential and should be made many months in advance of your trip. Along the 100-Mile Wilderness, lean-tos are on a first come, first served basis; low impact camping is allowed along this stretch of the AT.

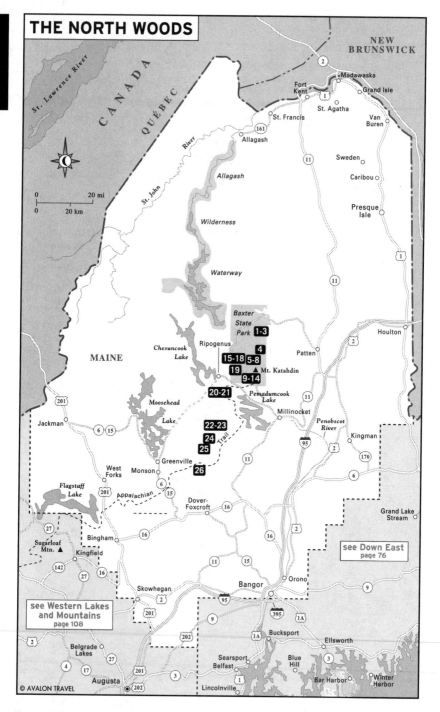

THE NORTH WOODS

MAINE

❶ SOUTH BRANCH FALLS
1 mi/1 hr 👥2 ⛰8

in northern Baxter State Park

A scenic leg stretcher after the long drive to Baxter, the South Branch Falls Trail, near South Branch Pond Campground, is a short, easy trek to cascading waterfalls along South Branch Pond Brook.

Pick up the trailhead at a small turnoff parking area on the west side of South Branch Pond Road, approximately 1.3 miles south of the Tote Road junction. Follow the blue blazes and descend gently through a mixed forest of dense poplar and birch (a good place to test the effectiveness of the bug repellant you've hopefully applied). As the sound of rushing water grows louder, the trail (at 0.4 mile) makes a sudden—and steep—descent out of the woods and into the deep ravine carved out by the South Falls Pond Brook. Carefully make your way along a series of rocky ledges as the trail takes you down to the brook and the falls. The falls appear as a series of cascades formed by water shooting out from between the ledges. The largest fall drops four feet and forms an inviting pool—the perfect spot for a quick dip. Other short side trails take you to different viewing points along the picturesque ravine. Return the way you came.

User Groups: Hikers only. No dogs, horses, mountain bikes, or wheelchair facilities.

Permits: No permits required. An entrance fee of $13 per vehicle is charged at the gatehouse, but vehicles bearing Maine registration enter at no charge. Parking in the park is free.

Maps: A waterproof trail map of Baxter State Park is available from the Appalachian Mountain Club (Rangeley–Stratton/Baxter State Park–Katahdin map, $7.95). For a topographic map, request Wassataquoik Lake and the Traveler from the USGS.

Directions: Trailhead is most easily accessed using Baxter State Park's northern Matagamon Gate entrance. From the junction of Routes 11 and 159 in Patten, drive west on Route 159 (Shin Pond Road) for 10 miles. At Shin Pond, Route 159 becomes Grand Lake Road, a private park access road that is open for public use. Stay on Grand Lake Road, following the road for 14 miles to reach the entrance for Baxter State Park. From the gatehouse, drive 7.3 miles along Tote Road (the park's perimeter road) and turn left at the sign for South Branch Pond Campground. Drive 1.3 miles to a parking turnout on the right.

Baxter State Park is open May 15–November 1 and December 1–March 31. During the summer season, the Matagamon Gate is open 6 A.M.–10 P.M.; the park's Togue Pond Gate is open 6 A.M.–10 P.M.—though it may open as early as 5 A.M. at the discretion of the park director.

GPS Coordinates: 46.1155 N, 68.9070 W

Contact: Baxter State Park, 64 Balsam Dr., Millinocket, ME 04462-2190, 207/723-5140, www.baxterstateparkauthority.com.

❷ NORTH TRAVELER MOUNTAIN
5 mi/3.5 hr 👥3 ⛰10

in northern Baxter State Park

BEST (

The superstar of Baxter's northern mountains is the Traveler (3,541 ft.), a sprawling, five-peaked ancient volcano rising high above Pogy Notch. North Traveler (3,144 ft.) is the most popular of the Traveler summits and its trailhead is easily accessed from the South Branch Pond Campground. With much of the mountain left denuded by a massive fire over a century ago, North Traveler is a rugged, somewhat rocky climb along mostly uncovered ridges. A total elevation gain of more than 2,000 feet, North Traveler's sweeping views rank among Baxter's most scenic.

From the South Branch Pond Campground parking area, walk the road into the campground. North Traveler defines the skyline to the east, or left, just above the Lower South Branch Pond. Bear left after entering the campground and pass several sites before reaching a large signpost for the Pogy Notch trailhead. Here, turn right (south) and follow Pogy Notch 0.1 mile to a well-marked trail junction. North Traveler Trail is to the left, a blue-blazed trail that begins with a fairly steep ascent along the edge of North Ridge (Pogy Notch is also blue-blazed, so be sure to look for the North Traveler Trail sign). Less than a half mile from the trailhead, forest cover ends and the trail emerges onto open ledges with excellent views of the two South Branch Ponds, across to the South Branch Mountains, and south toward Katahdin. The vistas only improve as you continue up the uncovered ridge, but loose stones and areas of rocky terrain can make footing difficult (especially around the 0.8 mile mark). After leveling out for a short stretch, the trail climbs again, passing through a grove of stunted birch trees and eventually to a luscious upland meadow (at 2.0 miles). Continue following the blazes and cairns to the broad summit, where stunning views are seen in every direction, including north to the wilderness and south to the main summit of the Traveler. Descend the way you came.

User Groups: Hikers only. No dogs, horses, mountain bikes, or wheelchair facilities. Trail should not be attempted in winter except by hikers experienced in mountaineering and prepared for severe weather; not suitable for skis.

Permits: No permits required. An entrance fee of $13 per vehicle is charged at the gatehouse, but vehicles bearing Maine registration enter at no charge. Parking in the park is free.

Maps: A waterproof trail map of Baxter State Park is available from the Appalachian Mountain Club (Rangeley–Stratton/Baxter State Park–Katahdin map, $7.95). For a topographic map, request Wassataquoik Lake and the Traveler from the USGS.

Directions: The trailhead is most easily accessed using Baxter State Park's northern Matagamon Gate entrance. From the junction of Routes 11 and 159 in Patten, drive west on Route 159 (Shin Pond Road) for 10 miles. At Shin Pond, Route 159 becomes Grand Lake Road, a private access road that is open for public use. Stay on Grand Lake Road, following the road for 14 miles to reach the entrance of Baxter State Park. From the gatehouse, drive 7.3 miles along Tote Road (the park's perimeter road) and turn left at the sign for South Branch Pond Campground. Drive 2.3 miles to the parking area at the end of the road.

Baxter State Park is open May 15–November 1 and December 1–March 31. During the summer season, the Matagamon Gate is open 6 A.M.–10 P.M.; the park's Togue Pond Gate is open 6 A.M.–10 P.M.—though it may open as early as 5 A.M. at the discretion of the park director. The road is not maintained to the trailhead in winter.

GPS Coordinates: 46.1079 N, 68.8979 W

Contact: Baxter State Park, 64 Balsam Dr., Millinocket, ME 04462-2190, 207/723-5140, www.baxterstateparkauthority.com.

3 TRAVELER LOOP
10.5 mi/10 hr

in northern Baxter State Park

The Traveler (3,541 ft.), along Baxter's northeast boundary, is a rocky, exposed mountain rivaled only by Katahdin for its unique features, stunning views, and difficulty in climbing—the loose rock found so abundantly here quickly becomes treacherous when wet. Bagging three of the mountain's five peaks, including the Traveler's tallest summit, this loop hike makes use of one of the park's newest trails, the challenging Traveler Trail. Opened in 2005, Traveler Trail connects Peak of the Ridges (3,225 ft.) with the Traveler's main summit and then turns north to reach the North Traveler summit (3,152 ft.). Because of the hike's length, you will want to start this one very early in the day. The complete loop nets an elevation gain of 3,700 feet from the Pogy Notch trailhead.

Leaving the South Branch Pond

Campground parking area, walk the road into the campground. Bear left after entering camp and pass several campsites before reaching a large signpost for the Pogy Notch Trail. Turn right (south) onto the blue-blazed Pogy Notch Trail. After a mile, the trail passes a junction with the Howe Brook Trail and then crosses an often-dry streambed. Reach another trail junction at 1.5 miles and turn left onto the Center Ridge Trail (also blue-blazed). Begin with a relentless and steep climb over loose rock for the first 0.7 mile. The ascent then levels out as the trail makes a more gradual climb up an open ridge. Enjoy magnificent views of the two South Branch Ponds, across to the South Branch Mountains and south toward Katahdin. At 1.2 miles, the trail becomes rocky and somewhat steep again, forcing you to scramble across an extensive talus field to reach the Peak of the Ridges summit, 2.1 miles from the Center Ridge trailhead.

Leave the summit via the Traveler Trail (blue-blazed), descending east along a sharp ridge of exposed volcanic rhyolite. At 0.7 mile from the Traveler trailhead, reach a large alpine meadow. At the meadow's eastern edge, the trail begins the ascent towards the Traveler summit, pushing its way up a steep talus slope before reaching the mountain's highest peak, a total hiking distance of 1.4 miles from Peak of the Ridges. On the open summit, enjoy panoramic views in all directions, including south to Katahdin and north into the wilderness. To reach North Traveler, the Traveler Trail continues north for another 2.9 miles. Leaving the summit, the trail descends, losing a total elevation of 800 feet over the next half mile. A forested col awaits at the end of this downward progression and the beginning of another long, rocky ridge—the trail's ascent to North Traveler starts here. Completely above the tree line all the way to the North Traveler peak, the views are expansive in all directions. The Traveler Trail ends at North Traveler summit. Return to the campground using the North Traveler and Pogy Notch

trails (see *North Traveler Mountain* listing in this chapter).

User Groups: Hikers only. No dogs, horses, mountain bikes, or wheelchair facilities. Trail should not be attempted in winter except by hikers experienced in mountaineering and prepared for severe weather; not suitable for skis.

Permits: No permits required. An entrance fee of $13 per vehicle is charged at the gatehouse, but vehicles bearing Maine registration enter at no charge. Parking in the park is free.

Maps: A waterproof trail map of Baxter State Park is available from the Appalachian Mountain Club (Rangeley–Stratton/Baxter State Park–Katahdin map, $7.95). For a topographic map, request Wassataquoik Lake and the Traveler from the USGS.

Directions: Trailhead is most easily accessed using Baxter State Park's northern Matagamon Gate entrance. From the junction of Routes 11 and 159 in Patten, drive west on Route 159 (Shin Pond Road) for 10 miles. At Shin Pond, Route 159 becomes Grand Lake Road, a private access road that is open for public use. Stay on Grand Lake Road, following the road for 14 miles to reach the entrance of Baxter State Park. From the gatehouse, drive for 7.3 miles along Tote Road (the park's perimeter road) and turn left at the sign for South Branch Pond Campground. Drive 2.3 miles to the parking area at the end of the road.

Baxter State Park is open May 15–November 1 and December 1–March 31. During the summer season, the Matagamon Gate is open 6 A.M.–10 P.M.; the park's Togue Pond Gate is open 6 A.M.–10 P.M.—though it may open as early as 5 A.M. at the discretion of the park director. The road is not maintained to the trailhead in winter.

GPS Coordinates: 46.1079 N, 68.8979 W

Contact: Baxter State Park, 64 Balsam Dr., Millinocket, ME 04462-2190, 207/723-5140, www.baxterstateparkauthority.com.

MAINE

❹ RUSSELL POND/DAVIS POND LOOP

19 mi/3 days   👣4 ⛰9

in central Baxter State Park

BEST (

Visitors to this magnificent park who hike only Katahdin—especially on a busy summer weekend—may not get a true sense of Baxter's remoteness. This loop, spread out over three days to take advantage of two excellent backcountry camping areas at Russell and Davis Ponds, wanders away from the park's popular peaks and brings you deep into the wilderness and solitude of Baxter's central section. The only steep stretches of this hike are the climbs to Davis Pond in the Northwest Basin and above Davis Pond to the Northwest Plateau, and the descent off Hamlin Peak. Much of this loop is easy hiking that fit backpackers can accomplish in a few hours of hiking per day.

From the parking area at Roaring Brook Campground, walk past the ranger's cabin and follow a well-worn path for about fifty yards to the trail junction. Russell Pond Trail turns right and is a relatively flat seven-mile hike north to Russell Pond Campground. A ranger is on duty at Russell Pond and canoe rentals are available. Listen for early morning or evening splashes in the pond—it's probably a moose grazing on some underwater foliage.

Day two, the hike follows the Northwest Basin Trail. To find the trailhead, double back on the Russell Pond Trail for 0.1 mile to reach a trail junction—take Northwest Basin Trail on the right (heading southwest). Climb gradually for the next five miles, passing such trail features as rock-strewn Wassataquoik Stream, the site of an old logging camp, and a large heath-covered knoll, a glacial *roche moutonnée*. At 5.2 miles, and about 1,700 feet uphill, is the Davis Pond lean-to (sleeps four).

The final day takes you up the Northwest Basin Trail onto the rocky, alpine Northwest Plateau area. At 2.2 miles past Davis Pond, come to a trail junction. Turn left onto the Hamlin Ridge Trail, soon passing over Hamlin Peak (4,751 ft.), one of Maine's 14 4,000-footers. The trail then descends along the open, rocky Hamlin Ridge, heading almost due east. Enjoy constant views down into the soaring, cliff-ringed North Basin to your left (north) and toward Katahdin on the right (south). About two miles from Hamlin Peak, reach a trail junction with the North Basin Trail. Turn left, following the North Basin Trail a short distance to the junction with the North Basin Cutoff. Here, turn right and follow the cutoff a bit more than a half mile to the Chimney Pond Trail. Turn left and follow the Chimney Pond Trail another 2.3 miles back to Roaring Brook Campground.

Advance reservations for campsites are strongly recommended. Russell Pond has a bunkhouse (capacity 13), four tent sites, and four lean-tos (capacity 4–8); Davis Pond has one lean-to (capacity 4).

User Groups: Hikers only. No dogs, horses, mountain bikes, or wheelchair facilities. This trail should not be attempted in winter.

Permits: No permits required. An entrance fee of $13 per vehicle is charged at the gatehouse, but vehicles bearing Maine registration can enter at no charge. Parking in the park is free.

Maps: A waterproof trail map of Baxter State Park is available from the Appalachian Mountain Club (Rangeley–Stratton/Baxter State Park–Katahdin map, $7.95). For a topographic map, ask the USGS for Mount Katahdin and Katahdin Lake.

Directions: From Millinocket, head west on Central Street/Route 11/Route 157 toward State Street. Turn right at Katahdin Avenue and follow briefly before turning left at Bates Street. This street becomes Millinocket Road. After 7.4 miles, bear right at a fork onto Baxter Park Road. Follow another 8.4 miles before reaching the park's Togue Pond gate. Just beyond the gatehouse, take the right fork on the gravel Tote Road (the park's perimeter road) and drive 8.1 miles to Roaring Brook Campground. The Russell Pond Trail begins

MAINE

beside the ranger station (where there is a hiker register).

Baxter State Park is open May 15–November 1 and December 1–March 31. During the summer season, the park's Togue Pond Gate is open 6 A.M.–10 P.M.—though it may open at 5 A.M. at the discretion of the park director; the Matagamon Gate is open 6 A.M.–10 P.M. GPS Coordinates: 45.9204 N, 68.8577 W **Contact:** Baxter State Park, 64 Balsam Dr., Millinocket, ME 04462-2190, 207/723-5140, www.baxterstateparkauthority.com.

5 SOUTH TURNER MOUNTAIN
4 mi/3 hr   ▓4 ▲9

in southern Baxter State Park

Though just 3,122 feet in elevation, South Turner's craggy summit gives a rare view of the entire Katahdin massif from the east side. Be prepared to spot moose and other wildlife, but not too many people, en route to the top of this mountain near Sandy Stream Pond. South Turner is so overshadowed by the big mountain to the southwest that many hikers don't even know about it—enhancing your chances of summiting in solitude. A scenically rewarding hike, the South Turner Trail is a moderate climb of 1,638 feet from the trailhead at Roaring Brook Campground.

Leaving the parking area near the ranger station at Roaring Brook Campground, follow the Russell Pond Trail north for a quarter mile to reach a trail junction. Turn right to follow the South Turner Mountain/Sandy Stream Pond Trail. You soon reach Sandy Stream Pond's southeast shore, which the trail follows (be on the lookout for moose and other wildlife in the early morning or evening hours). Coming around to the pond's far end (0.7 mile from Roaring Brook Campground), the South Turner Mountain Trail turns right and soon begins a steep climb through dense forest. Approaching the summit, the trail's final

stretch breaks out of the trees to unparalleled views of Katahdin's open cirques. Descend the same way you came.

User Groups: Hikers only. No dogs, horses, mountain bikes, or wheelchair facilities. This trail may be difficult to snowshoe in winter and is not suitable for skis.

Permits: No permits required. An entrance fee of $13 per vehicle is charged at the gatehouse, but vehicles bearing Maine registration can enter at no charge.

Maps: A waterproof trail map of Baxter State Park is available from the Appalachian Mountain Club (Rangeley–Stratton/Baxter State Park–Katahdin map, $7.95). For a topographic map, ask the USGS for Mount Katahdin and Katahdin Lake.

Directions: From Millinocket, head west on Central Street/Route 11/Route 157 toward State Street. Turn right at Katahdin Avenue and follow briefly before turning left at Bates Street. This street becomes Millinocket Road. After 7.4 miles, bear right at the fork for Baxter Park Road. Follow another 8.4 miles before reaching the park's Togue Pond gate. Just beyond the gatehouse, take the right fork on the gravel Tote Road (the park's perimeter road) and drive 8.1 miles to Roaring Brook Campground. The Russell Pond Trail begins beside the ranger station (where there is a hiker register).

Baxter State Park is open May 15–November 1 and December 1–March 31. During the summer season, the park's Togue Pond Gate is open 6 A.M.–10 P.M.—though it may open at 5 A.M. at the discretion of the park director; the Matagamon Gate is open 6 A.M.–10 P.M. The road is not maintained to the trailhead in winter, but it can be skied. GPS Coordinates: 45.9204 N, 68.8577 W **Contact:** Baxter State Park, 64 Balsam Dr., Millinocket, ME 04462-2190, 207/723-5140, www.baxterstateparkauthority.com.

MAINE

6 SANDY STREAM POND/ WHIDDEN PONDS LOOP
2.3 mi/1 hr 🏃1 ⛰8

in southern Baxter State Park

BEST (

This relatively flat, easy loop near Roaring Brook Campground hits two ponds where moose are often seen, especially early in the morning or around dusk (when the animals are most active). Mainly a hike to take in the natural beauty of Baxter's unspoiled pond ecosystems, the ramble leads to a terrific view across the southernmost of the Whidden Ponds toward the North Basin of Hamlin and Howe Peaks. Beginning in early September, the hardwood forest of birch, ash, and beech ringing the ponds blazes with autumn color, a nice contrast to Baxter's almost unbroken sea of evergreens. Hike this loop in the morning or afternoon if you seek solitude, as pond trails are popular early evening strolls for campers at Roaring Brook.

From the ranger station at Roaring Brook Campground, follow the Russell Pond Trail a brief 0.1 mile, turning right at a marked junction onto the South Turner Mountain Trail/ Sandy Stream Pond Trail. The trail hugs the southeast shore of Sandy Stream Pond, with short spur trails leading to picturesque viewing points. As you come around the far end of the pond, the South Turner Mountain Trail leads right; this hike turns left onto the Whidden Pond Trail, following it for a mile to the first of the Whidden Ponds (also the largest and the only one directly accessed by a trail). The trail ends at a junction with the Russell Pond Trail, but you can still see more of Whidden Pond. Turn right and follow the Russell Pond Trail for 0.2 mile, walking along the shore for views toward North Basin. Turn back (south) on the Russell Pond Trail for an easy one-mile hike back to Roaring Brook Campground.

User Groups: Hikers only. No dogs, horses, mountain bikes, or wheelchair facilities. This trail should not be attempted in winter except by experienced skiers or snowshoers prepared for severe winter weather.

Permits: No permits required. An entrance fee of $13 per vehicle is charged at the gatehouse, but vehicles bearing Maine registration can enter at no charge.

Maps: A waterproof trail map of Baxter State Park is available from the Appalachian Mountain Club (Rangeley–Stratton/Baxter State Park–Katahdin map, $7.95). For a topographic map, ask the USGS for Mount Katahdin and Katahdin Lake.

Directions: From Millinocket, head west on Central Street/Route 11/Route 157 toward State Street. Turn right at Katahdin Avenue and follow briefly before turning left at Bates Street. This street becomes Millinocket Road. After 7.4 miles, bear right at the fork for Baxter Park Road. Follow another 8.4 miles before reaching the park's Togue Pond gate. Just beyond the gatehouse, take the right fork on the gravel Tote Road (the park's perimeter road) and drive 8.1 miles to Roaring Brook Campground. The Russell Pond Trail begins beside the ranger station (where there is a hiker register).

Baxter State Park is open May 15–November 1 and December 1–March 31. During the summer season, the park's Togue Pond Gate is open 6 A.M.–10 P.M.—though it may open at 5 A.M. at the discretion of the park director; the Matagamon Gate is open 6 A.M.–10 P.M. The road is not maintained to the trailhead in winter, but it can be skied.

GPS Coordinates: 45.9204 N, 68.8577 W

Contact: Baxter State Park, 64 Balsam Dr., Millinocket, ME 04462-2190, 207/723-5140, www.baxterstateparkauthority.com.

7 HAMLIN PEAK
10.2 mi/6 hr 🏃5 ⛰10

in southern Baxter State Park

Hamlin Peak, at 4,751 feet, is Maine's second highest peak and one of 14 4,000-footers in the state, though it's also considered part of the Katahdin massif. Swarms of hikers climb Katahdin on summer weekends, but far fewer venture up onto Hamlin—and they are missing a lot. The constant views along the Hamlin Ridge, both into the North Basin and back toward the South Basin and Katahdin, are among the most magnificent in Baxter. This 9.5-mile round-trip hike climbs about 3,200 feet in elevation and is fairly strenuous.

From Roaring Brook Campground, follow the Chimney Pond Trail an easy 2.3 miles to a trail junction just beyond the Basin Ponds. Turn right onto the North Basin Cutoff, which ascends steadily for approximately 0.6 mile before coming to another junction. A short distance to the right (0.1 mile) is Blueberry Knoll and views into the North Basin. Experienced hikers will see that it's possible to bushwhack down to the pair of tiny ponds on the North Basin floor and explore that rugged glacial cirque. This hike, however, turns left (southwest) onto the North Basin Trail. Follow the North Basin Trail for 0.2 mile and then take a right to begin ascending the Hamlin Ridge Trail. Two miles farther you reach Hamlin Peak, a mound of rocks slightly higher than the vast surrounding tableland, or plateau. Descend the way you came.

Special note: For visitors making this peak part of an extended stay at Baxter State Park, another enjoyable way of hiking Hamlin is from Chimney Pond Campground, which is 3.3 miles from Roaring Brook Campground via the Chimney Pond Trail. Backpack in to Chimney Pond, and hike Hamlin Peak via the Chimney Pond, North Basin, and Hamlin Ridge trails (four miles, 2.5 hours). Chimney Pond is a good staging point for hikes of Katahdin, or even for beginning the Russell Pond/Davis Pond backpacking loop in the reverse direction.

User Groups: Hikers only. No dogs, horses, mountain bikes, or wheelchair facilities. This trail should not be attempted in winter except by experienced skiers or snowshoers prepared for severe winter weather.

Permits: No permits required. An entrance fee of $13 per vehicle is charged at the gatehouse, but vehicles bearing Maine registration can enter at no charge.

Maps: A waterproof trail map of Baxter State Park is available from the Appalachian Mountain Club (Rangeley–Stratton/Baxter State Park–Katahdin map, $7.95). For a topographic map, ask the USGS for Mount Katahdin and Katahdin Lake.

Directions: From Millinocket, head west on Central Street/Route 11/Route 157 toward State Street. Turn right at Katahdin Avenue and follow briefly before turning left at Bates Street. This street becomes Millinocket Road. After 7.4 miles, bear right at the fork for Baxter Park Road. Follow another 8.4 miles before reaching the park's Togue Pond gate. Just beyond the gatehouse, take the right fork on the gravel Tote Road (the park's perimeter road) and drive 8.1 miles to Roaring Brook Campground. The Chimney Pond Trail begins beside the ranger station (where there is a hiker register).

Baxter State Park is open May 15–November 1 and December 1–March 31. During the summer season, the park's Togue Pond Gate is open 6 A.M.–10 P.M.—though it may open at 5 A.M. at the discretion of the park director; the Matagamon Gate is open 6 A.M.–10 P.M. The road is not maintained to the trailhead in winter, but it can be skied. GPS Coordinates: 45.9204 N, 68.8577 W

Contact: Baxter State Park, 64 Balsam Dr., Millinocket, ME 04462-2190, 207/723-5140, www.baxterstateparkauthority.com.

8 KATAHDIN: KNIFE EDGE LOOP

9.3 mi/9 hr   🏃5 ⛰10

in southern Baxter State Park

Truly a mountain experience like no other in New England, this hike is the best way to take in as much of Maine's greatest mountain as possible in a day. Offering an elevation gain of 3,800 feet and made up almost entirely of rugged terrain, the loop encompasses Chimney Pond (set deep in the vast glacial cirque known as the South Basin), a challenging scramble up the Cathedral Trail, Katahdin's four peaks, the infamous Knife Edge arête, and the open Keep Ridge. Don't underestimate its length, difficulty, or dangers: Since the park started keeping records in 1926, 44 hiker deaths have occurred on Katahdin, usually the result of falls or lightning strikes.

From the parking area at Roaring Brook Campground, follow the fairly easy Chimney Pond Trail 3.3 miles east to the pond camping area (many visitors make this hike and go no farther because the views from Chimney Pond are so beautiful). Behind the Chimney Pond ranger station, pick up the Cathedral Trail, which climbs steeply up a rockslide and the right flank of Katahdin's sweeping head wall, passing the three prominent stone buttresses known as the Cathedrals. You can scramble off trail onto each of the Cathedrals for great South Basin views.

At 1.4 miles from the Cathedral trailhead, bear left where the trail forks, soon reaching a junction (in 0.1 miles) with the Saddle Trail and the more level ground of the Katahdin Tableland (at 1.5 miles). Turn left (southeast) onto the Saddle Trail and walk 0.2 mile to the main summit, Baxter Peak, where a large sign marks the highest point in Maine (5,267 ft.) and the Appalachian Trail's northern terminus. If high winds or the threat of thunderstorms have not forced rangers to temporarily close the next leg of the loop, continue straight over the summit (southeast) and onto the Knife Edge Trail, an increasingly narrow, rocky ridge that runs 1.1 miles across the top of South Basin to Pamola Peak. The Knife Edge Trail first hooks left to reach South Peak before beginning the precipitous 0.8-mile stretch to Pamola Peak. At times, the footpath is barely two feet wide, with sharp drops to either side. At Chimney Peak, scramble down the vertical wall of a ridge cleft, a spot known

© PETE LORD

High atop Katahdin's South Basin, hikers negotiate the narrow, rocky terrain of the Knife Edge Trail.

to intimidate more than a few hikers. Then you scramble up the other side (not as difficult) onto Pamola Peak. From here, turn right (east) on the Helon Taylor Trail, which descends the Keep Ridge, much of it open, for 3.1 miles to the Chimney Pond Trail. Turn right and walk 0.1 mile back to Roaring Brook Campground.

User Groups: Hikers only. No dogs, horses, mountain bikes, or wheelchair facilities. This trail should not be attempted in winter except by hikers experienced in mountaineering and prepared for severe winter weather, and is only suitable for skis as far as Chimney Pond.

Permits: No permits required. An entrance fee of $13 per vehicle is charged at the gatehouse, but vehicles bearing Maine registration can enter at no charge.

Maps: A waterproof trail map of Baxter State Park is available from the Appalachian Mountain Club (Rangeley–Stratton/Baxter State Park–Katahdin map, $7.95). For a topographic map, ask the USGS for Mount Katahdin and Katahdin Lake.

Directions: From Millinocket, head west on Central Street/Route 11/Route 157 toward State Street. Turn right at Katahdin Avenue and follow briefly before turning left at Bates Street. This street becomes Millinocket Road. After 7.4 miles, bear right at the fork for Baxter Park Road. Follow another 8.4 miles before reaching the park's Togue Pond gate. Just

MAINE

beyond the gatehouse, take the right fork on the gravel Tote Road (the park's perimeter road) and drive 8.1 miles to Roaring Brook Campground. The Chimney Pond Trail begins beside the ranger station (where there is a hiker register).

Baxter State Park is open May 15–November 1 and December 1–March 31. During the summer season, the park's Togue Pond Gate is open 6 A.M.–10 P.M.—though it may open at 5 A.M. at the discretion of the park director; the Matagamon Gate is open 6 A.M.–10 P.M. The road is not maintained to the trailhead in winter, but it can be skied.

GPS Coordinates: 45.9204 N, 68.8577 W

Contact: Baxter State Park, 64 Balsam Dr., Millinocket, ME 04462-2190, 207/723-5140, www.baxterstateparkauthority.com.

9 KATAHDIN: SADDLE TRAIL
11 mi/7 hr   🏃5 ⛰10

in southern Baxter State Park

By using the high plateau of the Katahdin Tableland for almost half its ascent to Baxter Peak (5,267 ft.), the Saddle Trail, a total climb of 2,353 feet from its trailhead at Chimney Pond Campground, is the most gradual approach to the top of Katahdin. The strenuous part of this summit trail comes at the very beginning—a steep scramble up the loose gravel and rock of the Saddle Slide.

From the Roaring Brook Campground parking area, proceed into the campground to pick up the westbound Chimney Pond Trail (look for the large trail signpost in the middle of the camp near the ranger's station). Follow the well-worn trail, a former tote road, for 3.3 miles to Chimney Pond Campground (2,914 ft.). Find the Saddle trailhead near the ranger's station in the middle of the campground (look for the large trail signpost) and proceed west. The blue-blazed trail ascends gradually through dense conifer cover before breaking out of the woods (at 1.0 mile) and

beginning the steep ascent up the Saddle Slide. It's a vigorous scramble for the next 0.2 mile as you make your way among giant granite boulders and loose rock, the result of a landslide that took place in 1893. Pay attention to your footing and keep an eye on the progress of those ahead of you—accidentally dislodge a rock and it's easy to send a sizeable stone hurtling down towards an unsuspecting hiker. Reaching the Tableland (4,300 ft.), the trail soon comes to a junction. Bear left to stay on the Saddle Trail and continue one more mile towards Baxter Peak, passing two other trail junctions before standing on Katahdin's summit. Return the way you came.

User Groups: Hikers only. No wheelchair facilities. Bikes, dogs, and horses are prohibited. This trail should not be attempted in winter except by hikers experienced in mountaineering and prepared for severe winter weather, and is only suitable for skis as far as Chimney Pond.

Permits: No permits required. An entrance fee of $13 per vehicle is charged at the gatehouse, but vehicles bearing Maine registration can enter at no charge.

Maps: A waterproof trail map of Baxter State Park is available from the Appalachian Mountain Club (Rangeley–Stratton/Baxter State Park–Katahdin map, $7.95). For a topographic map, ask the USGS for Mount Katahdin and Katahdin Lake.

Directions: From Millinocket, head west on Central Street/Route 11/Route 157 toward State Street. Turn right at Katahdin Avenue and follow briefly before turning left at Bates Street. This street becomes Millinocket Road. After 7.4 miles, bear right at the fork for Baxter Park Road. Follow another 8.4 miles before reaching the park's Togue Pond gate. Just beyond the gatehouse, take the right fork on the gravel Tote Road (the park's perimeter road) and drive 8.1 miles to the parking area at Roaring Brook Campground. The Chimney Pond Trail begins beside the ranger station (where there is a hiker register).

Baxter State Park is open May 15–November

MAINE

1 and December 1–March 31. During the summer season, the park's Togue Pond Gate opens is open 6 A.M.–10 P.M.—though it may open at 5 A.M. at the discretion of the park director; the Matagamon Gate is open 6 A.M.–10 P.M. The road is not maintained to the trailhead in winter, but it can be skied. GPS Coordinates: 45.9159 N, 68.9126 W
Contact: Baxter State Park, 64 Balsam Dr., Millinocket, ME 04462-2190, 207/723-5140, www.baxterstateparkauthority.com.

⓾ KATAHDIN: ABOL TRAIL
7.6 mi/7 hr   🥾5 △10

in southern Baxter State Park

This trail follows the path of the 1816 Abol landslide, and may be the oldest existing route up the 5,267-foot Katahdin. Ascending the massif from the southwest, Abol Trail is the shortest way to Katahdin's main summit, Baxter Peak, but by no means easy: It climbs 4,000 feet, and the slide's steepness and loose rock make for an arduous ascent, complicated by the possibility of falling rock. And descending this trail is harder than going up, though not impossible (but it can be very rough going on the knees).

From the Abol Campground day-use parking area, find the prominently marked Abol trailhead at the northern end of the campground. The trail leads through woods for more than a mile to the broad slide base. Pick your way carefully up the slide; watch for falling rock caused by hikers above, and take care not to kick anything down onto hikers below. At 2.6 miles, the trail reaches the level ground of the Tableland, a beautiful, sprawling alpine plateau. At 2.8 miles, near Thoreau Spring, the blue-blazed Abol Trail connects with the Hunt Trail. Turn right on the white-blazed Hunt Trail for the final mile to Baxter Peak, both Katahdin's summit and the Appalachian Trail's northern terminus. By shuttling vehicles between Abol

and Katahdin Stream Campgrounds, you can ascend the Abol and descend the Hunt Trail (adding 1.4 miles to your trek). Otherwise, descend the way you came.
User Groups: Hikers only. No wheelchair facilities. Bikes, dogs, and horses are prohibited. This trail should not be attempted in winter except by hikers experienced in mountaineering and prepared for severe winter weather; not suitable for skis.
Permits: No permits required. An entrance fee of $13 per vehicle is charged at the gatehouse, but vehicles bearing Maine registration can enter at no charge.
Maps: A waterproof trail map of Baxter State Park is available from the Appalachian Mountain Club (Rangeley–Stratton/Baxter State Park–Katahdin map, $7.95). For a topographic map, ask the USGS for Mount Katahdin and Katahdin Lake.
Directions: From Millinocket, head west on Central Street/Route 11/Route 157 toward State Street. Turn right at Katahdin Avenue and follow briefly before turning left at Bates Street. This street becomes Millinocket Road. After 7.4 miles, bear right at the fork for Baxter Park Road. Follow another 8.4 miles before reaching the park's Togue Pond gate. Just beyond the gatehouse, take the right fork on the gravel Tote Road (the park's perimeter road) and drive 5.7 miles to Abol Campground and day-use parking on the left, opposite the campground entrance.

Baxter State Park is open May 15–November 1 and December 1–March 31. During the summer season, the park's Togue Pond Gate is open 6 A.M.–10 P.M.—though it may open at 5 A.M. at the discretion of the park director; the Matagamon Gate is open 6 A.M.–10 P.M. The road is not maintained to the trailhead in winter, but it can be skied. GPS Coordinates: 45.8740 N, 68.9660 W
Contact: Baxter State Park, 64 Balsam Dr., Millinocket, ME 04462-2190, 207/723-5140, www.baxterstateparkauthority.com.

11 LITTLE ABOL FALLS
1.6 mi/1 hr

in southern Baxter State Park

Leaving from the Abol Campground in the shadow of Katahdin's soaring south wall, this easy walk along a path of packed dirt and gravel ascends gently 0.8 mile to a scenic waterfall on a branch of Abol Stream. With a shear drop of 15 feet, the fall forms a pleasant pool—and a popular swimming hole. Nearby campers and day hikers on their way back down the mountain flock to the cooling waters, especially on hot summer days. If you want some solitude at the falls, try going in the early morning.

From the Abol Campground parking area, walk up the campground road. The Little Abol Falls Trail begins at the upper end of the campground, between lean-tos #8 and #10. Follow the well-worn path and take in views of the southwest side of Katahdin, including Abol Slide. At 0.8 mile, reach the stream and follow alongside it as the water makes a sudden drop to the pool below. The trail takes you down to the pool. Return the way you came.

User Groups: Hikers only. No wheelchair facilities. Bikes, dogs, and horses are prohibited.

Permits: No permits required. An entrance fee of $13 per vehicle is charged at the gatehouse, but vehicles bearing Maine registration can enter at no charge.

Maps: A waterproof trail map of Baxter State Park is available from the Appalachian Mountain Club (Rangeley–Stratton/Baxter State Park–Katahdin map, $7.95). For a topographic map, ask the USGS for Mount Katahdin and Katahdin Lake.

Directions: From Millinocket, head west on Central Street/Route 11/Route 157 toward State Street. Turn right at Katahdin Avenue and follow briefly before turning left at Bates Street. This street becomes Millinocket Road. After 7.4 miles, bear right at the fork for Baxter Park Road. Follow another 8.4 miles before reaching the park's Togue Pond gate. Just beyond the gatehouse, take the right fork on the gravel Tote Road (the park's perimeter road) and drive 5.7 miles to Abol Campground and day-use parking on the left, opposite the campground entrance.

Baxter State Park is open May 15–November 1 and December 1–March 31. During the summer season, the park's Togue Pond Gate is open 6 A.M.–10 P.M.—though it may open at 5 A.M. at the discretion of the park director; the Matagamon Gate is open 6 A.M.–10 P.M. The road is not maintained to the trailhead in winter, but it can be skied.

GPS Coordinates: 45.8740 N, 68.9616 W

Contact: Baxter State Park, 64 Balsam Dr., Millinocket, ME 04462-2190, 207/723-5140, www.baxterstateparkauthority.com.

12 KATAHDIN: HUNT TRAIL
10 mi/8 hr

in southern Baxter State Park

Ascending the Katahdin massif (5,267 ft.) from the southwest, the rugged Hunt Trail gains 4,100 feet in elevation from its trailhead near Katahdin Stream Campground, much of it above timberline. The final stretch of the Appalachian Trail for northbound through-hikers on their way to the mountain's Baxter Peak summit, the Hunt Trail ends the epic 2,174-mile journey with a number of outstanding features: waterfalls, boulder fields, an expansive tableland, almost limitless views, and the chance to stand atop the highest spot in Maine. This was the same trail 19th century naturalist Henry David Thoreau used on his climb to Katahdin (described in his book, *The Maine Woods*). Thoreau wrote about the solitude of his ascent, but you probably won't be able to do the same. From the start of the warm weather hiking season in July until its end on October 15, the Hunt Trail is one of the most heavily trafficked in the whole of Baxter.

Pick up the white-blazed Hunt Trail at the

northeast end of Katahdin Stream Campground. Running parallel to Katahdin Stream for the first mile, the climb here is gradual and mainly forest covered. At 2.8 miles from the campground, the trail abruptly breaks out above the trees and the ascent quickly steepens. Around the three-mile mark, iron rungs drilled into the stone help you scale a short, vertical rock face.

Topping the rocky, open ridge crest, the trail reaches the Tableland, a mile-wide plateau at about 4,500 feet, a tundra littered with rocks. The trail passes Thoreau Spring near the Abol Trail junction before finally ascending to the main summit, panoramic Baxter Peak. A large sign marks the Appalachian Trail's northern terminus. Some 2,000 feet below is the blue dot of Chimney Pond. To the right (east) is the serrated crest of the Knife Edge, and to the north lie Hamlin Peak, the Howe Peaks, and the vast Baxter Park wilderness. Descend the same way you came up.

User Groups: Hikers only. No wheelchair facilities. Bikes, dogs, and horses are prohibited. This trail should not be attempted in winter except by hikers experienced in mountaineering and prepared for severe winter weather; not suitable for skis.

Permits: No permits required. An entrance fee of $13 per vehicle is charged at the gatehouse, but vehicles bearing Maine registration can enter at no charge.

Maps: A waterproof trail map of Baxter State Park is available from the Appalachian Mountain Club (Rangeley–Stratton/Baxter State Park–Katahdin map, $7.95). For a topographic map, ask the USGS for Mount Katahdin and Katahdin Lake.

Directions: From Millinocket, head west on Central Street/Route 11/Route 157 toward State Street. Turn right at Katahdin Avenue and follow briefly before turning left at Bates Street. This street becomes Millinocket Road. After 7.4 miles, bear right at the fork for Baxter Park Road. Follow another 8.4 miles before reaching the park's Togue Pond gate. Just beyond the gatehouse, take the right fork on the gravel Tote Road (the park's perimeter road) and drive eight miles to Katahdin Stream Campground. Turn right onto the campground road and continue 0.1 mile to the day-use parking area.

Baxter State Park is open May 15–November 1 and December 1–March 31. During the summer season, the park's Togue Pond Gate is open 6 A.M.–10 P.M.—though it may open at 5 A.M. at the discretion of the park director; the Matagamon Gate is open 6 A.M.–10 P.M. The road is not maintained to the trailhead in winter, but it can be skied.

GPS Coordinates: 45.8873 N, 68.9983 W

Contact: Baxter State Park, 64 Balsam Dr., Millinocket, ME 04462-2190, 207/723-5140, www.baxterstateparkauthority.com.

13 KATAHDIN STREAM FALLS
2.4 mi/1.5 hr

in southern Baxter State Park

A popular stopping off point for hikers ascending (and descending) Katahdin along the Hunt Trail, Katahdin Stream Falls tumbles about 50 feet and is visible from the trail after an easy walk of just over a mile up from the Hunt trailhead. Leaving the Katahdin Stream Campground parking area, follow the white blazes of the Hunt Trail, which is the Appalachian Trail's final stretch. It ascends easily through the woods. After passing a junction with the Owl Trail at the one-mile mark, continue 0.1 mile and cross on a wooden bridge over Katahdin Stream. Just 0.1 mile farther, a short spur trail leads to the waterfall. Enjoy the cascading spray and head back the way you came.

User Groups: Hikers only. No wheelchair facilities. Bikes, dogs, and horses are prohibited. This trail should not be attempted in winter except by hikers experienced in mountaineering and prepared for severe winter weather; not suitable for skis.

Permits: No permits required. An entrance fee of $13 per vehicle is charged at the gatehouse, but vehicles bearing Maine registration can enter at no charge.

Maps: A waterproof trail map of Baxter State Park is available from the Appalachian Mountain Club (Rangeley–Stratton/Baxter State Park–Katahdin map, $7.95). For a topographic map, ask the USGS for Mount Katahdin and Katahdin Lake.

Directions: From Millinocket, head west on Central Street/Route 11/Route 157 toward State Street. Turn right at Katahdin Avenue and follow briefly before turning left at Bates Street. This street becomes Millinocket Road. After 7.4 miles, bear right at the fork for Baxter Park Road. Follow another 8.4 miles before reaching the park's Togue Pond gate. Just beyond the gatehouse, take the right fork on the gravel Tote Road (the park's perimeter road) and drive eight miles to Katahdin Stream Campground. Turn right onto the campground road and continue 0.1 mile to the day-use parking area.

Baxter State Park is open May 15–November 1 and December 1–March 31. During the summer season, the park's Togue Pond Gate is open 6 A.M.–10 P.M.—though it may open at 5 A.M. at the discretion of the park director; the Matagamon Gate is open 6 A.M.–10 P.M. The road is not maintained to the trailhead in winter, but it can be skied.

GPS Coordinates: 45.8873 N, 68.9983 W

Contact: Baxter State Park, 64 Balsam Dr., Millinocket, ME 04462-2190, 207/723-5140, www.baxterstateparkauthority.com.

14 THE OWL

6 mi/6 hr   🥾5   ⛰10

in southern Baxter State Park

One of the most arduous hikes in Baxter State Park and one of its best-kept secrets, this six-mile round-tripper climbs some 2,600 feet to the 3,736-foot summit of the Owl, visible from the Hunt Trail/Appalachian Trail ridge on neighboring Katahdin.

From the day-use parking area at Katahdin Stream Campground, follow the white blazes of the Hunt Trail, the Appalachian Trail's final stretch, and ascend easily through the woods. After one mile, turn left at the sign for the Owl Trail, and if your timing is right, you're in for a sweet treat—the trail here is lined with ripe blueberries in late August and early September. In less than a mile from the Hunt Trail, cross a boulder field. Continue on and about 0.2 mile below the summit, you emerge onto an open ledge with a great view down into the Katahdin Stream ravine and across to Katahdin. Some hikers may want to turn around from here because the trail grows increasingly difficult and exposed.

If you decide to persevere, scramble up rocks to a second ledge, where a boulder perches at the brink of a precipice (is this a watchful owl perched on its branch?). After another short scramble, you reach the level shoulder of the Owl. The trail follows the crest of that narrow ridge, ducking briefly through a subalpine forest and ascending slightly to the bare ledges at the summit, where there are sweeping views in every direction. An example of Baxter's famed striped forest (alternating waves of old and new growth forest) is visible to the west. Katahdin dominates the skyline to the east; the Northwest Plateau lies to the northeast; the Brothers, Coe, and O-J-I to the west; and the wilderness lakes along the Appalachian Trail to the south. Descend along the same route.

User Groups: Hikers only. No wheelchair facilities. Bikes, dogs, and horses are prohibited. This trail should not be attempted in winter except by hikers experienced in mountaineering and prepared for severe winter weather; not suitable for skis.

Permits: No permits required. An entrance fee of $13 per vehicle is charged at the gatehouse, but vehicles bearing Maine registration can enter at no charge.

Maps: A waterproof trail map of Baxter State Park is available from the Appalachian

MAINE

Mountain Club (Rangeley–Stratton/Baxter State Park–Katahdin map, $7.95). For topographic area maps, request Doubletop Mountain and Mount Katahdin from the USGS.

Directions: From Millinocket, head west on Central Street/Route 11/Route 157 toward State Street. Turn right at Katahdin Avenue and follow briefly before turning left at Bates Street. This street becomes Millinocket Road. After 7.4 miles, bear right at the fork for Baxter Park Road. Follow another 8.4 miles before reaching the park's Togue Pond gate. Just beyond the gatehouse, take the right fork on the gravel Tote Road (the park's perimeter road) and drive eight miles to Katahdin Stream Campground. Turn right onto the campground road and continue 0.1 mile to the day-use parking area.

Baxter State Park is open May 15–November 1 and December 1–March 31. During the summer season, the park's Togue Pond Gate is open 6 A.M.–10 P.M.—though it may open at 5 A.M. at the discretion of the park director; the Matagamon Gate is open 6 A.M.–10 P.M. The road is not maintained to the trailhead in winter, but it can be skied.

GPS Coordinates: 45.8873 N, 68.9983 W

Contact: Baxter State Park, 64 Balsam Dr., Millinocket, ME 04462-2190, 207/723-5140, www.baxterstateparkauthority.com.

15 NORTH BROTHER
9.0 mi/6 hr   ⚎4 ⛰10

in southern Baxter State Park

At 4,143 feet, Maine's seventh-highest mountain has a fairly extensive summit area above the tree line and the excellent views from the peak encompass Katahdin to the southeast, the remote Northwest Plateau and Basin to the east, Fort and Traveler mountains to the north, Doubletop to the west, and the wild, trail-less area known as the Klondike to the immediate south. The hike gains about 2,900 feet in elevation.

From the Slide Dam Picnic Area parking lot, follow the gently ascending Marston Trail almost due west for 1.2 miles. Reaching a trail junction, the Marston Trail turns sharply left (north) and continues on to a small pond (at 2.2 miles from the trailhead). Here, the climb becomes suddenly steep and relentless as you ascend a basin wall, a strenuous 0.7 mile. At the top of the basin, the trail flattens out for the next 0.8 mile before dropping into a sag between North and South Brother and reaching another junction. To the right (south) is the summit trail for South Brother (3,930 feet). To reach the summit of North Brother, turn left and climb another 0.8 mile. A good example of Baxter's famous striped forest (alternating waves of old and new growth forest) is visible between South and North Brother. Return the same way you hiked up.

Special note: You can combine this hike with the hike up Mount Coe, and bag South Brother as well, in a loop of 9.4 miles. The best route is to ascend the Mount Coe slide, hitting Coe first, then continuing on the Mount Coe Trail to South Brother, and finally bagging North Brother, then descending the Marston Trail. (See the *Mount Coe* listing in this chapter.)

User Groups: Hikers only. No wheelchair facilities. Bikes, dogs, and horses are prohibited. This trail should not be attempted in winter except by hikers experienced in mountaineering and prepared for severe winter weather; not suitable for skis.

Permits: No permits required. An entrance fee of $13 per vehicle is charged at the gatehouse, but vehicles bearing Maine registration can enter at no charge.

Maps: A waterproof trail map of Baxter State Park is available from the Appalachian Mountain Club (Rangeley–Stratton/Baxter State Park–Katahdin map, $7.95). For topographic area maps, request Doubletop Mountain and Mount Katahdin from the USGS.

Directions: From Millinocket, head west on Central Street/Route 11/Route 157 toward State Street. Turn right at Katahdin Avenue and follow briefly before turning left at Bates Street. This street becomes Millinocket Road. After 7.4 miles, bear right at the fork for Baxter Park Road. Follow another 8.4 miles before reaching the park's Togue Pond gate. Just beyond the gatehouse, take the gravel Tote Road's left fork and drive 13.5 miles to a parking area on the right for the Marston Trail.

Baxter State Park is open May 15–November 1 and December 1–March 31. During the summer season, the park's Togue Pond Gate is open 6 A.M.–10 P.M.—though it may open at 5 A.M. at the discretion of the park director; the Matagamon Gate is open 6 A.M.–10 P.M. The road is not maintained to the trailhead in winter, but it can be skied.

GPS Coordinates: 45.9406 N, 69.0433 W

Contact: Baxter State Park, 64 Balsam Dr., Millinocket, ME 04462-2190, 207/723-5140, www.baxterstateparkauthority.com.

16 MOUNT COE
6.6 mi/6 hr

in southern Baxter State Park

Mount Coe's 3,764-foot summit has a sweeping view of the southern end of Baxter State Park, including east over the trail-less wilderness area of the Klondike and on toward Katahdin and the Northwest Plateau. This 6.6-mile out-and-back hike ascends about 2,500 feet.

From the Slide Dam Picnic Area parking lot, follow the Marston Trail for 1.2 miles to a trail junction. Bear right here onto the Mount Coe Trail. It ascends easily at first, reaching the foot of the Mount Coe rockslide, still in the forest, within a quarter of a mile. The trail emerges about a mile farther onto the open, broad scar of the slide, and for the next half mile climbs the slide's steep slabs and loose stone; this section becomes treacherous when wet, with the potential for injurious falls. Watch closely for the blazes and rock cairns because the trail zigzags several times across the slide.

Near the top of the slide, a side trail—easy to overlook—branches right, leading 0.7 mile to the Mount O-J-I summit. This hike continues straight up the slide, enters the scrub forest, and reaches the Mount Coe summit 3.3 miles from the Marston trailhead. This hike descends the same way you came.

User Groups: Hikers only. No wheelchair facilities. Bikes, dogs, and horses are prohibited. This trail should not be attempted in winter except by hikers experienced in mountaineering and prepared for severe winter weather, and is not suitable for skis.

Permits: No permits required. An entrance fee of $13 per vehicle is charged at the gatehouse, but vehicles bearing Maine registration can enter at no charge.

Maps: A waterproof trail map of Baxter State Park is available from the Appalachian Mountain Club (Rangeley–Stratton/Baxter State Park–Katahdin map, $7.95). For topographic area maps, request Doubletop Mountain and Mount Katahdin from the USGS.

Directions: From Millinocket, head west on Central Street/Route 11/Route 157 toward State Street. Turn right at Katahdin Avenue and follow briefly before turning left at Bates Street. This street becomes Millinocket Road. After 7.4 miles, bear right at the fork for Baxter Park Road. Follow another 8.4 miles before reaching the park's Togue Pond gate. Just beyond the gatehouse, take the gravel Tote Road's left fork and drive 13.5 miles to a parking area on the right for the Marston Trail.

Baxter State Park is open May 15–November 1 and December 1–March 31. During the summer season, the park's Togue Pond Gate is open 6 A.M.–10 P.M.—though it may open at 5 A.M. at the discretion of the park director; the Matagamon Gate is open 6 A.M.–10 P.M. The road is not maintained to the trailhead in winter, but it can be skied.

GPS Coordinates: 45.9406 N, 69.0433 W

Contact: Baxter State Park, 64 Balsam Dr., Millinocket, ME 04462-2190, 207/723-5140, www.baxterstateparkauthority.com.

MAINE

17 MOUNT O-J-I
5.8 mi/6 hr

in southern Baxter State Park

O-J-I takes its name from the shapes of three slides that—when seen from the southwest—resemble those letters (although the slides have expanded and the letters have become obscured in recent decades). This 5.8-mile loop up 3,410-foot Mount O-J-I is a very strenuous hike. It climbs about 2,300 feet, but more significantly, involves fairly serious scrambling. The South Slide trail to the summit is steep, with lots of loose rock and slabs that are hazardous when wet. Hiking time can vary greatly depending upon your comfort level on exposed rock. But you enjoy extensive views from the slides to the west and south, and excellent views from points near the summit.

From the Foster Field parking area, walk the road toward Foster Field for about 50 feet and turn right onto the South Slide Trail. For the first 0.4 mile the terrain is flat, crossing wet areas. At 1.8 miles from the trailhead, the slide begins. Ascend steeply and scramble your way up the loose rock, carefully following the trail's cairns and blue blazes. At 2.4 miles, the trail reaches the head of the slide and reenters the woods for a more gradual climb. Pass a trail junction at 2.7 miles (you can follow the O-J-I Link trail here to use neighboring Mount Coe as an alternate descent route). Continue on 0.1 mile and pass another trail junction (a short spur to a scenic overlook). At 2.9 miles from the trailhead, reach the summit of O-J-I, with excellent views of the wild Klondike Basin area of Baxter, Mount Coe, and the west side of Katahdin. Return the way you came.

User Groups: Hikers only. No wheelchair facilities. Bikes, dogs, and horses are prohibited. This trail should not be attempted in winter except by hikers experienced in mountaineering and prepared for severe winter weather; not suitable for skis.

Permits: No permits required. An entrance fee

of $13 per vehicle is charged at the gatehouse, but vehicles bearing Maine registration can enter at no charge.

Maps: A waterproof trail map of Baxter State Park is available from the Appalachian Mountain Club (Rangeley–Stratton/Baxter State Park–Katahdin map, $7.95). For topographic area maps, request Doubletop Mountain and Mount Katahdin from the USGS.

Directions: From Millinocket, head west on Central Street/Route 11/Route 157 toward State Street. Turn right at Katahdin Avenue and follow briefly before turning left at Bates Street. This street becomes Millinocket Road. After 7.4 miles, bear right at the fork for Baxter Park Road. Follow another 8.4 miles before reaching the park's Togue Pond gate. Just beyond the gatehouse, take the gravel Tote Road's left fork and drive 10.5 miles to a day-use parking area, just before Foster Field.

Baxter State Park is open May 15–November 1 and December 1–March 31. During the summer season, the park's Togue Pond Gate is open 6 A.M.–10 P.M.—though it may open at 5 A.M. at the discretion of the park director; the Matagamon Gate is open 6 A.M.–10 P.M. The road is not maintained to the trailhead in winter, but it can be skied.

GPS Coordinates: 45.9036 N, 69.0372 W

Contact: Baxter State Park, 64 Balsam Dr., Millinocket, ME 04462-2190, 207/723-5140, www.baxterstateparkauthority.com.

18 DOUBLETOP MOUNTAIN
6 mi/5.5 hr

in southern Baxter State Park

Measuring 3,488 feet, Doubletop Mountain's distinctive high ridge stands out prominently from various points around Baxter State Park's south end, rising like an upturned ax blade above the narrow valley of Nesowadnehunk Stream. Much of the quarter mile of ridge connecting the north and south peaks lies above the tree line, affording outstanding views of

MAINE

Katahdin to the east, the cluster of peaks immediately north that include the Brothers, Coe, and O-J-I, and the wilderness lakes to the south. This six-mile hike ascends about 2,200 feet.

From the Nesowadnehunk Campground parking area, follow the road into the campground and past campsites. At half a mile in, the road ends at the Doubletop trailhead. The trail is flat until crossing a stream at 1.2 miles. Here begins a very steep climb of almost two miles, leveling out briefly on the mountain's north shoulder, and then ascending again. After climbing a short iron ladder, you emerge above the forest, a few steps from the North Peak of Doubletop (3,488 ft.). The trail drops off that summit to the west, then turns south and follows the ridge for 0.2 mile to the lower South Peak. Return the same way you hiked up.

User Groups: Hikers only. No wheelchair facilities. Bikes, dogs, and horses are prohibited. This trail should not be attempted in winter except by hikers experienced in mountaineering and prepared for severe winter weather; not suitable for skis.

Permits: No permits required. An entrance fee of $13 per vehicle is charged at the gatehouse, but vehicles bearing Maine registration can enter at no charge.

Maps: A waterproof trail map of Baxter State Park is available from the Appalachian Mountain Club (Rangeley–Stratton/Baxter State Park–Katahdin map, $7.95). For topographic area maps, request Doubletop Mountain and Mount Katahdin from the USGS.

Directions: From Millinocket, head west on Central Street/Route 11/Route 157 toward State Street. Turn right at Katahdin Avenue and follow briefly before turning left at Bates Street. This street becomes Millinocket Road. After 7.4 miles, bear right at the fork for Baxter Park Road. Follow another 8.4 miles before reaching the park's Togue Pond gate. Just beyond the gatehouse, take the gravel Tote Road's left fork and drive 16.9 miles, then turn left into the Nesowadnehunk Field

Campground. Drive 0.3 mile to the parking area on the right.

Baxter State Park is open May 15–November 1 and from December 1–March 31. During the summer season, the park's Togue Pond Gate is open 6 A.M.–10 P.M.—though it may open at 5 A.M. at the discretion of the park director; the Matagamon Gate is open 6 A.M.–10 P.M. The road is not maintained to the trailhead in winter, but it can be skied. GPS Coordinates: 45.9736 N, 69.0755 W

Contact: Baxter State Park, 64 Balsam Dr., Millinocket, ME 04462-2190, 207/723-5140, www.baxterstateparkauthority.com.

19 KIDNEY POND LOOP
3.1 mi/1.5 hr   🚶1 ⛺8

in southern Baxter State Park

BEST (

This easy 3.1-mile loop around Kidney Pond offers a chance to see moose and pondlife, and comes with good views across the pond toward Katahdin, Doubletop, and O-J-I. Side paths lead to such scenic viewing spots as the Colt's Point peninsula; other paths radiate outward from the loop trail, leading the way to Rocky Pond and other nearby ponds. This is the perfect spot for a family outing to Baxter: Summertime nature programs for kids (run by park staff) often take place in and around the Kidney Pond area.

From the rear of the parking area for Kidney Pond Campground, pick up the trailhead at a sign for the Kidney Pond Loop. The trail follows the pond's shore at first, then skirts wide of it into the woods at its southern end. Pass through mixed forest (a great place to find and identify animal tracks), follow and cross a shallow stream, and eventually reach the campground road. Turn left on the road and walk the quarter mile back to the parking area.

User Groups: Hikers only. No wheelchair facilities. Bikes, dogs, and horses are prohibited.
Permits: No permits required. An entrance fee

© PETE LORD

Moose are a common sight in Maine's North Woods.

of $13 per vehicle is charged at the gatehouse, but vehicles bearing Maine registration can enter at no charge.

Maps: A waterproof trail map of Baxter State Park is available from the Appalachian Mountain Club (Rangeley–Stratton/Baxter State Park–Katahdin map, $7.95). For topographic area maps, request Doubletop Mountain from the USGS.

Directions: From Millinocket, head west on Central Street/Route 11/Route 157 toward State Street. Turn right at Katahdin Avenue and follow briefly before turning left at Bates Street. This street becomes Millinocket Road. After 7.4 miles, bear right at the fork for Baxter Park Road. Follow another 8.4 miles before reaching the park's Togue Pond gate. Just beyond the gatehouse, take the dirt perimeter road's left fork and drive 10.6 miles, then turn left at a sign for Kidney Pond Camps. Drive 1.1 miles to the parking area.

Baxter State Park is open May 15–November 1 and December 1–March 31. During the summer season, the park's Togue Pond Gate is open 6 A.M.–10 P.M.—though it may open at 5 A.M. at the discretion of the park director; the Matagamon Gate is open 6 A.M.–10 P.M. The road is not maintained to the trailhead in winter, but it can be skied.

GPS Coordinates: 45.8929 N, 69.0482 W

Contact: Baxter State Park, 64 Balsam Dr., Millinocket, ME 04462-2190, 207/723-5140, www.baxterstateparkauthority.com.

20 POLLYWOG GORGE
3.8 mi/2.5 hr

southwest of Baxter State Park

What's to see in the North Woods outside Baxter State Park? This pleasant hike makes a 3.8-mile loop through scenic Pollywog Gorge, a small ledge high above the rushing waters of Pollywog Stream. Starting and finishing on a 1.2-mile stretch of logging road within the 100-Mile Wilderness, this hike also follows parts of the Appalachian Trail (AT).

From the roadside parking just before the bridge over Pollywog Stream, turn left (southbound) on the AT and follow it one mile to a side path leading to the gorge overlook. Continue south on the AT through woods and around Crescent Pond to the logging road, 2.6 miles from the hike's start. Turn left and follow the road 1.2 miles back to the bridge.

The Rainbow Stream lean-to is located 2.4 miles north on the AT from the Pollywog Stream bridge (not along this hike). It's legal to camp anywhere along the AT in the 100-Mile Wilderness; low-impact camping is encouraged.

User Groups: Hikers only. No wheelchair facilities. Dogs are discouraged along the Appalachian Trail in Maine. Bikes and horses are prohibited. This trail should not be attempted in winter except by hikers prepared for severe winter weather, and is not suitable for skis.

Permits: No permits required.

Maps: For a trail map, refer to map 1 in the *Map and Guide to the Appalachian Trail in Maine,* a set of seven maps and a guidebook for $25.00 from the Maine Appalachian Trail Club. For a topographic area map, request Rainbow Lake West from the USGS.

Directions: From the junction of Routes 11 and 157 in Millinocket, head south on Route 11 for 15.5 miles. Cross over Bear Brook and turn west onto private, gravel Jo-Mary Road, which isn't passable at certain times of year due to snow or muddy conditions. In 0.2 mile, pass through a gate and pay a vehicle toll. Continue six miles from the gate and bear right at a sign for the Appalachian Trail. Follow that road another 20.2 miles (ignoring unimproved roads diverging from it) to where the AT crosses Pollywog Stream on a bridge; park at the roadside.

GPS Coordinates: 45.7793 N, 69.1725 W

Contact: Maine Appalachian Trail Club, P.O. Box 283, Augusta, ME 04332-0283, www.matc.org.

fording the East Branch of Pleasant River at mile 47 of the 100-Mile Wilderness

21 100-MILE WILDERNESS
99.4 mi one-way/9-10 days

👫5 ⛰10

between Monson and Baxter State Park

BEST (

From its starting point just north of Monson on Route 15 to where it ends at the West Branch of the Penobscot River outside Baxter State Park's southern boundary, the 100-Mile Wilderness stretch of the Appalachian Trail runs for 99.4 miles without crossing a paved or public road. (The trail is, however, bisected by a number of private logging roads.) A land of dense forest, wandering streams, and rugged hills, and home to moose, bears, and countless other species of northern wildlife, the Wilderness still constitutes one of the most remote backpacking experiences possible in New England. It's busiest in August and early September when the weather is warm and drier, the mosquitoes have dissipated somewhat, and Appalachian Trail through-hikers arrive on the last long leg of their journey towards Katahdin. Hit the trail in July or early October and you may find yourself making the 99.4-mile trek in almost complete solitude.

The number of days spent on this trail can vary greatly. Generally, the southern half, below Crawford Pond, is more mountainous and rugged; and from Crawford north the trail covers easier, flatter terrain around several vast wilderness lakes. If you do plan to hike the entire 99.4-mile stretch, bringing along water filtration/purification equipment is a must. The trail is well-marked with the white blazes of the Appalachian Trail (AT) and there are signs at many junctions.

From the parking turnout area north of Monson on Route 15 (mile 0), the AT enters the woods at a well-marked trail sign. Traversing relatively easy terrain past a number of small ponds, the trail soon reaches one of the many lean-tos scattered along the trail. Here, Leeman Brook lean-to (mile 3.0), sleeps six and sits above a small gorge. Continuing north, the trail crosses a logging road (at mile 4.2; passing logging trucks have the right of way on all logging roads, so show caution) and then pushes on to reach the top of 60-foot Little Wilson Falls (mile 6.6), one of the highest waterfalls along the AT. The trail turns sharply right, following the rim of the long, deep gorge below the falls, then descends steeply, eventually fording Little Wilson Stream (mile 6.8) with a good view upstream into the gorge. Turn left onto a gravel logging road (mile 7.2) and follow it for 100 yards, and then turn right into the woods. At the Big Wilson logging road (mile 9.1), turn left, follow it for 0.6 mile; then turn right off the road (mile 9.7) and ford Big Wilson Stream, which can be difficult in high water. A bridge across the stream is available 1.5 miles downstream. After crossing the bridge, take the unmarked path 1.5 miles back upstream to rejoin the AT. At mile 10, cross the Canadian Pacific Railroad line.

Less than a half mile from the railroad

right-of-way, a short side path leads right to the Wilson Valley lean-to (mile 10.4), which sleeps six; there is water at a nearby spring. The trail then continues on for the next five miles, fording Wilbur Brook (mile 13.6) and Vaughn Stream (mile 13.7) above a spectacular 20-foot waterfall that drops into a broad pool. At a logging road (mile 14.2), turn right and walk 100 yards and then left again into the woods. Ford Long Pond Stream (mile 14.3), walk alongside narrow pools and flumes of smooth rock, and then reach a short side path at 15 miles that leads left to Slugundy Gorge, a scenic gorge and falls. Just beyond, another side path leads left 150 yards to the Long Pond Stream lean-to, which sleeps eight; get water from the nearby brook.

Beyond the shelter, the AT begins the steep climb of Barren Mountain. At mile 16.2, a side path leads to the right about 250 feet to the top of the Barren Slide, from which there are excellent views south of Lake Onawa and Borestone Mountain. Following the ridge, the trail reaches the 2,670-foot summit of Barren Mountain (mile 18.2), which offers sweeping views, particularly south and west; also here is an abandoned fire tower. Dropping back into the woods, you pass a side trail (mile 19.1) leading right 0.3 mile to the beautiful tarn called Cloud Pond and a nearby lean-to; water can be obtained from a spring or the pond.

Continuing along the Barren-Chairback Ridge, the trail bounces over rugged terrain, passing over the wooded 2,383-foot summit of Fourth Mountain (mile 21.2) and a side path leading right 0.2 mile to West Chairback Pond (mile 24.3). Just beyond that path, the AT crosses a good stream where you may want to load up on water if you're planning to stay at the Chairback Gap lean-to, where the spring may run dry in late summer. The trail climbs steeply over Columbus Mountain, then drops into Chairback Gap, passing in front of the lean-to there; the spring is about 200 yards downhill along the trail. The trail then ascends to the top of 2,219-foot Chairback Mountain (mile 26.5), traversing its long, open crest with

excellent views west and north. At the end of the ridge, the trail descends a very steep slope (mile 26.6) of loose talus, trending left near its bottom. It passes over open ledges (mile 26.9) with views back to Chairback Mountain. At mile 29.9, cross a wide logging road; half a mile to the right (east) is a parking area heavily used by day visitors to Gulf Hagas. The road continues east for 7.1 miles to the Katahdin Iron Works Museum.

The AT passes through woods onward to the West Branch of Pleasant River (mile 30.4), a wide channel that might be knee-deep during an August trip, but could be dangerous at high water. (Before fording the river, you will notice a blue-blazed trail; this leads back to the parking area on the logging road.) After crossing the river, the AT follows easy ground through a forest of tall white pines; a short side path (mile 30.7) leads right to the Hermitage, a stand of white pines up to 130 feet tall. At mile 32, the AT hooks right, and a blue-blazed trail leads straight ahead to the 5.2-mile loop through Gulf Hagas, one of the most scenic areas along the AT's Maine corridor and a very worthwhile detour if you have the time (see the *Gulf Hagas* listing in this chapter). The AT ascends steadily northward for 4.2 miles, following Gulf Hagas Brook to the Carl A. Newhall lean-to and tent sites; the lean-to, accessed by a short side path off the AT (mile 35.9), sleeps six, and water is available from the brook. Climbing steeply, the trail passes over the 2,683-foot summit of Gulf Hagas Mountain (mile 36.8), where there are limited views to the west from just north of the true summit, and then descends to the Sidney Tappen Campsite (mile 37.7) for tents only; a nearby spring provides water. Continue north along the arduous ridge, over 3,178-foot West Peak (mile 38.4), with limited views, and the wooded summit of 3,244-foot Hay Mountain (mile 40.0).

At mile 40.6, the White Brook Trail departs to the right (east), descending 1.9 miles to logging roads that eventually link with the road to Katahdin Iron Works. The AT then climbs to the highest point on the ridge and one of the finest views along the 100-Mile Wilderness, the 3,654-foot summit of White Cap Mountain (mile 41.7), where you get your first view on this hike of Mount Katahdin to the north. White Cap is the last big peak in the 100-Mile Wilderness. Descending north off White Cap and passing an open ledge with another good view toward Katahdin (mile 42.5), the trail reaches the Logan Brook lean-to (mile 43.1), which sleeps six. Cross a gravel road (mile 44.7) to reach another lean-to (mile 46.8). The trail fords the East Branch of Pleasant River (mile 47.0), which could be difficult at high water, and then climbs over 2,017-foot Little Boardman Mountain (mile 50.2).

Descending easily, the AT crosses the dirt Kokadjo-B Pond Road (mile 51.6), enters the woods, and soon reaches the east shore of Crawford Pond (mile 51.7). Heading slightly northward along an old woods road, the AT reaches a side path (mile 54.8) leading 150 feet to the right to the Cooper Brook Falls lean-to and the spectacular cascades along Cooper Brook. Continuing along, the trail crosses the dirt Jo-Mary Road (mile 58.5) beside a bridge over Cooper Brook. To reach Route 11, turn right (east) and follow Jo-Mary Road for 12 miles. To keep on the AT, cross the road and reenter the woods.

Now passing through mainly flat, easy terrain, the AT crosses a gravel road (mile 61.4), fords several streams in succession (mile 61.5), crosses another old logging road (mile 62.0), and reaches a short side path (mile 62.7), veering right to the Antlers Campsite, a tenting area set amid red pines on a land point jutting into vast Lower Jo-Mary Lake. From that junction, the AT hooks left and swings around the lake's west shore to a junction with the Potaywadjo Ridge Trail (mile 64.2), which leads left. Ascend steadily for one mile to broad, open ledges on Potaywadjo Ridge, with sweeping views of the lakes and mountains to the south and east. This is one of the finest viewpoints in the northern half of the 100-Mile Wilderness and a great place for picking blueberries in late August. From that junction, the AT ascends the wooded end of the ridge and then drops to the Potaywadjo Spring lean-to (mile 66.2), which sleeps six. Following easy terrain again, the AT passes a junction with a side path (mile 66.8) leading a short distance to the shore of Pemadumcook Lake, where you get an excellent view across the water to Katahdin. Cross Deer Brook (mile 68.0), an old logging road (mile 68.8), and then ford a tributary of Nahmakanta Stream (mile 68.9). A high-water bypass trail 0.2 mile long diverges from the AT (mile 69.3) and then rejoins it (mile 69.4). At mile 70, you ford Tumbledown Dick Stream.

The AT parallels Nahmakanta Stream, where footing grows difficult over many rocks and roots, and then crosses a gravel road (mile 73.4); to reach Route 11, you would turn left (southwest) and continue 24 miles on this gravel road to the Jo-Mary Road. The AT crosses the gravel road and reenters the woods. At mile 73.8, the AT reaches the south shore of Nahmakanta Lake near a short side path leading to a gravel beach. It follows the lakeshore, skirting into the woods and out onto the rocky shore to a short side path (mile 76.0) leading right to a sandy beach; the path emerges at one end of the beach, near a small spring. From here, the AT crosses Wadleigh Stream (mile 76.3) and then reaches the Wadleigh Stream lean-to (mile 76.4), which sleeps six; the nearby stream provides water. The trail then makes a steep ascent up Nesuntabunt Mountain; from its north summit (mile 78.3), a short side path leads to an open ledge with an excellent view from high above Nahmakanta Lake toward Katahdin. Descending somewhat more moderately off Nesuntabunt, the AT crosses a logging road (mile 79.5); to the north, it's 1.2 miles to Pollywog Bridge, and to the south it's 25.2 miles to Route 11. This hike crosses the logging road and reenters the woods.

After circling Crescent Pond (mile 80.1), the AT passes a short side path (mile 81.1) leading left to a rather exposed ledge high above Pollywog Gorge. It then parallels Pollywog Stream to a logging road (mile 82.1); to reach Route 11, you would turn south and follow the road 26.4 miles. The AT turns left and crosses the stream on a bridge. Walk past a dirt road branching right and reenter the woods to the right. The trail follows a picturesque gorge along Rainbow Stream for about two miles and then reaches the Rainbow Stream lean-to (mile 84.5), which sleeps six; water is available from the stream. From here, easy terrain leads to a small clearing (mile 89.8); to the right, a short path leads to tent sites at the Rainbow Spring Campsite, and to the left, it's just a short walk to the spring and Rainbow Lake. Continuing along the big lake's shore, the AT reaches the Rainbow Mountain Trail at mile 90, which bears right and climbs a fairly easy 1.1 miles to the bare summit of Rainbow Mountain with excellent views, especially toward Katahdin.

The AT continues to the east end of Rainbow Lake (mile 91.7), passes a side path (mile 91.8) leading right 0.1 mile to Little Beaver Pond and 0.4 mile to Big Beaver Pond, and then ascends to Rainbow Ledges (mile 93.5); from various points along the ledges you get long views south and northeast to Katahdin. Descending easily, the AT fords Hurd Brook (mile 96.0), which can be difficult when the water is high, and reaches the Hurd Brook lean-to on the other side of the brook; it sleeps six, and water is available from the brook. From here, the trail rolls through fairly easy terrain to Golden Road (mile 99.3). Turn right and follow the road to Abol Bridge (mile 99.4), the terminus of this memorable trek.

There are numerous shelters along the Appalachian Trail, and it's legal to camp anywhere along the AT in the 100-Mile Wilderness; low-impact camping is encouraged.

User Groups: Hikers only. Dogs are discouraged along the Appalachian Trail in Maine. No bikes, horses, or wheelchair facilities. This trail should not be attempted in winter except by hikers prepared for severe winter weather; not suitable for skis.

Permits: A fee is charged for access to privately owned Golden Road; it has been $10 per vehicle in the past, but could change.

Maps: For a trail map, refer to maps 1, 2, and 3 in the *Map and Guide to the Appalachian Trail in Maine,* a set of seven maps and a guidebook for $25.00 from the Maine Appalachian Trail Club. For topographic area maps, request Rainbow Lake East, Rainbow Lake West, Wadleigh Mountain, Nahmakanta Stream, Pemadumcook Lake, Jo-Mary Mountain, Big Shanty Mountain, Silver Lake, Barren Mountain East, Barren Mountain West, Monson East, and Monson West from the USGS.

Directions: You need to shuttle two vehicles for this trip. From Millinocket, drive on Route 157 west through East Millinocket to Millinocket Road. Follow signs for Baxter State Park. About a mile before the park entrance, bear left onto Golden Road, a private logging road where you pass through a gate and pay a toll. Continue about seven miles to the private campground at Abol Bridge. Drive over the bridge and park in the dirt lot on the left, about 0.1 mile east of where the Appalachian Trail emerges at the road. Drive a second vehicle to Monson, and pick up Route 15 north for 3.5 miles to a large turnout on the right and the trailhead for the Appalachian Trail.

A fee-based shuttle to road crossings along the Appalachian Trail, as well as other hiker services, is offered by Shaw's Lodging in Monson, 207/997-3597, www.shawslodging. com. A hiker shuttle, free Kennebec River ferry service, and other hiker services along the Appalachian Trail in Maine are also provided by Rivers and Trails, 207/663-4441 or (in Maine only) 888/356-2863, www.riversandtrails.com.

GPS Coordinates: 45.3362 N, 69.5591 W

Contact: Maine Appalachian Trail Club, P.O. Box 283, Augusta, ME 04332-0283, www. matc.org.

22 HALF A 100-MILE WILDERNESS

47.8 or 51.6 mi one-way/4-6 days

👣 4 ⛰ 10

between Monson and Baxter State Park

BEST (

Backpackers seeking one of the most remote experiences possible in New England, but who don't have the time to hike the entire 100-Mile Wilderness—the stretch of the Appalachian Trail (AT) in northern Maine that crosses no paved or public road for 99.4 miles—can instead backpack "half a wilderness." The AT crosses the dirt Kokadjo-B Pond Road, identified on some maps as Johnson Pond Road, a logical place to begin or conclude a trek of either the northern or southern half of the 100-Mile Wilderness. The 51.6 trail miles from this logging road south to Route 15 are characterized by rugged hiking over a landscape dominated by low mountains boasting sporadic but long views of the forested landscape. The 47.8 miles of trail north to Golden Road at Abol Bridge have an entirely different personality, traversing mostly flat, low terrain around sprawling wilderness lakes. The southern portion can take five days or more; the northern is easier and can be done in four days by fit hikers. (See the trail notes in the *100-Mile Wilderness* listing in this chapter for a detailed description of both options.)

There are numerous shelters along the Appalachian Trail, and it's legal to camp anywhere along the AT in the 100-Mile Wilderness; low-impact camping is encouraged.

User Groups: Hikers only. No wheelchair facilities. Dogs are discouraged along the Appalachian Trail in Maine. Bikes and horses are prohibited. This trail should not be attempted in winter except by hikers prepared for severe winter weather; not suitable for skis.

Permits: A fee is charged for access to privately owned Golden Road; it has been $10 per vehicle in the past, but could change.

Maps: For a trail map, refer to maps 1, 2, and 3 in the *Map and Guide to the Appalachian Trail in Maine,* a set of seven maps and a guidebook for $25.00 from the Maine Appalachian Trail Club. For topographic area maps, request Rainbow Lake East, Rainbow Lake West, Wadleigh Mountain, Nahmakanta Stream, Pemadumcook Lake, Jo-Mary Mountain, Big Shanty Mountain, Silver Lake, Barren Mountain East, Barren Mountain West, Monson East, and Monson West from the USGS.

Directions: You need to shuttle two vehicles for this trip. To backpack the northern half of the 100-Mile Wilderness, from Millinocket take Route 157 west through East Millinocket to Millinocket Road. Follow signs for Baxter State Park. About a mile before the park entrance, bear left onto Golden Road, a private logging road where you pass through a gate and pay a toll. Continue about seven miles to the private campground at the Abol Bridge over the West Branch of the Penobscot River. Drive over the bridge and park in the dirt lot on the left, about 0.1 mile east of where the Appalachian Trail emerges at the road. Drive a second vehicle back to Millinocket. From the junction of Routes 11 and 157, go south on Route 11 for 15.5 miles and turn right (west) onto gravel Jo-Mary Road. Continue 0.2 mile and pass through a gate where a vehicle toll is collected. Proceed another six miles and bear left at a fork, following the sign for Gauntlet Falls/B-Pond (ignore the sign for the Appalachian Trail, which is also reached via the right fork). Continuing another 2.6 miles, bear right where the B-Pond Road branches left. At 14.6 miles from Route 11, the AT crosses the road 0.1 mile south of Crawford Pond; park off the road.

To backpack the southern half of the 100-Mile Wilderness, leave one car at the AT crossing of the logging road near Crawford Pond, then return to Route 11 and drive south to Monson. Pick up Route 15 north for 3.5 miles to a large turnout on the right and the trailhead for the Appalachian Trail at the 100-Mile Wilderness's southern end.

A fee-based shuttle to road crossings along the Appalachian Trail, as well as other hiker services, is offered by Shaw's Lodging in Monson, 207/997-3597, www.shawslodging.com. A hiker shuttle, free Kennebec River ferry service, and other hiker services along the Appalachian Trail in Maine are also provided by Steve Longley of Rivers and Trails, 207/663-4441 or (in Maine only) 888/356-2863, www.riversandtrails.com. GPS Coordinates: 45.3362 N, 69.5591 W **Contact:** Maine Appalachian Trail Club, P.O. Box 283, Augusta, ME 04332-0283, www.matc.org.

23 WHITE CAP MOUNTAIN
23 mi/2-3 days   🏃4 ⛰10

between Monson and Baxter State Park

At 3,654 feet, White Cap Mountain is the tallest peak in the 100-Mile Wilderness, the 99.4-mile stretch of the Appalachian Trail (AT) through northern Maine not crossed by paved or public roads. White Cap is also the last big peak in the Wilderness for northbound hikers and offers excellent views, especially toward Katahdin. A remote summit, White Cap can be reached on a two- or three-day trek via the logging road that accesses the AT.

From the logging road parking area, find the blue-blazed access trail on the north side of the pull-off and follow 0.2 mile to the white-blazed Appalachian Trail at the West Branch of the Pleasant River. You must ford this normally knee-deep channel of about 80 feet across to continue on (bring a pair of sandals or old sneakers for this stony crossing). The AT then continues over easy ground and among giant pines to the junction with the Gulf Hagas Trail, 1.3 miles from the river (see the *Gulf Hagas* listing in this chapter). The AT turns sharply right and ascends steadily northward for 4.2 miles, following Gulf Hagas Brook through dense forest to the Carl A. Newhall lean-to and tent sites, reached by a short side path off the AT; the lean-to sleeps six, and water is available from the brook.

Climbing steeply, the trail passes over the 2,683-foot summit of Gulf Hagas Mountain 6.6 miles from the road, where there are limited views to the west from just north of the true summit. After descending to the Sidney Tappen Campsite, the AT yo-yos north along the arduous ridge, over 3,178-foot West Peak (mile 8.2), with limited views, and the wooded summit of 3,244-foot Hay Mountain (mile 9.8). The trail dips again, passing a junction at 10.4 miles with the White Brook Trail (which descends east 1.9 miles to logging roads that eventually link with the road to Katahdin Iron Works). The AT then climbs to the White Cap summit. Enjoy impressive views towards Katahdin and return the way you came.

The Carl A. Newhall lean-to, with tent sites, is located 5.7 miles north on the AT from the parking area; and the Sidney Tappen Campsite, for tents only, lies 1.8 miles farther north. It's legal to camp anywhere along the AT in the 100-Mile Wilderness; low-impact camping is encouraged.

User Groups: Hikers only. No wheelchair facilities. Dogs are discouraged along the Appalachian Trail in Maine. Bikes and horses are prohibited. This trail should not be attempted in winter except by hikers experienced in mountaineering and prepared for severe winter weather; not suitable for skis.

Permits: No permits required.

Maps: For a trail map, refer to map 2 in the *Map and Guide to the Appalachian Trail in Maine,* a set of seven maps and a guidebook for $25.00 available from the Maine Appalachian Trail Club. For topographic area maps, request Hay Mountain, Big Shanty Mountain, Barren Mountain East, and Silver Lake from the USGS.

Directions: From Route 11, 5.5 miles north of Brownville Junction and 25.6 miles south of Millinocket, turn west onto a gravel road at a sign for Katahdin Iron Works. Follow it nearly seven miles to a gate where an entrance fee is collected. Beyond the gate, cross the bridge and turn right. Drive three miles, bear left at a fork, and then continue another 3.7 miles. As the road curves to the left, look for the parking area on the right (half a mile before the road's crossing of the Appalachian Trail).

This section of the Appalachian Trail is reached via a private logging road, and a nominal per-person toll is collected; children under 15 enter free. The access road isn't passable at certain times of year due to snow or muddy conditions.

GPS Coordinates: 45.4635 N, 69.2068 W

Contact: Maine Appalachian Trail Club, P.O. Box 283, Augusta, ME 04332-0283, www.matc.org.

24 GULF HAGAS
8 mi/5.5 hr ⚠️ 3 △ 10

between Monson and Baxter State Park

BEST (

Known as Maine's Little Grand Canyon, Gulf Hagas is a deep, narrow canyon along the West Branch of the Pleasant River and not far from the 32-mile mark along the 100-Mile Wilderness. Taking in the sheer slate walls that drop for hundreds of feet into a boulder-choked, impassable river, it's easy to understand why the Abenaki gave it the name "hagas," their word for "evil place." The blue-blazed loop trail through the gulf is a 5.2-mile detour off the Appalachian Trail in the 100-Mile Wilderness, but the round-trip hike from the parking area is 8 miles. This trail goes through very little elevation gain or loss, but runs constantly up and down over rugged, rocky terrain; your hike could easily take more than the estimated 5.5 hours, especially when you start hanging out at the many waterfalls and clifftop viewpoints. Be forewarned: This is a very popular hike in summer, so expect crowds.

From the parking area, follow the blue-blazed access trail 0.2 mile to the white-blazed Appalachian Trail (AT) at the West Branch of the Pleasant River, a normally knee-deep channel about 80 feet across, which you must ford (bring a pair of sandals or old sneakers for this stony crossing to make it easier on the

feet). Continue along the wide, flat AT and pass a side trail 0.2 mile from the river that leads to campsites at Hay Brook. At 0.3 mile, another side path leads about 200 feet into the Hermitage, a grove of ancient white pine trees, some as tall as 130 feet. The AT continues over easy ground among other giant pines to the junction with the Gulf Hagas Trail, 1.3 miles from the river. The AT turns sharply right, but continue straight onto the blue-blazed trail, immediately crossing Gulf Hagas Brook. Bear left onto the loop trail. At 0.1 mile, a side path leads left to beautiful Screw Auger Falls on Gulf Hagas Brook. At 0.2 mile, another side path leads to the bottom of Screw Auger. (The brook continues down through a series of cascades and pools, including some spots ideal for swimming.)

The Gulf Hagas Trail continues down to the canyon rim, weaving in and out of the forest to views from the canyon rim and dropping down to the riverbank in places. Significant features along the rim include Hammond Street Pitch, a view high above the river, reached on a short path at 0.7 mile; the Jaws Cascades (seen from side paths or views at 1.2, 1.4, and 1.5 miles); Buttermilk Falls at 1.8 miles; Stair Falls at 1.9 miles; Billings Falls at 2.7 miles; and a view down the gulf from its head at 2.9 miles. Three miles into the loop, turn right onto the Pleasant River Road, an old logging road that is at first a footpath but widens over the 2.2 miles back to the start of this loop. The logging road provides much easier walking and a faster return route than doubling back along the gulf rim.

User Groups: Hikers only. No wheelchair facilities. Dogs are discouraged along the Appalachian Trail in Maine. Bikes and horses are prohibited. Portions of this trail are difficult to ski or snowshoe.

Permits: No permits required.

Maps: For a trail map, refer to map 2 in the *Map and Guide to the Appalachian Trail in Maine,* a set of seven maps and a guidebook for $25.00 available from the Maine Appalachian Trail Club. For topographic area maps, request Barren Mountain East and Silver Lake from the USGS.

Directions: From Route 11, 5.5 miles north of Brownville Junction and 25.6 miles south of Millinocket, turn west onto a gravel road at a sign for Katahdin Iron Works. Follow it nearly seven miles to a gate where an entrance fee is collected. Beyond the gate, cross the bridge and turn right. Drive 3 miles, bear left at a fork, and then continue another 3.7 miles to a parking area (half a mile before the road crosses the Appalachian Trail).

Gulf Hagas is reached via a private logging road, and a nominal per-person toll is collected; children under 15 enter free. The access roads are not passable at certain times of year due to snow or muddy conditions.

GPS Coordinates: 45.4635 N, 69.2067 W

Contact: Maine Appalachian Trail Club, P.O. Box 283, Augusta, ME 04332-0283, www.matc.org.

25 BARREN MOUNTAIN AND SLUGUNDY GORGE

8 mi/6 hr   🏃4 ⛰10

northeast of Monson

By employing dirt logging roads to access this stretch of the Appalachian Trail (AT), you can make a one-day or an overnight hike into this picturesque and varied area of the 100-Mile Wilderness. What's here? The round-trip hike to the summit of Barren Mountain entails 8 demanding miles round-trip and 2,000 feet of climbing, but it's just 1.6 miles round-trip to picturesque Slugundy Gorge. Barren and Slugundy are reached by walking north on the AT. The one caveat about this hike is that Long Pond Stream can be very difficult to cross, so it's best to go in late summer or early fall, when water levels are down.

From the Bodfish Farm–Long Pond Tote Road, turn right (north) onto the AT. Within 0.1 mile, ford Long Pond Stream. The trail parallels pools and flumes in the stream for

more than half a mile; after it turns uphill, a short side path leads left to Slugundy Gorge, a scenic gorge and falls. Just beyond, another side path leads left 150 yards to the Long Pond Stream lean-to. Behind the shelter, the AT begins the steep Barren Mountain climb. At two miles, a side path leads right about 250 feet to the top of the Barren Slide, from which there are excellent views south of Lake Onawa and Borestone Mountain. Following the ridge, the trail reaches the aptly named, 2,670-foot summit of Barren Mountain two miles beyond the slide, where there are sweeping views, particularly south and west; an abandoned fire tower stands at the summit. Continuing north on the AT for 0.9 mile brings you to a side trail leading right 0.3 mile to the beautiful tarn called Cloud Pond and the nearby lean-to, but to finish this hike, turn around and hike back the way you came.

The Long Pond Stream lean-to is along the Appalachian Trail 0.9 mile into this hike, and the Cloud Pond lean-to lies 1.2 miles beyond the summit of Barren Mountain. It's legal to camp anywhere along the AT in the 100-Mile Wilderness; low-impact camping is encouraged.

User Groups: Hikers only. No wheelchair facilities. Dogs are discouraged along the Appalachian Trail in Maine. Bikes and horses are prohibited. Portions of this trail are difficult to ski or snowshoe.

Permits: Parking and access are free.

Maps: For a trail map, refer to map 3 in the *Map and Guide to the Appalachian Trail in Maine*, a set of seven maps and a guidebook for $25.00 from the Maine Appalachian Trail Club. For topographic area maps, request Monson East, Barren Mountain West, and Barren Mountain East from the USGS.

Directions: From the center of Monson, drive half a mile north on Route 15 and turn right onto Elliottsville Road. Continue 7.8 miles to Big Wilson Stream, cross the bridge, and then turn left onto a dirt road. Drive another 2.8 miles to the Bodfish Farm, bear left at a fork and go 2.9 miles farther to where the white-blazed Appalachian Trail crosses the dirt road, known as the Bodfish Farm–Long Pond Tote Road; park at the roadside.

The dirt roads from Monson aren't passable at certain times of year due to snow or muddy conditions.

GPS Coordinates: 45.4168 N, 69.4203 W

Contact: Maine Appalachian Trail Club, P.O. Box 283, Augusta, ME 04332-0283, www. matc.org.

26 BORESTONE MOUNTAIN
4.5 mi/3.5 hr   🏃3 ⛰9

in Borestone Mountain Audubon Sanctuary

Borestone Mountain (1,947 ft.) is a small, rugged peak located within a Maine Audubon Sanctuary just below the southern boundary of the 100-Mile Wilderness. Because the last timber harvest here was more than a century ago, the dense forest cover makes the mountain an attractive habitat for certain wildlife. Some of Maine's most coveted warblers spend their summer here—blackburnian and cape may nest in the coniferous canopy and goshawks wing through the mature deciduous woods to prey on grouse. Even pine martins are regularly seen by sanctuary staff. Expect lots of hikers with binoculars trained skyward while on this climb.

From the trailhead at the Bodfish Farm Road parking area, follow the gently ascending green-blazed Base Trail for 0.8 mile to the sanctuary's visitors center. Stop at the visitors center (9 A.M.–dusk daily, Memorial Day–October) to pay the entry fee for trail use. Here, you will also find nature displays, a gift shop, and restrooms.

Leaving the visitors center, the green-blazed Summit Trail crosses the outlet of Sunrise Pond (at the pond's southeastern end). Steadily ascending with good cover, you will notice the trail becoming rough and slippery about 1.1 miles out from the visitors center. Be prepared to scramble at the steepest sections. The trail keeps up a steady ascent and at 1.75 miles, you reach West Peak. Continue on for 0.25 mile down to a saddle and then climb a barren ledge to East Peak, the mountain's true summit. From here, look down on nearby Lake Onawa and across to 2,660-foot Barren Mountain. Return to the trailhead by the same route.

User groups: Hikers and leashed dogs only. No mountain bikes or horses. Sanctuary visitors center is fully accessible for wheelchairs (reach the center from a separate access road). This trail should not be attempted in winter.

Permits: Parking is free. Trail day pass fees are $4 adults and $3 students, children under 6 free (group rates available).

Maps: For a map of Borestone and the Boreston Mountain Audubon Sanctuary, contact Maine Audubon. For a topographic area map, request Barren Mountain East quad from the USGS.

Directions: From Monson, take Maine Routes 6 and 15 north 0.6 mile to Elliotsville Road. Turn right and continue on Elliotsville Road for 7.8 miles. After the bridge over Big Wilson Stream, turn left on Bodfish Farm Road and immediately cross the Canadian Pacific Railroad tracks. The trailhead is 0.1 mile past the railroad tracks and is well marked. Park across the road from the trailhead and make sure to leave your car out of the way of traffic.

GPS Coordinates: 45.3778 N, 69.4302 W

Contact: Maine Audubon, 20 Gilsland Farm Rd., Falmouth, ME 04105, 207/781-09, www. maineaudubon.org.

DOWN EAST

© PETER DAME

BEST HIKES

As Maine's jagged coastline stretches north and

east toward Canada, the bucolic landscape gives way to soaring granite cliffs and tall mountains so close to the roiling waters of the Atlantic, they seem to rear up from the sea itself. Here, too, are coastal meadows, salt marshes, cobblestone beaches, sky-high pine forests, and crystal-clear inland lakes. In New England and beyond – and whether you are an expert hiker, novice, or have kids in tow when you hit the trail – Down East harbors some of the best coastal hiking you'll find anywhere.

State parks dot the region and are excellent destinations for a day hike (especially Camden Hills State Park and Lubec's Quoddy Head), but Down East's centerpiece is Acadia National Park. Occupying 47,633 acres of granite-domed mountains, woodlands, lakes, ponds, and ocean shoreline, mostly on Mount Desert Island, Acadia is one of the country's smallest, yet most popular, national parks. Glaciers carved a unique landscape here of mountains rising as high as 1,500 feet virtually out of the ocean – most of them thrusting bare summits into the sky – and innumerable islands, bays, and coves that collaborate to create a hiking environment unlike any other. Designated with national park status in 1919, thanks in part to land donations from the area's wealthy summer residents (among them John D. Rockefeller), Acadia was the first national park established east of the Mississippi.

With more than 120 miles of hiking trails and 45 miles of gravel carriage roads, Acadia boasts almost endless possibilities for hiking, horseback riding, and mountain biking. Many of the park's most popular treks are relatively short in length, leading to spectacularly long views of mountains, ocean, and islands. And although some trails are steep and rugged, the majority of hikes in Acadia are suitable for younger children. All trails in Acadia are blue-blazed and cairns are frequent along rockier trails; trailheads are marked by signposts.

Isle au Haut (pronounced "eye la ho" locally), the outermost island in Penobscot Bay, serves as a remote outpost of Acadia National Park. Reached only by a small mail boat ferry from the mainland, the island is home to approximately 65 year-round residents who live on the edge of the parklands. Isle au Haut's many seasonal visitors have access to 18 miles of hiking trails on rocky coastline and low hills, with trailheads easily reached from the ferry landing at Duck Harbor.

Equal to the rugged beauty of the region's geography is Down East's eclectic mix of flora and fauna. Its cold, nutrient-rich seawater, high tidal ranges, and shoreline spruce forests create a unique boreal coastline — more similar to the fjords of northern Scandinavia than the sandy spits of southern New England. Thick with red spruce and white pine, Down East's forests are home to white-tail deer, red foxes, snowshoe hares, beavers, otters, and even the occasional moose; seabirds, hawks, peregrine falcons, and breeding warblers are just some of the many avian species spotted in the area. And a real treat for wildlife lovers: Look offshore almost anywhere along the coast and spot playful harbor seals sunning themselves at low tide. (Harbor seal populations are highest in spring and summer.)

July and August are crowded months on Mount Desert Island. May, June, September, and October are much less crowded; spring tends to be cool and sometimes rainy, while fall is drier, with its share of both warm and cool days. State parks in Maine don't see anywhere near the crowds of Acadia during the tourist season, making them a good alternative for those who want to enjoy Down East's scenic splendor in relative solitude. In winter, trails are almost empty of all but the hardiest of hikers as the weather turns brutally windy and cold, with frequent storms lashing the coast. Still, state parks and parts of Acadia do provide access year-round.

MAINE

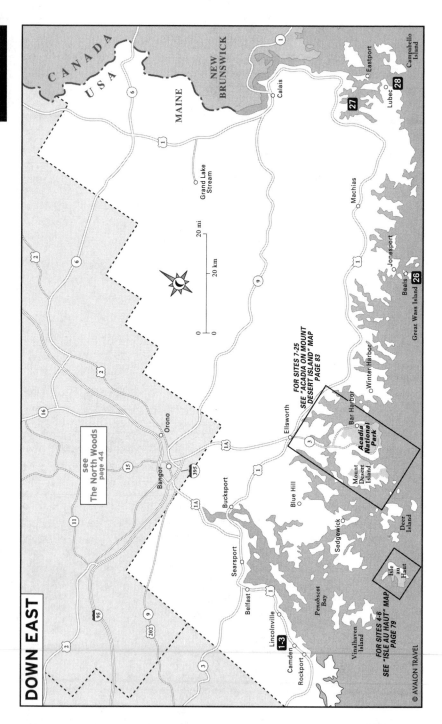

DOWN EAST

CANADA

U S A

MAINE

NEW BRUNSWICK

Calais

Eastport

Campobello Island

Lubec

28

27

Machias

Grand Lake Stream

Jonesport

20 mi

20 km

Beals

Great Wass Island

26

FOR SITES 7-25
SEE "ACADIA ON MOUNT DESERT ISLAND" MAP
PAGE 83

Winter Harbor

Ellsworth

Bar Harbor

Acadia National Park

Mount Desert Island

Orono

see
The North Woods
page 44

Bangor

Bucksport

Blue Hill

Sedgewick

Deer Island

Isle au Haut

Searsport

Penobscot Bay

Belfast

Vinalhaven Island

Lincolnville

1-3

Camden

Rockport

FOR SITES 4-6
SEE "ISLE AU HAUT" MAP
PAGE 79

© AVALON TRAVEL

1 MAIDEN CLIFF
2 mi/1.5 hr

in Camden Hills State Park

Tucked away along the northwest edge of Camden Hills State Park, the 800-foot Maiden Cliff soars high above sprawling Megunticook Lake and offers extensive views of the hills to the west. While it's a nice trek anytime, think about saving this hike for late in the day, when the sinking sun shoots sparkling rays across the lake and surrounding hills. For hikers who are new to Camden Hills State Park, a curious site on the cliff is the large wooden cross planted right at the cliff's edge. As a plaque near the cross explains, it commemorates the spot where a young girl named Elenora French fell to her death in 1864. According to local legend, she was attempting to catch her windblown hat when she fell over the almost sheer drop.

From the parking lot, follow the wide Maiden Cliff Trail, ascending steadily through the woods for a half mile. Bear right on the Ridge Trail, reaching an open area and the junction with the Scenic Trail in 0.3 mile. Turn left (northwest) on the Scenic Trail, following the cliff tops with outstanding views for nearly a quarter mile. The trail then dips back into the woods again to reach a junction with the Maiden Cliff Trail (marked by a sign) in another quarter mile. Continue ahead 100 feet to the cross and plaque. From here, double back and descend the Maiden Cliff Trail for nearly a mile to the parking lot.

User Groups: Hikers and leashed dogs. No bikes, horses, or wheelchair facilities.

Permits: Because the Maiden Cliff Trailhead is located outside the Camden Hills State Park perimeter, parking and access are free.

Maps: A basic trail system map, suitable for this hike, is available at the state park entrance on U.S. 1, two miles north of the Route 52 junction in Camden. For topographic area maps, request Camden and Lincolnville from the USGS.

Directions: From the junction of Route 52 and U.S. 1 in Camden, drive west on Route 52 for three miles to a parking area on the right (just before Megunticook Lake). The Maiden Cliff Trail begins at the back of the lot.

GPS Coordinates: 44.2822 N, 69.1018 W

Contact: Camden Hills State Park, 280 Belfast Rd., Camden, ME 04843, 207/236-3109 in season, 207/236-0849 off-season. Maine Department of Conservation, Bureau of Parks and Lands, 286 Water St., Key Bank Plaza, 3rd and 5th floors, Augusta, ME 04333-0022, 207/287-3821, www.maine.gov/doc/parks.

2 MOUNT MEGUNTICOOK TRAVERSE
4.75 mi one-way/3 hr

in Camden Hills State Park

Across the 5,500 acres of Camden Hills State Park, countless miles of hiking trails follow the coast and weave through the Megunticook Mountain range above the town of Camden, where the hills rise from near sea level to reach soaring heights. This fairly easy traverse of Mount Megunticook (1,380 ft.), the highest mountain in Camden Hills, combines good views from dramatic Maiden Cliff and scenic Ocean Lookout with a pleasant walk along Megunticook's mostly wooded ridge. A one-way traverse through the park, the hike climbs just over 1,000 feet.

From the parking area on Mount Battie Road, follow the Mount Megunticook Trail on a relentlessly uphill mile to Ocean Lookout. The trail's blue blazes start appearing at the hike's half-mile mark; stone stairs built into the hillside also start here to help with footing on the trail's steeper section. Reaching the lookout, take in terrific views south and east of the Camden area and even spot the famous windjammer ships cruising Penobscot Bay. Continue northwest on the Ridge Trail (look for the marker), passing over the wooded summit of Megunticook, a half mile beyond

Ocean Lookout. Continue over the summit on the Ridge Trail, and begin the relatively flat ridge walk. Approximately one mile past the summit, stay left on the Ridge Trail where Zeke's Trail branches right; then a half mile farther, stay right where the Jack Williams Trail enters from the left. Two miles past the summit, walk straight onto the Scenic Trail, following the open cliff tops with views of Megunticook Lake and the hills to the west. Dipping briefly into the woods again, in another 0.25 mile, you reach the Maiden Cliff Trail (marked by a sign). Before descending on the Maiden Trail, continue ahead 100 feet to Maiden Cliff; here a large wooden cross marks the spot where a young girl named Elenora French fell to her death in 1864. The cliffs seem to drop almost straight down into the lake. Double back and descend the Maiden Cliff Trail for nearly a mile to the parking lot on Route 52.

User Groups: Hikers and leashed dogs. No bikes, horses, or wheelchair facilities.

Permits: Parking and access are free at the Maiden Cliff Trailhead. To reach the Ocean Lookout/Mount Megunticook Trailhead, a fee of $3 per adult Maine resident/$4.50 per adult nonresident (age 12 and over) is charged at the state park entrance; senior citizens pay $1.50 and children under 12 years old enter free. The park season is May 15–October 15, although trailheads are accessible year-round. No staff is on duty and no fee is collected off-season.

Maps: A basic trail system map, suitable for this hike, is available at the state park entrance. For topographic area maps, request Camden and Lincolnville from the USGS.

Directions: Two vehicles must be shuttled at either end of this hike. From the junction of Route 52 and U.S. 1 in Camden, drive west on Route 52 for three miles to a parking area on the right (just before Megunticook Lake). The Maiden Cliff Trail begins at the back of the lot. Leave one vehicle there. Drive back to Camden and head north on U.S. 1 for two miles to the state park entrance on the left.

Past the entrance gate, turn left on Mount Battie Road and then right into a parking lot marked with a sign reading "Hikers Parking." The Mount Megunticook Trail begins at the back of the lot.

GPS Coordinates: 44.2311 N, 69.0470 W

Contact: Camden Hills State Park, 280 Belfast Rd., Camden, ME 04843, 207/236-3109 in season, 207/236-0849 off-season. Maine Department of Conservation, Bureau of Parks and Lands, 286 Water St., Key Bank Plaza, 3rd and 5th floors, Augusta, ME 04333-0022, 207/287-3821, www.maine.gov/doc/parks.

❸ OCEAN LOOKOUT
2 mi/1.5 hr 👫2 ⛰8

in Camden Hills State Park

Popular because of its wide views of the Camden area and the Penobscot Bay islands, this relatively easy hike leads to Ocean Lookout (1,300 ft.), a scenic open ridge on the otherwise wooded Mount Megunticook. Ocean Lookout makes for an enjoyable outing with adventurous kids or new hikers up for a challenge; the short, but relentlessly steady climb comes with a net elevation gain of almost a thousand feet.

From the parking area, pick up the Mount Megunticook Trail in the rear of the parking area at the trail marker. Initially an old woods road, in its first half mile, the trail enters a dense mixed forest, passes two trail junctions, and crosses a footbridge over a brisk stream. Blue blazes on the trees start to appear soon after the bridge crossing. Continue to follow the blazes as the trail steadily—and somewhat steeply—ascends to Ocean Lookout; stone steps at various spots along the trail make for easier footing. The wooded summit of 1,380-foot Mount Megunticook lies a half mile farther north on the Ridge Trail (see *Mount Megunticook Traverse* listing in this chapter), but this hike ends at the lookout. After you've taken in the bucolic beauty of Penobscot Bay, return the same way you came.

User Groups: Hikers and leashed dogs. No bikes, horses, or wheelchair facilities.

Permits: A fee of $3 per adult Maine resident/$4.50 per adult nonresident (age 12 and over) is charged at the state park entrance; senior citizens pay $1.50 and children under 12 years old enter free. The park season is May 15–October 15, although trailheads are accessible year-round. No staff is on duty and no fee is collected off-season.

Maps: A basic trail system map, suitable for this hike, is available at the state park entrance. For topographic area maps, request Camden and Lincolnville from the USGS.

Directions: The entrance to Camden Hills State Park is along U.S. 1, two miles north of the Route 52 junction in Camden. After passing through the entrance gate, turn left on Mount Battie Road and then right into a parking lot marked with a sign reading "Hikers Parking." The Mount Megunticook Trail begins at the back of the lot.

GPS Coordinates: 44.2311 N, 69.0470 W

Contact: Camden Hills State Park, 280 Belfast Rd., Camden, ME 04843, 207/236-3109 in season, 207/236-0849 off-season. Maine Department of Conservation, Bureau of Parks and Lands, 286 Water St., Key Bank Plaza, 3rd and 5th floors, Augusta, ME 04333-0022, 207/287-3821, www.maine.gov/doc/parks/index.html.

4 ISLE AU HAUT: EBEN'S HEAD

1 mi/0.75 hr

in Acadia National Park on Isle au Haut

BEST (

The Penobscot Bay outpost of Isle au Haut lies 15 miles southwest of Mount Desert Island. Home to a rural fishing village, complete with schoolhouse and post office, the island's six-mile long and two-mile wide expanse makes up a very remote section of Acadia National Park. Accessible only by a 45-minute mail boat

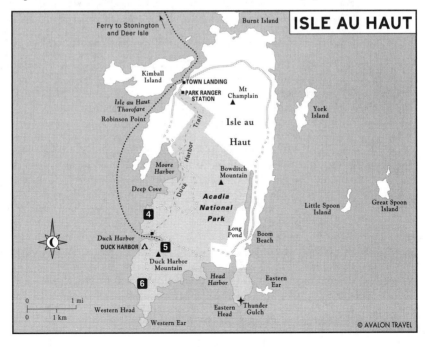

ISLE AU HAUT

© AVALON TRAVEL

VISITING ACADIA NATIONAL PARK AND ISLE AU HAUT

The park entrance fee to Acadia National Park is $20 per vehicle for a seven-day pass June 23–October 31, or $5 for walkers, bicyclists, or motorcyclists. The park entrance fee for vehicles is $10 May 1–June 22. A one-year vehicle pass costs $40. The Island Explorer shuttle bus provides free transportation from local lodges and campgrounds to points within the park and across Mount Desert Island late June–mid-October; contact Downeast Transportation, 207/667-5796, www.exploreacadia.com/index.html. Camping reservations can be made by calling 800/365-2267 or through the park's website. There are two campgrounds in Acadia: Blackwoods Campground, off Route 3 just south of Cadillac Mountain and east of Seal Harbor, is open year-round; Seawall Campground, off Route 102A east of Bass Harbor, opens in late June and closes after Labor Day.

Isle au Haut can be visited on a day trip or for overnight stays. A conveniently located campground near the ferry landing offers five lean-to shelters and a water pump. Lean-tos can be reserved May 15–October 15 by contacting the park; reservations are required. Reservations requests cannot be postmarked or made in person at park headquarters before April 1. Camping reservations cost $25 per site, regardless of the number of nights. Camping is limited to three nights mid-June–mid-September, and five nights the rest of the year. You can pitch a tent inside the lean-to only (which is advised in early summer, when the mosquitoes are vicious). Park rangers discourage bikes because of the limited roads, and bikes are prohibited from hiking trails. No wheelchair facilities are available.

ride from Stonington (no car ferry service is available), Isle au Haut rewards those who make the trip with plentiful trails, tall spruce forests, cobblestone beaches, and unobstructed ocean views. This hike leads to Eben's Head, a rocky bluff jutting into the ocean at the mouth of Duck Harbor, opposite the boat landing. For campers on the island, there is no nicer spot to watch the sunrise or sunset.

From the boat landing at Duck Harbor, turn left on the trail toward the water pump. Pass the trail branching right for the campground and continue straight onto Western Head Road. Follow it past the water pump and out to the main road. Turn left and follow the dirt main road around Duck Harbor. About 0.1 mile after the main road turns inland, you'll pass the Duck Harbor Trail on the right; then turn left onto the Eben's Head

Trail, which leads through woods out to that rocky bluff visible from the boat landing. Explore the rocky cove around Eben's Head, where interesting pools form at low tide. Return the way you came.

The Duck Harbor Campground has five lean-to shelters that can sleep up to six people each, and each lean-to site has a fire ring and picnic table. The lean-to shelters can be reserved May 15–October 15 by contacting the park (www.nps.gov/acad); reservations are required. Reservation requests cannot be postmarked or made in person at park headquarters before April 1. Camping reservations cost $25 per site, regardless of the number of nights.

User Groups: Hikers and dogs. Dogs must be leashed in the park and are prohibited in the campground. No bikes, horses, or wheelchair facilities.

Permits: No permits required.

Maps: A basic map of island trails and roads, suitable for this hike, is issued free to visitors arriving on the ferry or to those with camping reservations. The park website also has a map of Isle au Haut. Good trail maps of the area are the waterproof Acadia National Park (map 212) for $11.95 from Trails Illustrated (800/962-1643, www.natgeomaps.com/ti_212) and the Hiking and Biking Map to Acadia National Park and Mount Desert Island, $7.95 in waterproof Tyvek, from the Appalachian Mountain Club. For topographic island maps, request Isle au Haut West and Isle au Haut East from the USGS.

Directions: Isle au Haut is reached by mail boat/ferry from Stonington, Maine, to Duck Harbor, the starting point for the four Isle au Haut hikes described in this chapter. Round-trip cost is $35 for adults and $19 for children under age 12. The ferry is a small boat and does not transport motor vehicles (bikes are allowed).

To reach the dock where the ferry departs for Isle au Haut, take Route 15 to Main Street in Stonington and turn left at Bartlett's Market; the ferry landing is past the firehouse, at the end of the pier. GPS Coordinates: 44.1578 N, 68.6643 W

Contact: Acadia National Park, P.O. Box 177, Eagle Lake Rd., Bar Harbor, ME 04609-0177, 207/288-3338, www.nps.gov/acad. Friends of Acadia, P.O. Box 45, 43 Cottage St., Bar Harbor, ME 04609, 207/288-3340 or 800/625-0321, www.friendsofacadia.org. Isle au Haut Boat Company, P.O. Box 709, Sea Breeze Ave., Stonington, ME 04651, 207/367-5193, www.isleauhaut.com.

5 ISLE AU HAUT: DUCK HARBOR MOUNTAIN/ MERCHANT POINT LOOP
4.5 mi/2.5 hr   🏃3 ⛰9

in Acadia National Park on Isle au Haut

Taking you out to rugged coastline, scenic coves, and jutting Merchant Point, this loop

offers another way of hiking Duck Harbor Mountain. Try to time this hike for low tide when harbor seals are most likely to be seen lounging on off-shore rock outcroppings. Penobscot Bay is home to harbor and grey seals, as well as a few species of "ice seals" that occasionally wander south from subarctic regions. This hike traverses the mountain in the opposite direction from the Western Head Loop (see *Isle au Haut: Western Head Loop* listing in this chapter). It's easier going up the mountain from this side, so hikers squeamish about the rock scrambling on the Western Head side can hike up this way for the views, then just double back to Duck Harbor.

From the boat landing at Duck Harbor, turn left on the trail toward the water pump. Pass the trail branching right for the campground, and continue straight until you reach Western Head Road. Bearing left along the road, it's about 200 yards to the water pump (if you need water). For this hike, turn right on the grassy Western Head Road and follow it about a quarter mile, then turn left at the sign for the Duck Harbor Mountain Trail. Follow it a little more than a mile over several open ledges with commanding views of Isle au Haut's southern end. Reaching the trail's terminus at Squeaker Cove, turn left onto the Goat Trail, which moves in and out between woods and the coast. In less than a mile you reach a trail junction; left leads back to the dirt main road (where you would turn left for Duck Harbor), but bear right on a trail out to the rocky protrusion of Merchant Point (a great lunch spot). From Merchant Point, the trail turns back into the forest, crosses a marshy area, and reaches the main road. Turn left and follow the road a bit more than a mile to the head of Duck Harbor. Turn left onto Western Head Road, passing the water pump on the way back to the landing.

The Duck Harbor Campground has five lean-to shelters that can sleep up to six people each, and each lean-to site has a fire ring and picnic table. The lean-to shelters can be

MAINE

reserved May 15–October 15 by contacting the park (www.nps.gov/acad); reservations are required. Reservation requests cannot be postmarked or made in person at park headquarters before April 1. Camping reservations cost $25 per site, regardless of the number of nights.

User Groups: Hikers and dogs. Dogs must be leashed in the park and are prohibited from the campground. No wheelchair facilities. The island rarely gets enough snow for winter activities. Bikes, horses, and hunting are prohibited.

Permits: No permits required.

Maps: A basic map of island trails and roads is issued free to visitors arriving on the ferry or to those with camping reservations. The park website also has a map of Isle au Haut. Good trail maps of the area are the waterproof Acadia National Park (map 212) for $11.95 from Trails Illustrated (800/962-1643, www.natgeomaps.com/ti_212) and the Hiking and Biking Map to Acadia National Park and Mount Desert Island, $7.95 in waterproof Tyvek, from the Appalachian Mountain Club. For topographic island maps, request Isle au Haut West and Isle au Haut East from the USGS.

Directions: To reach the dock where the ferry departs for Isle au Haut, take Route 15 to Main Street in Stonington and turn left at Bartlett's Market; the ferry landing is past the firehouse, at the end of the pier. The round-trip cost is $35 for adults and $19 for children under age 12. The ferry is a small boat and does not transport motor vehicles (bikes are allowed).

GPS Coordinates: 44.1578 N, 68.6643 W

Contact: Acadia National Park, P.O. Box 177, Eagle Lake Rd., Bar Harbor, ME 04609-0177, 207/288-3338, www.nps.gov/acad. Friends of Acadia, P.O. Box 45, 43 Cottage St., Bar Harbor, ME 04609, 207/288-3340 or 800/625-0321, www.friendsofacadia.org. Isle au Haut Boat Company, P.O. Box 709, Sea Breeze Ave., Stonington, ME 04651, 207/367-5193, www.isleauhaut.com.

6 ISLE AU HAUT: WESTERN HEAD LOOP

5 mi/3 hr

in Acadia National Park on Isle au Haut

BEST (

If you have time for just one hike on Isle au Haut, this is the one to take. It follows the stunning rocky coast around Western Head, offers the opportunity at low tide to wander onto the tiny island known as Western Ear, and climbs over 314-foot Duck Harbor Mountain, which boasts the best views on the island. Although much of the hike is relatively flat, the trail is fairly rugged in places.

From the boat landing at Duck Harbor, follow the trail leading left toward the water pump. Pass the trail branching right for the campground and continue straight until reaching Western Head Road. Bearing left along the road, it's about 200 yards to the water pump (if you need water). For this hike, take the grassy road to the right and follow it for less than a mile. Turn right onto the Western Head Trail, which reaches the coast within about a half mile. The trail turns left (south) and follows the rugged coast out to the point at Western Head, where that trail ends and the Cliff Trail begins. At low tide, you can walk across the narrow channel out to Western Ear. Be careful not to get trapped out there, or you'll have to wait hours for the tide to go out again.

The Cliff Trail heads northward into the woods, alternately following more rugged coastline and turning back into the forest to skirt steep cliffs. It reaches the end of Western Head Road in less than a mile. Turn left and follow the road about a quarter mile. When you see a cove on your right, turn right (watch for the trail sign, which is somewhat hidden) onto the Goat Trail. (The Western Head Road leads directly back to the Duck Harbor landing, a hike of less than two miles, and is a good option for hikers who want to avoid the steep rock scrambling on Duck Harbor Mountain.) Follow the Goat Trail along the coast for less than a half mile. At scenic Squeaker Cove,

MAINE

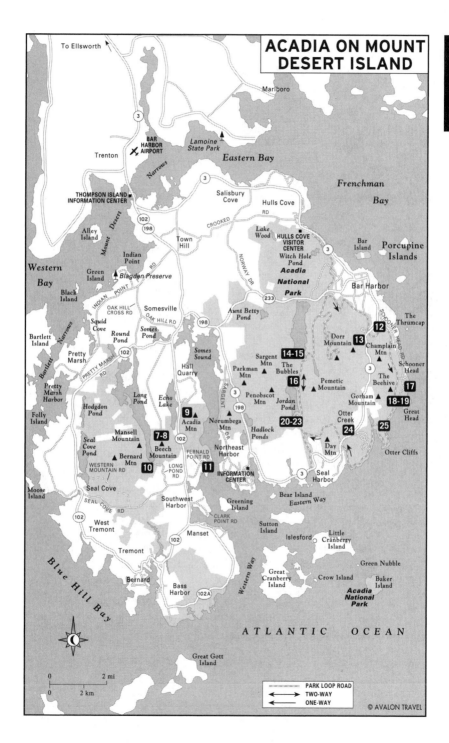

ACADIA ON MOUNT DESERT ISLAND

To Ellsworth

Marlboro

3

BAR HARBOR AIRPORT

Lamoine State Park

Trenton

Eastern Bay

Frenchman Bay

3

Salisbury Cove

Hulls Cove

THOMPSON ISLAND INFORMATION CENTER

102
198

Town Hill

HULLS COVE RD

Lake Wood

HULLS COVE VISITOR CENTER

Witch Hole Pond

Acadia National Park

Bar Island

Porcupine Islands

Alley Island

Green Island

Blagden Preserve

Indian Point

CROOKED RD

NORWAY DR

3

Bar Harbor

Western Bay

Black Island

INDIAN POINT RD

OAK HILL CROSS RD

Somesville

OAK HILL RD

Aunt Betty Pond

233

The Thrumcap

Bartlett Island

Squid Cove

Round Pond

Somes Pond

198

Dorr Mountain

13

12

Champlain Mtn

Schooner Head

Pretty Marsh

102

PRETTY MARSH RD

Somes Sound

Hall Quarry

Sargent Mtn

14-15

The Bubbles

Parkman Mtn

16

Pemetic Mountain

3

The Beehive

17

Pretty Marsh Harbor

Hodgdon Pond

Long Pond

Echo Lake

SARGENT DR

Penobscot Mtn

Jordan Pond

Gorham Mountain

18-19

Folly Island

9

Acadia Mtn

198

20-23

Otter Creek

Great Head

Seal Cove Pond

Mansell Mountain

7-8

Beech Mountain

Norumbega Mtn

Hadlock Ponds

24

25

Day Mtn

Moose Island

Bernard Mtn

10

WESTERN MOUNTAIN RD

LONG POND RD

FERNALD POINT RD

Northeast Harbor

11

INFORMATION CENTER

Otter Cliffs

SEAL COVE RD

Seal Cove

Southwest Harbor

Greening Island

Bear Island

Eastern Way

Seal Harbor

3

West Tremont

102

CLARK POINT RD

Manset

Sutton Island

Islesford

Little Cranberry Island

Green Nubble

Tremont

Western Way

Bernard

102

Bass Harbor

102A

Great Cranberry Island

Crow Island

Baker Island

Acadia National Park

Blue Hill Bay

ATLANTIC OCEAN

Great Gott Island

0   2 mi
0   2 km

PARK LOOP ROAD
TWO-WAY
ONE-WAY

© AVALON TRAVEL

MAINE

© LINDA MINER

lobster traps washed up on shore, Isle au Haut

turn left onto the Duck Harbor Mountain Trail; from here it's a bit more than a mile back to the Duck Harbor landing. The trail grows steep, involving somewhat exposed scrambling up rock slabs, and traverses several open ledges on Duck Harbor Mountain, with terrific long views of Isle au Haut Bay to the west (including Vinalhaven Island, the nearest piece of land across Isle au Haut Bay) and the Penobscot Bay islands and peninsulas to the north. The trail then descends to Western Head Road; turn right for Duck Harbor.

The Duck Harbor Campground has five lean-to shelters that can sleep up to six people each, and each lean-to site has a fire ring and picnic table. The lean-to shelters can be reserved May 15–October 15 by contacting the park (www.nps.gov/acad); reservations are required. Reservation requests cannot be postmarked or made in person at park headquarters before April 1. Camping reservations cost $25 per site, regardless of the number of nights.

User Groups: Hikers and dogs. Dogs must be leashed in the park and are prohibited from the campground. No bikes, horses, or wheelchair facilities.

Permits: No permits required.

Maps: A basic map of island trails and roads is issued free to visitors arriving on the ferry or to those with camping reservations. The park website also has a map of Isle au Haut. Good trail maps of the area are the waterproof Acadia National Park (map 212) for $11.95 from Trails Illustrated (800/962-1643, www.natgeomaps.com/ti_212) and the Hiking and Biking Map to Acadia National Park and Mount Desert Island, $7.95 in waterproof Tyvek, from the Appalachian Mountain Club. For topographic island maps, request Isle au Haut West and Isle au Haut East from the USGS.

Directions: To reach the dock where the ferry departs for Isle au Haut, take Route 15 to Main Street in Stonington and turn left at Bartlett's Market; the ferry landing is past the firehouse, at the end of the pier. The round-trip cost is $35 for adults and $19 for children under age 12. The ferry is a small boat and does not transport motor vehicles (bikes are allowed).

GPS Coordinates: 44.1578 N, 68.6643 W

Contact: Acadia National Park, P.O. Box 177, Eagle Lake Rd., Bar Harbor, ME 04609-0177, 207/288-3338, www.nps.gov/acad. Friends of Acadia, P.O. Box 45, 43 Cottage St., Bar Harbor, ME 04609, 207/288-3340 or 800/625-0321, www.friendsofacadia.org. Isle au Haut Boat Company, P.O. Box 709, Sea Breeze Ave., Stonington, ME 04651, 207/367-5193, www.isleauhaut.com.

7 BEECH MOUNTAIN
1.2 mi/1 hr   👥2 ⛰9

in Acadia National Park

A bit off the beaten path, Beech Mountain (841 ft.), on Mount Desert Island's quieter western end, offers excellent long views without the crowded trail conditions that so frequently plague popular attractions on the east side of Acadia. Steep in sections, this loop hike takes you to open cliff ridges dropping to the shores of Long Pond and an abandoned fire tower summit; the route makes for an elevation gain of 832 feet. Best of all on Beech, if you long for a slice of solitude in this highly visited national park, you have a good chance of finding it here.

Pick up the Beech Mountain Trail where it leaves from a signpost in the parking area. Only steps into this hike the well-worn footpath reaches a fork. The loop can be hiked in either direction, but for best views, bear left. Heading steeply uphill through mixed birch and pine forest, you soon emerge onto an open ledge with terrific views east and north: from the islands south of Mount Desert to Acadia, Sargent, and Penobscot mountains and the myriad waterways to the north. A short distance farther up the trail is the summit, where trees block any view, but you can climb one flight of stairs on the closed fire tower for a 360-degree view. Beyond the summit, bear right onto the descent trail, which offers magnificent views over Long Pond and all the way to Camden Hills.

User Groups: Hikers and leashed dogs. No bikes, horses, or wheelchair facilities.

Permits: The park entrance fee is $20 per vehicle for a seven-day pass June 23–October 31, or $5 for walkers, bicyclists, or motorcyclists. The park entrance fee for vehicles is $10 May 1–June 22. A one-year vehicle pass costs $40. For U.S. citizens and residents over the age of 62, a lifetime Senior Pass is available for $10.

Maps: A basic park map is available at the visitors center and the park website (www.nps.gov/acad). Good trail maps of the area are the waterproof Acadia National Park (map 212) for $11.95 from Trails Illustrated (800/962-1643, www.natgeomaps.com/ti_212) and the Hiking and Biking Map to Acadia National Park and Mount Desert Island, $7.95 in waterproof Tyvek, from the Appalachian Mountain Club.

For a topographic area map, request Southwest Harbor from the USGS.

Directions: From the junction of Routes 198 and 102 in Somesville, drive south on Route 102 for 0.8 mile and turn right onto Pretty Marsh Road at the sign for Beech Mountain and the Beech Cliffs. Drive 0.2 mile, turn left onto Beech Hill Road, and then drive 3.1 miles to the parking lot at the end of the road. The trailhead is on the right as you enter. The park visitors center is located north of Bar Harbor at the junction of Route 3 and the start of the Park Loop Road.

GPS Coordinates: 44.3155 N, 68.3435 W

Contact: Acadia National Park, P.O. Box 177, Eagle Lake Rd., Bar Harbor, ME 04609-0177, 207/288-3338, www.nps.gov/acad. Friends of Acadia, P.O. Box 45, 43 Cottage St., Bar Harbor, ME 04609, 207/288-3340 or 800/625-0321, www.friendsofacadia.org.

🗗 BEECH AND CANADA CLIFFS
0.7 mi/0.75 hr   🏃1 ⛰8

in Acadia National Park

With very little effort required, the soaring cliffs above Echo Lake provide extraordinary views of Somes Sound and the St. Sauveur mountains to the east, the Gulf of Maine and the Cranberry Isles to the south, and Beech Mountain with its fire tower to the west.

From the parking lot, the almost flat Cliffs Trail quickly leads to the crest of land rising up from Echo Lake and to a trail junction. To the right is the trail to the Canada Cliffs, to the left the trail to the Beech Cliffs. Both entail a short walk of mere steps to some very worthwhile views. Explore both if you can, though Beech Cliffs may be closed in late spring and early summer to protect nesting peregrine falcons. The Canada Cliffs should be open all year. Once you've taken in the rugged majesty, retrace your steps back to the trail junction and parking area.

MAINE

User Groups: Hikers and leashed dogs. No bikes, horses, or wheelchair facilities.

Permits: The park entrance fee is $20 per vehicle for a seven-day pass June 23–October 31, or $5 for walkers, bicyclists, or motorcyclists. The park entrance fee for vehicles is $10 May 1–June 22. A one-year vehicle pass costs $40. For U.S. citizens and residents over the age of 62, a lifetime Senior Pass is available for $10.

Maps: A basic park map is available at the visitors center and the park website (www.nps. gov/acad). Good trail maps of the area are the waterproof Acadia National Park (map 212) for $11.95 from Trails Illustrated (800/962-1643, www.natgeomaps.com/ti_212) and the Hiking and Biking Map to Acadia National Park and Mount Desert Island, $7.95 in waterproof Tyvek, from the Appalachian Mountain Club. For a topographic area map, request Southwest Harbor from the USGS.

Directions: From the junction of Routes 198 and 102 in Somesville, drive south on Route 102 for 0.8 mile and turn right onto Pretty Marsh Road at the sign for Beech Mountain and the Beech Cliffs. Continue 0.2 mile, turn left onto Beech Hill Road, and then drive 3.1 miles to the parking lot at the end of the road; the trailhead is on the left as you enter. The park visitors center is located north of Bar Harbor at the junction of Route 3 and the start of the Park Loop Road. GPS Coordinates: 44.3155 N, 68.3435 W

Contact: Acadia National Park, P.O. Box 177, Eagle Lake Rd., Bar Harbor, ME 04609-0177, 207/288-3338, www.nps.gov/acad. Friends of Acadia, P.O. Box 45, 43 Cottage St., Bar Harbor, ME 04609, 207/288-3340 or 800/625-0321, www.friendsofacadia.org.

9 ACADIA MOUNTAIN
2.5 mi/1.5 hr

in Acadia National Park

Acadia Mountain (655 ft.) is the biggest hill on the west side of Somes Sound, the 168-foot

deep salt water gorge that nearly bisects the island—and the only true fjord in the eastern United States. From the park's namesake peak are excellent views of the sound, the towns of Northeast Harbor and Southwest Harbor, and the islands south of Mount Desert. Although it's a bit of a scramble on the way up, climbing about 500 feet, this easy hike is a good one for young children.

From the turnout, cross the highway to the trail. It soon forks; stay left, and in the next mile, cross a fire road (your route of descent) and proceed to the open, rocky ledges at the summit. The trail continues past the summit to even better views from ledges atop the mountain's east face. The trail then turns right, descending steep ledges with good views, and reaches a junction with the fire road (which resembles a trail here). Turn right, and the road soon widens. Just before reaching the highway, turn left onto the Acadia Mountain Trail, which leads back to the start.

User Groups: Hikers and leashed dogs. No bikes, horses, or wheelchair facilities.

Permits: The park entrance fee is $20 per vehicle for a seven-day pass June 23–October 31, or $5 for walkers, bicyclists, or motorcyclists. The park entrance fee for vehicles is $10 May 1–June 22. A one-year vehicle pass costs $40. For U.S. citizens and residents over the age of 62, a lifetime Senior Pass is available for $10.

Maps: A basic park map is available at the visitors center and the park website (www.nps. gov/acad). Good trail maps of the area are the waterproof Acadia National Park (map 212) for $11.95 from Trails Illustrated (800/962-1643, www.natgeomaps.com/ti_212) and the Hiking and Biking Map to Acadia National Park and Mount Desert Island, $7.95 in waterproof Tyvek, from the Appalachian Mountain Club. For a topographic area map, request Southwest Harbor from the USGS.

Directions: From the junction of Routes 198 and 102 in Somesville, drive south on Route 102 for 3.4 miles to a turnout on the right at the trailhead for Acadia Mountain (look for the sign marker). The park visitors center is located

north of Bar Harbor at the junction of Route 3 and the start of the Park Loop Road.
GPS Coordinates: 44.3227 N, 68.3324 W
Contact: Acadia National Park, P.O. Box 177, Eagle Lake Rd., Bar Harbor, ME 04609-0177, 207/288-3338, www.nps.gov/acad. Friends of Acadia, P.O. Box 45, 43 Cottage St., Bar Harbor, ME 04609, 207/288-3340 or 800/625-0321, www.friendsofacadia.org.

10 BERNARD AND MANSELL MOUNTAINS
3.7 mi/2.5 hr   🚶4 ⛰7

in Acadia National Park

While Bernard (1,071 ft.) and Mansell (949 ft.) are the two highest mountains on Mount Desert Island's west side, their summits are wooded, so these trails lack the spectacular views of other peaks in Acadia National Park. Still, this loop offers a scenic walk through the woods, is fairly challenging, lacks crowds of any kind, and does take you past a few good views of the bays and Long Pond. The cumulative elevation gain on this 3.7-mile hike is about 1,200 feet.

From the parking area, hike west on the Long Pond Trail, soon bearing left onto the Cold Brook Trail. In less than a half mile, cross Gilley Field and follow a road a short distance to the Sluiceway Trail on the right. It climbs fairly steeply to the South Face Trail, where you turn left for the Bernard Mountain summit, a few minutes' walk away. Backtrack and follow the trail down into Great Notch and straight ahead to the summit of Mansell Mountain. Continue over the summit, picking up the Perpendicular Trail, which descends the rugged east face of Mansell, often passing below low cliffs, to the Long Pond Trail. Turn right for the parking area.
User Groups: Hikers and leashed dogs. No bikes, horses, or wheelchair facilities.
Permits: The park entrance fee is $20 per vehicle for a seven-day pass June 23–October 31,

or $5 for walkers, bicyclists, or motorcyclists. The park entrance fee for vehicles is $10 May 1–June 22. A one-year vehicle pass costs $40. For U.S. citizens and residents over the age of 62, a lifetime Senior Pass is available for $10.
Maps: A basic park map is available at the visitors center and the park website (www.nps.gov/acad). Good trail maps of the area are the waterproof Acadia National Park (map 212) for $11.95 from Trails Illustrated (800/962-1643, www.natgeomaps.com/ti_212) and the Hiking and Biking Map to Acadia National Park and Mount Desert Island, $7.95 in waterproof Tyvek, from the Appalachian Mountain Club. For a topographic area map, request Southwest Harbor from the USGS.
Directions: From Route 102 in Southwest Harbor, turn west onto Seal Cove Road. Take a right onto Long Pond Road and follow it to the parking area at the south end of Long Pond (and a great view of the pond). The park visitors center is located north of Bar Harbor at the junction of Route 3 and the start of the Park Loop Road.
GPS Coordinates: 44.2991 N, 68.3493 W
Contact: Acadia National Park, P.O. Box 177, Eagle Lake Rd., Bar Harbor, ME 04609-0177, 207/288-3338, www.nps.gov/acad. Friends of Acadia, P.O. Box 45, 43 Cottage St., Bar Harbor, ME 04609, 207/288-3340 or 800/625-0321, www.friendsofacadia.org.

11 FLYING MOUNTAIN
0.6 mi/0.5 hr   🚶2 ⛰8

in Acadia National Park

Nearly bisecting Mount Desert Island, the glacially carved fjord, Somes Sound, is one of Acadia's most distinctive features. This short hike up Flying Mountain, a hill that rises just 284 feet above Somes (rhymes with homes), offers surprisingly nice views of the fjord from open ledges. The relatively small effort needed to reach this direct perch makes this a good hike for beginners and kids.

From the parking area, pick up the Flying Mountain Trail at the signpost. Ascending steadily from the start, the last stretch could seem a bit steep for some. Once on the ledges, be sure to continue to the true summit, marked by a signpost, where the views are often even better than those you see when you first reach the ledges. Retrace your steps to return to your car.

User Groups: Hikers and leashed dogs. No bikes, horses, or wheelchair facilities.

Permits: The park entrance fee is $20 per vehicle for a seven-day pass June 23–October 31, or $5 for walkers, bicyclists, or motorcyclists. The park entrance fee for vehicles is $10 May 1–June 22. A one-year vehicle pass costs $40. For U.S. citizens and residents over the age of 62, a lifetime Senior Pass is available for $10.

Maps: A basic park map is available at the visitors center and the park website (www.nps.gov/acad). Good trail maps of the area are the waterproof Acadia National Park (map 212) for $11.95 from Trails Illustrated (800/962-1643, www.natgeomaps.com/ti_212) and the Hiking and Biking Map to Acadia National Park and Mount Desert Island, $7.95 in waterproof Tyvek, from the Appalachian Mountain Club. For a topographic area map, request Southwest Harbor from the USGS.

Directions: From the junction of Routes 198 and 102 in Somesville, go south on Route 102 for 5.4 miles and turn left on Fernald Point Road. Drive one mile to a parking area on the left. The park visitors center is north of Bar Harbor, at the junction of Route 3 and Park Loop Road.

GPS Coordinates: 44.2994 N, 68.3162 W

Contact: Acadia National Park, P.O. Box 177, Eagle Lake Rd., Bar Harbor, ME 04609-0177, 207/288-3338, www.nps.gov/acad. Friends of Acadia, P.O. Box 45, 43 Cottage St., Bar Harbor, ME 04609, 207/288-3340 or 800/625-0321, www.friendsofacadia.org.

12 ACADIA TRAVERSE

13.5 mi one-way/10 hr

in Acadia National Park

Only have a day to spend at Acadia? If you are physically up for it, this traverse of Mount Desert Island's east side hits the park's six major peaks and spends much of the route above the trees, with sweeping views from a succession of long, open ridges. It's a long day: including time spent on short rest stops (but not including time spent shuttling vehicles), you may be out for 10 hours, finishing just before sunset. The cumulative elevation gain is about 4,700 feet—more than hiking up Mount Washington. And many of these trails—particularly the Beechcroft, the Cadillac Mountain West Face, and a section of the Penobscot Mountain Trail—are very steep. There are water sources on top of Cadillac Mountain and at the Jordan Pond House for refilling bottles.

Follow the Bear Brook Trail south to the summit of Champlain Mountain; within minutes of setting out, you enjoy views of the Frenchman Bay islands. Turn right (west) and descend the Beechcroft Trail 0.8 mile to the small pond called the Tarn (crossing Route 3). Ascend the steep Dorr Mountain East Face Trail, then turn right (north) onto the Dorr Mountain Trail and reach the open summit of Dorr (approximately one mile from the Tarn). Passing north over the summit, the trail becomes the North Ridge Trail and reaches a junction in 0.1 mile. Here, take a left for the Dorr Mountain Notch Trail. The trail dips 0.4 mile into the shallow but spectacular notch between Dorr and Cadillac Mountains and then climbs the open slope for half a mile to the Cadillac Mountain summit.

Descend the Cadillac Mountain South Ridge Trail for half a mile to the Cadillac Mountain West Face Trail, which drops very steeply for nearly a mile to a parking lot at the north end of Bubble Pond. Follow the carriage road south roughly 0.1 mile; then turn right onto the Pemetic Mountain Trail and take it over Pemetic's summit, 1.3 miles from Bubble Pond. Continue south over the long, rocky ridge for just over half a mile and then bear right onto the Pemetic West Cliff Trail. That trail descends 0.6 mile to the Pond Trail; turn right onto the Jordan Pond Trail, and descend easily another 0.4 mile to the Park Loop Road. Cross the road, enter the woods, and turn left on a trail to the Jordan Pond House. The Penobscot Mountain Trail begins behind the Jordan Pond House and leads 1.5 miles to the summit of Penobscot, at one point going straight up steep, rocky terrain. From the open summit of Penobscot, the Sargent Pond Trail heads northwest. Winding past Sargent Pond, the trail comes to a tiny alpine pond nestled among the conifers where it reaches a junction. Turn right (north) onto the Sargent Mountain South Ridge Trail, gradually climbing the long ridge to the 1,373-foot summit, a mile beyond Penobscot's, for the final panoramic view of this hike.

Descend west on the Grandgent Trail (be careful not to confuse it with the Sargent Mountain North Ridge Trail, which will add mileage to your hike at a time when you don't want it) for just over a mile to the top of little Parkman Mountain. (Note the trail signs before starting down off Sargent. Grandgent leaves from the summit heading due west. If you find yourself walking north, chances are you are on the North Ridge Trail.) Turn left onto the Parkman Mountain Trail, descending southward. You cross two carriage roads; at the second crossing, turn right and follow that carriage road a short distance to a connector leading left to the parking area on Route 198, a mile from the Parkman summit. Then take off your boots and vigorously massage your feet.

User Groups: Hikers and leashed dogs. No bikes, horses, or wheelchair facilities.

Permits: The park entrance fee is $20 per vehicle for a seven-day pass June 23–October 31, or $5 for walkers, bicyclists, or motorcyclists. The park entrance fee for vehicles is $10 May 1–June 22. A one-year vehicle pass costs $40. For U.S. citizens and residents over the age of 62, a lifetime Senior Pass is available for $10.

Maps: A basic park map is available at the visitors center and the park website (www.nps.gov/acad). Good trail maps of the area are the waterproof Acadia National Park (map 212) for $11.95 from Trails Illustrated (800/962-1643, www.natgeomaps.com/ti_212) and the Hiking and Biking Map to Acadia National Park and Mount Desert Island, $7.95 in waterproof Tyvek, from the Appalachian Mountain Club. For a topographic area map, request Seal Harbor from the USGS.

Directions: Two vehicles are needed for this traverse. Leave one vehicle at the northernmost of the two parking areas north of Upper Hadlock Pond along Route 198 in Northeast Harbor. Then drive to the hike's start, a turnout on the Park Loop Road at the Bear Brook Trail, 0.2 mile past a picnic area. If you're traveling with a group of friends, you might leave a third vehicle roughly halfway through the hike, at either the Bubble Pond or Jordan Pond parking areas, in case you can't finish the hike. The park visitors center is located north of Bar Harbor at the junction of Route 3 and the start of the Park Loop Road.

GPS Coordinates: 44.3602 N, 68.1983 W

Contact: Acadia National Park, P.O. Box 177, Eagle Lake Rd., Bar Harbor, ME 04609-0177, 207/288-3338, www.nps.gov/acad. Friends of Acadia, P.O. Box 45, 43 Cottage St., Bar Harbor, ME 04609, 207/288-3340 or 800/625-0321, www.friendsofacadia.org.

13 DORR AND CADILLAC MOUNTAINS
3 mi/2 hr   🏃4 ⛰10

in Acadia National Park

BEST (

This moderate hike combines the highest peak on Mount Desert Island, 1,530-foot Cadillac Mountain, with its neighbor to the east, 1,270-foot Dorr, a mountain just as scenic but far less crowded. For much of this hike, you enjoy continuous views that take in Champlain Mountain, the islands of Frenchman Bay, and the rugged terrain atop Dorr and Cadillac. While just three miles long, this hike's cumulative elevation gain exceeds 1,500 feet.

From the parking area, turn left onto the Jessup Path and right onto the Dorr Mountain East Face Trail, which ascends numerous switchbacks up the steep flank of the mountain. Turn left onto the Dorr Mountain Trail; the trail actually passes just north of Dorr's true summit, which is reached by walking a nearly flat 0.1 mile south on the Dorr Mountain South Ridge Trail. Double back and turn left (west) onto the Dorr Mountain Notch Trail, which drops into the rugged—though not very deep—notch between Dorr and Cadillac. (This distinctive notch is visible from Route 3 south of the Tarn.) Follow the trail up the open east slope of Cadillac to the summit. Descend the way you came, but instead of turning right onto the Dorr Mountain East Face Trail, continue straight on the somewhat more forgiving Dorr Mountain Trail and then turn right onto the Jessup Path for the parking area.

User Groups: Hikers and leashed dogs. No bikes, horses, or wheelchair facilities.

Permits: The park entrance fee is $20 per vehicle for a seven-day pass June 23–October 31, or $5 for walkers, bicyclists, or motorcyclists. The park entrance fee for vehicles is $10 May 1–June 22. A one-year vehicle pass costs $40. For U.S. citizens and residents over the age of 62, a lifetime Senior Pass is available for $10.

Maps: A basic park map is available at the visitors center and the park website (www.nps.gov/acad). Good trail maps of the area are the waterproof Acadia National Park (map 212) for $11.95 from Trails Illustrated (800/962-1643, www.natgeomaps.com/ti_212) and the Hiking and Biking Map to Acadia National Park and Mount Desert Island, $7.95 in waterproof Tyvek, from the Appalachian Mountain Club. For a topographic area map, request Seal Harbor from the USGS.

Directions: Take Route 3 south from Bar Harbor or north from Blackwoods Campground, and turn into the parking area at the Tarn, just

south of the Sieur de Monts entrance to the Park Loop Road. The park visitors center is located north of Bar Harbor, at the junction of Route 3 and the start of the Park Loop Road.

GPS Coordinates: 44.3556 N, 68.2048 W

Contact: Acadia National Park, P.O. Box 177, Eagle Lake Rd., Bar Harbor, ME 04609-0177, 207/288-3338, www.nps.gov/acad. Friends of Acadia, P.O. Box 45, 43 Cottage St., Bar Harbor, ME 04609, 207/288-3340 or 800/625-0321, www.friendsofacadia.org.

1.4 JORDAN POND/EAGLE LAKE/BUBBLE POND CARRIAGE ROAD LOOP

11.5 mi/6 hr   🥾5 ⛰9

in Acadia National Park

This moderately hilly loop is one of the best carriage road trails in the park, passing high above Jordan Pond, circling Eagle Lake, and cruising along the western shore of Bubble Pond. Some may opt to bike this loop, but taking to the trail on foot gives you a better opportunity to savor every detail of this particularly lovely section of Acadia.

From the Bubble Pond parking area, follow the carriage road north along Eagle Lake. At the lake's northwest corner, turn left and follow the carriage road along the lake's western shore. After angling away from the lake (around Conners Nubble), turn right, then left, soon passing above Jordan Pond. At the pond's south end, turn left and cross the Park Loop Road. Follow this carriage road all the way back to Bubble Pond. Along the way, you pass a carriage road leading to the right across a bridge over the Loop Road; the loop beginning across the bridge climbs Day Mountain, a fun, if challenging, ride up and a fast ride down for mountain bikers who have the time and energy to add a few miles to this trail's distance.

User Groups: Hikers, bikers, leashed dogs,

skiers, and snowshoers. No wheelchair facilities. Horses and hunting are prohibited.

Permits: The park entrance fee is $20 per vehicle for a seven-day pass June 23–October 31, or $5 for walkers, bicyclists, or motorcyclists. The park entrance fee for vehicles is $10 May 1–June 22. A one-year vehicle pass costs $40. For U.S. citizens and residents over the age of 62, a lifetime Senior Pass is available for $10.

Maps: A basic park map is available at the visitors center and the park website (www.nps.gov/acad). Good trail maps of the area are the waterproof Acadia National Park (map 212) for $11.95 from Trails Illustrated (800/962-1643, www.natgeomaps.com/ti_212) and the Hiking and Biking Map to Acadia National Park and Mount Desert Island, $7.95 in waterproof Tyvek, from the Appalachian Mountain Club. For topographic area maps, request Seal Harbor and Southwest Harbor from the USGS.

Directions: Take Route 3 south from Bar Harbor to Seal Harbor. Turn right at the Acadia National Park entrance and left on the Park Loop Road, following it 2.6 miles past the Jordan Pond parking area to the Bubble Pond parking area. From the park visitors center, follow the Park Loop Road south. Where it splits, turn right for the Bubble Pond parking area. You can bike to the start from Blackwoods Campground, adding about seven miles round-trip: Bike Route 3 toward Seal Harbor and where the highway crosses a bridge over the Park Loop Road, carry your bike down a footpath to the Loop Road and follow it north. Just before the Jordan Pond House, turn right onto this carriage road loop. The park visitors center is north of Bar Harbor at the junction of Route 3 and Park Loop Road.

GPS Coordinates: 44.3354 N, 68.2510 W

Contact: Acadia National Park, P.O. Box 177, Eagle Lake Rd., Bar Harbor, ME 04609-0177, 207/288-3338, www.nps.gov/acad. Friends of Acadia, P.O. Box 45, 43 Cottage St., Bar Harbor, ME 04609, 207/288-3340 or 800/625-0321, www.friendsofacadia.org.

15 CADILLAC MOUNTAIN: WEST FACE TRAIL
2.8 mi/2.5 hr 4 9

in Acadia National Park

This trail offers the most direct and difficult route up Mount Desert Island's highest peak, 1,530-foot Cadillac Mountain. It involves a great deal of scrambling over steep slabs of open rock, relentlessly strenuous hiking, and about 1,200 feet of elevation gain. Descending may be more difficult than ascending. Much of the trail lies in the woods, but the occasional views—which become more frequent as you climb higher—down to Bubble Pond and of the deep cleft separating Cadillac and Pemetic Mountains are spectacular.

From the parking area, cross the carriage road and pick up the Cadillac Mountain West Face Trail at the north end of Bubble Pond. The trail rises sharply from the very beginning, following a rocky uphill path towards a large grove of cedar trees. Skirting left through the grove, the trail soon emerges onto the mountain's exposed face, a series of granite slabs broken only by patches of scrub vegetation. With so much rock, it's easy to lose the trail here; rely on the frequent trail cairns to help keep you on course. Wide-open, bird's eye views of the ocean and surrounding parkland may take your mind off the steep ascent. In just under a mile from the trailhead (and after a bit of a rock scramble at the very end), you top out on the mountain's South Ridge. Turn left onto the Cadillac Mountain South Ridge Trail and follow it to the summit. Head back along the same route.

User Groups: Hikers and leashed dogs. No bikes, horses, or wheelchair facilities.

Permits: The park entrance fee is $20 per vehicle for a seven-day pass June 23–October 31, or $5 for walkers, bicyclists, or motorcyclists. The park entrance fee for vehicles is $10 May 1–June 22. A one-year vehicle pass costs $40. For U.S. citizens and residents over the age of 62, a lifetime Senior Pass is available for $10.

MAINE

© LINDA MINER

looking toward The Bubbles from the southern end of Jordan Pond, Acadia National Park

Maps: A basic park map is available at the visitors center and the park website (www.nps.gov/acad). Good trail maps of the area are the waterproof Acadia National Park (map 212) for $11.95 from Trails Illustrated (800/962-1643, www.natgeomaps.com/ti_212) and the Hiking and Biking Map to Acadia National Park and Mount Desert Island, $7.95 in waterproof Tyvek, from the Appalachian Mountain Club. For topographic area maps, request Seal Harbor and Southwest Harbor from the USGS.

Directions: Take Route 3 south from Bar Harbor to Seal Harbor. Turn right at the Acadia National Park entrance and left on the Park Loop Road, following it 2.6 miles past the Jordan Pond parking area to the Bubble Pond parking area. Or from the park visitors center, follow the Park Loop Road south. Where it splits, turn right for the Bubble Pond parking area. The park visitors center is located north of Bar Harbor at the junction of Route 3 and Park Loop Road.

GPS Coordinates: 44.3354 N, 68.2510 W

Contact: Acadia National Park, P.O. Box 177, Eagle Lake Rd., Bar Harbor, ME 04609-0177,

207/288-3338, www.nps.gov/acad. Friends of Acadia, P.O. Box 45, 43 Cottage St., Bar Harbor, ME 04609, 207/288-3340 or 800/625-0321, www.friendsofacadia.org.

16 THE BUBBLES/EAGLE LAKE LOOP

4.2 mi/2 hr   🥾4 ⛰️10

in Acadia National Park

BEST (

The Bubbles, the two 800-foot rounded peaks near the north shore of Jordan Pond really do look like twin pockets of air rising up from the pond's surface. This loop takes you to open ledges atop both North and South Bubble, with excellent views of Jordan Pond and the steep hills enclosing it. The loop also leads to Conners Nubble—a commanding overlook of Eagle Lake to the north of the Bubbles—and finishes with a walk along the rocky shore of Eagle Lake. A popular destination for summer tourists to Acadia, this loop may be at its best in September when the Bubbles glow with autumn color—an eye-popping treat for post-

Labor Day visitors to the park. For a shorter walk, the round-trip hike to the summit of North Bubble alone is 1.2 miles.

From the Bubble Rock parking area, the Bubble-Pemetic Trail heads west, then northwest through the woods, then turns sharply left, and climbs to the saddle between North and South Bubble within a half mile. Turn left to quickly reach the summit of South Bubble. Backtrack and ascend the North Bubble Trail to that summit, which is higher than the South Bubble summit. Continue over North Bubble, crossing a carriage road, to reach Conners Nubble in another mile. After taking in the view, descend and turn right onto the Eagle Lake Trail, dropping quickly to hug the lakeshore. At approximately 3.0 miles into this hike, turn right on the Jordan Pond Carry Trail and follow for about a mile back to the Bubble-Pemetic Trail, the return route to the parking area.

User Groups: Hikers and leashed dogs. No bikes, horses, or wheelchair facilities.

Permits: The park entrance fee is $20 per vehicle for a seven-day pass June 23–October 31, or $5 for walkers, bicyclists, or motorcyclists. The park entrance fee for vehicles is $10 May 1–June 22. A one-year vehicle pass costs $40. For U.S. citizens and residents over the age of 62, a lifetime Senior Pass is available for $10.

Maps: A basic park map is available at the visitors center and the park website (www.nps. gov/acad). Good trail maps of the area are the waterproof Acadia National Park (map 212) for $11.95 from Trails Illustrated (800/962-1643, www.natgeomaps.com/ti_212) and the Hiking and Biking Map to Acadia National Park and Mount Desert Island, $7.95 in waterproof Tyvek, from the Appalachian Mountain Club. For topographic area maps, request Seal Harbor and Southwest Harbor from the USGS.

Directions: Drive on Route 3 south from Bar Harbor to Seal Harbor. Turn right at the Acadia National Park entrance and left on the Park Loop Road, following it to the Bubble Rock

parking area, 1.6 miles past the Jordan Pond parking area. Or from the park visitors center, follow the Park Loop Road south. Where it splits, turn right for the Bubble Rock parking area. The park visitors center is located north of Bar Harbor, at the junction of Route 3 and the start of the Park Loop Road.

GPS Coordinates: 44.3354 N, 68.2510 W

Contact: Acadia National Park, P.O. Box 177, Eagle Lake Road, Bar Harbor, ME 04609-0177, 207/288-3338, www.nps.gov/acad. Friends of Acadia, P.O. Box 45, 43 Cottage St., Bar Harbor, ME 04609, 207/288-3340 or 800/625-0321, www.friendsofacadia.org.

17 GREAT HEAD
1.6 mi/1 hr   🏃1 ⛰9

in Acadia National Park

BEST (

This short, easy walk ascends 324 feet to the tops of tall cliffs rising virtually out of the ocean, offering spectacular views that stretch from the islands of Frenchman Bay to Otter Cliffs. It's a popular hike, but like many popular hikes, it tends to attract most folks during the day. Come here in the early morning or late afternoon for a less crowded visit. And this hike even gets a celebrity endorsement! Domestic mogul Martha Stewart, who owns a summer house nearby in Seal Harbor, calls Great Head her favorite hike in all of Acadia. When in the area, she often finds her way here to watch the sunrise.

From the parking area, follow the wide gravel path into the woods, soon reaching a trail entering from the left—the way this loop returns. Continue straight ahead, passing above Sand Beach (a trail leads down to the beach) and then ascending slightly. Where the trail forks, be sure to stay to the right, soon emerging at the cliffs. To return, follow the blue blazes north back to the gravel path and then turn right to head back to the parking area.

User Groups: Hikers and leashed dogs. No bikes, horses, or wheelchair facilities.

MAINE

Permits: The park entrance fee is $20 per vehicle for a seven-day pass June 23–October 31, or $5 for walkers, bicyclists, or motorcyclists. The park entrance fee for vehicles is $10 May 1–June 22. A one-year vehicle pass costs $40. For U.S. citizens and residents over the age of 62, a lifetime Senior Pass is available for $10.

Maps: A basic park map is available at the visitors center and the park website (www.nps.gov/acad). Good trail maps of the area are the waterproof Acadia National Park (map 212) for $11.95 from Trails Illustrated (800/962-1643, www.natgeomaps.com/ti_212) and the Hiking and Biking Map to Acadia National Park and Mount Desert Island, $7.95 in waterproof Tyvek, from the Appalachian Mountain Club. For a topographic area map, request Seal Harbor from the USGS.

Directions: Drive on the Park Loop Road to the east side of Mount Desert Island, past the Precipice parking area. Immediately before the Loop Road entrance station (fee charged), turn left onto an unmarked road. Drive 0.2 mile, turn right, drive another 0.4 mile, and pull into a parking area on the left. The park visitors center is located north of Bar Harbor at the junction of Route 3 and the start of Park Loop Road.

GPS Coordinates: 44.3294 N, 68.1840 W

Contact: Acadia National Park, P.O. Box 177, Eagle Lake Rd., Bar Harbor, ME 04609-0177, 207/288-3338, www.nps.gov/acad. Friends of Acadia, P.O. Box 45, 43 Cottage St., Bar Harbor, ME 04609, 207/288-3340 or 800/625-0321, www.friendsofacadia.org.

18 THE BEEHIVE
1.3 mi/1.5 hr

in Acadia National Park

The climb up the cliffs on the Beehive's east face looks as if it's strictly for technical rock climbers when you stare up at it from the Sand Beach parking lot. The trail zigs and zags up ledges on the nearly vertical face, requiring hand-and-foot scrambling and the use of iron ladder rungs drilled into the rock. Though it's a fairly short climb, and just a half-mile walk some 400 feet uphill, this trail is not for anyone in poor physical condition or uncomfortable with exposure and heights. On the other hand, it's a wonderful trail for hikers looking for a little adventure. All the way up, you're treated to unimpeded views over Frenchman Bay and the coast, from Sand Beach and Great Head south to Otter Cliffs. On the summit, you look north to Champlain Mountain and northwest to Dorr and Cadillac Mountains.

From the parking area, cross the Loop Road and walk a few steps to the right to the Bowl Trail. You will soon turn onto the Beehive Trail and follow it to the summit. Continuing over the summit, turn left onto the Bowl Trail and make the easy descent back to the Loop Road. A very scenic and popular 3.7-mile loop links this with the Gorham Mountain Trail and Ocean Path (see *Gorham Mountain* and *Ocean Path* listings in this chapter).

User Groups: Hikers and leashed dogs. No bikes, horses, or wheelchair facilities.

Permits: The park entrance fee is $20 per vehicle for a seven-day pass June 23–October 31, or $5 for walkers, bicyclists, or motorcyclists. The park entrance fee for vehicles is $10 May 1–June 22. A one-year vehicle pass costs $40. For U.S. citizens and residents over the age of 62, a lifetime Senior Pass is available for $10.

Maps: A basic park map is available at the visitors center and the park website (www.nps.gov/acad). Good trail maps of the area are the waterproof Acadia National Park (map 212) for $11.95 from Trails Illustrated (800/962-1643, www.natgeomaps.com/ti_212) and the Hiking and Biking Map to Acadia National Park and Mount Desert Island, $7.95 in waterproof Tyvek, from the Appalachian Mountain Club. For a topographic area map, request Seal Harbor from the USGS.

Directions: Drive the Park Loop Road to the east side of Mount Desert Island and the large parking area at Sand Beach, half a mile south of the entrance station. The park visitors center is located north of Bar Harbor, at the junction of Route 3 and the start of the Park Loop Road.

GPS Coordinates: 44.3310 N, 68.1851 W

Contact: Acadia National Park, P.O. Box 177, Eagle Lake Rd., Bar Harbor, ME 04609-0177, 207/288-3338, www.nps.gov/acad. Friends of Acadia, P.O. Box 45, 43 Cottage St., Bar Harbor, ME 04609, 207/288-3340 or 800/625-0321, www.friendsofacadia.org.

19 OCEAN PATH

3.6 mi/2 hr

in Acadia National Park

This is one of the most popular hikes in the national park and for good reason. The Ocean Path follows the rugged shoreline from Sand Beach to Otter Point, passing over the top of Otter Cliffs—the island's tallest cliffs, popular with rock climbers. About midway along this trail is the famous Thunder Hole, where incoming waves crash into a channel-like pocket in the rocks, trapping air to create a loud and deep popping noise; it's most impressive around high tide.

From the parking area, the trail veers right. The shore here is mostly rocky, but constantly changes character over the course of this trail—some beaches are covered exclusively with small, round stones, others only with large rocks. As it approaches Otter Cliffs, the trail enters a small woods (across the road from another parking lot) and emerges atop Otter Cliffs. The trail continues beyond the cliffs to Otter Point, where it was extended a short distance in recent years to include a particularly scenic section right along the shore at Otter Point. Hike back along the same route.

Special Note: In the event of stormy weather or strong tidal surges, avoid this hike. In 2009, several people were dragged into the ocean near Otter Point by powerful waves,

the remnants of a passing hurricane. Always heed surf warnings issued by rangers and other park personnel.

User Groups: Hikers and leashed dogs. No bikes, horses, or wheelchairs.

Permits: The park entrance fee is $20 per vehicle for a seven-day pass June 23–October 31, or $5 for walkers, bicyclists, or motorcyclists. The park entrance fee for vehicles is $10 May 1–June 22. A one-year vehicle pass costs $40. For U.S. citizens and residents over the age of 62, a lifetime Senior Pass is available for $10.

Maps: A basic park map is available at the visitors center and the park website (www.nps.gov/acad). Good trail maps of the area are the waterproof Acadia National Park (map 212) for $11.95 from Trails Illustrated (800/962-1643, www.natgeomaps.com/ti_212) and the Hiking and Biking Map to Acadia National Park and Mount Desert Island, $7.95 in waterproof Tyvek, from the Appalachian Mountain Club. For a topographic area map, request Seal Harbor from the USGS.

Directions: Drive on the Park Loop Road to Mount Desert Island's east side and the large parking area at Sand Beach, half a mile south of the entrance station. The park visitors center is located north of Bar Harbor at the junction of Route 3 and the start of the Park Loop Road.

GPS Coordinates: 44.3310 N, 68.1851 W

Contact: Acadia National Park, P.O. Box 177, Eagle Lake Rd., Bar Harbor, ME 04609-0177, 207/288-3338, www.nps.gov/acad. Friends of Acadia, P.O. Box 45, 43 Cottage St., Bar Harbor, ME 04609, 207/288-3340 or 800/625-0321, www.friendsofacadia.org.

20 PENOBSCOT AND SARGENT MOUNTAINS

4.5 mi/3 hr

in Acadia National Park

While nearly everyone who comes to Acadia National Park knows of Cadillac Mountain, few have heard of—and even fewer will actually hike—Penobscot and Sargent Mountains, which rise abruptly from the west shore of Jordan Pond. Yet the elevations of Sargent at 1,373 feet and Penobscot at 1,194 feet rank them as the second- and fifth-highest peaks on Mount Desert Island. And the ridge connecting them pushes nearly as much area above the trees as Cadillac's scenic South Ridge. For much of this 4.5-mile hike, which climbs more than 1,200 feet in elevation, you enjoy long views east to the Pemetic and Cadillac Mountains, south to the many offshore islands, and west across Somes Sound and Penobscot Bay to the Camden Hills.

From the parking area, head down the dirt access road toward Jordan Pond and turn left onto a trail leading about 50 yards to the Jordan Pond House. The Penobscot Mountain Trail begins behind the Jordan Pond House, soon ascending steep ledges that require some scrambling. After a rugged half mile, the trail reaches Penobscot's ridge, where the terrain flattens out somewhat and the hiking gets much easier. At 1.6 miles from the trailhead, the Penobscot summit is reached. Staying on the Penobscot Trail as it leaves the summit, in another 0.5 mile, dip into a small saddle between the mountains, soon reaching a trail junction. Here, turn left onto the Sargent Pond Trail, passing the small pond in the woods. Turn right onto the Sargent Mountain South Ridge Trail, ascending the long slope to the summit, marked by a pile of rocks. Just beyond the summit, turn right onto the Jordan Cliffs Trail, which traverses above the cliffs visible from Jordan Pond. Cross a carriage road and turn left onto the Penobscot Mountain Trail to return.

User Groups: Hikers and leashed dogs. No bikes, horses, or wheelchair facilities.

Permits: The park entrance fee is $20 per vehicle for a seven-day pass June 23–October 31, or $5 for walkers, bicyclists, or motorcyclists. The park entrance fee for vehicles is $10 May 1–June 22. A one-year vehicle pass costs $40. For U.S. citizens and residents over the age of 62, a lifetime Senior Pass is available for $10.

Maps: A basic park map is available at the visitors center and the park website (www.nps. gov/acad). Good trail maps of the area are the waterproof Acadia National Park (map 212) for $11.95 from Trails Illustrated (800/962-1643, www.natgeomaps.com/ti_212) and the Hiking and Biking Map to Acadia National Park and Mount Desert Island, $7.95 in waterproof Tyvek, from the Appalachian Mountain Club. For a topographic area map, request Southwest Harbor from the USGS.

Directions: Take Route 3 south from Bar Harbor to Seal Harbor. Turn right at the Acadia National Park entrance and left on the Park Loop Road, following it to the Jordan Pond parking area. Or from the park visitors center, follow the Park Loop Road south. Where it splits, turn right and continue to the Jordan Pond parking area. The park visitors center is located north of Bar Harbor, at the junction of Route 3 and the start of the Park Loop Road. GPS Coordinates: 44.3205 N, 68.2526 W

Contact: Acadia National Park, P.O. Box 177, Eagle Lake Rd., Bar Harbor, ME 04609-0177, 207/288-3338, www.nps.gov/acad. Friends of Acadia, P.O. Box 45, 43 Cottage St., Bar Harbor, ME 04609, 207/288-3340 or 800/625-0321, www.friendsofacadia.org.

21 JORDAN POND/SARGENT MOUNTAIN CARRIAGE ROAD LOOP

16 mi/8 hr　　　　　🥾5 ⛰9

in Acadia National Park

Jordan Pond and the nearby lakes and wooded hills are popular destinations within Acadia, and this moderately hilly loop makes for a pleasant long-distance hike over several miles of broken-stone pathways. Part of the park's 45-mile carriage road system, the winding lanes were the brainchild of John D. Rockefeller as a way to encourage non-vehicular use of the park. This route could also make for an idyllic afternoon of biking or horseback riding,

MAINE

© JAROSLAW TRAPSZO

Rosa rugosa (beach rose) flourishes along Acadia's carriage roads.

but for hikers, walking the carriage roads may be the best way to cover a wide swath of parkland without coming in contact with Acadia's often traffic-choked auto access roads.

For navigation ease, carriage road intersections within Acadia National Park are marked with numbered signposts. From the Jordan Pond parking area, go south on the Park Loop Road a short distance to a right turn onto the first carriage road you reach. Within a few feet, you will see a signpost marked 16. Here, take a right onto another carriage road and continue, passing intersections with carriage roads 15 and 14, and soon ascending a gradual slope above Jordan Pond. At approximately two miles into the hike, an intersection is reached at signpost 10. Turn right and in another 0.1 mile turn left at signpost 8 to follow the northwest shoreline of Eagle Lake. After 1.9 miles on this road, turn left at signpost 9.

Winding through the woods for 2.5 miles, the road passes secluded Aunt Betty

Pond—there's a view across the pond toward Sargent Mountain—and eventually contours around Sargent. Turn right at signpost 11 and in another 3.3 miles, pass almost straight through the intersection at signpost 13, heading south to pass Upper Hadlock Pond (on the right). At 1.5 miles past signpost 13, the carriage road makes a U-turn, passing by signpost 18. At signpost 19, take a right, travel a brief 0.9 mile, and then take a left at signpost 20. In another 1.2 miles, bear left at signpost 21 and in one more mile, take a right at signpost 14 to return to Jordan Pond. Pass signpost 15 to again reach signpost 16. Turn left at 16 to reach the Park Loop Road and the Jordan Pond Parking area.

User Groups: Hikers, bikers, leashed dogs, and horses. No wheelchair facilities. Hunting is prohibited.

Permits: The park entrance fee is $20 per vehicle for a seven-day pass June 23–October 31, or $5 for walkers, bicyclists, or motorcyclists. The park entrance fee for vehicles is $10 May 1–June 22. A one-year vehicle pass costs $40. For U.S. citizens and residents over the age of 62, a lifetime Senior Pass is available for $10.

Maps: A basic park map is available at the visitors center and the park website (www.nps. gov/acad). Good trail maps of the area are the waterproof Acadia National Park (map 212) for $11.95 from Trails Illustrated (800/962-1643, www.natgeomaps.com/ti_212) and the Hiking and Biking Map to Acadia National Park and Mount Desert Island, $7.95 in waterproof Tyvek, from the Appalachian Mountain Club. For a topographic area map, request Southwest Harbor from the USGS.

Directions: Take Route 3 south from Bar Harbor to Seal Harbor. Turn right at the Acadia National Park entrance and left on the Park Loop Road, following it to the Jordan Pond parking area. You can bike to the start from Blackwoods Campground, adding about seven miles round-trip: Bike Route 3 toward Seal Harbor, and where the highway crosses a bridge over the Park Loop Road, carry your bike down a footpath to the Loop Road; then follow it north and turn left onto a carriage path just before the Jordan Pond House. The park visitors center is located north of Bar Harbor at the junction of Route 3 and the start of the Park Loop Road.

GPS Coordinates: 44.3205 N, 68.2526 W

Contact: Acadia National Park, P.O. Box 177, Eagle Lake Rd., Bar Harbor, ME 04609-0177, 207/288-3338, www.nps.gov/acad. Friends of Acadia, P.O. Box 45, 43 Cottage St., Bar Harbor, ME 04609, 207/288-3340 or 800/625-0321, www.friendsofacadia.org.

22 JORDAN POND LOOP

3.3 mi/1.5 hr

in Acadia National Park

BEST (

In a park filled with so many glacier-carved lakes and ponds, Jordan Pond, on the western side of Park Loop Road, is perhaps the loveliest. This fairly flat trail loops around the scenic pond, allowing for constant gazing across the water to the steep mountainsides surrounding its peaceful waters—from the cliffs and rounded humps of the Bubbles to the wooded slopes of Penobscot and Pemetic Mountains. The easiest walking is along the pond's east shore; on the northeast and especially the northwest shores, the trail crosses areas of boulders that require some scrambling and rock-hopping. Although these patches are not too difficult to navigate, you can avoid them altogether by hiking in a counterclockwise direction and turning back upon reaching these sections.

From the Jordan Pond parking area, continue down the dirt road to the shore and turn right onto the wide gravel path of the Jordan Pond Shore Trail. At the pond's southwest corner, the trail reaches a carriage road; turn left over a bridge, then immediately left onto the trail again, soon reaching the famous view of the Bubbles from the pond's south end. Just beyond that, the trail completes the

loop at the dirt access road. Turn right for the parking lot.

User Groups: Hikers and leashed dogs. Bikes and horses allowed on carriage roads only. With assistance, some wheelchair users may be able to negotiate the east side of this hike. Contact the park for more information about accessibility at Acadia.

Permits: The park entrance fee is $20 per vehicle for a seven-day pass June 23–October 31, or $5 for walkers, bicyclists, or motorcyclists. The park entrance fee for vehicles is $10 May 1–June 22. A one-year vehicle pass costs $40. For U.S. citizens and residents over the age of 62, a lifetime Senior Pass is available for $10.

Maps: A basic park map is available at the visitors center and the park website (www.nps. gov/acad). Good trail maps of the area are the waterproof Acadia National Park (map 212) for $11.95 from Trails Illustrated (800/962-1643, www.natgeomaps.com/ti_212) and the Hiking and Biking Map to Acadia National Park and Mount Desert Island, $7.95 in waterproof Tyvek, from the Appalachian Mountain Club. For topographic area maps, request Seal Harbor and Southwest Harbor from the USGS.

Directions: Take Route 3 south from Bar Harbor to Seal Harbor. Turn right at the Acadia National Park entrance and left on the Park Loop Road, following it to the Jordan Pond parking area. Or from the park visitors center, follow the Park Loop Road south. Where it splits, turn right for the Jordan Pond parking area. The park visitors center is located north of Bar Harbor at the junction of Route 3 and the start of the Park Loop Road.

GPS Coordinates: 44.3205 N, 68.2526 W

Contact: Acadia National Park, P.O. Box 177, Eagle Lake Rd., Bar Harbor, ME 04609-0177, 207/288-3338, www.nps.gov/acad. Friends of Acadia, P.O. Box 45, 43 Cottage St., Bar Harbor, ME 04609, 207/288-3340 or 800/625-0321, www.friendsofacadia.org.

MAINE

23 PEMETIC MOUNTAIN
3.3 mi/2.5 hr   👫3 △10

in Acadia National Park

Pemetic Mountain, situated between Jordan Pond to the west and Bubble Pond and Cadillac Mountain to the east, thrusts a long, open ridge of rock into the sky. Its summit, at 1,284 feet, offers sweeping views—but it's the walk along the ridge that makes this hike memorable. The views take in Cadillac, Penobscot, and Sargent Mountains, the islands south of Mount Desert, and Jordan Pond, and offer a unique perspective on the Bubbles. The elevation gain is just under 1,000 feet.

From the Jordan Pond parking area, follow the dirt access road to the southeast shore of Jordan Pond. Turn left, follow the Jordan Pond Shore Trail a short distance, and then turn left onto the Pond Trail. Cross the Park Loop Road and in less than a half mile, turn left onto the Pemetic Mountain West Cliff Trail, ascending the ridge. At the junction with the Pemetic Mountain Trail, turn left (north) and proceed to the summit. Double back and follow the Pemetic Mountain Trail all the way to the Pond Trail, then turn right to go back the way you came.

User Groups: Hikers and leashed dogs. No bikes, horses, or wheelchair facilities.

Permits: The park entrance fee is $20 per vehicle for a seven-day pass June 23–October 31, or $5 for walkers, bicyclists, or motorcyclists. The park entrance fee for vehicles is $10 May 1–June 22. A one-year vehicle pass costs $40. For U.S. citizens and residents over the age of 62, a lifetime Senior Pass is available for $10.

Maps: A basic park map is available at the visitors center and the park website (www.nps.gov/acad). Good trail maps of the area are the waterproof Acadia National Park (map 212) for $11.95 from Trails Illustrated (800/962-1643, www.natgeomaps.com/ti_212) and the Hiking and Biking Map to Acadia National Park and Mount Desert Island, $7.95

in waterproof Tyvek, from the Appalachian Mountain Club. For topographic area maps, request Seal Harbor and Southwest Harbor from the USGS.

Directions: Take Route 3 south from Bar Harbor to Seal Harbor. Turn right at the Acadia National Park entrance and left on the Park Loop Road, following it to the Jordan Pond parking area. Or from the park visitors center, follow the Park Loop Road south. Where it splits, turn right and continue to the Jordan Pond parking area. The park visitors center is located north of Bar Harbor at the junction of Route 3 and the start of the Park Loop Road.

GPS Coordinates: 44.3205 N, 68.2526 W

Contact: Acadia National Park, P.O. Box 177, Eagle Lake Rd., Bar Harbor, ME 04609-0177, 207/288-3338, www.nps.gov/acad. Friends of Acadia, P.O. Box 45, 43 Cottage St., Bar Harbor, ME 04609, 207/288-3340 or 800/625-0321, www.friendsofacadia.org.

24 CADILLAC MOUNTAIN: SOUTH RIDGE TRAIL
7 mi/4 hr   👫5 △10

in Acadia National Park

BEST (

The long, spectacular, wide-open South Ridge on the highest peak on Mount Desert Island—1,530-foot Cadillac Mountain—affords one of the longest and most scenic hikes in Acadia National Park. How many mountain ridges offer views not only of surrounding hills, but also of the ocean and a profusion of islands? A relatively short and somewhat steep hike through the woods brings you onto the broad ridge; then you have a long, uphill walk accompanied by sweeping views all the way to the summit. This seven-mile round-tripper climbs about 1,300 feet, making it one of the most challenging outings in the park. For campers staying at nearby Blackwoods Campground, make the easy mile-long climb to Eagles Crag (702 ft.) in the moments just before dawn and come prepared for an unbelievable sunrise. As the highest point on the North Atlantic seaboard, Cadillac Mountain is one of the first places in the United States to greet the rising sun.

From the roadside parking area, pickup the Cadillac Mountain South Ridge Trail as it enters the woods about 50 yards past the campground entrance road on the right (look for the trail marker). Starting off as a pleasant uphill walk through the woods, at 1.0 mile from Route 3, take the loop trail out to Eagles Crag (702 ft.), which offers views to the east; the loop trail rejoins the South Ridge Trail in 0.2 mile. Continuing up the South Ridge Trail, by 1.5 miles, the trail breaks out above the trees to views west to Pemetic and Sargent Mountains, and east and south to Frenchman Bay and numerous islands. At three miles, the trail passes a junction with the Cadillac Mountain West Face Trail (which descends left, or west), reaches a switchback in the paved summit road, and veers right, winding another half mile to the summit. Return the same way you came.

User Groups: Hikers and leashed dogs. No bikes, horses, or wheelchair facilities.

Permits: The park entrance fee is $20 per vehicle for a seven-day pass June 23–October 31, or $5 for walkers, bicyclists, or motorcyclists. The park entrance fee for vehicles is $10 May 1–June 22. A one-year vehicle pass costs $40. For U.S. citizens and residents over the age of 62, a lifetime Senior Pass is available for $10.

Maps: A basic park map is available at the visitors center and the park website (www.nps.gov/acad). Good trail maps of the area are the waterproof Acadia National Park (map 212) for $11.95 from Trails Illustrated (800/962-1643, www.natgeomaps.com/ti_212) and the Hiking and Biking Map to Acadia National Park and Mount Desert Island, $7.95 in waterproof Tyvek, from the Appalachian Mountain Club. For a topographic area map, request Seal Harbor from the USGS.

Directions: Take Route 3 south from Bar Harbor to the Blackwoods Campground entrance. The Cadillac Mountain South Ridge Trail enters the woods on the right about 50 yards past the campground entrance road; there is parking at the roadside. Campers in Blackwoods can pick up the trail at the west end of the campground's south loop (adding 1.4 miles to the hike's round-trip distance). The park visitors center is located north of Bar Harbor, at the junction of Route 3 and the start of the Park Loop Road.

GPS Coordinates: 44.3132 N, 68.2144 W

Contact: Acadia National Park, P.O. Box 177, Eagle Lake Rd., Bar Harbor, ME 04609-0177, 207/288-3338, www.nps.gov/acad. Friends of Acadia, P.O. Box 45, 43 Cottage St., Bar Harbor, ME 04609, 207/288-3340 or 800/625-0321, www.friendsofacadia.org.

25 GORHAM MOUNTAIN
2 mi/1.5 hr   🏃2 ⛰10

in Acadia National Park

On the southeastern edge of Mount Desert Island, this spectacular and all-too-brief climb along the open ridge of Gorham Mountain leads to continuous views of Acadia's coast and countless islands spun out across the bay. At 525 feet in elevation, Gorham is but a tiny hill compared to some of the park's loftier peaks. But because of Gorham's coastal location, the close views of the roiling sea are intimate and truly powerful. Reaching the rocky crown in just a mile, the trail grows rugged in spots as it nears the Cadillac Cliffs.

From the parking area, follow the Gorham Mountain Trail, at first an easy steady climb through a spruce forest. As the trees give way to a gradually steepening granite ascent, the trail reaches a split. Bear left to continue on the Gorham Mountain Trail. Or, for a more rugged route, bear right to follow the Cadillac Cliffs Trail, passing below the cliffs with rocky outcroppings overhead in places and loose rock underfoot. Some love this kind of trail adventure; others abhor it. Whichever path you take, the two trails rejoin just below the summit. Drink in the views from the top and then retrace your steps. (For better footing, even adventurers should consider descending the Gorham Mountain Trail all the way down.)

User Groups: Hikers and leashed dogs. No bikes, horses, or wheelchair facilities.

Permits: The park entrance fee is $20 per vehicle for a seven-day pass June 23–October 31, or $5 for walkers, bicyclists, or motorcyclists. The park entrance fee for vehicles is $10 May 1–June 22. A one-year vehicle pass costs $40. For U.S. citizens and residents over the age of 62, a lifetime Senior Pass is available for $10.

Maps: A basic park map is available at the visitors center and the park website (www.nps. gov/acad). Good trail maps of the area are the waterproof Acadia National Park (map 212) for $11.95 from Trails Illustrated (800/962-1643, www.natgeomaps.com/ti_212) and the Hiking and Biking Map to Acadia National Park and Mount Desert Island, $7.95 in waterproof Tyvek, from the Appalachian Mountain Club. For a topographic area map, request Seal Harbor from the USGS.

Directions: Take the Park Loop Road to the east side of Mount Desert Island and the parking area at the Gorham Mountain Trail and Monument Cove, south of Sand Beach and north of Otter Cliffs. The park visitors center is located north of Bar Harbor at the junction of Route 3 and the start of the Park Loop Road.

GPS Coordinates: 44.3167 N, 68.1913 W

Contact: Acadia National Park, P.O. Box 177, Eagle Lake Rd., Bar Harbor, ME 04609-0177, 207/288-3338, www.nps.gov/acad. Friends of Acadia, P.O. Box 45, 43 Cottage St., Bar Harbor, ME 04609, 207/288-3340 or 800/625-0321, www.friendsofacadia.org.

🄯 GREAT WASS ISLAND
5 mi/2.5 hr   🚶2 ⛰8

in Jonesport

BEST (

Connected to mainland Jonesport by bridge, Great Wass Island, covering six square miles,

is the biggest island in the Great Wass Archipelago, a chain of over 43 hunks of rock extending far off the Down East coast. Much of Great Wass is a Nature Conservancy preserve, open to the public for hiking and birdwatching. The island's windswept, North Atlantic terrain, kept cold by the currents of the nearby Bay of Fundy, makes it a popular nesting grounds for virtually all boreal (subartic) birds in the state of Maine, including palm warblers, boreal chickadees, spruce grouse, yellow-bellied flycatchers, and black beak woodpeckers. Nesting takes place continuously during the warmer summer months. You can also see large numbers of harbor seals lounging at low tide just offshore. And on clear days, look far offshore for a glimpse of the distant Moose Peak lighthouse, built in 1851 on a remote island to the east (and still in operation). This loop of about five miles takes you deep into the island's boreal forest of jack pine and spruce and out to open, rocky ledges for breathtaking views.

From the parking area, leave on the unmarked trail (a well-worn path). In approximately 100 yards, the trail reaches a fork. Bear right on the Little Cove Trail; the Mud Hole Trail to the left is the one you will return on. For the next two miles, wander along the Little Cove Trail as it passes through a lush boreal forest of cold-loving conifers. Carpeting the forest floor is a velvety, electric green moss that springs underfoot. It's beautiful, but when wet, the moss can be very slippery. Breaks in tree cover give way along the trail in various places to open ledges of the island's best bog areas. Reaching the crashing shoreline, a red marker and cairn indicate the end of the trail. Turn left and follow the shore about a half-mile to another cairn and red marker at Mud Hole Point. The Mud Hole Trail follows a narrow cove for its first half-mile and is a good place for birding and seal watching. Reentering the boreal forest, the hike continues as a pleasant woods walk until reaching the junction with the Little Cove Trail. Turn right to return 100 yards back to the parking area.

Special Note: The rocky stretch of shore connecting the two trails may be tricky for some, especially at hide tide when the rocks will most likely be wet. If necessary, turn back and return to your car on the Little Cove Trail.

User Groups: Hikers and leashed dogs. No bikes, horses, or wheelchair facilities.

Permits: Parking and access are free.

Maps: A free trail map is available at the trailhead. For a topographic area map, request Great Wass Island from the USGS.

Directions: Cross the bridge from Jonesport to Beals Island (across from Tall Barney's Restaurant). Turn left at the end of the bridge, continue through one stop sign and cross a short causeway to Great Wass Island; make the first right immediately after the causeway and continue for 2.6 miles on a road that turns to gravel. Look for the Nature Conservancy parking lot on the left.

GPS Coordinates: 44.5060 N, 67.6004 W

Contact: The Nature Conservancy of Maine, 4 Maine St., Brunswick, ME 04011, 207/729-5181.

27 COBSCOOK BAY STATE PARK

1.8 mi/1 hr   🏃1 ⛰8

in Edmunds Township

The Cobscook Bay estuary is a narrow opening to the sea that simply teems with wildlife. Eagles, ospreys, seals, otters, and even the occasional bear enjoy the bay's abundant fish populations, including smelt, alewives, shad, sea-run brook trout, striped bass and Atlantic salmon. Also found here are shellfish, marine worms, and other estuarine creatures. The park itself is an 888-acre peninsula thrust out into the bay, with trails providing good opportunities to observe the ebb and flow of the region's impressive tides. Cobscook, the Maliseet-Passamaquoddy tribal word for "boiling tides," aptly describes this setting where the tidal range averages 24 feet and can reach 28

feet (compared to a 9-foot average tide along Maine's southernmost coast). This trail leads to one of the park's largest coves and is an excellent place for nature observation and bird-watching.

From the parking area near the campground, pick up the Nature Trail, marked with a sign. Follow the trail an easy 0.6 mile to reach the shore of Cobscook's Burnt Cove. Come here in fall and at low tide, large groups of shorebirds can be seen along the mudflats and eel grass, a rest and refueling stop during seasonal migrations. Burnt Cove and other coves in the bay support a quarter of Maine's wintering black ducks and the state's highest concentration of bald eagles. (Be sure to ask for the free birding list for Cobscook Bay available at the park entrance.) Continue on the Nature Trail for another 0.3 mile to where it ends at the campground. Retrace your steps back to the parking area. Before you leave, cross the park access road and make a quick 0.4 mile round-trip to the park's fire tower lookout for long views of the bay.

User Groups: Hikers and leashed dogs. No bikes, horses, or wheelchair facilities.

Permits: A fee of $3 per adult Maine resident or $4.50 per adult nonresident (age 12 and over) is charged at the state park entrance; senior citizens pay $1.50 and children under 12 years old enter free. The park season is May 15–October 15, although trailheads are accessible year-round. No staff is on duty and no fee is collected off-season.

Maps: A free trail map, suitable for this hike, is available at the state park entrance. For a topographic map of trails, request Eastport from the USGS.

Directions: Take U.S. 1 to Edmunds and look for park signs marking the turnoff onto South Edmunds Road. The main park entrance is on the right 0.5 mile from the turnoff.

GPS Coordinates: 44.8505 N, 67.1544 W

Contact: Cobscook Bay State Park, 40 South Edmunds Rd., Edmunds Township, ME 04628, 207/726-4412, www.maine.gov/doc/parks/index.html.

28 QUODDY HEAD STATE PARK

3.6 mi/2 hr   🏃2 ⛰9

in Lubec

Quoddy Head State Park is a rugged, 541-acre stretch of coast at the tip of America's easternmost peninsula, capped by the West Quoddy Head Light, the easternmost lighthouse in the United States. Trails through the park lead to some of Maine's best wildlife-watching areas. In summer, you may spot humpback, minke, and finback whales offshore, along with rafts of eider, scoter, and old squaw ducks. This loop hike, over relatively flat terrain, follows the open shoreline west to Carrying Place Cove, another popular birding spot, before turning inland to reach a subartic heath bog.

From the parking area, explore West Quoddy Head Light, just across South Lubec Road. Commissioned by President Thomas Jefferson, West Quoddy Head Light was first built in 1808. The present tower and house date back to 1858 and were staffed by resident lightkeepers until 1988 when the U.S. Coast Guard installed an automated light. West Quoddy Head's distinct red and white striped exterior set against a background of crashing surf is near postcard perfect; don't forget the camera on this hike.

Leaving West Quoddy Head, cross back over South Lubec Road and walk through the parking area to pick up the Coastal Trail (marked with a sign). Treading along on a dirt path just above the shore for 1.6 miles, you'll reach especially scenic lookouts at Gulliver's Hole and High Ledge (both about 0.3 mile into the hike). At Green Point you'll reach another scenic lookout, about 0.6 mile into the hike; a short spur path leads down onto the pebbled beach. Reaching Carrying Place Cove, the Coastal Trail turns inland and becomes the Thompson Trail. After a 1.1-mile stroll through scrub forest, the Thompson Trail reaches a junction with the Bog Trail. Turn left and follow the boardwalk to this unusual coastal plateau bog; subarctic and arctic plants rarely seen south of Canada are able to grow here in thriving abundance. Shrubs predominate, particularly black crowberry, baked appleberry, and Labrador tea, along with carnivorous plants such as pitcher plants and sundew. Backtrack from the bog to the Thompson Trail and turn left for another 0.4 mile back to the picnic and parking area.

User Groups: Hikers and leashed dogs. No bikes or horses. Wheelchair facilities are limited to the grounds at West Quoddy Head Light.

Permits: A fee of $2 per adult Maine resident or $3 per adult nonresident (age 12 and over) is charged at the state park entrance; senior citizens pay $1 and children under 12 years old enter free. The park season is May 15–October 15, although trailheads are accessible year-round. No staff is on duty and no fee is collected off-season.

Maps: A free trail map, suitable for this hike, is available at the state park entrance. For a topographic map of trails, request Lubec from the USGS.

Directions: From Route 189 in downtown Lubec, turn right on South Lubec Road and follow two miles to a fork, bear left and continue two miles to the park entrance and adjacent picnic area. Handicap parking is available next to the lighthouse visitors center. GPS Coordinates: 44.8167 N, 66.9495 W

Contact: Quoddy Head State Park, 973 South Lubec Rd., Lubec, ME 04652, 207/733-0911, www.maine.gov/doc/parks/index.html.

WESTERN LAKES AND MOUNTAINS

© MIKE SINGER

BEST HIKES

Southernmost Maine is a true microcosm of the

state's best natural features. The hikes in this chapter take you to rugged mountains and wild river valleys, densely forested hills, serene lakes, and even a few stops along Maine's jagged ocean coastline. Some of the state's biggest and most popular hiking destinations are here, peaks such as Bigelow Mountain and the summits of the Saddleback Range. Low mountains in the area are no less spectacular, with smaller hills such as Pleasant Mountain and Tumbledown Mountain providing excellent long views for only moderate effort.

Many of the hikes in the western part of the state lie on or very near the Appalachian Trail; others lead to beautiful waterfalls, including Screw Auger Falls and Step Falls, two especially breathtaking cascades in Grafton Notch. The majority of the trails are within minutes of popular tourist areas on Rangeley Lakes and Sebago Lake; even New Hampshire's North Conway makes an easy access point for the Maine continuation of the White Mountain National Forest. And for those seeking truly rugged adventure, Western Maine is a backpacker's paradise and home to some of New England's premier long distance routes, including the 30-mile trek through the Mahoosuc Range.

The southeast coast is dominated by Portland, Maine's largest city. Hikes in this area get you away from the hustle and bustle of the city to catch glimpses of the seacoast's forests, hills, and miles of rocky shoreline. A hidden gem in this area is Vaughn Woods State Park in South Berwick. Here, hundred-year-old trees tower over the shady, pine needle–covered forest floor on this beautiful woods walk along the Salmon River.

At higher elevations and close to the coast, summer temperatures are more moderate than inland locations; but are also less predictable. Inland from the coast, it's blackfly country, with swarms of the pesky insects arriving by June; joined in early July with an equally thick mosquito population. The warm weather hiking season extends into October in the western hills – and into November or even December along the coast. Pine trees and hemlock cover much of this land, but stands of birch still coat the landscape in a golden glow starting in September.

Winter access gets trickier on many of these hikes. In western Maine, some roads, such as Route 113 through Evans Notch, are not maintained in winter, and others simply are often covered with ice and snow. Many of the trails in this part of the state see little or no visitors in winter, meaning you'll probably be breaking trail through snow, without the security of knowing other people might come along to help you out in case of an emergency. That can be exciting, but it's certainly riskier. Along the southeast coast, heavy nor'easter snowstorms and biting wind mark most of the winter months. Still, on the occasional sunny, calm day, walking the Bay Cove Trail in Portland is the best antidote around for a bad case of cabin fever.

A few hikes are on private land left open to public use in keeping with a long-standing tradition in Maine – a state where more than 90 percent of the total land area is privately held. Explore these places with the understanding that you alone are responsible for yourself. Bear in mind that while most of these private-land trails have been open to public use for many years, access can be restricted or denied at any time. Respect private property when on it, obey No Trespassing signs, and assume that hunting is allowed in season unless posted otherwise.

MAINE

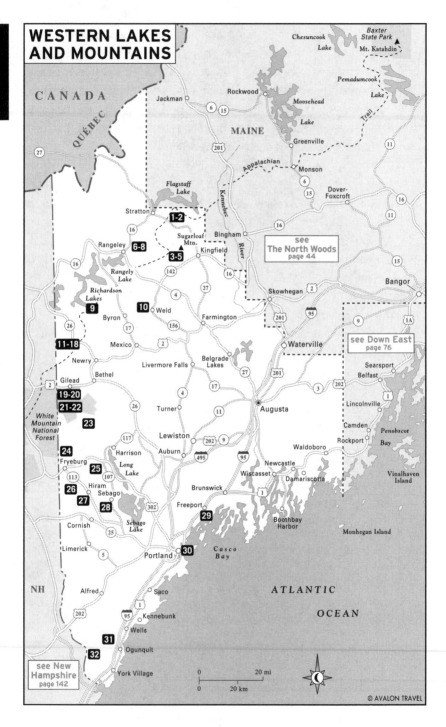

WESTERN LAKES AND MOUNTAINS

CANADA

QUÉBEC

MAINE

Baxter State Park
Mt. Katahdin

Chesuncook Lake

Pemadumcook Lake

Trail

Rockwood

Jackman

6 · 15

Moosehead Lake

Greenville

201

Appalachian

Monson

6

15

Dover-Foxcroft

16

11

11

Bangor

Flagstaff Lake

Stratton

1-2

Kennebec

Bingham

16

see
The North Woods
page 44

16

Sugarloaf Mtn.

6-8

Rangeley

3-5

Kingfield

142

River

16

15

Skowhegan

2

95

1A

9

Rangely Lake

4

27

Farmington

201

Richardson Lakes

9

Byron

10

Weld

156

Mexico

17

2

201

Waterville

see Down East
page 76

26

Newry

Livermore Falls

Belgrade Lakes

27

Searsport

Belfast

11-18

Gilead

Bethel

26

4

17

201

3

202

Lincolnville

Camden

1

19-20

21-22

Turner

11

Augusta

Rockport

Penobscot Bay

23

Lewiston

202

9

Waldoboro

White Mountain National Forest

117

Auburn

495

95

Newcastle

Vinalhaven Island

24

Harrison

Long Lake

Wiscasset

Damariscotta

Fryeburg

25

107

Brunswick

113

Hiram

26

Sebago

27

28

302

Freeport

29

Cornish

Sebago Lake

Boothbay Harbor

Monhegan Island

Limerick

5

25

Portland

30

Casco Bay

NH

Alfred

Saco

ATLANTIC

202

95

Kennebunk

OCEAN

31

Wells

32

Ogunquit

see New Hampshire
page 142

York Village

0   20 mi

0   20 km

© AVALON TRAVEL

❶ BIGELOW RANGE

16.7 mi one-way/2 days 🏃5 ⛺10

east of Stratton

A darling of Maine hikers, Bigelow Mountain is unquestionably one of the two or three most spectacular peaks in the state; only Katahdin and Bigelow's neighbor to the south, the Saddleback Range, warrant comparison. Reflecting the state's affection for this range, Maine voters supported a grassroots movement and in 1976 created the Bigelow Preserve, a 35,000-acre park encompassing the entire Bigelow Range—including about 17 miles of the Appalachian Trail—and 21 miles of shoreline on sprawling Flagstaff Lake. Both of Bigelow's summits rise well above the tree line, affording long views in every direction. On rare clear days, you can see north to Katahdin and southwest to Mount Washington. This 16.7-mile, two-day backpacking trip traverses the entire Bigelow Mountain range along the Appalachian Trail (AT). The distance is moderate for two days, but don't underestimate the trail's ruggedness.

From East Flagstaff Road, follow the white blazes of the AT southbound, passing a blue-blazed side trail at 1.4 miles that leads 0.1 mile to the Little Bigelow lean-to, where there is a good spring and tent space. From there, the AT climbs steadily until cresting the eastern end of the long, low ridge of Little Bigelow Mountain three miles from the road. There are excellent views from open ledges west toward Bigelow Mountain and the ski area at Sugarloaf Mountain, across the Carrabassett Valley. For those looking for a day hike only, this is a logical point of descent (a total round-trip of six miles).

Dipping back into the forest, the trail then follows the relatively flat, wooded ridge top, passing another open ledge with a view of Bigelow and Flagstaff Lake at 4.5 miles. It then descends about 1,000 feet over less than two miles into Safford Notch, where the forested floor is littered with giant boulders, some of them stacked dramatically atop one another.

At 6.3 miles from East Flagstaff Road, a side trail leads left (southwest) 0.3 mile to tent platforms at the Safford Notch campsite. Just 0.1 mile farther down the AT, the Safford Brook Trail exits right (north), leading 2.2 miles to East Flagstaff Road (and 2.5 miles to Flagstaff Lake). The AT climbs steeply out of Safford Notch, over and around boulders, gaining about 2,000 feet in elevation over two miles to Bigelow's east summit, 4,088-foot Avery Peak. On the way up Avery, the trail passes a side path at 7.5 miles that leads 0.1 mile to an excellent view east and north from atop the cliff called the "Old Man's Head." Beyond that side path, the AT ascends the crest of a narrow, wooded ridge, breaking out of the trees for the final 0.1 mile up Avery Peak. Passing over Avery, the trail descends into the wooded col between the summits, reaching the Avery tenting area at 8.7 miles. There is a water source here, but don't rely on it; by mid-summer, the spring is often dried out.

From the col, the ascent grows fairly steep up West Peak, Bigelow's true summit at 4,145 feet (0.7 mile from Avery Peak). The AT descends to and follows the up-and-down ridge connecting Bigelow to the 3,805-foot summit of South Horn, where you get a good view to the west from directly above Horns Pond. Just 0.1 mile farther, a side trail leads 0.2 mile to the summit of North Horn (3,792 ft.). Continue steeply downhill on the AT, reaching the Horns Pond lean-tos and tent sites at 11.6 miles from East Flagstaff Road and half a mile from South Horn. Horns Pond is a scenic tarn nestled in a tiny bowl at about 3,200 feet on Bigelow's west slope. From here, the AT climbs slightly out of the bowl, passing the junction with the Horns Pond Trail 0.2 mile south of Horns Pond and a short side path to a pond overlook at 0.3 mile. The trail then descends steadily, swinging south and passing the Bigelow Range Trail junction nearly two miles from Horns Pond, to the Cranberry Stream campsite at 14.8 miles (3.2 miles south of Horns Pond and 1.9 miles north of Route 27/16). At 15.8 miles, the AT crosses

MAINE

MAINE

Stratton Brook on a bridge before reaching Route 27/16 at mile 16.7 of this trip, 5.1 miles from Horns Pond.

Special note: The traverse of this range ranks among the most popular backpacking treks in New England. Especially during the warmer months, the campsites and shelters fill quickly, even during the week. Bringing a tent is recommended. Also, above the tree line take care to walk only on the trail as fragile alpine vegetation is easily trampled.

Camp at existing camping areas and shelters: Little Bigelow lean-to at 1.4 miles south of East Flagstaff Road, Safford Notch campsite at 6.3 miles, Avery tenting area at 8.7 miles, Horns Pond lean-tos and tent sites at 11.6 miles, and the Cranberry Stream campsite at 14.8 miles.

User Groups: Hikers only. No wheelchair facilities. Dogs are discouraged along the Appalachian Trail in Maine. Bikes and horses are prohibited. This trail should not be attempted in winter except by hikers experienced in mountaineering and prepared for severe winter weather, and is not suitable for skis.

Permits: Parking, access, and camping are free. Backcountry camping accommodations are available on a first-come, first-served basis.

Maps: A free contour map of trails in the Bigelow Preserve is available at some trailheads and from the Maine Bureau of Public Lands. Detailed trail maps are available from the Maine Appalachian Club (Kennebec River to Maine Highway 27, $8) and the Appalachian Mountain Club (Rangeley–Stratton/Baxter State Park–Katahdin, $7.95 in waterproof Tyvek). For topographic area maps, request Little Bigelow Mountain, the Horns, Sugarloaf Mountain, and Poplar Mountain from the USGS.

Directions: You need to shuttle two vehicles for this trip. To do the hike from north to south, as described here, leave one vehicle at the junction of the Appalachian Trail and Routes 27 and 16, 5.3 miles south of where Routes 27 and 16 split in Stratton and 16

miles north of where Routes 27 and 16 split in Kingfield. Then drive on Route 16 east to North New Portland. Turn left (north) in front of the country store onto Long Falls Dam Road and follow it for 17.4 miles. Bear left onto the dirt Bog Brook Road. Drive 0.7 mile, bear left onto the dirt East Flagstaff Road, and drive 0.1 mile. Park either in the gravel pit on the right or at the roadside where the Appalachian Trail crosses the road just beyond the pit.

GPS Coordinates: 45.1361 N, 70.1597 W

Contact: Maine Department of Conservation, Bureau of Parks and Lands, 286 Water St., Key Bank Plaza, 3rd and 5th floors, Augusta, ME 04333-0022, 207/287-3821, www.state.me.us/doc/parks. Maine Appalachian Trail Club, P.O. Box 283, Augusta, ME 04332-0283, www.matc.org. Appalachian Mountain Club, 5 Joy St., Boston, MA 02108, 617/523-0655, www.outdoors.org. For information about a hiker shuttle, free Kennebec River ferry service, and other hiker services along the Appalachian Trail in Maine, contact Steve Longley, P.O. Box 90, Rte. 201, The Forks, ME 04985, 207/663-4441, 207/246-4642, or 888/356-2863 (in Maine only), www.riversandtrails.com.

🄯 BIGELOW MOUNTAIN
13.8 mi/10.5 hr or 1-2 days
🏃5 🄰10

east of Stratton

This hike up one of Maine's most spectacular and popular mountains, Bigelow, can be accomplished in a single long day by fit hikers getting an early start. But there are two camping areas along the trail that offer the option of a two-day trip, leaving your heavy pack behind for the day hike to Bigelow's summits. The cumulative elevation gained by hitting both of Bigelow's summits is nearly 4,000 feet, much of it above the tree line. Dress appropriately for rapidly changing weather conditions and stick to the trail to avoid trampling fragile alpine vegetation.

For the Bigelow summit hike, begin at Stratton Brook Pond Road and follow the white blazes of the Appalachian Trail (AT) northbound into the woods. Within a quarter mile you will cross a logging road and Stratton Brook on a bridge. The AT ascends steadily, passing the Cranberry Stream campsite at 1.1 miles and a junction with the Bigelow Range Trail at 2.4 miles. Stay on the AT, which swings east and climbs past a short side trail out to ledges above Horns Pond at four miles, and then passes the Horns Pond Trail junction 0.1 mile farther. The trail drops slightly into the bowl, home to the tiny mountain tarn called Horns Pond and a camping area with two lean-tos and tent sites, at 4.3 miles.

The AT climbs steeply for the next half mile, passing a side trail leading 0.2 mile to North Horn (3,792 ft.) at 4.7 miles and reaching the South Horn summit (3,805 ft.) at 4.8 miles, with a good view over Horns Pond and north to Flagstaff Lake. Descending steeply off South Horn, you follow an up-and-down ridge for more than a mile. Then climb steeply to West Peak, Bigelow's true summit at 4,145 feet, 6.9 miles in. The rocky, open summit affords views in every direction: north over Flagstaff Lake and the wilderness of the North Woods, all the way to Katahdin on a clear day, and southwest to Mount Washington when conditions are right. For this hike, turn around and descend the same way you came. To reach 4,088-foot Avery Peak, continue northbound on the AT, dropping into the saddle between Bigelow's two summits, passing the Avery tenting area at 7.2 miles, and then climbing to the open summit of Avery Peak. Hiking to Avery and back adds 1.4 miles and an hour (possibly more) to this hike's distance.

Special note: To make a loop hike of about 12.5 miles instead of this route over Bigelow's two summits, go up the Fire Warden's Trail, which begins a little more than a half mile beyond the Appalachian Trail crossing of Stratton Brook Pond Road. Climb the Fire Warden's Trail for 3.5 miles to Avery col, turn right (northbound) on the AT for 0.4 mile to Avery Peak, then turn around and descend the AT southbound for nearly eight miles to Stratton Brook Road. Turn left and walk the road for 0.5 mile to complete the loop. The upper half mile of the Fire Warden's Trail is very steep and severely eroded.

Camp at existing camping areas and shelters, which along this route include the Cranberry Stream campsite 1.1 miles from Stratton Brook Pond Road, the Horns Pond lean-tos and tent sites at 4.3 miles, and the Avery tenting area at 7.2 miles. Bigelow Mountain ranks among the most popular peaks in New England. Especially during the warmer months, the campsites and shelters fill quickly, even during the week. Bringing a tent is recommended.

User Groups: Hikers only. Bikes and horses are prohibited; no wheelchair facilities. Dogs are discouraged along the Appalachian Trail in Maine. This trail should not be attempted in winter except by hikers experienced in mountaineering and prepared for severe winter weather, and is not suitable for skis.

Permits: Parking, access, and camping are free. Backcountry camping accommodations are available on a first-come, first-served basis.

Maps: A free contour map of trails in the Bigelow Preserve is available at some trailheads and from the Maine Bureau of Public Lands. Detailed trail maps are available from the Maine Appalachian Club (Kennebec River to Maine Highway 27, $8) and the Appalachian Mountain Club (Rangeley–Stratton/Baxter State Park–Katahdin, $7.95 in waterproof Tyvek). For topographic area maps, request Horns and Sugarloaf Mountain from the USGS.

Directions: From the intersection of Routes 27 and 16 in Stratton (where the two roads join), drive east on Route 27/16 for approximately five miles to Stratton Brook Pond Road. Turn left (north) and drive 1.4 miles

MAINE

to where the AT crosses the dirt road; park at the roadside.

GPS Coordinates: 45.1097 N, 70.3636 W

Contact: Maine Department of Conservation, Bureau of Parks and Lands, 286 Water St., Key Bank Plaza, 3rd and 5th floors, Augusta, ME 04333-0022, 207/287-3821, www.state. me.us/doc/parks. Maine Appalachian Trail Club, P.O. Box 283, Augusta, ME 04332-0283, www.matc.org. Appalachian Mountain Club, 5 Joy St., Boston, MA 02108, 617/523-0655, www.outdoors.org.

3 SUGARLOAF MOUNTAIN
5.8 mi/4.5 hr   🏃5 ⛰9

south of Stratton

Maine's third-highest peak at 4,237 feet, Sugarloaf's barren summit offers long views in every direction. On a clear day, you can see Mount Washington in New Hampshire to the southwest and all the way to Katahdin in the far north. Like any high, exposed peak, this can be a rough place in foul weather: prepare for the possibility of swirling fog and biting wind, even when conditions at the trailhead are hot and sunny. Sugarloaf Mountain is also one of Maine's most popular downhill ski areas. But this day hike of Sugarloaf, via the Appalachian Trail (AT), is a rugged, 5.8-mile route that shows very little evidence of the resort. It's only when you reach the summit that you see a cluster of ski area buildings. The climb's net elevation gain is approximately 2,000 feet.

From Caribou Valley Road, follow the white-blazed AT to the left (south), immediately crossing the South Branch of the Carrabassett River, which can be dangerous at times of high water. The AT then climbs very steeply up Sugarloaf Mountain, involving short stretches of tricky scrambling up a heavily eroded trail. The trail emerges from the woods high on the north slope of Sugarloaf, with views to South and North Crocker across the valley. It reenters the woods and then reaches a junction with

the Sugarloaf Mountain Trail 2.3 miles from Caribou Valley Road. Turn left onto that trail and follow its rocky path steeply uphill for 0.6 mile to the exposed Sugarloaf summit, where there are ski area buildings and long views in every direction. Descend the same route back to the road.

Special note: Sugarloaf can be linked with Spaulding Mountain by continuing on the AT southbound, a 10.2-mile round-trip from Caribou Valley Road. An ambitious hiker can continue on to Mount Abraham, making a 17.4-mile day hike or a two-day backpacking trip. (See *Spaulding Mountain* and *Mount Abraham* listings in this chapter for more details.)

User Groups: Hikers only. Bikes and horses are prohibited; no wheelchair facilities. Dogs are discouraged along the Appalachian Trail in Maine. Access to this trail by car during the winter may be limited since Caribou Valley Road may not be plowed; however, it could be skied as far as the AT crossing. Hiking Sugarloaf should not be attempted in winter except by hikers experienced in mountaineering and prepared for severe winter weather.

Permits: Parking, access, and camping are free. Backcountry camping accommodations are available on a first-come, first-served basis.

Maps: Detailed trail maps are available from the Maine Appalachian Club (Maine Highway 27 to Maine Highway 17, $8) and the Appalachian Mountain Club (Rangeley–Stratton/Baxter State Park–Katahdin, $7.95 in waterproof Tyvek). For a topographic area map, request Sugarloaf Mountain from the USGS.

Directions: From Route 27/16 in Bigelow (listed on some maps as Carrabassett), about a mile west of the entrance to the Sugarloaf USA ski resort, turn south (left) onto the dirt Caribou Valley Road. Drive 4.3 miles to the Appalachian Trail crossing and park at the roadside. The dirt Caribou Valley Road was improved in recent years all the way to the AT crossing and is now passable for cars during the warm months.

GPS Coordinates: 45.0808 N, 70.3394 W
Contact: Maine Appalachian Trail Club, P.O.
Box 283, Augusta, ME 04332-0283, www.
matc.org. Appalachian Mountain Club, 5 Joy
St., Boston, MA 02108, 617/523-0655, www.
outdoors.org.

❹ SPAULDING MOUNTAIN
9 mi/7 hr   🥾5 ⛰8

south of Stratton

At 4,010 feet, Spaulding offers good—if not
spectacular—views towards neighboring
Sugarloaf Mountain and Mount Abraham.
Reaching Spaulding actually requires a partial
climb up Sugarloaf and the best feature on this
hike may be the route's fairly flat ridge walk
from Sugarloaf to Spaulding, a quiet stretch of
trail through a lush forest of hemlock, ferns,
and moss. Keep quiet and watch for wildlife
here—one intrepid hiker tells of running into
a bull moose with a 26-point rack while out
on Spaulding one crisp day in fall. He and his
companions estimated the antlers spanned
nearly six feet. The total elevation on this hike
is slightly more than 2,000 feet.

From Caribou Valley Road, turn left (south)
on the AT, immediately crossing the South
Branch of the Carrabassett River, which can
be dangerous at times of high water. The trail
climbs very steeply up Sugarloaf Mountain,
involving short stretches of tricky scrambling
on a heavily eroded trail. It breaks out of the
woods high on Sugarloaf's north slope, with
views to South and North Crocker across the
valley. It reenters the woods and then reaches
a junction with the Sugarloaf Mountain Trail,
2.3 miles from Caribou Valley Road. From
the Sugarloaf Mountain Trail junction, follow the AT along the fairly flat ridge from
Sugarloaf to Spaulding. About 0.1 mile south
of the Sugarloaf Mountain Trail junction, a
side path leads about 40 feet to a good view.
The AT continues along the wooded ridge
to a junction with the Spaulding Mountain

Trail, 4.4 miles from Caribou Valley Road.
That trail leads 0.1 mile uphill to Spaulding's
summit. Return the way you came.

The Spaulding Mountain lean-to is located
down a short side path off the AT, 5.2 miles
south of Caribou Valley Road and 0.8 mile
south of the Spaulding Mountain Trail/Ap-
palachian Trail junction.
User Groups: Hikers only. Bikes and horses
are prohibited; no wheelchair facilities. Dogs
are discouraged along the Appalachian Trail
in Maine.
Permits: Parking, access, and camping are
free. Backcountry camping accommodations
are available on a first-come, first-served
basis.
Maps: Detailed trail maps are available from the
Maine Appalachian Club (Maine Highway 27
to Maine Highway 17, $8) and the Appalachian
Mountain Club (Rangeley–Stratton/Baxter
State Park–Katahdin, $7.95 in waterproof
Tyvek). For a topographic area map, request
Sugarloaf Mountain from the USGS.
Directions: From Route 27/16, about a mile
west of the entrance to the Sugarloaf USA ski
resort in Bigelow (also listed as Carrabassett
on some maps), turn left (south) onto the dirt
Caribou Valley Road. Drive 4.3 miles to the
Appalachian Trail crossing and park at the
roadside. The dirt Caribou Valley Road was
improved in recent years all the way to the
AT crossing.
GPS Coordinates: 45.0808 N, 70.3394 W
Contact: Maine Appalachian Trail Club, P.O.
Box 283, Augusta, ME 04332-0283, www.
matc.org. Appalachian Mountain Club, 5 Joy
St., Boston, MA 02108, 617/523-0655, www.
outdoors.org.

❺ MOUNT ABRAHAM
16 mi/12 hr or 1-2 days   🥾5 ⛰10

south of Stratton

Mount Abraham boasts one of the largest alpine
areas in Maine, with more than four miles of

ridge above the tree line featuring excellent panoramic views. But because Appalachian Trail (AT) hikers have to make a 3.4-mile detour to climb Abraham, it attracts fewer visitors than some peaks in western Maine, such as neighboring Saddleback Mountain. This 16-mile hike to bag one of Maine's 14 4,000-footers is difficult and long—a conceivable one-day goal for fit hikers getting an early start at a time of year that affords lots of daylight, but it also makes for a satisfying two-day trip in relative solitude. The cumulative elevation gain on the round-trip is about 3,200 feet.

From Caribou Valley Road, turn left (southbound) on the AT, immediately crossing the South Branch of the Carrabassett River, which can be dangerous at times of high water. The trail then climbs very steeply up Sugarloaf Mountain, involving short stretches of tricky scrambling up a heavily eroded trail. The trail emerges from the woods high on the north slope of Sugarloaf, with views to South and North Crocker across the valley. It reenters the woods and then reaches a junction with the Sugarloaf Mountain Trail 2.3 miles from Caribou Valley Road. (For a scenic 1.2-mile detour off this hike, follow that rocky trail steeply uphill to the exposed 4,237-foot Sugarloaf summit, Maine's third-highest peak, where there are ski area buildings and long views in every direction.) From the Sugarloaf Mountain Trail junction, follow the AT along the fairly flat ridge that connects Sugarloaf to Spaulding Mountain—a quiet stretch through a lush forest of hemlock, ferns, and moss. About 0.1 mile south of the Sugarloaf Mountain Trail junction, a side path leads some 40 feet to a good view. The AT continues along the wooded ridge to a junction with the Spaulding Mountain Trail, 4.4 miles from Caribou Valley Road. (That trail, which is not included in this hike's distance, leads 0.1 mile uphill to Spaulding's 4,010-foot summit, where three short side paths lead to limited views toward Sugarloaf and Abraham.) From the Spaulding Mountain Trail junction, the AT descends 0.8 mile to a side path leading

150 feet to the Spaulding Mountain lean-to, where there is space for tents.

The AT follows moderate terrain southward, reaching the Mount Abraham Trail 1.1 miles from the Spaulding lean-to. On this blue-blazed trail, it's 1.7 miles one-way to Abraham's 4,043-foot summit. Although it's relatively flat for the first half mile, the trail—after emerging from the woods—climbs over three bumps on a ridge, crossing rough talus slopes. From the summit, marked by the rusting remains of an old fire tower, the Horn and Saddleback Mountain are visible to the southwest, and the Bigelow Range can be seen to the north. About 30 feet from the tower, along the Fire Warden's Trail, there is a primitive stone shelter with a shingled roof and enough space under its very low ceiling for a few people to crawl inside; not a very roomy spot, but good for an emergency shelter. About 100 feet beyond the summit stand several tall cairns. For this hike, return to Caribou Valley Road via the same route you took up.

The Spaulding Mountain lean-to is located down a short side path off the AT, 5.2 miles south of Caribou Valley Road.

User Groups: Hikers only. Bikes and horses are prohibited; no wheelchair facilities. Dogs are discouraged along the Appalachian Trail in Maine. The Caribou Valley Road may not be plowed in winter to provide access to this trail, though it could be skied as far as the AT crossing. Hiking Abraham should not be attempted in winter except by hikers experienced in mountaineering and prepared for severe winter weather.

Permits: Parking, access, and camping are free. Backcountry camping accommodations are available on a first-come, first-served basis.

Maps: Detailed trail maps are available from the Maine Appalachian Club (Maine Highway 27 to Maine Highway 17, $8) and the Appalachian Mountain Club (Rangeley–Stratton/Baxter State Park–Katahdin, $7.95 in waterproof Tyvek). For topographic area maps, request Sugarloaf Mountain and Mount Abraham from the USGS.

Directions: From Route 27/16, about a mile west of the entrance to the Sugarloaf USA ski resort in Bigelow (also listed as Carrabassett on some maps), turn left (south) onto the dirt Caribou Valley Road. Drive 4.3 miles to the Appalachian Trail crossing and park at the roadside. The dirt Caribou Valley Road was improved in recent years all the way to the AT crossing and is now passable for cars during the warm months.

GPS Coordinates: 45.0808 N, 70.3394 W

Contact: Maine Appalachian Trail Club, P.O. Box 283, Augusta, ME 04332-0283, www.matc.org. Appalachian Mountain Club, 5 Joy St., Boston, MA 02108, 617/523-0655, www.outdoors.org.

6 SADDLEBACK RANGE
32.2 mi one-way/3-4 days
🏃 5 ⛰ 10

east of Rangeley

BEST (

The Saddleback Range stands out as one of the three premier mountain ranges in Maine—the other two being the greater Katahdin region and the Bigelow Range—and a multiday traverse of its peaks is as rugged, varied, and scenic a mountain experience as can be had anywhere in New England. Seven of the eight summits rise above 4,000 feet, and four of them thrust extensive areas above the tree line, offering long, panoramic views. Three miles of ridge above the trees extend from Saddleback Mountain to the Horn. Wintry storms with dangerously high winds occur year-round, so avoid this exposed ground if bad weather threatens. This traverse could be accomplished in three days. If you allow time to make the side trips to Sugarloaf Mountain and Mount Abraham, you are likely to be out on the trail for four days. Both side trips add to this hike's 32.2-mile distance.

From Route 16/27, follow the white blazes of the Appalachian Trail southbound. It rises gently at first and never grows more than moderately steep before reaching the wooded North Crocker Mountain summit (4,168 ft.), 5.2 miles from the highway. There are limited views over the tops of low spruce trees. A better view is along the AT just south of the

nearing the summit of Saddleback Mountain

summit, looking toward Sugarloaf Mountain and Mount Abraham. Continuing south on the AT, you drop into the shallow col between the two summits of Crocker, then climb to the top of South Crocker (4,010 ft.), a mile away from North Crocker. The actual summit is reached via a 100-foot side path off the AT. An open ledge there affords a limited view toward Sugarloaf and Abraham.

Descending south, the AT crosses an open slope of loose, broken rocks with views north and east toward the Bigelow Range. Footing becomes difficult descending the steep and very loose final half mile to Crocker Cirque campsite, just over a mile from South Crocker's summit and 7.3 miles from Route 27/16. One mile farther south, the AT crosses the dirt Caribou Valley Road (which was improved in recent years all the way to the AT crossing, providing another access to the AT; Route 16/27 is 4.3 miles down Caribou Valley Road). From the road, the AT immediately crosses the South Branch of the Carrabassett River—which can be dangerous at times of high water—then climbs very steeply up Sugarloaf Mountain, involving short stretches of tricky scrambling. The trail emerges from the woods high on Sugarloaf's north slope, with views of the Crockers across the valley. It reenters the woods and then reaches a junction with the Sugarloaf Mountain Trail 3.3 miles south of Crocker Cirque campsite (and 2.3 miles from Caribou Valley Road); this rocky trail leads steeply uphill 0.6 mile to the exposed 4,237-foot Sugarloaf summit, Maine's third-highest peak, where there are ski area buildings and long views in every direction. From the Sugarloaf Mountain Trail junction, the AT follows the fairly flat ridge connecting Sugarloaf to Spaulding Mountain—a quiet trail stretch through a lush forest of hemlock, ferns, and moss. About 0.1 mile south of the Sugarloaf Mountain Trail junction, a side path leads about 40 feet to a good view. The AT continues along the wooded ridge to a junction with the Spaulding Mountain Trail, 5.4 miles from Crocker Cirque campsite; this trail leads 0.1

mile uphill to Spaulding's 4,010-foot summit, where three short side paths lead to limited views toward Sugarloaf and Abraham.

From the Spaulding Mountain Trail junction, the AT descends 0.8 mile to a side path leading 150 feet to the Spaulding Mountain lean-to, where there is also space for tents. The AT follows moderate terrain south, reaching the Mount Abraham Trail 1.1 miles from the Spaulding lean-to. On this blue-blazed trail, it's 1.7 miles one-way to the 4,043-foot Abraham summit. Although it's relatively flat for the first half mile, after emerging from the woods, the trail climbs over three bumps on a ridge, crossing talus slopes reminiscent of bigger mountains like Washington or Katahdin. The views from Abraham are among the best in the range. From the Mount Abraham Trail junction, the AT southbound passes a view toward Abraham within 0.2 mile and then passes over the wooded top of Lone Mountain in a mile.

Descending, the trail follows and then crosses beautiful Perham Stream (immediately after crossing a logging road), its narrow current choked with moss-covered rocks. The AT crosses a second logging road and, 1.2 miles from Perham Stream, crosses another gem, Sluice Brook, which parallels the trail for 0.7 mile before pouring through a narrow flume. The trail crosses a gravel road and descends very steeply to Orbeton Stream, 5.3 miles from the Spaulding lean-to; fording can be difficult in high water. From Orbeton, the AT makes one of its steepest and most arduous ascents in this range, more than two miles to the open ledges of Poplar Ridge, where there are views to the south and east. A half mile beyond the ledges is the Poplar Ridge lean-to (a small brook provides water, but may be dried out by late summer).

From the shelter, the AT climbs steadily 1.4 miles to the open summit of Saddleback Junior (3,655 ft.), with excellent views in all directions. Follow white blazes and cairns across the Saddleback Junior top, descend about 500 feet, and then climb steeply 1,000 feet to the open, 4,041-foot summit of the Horn, two miles from Saddleback Junior. Again the views are spectacular, encompassing the Rangeley Lake area and Saddleback Mountain to the west, and extending north to Katahdin and southwest to Washington on a clear day.

Descend south on the AT, crossing mostly open ground with nonstop views, and then ascend Saddleback's ledges to the lower of its two summits. Walk the easy ridge to the true summit, at 4,120 feet, 1.6 miles from the Horn's summit. Continuing south, the AT drops back into the woods a mile below the summit and then crosses a logging road nearly a mile below the tree line. The trail crosses a stream 0.2 mile beyond the logging road and crosses Saddle-back Stream 0.6 mile farther. At 3.7 miles from Saddleback's summit, a side path leads a short distance to the Caves, actually passageways through giant boulders that have cleaved from the cliff above over the eons. Just 0.2 mile past the Caves, the trail reaches the Piazza Rock lean-to area, a popular backcountry campsite less than two miles from Route 4. There are tent sites and a large shelter, but this place fills quickly on weekends. A side path off the AT leads about 200 yards uphill to Piazza Rock, an enormous horizontal slab protruding improbably from the cliff. You can follow the trail up onto the slab with a little scrambling. From the lean-to area, the AT descends south for 1.8 miles to Route 4, this hike's terminus.

There are three lean-to shelters and one campsite along this section of the Appalachian Trail: the Crocker Cirque campsite, with three tent platforms, lies 0.1 mile down a side path off the AT, 7.3 miles south of Route 27/16; the Spaulding Mountain lean-to is located down a short side path off the AT, 6.2 miles south of the Crocker Cirque campsite; the Poplar Ridge lean-to sits along the AT, eight miles south of the Spaulding Mountain lean-to; and the Piazza Rock lean-to lies on a short side path off the AT, 8.9 miles south of the Poplar Ridge lean-to.

User Groups: Hikers only. Bikes and horses are prohibited; no wheelchair facilities. Dogs are discouraged along the Appalachian Trail in Maine. This trail should not be attempted in winter except by hikers experienced in mountaineering and prepared for severe winter weather, and is not suitable for skis.

Permits: Parking, access, and camping are free. Backcountry camping accommodations are available on a first-come, first-served basis.

Maps: Detailed trail maps are available from the Maine Appalachian Club (Maine Highway 27 to Maine Highway 17, $8) and the Appalachian Mountain Club (Rangeley–Stratton/ Baxter State Park–Katahdin, $7.95 in waterproof Tyvek). For topographic area maps, request Sugarloaf Mountain, Black Nubble, Mount Abraham, Redington, and Saddleback Mountain from the USGS.

Directions: You need to shuttle two vehicles for this backpacking trip. To do the hike from north to south, as described here, leave one vehicle where the Appalachian Trail crosses Route 4, about 12 miles north of the junction of Routes 4 and 142 in Phillips and 10.1 miles south of the junction of Routes 4 and 16. Then drive to the hike's start, where the AT crosses Route 27/16, 5.3 miles east of where Routes 27 and 16 join in Stratton and 16 miles west of where Routes 27 and 16 split in Kingfield. GPS Coordinates: 45.1035 N, 70.3556 W

Contact: Maine Appalachian Trail Club, P.O. Box 283, Augusta, ME 04332-0283, www. matc.org. Appalachian Mountain Club, 5 Joy St., Boston, MA 02108, 617/523-0655, www.outdoors.org. For information about a hiker shuttle and other hiker services along the Appalachian Trail in Maine, contact Steve Longley, P.O. Box 90, Rte. 201, The Forks, ME 04985, 207/663-4441 or 888/356-2863 (in Maine only), www.riversandtrails.com.

⁊ SADDLEBACK MOUNTAIN AND THE HORN

13.4 mi/8.5 hr   🏃5 ⛺10

southeast of Rangeley

BEST (

Saddleback Mountain rises to 4,120 feet, offering some of the best views in the state from

MAINE

its summit and from the open, three-mile ridge linking it and its neighboring 4,000-footer, the Horn. A round-trip hike on the Appalachian Trail (AT) from Route 4 to the true Saddleback summit—the first of its two summits reached from this direction—is a strenuous 10.2-mile day hike. Continuing to the Horn makes the round-trip distance a very challenging 13.4 miles, with a cumulative 3,800 feet of uphill. Although these are among the most sought-after Maine summits, avoid this exposed ridge in inclement weather. Also carry plenty of water, as there is no water source above the outlet to Moose and Deer Pond.

From Route 4, follow the white blazes of the AT northbound. Within 0.1 mile, the trail crosses a bridge over Sandy River and then climbs steadily to the Piazza Rock lean-to and camping area, 1.8 miles from the road (a very popular destination among weekend backpackers). A side path off the AT leads about 200 yards uphill to Piazza Rock, an enormous horizontal slab protruding improbably from the cliff. You can follow the trail up onto the slab with a little scrambling. Following the AT 0.2 mile north of the camping area, pass another side path leading a short distance to the Caves, actually passageways through giant boulders that have cleaved from the cliff above over the eons. Just over a mile beyond the Caves side path, the AT crosses Saddleback Stream, and 0.6 mile farther it crosses the Moose and Deer Pond outlet, the last water source on this hike. At 4.7 miles from Route 4, the trail emerges above the tree line on Saddleback and ascends the open ridge another mile to the summit. Views here are spectacular, encompassing the Rangeley Lake area to the west, the Horn to the northeast, and extending north to Katahdin and southwest to Washington on a clear day. The AT continues down into the slight saddle that gives the mountain its name, over Saddleback's second summit, and then drops more steeply over ledges for several hundred feet into the col between Saddleback and the Horn. It turns upward again, climbing gently to the 4,041-foot summit of the Horn, 1.6

miles from Saddleback's summit, where again the views are long in every direction. The AT continues north, but this hike returns via the same route you came.

The Piazza Rock lean-to and camping area is reached via a short side path off the Appalachian Trail, 1.8 miles north of Route 4.

User Groups: Hikers only. Bikes and horses are prohibited; no wheelchair facilities. Dogs are discouraged along the Appalachian Trail in Maine. This trail should not be attempted in winter except by hikers experienced in mountaineering and prepared for severe winter weather, and is not suitable for skis.

Permits: Parking, access, and camping are free. Backcountry camping accommodations are available on a first-come, first-served basis.

Maps: Detailed trail maps are available from the Maine Appalachian Club (Maine Highway 27 to Maine Highway 17, $8) and the Appalachian Mountain Club (Rangeley–Stratton/Baxter State Park–Katahdin, $7.95 in waterproof Tyvek). For topographic area maps, request Redington and Saddleback Mountain from the USGS.

Directions: Park in the roadside turnout where the AT crosses Route 4, about 12 miles north of the junction of Routes 4 and 142 in Phillips and 10.1 miles south of the junction of Routes 4 and 16 in Rangeley.

GPS Coordinates: 44.8910 N, 70.5371 W

Contact: Maine Appalachian Trail Club, P.O. Box 283, Augusta, ME 04332-0283, www.matc.org. Appalachian Mountain Club, 5 Joy St., Boston, MA 02108, 617/523-0655, www.outdoors.org.

⑧ PIAZZA ROCK AND THE CAVES
4 mi/3 hr   🏃2 △8

southeast of Rangeley

Many Appalachian Trail (AT) hikers continue beyond Piazza Rock and the Caves on their way to bag Saddleback Mountain and the Horn. But these two interesting geological formations just a couple miles from the road offer a wonderful destination for a short hike that climbs little more than a few hundred feet—it's especially suited for children. Piazza Rock is an enormous horizontal slab protruding improbably from the cliff. The Caves are interesting passageways through giant boulders that have cleaved from the cliff above over the eons. The lean-to and camping area nearby provides the option of an overnight trip, though the area is very popular and fills quickly on summer and fall weekends.

From Route 4, follow the white blazes of the AT northbound. Within 0.1 mile, the trail crosses a bridge over Sandy River and then climbs steadily to the Piazza Rock lean-to, 1.8 miles from the highway. Turn left on a side path that leads about 200 yards uphill to Piazza Rock. You can follow the trail up onto the slab with a little scrambling. Returning to the AT, follow the trail another 0.2 mile north to a short spur path leading to the Caves. Hike back to your vehicle the same way you came.

The Piazza Rock lean-to and camping area is reached via a short side path off the Appalachian Trail, 1.8 miles north of Route 4.

User Groups: Hikers only. Bikes and horses are prohibited; no wheelchair facilities. Dogs are discouraged along the Appalachian Trail in Maine. This trail is not suitable for skis.

Permits: Parking, access, and camping are free. Backcountry camping accommodations are available on a first-come, first-served basis.

Maps: Detailed trail maps are available from the Maine Appalachian Club (Maine Highway 27 to Maine Highway 17, $8) and the Appalachian Mountain Club (Rangeley–Stratton/Baxter State Park–Katahdin, $7.95 in waterproof Tyvek). For topographic area maps, request Redington and Saddleback Mountain from the USGS.

Directions: Park in the roadside turnout where the AT crosses Route 4, about 12 miles north of the junction of Routes 4 and 142 in Phillips and 10.1 miles south of the junction of Routes 4 and 16 in Rangeley.

GPS Coordinates: 44.8910 N, 70.5371 W

Contact: Maine Appalachian Trail Club, P.O. Box 283, Augusta, ME 04332-0283, www.matc.org. Appalachian Mountain Club, 5 Joy St., Boston, MA 02108, 617/523-0655, www.outdoors.org.

9 OLD BLUE MOUNTAIN
5.6 mi/4 hr   🥾5 ⛰9

north of Andover

From the first steps up this remote stretch of the Appalachian Trail (AT) to the dazzling 360 degree views atop the 3,600-foot summit of Old Blue Mountain, this is a hike without a dull moment. Moose travel freely through the hardwood forest here, and, without the heavy boot traffic on the trail, you might even see the reclusive black bear lumbering nearby—or at least come across scat and prints. The best time to hike Old Blue is between July and early October—but be prepared for any type of weather. Even in late May and early June, the mountain's weather can feel more like March. The elevation gain is about 2,200 feet.

The AT leaves South Arm Road (look for a sign a few steps in from the road) and its first mile climbs steeply above spectacular Black Brook Notch. Atop the cliffs, watch for an open ledge to the trail's right with an unobstructed view of the notch. At approximately two miles out from the trailhead, the AT then meanders to the summit through dense woods, at one point offering a good view toward Old Blue's summit. The summit itself is a broad plateau covered with scrub trees and offering views in all directions. Visible to the south are the Mahoosucs and the slopes of the Sunday River Ski Area; to the northeast are the Saddleback Range and Bigelow Mountain. Descend the same way you came.

User Groups: Hikers only. Bikes and horses

MAINE

are prohibited; no wheelchair facilities. Dogs are discouraged along the Appalachian Trail in Maine. This trail should not be attempted in winter except by hikers experienced in mountaineering and prepared for severe winter weather, and is not suitable for skis.

Permits: Parking, access, and camping are free. Backcountry camping accommodations are available on a first-come, first-served basis.

Maps: A detailed trail map of this portion of the Appalachian Trail is available from the Maine Appalachian Club (Maine Highway 17 to Maine–New Hampshire State Line,$8). For topographic area maps, request Metallak Mountain and Andover from the USGS.

Directions: From the junction of Routes 5 and 120 in Andover, head east on Route 120 for half a mile and then turn left onto South Arm Road. Drive another 7.7 miles into Black Brook Notch to where the AT crosses the road. Park at the roadside.

GPS Coordinates: 44.7219 N, 70.7856 W

Contact: Maine Appalachian Trail Club, P.O. Box 283, Augusta, ME 04332-0283, www.matc.org. Appalachian Trail Conference, 799 Washington St., P.O. Box 807, Harpers Ferry, WV 25425-0807, 304/535-6331, www.appalachiantrail.org.

10 TUMBLEDOWN MOUNTAIN BROOK TRAIL
3.8 mi/3 hr   🏃4 ⛰10

northwest of Weld

With a 700-foot cliff on its south face, a pristine alpine pond, and more than a half mile of open, rocky ridge, Tumbledown Mountain seems far taller than 3,068 feet. The views from the ridge and two peaks (East and West) take in a landscape of mountains and lakes offering few, if any, signs of human presence. The long views stretch far to the east, south, and west, all the way to Mount Washington and the White Mountains in New Hampshire

(the tall ridge looming in the distance to the southwest). There are other trails to the top of Tumbledown, but this one is significantly easier and more appropriate for children and casual hikers, though it still climbs approximately 1,900 feet. All trail junctions are marked with signs.

From the parking area, the Brook Trail follows an old logging road for its first mile and then climbs more steeply for the next half mile to Tumbledown Pond, a scenic alpine tarn tucked amid Tumbledown's three summits (East, West, and North Peaks). From the pond, turn left (west) on the Tumbledown Ridge Trail and hike up a moderately steep, open ridge of rock for 0.4 mile to East Peak, where there are sweeping mountain views to the east, south, and west, all the way to Mount Washington.

This hike ends here and returns the way you came. But to reach West Peak—the true summit at 3,068 feet—follow the Tumbledown Ridge Trail another 0.3 mile west; it drops down into the saddle between the peaks and then climbs the rocky ridge to West Peak (adding 0.6 mile to this hike's distance).

User Groups: Hikers and dogs. Not suitable for bikes or horses; no wheelchair facilities.

Permits: Parking and access are free.

Maps: For a contour map of trails, obtain the Camden–Pleasant–Weld/Mahoosuc–Evans map, $7.95 in waterproof Tyvek, from the Appalachian Mountain Club. For topographic area maps, request Weld, Madrid, Roxbury, and Jackson Mountain from the USGS.

Directions: From the junction of Routes 142 and 156 in Weld, drive 2.4 miles north on Route 142 to Weld Corner. Turn left onto West Side Road at the Mount Blue State Park sign. Continue a half mile and bear right on a dirt road. Drive 2.3 miles on that road, passing the Mountain View Cemetery, and then bear right again on another dirt road, heading toward Byron Notch. From that intersection, it's 1.6 miles to the Brook Trail; park at the roadside.

Contact: Tumbledown Conservation Alliance, P.O. Box 24, Weld, ME 04285, www.

tumbledown.org. Appalachian Mountain Club, 5 Joy St., Boston, MA 02108, 617/523-0655, www.outdoors.org.

11 TABLE ROCK, GRAFTON NOTCH

2.5 mi/1.5 hr   4   9

in Grafton Notch State Park

Flanked to the south by Old Speck Mountain and to the north by Baldpate Mountain, Grafton Notch takes a deep bite out of this western Maine stretch of the Appalachians and marks the northern terminus of the Mahoosuc Range. Perched hundreds of feet up Baldpate Mountain, the broad, flat Table Rock overlooks the notch. Visible from Route 26, Baldpate affords commanding views of the notch and Old Speck. This 2.5-mile loop over Table Rock employs the Appalachian Trail and the orange-blazed Table Rock Trail, which ascends very steeply and relentlessly for a mile. The vertical ascent above Grafton Notch is nearly 1,000 feet.

From the parking lot, pick up the white-blazed Appalachian Trail (AT) heading north, crossing the highway. After reentering the woods, follow the AT for 0.1 mile and then turn right at the sign for Table Rock. The orange-blazed trail almost immediately grows steep, emerging a mile later at the so-called slab caves, which are actually intriguing cavities amid boulders rather than true caves. The trail turns right and circles around and up onto Table Rock. To descend, walk off the back of Table Rock, following a blue-blazed trail for a half mile to the left until reaching the AT. Turn left (south), and follow the AT nearly a mile back to Route 26. Cross the highway to the parking lot.

Special Note: For those looking for a more moderate climb to Table Rock (but skipping the slab caves), reverse the descent route, following the AT for a mile to the blue-blazed spur trail leading another half mile to Table Rock.

User Groups: Hikers only. Bikes and horses are prohibited; no wheelchair facilities. Dogs are discouraged along the Appalachian Trail in Maine. This trail would be difficult to snowshoe and is not suitable for skis.

Permits: Visitors using the parking lot at this trailhead are asked to pay a self-service fee of $2 per adult Maine resident/$3 per adult nonresident and $1 per child. There is a box beside the parking lot.

Maps: A very basic map of Grafton Notch State Park trails is available from park rangers, who are usually on duty at high-traffic areas such as Screw Auger Falls; it can also be obtained through the park office or the Maine Bureau of Parks and Lands. A detailed trail map is available from the Maine Appalachian Trail Club (Maine Highway 17 to Maine–New Hampshire State Line, $8). For a topographic area map, request Old Speck Mountain from the USGS.

Directions: This hike begins from a large parking lot (marked by a sign labeled Hiking Trail) where the Appalachian Trail crosses Route 26 in Grafton Notch State Park, 6.7 miles north of the sign at the state park's southern entrance and 1.8 miles south of the sign at the state park's northern entrance. Grafton Notch borders Route 26 between Upton and Newry. Grafton Notch State Park is open May 15–October 15, though the trails are accessible year-round.

GPS Coordinates: 44.6199 N, 70.9543 W

Contact: Grafton Notch State Park, 1941 Bear River Rd., Newry, ME 04261, 207/824-2912 or 207/624-6080 off-season. Maine Department of Conservation, Bureau of Parks and Lands, 286 Water St., Key Bank Plaza, 3rd and 5th floors, Augusta, ME 04333-0022, 207/287-3821, www.state.me.us/doc/parks. Maine Appalachian Trail Club, P.O. Box 283, Augusta, ME 04332-0283, www.matc.org.

12 MOTHER WALKER FALLS
0.2 mi/0.25 hr   🚶1 ⛰7

in Grafton Notch State Park

Southeast of Grafton Notch, this short walk on an easy, wide path leads to viewpoints above Mother Walker Falls, an impressive gorge in the park cut by the erosive action of the Bear River.

From the turnout, walk down the stairs. A gravel path leads both to the right and to the left, and both directions lead a short distance to views into the narrow gorge, in which roaring water drops through several short steps for 100 yards or more. To the right, the walkway ends at a fence (and is a good choice if you have young kids in tow). If you go left, there is no fence, allowing greater liberty to explore the gorge. However, dense forest cover and rugged terrain here obscure any long views.

User Groups: Hikers and leashed dogs. This trail is not suitable for bikes or horses; no wheelchair facilities.

Permits: Parking and access are free.

Maps: Although no map is needed for this walk, a very basic map of Grafton Notch State Park trails is available from park rangers, who are usually on duty at Screw Auger Falls; it can also be obtained through the park office or the Maine Bureau of Parks and Lands. For a topographic area map, request Old Speck Mountain from the USGS.

Directions: This hike begins from a roadside turnout marked by a sign for Mother Walker Falls, on Route 26 in Grafton Notch State Park, 2.2 miles north of the sign at the state park's southern entrance and 6.3 miles south of the sign at the state park's northern entrance.

GPS Coordinates: 44.5814 N, 70.9253 W

Contact: Grafton Notch State Park, 1941 Bear River Rd., Newry, ME 04261, 207/824-2912 or 207/624-6080 off-season. Maine Department of Conservation, Bureau of Parks and Lands, 286 Water St., Key Bank Plaza, 3rd and 5th floors, Augusta, ME 04333-0022, 207/287-3821, www.state.me.us/doc/parks.

13 SCREW AUGER FALLS
0.1 mi/0.25 hr   🚶1 ⛰9

in Grafton Notch State Park

BEST (

As the Bear River pours over smooth stone slabs, it tumbles through an impressive waterfall and a tight gorge of water-sculpted rock before stopping momentarily to form a pleasant pool of water. Sitting in the heart of 3,192-acre Grafton Notch State Park, Screw Auger Falls is a popular swimming hole for families and a scenic attraction for tourists. The gorge lies just a few minutes' stroll down a flat walkway from the parking lot. The short walk is well-marked and wheelchair-accessible.

User Groups: Hikers, wheelchair users, and leashed dogs. This trail is not suitable for bikes or horses.

Permits: Parking and access are free.

Maps: Although no map is needed for this walk, a very basic map of Grafton Notch State Park trails is available from park rangers, who are usually on duty at Screw Auger Falls; it can also be obtained through the park office or the state Bureau of Parks and Lands. For a topographic area map, request Old Speck Mountain from the USGS.

Directions: This hike begins from a large parking lot marked by a sign for Screw Auger Falls, on Route 26 in Grafton Notch State Park, one mile north of the sign at the state park's southern entrance and 7.5 miles south of the sign at the state park's northern entrance.

GPS Coordinates: 44.5832 N, 70.9031 W

Contact: Grafton Notch State Park, 1941 Bear River Rd., Newry, ME 04261, 207/824-2912 or 207/624-6080 off-season. Maine Department of Conservation, Bureau of Parks and Lands, 286 Water St., Key Bank Plaza, 3rd and 5th floors, Augusta, ME 04333-0022, 207/287-3821, www.state.me.us/doc/parks.

14 EYEBROW TRAIL

2.3 mi/1.5 hr

in Grafton Notch State Park

The Eyebrow Trail is a rugged side loop off the Appalachian Trail that offers a spectacular Grafton Notch view from the crest of Old Speck Mountain's towering cliffs, visible from the parking lot. Be forewarned: Parts of the trail are severely eroded and could be unpleasant, especially in wet weather. The elevation gain is about 1,000 feet.

From the parking lot, walk southbound on the white-blazed AT for about 100 yards and then bear right onto the orange-blazed Eyebrow Trail. The trail climbs very steeply over rugged terrain—at one point traversing an exposed slab of rock that could be dangerous when wet or icy. A bit more than a mile from the trailhead, the Eyebrow Trail passes over a series of four ledges. The view of Grafton Notch from the first ledge, a small overlook, is pretty good; the third ledge's view is largely obscured by trees. But from the second and fourth ledges you get an excellent, cliff-top view of Grafton Notch. The summit of Old Speck Mountain looms high to the right, Table Rock is distinguishable on the face of Baldpate Mountain directly across the notch, and Sunday River Whitecap rises prominently to the southeast. After enjoying the view, continue along the Eyebrow Trail 0.1 mile to its upper junction with the AT. Turn left and descend the AT for 1.1 miles back to the trailhead.

User Groups: Hikers only. Bikes and horses are prohibited; no wheelchair facilities. Dogs are discouraged along the Appalachian Trail in Maine. This trail should not be attempted in winter except by hikers experienced in mountaineering and prepared for severe winter weather, and is not suitable for skis.

Permits: Visitors using the parking lot at this trailhead are asked to pay a self-service fee of $2 per adult Maine resident/$3 per adult nonresident and $1 per child. There is a box beside the parking lot. The Old Speck summit

and northeast slopes are within Grafton Notch State Park in Maine.

Maps: Detailed trail maps are available from the Appalachian Mountain Club (Camden–Pleasant–Weld/Mahoosuc–Evans, $7.95 in waterproof Tyvek) and Maine Appalachian Trail Club (Maine Highway 17 to Maine–New Hampshire State Line, $8). For a topographic area map, request Old Speck Mountain from the USGS.

Directions: Park in the large parking lot located where the white-blazed Appalachian Trail crosses Route 26 (marked by a sign labeled Hiking Trail), 6.7 miles north of the sign at the state park's southern entrance and 1.8 miles south of the sign at the state park's northern entrance. Grafton Notch State Park is open May 15–October 15, though the trails are accessible year-round.

GPS Coordinates: 44.6385 N, 70.9566 W

Contact: Grafton Notch State Park, 1941 Bear River Rd., Newry, ME 04261, 207/824-2912 or 207/624-6080 off-season. Maine Department of Conservation, Bureau of Parks and Lands, 286 Water St., Key Bank Plaza, 3rd and 5th floors, Augusta, ME 04333-0022, 207/287-3821, www.state.me.us/doc/parks. Maine Appalachian Trail Club, P.O. Box 283, Augusta, ME 04332-0283, www.matc. org. Appalachian Mountain Club, 5 Joy St., Boston, MA 02108, 617/523-0655, www. outdoors.org.

15 STEP FALLS PRESERVE

1 mi/0.5 hr

south of Grafton Notch State Park, in Newry

BEST (

Step Falls is a steeply descending series of cascades and pools on the frothing white waters of Wight Brook. With a total drop of over 250 feet, it is one of the highest falls in Maine. A lodge and tourist cabins once stood in the area, advertising Step Falls as one of the most beautiful natural areas in western Maine. In 1909, the main lodge burned and the tourist operation disintegrated. Owned by the Nature Conservancy since 1962, forest cover has rebounded along Wight Brook, giving the falls a real sense of wild ruggedness.

From the parking lot, follow the obvious, white-blazed trail for a half mile along Wight Brook. (Considered a "braided brook" geologically, the Wight's rocky, foamy waters make an excellent environment for brook trout.) The trail is an easy, flat walk; take care not to wander off it onto false trails because such roaming tramples vegetation. Explore the base of the falls and head a bit further up to see the deep plunge pools formed by the action of ice and water splitting the underlying granite. Return the same way.

User Groups: Hikers and dogs. No bikes, horses, or wheelchair facilities.

Permits: Parking and access are free.

Maps: No map is needed for this easy walk. But for a topographic area map, request Old Speck Mountain from the USGS.

Directions: This hike begins from a large dirt parking lot off Route 26, 0.6 mile south of the Grafton Notch State Park southern entrance. Watch for a dirt road, marked by a small sign,

on the south side of a small bridge over Wight Brook; it leads 100 feet to the parking area. The preserve is open dawn–dusk.
GPS Coordinates: 44.5695 N, 70.8714 W
Contact: The Nature Conservancy Maine Chapter, Fort Andross, 14 Maine St., Suite 401, Brunswick, ME 04011, www.nature. org.

16 OLD SPECK MOUNTAIN
7.6 mi/5 hr   🏃4 ⛰️7

in Grafton Notch State Park

This 7.6-mile round-trip hike brings you to the summit of Maine's fourth-highest peak and at a height of 4,180 feet, one of the state's 14 4,000-footers. Old Speck's summit lacked views until a fire tower was built there in 1999, replacing an old, unsafe tower. Now you can climb the tower for stunning, 360-degree views. There are also views along the Old Speck Trail, which coincides with the Appalachian Trail (AT), from the shoulder of Old Speck out over the vast sweep of woodlands to

© D TALBOT/WWW.GHOSTFLOWERS.COM

the view southeast across Mahoosuc Notch to the Northern Presidentials from the summit of Old Speck Mountain

the north. This hike's other attractions are the brook cascades, which the trail parallels lower on the mountain. The popular Grafton Notch hike climbs about 2,700 feet in elevation.

From the parking lot in Grafton Notch, follow the white blazes of the AT/Old Speck Trail southbound, following the playful waters of the dropping cascades. (The relaxing sound of falling water may help distract you from the steepness of the trail.) Leaving the brook behind by 1.5 miles, the trail continues relentlessly uphill. At 3.5 miles, reach a junction with the Mahoosuc Trail. Here, turn left on the Mahoosuc for the easy, final 0.3-mile climb to Old Speck's summit. Head back along the same route.

User Groups: Hikers only. Bikes and horses are prohibited; no wheelchair facilities. Dogs are discouraged along the Appalachian Trail in Maine. This trail should not be attempted in winter except by hikers experienced in mountaineering and prepared for severe winter weather, and is not suitable for skis.

Permits: Visitors using the parking lot at this trailhead are asked to pay a self-service fee of $3 per adult Maine resident/$2 per adult nonresident and $1 per child. There is a box beside the parking lot. The Old Speck summit and northeast slopes are within Grafton Notch State Park in Maine.

Maps: Detailed trail maps are available from the Appalachian Mountain Club (Camden–Pleasant–Weld/Mahoosuc–Evans, $7.95 in waterproof Tyvek) and the Maine Appalachian Trail Club (Maine Highway 17 to Maine–New Hampshire State Line, $8). For a topographic area map, request Old Speck Mountain from the USGS.

Directions: Grafton Notch State Park borders Route 26 between Upton and Newry. Park in the large parking lot located where the white-blazed Appalachian Trail crosses Route 26 (marked by a sign labeled Hiking Trail), 6.7 miles north of the sign at the state park's southern entrance and 1.8 miles south of the sign at the state park's northern entrance. Grafton Notch State Park is open May

15–October 15, though the trails are accessible year-round.

GPS Coordinates: 44.5901 N, 70.9443 W
Contact: Grafton Notch State Park, 1941 Bear River Rd., Newry, ME 04261, 207/824-2912 or 207/624-6080 off-season. Maine Department of Conservation, Bureau of Parks and Lands, 286 Water St., Key Bank Plaza, 3rd and 5th floors, Augusta, ME 04333-0022, 207/287-3821, www.state.me.us/doc/parks. Appalachian Mountain Club Pinkham Notch Visitor Center, P.O. Box 298, Gorham, NH 03581, 603/466-2721, www.outdoors.org. Maine Appalachian Trail Club, P.O. Box 283, Augusta, ME 04332-0283, www.matc.org.

17 MAHOOSUC NOTCH
6.5 mi/6 hr   🏃5 ⛰10

south of Grafton Notch State Park

Strewn about on the floor of this deep, wild notch is a maze of stone and cavelike passages, formed by giant boulders which, over the eons, have fallen from the towering cliffs of Mahoosuc and Fulling Mill Mountains. Mahoosuc Notch can be hiked via the Notch Trail from Success Pond Road when the road is passable; it's 6.5 miles round-trip, climbs a cumulative 1,300 feet or so, and can easily take several hours; in many circles, the rocky obstacle course is known as one of the Appalachian Trail's most difficult miles. The shady notch is often much cooler than surrounding terrain; be sure to dress in layers, even in mid-summer.

From the Success Pond Road parking area, follow the Notch Trail as it ascends gently eastward through heavy cover of mixed forest. At 2.2 miles, it reaches a junction with the Mahoosuc Trail, which then coincides with the Appalachian Trail (AT). Bear left (northbound) on the AT, soon entering the boulder realm of the notch. Picking and crawling your way through the boulder field, carefully watch for white blazes to guide your next turn. Upon reaching the opposite end—you will know when you're through it—turn around and return the way you came, again watching for the white blazes.

For a two- or three-day loop that incorporates the notch and allows you to avoid backtracking through the notch, see *The Mahoosuc Range* hike in this chapter.

User Groups: Hikers only. Bikes and horses are prohibited; no wheelchair facilities. Dogs are discouraged along the Appalachian Trail in Maine.

Permits: Parking and access are free.

Maps: Detailed trail maps are available from the Appalachian Mountain Club (Camden–Pleasant–Weld/Mahoosuc–Evans, $7.95 in waterproof Tyvek) and the Maine Appalachian Trail Club (Maine Highway 17 to Maine–New Hampshire State Line, $8). For topographic area maps, request Success Pond and Old Speck Mountain from the USGS.

Directions: The Mahoosuc Notch Trail begins at a parking area off the dirt Success Pond Road, which runs south from Route 26, 2.8 miles north of where the white-blazed Appalachian Trail crosses the highway in Grafton Notch State Park. From Route 26, follow the twisting road for several miles, dipping over the state line and then back again to reach a left hand turn for the trailhead (look for the Notch Trail signpost). To access Success Pond Road from the south, drive north on Route 16 from its southern junction with U.S. 2 in Gorham, New Hampshire, for about 4.5 miles and turn east on the Cleveland Bridge across the Androscoggin River in Berlin, New Hampshire. Bear left onto Unity Street; go through the traffic light 0.7 mile from Route 16, and then continue 0.1 mile and bear right onto Hutchins Street. Drive 0.8 mile farther and turn sharply left, passing the paper company mill yard. Just 0.3 mile farther, turn right onto Success Pond Road. From Hutchins Street, it's about 11 miles to the trailhead parking area on the right at the Notch Trail sign. Success Pond Road, a private logging road that parallels the Mahoosuc Range on its west side, isn't

maintained in winter and may not be passable due to mud in spring.

GPS Coordinates: 44.5386 N, 71.0259 W

Contact: Appalachian Mountain Club Pinkham Notch Visitor Center, P.O. Box 298, Gorham, NH 03581, 603/466-2721, www.outdoors.org. Maine Appalachian Trail Club, P.O. Box 283, Augusta, ME 04332-0283, www.matc.org.

18 THE MAHOOSUC RANGE

30.6 mi one-way/4-5 days

🏃🏃5 ⚠10

between Shelburne, New Hampshire, and Grafton Notch State Park

BEST (

If you like the rugged adventure of a multi-day backpacking trek, you will love the journey offered by this wild, remote string of hills straddling the Maine–New Hampshire border; much of the route takes place on the Appalachian Trail (AT). Only one peak in the Mahoosucs—Old Speck—rises above 4,000 feet, but there's nary a flat piece of earth through the entire range. Read: Very tough hiking. Among the highlights are the ridge walk over Goose Eye Mountain, and Mahoosuc Notch, a boulder-strewn cleft in the range, often referred to as one of the most difficult miles on the Appalachian Trail. The route stretches from U.S. 2 in Shelburne, New Hampshire, to Grafton Notch, Maine, a 30.6-mile outing that can easily take five days. For a shorter trip, consider a two- or three-day hike from Grafton Notch to either the Mahoosuc Notch Trail (see the *Mahoosuc Notch* listing in this chapter) or the Carlo Col Trail.

The Centennial Trail, blazed in 1976 to commemorate the 100th anniversary of the Appalachian Mountain Club, is actually an old logging road and a shorter section of the Appalachian Trail. Leaving from the parking area, the familiar white blazes of the AT mark the Centennial Trailhead. Beginning on an old woods road, the Centennial Trail ascends steadily, and steeply at times, to the Mount Hayes eastern summit at 2.8 miles, which offers good views of the Carter–Moriah Range and the northern Presidentials to the south and southwest. At 3.1 miles, turn right (north) on the Mahoosuc Trail, which coincides with the white-blazed Appalachian Trail. (Just 0.2 mile to the left is a good view from the Mount Hayes summit.) At 4.9 miles, the AT passes over the open summit of Cascade Mountain and at 6.1 miles a side path leads 0.2 mile to the Trident Col campsite. The AT skirts Page Pond at 7.1 miles, and at 7.7 miles a side path leads to views from Wocket Ledge. At 8.8 miles, the trail runs along the north shore of Dream Lake; at the lake's far end, the Peabody Brook Trail diverges right, leading 3.1 miles south to North Road. (The Dryad Falls Trail branches east from the Peabody Brook Trail 0.1 mile from the AT and leads 1.8 miles to the Austin Brook Trail.) At 11 miles, the AT descends to Gentian Pond and a lean-to near its shore.

Continuing northbound, the trail climbs steeply up Mount Success, reaching the summit at 13.8 miles. After the Success Trail diverges left (west) at 14.4 miles (leading 2.4 miles to Success Pond Road), the AT descends steeply and then climbs to the Carlo Col Trail junction at 16.2 miles. (That trail leads 0.2 mile to the Carlo Col shelter and 2.6 miles west to Success Pond Road.) At 16.6 miles the AT passes over Mount Carlo's open summit, descends, and then climbs—very steeply near the top—to Goose Eye Mountain's high ridge at 18 miles. Walk the open ridge to the left a short distance for the terrific view from the west peak, where the Goose Eye Trail diverges left (west), leading 3.1 miles to Success Pond Road. Then turn north again on the AT, descend, and follow it as it skirts the 3,794-foot east peak, around which the AT was rerouted in the 1990s because of damage by hikers to fragile alpine vegetation on its summit. (The two Wright Trail branches reach the AT immediately south and north of the east peak, both leading east about four miles to the Sunday River Ski Area road in Ketchum.) Descend again, climb over the summit of North Peak at 19.6 miles, and reach the Full Goose shelter at 20.6 miles. The AT climbs steeply north from the shelter to the barren South Peak summit, with views in nearly every direction. It swings left and then descends steeply to the junction with the Mahoosuc Notch Trail at 22.1 miles (the trail leads 2.2 miles west to Success Pond Road).

The next trail mile traverses the floor of Mahoosuc Notch, flanked by tall cliffs that usually leave the notch in cool shadow. Follow the white blazes carefully through the jumbled terrain of boulders, where carrying a backpack can be very difficult. At the notch's far end, at 23.1 miles, the AT swings uphill for the sustained climb of Mahoosuc Arm, passes ledges with good views, and then drops downhill to beautiful Speck Pond—at 3,430 feet, it's one of the highest ponds in Maine. There is a lean-to just above the pond's shore, at 25.7 miles; nearby, the Speck Pond Trail descends west 3.6 miles to Success Pond Road. From the shelter, the AT ascends north up Old Speck Mountain, traversing open ledges with excellent views to the south, then reentering the woods to reach a junction with the Old Speck Trail at 26.8 miles (where the Mahoosuc Trail ends). From that junction, the Old Speck Trail continues straight ahead 0.3 mile over easy ground to the 4,180-foot summit of Old Speck, where a fire tower offers glorious 360-degree views. The AT coincides with the Old Speck Trail for the circuitous, 3.5-mile descent to Grafton Notch, culminating at the parking lot.

Camping is permitted only at the five backcountry campsites along the Appalachian Trail through the Mahoosuc Range (Trident Col, Gentian Pond, Carlo Col, Full Goose, and Speck Pond). Backpackers stay in the shelters or use the tent platforms; all sites are free of charge except Speck Pond, which charges a caretaker fee of $8 per person per night. The Old Speck summit and northeast slopes are within Grafton Notch State Park in Maine, but the rest of the Mahoosucs are on private

MAINE

property and not a part of the White Mountain National Forest.

User Groups: Hikers only. Bikes and horses are prohibited; no wheelchair facilities. Dogs are discouraged along the Appalachian Trail in Maine. This trail should not be attempted in winter except by hikers experienced in mountaineering and prepared for severe winter weather.

Permits: Parking and access are free. All backcountry camping accommodations are free on a first-come, first-served basis, with the exception of Speck Pond. Campers at Speck Pond pay a cash-only caretaker fee of $8 per person, per night.

Maps: The best trail map for this route is the Camden–Pleasant–Weld/Mahoosuc–Evans map, $7.95 in waterproof Tyvek, available from Appalachian Mountain Club. The map available from the Main Appalachian Trail Club (Maine Highway 17 to Maine–New Hampshire State Line, $8) covers just the AT in Maine. For topographic area maps, request Berlin, Shelburne, Success Pond, Gilead, and Old Speck Mountain from the USGS.

Directions: You need to shuttle two vehicles for this backpacking trip. To hike the range from south to north, as described here, leave one vehicle in the large parking lot located where the white-blazed Appalachian Trail crosses Route 26 in Grafton Notch State Park (marked by a sign labeled Hiking Trail), 6.7 miles north of the sign at the state park's southern entrance and 1.8 miles south of the sign at the state park's northern entrance. To reach the start of this hike, turn north off U.S. 2 onto North Road in Shelburne, New Hampshire, about 3.2 miles east of the southern junction of U.S. 2 and Route 16 in Gorham. Cross the Androscoggin River, turn left onto Hogan Road, and continue 0.2 mile to a small parking area for the Centennial Trail.

GPS Coordinates: 44.5907 N, 70.9461 W

Contact: Grafton Notch State Park, 1941 Bear River Rd., Newry, ME 04261, 207/824-2912 or 207/624-6080 off-season. Maine Department of Conservation, Bureau of Parks and Lands, 286 Water St., Key Bank Plaza, 3rd and 5th floors, Augusta, ME 04333-0022, 207/287-3821, www.state.me.us/doc/parks. Appalachian Mountain Club Pinkham Notch Visitor Center, P.O. Box 298, Gorham, NH 03581, 603/466-2721, www.outdoors.org. Maine Appalachian Trail Club, P.O. Box 283, Augusta, ME 04332-0283, www.matc.org.

🄳🄳 THE ROOST

1 mi/0.75 hr

in White Mountain National Forest, south of Gilead

Tucked away in the more remote Evans Notch is the Roost (1,374 ft.), a rocky outcropping above the Wild River with nice, though partially obscured, views west towards Mount Washington and Mount Clay. From the turnout, walk south across the bridge and turn left (east) on the Roost Trail. Cross two small brooks within the first quarter mile and then walk an old woods road. Less than a half mile from the trailhead, turn left (where indicated by an arrow and yellow blazes). Cross a brook and climb steeply uphill for the final 0.2 mile to the rocky knob of a summit; the views here are largely obstructed by trees. Follow the view sign and trail downhill for 0.1 mile to open ledges with a good view looking west over the Wild River Valley. This is a nice place to watch the sunset. Turn around and return the way you came. The elevation gain is about 500 feet.

User Groups: Hikers and dogs. This trail is not suitable for bikes or horses; no wheelchair facilities. Hunting is allowed in season. It is possible to ski and snowshoe this route; snow-covered trail conditions can be found here as early as late October and last some years through April, depending on weather conditions.

Permits: Parking and access are free.

Maps: For a contour map of trails, get the Map of Cold River Valley and Evans Notch, available from the Chatham Trails Association for $5, or the Appalachian Mountain Club's Carter Range–Evans Notch/North Country–Mahoosuc map ($7.95 in waterproof Tyvek). For a topographic area map, request Speckled Mountain from the USGS.

Directions: Drive to a turnout just north of the bridge over Evans Brook on Route 113, 3.7 miles south of the junction of Route 113 and U.S. 2 in Gilead and 7 miles north of where Route 113 crosses the Maine–New Hampshire border.

Route 113 through Evans Notch is not maintained in winter. In fact, gates are used to close off a 9.1-mile stretch of the highway. But you can drive to parking areas near the gates and ski or snowshoe the road beyond the gates to access this area. The northern gate on Route 113 is 1.6 miles south of the junction of U.S. 2 and Route 133 in Gilead. The southern gate sits on the Maine–New Hampshire line, 0.2 mile south of Brickett Place in North Chatham and immediately north of the White Mountain National Forest Basin Recreation Area entrance. The distance given for this hike is from the trailhead.

GPS Coordinates: 44.3592 N, 70.9847 W

Contact: Chatham Trails Association, 22 Grove Pl., Unit 29, Winchester, MA 01890, http://snebulos.mit.edu/orgs/cta. Appalachian Mountain Club Pinkham Notch Visitor Center, P.O. Box 298, Gorham, NH 03581, 603/466-2721, www.outdoors.org. White Mountain National Forest Supervisor, 719 North Main St., Laconia, NH 03246, 603/528-8721, TDD for the hearing impaired 603/528-8722, www.fs.fed.us/r9/white.

20 MOUNT CARIBOU

7.3 mi/4.5 hr 🏃5 ⛰9

in White Mountain National Forest, south of Gilead

This scenic 7.3-mile loop leads you past beautiful waterfalls and cascades to the top

of Mount Caribou, a hill with unusually excellent summit views for its 2,828-foot elevation. Caribou is part of the Caribou–Speckled Mountain Wilderness of the White Mountain National Forest. From this more isolated peak, take in a scenic vista that stretches north to the Androscoggin River Valley and south to the Speckled Mountain range peaks of Haystack, Butters, and Durgin Mountains. This loop gains more than 1,800 feet in elevation.

The Caribou Trail–Mud Brook Trail loop begins and ends at the parking area; this 7.3-mile hike follows it clockwise. Yellow blazes mark both trails only sporadically, though the paths are well used and obvious (except when covered with snow). Hike north (left from the parking area) on the Caribou Trail, crossing a wooden footbridge over a brook at 0.3 mile. About a half mile past the footbridge, the trail crosses Morrison Brook and trends in a more easterly direction—making several more stream crossings over the next two miles, some of which could be difficult at high water times. One stretch of about a half mile makes five crossings near several waterfalls and cascades, including 25-foot Kees Falls. Three miles from the trailhead, the Caribou Trail reaches a junction with the Mud Brook Trail, marked by a sign. Turn right (south) on the Mud Brook Trail and follow it a half mile, climbing steadily, to the open ledges of the summit. From various spots on the ledges you enjoy views of western Maine's low mountains and lakes in virtually every direction. Numerous false trails lead through the summit's scrub brush, so take care to follow cairns and faint yellow blazes over the summit, continuing on the Mud Brook Trail. A half mile below the summit, the trail traverses a cliff top with a good view east. From the summit, it's nearly four miles back to the parking area. Along its lower two miles, the trail parallels and twice crosses Mud Brook.

User Groups: Hikers and dogs. This trail is not suitable for bikes or horses; no wheelchair facilities. It is possible to ski and snowshoe this route; snow-covered trail conditions can

MAINE

MAINE

be found here as early as late October and last some years through April, depending on weather conditions.

Permits: Parking and access are free.

Maps: For a contour map of trails, get the Map of Cold River Valley and Evans Notch for $5 from the Chatham Trails Association or the Carter Range–Evans Notch/North Country–Mahoosuc map, $7.95 in waterproof Tyvek, available from the Appalachian Mountain Club. For a topographic area map, request Speckled Mountain from the USGS.

Directions: The hike begins from a parking lot on Route 113, 4.8 miles south of its junction with U.S. 2 in Gilead and 5.9 miles north of where Route 113 crosses the Maine–New Hampshire border.

Route 113 through Evans Notch is not maintained in winter and gates are used to close off a 9.1-mile stretch of the highway. But you can drive to parking areas near the gates and ski or snowshoe the road beyond the gates to access this area. The northern gate on Route 113 is 1.6 miles south of the junction of U.S. 2 and Route 133 in Gilead. The southern gate sits on the Maine–New Hampshire line, 0.2 mile south of Brickett Place in North Chatham and immediately north of the White Mountain National Forest Basin Recreation Area entrance. The distance given for this hike is from the trailhead.

GPS Coordinates: 44.3470 N, 70.9803 W

Contact: Chatham Trails Association, 22 Grove Pl., Unit 29, Winchester, MA 01890, http://snebulos.mit.edu/orgs/cta. Appalachian Mountain Club Pinkham Notch Visitor Center, P.O. Box 298, Gorham, NH 03581, 603/466-2721, www.outdoors.org. White Mountain National Forest Supervisor, 719 North Main St., Laconia, NH 03246, 603/528-8721, TDD for the hearing impaired 603/528-8722, www.fs.fed.us/r9/white.

21 EAST ROYCE
3.0 mi/2 hr

in White Mountain National Forest, south of Gilead

Explore another small, rugged mountain overlooking the state line. The hike up East Royce (3,114 feet) makes several stream crossings, passing picturesque waterfalls and cascades, as it ascends the relentlessly steep mountainside. The uphill effort is worth it, though, as the East Royce summit offers sweeping views west to the dramatic cliffs of West Royce and the peaks of South and North Baldface in New Hampshire, and the lakes and lower hills of western Maine. The hike ascends about 1,700 feet.

From the parking lot, follow the East Royce Trail a steep 1.5 miles, crossing over, and then following, the cascading Evans Brook. Leaving the brook, the Royce Connector Trail enters from the left. Here, turn right to stay with the East Royce Trail, reaching open ledges that involve somewhat exposed scrambling within a quarter mile, and the summit just 0.1 mile farther. Return the way you came.

Special note: Across Route 113 from the parking area, the Spruce Hill Trail enters the woods beside a series of cascades worth checking out when the water is high.

User Groups: Hikers and dogs. This trail is not suitable for bikes or horses; no wheelchair facilities. It is possible to ski and snowshoe this route; snow-covered trail conditions can be found here as early as late October and last some years through April, depending on weather conditions.

Permits: Parking and access are free.

Maps: For a contour map of trails, get the Map of Cold River Valley and Evans Notch for $5 from the Chatham Trails Association or the Carter Range–Evans Notch/North Country–Mahoosuc map, $7.95 in waterproof Tyvek, from the Appalachian Mountain Club. For a topographic area map, request Speckled Mountain from the USGS.

Directions: The East Royce Trail begins at a parking lot on the west side of Route 113, 7.6 miles south of the junction of U.S. 2 and Route 113 in Gilead and 3.1 miles north of where Route 113 crosses the Maine–New Hampshire border.

Route 113 through Evans Notch is not maintained in winter, and gates are used to close off a 9.1-mile stretch of the highway. But you can drive to parking areas near the gates and ski or snowshoe the road beyond the gates to access this area. The northern gate on Route 113 is 1.6 miles south of the junction of U.S. 2 and Route 133 in Gilead. The southern gate sits on the Maine–New Hampshire line, 0.2 mile south of Brickett Place in North Chatham and immediately north of the White Mountain National Forest Basin Recreation Area entrance. The distance given for this hike is from the trailhead.

GPS Coordinates: 44.3104 N, 70.9865 W

Contact: Chatham Trails Association, 22 Grove Pl., Unit 29, Winchester, MA 01890, http://snebulos.mit.edu/orgs/cta. Appalachian Mountain Club Pinkham Notch Visitor Center, P.O. Box 298, Gorham, NH 03581, 603/466-2721, www.outdoors.org. White Mountain National Forest Supervisor, 719 North Main St., Laconia, NH 03246, 603/528-8721, TDD for the hearing impaired 603/528-8722, www.fs.fed.us/r9/white.

22 SPECKLED AND BLUEBERRY MOUNTAINS
7.9 mi/5 hr   🥾5 ⛰9

in White Mountain National Forest, south of Gilead

From the bald, rocky crown of Speckled Mountain (2,906 ft.), the views are spectacular in almost every direction. But this hike is a twofer, taking you to the open ridge and ledges of Blueberry Mountain (1,781 ft.) and to a wide panorama of lakes and hills stretching to the south and east and back into Evans

Notch. With a cumulative elevation gain of 2,400 feet, much of this hike, especially along the Blueberry Ridge Trail, makes for rugged a trip.

From the parking area, pick up the Bickford Brook Trail. At 0.6 mile, turn right at the sign for the Blueberry Ridge Trail. Immediately the trail makes a stream crossing at a narrow gorge that can be dangerous during high water. (If the stream is impassable or if you would prefer a less strenuous hike to the summit of Speckled Mountain, skip this trail and follow the Bickford Brook Trail all the way to the summit, an 8.6-mile round-trip.) Continue up the Blueberry Ridge Trail for 0.7 mile to a junction with the Lookout Loop, a half-mile detour out to the scenic ledges of the Blueberry Mountain cliffs. The Lookout Loop rejoins the Blueberry Ridge Trail; follow it to the right. It then ascends the two-mile ridge, much of it open, with wide views over your shoulder of the peaks across Evans Notch: East and West Royce, Meader, and North and South Baldface. At the upper junction with the Bickford Brook Trail, turn right (east) joining the trail for the easy half-mile hike to the Speckled summit. Descend via the Bickford Brook Trail all the way back (4.3 miles) to the parking area.

User Groups: Hikers and dogs. This trail is not suitable for bikes or horses; no wheelchair facilities. It is possible to ski and snowshoe this route; snow-covered trail conditions can be found here as early as late October and last some years through April, depending on weather conditions.

Permits: Parking and access are free.

Maps: For a contour map of trails, get the Map of Cold River Valley and Evans Notch for $5 from the Chatham Trails Association or the Carter Range–Evans Notch/North Country–Mahoosuc map, $7.95 in waterproof Tyvek, available from the Appalachian Mountain Club. For a topographic area map, request Speckled Mountain from the USGS.

Directions: This hike begins at Brickett Place, a parking area beside a brick building on

MAINE

Route 113 in North Chatham, 0.2 mile north of where Route 113 crosses the Maine–New Hampshire border and 10.5 miles south of the junction of Route 113 and U.S. 2 in Gilead.

Route 113 through Evans Notch is not maintained in winter, and gates are used to close off a 9.1-mile stretch of the highway. But you can drive to parking areas near the gates and ski or snowshoe the road beyond the gates to access this area. The northern gate on Route 113 is 1.6 miles south of the junction of U.S. 2 and Route 133 in Gilead. The southern gate sits on the Maine–New Hampshire line, 0.2 mile south of Brickett Place in North Chatham and immediately north of the White Mountain National Forest Basin Recreation Area entrance. The distance given for this hike is from the trailhead.

GPS Coordinates: 44.2740 N, 71.0033 W

Contact: Chatham Trails Association, 22 Grove Pl., Unit 29, Winchester, MA 01890, http://snebulos.mit.edu/orgs/cta. Appalachian Mountain Club Pinkham Notch Visitor Center, P.O. Box 298, Gorham, NH 03581, 603/466-2721, www.outdoors.org. White Mountain National Forest Supervisor, 719 North Main St., Laconia, NH 03246, 603/528-8721, TDD for the hearing impaired 603/528-8722, www.fs.fed.us/r9/white.

23 SABATTUS MOUNTAIN
1.5 mi/1 hr

outside Center Lovell

This short but popular local hike leads to the top of a sheer drop of hundreds of feet, providing wide views of nearly unbroken forest and mountains, including Pleasant Mountain to the south and the White Mountains to the east. This is a great hike for young children and fall foliage lovers. Follow the wide trail, which ascends steadily—and at times steeply—for 0.75 mile to the summit. Walk the cliff top to the right for the best views of the Whites. Return the same way.

User Groups: Hikers and dogs. This trail is not suitable for bikes or horses; no wheelchair facilities.

Permits: Parking and access are free.

Maps: No map is needed for this hike. The Camden–Pleasant–Weld/Mahoosuc–Evans map shows the location of Sabattus Mountain, but not its trail; the map is made of waterproof Tyvek and costs $7.95 from the Appalachian Mountain Club. For a topographic area map, request Center Lovell from the USGS.

Directions: From the Center Lovell Inn on Route 5 in Center Lovell, drive north for 0.2 mile on Route 5 and turn right on Sabattus Road. Continue for 1.5 miles and then bear right on the dirt Sabattus Mountain Road. Park in a small dirt lot or at the roadside 0.3 mile farther. The trail begins across the road from the lot.

GPS Coordinates: 44.1922 N, 70.8607 W

Contact: Maine Department of Conservation, Bureau of Parks and Lands, 286 Water St., Key Bank Plaza, 3rd and 5th floors, Augusta, ME 04333-0022, 207/287-3821, www.state.me.us/doc/parks.

24 JOCKEY CAP
0.4 mi/0.5 hr

in Fryeburg

This short walk in Fryeburg—just down the road from North Conway, New Hampshire—leads to the top of what a sign along the trail describes as "the largest boulder in the United States." While that claim's veracity might be questionable, the hike does nonetheless provide a nice walk to a good view of the surrounding countryside, including Mounts Washington and Chocorua in the White Mountains.

Find the entrance gate to the Jockey Cap Trail between the Jockey Cap cabins and country store. Follow the wide and obvious trail into the woods. As the rocky face of Jockey Cap comes into view through the trees, the trail circles to the left around the boulder and emerges from the woods at a spot where you can safely walk up onto the cap. Return the same way.

User Groups: Hikers and dogs. No wheelchair facilities. This trail is not suitable for bikes, horses, or skis.

Permits: Parking and access are free.

Maps: No map is needed for this short walk, but for a topographic area map, request Fryeburg from the USGS.

Directions: From the junction of U.S. 302, Route 5, and Route 113 in Fryeburg, drive east on U.S. 302 for one mile and park at the Jockey Cap Country Store on the left. The Jockey Cap Trail begins at a gate between the store and the cabins to the right. The trail is open to the public year-round.

GPS Coordinates: 44.0216 N, 70.9622 W

Contact: This trail crosses private land owned by Quinn's Jockey Cap Country Store and Motel, 207/935-2306, www.quinnsjockeycap.com, and land owned by the town of Fryeburg and managed by its recreation department, 207/935-3933.

25 PLEASANT MOUNTAIN
5.7 mi/3.5 hr

between Fryeburg, Denmark, and Bridgeton

Yes, it's a very pleasant trek to the top of Pleasant Mountain, one of the defining landmarks of the Sebago Lake region. Rising barely more than 2,000 feet above sea level, the mountain's ridge walk takes you through beautiful forest, over open ledges, and to several distinct summit humps, including excellent views from Big Bald Peak and Pleasant's main summit. This loop hike's cumulative elevation gain is about 1,600 feet.

From the turnout, pick up the Bald Peak Trail and begin a steady ascent beside a stream; watch for short waterfalls and a miniature flume. At 0.7 mile, the Sue's Way Trail and North Ridge Trail enter from the right, but stay left, climbing a steep 0.3 mile to Big Bald

Peak. From here, follow the Bald Peak Trail southward along the ridge, with excellent views. After 1.2 miles on the ridge, the Bald Peak Trail reaches a junction with the Fire Warden's Trail. Turn left here and proceed another 0.2 mile to the 2006-foot summit of Pleasant Mountain. Continue over the summit to pick up the Ledges Trail, which descends 1.8 miles along open ledges with terrific views to the south. The only downside to this descent route is found along the lower sections of this trail, which can be muddy and running with water. At the road, if you did not shuttle two vehicles, turn left and walk 1.5 miles to the Bald Peak Trailhead.

User Groups: Hikers and dogs. This trail is not suitable for bikes or horses; no wheelchair facilities.

Permits: Parking and access are free.

Maps: The area map Camden–Pleasant–Weld/Mahoosuc–Evans map, $7.95 in waterproof Tyvek, available from the Appalachian Mountain Club, shows this hike. The Loon Echo Land Trust offers a free, detailed map of trails in the Pleasant Mountain area, available for download on its website. For a topographic area map, request Pleasant Mountain from the USGS.

Directions: From the junction of U.S. 302 and Route 93, west of Bridgeton, drive 4.5 miles west on U.S. 302 and turn left onto Mountain Road (heading toward the Shawnee Peak Ski Area). Drive another 1.8 miles to a turnout at the Bald Peak Trailhead (marked by a sign on the right). If you have two vehicles, leave one at the Ledges Trailhead (marked by a sign) 1.5 miles farther down the road. Otherwise, you walk that stretch of road to finish this loop.

GPS Coordinates: 44.0457 N, 70.8032 W

Contact: Loon Echo Land Trust, 1 Chase St., Bridgton, ME 04009, 207/647-4352, www.loonecholandtrust.org. Appalachian Mountain Club, 5 Joy St., Boston, MA 02108, 617/523-0655, www.outdoors.org.

MAINE

26 BURNT MEADOW MOUNTAIN

2.4 mi/2 hr   🚶3 ⛰7

outside Brownfield

A nice, short local hike, this hill near Brownfield has an open summit with views in almost every direction, from the White Mountains to the lakes of western Maine. Burnt Meadow was a ski area in the 1960s and 1970s and remnants of the ski operation can still be seen, though forest cover has all but completely taken back the bare slopes and runs that once stood here. Technically abandoned property that is opened to the public for recreational use, trails are maintained by volunteers from the Maine Appalachian Trail Club. This hike gains about 1,200 feet in elevation.

From the parking area, walk uphill to the old T-bar of a former ski area. Turn left and follow the T-bar and a worn footpath uphill. Ignore the sign with an arrow pointing to the right, which you encounter within the first half mile, and continue straight ahead under the T-bar. The trail grows quite steep, with lots of loose stones and dirt. Footing may become very tricky here in spring. Where the T-bar ends in a small clearing, turn left onto a trail marked by blue blazes, which leads at a more moderate angle to the summit. Watch for a good view from ledges on the left before reaching the summit. The broad top of Burnt Meadow Mountain offers views to the west, north, and south; continue over it and you get views to the south and east. Descend the way you came.

User Groups: Hikers and dogs. This trail is not suitable for bikes or horses; no wheelchair facilities.

Permits: Parking and access are free.

Maps: A trail map of Burnt Meadow Mountain can be found in the Maine Atlas, map 4 (Delorme Publishing). For a topographic area map, request Brownfield from the USGS.

Directions: From the junction of Route 5/113 and Route 160 in East Brownfield, turn west

on Route 160 and continue 1.1 miles. Turn left, staying on Route 160, and continue another 0.3 mile. Turn right onto the paved Fire Lane 32 (shown as Ski Area Road on some maps). The parking area is 0.2 mile farther. The trailhead isn't marked, but there's an obvious parking area. The trail starts at the parking area's right side.

GPS Coordinates: 43.9361 N, 70.9038 W

Contact: Maine Appalachian Trail Club, P.O. Box 283, Augusta, ME 04332-0283, www. matc.org.

27 MOUNT CUTLER

2.6 mi/1.5 hr   🚶2 ⛰8

in Hiram

Rising abruptly from the floor of the Saco River Valley, Mount Cutler (1,232 ft.) is a short but rugged hike to views almost directly above the village of Hiram and west to the White Mountains. In its 1.3-mile route to the top, this hike climbs a steep 1,000 feet from the trailhead.

From the parking area, cross the railroad tracks, turn left, and then enter the woods on the right at a wide trail. Soon you branch right onto a red-blazed trail. The blazes appear sporadically at times, and on rocks rather than on trees higher up the mountain, making the trail potentially difficult to follow (particularly in winter). The trail ascends steep ledges overlooking the town of Hiram and grows narrow; care is needed over the ledges. But once you gain the ridge, the walking grows much easier as you pass through forests with a mix of hardwoods and hemlocks and traverse open areas with sweeping views. The east summit ledges, with views of the Saco Valley, are a good destination for a round-trip hike of about 1.5 miles. Continue on the trail along the ridge and into a saddle, where there's a birch tree grove. A faint footpath leads up the left side of the slope to the main summit, which is wooded. Just beyond it and to the right, however, is an open area with great views toward Pleasant Mountain and the White Mountains. Descend the way you came.

User Groups: Hikers and dogs. No wheelchair facilities. This trail is not suitable for bikes or horses.

Permits: Parking and access are free.

Maps: A trail map of Burnt Meadow Mountain can be found in the Maine Atlas, map 4 (Delorme Publishing). For topographic area maps, request Hiram and Cornish from the USGS.

Directions: From the junction of Route 117 and Route 5/113 in Hiram, drive over the concrete bridge; take an immediate left and then a right onto Mountain View Avenue. Drive about 0.1 mile and park at the roadside near the railroad tracks.

GPS Coordinates: 43.8778 N, 70.8052 W

Contact: Maine Appalachian Trail Club, P.O. Box 283, Augusta, ME 04332-0283, www.matc.org.

28 DOUGLAS HILL

1.2 mi/0.5 hr   🥾2 ⛰7

south of Sebago

A short, scenic walk to the hill's open summit and its stone tower gives you expansive views of Sebago Lake, Pleasant Mountain, and the mountains to the northwest as far as Mount Washington. This 169-acre preserve, formerly owned by The Nature Conservancy, is now owned by the town of Sebago.

From the registration box, walk through the stone pillars, follow the yellow-blazed Woods Trail a short distance, and then bear left onto the Ledges Trail (also blazed yellow). This trail leads over interesting open ledges with good views, though they are slick when wet. At the summit, climb the stone tower's steps; on top is a diagram identifying the distant peaks. A nature trail, blazed orange, makes a 0.75-mile loop off the summit and returns to it. Descend back to the parking lot via the

Woods Trail, which is a more direct descent than the Ledges Trail.

User Groups: Hikers only. No wheelchair facilities. This trail is not suitable for bikes or horses and is not open in winter. Dogs are prohibited.

Permits: Parking and access are free; just register at the trailhead.

Maps: A free guide and map to Douglas Hill is available at the trailhead registration box. For topographic area maps, request Steep Falls and North Sebago from the USGS.

Directions: From the junction of Routes 107 and Macks Corner Road in East Sebago, drive a half mile north on Route 107 and turn left onto Douglas Hill Road (which is one mile south of Sebago center). On some maps, the road is not labeled. Drive 0.8 mile to a hilltop and take a sharp left. In another half mile, turn left into a small parking area. The preserve is open only during daylight hours.

GPS Coordinates: 43.8741 N, 70.6985 W

Contact: Sebago Town Hall, 406 Bridgton Rd., Sebago, ME 04029, 207/787-8884.

29 WOLFE'S NECK WOODS

2 mi/1 hr   🥾1 ⛰8

in Freeport

A five minute drive from Freeport's busy shopping district, the marshes, forests, and open fields of Wolfe's Neck State Park are a welcome pocket of calm in the midst of what can be a very crowded tourist city. (Plus, it's a great place to try out some of that hiking gear you just loaded up on at L.L.Bean.) This flat loop of approximately two miles winds through the Wolfe's Neck Woods, taking you to many of the park's best features, including a white pine forest, salt marshes, and the rocky shorelines of Casco Bay and the Harraseeket River estuary. The White Pine Trail portion of this hike is wheelchair accessible.

From the parking area, pick up the White Pine Trail, a level, universally accessible trail that leads deep into a tall forest of pine and hemlock. Meandering a bit at first, the trail reaches the marshy shore of Casco Bay within 0.2 mile. Interpretative panels explain sites along the trail, including information about the park's signature resident: the osprey. Nearby Googins Island (just offshore and clearly visible from the trail) is a popular northern nesting ground for the graceful bird. Dozens can be seen summering on the island; bring binoculars for the best views of young osprey taking flight for perhaps the very first time. The Casco Bay Trail, a footpath, continues on past the island overlook; those who wish to stay on the universally accessible path can turn right to return to the parking area (The White Pine Trail loop is approximately 0.4 mile long). Following the shores of the bay for another 0.3 mile, the trail turns inland and becomes the Harraseeket River Trail. In less than a half mile, the trail brings you to the shores of the Harraseeket River. Hugging the shoreline for approximately 0.2 mile, the trail offers nice views west toward Freeport. Turning inland again, follow the trail another 0.3 mile back to the parking area.

User Groups: Hikers, leashed dogs, and wheelchairs. No bikes or horses.

Permits: Visitors to Wolfe's Neck Woods pay $3 per adult Maine resident/$4.50 per adult nonresident and $1.50 per child May–October. Trails are still open in the off-season.

Maps: A trail map and informational brochure is available at the trailhead. For a topographic area map, request Freeport from the USGS.

Directions: From downtown Freeport, drive 4.5 miles east on Route 1 to a right turn at Bow Street. Follow a short distance to Wolfe Neck Road and the park entrance.

GPS Coordinates: 43.8217 N, 70.0840 W

Contact: Wolfe's Neck Woods State Park, 426 Wolfe's Neck Rd., Freeport, ME 04032, 207/865-4465. Maine Department of Conservation, Bureau of Parks and Lands, 286 Water St., Key Bank Plaza, 3rd and 5th floors, Augusta, ME 04333-0022, 207/287-3821, www.state.me.us/doc/parks.

30 PORTLAND: BACK COVE TRAIL AND EASTERN PROMENADE
3.1 mi/1.5 hr

in Portland

BEST (

Portland is consistently rated as one of the healthiest places to live in the United States, and you'll see why as you join dozens of Portlanders for a walk or jog along the Back Cove Trail. Just off I-295, and not far from Portland's bustling city center, this wheelchair-accessible loop circles the beautiful shores of Back Cove and is an urban oasis for jogging, biking, and just strolling along taking in great views of the city skyline. The trail is a combination of stone dust and paved surfaces—mostly flat with a slight rise along the stretch that parallels I-295. And with its numerous benches along the trail and portable toilets available near both parking areas, it's a great place to bring kids. The loop is a popular recreation area for Portland locals—especially for early morning and late afternoon joggers.

Access the trail from either of the two parking lots—in Payson Park on the north end of the loop or from the Preble Street Extension on the south shore of Back Cove. A good route for views is to leave from Payson Park, bearing right on the trail (counterclockwise). On your left, for the first mile or so, is the Portland city skyline, a mix of old brick buildings and gleaming modern structures. Continuing to skirt the southern and eastern shores of the cove, views look over the pleasant water, eventually looping back to reach Payson Park.

Special Note: Before returning to Payson Park, the trail crosses a bridge over the watery entrance to Back Cove. On the southern end of the bridge, another wheelchair-accessible trail leads to the right. This is Eastern Promenade Trail, a two-mile loop along Casco Bay. The waterfront trail, part of an old rail line, offers spectacular harbor and ocean views. Approximately one mile from leaving Back Cove, the "Eastern Prom" reaches East End

MAINE

Beach and Fort Allen Park. The trail loops back from Fort Allen Park and eventually rejoins the main Eastern Prom for the return to Back Cove. The trailhead can also be accessed at the corner of Commercial and India Streets. To reach the East End Beach parking area, descend from Fort Allen Park down Cutter Street to the parking area.

User Groups: Hikers, leashed dogs, bikes, and wheelchairs. No horses.

Permits: Access and parking are free.

Maps: Trail maps of both Back Cove and the Eastern Promenade are available from Portland Trails. For topographic area maps, request Portland East and Portland West from the USGS.

Directions: To reach Payson Park and the parking area off Preble Street: From the intersection of Marginal Way and Forest Avenue/U.S. 302 in Portland, turn onto U.S. 302, heading west under I-293. After passing the highway exit ramps, take the first right onto Baxter Boulevard/Route 1 North. Follow 1.7 miles to

a right turn at Preble Street. The parking area is at the end of the street to the right.

GPS Coordinates: 43.6790 N, 70.2681 W

Contact: Portland Trails, 305 Commercial St., Portland, ME, 04101, 207/775.2411, www.trails.org.

₃₁ MOUNT AGAMENTICUS
1 mi/0.75 hr   👫₂ ⛰₇

west of Ogunquit

BEST (

Mount Agamenticus (known locally as Mount A) is famous as one of Maine's best sites for hawk-watching. Each fall, thousands of migrating hawks, including peregrine falcons, bald eagles, osprey, and northern goshawks, can be viewed from the summit. On an early October day with strong northwest winds, hundreds of raptors may soar over the mountain in just a few hours. This one-mile hike up and

© J.D. BROWN

On Mount Agamenticus, an interpretive panel identifies the far-off peaks of the White Mountains, including Mount Washington.

MAINE

down tiny Agamenticus (689 ft.) is an easy walk to a summit with a fire tower and two viewing platforms that offer 360-degree views of the Seacoast region and southern Maine and New Hampshire.

From the parking area at the base of Summit Road, follow the Ring Trail, an old woods road. Reaching a fork within 0.1 mile of the trailhead, bear left, crossing over Summit Road and soon reaching another junction. Here, turn right on the Blueberry Bluff Trail and continue uphill to the broad summit area. Mount A's summit is grassy and broad with two viewing platforms, a town recreation lodge, and fire tower; despite all this development, there's still plenty of room to picnic and just roam about. The only mar to this beautiful place is the very large (and very out of place) cell tower. Return the way you came or descend via Summit Road.

User Groups: Hikers and dogs. Parts of the trail are not suitable for bikes or horses. Refer to the map found at the trailhead for trails on the mountain open to biking and horseback riding. No wheelchair facilities on the trail. Summit Road leads to a level parking area with wheelchair access.

Permits: Parking and access are free.

Maps: A trail map and informational brochure is available at the trailhead. For topographic area maps, request York Harbor and North Berwick from the USGS.

Directions: From the corner of U.S. 1 and York Street in York, drive north on U.S. 1 for 4.1 miles to a left turn on Mountain Road. Follow 2.6 miles to a right turn on Summit Road (listed as the Mount A Road on some maps). Park in the turnouts at the base of the road. GPS Coordinates: 43.2169 N, 70.6922 W

Contact: York Parks and Recreation Department, 186 York St., York, ME 03909, 207/363-1040, www.parksandrec.yorkmaine.org. The Nature Conservancy Maine Chapter, Fort Andross, 14 Maine St., Suite 401, Brunswick, ME 04011, 207/729-5181, www.nature.org. The Nature Conservancy Southern Maine Field Office, 207/646-1788.

32 VAUGHAN WOODS
2 mi/1 hr

in South Berwick

A few miles east of Kittery and only a half mile from the village center of South Berwick, Vaughan Woods is a lush forest of pine and hemlock running for nearly one mile along the banks of the placid Salmon River. Seemingly oblivious to the development of the past century, trails in the area take you through stands of giant trees more than a hundred years old and to views of the historic Hamilton House, an 18th century mansion that was once the centerpiece of bustling farmlands.

From the parking area, walk towards the bathroom and leave on the River Run Trail. Heading downhill a short distance, the trail is immediately surrounded by soaring pines. Following a rocky stream dropping off to the left, the trail reaches the river within 0.1 mile. Bear left to stay on the River Run Trail, stepping carefully over exposed tree roots. Benches at scenic overlooks along the trail invite you to stop and gaze for a few moments at the bucolic beauty of the Salmon River, a tidal tributary of the Piscataqua River estuary. Across the water is the rural town of Rollinsford, New Hampshire, and in keeping with Vaughan's lost-in-time feel, all that's visible on the other shore is ancient farmland that's still in active use; on quiet days, you may even hear the mooing of a grazing dairy herd.

After a mile, the trail ends at the Bridle Path. Turn left and head uphill through the woods, passing the old Warren homesite, now marked with a plaque for one of the area's first inhabitants. Continue on the Bridle Path for the next mile back to the park area and enjoy the quiet solitude of the woods.

User Groups: Hikers, leashed dogs, and horses. No bikes or on-trail wheelchair facilities (the bathroom and picnic area are wheelchair accessible).

Permits: At the payment box at the entrance to the park, visitors pay a self-service fee of $2 per adult Maine resident/$3 per adult nonresident and $1 per child.

Maps: A trail map and informational brochure is available at the trailhead. For a topographic area map, request Dover East from the USGS.

Directions: From the intersection of Routes 4 and 236 in South Berwick, drive south on Route 236 for approximately a half mile. Turn right opposite the junior high school at Vine Street. Go about one mile to the intersection of Vine Street and Old Fields Road. Turn right and watch for the park entrance on the right.

GPS Coordinates: 43.2116 N, 70.8088 W

Contact: Vaughan Woods State Park, 28 Oldsfields Rd., South Berwick, ME 03908, 207/490-4079. Maine Department of Conservation, Bureau of Parks and Lands, 286 Water St., Key Bank Plaza, 3rd and 5th floors, Augusta, ME 04333-0022, 207/287-3821, www.state.me.us/doc/parks.

New Hampshire

NEW HAMPSHIRE

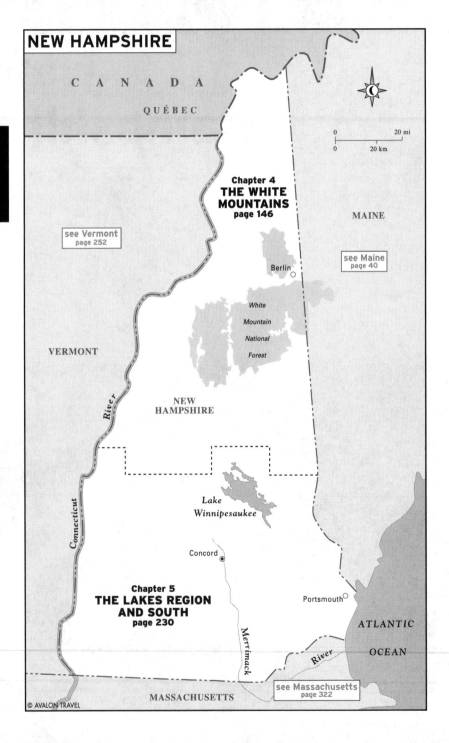

NEW HAMPSHIRE

C A N A D A

QUÉBEC

0   20 mi

0   20 km

Chapter 4
THE WHITE
MOUNTAINS
page 146

MAINE

see Vermont
page 252

see Maine
page 40

Berlin

White

Mountain

National

Forest

VERMONT

River

NEW
HAMPSHIRE

Lake
Winnipesaukee

Connecticut

Concord

Chapter 5
THE LAKES REGION
AND SOUTH
page 230

Portsmouth

ATLANTIC

OCEAN

Merrimack

River

see Massachusetts
page 322

MASSACHUSETTS

© AVALON TRAVEL

THE WHITE MOUNTAINS

© VINCENT VANNICOLA

BEST HIKES

Poet, naturalist, and avid hiker Henry David Thoreau

once observed, "thousands annually seek the White Mountains to be re-
freshed by their wild and primitive beauty." Change that figure to millions
and the famous New Englander's words are as true now as they were when
he wrote them over 150 years ago. Comprised of an 800,000-acre national
forest, countless state parks, seven soaring summits of over 5,000 feet,
and more than 1,200 miles of trails, this great alpine outcropping of the
Appalachian chain is, for many, simply the most spectacular range east
of the Rockies.

Besides the classic and popular summits of the Presidentials – including Mount Washington and Mount Adams – hiking "the Whites" takes
you from the dizzying heights of Franconia Ridge and Mount Chocorua
to the scenic lowlands of Zealand and Crawford Notches and to the largest federal wilderness in the Northeast (the Pemigewasset). Walks to
waterfalls, gorges, rock-strewn rivers, and quiet mountain ponds also
await – as well as the chance to glimpse moose, fox, deer, bear, and other
northern wildlife roaming freely across the landscape of mixed evergreen
and deciduous forest.

Many hikes in the White Mountains (Mounts Lincoln and Lafayette,
Mount Chocorua, Mount Moosilauke) are among the most popular in New
England. You are likely to find trails crowded with boots on nice weekends
in summer and fall – and even in winter. Some of the lower peaks (Welch
and Dickey, North Moat, Mount Willard) offer the best views per ounce
of sweat that you'll find anywhere, while still other summit climbs (Flume
and Tripyramid) rank among the region's most rugged and difficult. For
isolation, the hikes along the newly constructed Cohos Trail, a winding
162-mile footpath leading from the northern edge of the Presidentials

all the way to the Canadian border, is remote, backcountry summiting at its New England best.

Hikes to the bigger peaks of the Whites often entail more than 3,000 or even 4,000 feet of elevation gain, at least several miles round-trip, very rugged terrain, and the possibility of severe weather. Some of the worst weather conditions in North America have been recorded at the Mount Washington weather observatory and hikers must always be prepared for unpredictable changes in the weather at any time and in any season. The Pinkham Notch AMC visitors center offers updated weather conditions for Mount Washington and other major peaks.

In the White Mountain National Forest, fires are prohibited above timberline and camping is prohibited within a quarter mile of any hut or shelter except at authorized tent sites. Camping is permitted above timberline only where there exists a base of at least two feet of snow. Timberline is defined as that elevation at which trees are less than eight feet tall and is often indicated by trailside signs. Stay on the trail in the alpine zone (the area above timberline) to avoid damaging fragile alpine vegetation.

Along the Appalachian Trail as it passes through the White Mountains, dogs must be kept under control, and horses, bikes, hunting, and firearms are prohibited. Cross-country skiing and snowshoeing are allowed, though the trail is often too rugged for skiing. In areas where the Appalachian Trail crosses through New Hampshire state park land, dogs must be leashed.

Keep group sizes to no more than 10 people in any federal wilderness area in the White Mountain National Forest (a good guideline to follow in non-wilderness areas as well, because large groups disproportionately affect the land and the experience of other hikers). Contact the White Mountain National Forest for information on permits for larger groups.

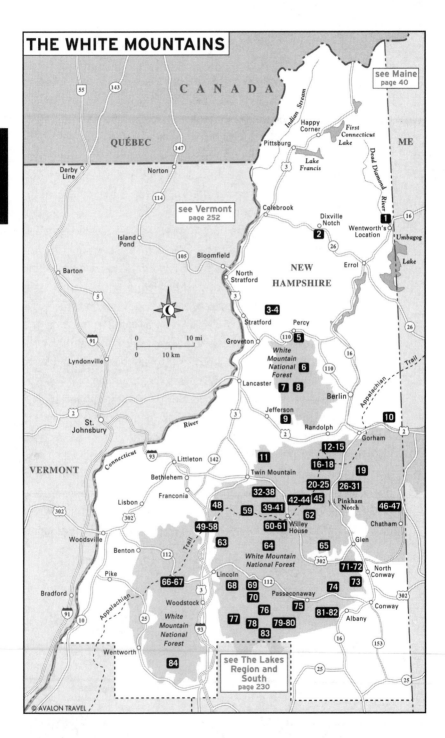

NEW HAMPSHIRE

THE WHITE MOUNTAINS

1 DIAMOND PEAKS
6.6 mi/3.5 hr   👥2 ▲7

in the Second College Grant near Wentworth's Location

Tucked away in the vast wilds of the North Country, this moderate trek to two of Diamond Mountain's three peaks (West Peak, 2,010 ft. and East Peak, 2,050 ft.) takes you to a scenic ridge rising high between the Dead Diamond and Magalloway Rivers. The land is part of the Second College Grant, a tract of land given by the state to Dartmouth College in 1807. Hikers not affiliated with the college are welcome on the trails, but will need to park outside the grant and walk or bike the 2.2 miles of flat road to the trailhead (making for a total hiking distance of 6.6 miles round-trip). The hike up Diamond Peaks climbs about 600 feet.

Across from the Dartmouth Forest Management Center, the yellow-blazed Diamond Peaks Trail begins at a sign on the right (east) side of the road. Bikes are prohibited on the trail, but can be left near the trailhead. The trail rises gently through the woods at first before beginning a short but steep ascent up the rocky hillside. At 0.3 mile, a spur trail on the left leads to Alice Ledge, a lookout with good views of the Dead Diamond River Valley. Turning sharply right, the main trail pushes almost due west, passing Linda Ledge (at 0.5 mile), before reaching West Peak at approximately one mile from the trailhead. Just below the peak's wooded summit is an open ledge overlooking precipitous cliffs. Continuing its ascent along the top of the cliffs, the trail offers several good views of the valley below and the surrounding wooded hills. In this fine spot for bird-watching, ravens and red-tailed hawks are frequently seen around the Diamond Peaks. The trail then ends in another 0.1 mile atop the tall cliffs of East Peak. Follow the same route back.

User Groups: Hikers and dogs. Bikes are prohibited past the trailhead. No horses or wheelchair facilities.

Permits: The hike is on private land within the Second College Grant, a township of nearly 27,000 acres owned by Dartmouth College in Hanover. The college uses gates to control access. A permit from the Outdoor Programs Office at Dartmouth College is required to park within the grant and is available only to persons affiliated with the college or its Outing Club. However, day use by the public is allowed, provided you park outside the grant.

Maps: The Outdoor Programs Office at Dartmouth College sells a waterproof contour trail map of the Second College Grant for $2. For a topographic area map, request Wilsons Mills from the USGS.

Directions: From the junction of Routes 16 and 26 in Errol, follow Route 16 north for 8.7 miles into Wentworth's Location. About 0.2 mile past the Mount Dustan Store in the Wentworth's Location village center, turn left at a small cemetery onto Dead Diamond Road, a gravel logging road; find the parking turnout in another 0.2 mile, just before the gate. Remember how far north you are—this road could be snow covered from mid-autumn well into spring and may be a mud bog until July. Follow it for 2.2 miles to the Forest Management Center.

GPS Coordinates: 44.8860 N, 71.0740 W

Contact: Dartmouth College Outdoor Programs Office, 119 Robinson Hall, Dartmouth College, Hanover, NH 03755, 603/646-2834, www.dartmouth.edu/~doc.

2 TABLE ROCK, DIXVILLE NOTCH
0.7 mi/1.5 hr   👥4 ▲10

in Dixville Notch State Park

Not for the faint of heart—or those afraid of heights, this hike takes you to the soaring precipice of spectacular Table Rock (2,510 ft.), a narrow promontory jutting out an incredible

100 feet from the north shoulder of Mount Gloriette, one of the mountains flanking narrow, winding Dixville Notch. Only four feet at its tip with sheer drops of up to 800 feet off either side, Table Rock is a lookout perch unlike any other in New England.

From the roadside trailhead, the trail climbs very steeply over difficult, rocky ground for 0.3 mile as it rises 600 feet to the cliff top. Once on the ledge, turn right with the trail, climbing uphill another 40 feet to walk the long gangplank of Table Rock. The giant buttress of shattered rock thrusting far out from the main cliff face rises hundreds of feet above the floor, with sheer drops off either side of the narrow walkway. Edging along Table Rock is an unnerving adventure for even the most experienced hikers. But if you stay put along the wider base of the ledge, you might be able to put anxiety aside as you take in panoramic views of the surrounding mountains and the Balsams, a grand resort hotel and Dixville Notch landmark. The Balsams maintains a crisscrossing network of trails in this area, leading to and from the hotel, but this hike descends the way you came—arguably more difficult and dangerous than the ascent because of the steepness and frequently wet rock.

User Groups: Hikers only. This trail is not suitable for bikes, dogs, or horses; no wheelchair facilities.

Permits: Parking and access are free.

Maps: A guidebook with map for the Cohos Trail, including information about Table Rock, is available from the Cohos Trail Association ($21.95). For a topographic area map, request Dixville Notch from the USGS.

Directions: From the main entrance to the Balsams Resort on Route 2, head east for 0.1 mile. Park in the ample turnout where a sign marks the Dixville Notch Heritage Trail start (behind the state park sign).

GPS Coordinates: 44.8651 N, 71.3010 W

Contact: The Cohos Trail Association, 266 Danforth Rd., Pittsburg, NH 03592, 603/363-8902, www.cohostrail.org. Dixville Notch State Park, Route 26, Dixville, NH 03576, 603/538-6707, www.nhstateparks.org.

3 SUGARLOAF MOUNTAIN
3.5 mi/2.5 hr   3 8

in Nash Stream State Forest

The North Country's 39,601-acre Nash Stream State Forest offers some of the most remote and lonely hiking in the Granite State—and on some sizable hills, no less. Sugarloaf fronts a large range of peaks that are virtually unknown to many hikers and that nearly rival in size the Pilot Range of the northern White Mountain National Forest to the south. Were the 3,701-foot bare rock summit of Sugarloaf just a few hundred feet taller, peak-baggers would flock here. As it is, the state forest sees few visitors. Even during prime hiking season don't be surprised if you find moose, deer, and other northern wildlife your only companions as you enjoy a vista of peaks stretching all the way north into Quebec. This 3.5-mile hike offers a net elevation gain of about 2,100 feet.

From the parking area, pick up the westbound Sugarloaf Trail, an old jeep road (look for the sign marker). Starting off as a gradual climb, at 0.2 mile, the trail comes to a fork. Here, bear right (the yellow-blazed trail bearing to the left is the Cohos Trail). Soon listing to the northwest, the trail begins to ascend steeply and without pause—a real calf-burner. At 1.2 miles, a sharp change of course faces you almost due north as the trail eases out somewhat and begins to skirt the summit. Changing direction again a short distance further, the trail turns left and heads south to reach the craggy summit ledges, a little more than 1.7 miles from the trailhead. Hike back the same way.

User Groups: Hikers and leashed dogs. This trail is not suitable for bikes or horses; no wheelchair facilities.

Permits: Parking and access are free.

Maps: A guidebook with map for the Cohos

Trail, including information about Sugarloaf Mountain, is available from the Cohos Trail Association ($21.95). For topographic area maps, request Tinkerville, Blue Mountain, Stratford, and Percy Peaks from the USGS. **Directions:** From the junction of Route 110 and U.S. 3 in Groveton, follow Route 110 east for 2.6 miles to Emerson Road. Turn left and drive 2.2 miles to a left hand turn onto the dirt Nash Stream Road. Continue a half mile to an open area with an oversized locator map posted on a sign. From the sign, follow Nash Stream Road another 4.6 miles, bear left, and continue 3.2 miles. Drive over a bridge and another 100 feet to a parking area on the left. Nash Stream Road is typically open Memorial Day–early November, depending on weather conditions.

GPS Coordinates: 44.7371 N, 71.4392 W

Contact: New Hampshire Division of Forests and Lands, P.O. Box 1856, Concord, NH 03302-1856, 603/271-3456, www.nhdfl.org. Cohos Trail Association, 266 Danforth Rd., Pittsburg, NH 03592, 603/363-8902, www.cohostrail.org.

◪ NORTH PERCY PEAK
4 mi/3 hr   🏃4 ⬛9

in Nash Stream State Forest

BEST (

Though located in the remote Nash Stream State Forest, direct road access makes the 3,418-foot North Percy Peak a bit more accessible than other trailheads in the Nash Stream region. A challenging climb over rock slabs that are dangerously slippery when wet, this hidden gem of a hike rewards you with long views in every direction from the mountain's scrub-covered summit. Hiking to the top of North Percy Peak offers a net elevation of about 2,200 feet.

From the parking area on Nash Stream Road, follow the orange-blazed Percy Peaks Trail as it begins a moderate ascent through hardwood forest, crossing a stream at 0.3 mile,

and then reaching a large boulder at the one-mile mark. Here, the trail turns left and quickly grows steep and rough as it reaches exposed slabs. At 1.2 miles, the trail comes to a junction with the former Slide Trail. Now officially closed due to unsafe conditions, the Slide Trail forges straight up the exposed slabs. This hike stays on Percy Peaks Trail as it angles southeast away from the slabs and rounds the peak to a col between North Percy and South Percy. At 1.7 miles, the trail passes a junction with the Cohos Trail and then takes a sharp left, emerging above the tree line and running at a steep angle up vast southern slabs another 0.5 mile to the summit. Remember where the trail reenters the woods at the tree line: Sporadic blazes and cairns and the landscape of scrub brush on the mountain's flat summit make it easy to lose the way back to the trail. Return the way you came.

User Groups: Hikers and leashed dogs. This trail is not suitable for bikes or horses; no wheelchair facilities.

Permits: Parking and access are free.

Maps: A guidebook with map for the Cohos Trail, including information about the Percy Peaks Trail, is available from the Cohos Trail Association ($21.95). For topographic area maps, request Tinkerville, Blue Mountain, Stratford, and Percy Peaks from the USGS.

Directions: From the junction of Route 110 and U.S. 3 in Groveton, follow Route 110 east for 2.6 miles to Emerson Road. Turn left and drive 2.2 miles to a left hand turn onto the dirt Nash Stream Road. Continue a half mile to an open area with an oversized locator map posted on a sign. From the sign, follow the Nash Stream Road another 2.2 miles to a turnout on the right. Nash Stream Road is typically open Memorial Day–early November, depending on weather conditions.

Contact: New Hampshire Division of Forests and Lands, P.O. Box 1856, Concord, NH 03302-1856, 603/271-3456. The Cohos Trail Association, 266 Danforth Rd., Pittsburg, NH 03592, 603/363-8902, www.cohostrail.org.

NEW HAMPSHIRE

NEW HAMPSHIRE

5 DEVIL'S HOPYARD
2.4 mi/1.5 hr

in the northern White Mountain National
Forest east of Lancaster and west of Berlin

A short detour off the Kilkenny Ridge Trail
leads to the wild and otherworldly Devil's
Hopyard, a small gorge almost completely
overgrown with moss, ferns, and trees. In the
middle of all this lush green, water cascades
and then rushes out of sight beneath massive
boulders—a sight that can make you think
you've stepped into some kind of emerald
fairyland. This short hike nets an easy elevation gain of 250 feet.

From the South Pond parking area, head
south on the Kilkenny Ridge Trail/Devil's
Hopyard Trail. (The two trails coincide for
the first 0.6 mile, but on many maps, only the
Kilkenny Ridge Trail is listed.) In 60 yards
after crossing the Devil's Hopyard stream, the
Devil's Hopyard Trail turns right (west) at a
signed trail junction and leaves the Kilkenny.
As the Devil's Hopyard Trail continues, the
path narrows and becomes somewhat rocky.
At 0.8 mile, the trail crosses the stream again
and soon enters the Hopyard gorge. Crossing over moss-covered rocks (which can be
very slippery even when not very wet), the
trail turns steep as it rises to the ledges above
the cascades (at 1.2 miles). Return the way
you came.

User Groups: Hikers and dogs. No bikes,
horses, or wheelchair facilities.

Permits: A permit is required for day use or
overnight parking at any White Mountain
National Forest trailhead. Permits are available
at several area stores and from the national
forest at a cost of $5 for seven consecutive days
or $20 per year. A $3 one-day permit can be
purchased at self-service stations at national
forest trailheads, but the permit is good only
for the trailhead at which it's purchased.

Maps: A waterproof area trail map is available from the Appalachian Mountain
Club (Carter Range–Evans Notch/North

Country–Mahoosuc, $9.95). For a topographic
map, request West Milan from the USGS.

Directions: From the intersection of U.S. 3
and Route 110 in Groveton, drive east on
Route 100 for approximately 10 miles to reach
a right hand turn for South Pond Road. Follow South Pond Road 0.7 mile to the White
Mountain National Forest South Pond Recreation Area; continue 0.2 mile to the parking
area and trailhead.

GPS Coordinates: 44.5971 N, 71.3675 W

Contact: White Mountain National Forest Headquarters, 71 White Mountain Dr.,
Campton, NH 03246, 603/536-6100, TDD
for hearing impaired 603/536-3665, www.
fs.fed.us/r9/white.

6 ROGERS LEDGE
10 mi/6 hr

in the northern White Mountain National
Forest east of Lancaster and west of Berlin

This long, though fairly easy, hike is a pleasant walk in the woods as it passes through a
relatively quiet area of the White Mountain
National Forest on the way to Rogers Ledge
(2,945 ft.) and its beautiful mountain views.
With a net elevation gain of about 1,500 feet
spread out over five miles, the rugged terrain
that dominates so much of the rest of this
region is relatively absent here, allowing you
more time to spot moose and bear tracks,
watch spotted salamanders and tree frogs
scamper from the trail, and catch sight of
such birds as the American redstart, black-
throated blue warbler, and red-eyed vireo—
some of the over 72 varieties of neotropical
migrant birds who summer in these parts of
the Whites.

From the parking area, follow the Mill
Brook Trail a relatively flat 3.8 miles to the
Kilkenny Ridge Trail. Turn right (north) and
walk this easy stretch of the Kilkenny 0.6 mile
to Rogers Ledge. At 2,945 feet, this high ledge
overlooks the Presidentials to the south, the

Pilot Range to the southwest, and Berlin and the Mahoosuc Range to the east. After enjoying the view, return the way you came. For those who wish to camp overnight before the return trip back, the Rogers Ledge Tentsite is located at the junction of the Kilkenny Ridge and Mill Brook trails.

User Groups: Hikers and dogs. No bikes, horses, or wheelchair facilities.

Permits: No backcountry permit is needed, but a permit is required for day use or overnight parking at any White Mountain National Forest trailhead. Permits are available at several area stores and from the national forest at a cost of $5 for seven consecutive days or $20 per year. A $3 one-day permit can be purchased at self-service stations at national forest trailheads, but the permit is good only for the trailhead at which it's purchased.

Maps: A waterproof area trail map is available from the Appalachian Mountain Club (Carter Range–Evans Notch/North Country–Mahoosuc, $9.95). For topographic area maps, request West Milan, Milan, Pliny Range, and Berlin from the USGS.

Directions: From the junction of Routes 16 and 110 in Berlin, drive north on Route 110 for approximately seven miles. At a sign for the U.S. Fish Hatchery, turn left onto York Pond Road. Follow the paved road to the hatchery and then follow the Mill Brook Trail signs to a small parking area at the end of a short dirt road behind the hatchery office. The entrance gate to the U.S. Fish Hatchery on York Pond Road is closed 4 P.M.–8 A.M., but not locked; close and pin the gate again after passing through if it is closed when you arrive.

GPS Coordinates: 44.4986 N, 71.3390 W

Contact: White Mountain National Forest Headquarters, 71 White Mountain Dr., Campton, NH 03246, 603/536-6100, TDD for hearing impaired 603/536-3665, www.fs.fed.us/r9/white.

◼ KILKENNY LOOP
18.5 mi/2 days   👣4 ⛰9

in the northern White Mountain National Forest east of Lancaster and west of Berlin

BEST (

This backpacking loop is good proof that even in a national forest as heavily used as the White Mountains, trails strewn with pine-needle duff and moss so untrod upon that it actually gives softly like a cushion underfoot, still exist—and exist in abundance. This two-day traverse of the Pilot Range, much of it on the Kilkenny Ridge Trail, takes place along the national forest's northernmost reaches. Far removed from population centers, the Pilot Range boasts no giant peaks to attract hikers, but it does offer the chance to revel in the solitude and quiet of the forest. This hike includes side trips to Rogers Ledge and the Horn, perhaps the two best views in the range, and offers a net elevation gain of about 4,000 feet.

From the small parking area behind the fish hatchery office, follow the gently rising Mill Brook Trail 3.8 miles to the Kilkenny Ridge Trail, passing through an extensive area of birch forest. Drop your packs and turn right (north) for the 1.2-mile side trip to Rogers Ledge, an open ledge atop cliffs with sweeping views south to the Presidentials, southwest to the unfolding Pilot Range, and southeast to Berlin's smokestacks and the Mahoosuc Range beyond. Double back to your packs and hike southwest on the Kilkenny Ridge Trail for 2.1 miles, much of it an easy walk, with a moderate hill climb just before you reach Unknown Pond and the intersection with the Unknown Pond Trail. The Unknown Pond Tentsite is on the left, a good place to camp for the night.

On the hike's second day, head back to the trail junction to rejoin the southbound Kilkenny Ridge Trail. Climbing steeply, the trail gains several hundred feet in elevation. At 1.7 miles from Unknown Pond, a side trail leads left (east) 0.3 mile to the craggy, 3,905-foot summit of the Horn, with expansive views in every direction. Reaching the very summit of the Horn requires a little hand and foot scrambling, but it's not too difficult.

Back on the Kilkenny Ridge Trail, continue southwest over the wooded summit of the Bulge (3,920 ft.) and on to the highest point on the ridge, 4,170-foot wooded summit of Mount Cabot, 2.8 miles from Unknown Pond. From Cabot's summit, the Kilkenny Ridge Trail coincides with the Mount Cabot Trail for 1.4 miles, with great views from an open ledge along the way. Where the two trails split, bear left (east) with the Kilkenny Ridge Trail and follow it for another 0.3 mile to the Bunnell Notch Trail. They coincide for 0.1 mile; where they split, stay left (east) on the Bunnell Notch Trail for another 2.6 miles. Turn left on the York Pond Trail and follow it 0.2 mile back to York Pond Road. From here, bear right and follow the road for two miles back to the fish hatchery parking area.

There are two backcountry campsites on the Kilkenny Ridge Trail: 0.1 mile north of the Mill Brook Trail junction and at Unknown Pond. There's also a cabin with bunks on the Kilkenny Ridge Trail 0.4 mile south of the Mount Cabot summit.

User Groups: Hikers and dogs. Trail is not suitable for bikes or horses. No wheelchair facilities.

Permits: No backcountry permit is needed, but a permit is required for day use or overnight parking at any White Mountain National Forest trailhead. Permits are available at several area stores and from the national forest at a cost of $5 for seven consecutive days or $20 per year. A $3 one-day permit can be purchased at self-service stations at national forest trailheads, but the permit is good only for the trailhead at which it's purchased.

Maps: A waterproof area trail map is available from the Appalachian Mountain Club (Carter Range–Evans Notch/North Country–Mahoosuc, $9.95). For topographic area maps, request West Milan, Milan, Pliny Range, and Berlin from the USGS.

Directions: You can either shuttle vehicles to either end of this hike or use one vehicle and hike two miles of road at the end of the trip. From the junction of Routes 16 and 110 in Berlin, drive north on Route 110 for about seven miles. At the U.S. Fish Hatchery sign, turn left onto York Pond Road. Follow the paved road to the hatchery and then follow signs for the Mill Brook Trail to a small parking area at the end of a short dirt road behind the hatchery office. The hike begins there and ends at the York Pond Trail, which begins two miles farther down York Pond Road.

The U.S. Fish Hatchery entrance gate on York Pond Road is closed 4 P.M.–8 A.M., but not locked; close and pin the gate again after passing through if it is closed when you arrive.

GPS Coordinates: 44.4986 N, 71.3390 W

Contact: White Mountain National Forest Headquarters, 71 White Mountain Dr., Campton, NH 03246, 603/536-6100, TDD for hearing impaired 603/536-3665, www.fs.fed.us/r9/white.

8 MOUNT CABOT

11.5 mi/7 hr   🏃4 ⛰8

in the northern White Mountain National Forest east of Lancaster and west of Berlin

Although Mount Cabot (4,170 ft.) has a wooded summit with no views, it attracts hikers for its status as the tallest peak in New Hampshire's North Country, the wild, hilly land of forests and lakes that stretches from the northern White Mountain all the way to the Canadian border. Bunnell Rock, an open ledge along this hike, and the Horn (3,905 ft.), one of Cabot's subsidiary peaks, offer broad views of this corner of the Pilot Range and add greatly to the hike's scenic quality. There is a net elevation gain of nearly 3,000 feet over the course of the hike.

From the parking area on York Pond Road, follow the York Pond Trail for 0.2 mile before bearing right onto the Bunnell Notch Trail.

For the next 2.9 miles, the gently descending Bunnell Notch Trail generally tracks along the north side of a stream and then ends at the junction with the Kilkenny Ridge Trail. Here, turn right, and follow the Kilkenny Ridge/Mount Cabot Trail uphill for 1.4 miles to the wooded summit of Mount Cabot, passing the great view from Bunnell Rock along the way. The Kilkenny Ridge Trail continues northward past Cabot's summit, bouncing up and down along a wooded ridge. It passes over the 3,920-foot summit of the Bulge, and, 1.1 miles from Cabot's summit, reaches a side path that leads 0.3 mile to the craggy, 3,905-foot summit of the Horn, which is reached by an easy scramble and offers great views of the Whites. Backtrack to the Kilkenny Ridge Trail, turn right (north), and descend, steeply at times, for 1.7 miles to Unknown Pond. Turn right (southeast), following the pond's shoreline briefly; where the Kilkenny Ridge Trail swings left (northeast), continue straight ahead on the Unknown Pond Trail, descending 3.3 miles to York Pond Road. Turn right and walk a short distance back to the York Pond Trail parking area.

User Groups: Hikers and dogs. No bikes, horses, or wheelchair facilities.

Permits: No backcountry permit is needed, but a permit is required for day use or overnight parking at any White Mountain National Forest trailhead. Permits are available at several area stores and from the national forest at a cost of $5 for seven consecutive days or $20 per year. A $3 one-day permit can be purchased at self-service stations at national forest trailheads, but the permit is good only for the trailhead at which it's purchased.

Maps: A waterproof area trail map is available from the Appalachian Mountain Club (Carter Range–Evans Notch/North Country–Mahoosuc, $9.95). For topographic area maps, request Pliny Range and Stark from the USGS.

Directions: From the junction of Routes 16 and 110 in Berlin, drive north on Route 110 for about seven miles and turn left onto York Pond Road at the U.S. Fish Hatchery sign. Follow the paved road to the hatchery and then continue about two miles farther to a small parking area on the right, just before the end of York Pond Road. The York Pond Trail begins at the end of the road. The U.S. Fish Hatchery entrance gate on York Pond Road is closed 4 P.M.–8 A.M., but not locked; close and pin the gate again after passing through if it is closed when you arrive. The York Pond Road has been plowed all the way to its end in recent winters, but check first with the White Mountain National Forest.

GPS Coordinates: 44.4963 N, 71.3593 W

Contact: White Mountain National Forest Headquarters, 71 White Mountain Dr., Campton, NH 03246, 603/536-6100, TDD for hearing impaired 603/536-3665, www.fs.fed.us/r9/white.

⑨ MOUNTS STARR KING AND WAUMBEK
7.2 mi/3.5 hr   🏃‍3 ⚠7

in the White Mountain National Forest near Jefferson

This trek along the Cohos Trail leads to two peaks in the Pliny Range: Mount Starr King (3,914 ft.), named for Thomas Starr King, a Boston pastor who wrote an early book on the White Mountains, and Mount Waumbek (4,006 ft.), one of the White Mountain's lesser known 4,000-footers and sometimes labeled on older maps as Pliny Major, the mountain's former name. This not-so-steep climb gains approximately 2,400 feet in elevation as it reaches the scenic top of Starr King; continuing to Waumbek adds another 200 feet of ascent.

From the access road parking area, look for the Starr King/Cohos Trail sign marker. The yellow-blazed trail ascends at a steady, but moderate grade for almost the entire length of its 2.6-mile push northeast to the Starr King summit. From a cleared area at the top, the

NEW HAMPSHIRE

site of a long gone summit shelter, sweeping views of the Whites, from the Presidential Range (southeast) to the Pemigewasset Wilderness peaks (south) and Franconia Ridge (southwest) are still stunning, even as they are being rapidly encroached upon by returning forest growth (scramble atop a boulder for the better views). The trail continues off the summit and onward for another mile on easy terrain to Mount Waumbek. The sporadically marked trail is almost completely in the woods and low trees obstruct any kind of view from the Waumbek summit. Still, for peak baggers, Waumbek is worth the boot mileage. From Waumbek's summit, the Kilkenny Ridge Trail/Cohos Trail leads east and north into the Pilot Range, toward Mount Cabot, Unknown Pond, and Rogers Ledge. This hike descends the same way you came.

User Groups: Hikers and dogs. No bikes, horses, or wheelchair facilities.

Permits: No backcountry permit is needed, but a permit is required for day use or overnight parking at any White Mountain National Forest trailhead. Permits are available at several area stores and from the national forest at a cost of $5 for seven consecutive days or $20 per year. A $3 one-day permit can be purchased at self-service stations at national forest trailheads, but the permit is good only for the trailhead at which it's purchased.

Maps: A waterproof area trail map is available from the Appalachian Mountain Club (Carter Range–Evans Notch/North Country–Mahoosuc, $9.95). For a topographic area map, request Pliny Range from the USGS.

Directions: From the junction of Route 115A and U.S. 2 in Jefferson, follow U.S. 2 east for 0.2 mile. Turn left up a narrow road at a sign for the Starr King Trail. The road ends in about 0.1 mile at a small parking area at the trailhead.

GPS Coordinates: 44.4194 N, 71.4654 W

Contact: White Mountain National Forest Headquarters, 71 White Mountain Dr., Campton, NH 03246, 603/536-6100, TDD for hearing impaired 603/536-3665, www.fs.fed.us/r9/white.

10 MAHOOSUC RANGE: GENTIAN POND
6 mi/3.5 hr 👥2 △8

in Shelburne

BEST (

Gentian Pond is a picturesque and quite large puddle of water tucked away in the evergreen woods of the rugged Mahoosucs. Go in June to see hundreds of rare white and pink lady's slippers in bloom along the trail and, if you have time, load up a backpack for two or three days and stay in the shelter at Gentian Pond—the dusk view southward to the Androscoggin Valley and the Carter-Moriah Range is fantastic. The shelter is also a good base for exploring the surrounding Mahoosuc Range. This out-and-back hike to the pond climbs about 800 feet uphill.

From the trailhead on North Road, pick up the northbound Austin Brook Trail, an old logging road. After a level two miles, the road narrows to a hiking trail as it begins to skirt the edge of a swampy area. At 2.5 miles, the trail turns sharply right, continuing its modest ascent before growing quite steep in its final 0.5 mile push to the pond and shelter. Just before the Gentian Pond shelter, the Austin Brook Trail meets the Appalachian Trail (also known along this stretch as the Mahoosuc Trail). Return the way you came.

Camping is only allowed at shelters and designated camping areas.

User Groups: Hikers and dogs. This trail is not suitable for bikes or horses; no wheelchair facilities.

Permits: Parking and access are free.

Maps: A waterproof area trail map is available from the Appalachian Mountain Club (Carter Range–Evans Notch/North Country–Mahoosuc, $9.95). For a topographic area map, request Shelburne from the USGS.

Directions: From the intersection of U.S. 2

and Route 16 in Gorham, head southeast on Main Street/Route 16 for 6.9 miles. Turn left at Meadow Road, crossing the Androscoggin River. In 0.9 mile, turn left on North Road and continue for another 0.5 mile. The trailhead is on the right (north) side of the road; park along the road. The Mahoosuc Range is on private property, not within the White Mountain National Forest.
GPS Coordinates: 44.4125 N, 71.0680 W
Contact: Appalachian Mountain Club Pinkham Notch Visitor Center, P.O. Box 298, Gorham, NH 03581, 603/466-2721, www. outdoors.org.

11 CHERRY MOUNTAIN: OWL'S HEAD TRAIL
3.8 mi/2.5 hr   🏃3 ⛰8

in the White Mountain National Forest south of Jefferson

Almost due west of the Presidential Range, the broad, open ledges of the Owl's Head (3,258 ft.) offer dramatic views of the Presidentials' soaring peaks. A climb with a net elevation gain of just under 2,000 feet, this hike takes place on a completed portion of the new Cohos Trail, a 162-mile footpath that will eventually run the entire length of Coos County, from the Presidentials (of which Cherry Mountain is technically a western outpost) to the Canadian border.

From the parking area on Route 115, the yellow-blazed Owl's Head Trail/Cohos Trail heads south, briefly entering a thin strip of woods before crossing a small brook and emerging into a cleared area. Head straight across the clearing to a post marker that reads "Path." The trail has been relocated a bit in this area in recent years due to heavy logging operations, so keep an eye out for signs of recent trail work and brush clearing. The hiking is fairly easy at first, crossing some logged areas—watch for cairns and trail markers. At 0.7 mile, the trail swings left (south)

towards the mountain and begins climbing at a moderate grade. About 1.8 miles from the road, the trail crests the Cherry Mountain ridge; walk a relatively flat 0.1 mile to the Owl's Head ledges. To the south, the trail continues on to Mount Martha (3,573 ft.), 0.8 mile farther, where there is a good view. This hike turns back from the Owl's Head ledges and returns to the trailhead along the same route.

User Groups: Hikers and dogs. Trail is not suitable for bikes or horses; no wheelchair facilities.

Permits: No backcountry permit is needed, but a permit is required for day use or overnight parking at any White Mountain National Forest trailhead. Permits are available at several area stores and from the national forest at a cost of $5 for seven consecutive days or $20 per year. A $3 one-day permit can be purchased at self-service stations at national forest trailheads, but the permit is good only for the trailhead at which it's purchased.

Maps: A waterproof area trail map is available from the Appalachian Mountain Club (Franconia–Pemigewasset Range, $9.95). For a guidebook and maps to the Cohos Trail, contact the Cohos Trail Association. For topographic maps, request Bethlehem and Mount Washington from the USGS.

Directions: From the junction of Route 115 and U.S. 3 in Carroll, follow Route 115 north 5.8 miles to the parking area on the right (with Stanley Slide historical marker).
GPS Coordinates: 44.3590 N, 71.4901 W
Contact: White Mountain National Forest Headquarters, 71 White Mountain Dr., Campton, NH 03246, 603/536-6100, TDD for hearing impaired 603/536-3665, www. fs.fed.us/r9/white. The Cohos Trail Association, 266 Danforth Road, Pittsburg, NH 03592, 603/363-8902, www.cohostrail.org.

NEW HAMPSHIRE

🔟🔁 MOUNTS ADAMS AND MADISON: THE AIR LINE

9.9 mi/8 hr   🏃5   ⛰10

in the White Mountain National Forest south of Randolph

This is the most direct route to the second-highest peak summit in New England—5,799-foot Mount Adams—though not necessarily the fastest. It follows the mountain's spectacular Durand Ridge, giving hikers extended views down into King Ravine, southwest across the prominent ridges on the northern flanks of Mounts Adams and Jefferson, and north across the Randolph Valley to the Pilot Range peaks. Some scrambling is necessary, and you need to be comfortable with exposure—there's an interesting little foot ledge traverse that can get your heart pumping. In good weather, this route allows a fit hiker the option of hitting both Adams and Madison in a day. The vertical ascent to Adams is nearly 4,500 feet, and Madison adds about another 500 feet.

From the parking lot at Appalachia, the Air Line heads almost due south as it makes a beeline to Adams's summit, passing straight through several trail junctions and coinciding briefly with the Randolph Path at 0.9 mile. Emerging above the tree line at three miles, the trail makes a sharp ascent up Durand Ridge, the rocky, bare crest of King Ravine (the ravine plunges to the right; this part of the trail is also called the Knife-edge). Still ascending steeply and without cover, the trail veers right and coincides with the Appalachian Trail/Gulfside Trail at 3.7 miles. A mere 70 yards later, the Air Line bears left for the final 0.6 mile push to the Mount Adams summit. Descend via the Air Line—or go for Madison's summit (5,366 ft.). To reach Madison from Adams's summit, backtrack 0.6 mile back to where the Air Line and AT/Gulfside Trail coincide. This time, stay on the AT heading northwest and in 0.2 mile reach the Madison AMC hut. From the hut, follow the AT (it now coincides with the Osgood Trail) another 0.5 mile to Madison's summit. To descend, retrace your steps to the Madison AMC hut and then head north on the Valley Way all the way back to the parking area, a return trip of 4.3 miles. While on the

alpine scrub growth

© PETER DAME

NEW HAMPSHIRE

Valley Way, be sure to take the side paths that parallel it past scenic Tama Fall and Gordon Fall, which are marked by signs not far from the trailhead and do not add any appreciable distance to this hike.

Note: Weather conditions, especially above the tree line, may change rapidly. In the event of bad weather, even the most expert of hikers should turn back. The Valley Way re-enters the woods more quickly than other trails and is the best escape route.

User Groups: Hikers and dogs. No wheelchair facilities. This trail should not be attempted in winter except by hikers experienced in mountaineering and prepared for severe winter weather, and is not suitable for bikes, horses, or skis.

Permits: Parking and access are free.

Maps: A waterproof area trail map is available from the Appalachian Mountain Club (Presidential Range, $9.95). For a topographic area map, request Mount Washington from the USGS.

Directions: From the junction of U.S. 2 and Route 16 in Gorham, follow U.S. 2 west for 2.1 miles. The Appalachia parking area is on the left (south), marked by a sign.

GPS Coordinates: 44.3709 N, 71.2893 W

Contact: White Mountain National Forest Headquarters, 71 White Mountain Drive, Campton, NH 03246, 603/536-6100, TDD for hearing impaired 603/536-3665, www.fs.fed.us/r9/white. The Appalachian Mountain Club Pinkham Notch Visitor Center has up-to-date weather and trail information about the Whites; call 603/466-2725.

13 MOUNT ADAMS: KING RAVINE

9.2 mi/8 hr   🏃5 ⛰10

in the White Mountain National Forest south of Randolph

BEST (

This route through King Ravine is one of the most difficult and spectacular hikes in the White Mountains and an adventurous way up the second-highest peak in New England: 5,799-foot Mount Adams. Besides involving hard scrambling over boulders and up the talus of a very steep ravine headwall, you will gain nearly 4,400 feet in elevation from the trailhead to Adams's summit.

From the Appalachia parking lot, pick up the Air Line Trail and follow it for 0.8 mile, ascending steadily but at an easy grade through mixed deciduous forest; at the trail junction with the Short Line, bear right. The Short Line parallels the cascading Cold Brook, drawing near the brook in spots—though much of the trail is separated from the brook by forest too dense to bushwhack through. Follow the Short Line for 1.9 miles—it coincides for nearly a half mile with the Randolph Path—until it joins the King Ravine Trail. Immediately after you turn onto the King Ravine Trail, a sign marks Mossy Fall on the right, a five-foot-tall waterfall that drops into a shallow pool. The forest here is dense but low, and you start getting views of the ravine walls towering high overhead. Beyond Mossy Fall, the trail grows much steeper, weaving amid massive boulders that have tumbled off the ravine cliffs over the eons. Scrambling atop one of these boulders offers an unforgettable view of King Ravine; the cabin visible on the western wall is Crag Camp, managed by the Randolph Mountain Club.

Just past the junction with the Chemin des Dames at 2.9 miles—a trail that scales the steep ravine wall to the left (east) to join the Air Line—the King Ravine Trail divides. To the right, the Subway will have you crawling through boulder caves, at times removing your pack to squeeze through narrow passages. To the left is an easier route known as the Elevated, which skirts most of the boulders and offers more ravine views. The two trails rejoin within about 200 yards. Soon afterward, the King Ravine Trail passes a trail junction with the Great Gully Trail and offers another choice of options: to the left, the main trail; to the right, a side loop through the Ice Caves, where ice tends to linger year-round. Again, these two paths rejoin within a short distance. The trail emerges completely from the trees and reaches the base of the King Ravine headwall at 3.4 miles. The King Ravine Trail grows its steepest up the headwall, basically following a talus slope. In just over 0.5 mile, the trail gains 1,100 feet in elevation, and footing is tricky on the sometimes-loose rocks.

Atop the headwall, the trail passes between rocky crags at a spot called the Gateway. On the other side, turn right on the Air Line and follow it for 0.6 mile over treeless alpine terrain to the Adams summit (4.6 miles from the Appalachia parking area), with stunning views in every direction. On the way down, you have the option of bagging the Mount Madison summit as well. (See the *Mounts Adams and Madison: the Air Line* listing in this chapter.) Descend via the Air Line; it's 4.3 miles back to the trailhead.

User Groups: Hikers and dogs. No bikes, horses, or wheelchair facilities. This trail should not be attempted in winter except by hikers experienced in mountaineering and prepared for severe winter weather.

Permits: Parking and access are free.

Maps: A waterproof area trail map is available from the Appalachian Mountain Club (Presidential Range, $9.95). For a topographic area map, request Mount Washington from the USGS.

Directions: From the junction of U.S. 2 and Route 16 in Gorham, follow U.S. 2 west for 2.1 miles. The Appalachia parking area is on the left (south), marked by a sign.

GPS Coordinates: 44.3709 N, 71.2893 W

Contact: White Mountain National Forest Headquarters, 71 White Mountain Drive, Campton, NH 03246, 603/536-6100, TDD for hearing impaired 603/536-3665, www. fs.fed.us/r9/white. Randolph Mountain Club, P.O. Box 279, Randolph, NH 03581, www. randolphmountainclub.org.

14 MOUNT ADAMS: LOWE'S PATH

9.6 mi/6 hr

in the White Mountain National Forest south of Randolph

This is the easiest route to the Mount Adams summit, which at 5,799 feet is the second-highest peak in New England and one of the most interesting. The trail has moderate grades and is well protected until timberline, but the last 1.5 miles are above the trees. It's also the oldest trail coming out of the Randolph Valley, cut in 1875–1876.

Lowe's Path ascends gently at first, making several crossings of brooks through an area often wet and muddy. After 2.5 miles you reach the Log Cabin, a Randolph Mountain Club shelter. Another 0.6 mile brings you to both the timberline and a spur trail branching left which leads 0.1 mile to the RMC's Gray Knob cabin. This trail junction also offers the hike's first sweeping views, with the Mount Jefferson Castellated Ridge thrusting its craggy teeth skyward and much of the White Mountains visible on a clear day. From here, Lowe's Path cuts through some krummholz (the dense stands of stunted and twisted conifers that grow at timberline) and then ascends barren talus, where it can be tricky to find the cairns. At 4.1 miles, the trail forces a scramble over a rock mound known as Adams 4 and then begins the final 0.7-mile uphill stretch to the 5,799-foot summit. From Adams's aery heights, hikers are rewarded with some of the best views in these mountains. To the south are Mounts Jefferson, Clay, and Washington and the vast Great Gulf Wilderness; to the north lies neighboring Mount Madison.

User Groups: Hikers and dogs. No bikes, horses, or wheelchair facilities. This trail should not be attempted in winter except by hikers experienced in mountaineering and prepared for severe winter weather.

Permits: Access is free. There is a parking

fee of $2 per day per vehicle at Lowe's Store parking lot.

Maps: A waterproof area trail map is available from the Appalachian Mountain Club (Presidential Range, $9.95). For a topographic area map, request Mount Washington from the USGS.

Directions: From the junction of U.S. 2 and Route 16 in Gorham, follow U.S. 2 west for 8.4 miles to Lowe's Store (on the right). Park at the store and cross U.S. 2. To the right (west) is a dirt driveway that leads about 50 yards to Lowe's Path (on the right).

GPS Coordinates: 44.3637 N, 71.3306 W

Contact: White Mountain National Forest Headquarters, 71 White Mountain Drive, Campton, NH 03246, 603/536-6100, TDD for hearing impaired 603/536-3665, www.fs.fed.us/r9/white. The Appalachian Mountain Club Pinkham Notch Visitor Center has up-to-date weather and trail information about the Whites; call 603/466-2725. Randolph Mountain Club, P.O. Box 279, Randolph, NH 03581, www.randolphmountainclub.org.

15 MOUNT MADISON: MADISON GULF AND WEBSTER TRAILS

11.5 mi/10 hr   🥾5 ⛰10

in the White Mountain National Forest south of Randolph

BEST (

The Madison headwall ascent on the Madison Gulf Trail is without question one of the most difficult hikes in New England. With its intimidating 11.5 miles round-trip and 4,000 feet of elevation gain, this hike also rates as one of the wildest hikes in these mountains—and you may well see no other hikers on the trail. Still, the rugged physical challenge and scenic reward from the top of Madison make this a butt kicker not to miss. Portions of the route coincide with the Appalachian Trail (AT).

From the parking area, follow the Great Gulf Link Trail a flat mile to the Great Gulf

Trail. Turn right and continue about three easy miles (passing the Osgood Trail junction in less than two miles); soon after a jog left in the trail, turn right (north) onto the Madison Gulf Trail. You are in the Great Gulf, the enormous glacial cirque nearly enclosed by the high peaks of the northern Presidentials, which loom around you. The Madison Gulf Trail grows increasingly steep, following the boulder-filled Parapet Brook through a dense forest for about two miles to the base of the formidable headwall. Crossing a lush, boggy area along a shelf at the headwall's base, you then attack the main headwall, a scramble over steep, exposed rock ledges that can be hazardous in wet weather.

After a strenuous mile, the trail reaches the flat saddle between Mounts Madison and Adams, where you find the AMC's Madison hut and Star Lake, a beautiful little tarn and one of the few true alpine ponds in the Whites. From the hut, turn right (east) on the Appalachian Trail/Osgood Trail leading to Madison's ridge-like summit (5,366 ft.). Continue over the summit and down the open AT/Osgood Trail for a half mile. The Daniel Webster Trail branches left (northeast) at Osgood Junction, heading diagonally down a vast talus slope to the woods, leading another 3.5 miles to the campground road in Dolly Copp. Turn right and walk 0.2 mile down the road to your car.

User Groups: Hikers and dogs. No bikes, horses, or wheelchair facilities. This trail should not be attempted in winter except by hikers experienced in mountaineering and prepared for severe winter weather.

Permits: No backcountry permit is needed, but a permit is required for day use or overnight parking at any White Mountain National Forest trailhead, as indicated by signs posted at most trailheads. Permits are available at several area stores and from the national forest at a cost of $5 for seven consecutive days or $20 per year. A $3 one-day permit can be purchased at self-service stations at national forest trailheads, but the permit is good only for the trailhead at which it's purchased.

NEW HAMPSHIRE

Maps: A waterproof area trail map is available from the Appalachian Mountain Club (Presidential Range, $9.95). For a topographic area map, request Mount Washington from the USGS.

Directions: From the Pinkham Notch Visitor Center, drive north on Route 16 approximately two miles to the entrance of the Dolly Copp Campground (on your left). Drive to the end of the campground road and park in the dirt lot at the start of the Great Gulf Link Trail. About a quarter mile before the parking lot, you pass the start of the Daniel Webster (scout) Trail, which is where you will end this hike. GPS Coordinates: 44.3236 N, 71.2187 W

Contact: White Mountain National Forest Headquarters, 71 White Mountain Drive, Campton, NH 03246, 603/536-6100, TDD for hearing impaired 603/536-3665, www. fs.fed.us/r9/white. The Appalachian Mountain Club Pinkham Notch Visitor Center has up-to-date weather and trail information about the Whites; call 603/466-2725.

© PETER DAME

Mount Jefferson's summit and Castellated Ridge (visible to the right of the summit)

16 MOUNT JEFFERSON: THE CASTELLATED RIDGE
10 mi/9 hr   5 ▲10

in the White Mountain National Forest south of Bowman

BEST (

The stretch of the Castle Trail above timberline ranks among the most spectacular ridge walks in New England—but you must work hard to get there, climbing some 4,200 feet on this 10-mile round-tripper. The Castellated Ridge narrows to a rocky spine jutting above the krummholz (the dense stands of stunted and twisted conifers that grow at timberline), with long, sharp drops off either side. The ridge acquired its name from the three castles, or towers, of barren rock you scramble over and around. This can be a dangerous place in nasty weather. But on a clear day, from Jefferson's summit (5,716 ft.), you can see almost all of the Whites and all the way to

Vermont's Green Mountains, and even beyond to New York's Adirondacks. You also walk briefly on the Appalachian Trail where it coincides with the Gulfside Trail north of Jefferson's summit.

From the parking area, follow the dirt driveway to the right for about 150 yards until you reach a somewhat hidden marker on the right where the Castle Trail enters the woods. The hiking is fairly easy at first, but in the first half mile there's a bridgeless crossing of the Israel River, which can be difficult at high water. Approximately one mile beyond the stream crossing, the trail passes the junction with the Israel Ridge Path on the left, on which you will return. The trail then ascends the ridge, growing steep and passing through an interesting subalpine forest before passing a junction with the Link at 3.5 miles out.

The Castle Trail requires scrambling from this point, reaching the first castle a quarter mile past the Link junction. Continue up the ridge to the vast talus field covering the upper flanks of Mount Jefferson, watching carefully for cairns. The trail follows a direct line to the summit, where twin rock mounds are separated by a short distance; the first you encounter, farther west, is the true summit, five miles from the trailhead.

Descend to the trail junction between the two summits, walk north on the Jefferson Loop Trail toward Mount Adams for 0.4 mile, and then continue on the Gulfside Trail for another 0.2 mile into Edmands Col. Bear left onto the Randolph Path, which then leads to the right (northeast) around the Castle Ravine headwall. At 0.7 mile from Edmands Col, the trail coincides briefly with the Israel Ridge Path. Where they split, stay to the left on the Israel Ridge Path, continuing approximately 0.5 mile to a junction with the Emerald Trail. If you have time, take a left on the Emerald Trail and make the worthwhile 20-minute detour to Emerald Bluff, which offers a stunning view of Castle Ravine. The Israel Ridge Path continues down into the woods, eventually rejoining the Castle Trail 2.5 miles below the Emerald Trail. Turn right and continue to the trailhead parking area, 1.3 miles ahead.

User Groups: Hikers and dogs. No bikes, horses, or wheelchair facilities. This trail should not be attempted in winter except by hikers experienced in mountaineering and prepared for severe winter weather.

Permits: No backcountry permit is needed, but a permit is required for day use or overnight parking at any White Mountain National Forest trailhead. Permits are available at several area stores and from the national forest at a cost of $5 for seven consecutive days or $20 per year. A $3 one-day permit can be purchased at self-service stations at national forest trailheads, but the permit is good only for the trailhead at which it's purchased.

Maps: A waterproof area trail map is available from the Appalachian Mountain Club (Presidential Range, $9.95). For a topographic area map, request Mount Washington from the USGS.

Directions: From the junction of U.S. 2 and Route 115 in Randolph, follow U.S. 2 east for 4.1 miles to the parking area on the right (south) side of the road.

GPS Coordinates: 44.3564 N, 71.3468 W

Contact: White Mountain National Forest Headquarters, 71 White Mountain Drive, Campton, NH 03246, 603/536-6100, TDD for hearing impaired 603/536-3665, www.fs.fed.us/r9/white. The Appalachian Mountain Club Pinkham Notch Visitor Center has up-to-date reports on weather in the Presidential Range; call 603/466-2721.

☷ MOUNT JEFFERSON: RIDGE OF THE CAPS

6.6 mi/5 hr   ☸4 ⛰10

in the White Mountain National Forest south of Jefferson

Beginning at an elevation of 3,008 feet, the highest trailhead accessed by a public road in the White Mountains, the Caps Ridge Trail provides the shortest route from a trailhead to a 5,000-foot summit in these mountains: five miles round-trip if you go up and down the Caps Ridge Trail. This hike extends the distance to 6.6 miles to make a loop and incorporate the spectacular Castellated Ridge. Despite the relatively short distance compared to other Presidential Range hikes, rugged trails and a net climb of 2,700 feet still make this alpine loop fairly strenuous.

Follow the Caps Ridge Trail, which rises steadily through conifer forest; at mile one, an open ledge offers sweeping views to the Ridge of the Caps above, the Castellated Ridge to the north, and the southern Presidentials to the south. You may also see the black smoke from the cog railway chugging up Mount Washington. Continue up the Caps Ridge Trail, immediately passing the junction with the Link trail, on which this route returns. The Caps Ridge Trail soon emerges from the woods and zigzags up the craggy ridge, with excellent views of most of the Whites. At 2.1

NEW HAMPSHIRE

miles, the trail passes through a junction with the Cornice Trail. Continue on for another 0.4 mile; when the ridge becomes less distinct in a sprawling talus slope, you are near Jefferson's summit, a pile of rocks rising to 5,716 feet above sea level.

For a five-mile total hike, descend the way you came. To continue on this hike, descend the other side of Jefferson's summit cone, follow the summit loop trail northward just a few steps, and then turn left (northwest) onto the Castle Trail (marked). Follow its cairns, descending at a moderate angle over the vast boulder fields of Jefferson, to the prominent Castellated Ridge. The trail follows close to the ridge crest, passing the three distinct stone castles along it. At 1.5 miles below the summit, turn left (south) on the Link, which wends a rugged—and in spots heavily eroded—path through dense forest for 1.6 miles back to the Caps Ridge Trail. Turn right (west) and descend a mile back to the trailhead.

User Groups: Hikers and dogs. No bikes, horses, or wheelchair facilities. This trail is not accessible in winter.

Permits: No backcountry permit is needed, but a permit is required for day use or overnight parking at any White Mountain National Forest trailhead. Permits are available at several area stores and from the national forest at a cost of $5 for seven consecutive days or $20 per year. A $3 one-day permit can be purchased at self-service stations at national forest trailheads, but the permit is good only for the trailhead at which it's purchased.

Maps: A waterproof area trail map is available from the Appalachian Mountain Club (Presidential Range, $9.95). For a topographic area map, request Mount Washington from the USGS.

Directions: From the junction of U.S. 2 and route 115 in Jefferson, follow U.S. 2 east a short distance to Valley Road. Turn right and follow the road more than a mile. Then turn left onto the gravel Jefferson Notch Road and continue on it for about four miles to the trailhead. From U.S. 302 in Bretton Woods, turn onto the Base Road at a sign for the Mount Washington Cog Railway and drive 5.6 miles. Then turn left on Jefferson Notch Road and follow it to Jefferson Notch. Or from U.S. 302 in Crawford Notch, 0.2 mile north of the visitor information center, turn onto Mount Clinton Road. Follow it 3.7 miles, cross Base Road, and continue straight ahead onto Jefferson Notch Road.

GPS Coordinates: 44.2961 N, 71.3536 W

Contact: White Mountain National Forest Headquarters, 71 White Mountain Drive, Campton, NH 03246, 603/536-6100, TDD for hearing impaired 603/536-3665, www.fs.fed.us/r9/white. The Appalachian Mountain Club Pinkham Notch Visitor Center has up-to-date reports on weather in the Presidential Range; call 603/466-2721.

18 PRESIDENTIAL RANGE TRAVERSE

20 mi one-way/2.5 days   👥5   ⛰10

in the White Mountain National Forest between Gorham and Crawford Notch

BEST (

This is the premier backpacking traverse in New England—in fact, nowhere else east of the Rockies can you hike a 15-mile ridge entirely above timberline. The route hits nine summits, seven of them higher than 5,000 feet—including New England's highest, 6,288-foot Mount Washington—and each with its own unique character. The route covers some very rugged terrain and is quite strenuous, with a cumulative vertical ascent of well over 8,000 feet. The task is complicated by the fact that the odds of having three straight days of good weather in these peaks may be only slightly better than those of winning the lottery. Finding appropriate campsites can be difficult, too, because of the White Mountain National Forest regulations that prohibit against camping above timberline. Skipping the side paths to summits and staying on the Gulfside Trail, Westside Trail, and

Crawford Path will reduce the distance slightly and the elevation gain significantly. Masochistic types have been known to attempt this traverse in a single day, a feat known in some circles as the Death March. From the junction of the Osgood and Daniel Webster Trails to the junction of the Crawford Path and the Webster Cliffs Trail, this hike coincides with the Appalachian Trail (AT).

From the parking area near the entrance to the Dolly Copp Campground, take the Daniel Webster-Scout Trail (marked), ascending moderately through the woods. Starting around the 2.0-mile mark, the trail grows rockier and increasingly steep until, at 2.9 miles, it begins a rough climb almost directly up a steep talus slope; scrambling will be necessary in parts. At 3.5 miles, the trail ascends open Osgood Ridge, with stunning views of the Great Gulf Wilderness and the peaks of the northern Presidentials. Approaching the ridge crest, the trail reaches Osgood Junction. Here, bear right on the Appalachian Trail/Osgood Trail and follow another 0.6 mile to the top of Mount Madison (a narrow ridge of boulders marks the summit). Continue over the summit on the AT/Osgood Trail a half mile down to the Madison AMC hut and turn left for the Star Lake Trail, a less-traveled footpath that passes the beautiful Star Lake tarn and winds a mile up the steep east side of 5,799-foot Mount Adams, the second-highest peak in New England. Adams has five distinct summits, several ridges and ravines, and excellent views. Descend via Lowe's Path nearly a half mile over an expansive talus field to the giant cairn at Thunderstorm Junction, where several trails meet.

From here, you can descend the Spur Trail a mile to the Randolph Mountain Club's Crag Camp cabin, or follow Lowe's Path for 1.3 miles to the Gray Knob cabin—both are good places to spend the night. To continue on, turn left (southwest) onto the Gulfside Trail. At 0.6 mile south of Thunderstorm Junction, you pass the Israel Ridge Path branching to the right toward the RMC's Perch camping

area. From Edmands Col (the saddle 1.3 miles south of Thunderstorm Junction), hike 0.2 mile southwest and bear right onto the Jefferson Loop Trail, climbing 0.4 mile to Mount Jefferson's top. Of its two summits, the westernmost (to your right from this direction) is the highest at 5,716 feet. The other summit is 11 feet lower.

Continue between the two summits on the loop trail and rejoin the Gulfside Trail. About 0.5 mile farther, after dipping down through Sphinx Col, bear left onto the Mount Clay Loop Trail. On a day when you see two dozen hikers on Jefferson, you may have Clay to yourself. This is probably because Clay is considered a shoulder of Mount Washington rather than a distinct peak. Yet, on Clay's broad 5,533-foot summit, you can observe abundant alpine wildflowers (particularly in the second half of June) and peer down the sheer headwall of the Great Gulf. The Clay Loop rejoins the Gulfside in 1.2 miles, and then it's another mile to the roof of New England, Washington's 6,288-foot summit, finishing via the Crawford Path. The summit has a visitors center with a cafeteria and bathrooms—seen by weary hikers as either a welcome respite or a blemish on this otherwise wild trek.

From the summit, turn southwest onto the Crawford Path and follow it 1.4 miles down to Lakes of the Clouds, the location of another AMC hut. Just south of the hut, bear right off the Crawford onto the Mount Monroe Loop Trail for the steep half-mile climb to its 5,372-foot summit (a great place to catch the sunset if you're staying at the Lakes hut). The Monroe Loop rejoins the Crawford Path southbound 0.3 mile past the summit. The Crawford then traverses the bump on the ridge known as Mount Franklin (5,001 ft.), also not considered a distinct summit. About two miles south of the Lakes hut, bear right for the loop over 4,760-foot Mount Eisenhower. A mile south of Eisenhower, follow the Webster Cliffs Trail 0.1 mile to the 4,312-foot summit of Mount Pierce, then double back and turn left on the Crawford Path, descending nearly three miles. Just before reaching U.S. 302 in Crawford Notch, turn right onto the Crawford Connector path leading 0.2 mile to the parking area on the Mount Clinton Road.

The Appalachian Mountain Club operates the Madison and Lakes of the Clouds huts, where a crew prepares meals and guests share bunkrooms and bathrooms. The Randolph Mountain Club operates two cabins on Mount Adams: Crag Camp (capacity 20) and the winterized Gray Knob (capacity 15), both of which cost $12 per person per night and are run on a first-come, first-served basis. The RMC also operates two open-sided shelters on Adams, the Perch (capacity 8, plus four tent platforms) and the Log Cabin (capacity 10), both of which cost $7 per night, with the fee collected by a caretaker. All shelters are open year-round.

User Groups: Hikers and dogs. No bikes, horses, or wheelchair facilities. This hike should not be attempted in winter except by hikers experienced in mountaineering and prepared for severe winter weather.

Permits: No backcountry permit is needed, but a permit is required for day use or overnight parking at any White Mountain National Forest trailhead, as indicated by signs posted at most trailheads. Permits are available at several area stores and from the national forest at a cost of $5 for seven consecutive days or $20 per year. A $3 one-day permit can be purchased at self-service stations at national forest trailheads, but the permit is good only for the trailhead at which it's purchased.

Maps: A waterproof area trail map is available from the Appalachian Mountain Club (Presidential Range, $9.95). For a topographic area map, request Mount Washington from the USGS.

Directions: From Gorham, drive 4.4 miles south on Route 16 to the U.S. Forest Service's Dolly Copp Campground (entrance on right), which is operated on a first-come, first-served basis. Drive to the end of the campground road to a dirt parking lot at the Great Gulf

Link trailhead. About a quarter mile before the parking lot is the start of the Daniel Webster-Scout Trail, which is where you begin this hike. Leave a second vehicle at the other end of this traverse, just off U.S. 302 in Crawford Notch State Park. The Crawford Path Trailhead parking area is on Mount Clinton Road, opposite the Crawford House site and just north of Saco Lake. The AMC-run hiker shuttle bus also provides service in this area to many popular trailheads and may be able to provide transportation for the return trip. GPS Coordinates: 44.3236 N, 71.2187 W

Contact: White Mountain National Forest Headquarters, 71 White Mountain Drive, Campton, NH 03246, 603/536-6100, TDD for hearing impaired 603/536-3665, www.fs.fed.us/r9/white. The Appalachian Mountain Club Pinkham Notch Visitor Center has up-to-date weather and trail information about the Whites; call 603/466-2725. For route information and to make reservations for the AMC-run hiker shuttle bus, call 603/466-2727.

19 THE CARTER-MORIAH RANGE

20 mi one-way/3 days

in the White Mountain National Forest between Pinkham Notch and Shelburne

BEST (

This section of the Appalachian Trail (AT) just might have you cursing one moment, uttering expressions of awe the next. This is a great three-day ridge walk on the AT, with excellent views of the Presidential Range to the west and the Wild River Valley to the east. The cumulative elevation gained on this 20-mile hike is more than 6,700 feet.

From the Appalachian Mountain Club Visitor Center, follow the Lost Pond Trail to the Wildcat Ridge Trail; turn left (east), and you will soon begin the steep climb to the ridge, passing over open ledges with commanding views of Mount Washington—a good destination for a short day hike. The first of Wildcat's five summits that you'll encounter— Peak E, 4,041 feet high—is a 3.8-mile round-trip hike of about three hours. The trail traverses the roller coaster Wildcat Ridge, up and down five humped summits with few views. Just beyond the final peak is a short spur trail to a view atop cliffs overlooking Carter Notch and the Carter Range that will make you eat all your nasty comments about this trail. Descend north a steep mile—including a traverse of about 25 feet across a loose, very steep rockslide area— turning right (east) onto the Nineteen-Mile Brook Trail for the final 0.2 mile into the notch and to the larger of two ponds there. Tent sites can be found near the junction of the Wildcat Ridge and Nineteen-Mile Brook Trails, or ask a caretaker at the AMC hut in Carter Notch about nearby sites.

Leaving from the notch, head north on the steep Carter-Moriah Trail, passing one ledge with a view of the entire notch from high above it. A bit more than a mile from the notch, the trail passes over the highest point on this ridge, Carter Dome, at 4,832 feet. Unfortunately, trees block any views. The trail continues nearly a mile to the rocky summit of Mount Hight (4,675 ft.)—the nicest summit in the range, with 360-degree views of the Presidentials and far into Maine to the east. From Hight, the Carter-Moriah Trail turns sharply left (west) a short distance, drops north down a steep slope into the forest for a half mile to Zeta Pass, then continues north over the wooded summits of South Carter and Middle Carter (2.7 miles from Mount Hight). As the ridge ascends gradually again toward North Carter, you break into the alpine zone and some of the best views on this hike, particularly west to Mount Washington. From the viewless summit of North Carter, the trail drops several hundred feet over rock ledges that require scrambling, passes over the hump known as Imp Mountain, and reaches the spur trail to the Imp campsite in two miles. Check out the view at sunset from the ledge just below the shelter.

Continuing north on the Carter-Moriah Trail, you cross over some open ledges on Imp Mountain before the trail ascends steadily onto the open southern ledges of Mount Moriah two miles from the shelter. A short distance farther, the Carter-Moriah Trail peels off left toward the town of Gorham. This hike continues on the AT, which at this point coincides with the Kenduskeag Trail—but drop your pack and make the short detour on the Carter-Moriah for the rocky scramble up the spur trail to Moriah's summit. Backtrack to the Kenduskeag (an Abenaki word meaning "a pleasant walk") and follow its often wet path 1.5 miles to the Rattle River Trail, where you'll turn left (north). The trail descends steeply at first, through a dense, damp forest, then levels out before reaching the Rattle River shelter in 2.5 miles. From there, it's less than two miles to a parking lot on U.S. 2 in Shelburne, the terminus of this traverse.

Backcountry campsites along this route are scarce, and camping is prohibited along much of the high ridge; bring adequate equipment for off-trail camping, which is permitted 200 feet away from any trails or water sources. Carry cash for camping overnight at the Appalachian Mountain Club hut in Carter Notch ($25 per person per night) or the AMC's Imp campsite ($8 per person per night).

User Groups: Hikers and dogs. No bikes, horses, or wheelchair facilities. This trail should not be attempted in winter except by hikers experienced in mountaineering and prepared for severe winter weather, and is not suitable for skis.

Permits: No backcountry permit is needed, but a permit is required for day use or overnight parking at any White Mountain National Forest trailhead. Permits are available at several area stores and from the national forest at a cost of $5 for seven consecutive days or $20 per year. A $3 one-day permit can be purchased at self-service stations at national forest trailheads, but the permit is good only for the trailhead at which it's purchased.

Maps: A waterproof area trail map is available

from the Appalachian Mountain Club (Carter Range–Evans Notch/North Country–Mahoosuc, $9.95). For a topographic area map, request Carter Dome from the USGS.

Directions: To shuttle two vehicles for this traverse, leave one at the hike's terminus, a parking area where the Appalachian Trail crosses U.S. 2, 3.6 miles east of the southern junction of U.S. 2 and Route 16 in Shelburne. The hike begins at the Appalachian Mountain Club Visitor Center on Route 16 in Pinkham Notch at the base of Mount Washington, 12 miles south of the junction with U.S. 2 in Gorham and about 8 miles north of Jackson. An AMC-run hiker shuttle bus also provides service in this area to select trailheads.

GPS Coordinates: 44.2564 N, 71.2525 W

Contact: White Mountain National Forest Headquarters, 71 White Mountain Drive, Campton, NH 03246, 603/536-6100, TDD for hearing impaired 603/536-3665, www. fs.fed.us/r9/white. The Appalachian Mountain Club Pinkham Notch Visitor Center has up-to-date weather and trail information about the Whites; call 603/466-2725. For information and reservations for the AMC-run hiker shuttle bus, call 603/466-2727.

20 MOUNT WASHINGTON: HUNTINGTON RAVINE AND THE ALPINE GARDEN
8 mi/8 hr   🥾5 ⛰10

in the White Mountain National Forest in Pinkham Notch

BEST (

Discard all your preconceived notions of difficult trails. Huntington Ravine has earned a reputation as the most difficult regular hiking trail in the White Mountains—and for good reason. The trail ascends the ravine headwall, involving very exposed scrambling up steep slabs of rock with significant fall potential. Inexperienced scramblers should shy away from this route and persons carrying a heavy pack may want to consider another way up

the mountain. The ravine is strictly a summer and early fall hike, and even in those seasons snow can fall, treacherous ice can form, or the steep rock slabs may be slick with water. The headwall, the Alpine Garden, and the top of the Lion Head all lie above the tree line and are exposed to the weather. This eight-mile loop, with a net elevation gain of 3,400 feet, will lead you through mountain terrain found on few other peaks east of the Rockies.

From the Appalachian Mountain Club Visitor Center, follow the wide Tuckerman Ravine Trail. Less than 1.5 miles up, the Huntington Ravine Trail diverges right (north); watch closely for it, because the sign may be partly hidden by trees, and the path is narrow and easily overlooked. This trail climbs steeply in spots and you get fleeting glimpses of the ravine headwall above. Within 1.5 miles from the Tuckerman Ravine Trail, you reach a flat, open area on the Huntington Ravine floor—and your first sweeping view of the massive headwall, riven by several ominous gullies separating tall cliffs. Novice hikers can reach this point without any trouble and the view of the ravine is worth it. Nearby is a first-aid cache bearing a plaque memorializing Albert Dow, a climber and mountain rescue volunteer killed by an avalanche in Huntington Ravine during a 1982 search for a pair of missing ice climbers.

The trail leads through a maze of giant boulders to the headwall base and then heads diagonally up the talus. On the headwall proper, the well-blazed trail ascends rock slabs, which may be wet, and sections of blocky boulders. Two miles from the Tuckerman Ravine Trail, you reach the top of the ravine and the broad tableland known as the Alpine Garden, where colorful wildflowers bloom mid-June–August.

By following the Huntington Ravine Trail a quarter mile farther, you can pick up the Nelson Crag Trail for the final mile to Washington's summit and then descend the Tuckerman Ravine and Lion Head Trails to rejoin this loop at the other side of the Alpine Garden—adding two miles and about 800 feet of ascent to this hike. But this hike takes a finer route—free from the tourists who flock to the summit via the auto road or cog railway—crossing the Alpine Garden to the Lion Head. Turn left (south) onto the Alpine Garden Trail, which traverses the mile-wide, tundra-like plain. In a short distance, you see to your left the top of a prominent cliff known as the Pinnacle, which is part of the Huntington Ravine headwall. The view from atop the Pinnacle merits the short detour, but take care to walk on rocks and not the fragile alpine vegetation—some plants found here are the only known of their kind. The sprawling boulder pile of the mountain's upper cone rises up on your right.

Once you're across the Alpine Garden, turn left (east) onto the Lion Head Trail. The flat trail follows the crest of a prominent buttress, above the cliffs that form the northern or right-hand wall of Tuckerman Ravine. There are numerous good views down into the ravine before the trail drops back into the woods again, descending steeply and eventually rejoining the Tuckerman Ravine Trail about two miles from the AMC Visitor Center. Turn left (east) and head down.

User Groups: Hikers only. No bikes, horses, or wheelchair facilities. This hike should not be attempted in winter except by hikers experienced in mountaineering and prepared for severe winter weather.

Permits: No backcountry permit is needed, but a permit is required for day use or overnight parking at any White Mountain National Forest trailhead. Permits are available at several area stores and from the national forest at a cost of $5 for seven consecutive days or $20 per year. A $3 one-day permit can be purchased at self-service stations at national forest trailheads, but the permit is good only for the trailhead at which it's purchased.

Maps: A waterproof area trail map is available from the Appalachian Mountain Club (Presidential Range, $9.95). For a topographic area map, request Mount Washington from the USGS.

Directions: The hike begins from the Appalachian Mountain Club Visitor Center on Route 16 in Pinkham Notch at the base of Mount Washington, 12 miles south of the junction of Route 16 and U.S. 2 in Gorham and about 8 miles north of Jackson. The trailhead is behind the visitors center.

GPS Coordinates: 44.2575 N, 71.2533 W

Contact: White Mountain National Forest Headquarters, 71 White Mountain Drive, Campton, NH 03246, 603/536-6100, TDD for hearing impaired 603/536-3665, www.fs.fed.us/r9/white. The Appalachian Mountain Club Pinkham Notch Visitor Center has up-to-date reports on weather in the Presidential Range; call 603/466-2721.

21 MOUNT WASHINGTON: THE LION HEAD
8.6 mi/7 hr   👥5 ⛰10

in the White Mountain National Forest in Pinkham Notch

The Lion Head Trail, a less-traveled route up New England's highest peak than the Tuckerman Ravine Trail in summer, is the standard route for a challenging winter ascent. The actual winter Lion Head Trail follows a different route than the summer trail to avoid avalanche hazard. Trail signs are posted in the appropriate places when each trail is opened or closed for the season. To check on the status of the changeover, call the AMC's Pinkham Notch Visitor Center.

From Pinkham Notch, pick up the wide Tuckerman Ravine Trail, follow it for 2.3 miles, and then turn right onto the Lion Head Trail. It soon begins steep switchbacks up the face of the Lion Head ridge, breaking out of the forest within a half mile of the Tuckerman Ravine Trail junction for excellent views of Pinkham Notch and the Carter Range across the notch. Shortly after leaving the forest, the trail crests the Lion Head for much flatter walking across the Alpine Garden, a tundra-like

© CYNTHIA CORDES

NEW HAMPSHIRE

looking up at Tuckerman Ravine, Mount Washington

plateau that's one of the best places in these mountains to view alpine wildflowers from late spring well into summer, depending on how long the snow lingers. To your left, the ridge drops away abruptly into Tuckerman Ravine; straight ahead lies Washington's summit, still more than 1,200 feet higher.

At 1.1 miles from the Tuckerman Ravine Trail, the Lion Head Trail crosses the Alpine Garden Trail and soon afterward begins climbing Mount Washington's summit cone. A half mile farther, turn right onto the Tuckerman Ravine Trail and follow it another 0.4 mile to Washington's summit. Descend the way you came.

User Groups: Hikers only. Trail is not suitable for bikes, dogs, or horses; no wheelchair facilities. This hike should not be attempted in winter except by hikers experienced in mountaineering and prepared for severe winter weather.

Permits: No backcountry permit is needed, but a permit is required for day use or overnight parking at any White Mountain National Forest trailhead. Permits are available at several area stores and from the national forest at a cost of $5 for seven consecutive days or $20 per year. A $3 one-day permit can be purchased at self-service stations at national forest trailheads, but the permit is good only for the trailhead at which it's purchased.

Maps: A waterproof area trail map is available from the Appalachian Mountain Club (Presidential Range, $9.95). For a topographic area map, request Mount Washington from the USGS.

Directions: The hike begins from the Appalachian Mountain Club Visitor Center on Route 16 in Pinkham Notch at the base of Mount Washington, 12 miles south of the junction of Route 16 and U.S. 2 in Gorham and about 8 miles north of Jackson. The trailhead is behind the visitors center.

GPS Coordinates: 44.2575 N, 71.2533 W

Contact: White Mountain National Forest Headquarters, 71 White Mountain Drive, Campton, NH 03246, 603/536-6100, TDD for hearing impaired 603/536-3665, www.fs.fed.us/r9/white. The AMC's Pinkham Notch Visitor Center has up-to-date reports on weather in the Presidential Range; call 603/466-2721.

22 MOUNT WASHINGTON: TUCKERMAN RAVINE
8.4 mi/7 hr   🥾5 △10

in the White Mountain National Forest in Pinkham Notch

BEST (

This trail is the standard route and most direct way up the 6,288-foot Mount Washington, the Northeast's highest peak, so it typically sees hundreds of hikers on nice weekends in summer and early autumn. It's also a busy place in spring, when skiers make the hike up into Tuckerman Ravine to ski its formidable headwall. Although the crowds can diminish the mountain experience, the ravine is stunningly scenic, an ascent of the headwall is a serious challenge, and reaching Washington's summit is an accomplishment sought by many. This is the common route for first-time hikers of Washington. The trail on the ravine headwall is sometimes closed due to ice; check on weather and conditions at the visitors center. While hiking the headwall, watch out for rocks kicked loose by hikers above you and be careful not to dislodge any rocks yourself. When you pass over the Mount Washington summit, you'll be walking on the Appalachian Trail. The elevation gained on this hike to the rooftop of New England is about 4,300 feet.

From behind the visitors center, the wide Tuckerman Ravine Trail ascends at a moderate grade, passing the short side path to Crystal Cascade within a half mile. As you continue up the Tuckerman Ravine Trail, you'll pass intersections with several trails. At 2.5 miles the trail reaches the floor of the ravine, a worthwhile destination in itself; to the right is the Lion Head and to the left the cliffs of Boott Spur. (From the Hermit Lake shelter, which is along the Tuckerman Ravine Trail, walk to the right less than a quarter mile for a striking reflection of Boott Spur in Hermit Lake.) The trail then climbs the headwall, reaching its lip a mile from Hermit Lake, and follows rock cairns nearly another mile to the summit. Although many hikers descend Tuckerman's headwall, an easier way down is via the Lion Head Trail, which diverges left from the Tuckerman Ravine Trail just below the summit and then rejoins it 0.1 mile below Hermit Lake.

User Groups: Hikers only. Trail is not suitable for bikes, dogs, or horses; no wheelchair facilities. This hike should not be attempted in winter except by hikers experienced in mountaineering and prepared for severe winter weather.

Permits: No backcountry permit is needed, but a permit is required for day use or overnight parking at any White Mountain National Forest trailhead. Permits are available at several area stores and from the national forest at a cost of $5 for seven consecutive days

or $20 per year. A $3 one-day permit can be purchased at self-service stations at national forest trailheads, but the permit is good only for the trailhead at which it's purchased.

Maps: A waterproof area trail map is available from the Appalachian Mountain Club (Presidential Range, $9.95). For a topographic area map, request Mount Washington from the USGS.

Directions: The hike begins from the Appalachian Mountain Club Visitor Center on Route 16 in Pinkham Notch, at the base of Mount Washington, 12 miles south of the junction of Route 16 and U.S. 2 in Gorham and about 8 miles north of Jackson. The trailhead is behind the visitors center.

GPS Coordinates: 44.2575 N, 71.2533 W

Contact: White Mountain National Forest Headquarters, 71 White Mountain Drive, Campton, NH 03246, 603/536-6100, TDD for hearing impaired 603/536-3665, www.fs.fed.us/r9/white. The Appalachian Mountain Club Pinkham Notch Visitor Center has up-to-date reports on weather in the Presidential Range; call 603/466-2721.

⓴ MOUNT WASHINGTON: AMMONOOSUC RAVINE/ JEWELL TRAIL
9.8 mi/7.5 hr   🏃5 ⛰10

in the White Mountain National Forest north of Crawford Notch

Like every other route to the 6,288-foot summit of Mount Washington, this loop hike offers great views, rough terrain, and the chance to run into some really nasty weather. A northeasterly approach to the mountain that uses the Appalachian Trail (AT) for part of its ascent, this climb traverses exposed ground from just below the Lakes of the Clouds hut until descending more than a half mile down the Jewell Trail; always bring warm, weatherproof clothes along for what can be very rapidly shifting conditions. And even on the sunniest of days, hikers should also watch out for tricky—and often wet—stretches on the Ammonoosuc Ravine's steep upper headwall as well as several brook crossings, some of which are impossible to ford in times of high water. This hike climbs about 3,800 feet in elevation.

From the parking lot, follow the moderately ascending Ammonoosuc Ravine Trail, passing picturesque Gem Pool about two miles out. For the next half mile, the trail makes a steep ascent of the headwall, passing several cascades and pools and good views back into Ammonoosuc Ravine. At three miles, you leave the last scrub vegetation behind and enter the alpine zone; take care to walk on rocks and not the fragile plant life. From the Lakes of the Clouds AMC hut (reached at 3.1 miles), the detour south to the 5,372-foot summit of Monroe adds a relatively easy one-mile round-trip and 360 feet of climbing to this hike.

To continue the hike, turn left (north) from the Lakes of the Clouds hut onto the Appalachian Trail/Crawford Path, which passes by the two tiny tarns that give the hut its name. It's 1.4 more miles and more than 1,000 vertical feet to the top of Washington, where there is a visitors center and amazing views. Descend the AT/Crawford Path from the summit for 0.2 mile and bear right with the AT, now coinciding with the Gulfside Trail heading north. Follow it 1.4 miles, walking the crest of the exposed ridge, passing the loop trail up Mount Clay, and finally reaching a junction with the Jewell Trail. Turn left and descend the Jewell for 3.7 miles, descending steep ground through several switchbacks at first, and then proceeding at a more moderate grade back to the parking area.

The Appalachian Mountain Club operates the Lakes of the Clouds hut, where a crew prepares meals and guests share bunkrooms and bathrooms.

User Groups: Hikers and dogs. No bikes, horses, or wheelchair facilities. This trail should not be attempted in winter except by hikers experienced in mountaineering and prepared for severe winter weather.

Permits: No backcountry permit is needed,

but a permit is required for day use or overnight parking at any White Mountain National Forest trailhead. Permits are available at several area stores and from the national forest at a cost of $5 for seven consecutive days or $20 per year. A $3 one-day permit can be purchased at self-service stations at national forest trailheads, but the pass is good only for the trailhead at which it's purchased.

Maps: A waterproof area trail map is available from the Appalachian Mountain Club (Presidential Range, $9.95). For a topographic area map, request Mount Washington from the USGS.

Directions: From the junction of U.S. 302 and U.S. 3 in Twin Mountain, drive east on U.S. 302 for 4.6 miles and turn left at signs for the Mount Washington Cog Railway. Continue 6.7 miles to a large parking lot on the right. Or from U.S. 302 in Crawford Notch, 0.2 mile north of the visitor information center, turn onto Mount Clinton Road (not maintained in winter). Follow it 3.7 miles and turn right. Continue 1.1 miles and turn right into the parking lot.

GPS Coordinates: 44.2699 N, 71.3498 W

Contact: White Mountain National Forest Headquarters, 71 White Mountain Drive, Campton, NH 03246, 603/536-6100, TDD for hearing impaired 603/536-3665, www. fs.fed.us/r9/white. The Appalachian Mountain Club Pinkham Notch Visitor Center has up-to-date reports on weather in the Presidential Range; call 603/466-2721. The Appalachian Mountain Club, 603/466-2727 for reservation and rate information.

24 MOUNTS WASHINGTON AND MONROE: CRAWFORD PATH

16.4 mi/11 hr   🏃4 ⛰10

in the White Mountain National Forest and Crawford Notch State Park

This is a hike typically covered in two days, with a stay at the AMC's Lakes of the Clouds

© VINCENT VANNICOLA

the AMC's Lakes of the Clouds hut in the saddle between Mounts Washington and Monroe

Crawford Cliff, with a good view of Crawford Notch.) From the connector trail junction, the Crawford Path ascends steadily, passing a short side path in 0.4 mile that leads to Gibbs Falls. Less than three miles from U.S. 302, the trail emerges from the forest and meets the Appalachian Trail/Webster Cliff Trail (turning right and walking about 150 yards south on that trail brings you to the 4,312-foot summit of Mount Pierce). From this point to Washington's summit, the Appalachian Trail and Crawford Path coincide; turn left on the now white-blazed trail or enjoy more level ground with views in all directions. A bit more than a mile from the Webster Cliffs Trail junction, the Mount Eisenhower loop trail diverges for the 0.4-mile climb to Eisenhower's 4,760-foot summit, then descends, steeply in spots, another 0.4 mile to rejoin the Crawford Path. Although bagging Eisenhower entails 300 feet of climbing and 0.2 mile more hiking than taking the Crawford Path around the summit, the view from its summit is worth the small effort. The AT/Crawford Path continues to ascend at a very gentle grade until, six miles from U.S. 302, the Mount Monroe Loop branches left for its two summits (from this direction, the second, or northernmost, summit is the highest).

It's the same distance, 0.7 mile, via either the Crawford Path or the Monroe Loop to where the two trails meet again north of Monroe, but the Monroe Loop involves another 350 feet of elevation gain and is much more exposed. From the northern junction of the trails, the Crawford Path leads a flat 0.1 mile to the Lakes of the Clouds hut. From there, it's a steady climb for 1.4 miles over very rocky terrain up the barren summit cone of Washington to the roof of New England. Return via the same route.

The Appalachian Mountain Club operates the Lakes of the Clouds hut in the saddle between the summits of Washington and Monroe, where a crew prepares meals and guests share bunkrooms and bathrooms.

User Groups: Hikers and dogs. No bikes, horses, or wheelchair facilities. This trail should not be

hut, but the gentle nature of the Crawford Path allows very fit hikers to do this in a day. The southern ridge of the Presidentials is far less rugged than the northern ridge, yet the views surpass those of most hikes in New England. Another draw: the Lakes of the Clouds, among the few true alpine tarns in the White Mountains. The 5,372-foot Mount Monroe rolls like a wave south from the 6,288-foot Mount Washington. If you do spend a night at the hut, make the short walk up onto Monroe to watch the sunset. Remember that weather changes quickly on these peaks and may even be radically different atop Washington than on the other summits. Even on a sunny September day in the valley, it's not unusual to encounter a snowstorm atop Washington.

From the parking area, follow the Crawford Connector 0.2 mile to the Crawford Path, considered the oldest continuously maintained footpath in the country. (Nearby, a side path leads left for 0.4 mile over rough ground to

attempted in winter except by hikers experienced in mountaineering and prepared for severe winter weather, and is not suitable for skis.

Permits: No backcountry permit is needed, but a permit is required for day use or overnight parking at any White Mountain National Forest trailhead. Permits are available at several area stores and from the national forest at a cost of $5 for seven consecutive days or $20 per year. A $3 one-day permit can be purchased at self-service stations at national forest trailheads, but the pass is good only for the trailhead at which it's purchased.

Maps: A waterproof area trail map is available from the Appalachian Mountain Club (Presidential Range, $9.95). For a topographic area map, request Mount Washington from the USGS.

Directions: From the Appalachian Mountain Club Highland Center on U.S. 302 in Crawford Notch, turn left onto U.S. 302 and drive north for less than 0.1 mile to a right turn for Mount Clinton Road. Follow the road only a short distance to the trailhead parking area. GPS Coordinates: 44.2200 N, 71.4100 W

Contact: White Mountain National Forest Headquarters, 71 White Mountain Drive, Campton, NH 03246, 603/536-6100, TDD for hearing impaired 603/536-3665, www.fs.fed.us/r9/white. The Appalachian Mountain Club Pinkham Notch Visitor Center has up-to-date reports on weather in the Presidential Range; call 603/466-2721. The Appalachian Mountain Club, 603/466-2727 for reservation and rate information, www.outdoors.org

25 MOUNT WASHINGTON: BOOT SPUR/GULF OF SLIDES

6.9 mi/5 hr   🏃5 ⛰10

in the White Mountain National Forest in Pinkham Notch

The summit of 6,288-foot Mount Washington, with its commercial development

and access by road and cog railway, may be a turn-off for some alpine purists. This climb—onto a high shoulder of Washington with views down into two of its ravines—skips the summit, but doesn't skimp on breathtaking scenery or natural beauty. The ascent to the high point named Boott Spur (5,500 ft.) is about 3,500 feet.

From the Appalachian Mountain Club Visitor Center, follow the Tuckerman Ravine Trail for nearly a half mile. Shortly after passing the side path to Crystal Cascade, turn left at a junction with the Boott Spur Trail. In another 1.7 miles, a side path leads a short distance right to Ravine Outlook, a worthy detour that takes you high above Tuckerman Ravine (but adds no appreciable mileage). Return to the Boott Spur Trail, which emerges from the woods nearly two miles from where it left the Tuckerman Ravine Trail. In another 0.2 mile, the trail passes between the halves of Split Rock and begins the 0.7-mile push to the open ridge known as Boott Spur, with excellent views down into Tuckerman Ravine. Although the grade is moderate, a few false summits along the steplike ridge deceive many hikers. Once atop the shoulder, approximately three miles from the Boott Spur Trailhead, turn left (south) onto the Davis Path and follow it for a half mile. Then turn left again (southeast) onto the Glen Boulder Trail, which circles around the rim of the Gulf of Slides, another of Washington's scenic ravines. Much of the Glen Boulder Trail is above the tree line, with long views to the south and good views east toward Wildcat Mountain and the Carter Range. At 1.5 miles from the Davis Path, you'll pass the Glen Boulder, an enormous glacial erratic set precariously on the mountainside. A bit more than a mile past the boulder, back down in the woods, turn left onto the Direttissima, the trail heading the last mile back to the visitors center parking lot.

User Groups: Hikers only. No bikes, dogs, horses, or wheelchair facilities. This trail should not be attempted in winter except by hikers experienced in mountaineering and prepared for severe winter weather.

Permits: No backcountry permit is needed, but a permit is required for day use or overnight parking at any White Mountain National Forest trailhead. Permits are available at several area stores and from the national forest at a cost of $5 for seven consecutive days or $20 per year. A $3 one-day permit can be purchased at self-service stations at national forest trailheads, but the pass is good only for the trailhead at which it's purchased.

Maps: A waterproof area trail map is available from the Appalachian Mountain Club (Presidential Range, $9.95). For a topographic area map, request Mount Washington from the USGS.

Directions: The hike begins from the Appalachian Mountain Club Visitor Center on Route 16 in Pinkham Notch, at the base of Mount Washington, 12 miles south of the junction of Route 16 and U.S. 2 in Gorham and about 8 miles north of Jackson. The trailhead is behind the visitors center.

GPS Coordinates: 44.2575 N, 71.2533 W

Contact: White Mountain National Forest Headquarters, 71 White Mountain Drive, Campton, NH 03246, 603/536-6100, TDD for hearing impaired 603/536-3665, www. fs.fed.us/r9/white. The Appalachian Mountain Club Pinkham Notch Visitor Center has up-to-date reports on weather in the Presidential Range; call 603/466-2721.

26 SQUARE LEDGE

1.2 mi/0.75 hr

in the White Mountain National Forest in Pinkham Notch

Square Ledge is the aptly named cliff that's obvious when you're standing in the parking lot at the Appalachian Mountain Club Visitor Center on Route 16 and looking due east across the road. The view from atop this cliff is one of the best you can get of Pinkham

Notch and the deep ravines on the east side of New England's highest peak, 6,288-foot Mount Washington. A good taste of White Mountains adventure for first time hikers, this route offers a bit of easy scrambling up the last six or eight feet of rock to get onto Square Ledge, with a total net climb of 400 feet.

From the Appalachian Mountain Club Visitor Center, cross Route 16 and walk south about 100 feet to where the Lost Pond Trail, a part of the white-blazed Appalachian Trail, crosses a bog on a boardwalk and enters the woods. About 50 feet into the woods, turn left on the blue-blazed Square Ledge Trail. The trail almost immediately crosses a ski trail and then ascends gradually through a mixed forest with lots of white birch trees. Watch for the sporadic blazes marking the trail, especially in winter, when the pathway may be less obvious. At 0.1 mile from the road, turn left and follow a side path 100 feet to Ladies Lookout, where you'll get a decent view toward Washington. Back on the Square Ledge Trail, continue through the woods, skirting around Hangover Rock—easy to recognize—then turn right and climb more steeply uphill. At 0.6 mile, scramble up the gully to the right of the cliffs and at the top of the gully, scramble up the rocks to the top of the ledge with excellent views towards Washington and Pinkham Notch. Return the way you came.

User Groups: Hikers and dogs. Dogs must be under control at all times. Trail is not suitable for bikes, horses, or wheelchairs.

Permits: No backcountry permit is needed, but a permit is required for day use or overnight parking at any White Mountain National Forest trailhead. Permits are available at several area stores and from the national forest at a cost of $5 for seven consecutive days or $20 per year. A $3 one-day permit can be purchased at self-service stations at national forest trailheads, but the permit is good only for the trailhead at which it's purchased.

Maps: A waterproof area trail map is available from the Appalachian Mountain Club (Presidential Range, $9.95). For a topographic area map, request Mount Washington from the USGS.

Directions: The hike begins from the Appalachian Mountain Club Visitor Center on Route 16 in Pinkham Notch, at the base of Mount Washington, 12 miles south of the junction of Route 16 and U.S. 2 in Gorham and about 8 miles north of Jackson. The trailhead is across the highway from the visitors center.

GPS Coordinates: 44.2565 N, 71.2523 W

Contact: White Mountain National Forest Headquarters, 71 White Mountain Drive, Campton, NH 03246, 603/536-6100, TDD for hearing impaired 603/536-3665, www. fs.fed.us/r9/white. The Appalachian Mountain Club Pinkham Notch Visitor Center has up-to-date reports on weather in the Presidential Range; call 603/466-2721.

27 MOUNT HIGHT/CARTER DOME/CARTER NOTCH

10 mi/7.5 hr   🏃5 ⛰10

in the White Mountain National Forest north of Pinkham Notch

This scenic 10-mile loop through the Carter Range, a series of rugged hills extending south of Gorham on the eastern side of Route 16, takes you over the summit of craggy Mount Hight (4,675 ft.); onto the ninth-highest peak in the Granite State, the 4,832-foot Carter Dome; and into a boulder-strewn mountain notch where towering cliffs flank a pair of tiny ponds. The hike climbs approximately 3,500 feet and coincides in portions with the Appalachian Trail.

From the parking turnout on the east side of Route 16, pick up the Nineteen-Mile Brook Trail at the trail marker and follow it southeast for an easy stretch. Just before two miles out, the trail reaches a junction. Turn left (east) onto the Carter Dome Trail. In about two miles, at Zeta Pass, head south (right), picking up the Carter-Moriah Trail, which coincides with the white-blazed Appalachian Trail (AT).

The trail climbs steeply, requiring some scrambling over rocks, to the bare summit of Mount Hight. There you have a 360-degree panorama of the Presidential Range dominating the skyline to the west, the Carters running north, and the lower hills of eastern New Hampshire and western Maine to the south and east. Continue south on the AT/Carter-Moriah Trail, over the viewless summit of Carter Dome, and descend into Carter Notch. There's a great view of the notch from open ledges before you start the knee-pounding drop. At the larger of the two Carter Lakes in the notch, two miles past Mount Hight, leave the AT and turn right (northwest) onto the Nineteen-Mile Brook Trail for the nearly four-mile walk back to the parking area.

User Groups: Hikers and dogs. Dogs must be under control. No bikes, horses, or wheelchair facilities.

Permits: No backcountry permit is needed, but a permit is required for day use or overnight parking at any White Mountain National Forest trailhead. Permits are available at several area stores and from the national forest at a cost of $5 for seven consecutive days or $20 per year. A $3 one-day permit can be purchased at self-service stations at national forest trailheads, but the pass is good only for the trailhead at which it's purchased.

Maps: A waterproof area trail map is available from the Appalachian Mountain Club (Carter Range–Evans Notch/North Country–Mahoosuc, $9.95). For a topographic area map, request Carter Dome from the USGS.

Directions: From the Appalachian Mountain Club Pinkham Notch Visitor Center, drive north on Route 16 approximately four miles to the parking turnout for the Nineteen-Mile Brook Trail on the right (a mile north of the Mount Washington Auto Road).

GPS Coordinates: 44.3021 N, 71.2208 W

Contact: White Mountain National Forest Headquarters, 71 White Mountain Drive, Campton, NH 03246, 603/536-6100, TDD for hearing impaired 603/536-3665, www. fs.fed.us/r9/white.

28 WILDCAT MOUNTAIN
8.5 mi/5.5 hr

in Pinkham Notch in the White Mountain National Forest

The summit of this 4,000-foot peak is wooded and uninteresting, but the walk along Nineteen-Mile Brook and the view from the top of the cliffs overlooking Carter Notch and the Carter Range—reached via a short spur trail just below Wildcat Mountain's 4,422-foot summit—make this hike very worthwhile. Because this end of Wildcat Mountain does not tend to lure many hikers, you might have that viewpoint to yourself. This hike climbs nearly 3,000 feet and coincides in portions with the Appalachian Trail.

From Route 16, the Nineteen-Mile Brook Trail ascends very gently toward Carter Notch, paralleling the wide, rock-strewn streambed and crossing two tributaries. Just 0.2 mile before the trail drops down into the notch—and 3.5 miles from Route 16—turn right onto the Wildcat Ridge Trail, also the white-blazed Appalachian Trail. The next 0.7 mile is a relentless climb up the steep, rocky east face of Wildcat Mountain; footing here is loose even in summer and often dangerously icy in winter. Upon reaching more level ground, shortly before topping the mountain's long summit ridge, watch for the spur trail branching left that leads about 30 feet to the top of the cliffs overlooking Carter Notch. Return to the parking area the way you came—and on the descent, if you still have energy to burn, the half-mile detour from the Nineteen-Mile Brook Trail junction down into Carter Notch is well worth the effort.

User Groups: Hikers and dogs. No bikes, horses, or wheelchair facilities.

Permits: No backcountry permit is needed, but a permit is required for day use or overnight parking at any White Mountain National Forest trailhead. Permits are available at several area stores and from the national forest at a cost of $5 for seven consecutive days

or $20 per year. A $3 one-day permit can be purchased at self-service stations at national forest trailheads, but the pass is good only for the trailhead at which it's purchased.

Maps: A waterproof trail map is available from the Appalachian Mountain Club (Presidential Range map or the Carter Range–Evans Notch/North Country–Mahoosuc map, $9.95 each). For a topographic area map, request Carter Dome from the USGS.

Directions: From the Appalachian Mountain Club Pinkham Notch Visitor Center, drive north on Route 16 approximately four miles to the parking turnout for the Nineteen-Mile Brook Trail on the right (a mile north of the Mount Washington Auto Road). GPS Coordinates: 44.3021 N, 71.2208 W

Contact: White Mountain National Forest Headquarters, 71 White Mountain Drive, Campton, NH 03246, 603/536-6100, TDD for hearing impaired 603/536-3665, www. fs.fed.us/r9/white.

29 CARTER NOTCH: WILDCAT RIVER TRAIL
8.6 mi/5 hr

in the White Mountain National Forest north of Jackson

This relatively easy hike accesses spectacular Carter Notch via a trail less traveled than the popular Nineteen-Mile Brook Trail (see the *Mount Hight/Carter Dome/Carter Notch* listing in this chapter) and takes you to the Carter Notch Appalachian Mountain Club hut. The trail nets an elevation gain of about 1,500 feet.

From the parking area, follow the Bog Brook Trail for 0.7 mile. Just after crossing the Wildcat River, which can be difficult at times of high water, the Bog Brook Trail bears right, but you will continue straight ahead onto the Wildcat River Trail. Follow it along the gorgeous river, then away from the river into the woods. It ascends steadily but gently, except for brief, steep pitches, for 3.6 miles from the Bog Brook Trail junction to the Appalachian Mountain Club hut in Carter Notch. After exploring the notch a bit, return the way you came.

User Groups: Hikers and dogs. No bikes, horses, or wheelchair facilities.

Permits: No backcountry permit is needed, but a permit is required for day use or overnight parking at any White Mountain National Forest trailhead. Permits are available at several area stores and from the national forest at a cost of $5 for seven consecutive days or $20 per year. A $3 one-day permit can be purchased at self-service stations at national forest trailheads, but the pass is good only for the trailhead at which it's purchased. Carry cash for camping overnight at the Appalachian Mountain Club hut in Carter Notch.

Maps: A waterproof area trail map is available from the Appalachian Mountain Club (Carter Range–Evans Notch/North Country–Mahoosuc, $9.95). For topographic area maps, request Jackson and Carter Dome from the USGS.

Directions: From Route 16A in Jackson, Route 16B loops through the north end of town, its two endpoints leaving Route 16A very near each other; take the left, or westernmost, endpoint of Route 16B and follow it uphill. Where Route 16B turns sharply right, continue straight ahead onto Carter Notch Road. Three miles after leaving Route 16B, just after a sharp left turn in the road, park at a turnout for the Bog Brook Trail.

GPS Coordinates: 44.2168 N, 71.1968 W

Contact: White Mountain National Forest Headquarters, 71 White Mountain Drive, Campton, NH 03246, 603/536-6100, TDD for hearing impaired 603/536-3665, www.fs.fed.us/r9/white.

30 LOST POND

2 mi/1 hr

in the White Mountain National Forest in Pinkham Notch

While this pond is no more lost than the popular Lonesome Lake on the other side of the Whites is lonesome, this is a nice short hike that's flat and offers opportunities for wildlife-viewing and a unique view of Mount Washington. The out-and-back route follows the Appalachian Trail (AT).

From the Appalachian Mountain Club Visitor Center, cross Route 16 and follow the white-blazed Appalachian Trail/Lost Pond Trail, less than 0.8 mile before reaching the pond. Immediately you will see signs of beaver activity—probably dams and a lodge—and, if you're lucky, a moose will be grazing in the swampy area to the left. About halfway around the pond, look across to a fine view of Washington above the still water. Return the way you came. Or for a little extra adventure, keep following the AT until it comes to a junction and turns to follow Wildcat Ridge Trail. You are now just minutes from the 70-foot tall Glen Ellis Falls, which can be reached by turning right (west) and crossing the Ellis River on the way toward Route 16; in spring and early summer, crossing the Ellis River between this trail junction and Route 16 can be difficult and dangerous. You can also reach some nice views of this valley and Mount Washington by turning left at this junction and climbing less than a mile up the Wildcat Ridge Trail. This hike returns the way you came.

User Groups: Hikers and dogs. No bikes, horses, or wheelchair facilities.

Permits: No backcountry permit is needed, but a permit is required for day use or overnight parking at any White Mountain National Forest trailhead. Permits are available at several area stores and from the national forest at a cost of $5 for seven consecutive days or $20 per year. A $3 one-day permit can be

purchased at self-service stations at national forest trailheads, but the pass is good only for the trailhead at which it's purchased.

Maps: Two waterproof area trail maps available from the Appalachian Mountain Club show this hike (Presidential Range map and Carter Range–Evans Notch/North Country–Mahoosuc map, $9.95 each). For topographic area maps, request Mount Washington, Carter Dome, Jackson, and Stairs Mountain from the USGS.

Directions: The hike begins from the Appalachian Mountain Club Visitor Center on Route 16 in Pinkham Notch, at the base of Mount Washington, 12 miles south of the junction of Route 16 and U.S. 2 in Gorham and about 8 miles north of Jackson. The trailhead is across the highway from the visitors center. GPS Coordinates: 44.2565 N, 71.2523 W

Contact: White Mountain National Forest Headquarters, 71 White Mountain Drive, Campton, NH 03246, 603/536-6100, TDD for hearing impaired 603/536-3665, www.fs.fed.us/r9/white. Appalachian Mountain Club Pinkham Notch Visitor Center, P.O. Box 298, Gorham, NH 03581, 603/466-2721, www.outdoors.org.

31 GLEN ELLIS FALLS
0.6 mi/0.75 hr

in the White Mountain National Forest south of Pinkham Notch

BEST (

Here's a scenic, short walk that's ideal for young children and enjoyable for adults. The trail descends steeply at times, but there are rock steps and a handrail. (Children will definitely need a steady hand of an adult to hold onto on the way down.) From the parking area, follow the wide gravel trail through a tunnel under Route 16. The trail descends steeply at times, but there are rock steps and a handrail. Continue along a well-worn path to the waterfall, a 70-foot tall wall of water that makes a single, sheer drop

before continuing on along the Glen Ellis River. Return the way you came. This is a popular walk with tourists and it's especially spectacular in late spring, when water flow is heaviest.

Special note: If you're coming from Lost Pond or Wildcat Mountain to see the falls (see the *Lost Pond* and *Carter Notch: Wildcat River Trail* listings in this chapter), be aware that the Wildcat River Trail makes a crossing of the Ellis River near Route 16 that can be treacherous in times of high water and unsafe for young children.

User Groups: Hikers and dogs. Not suitable for bikes, horses, or skis. No wheelchair facilities.

Permits: No backcountry permit is needed, but a permit is required for day use or overnight parking at any White Mountain National Forest trailhead. Permits are available at several area stores and from the national forest at a cost of $5 for seven consecutive days or $20 per year. A $3 one-day permit can be purchased at self-service stations at national forest trailheads, but the pass is good only for the trailhead at which it's purchased.

Maps: Two waterproof area trail maps available from the Appalachian Mountain Club show this hike (Presidential Range map and Carter Range–Evans Notch/North Country–Mahoosuc map, $9.95 each). For topographic area maps, request Mount Washington, Carter Dome, Jackson, and Stairs Mountain from the USGS.

Directions: The trail begins at a parking lot for Glen Ellis Falls off Route 16, less than a mile south of the Appalachian Mountain Club Visitor Center in Pinkham Notch. GPS Coordinates: 44.2456 N, 71.2533 W

Contact: White Mountain National Forest Headquarters, 71 White Mountain Drive, Campton, NH 03246, 603/536-6100, TDD for hearing impaired 603/536-3665, www.fs.fed.us/r9/white. Appalachian Mountain Club Pinkham Notch Visitor Center, P.O. Box 298, Gorham, NH 03581, 603/466-2721, www.outdoors.org.

NEW HAMPSHIRE

32 ZEALAND NOTCH/ WILLEY RANGE

17 mi/2–3 days 👣3 ⛰9

in the White Mountain National Forest southeast of Twin Mountain

Along the northeastern edge of the Pemigewasset Wilderness, this 17-mile loop passes through spectacular Zealand Notch and traverses the Willey Range, with a pair of 4,000-footers, lots of rugged terrain, and limited views marking this lesser known corner of the Whites. Best spread out over 2–3 days, the cumulative elevation gained is less than 3,000 feet.

From the Zealand Road parking lot, follow the Zealand Trail south, paralleling the Zealand River. At 2.3 miles, the A-Z Trail enters from the left; you will return on that trail. The Zealand Trail reaches a junction with the Twinway and the Ethan Pond Trail at 2.5 miles (the Appalachian Mountain Club's Zealand Falls hut lies 0.2 mile uphill on the Twinway). This hike bears left onto the Ethan Pond Trail, which runs for two miles to the opposite end of the notch, passing numerous overlooks through the trees. Reaching the Thoreau Falls Trail at 4.6 miles, bear right and follow it for 0.1 mile to Thoreau Falls, which tumbles more than 100 feet down through several steps. Backtrack and turn right (east) on the Ethan Pond Trail, which follows level ground for 2.5 miles to the side path leading left less than 0.1 mile to Ethan Pond and the shelter just above the pond.

A mile beyond the junction, turn left (north) onto the Willey Range Trail, which soon begins a steep and sustained climb of 1.1 miles up 4,285-foot Mount Willey, where there are some views from just below the summit. The trail continues north, dropping into a saddle, then ascending to the 4,340-foot summit of Mount Field—named for Darby Field, the first known person to climb Mount Washington—1.4 miles from Willey's summit. Field is wooded with no views. Just beyond the

summit, the Avalon Trail branches right, but stay left with the Willey Range Trail, descending steadily to the A-Z Trail, 0.9 mile from the summit of Field. Turn left (west), descending easily for 2.7 miles to the Zealand Trail. Turn right (north) and walk 2.5 miles back to the Zealand Road parking lot.

The Appalachian Mountain Club (AMC) operates the Zealand Falls hut year-round. The Zealand Falls hut is on the Twinway, 0.2 mile from the junction of the Zealand, Twinway, and Ethan Pond Trails and 2.7 miles from the end of Zealand Road. Contact the AMC for information on cost and reservations.

The AMC also operates the first-come, first-served Ethan Pond shelter. A caretaker collects the $8 per person nightly fee late spring–fall. The Ethan Pond shelter is located just off the Ethan Pond Trail, 7.3 miles from the Zealand Road parking lot along this hike's route.

User Groups: Hikers and dogs. No bikes, horses, or wheelchair facilities.

Permits: No backcountry permit is needed, but a permit is required for day use or overnight parking at any White Mountain National Forest trailhead. Permits are available at several area stores and from the national forest at a cost of $5 for seven consecutive days or $20 per year. A $3 one-day permit can be purchased at self-service stations at national forest trailheads, but the pass is good only for the trailhead at which it's purchased.

Maps: Two waterproof area trail maps are available from the Appalachian Mountain Club (Franconia–Pemigewasset Range map and Crawford Notch–Sandwich Range/Moosilauke–Kinsman map, $9.95 each). For a topographic area map, request Crawford Notch from the USGS.

Directions: From the junction of U.S. 3 and U.S. 302 in Twin Mountain, drive east on U.S. 302 for 2.3 miles and turn right onto Zealand Road. Continue 3.5 miles to a parking lot at the end of the road. Zealand Road is not maintained in winter; the winter parking lot is on U.S. 302, immediately east of Zealand Road.

GPS Coordinates: 44.2221 N, 71.4780 W

Contact: White Mountain National Forest Headquarters, 71 White Mountain Drive, Campton, NH 03246, 603/536-6100, TDD for hearing impaired 603/536-3665, www.fs.fed.us/r9/white. Appalachian Mountain Club Pinkham Notch Visitor Center, P.O. Box 298, Gorham, NH 03581, 603/466-2721, www.outdoors.org.

33 MOUNT HALE
4.6 mi/2.5 hr 👥4 ▲7

in the White Mountain National Forest southeast of Twin Mountain

This climb to the top of Mount Hale (4,054 ft.) offers a net elevation gain of approximately 2,300 feet. Compared to some of New Hampshire's other 4,000-footers, this might seem gentle, but don't assume this hike is a walk in the park: The Hale Brook Trail is a rugged, relentlessly steep 2.3 miles to the summit, passing cascades along the brook, including rocky sections that grow slick in the wet season. At the rapidly disappearing clearing atop Hale (the former site of a firetower is quickly being reclaimed by forest), you do get some views of the Sugarloafs to the north, the Presidential Range to the northeast, Zealand Notch to the southeast, and North and South Twin to the southwest. One curiosity about Hale is that rocks near its summit are magnetized and will interfere with a magnetic compass.

From the parking lot on Zealand Road, pick up the Hale Brook Trail (marked) heading southwest. Within the first half mile, the trail crosses over a cross-country ski trail and then rises at a steady pace until a crossing with Hale Brook at 0.8 mile. The trail continues to ascend, heading up the steep slope and re-crossing Hale Brook at 1.3 miles. Switchbacks in the trail help to reduce the grade somewhat and at 1.7 miles, another small brook is crossed. The trail heads almost due south before swinging to the right to ascend the wooded summit from

the east. This hike returns by descending the same trail, but another option is to create a loop of eight or nine miles—depending on whether you shuttle two vehicles—by descending on the Lend-a-Hand Trail from Hale's summit for 2.7 miles to the Twinway. Turn left on the Twinway, passing the Appalachian Mountain Club's Zealand Falls hut in 0.1 mile and reaching the Zealand Trail 0.3 mile farther. Turn left (north) on the Zealand Trail and follow its fairly flat course 2.5 miles back to Zealand Road. Unless you've shuttled a second vehicle to the Zealand Trail parking area, walk just over a mile down the road back to the parking area for the Hale Brook Trail.

You can make an enjoyable two-day outing of this loop—a great one for families—with a stay in the Zealand Falls hut. The Appalachian Mountain Club operates the Zealand Falls hut year-round. The Zealand Falls hut is on the Twinway, 0.2 mile from the junction of the Zealand, Twinway, and Ethan Pond Trails and 2.7 miles from the end of Zealand Road.

User Groups: Hikers and dogs. No bikes, horses, or wheelchair facilities.

Permits: No backcountry permit is needed, but a permit is required for day use or overnight parking at any White Mountain National Forest trailhead. Permits are available at several area stores and from the national forest at a cost of $5 for seven consecutive days or $20 per year. A $3 one-day permit can be purchased at self-service stations at national forest trailheads, but the pass is good only for the trailhead at which it's purchased.

Maps: A waterproof area trail map is available from the Appalachian Mountain Club (Franconia–Pemigewasset Range, $9.95). For a topographic area map, request Crawford Notch from the USGS.

Directions: From the junction of U.S. 3 and U.S. 302 in Twin Mountain, drive east on U.S. 302 for 2.3 miles and turn right onto Zealand Road. Continue 2.4 miles to a parking lot on the right. The winter parking lot is on U.S. 302, 0.1 mile east of Zealand Road. Zealand Road is not maintained in winter.

GPS Coordinates: 44.2367 N, 71.4867 W
Contact: White Mountain National Forest Headquarters, 71 White Mountain Drive, Campton, NH 03246, 603/536-6100, TDD for hearing impaired 603/536-3665, www.fs.fed.us/r9/white. Appalachian Mountain Club Pinkham Notch Visitor Center, P.O. Box 298, Gorham, NH 03581, 603/466-2721, www.outdoors.org.

34 ZEALAND NOTCH
7.6 mi/5 hr

in the White Mountain National Forest southeast of Twin Mountain

Partly due to the convenience provided by the Appalachian Mountain Club's Zealand Falls hut, but also simply because of its splendor, Zealand Notch ranks as one of the most-visited spots in the White Mountains year-round. Although the trail tends to be muddy and has a lot of slippery, exposed roots, this is a nice hike in summer and fall—and fairly easy, gaining only about 500 feet in elevation.

From the end of Zealand Road, follow the Zealand Trail south, paralleling the Zealand River. At 2.3 miles, the A-Z Trail diverges left. Continuing on the Zealand Trail, you reach the junction with the Twinway and the Ethan Pond Trail at 2.5 miles. The AMC's Zealand Falls hut lies 0.2 mile to the right on the Twinway (adding 0.4 mile to this hike's distance). This hike continues straight ahead on the Ethan Pond Trail and soon enters the narrow passageway of Zealand Notch. After about a mile, the trail breaks out of the woods and traverses a shelf across the boulder field left behind by an old rockslide; from this perch, the views of Zealand Notch are spectacular. Cross this open area to where the Ethan Pond Trail reenters the woods near the junction with the Zeacliff Trail, 1.3 miles from the Twinway/Zealand Trail junction. Return the way you came.

Special note: For the ambitious or those with more time because they are spending a night at the Zealand Falls hut, hiking all the way to Thoreau Falls would add 1.6 miles round-trip to this hike. Continue on the Ethan Pond Trail beyond the Zeacliff Trail junction for 0.7 mile, then bear right onto the Thoreau Falls Trail. In another 0.1 mile, the trail reaches the top of the falls, which drops more than 100 feet through several steps and creates a very impressive cascade of ice in winter.

The Appalachian Mountain Club operates the Zealand Falls hut year-round. The Zealand Falls hut is on the Twinway, 0.2 mile from the junction of the Zealand, Twinway, and Ethan Pond Trails and 2.7 miles from the end of Zealand Road.

User Groups: Hikers and dogs. No bikes, horses, or wheelchair facilities.

Permits: No backcountry permit is needed, but a permit is required for day use or overnight parking at any White Mountain National Forest trailhead. Permits are available at several area stores and from the national forest at a cost of $5 for seven consecutive days or $20 per year. A $3 one-day permit can be purchased at self-service stations at national forest trailheads, but the pass is good only for the trailhead at which it's purchased.

Maps: A waterproof area trail map is available from the Appalachian Mountain Club (Franconia–Pemigewasset Range, $9.95). For a topographic area map, request Crawford Notch from the USGS.

Directions: From the junction of U.S. 3 and U.S. 302 in Twin Mountain, drive east on U.S. 302 for 2.3 miles and turn right onto Zealand Road. Continue 3.5 miles to a parking lot at the end of the road. The winter parking lot is on U.S. 302, 0.1 mile east of Zealand Road. Zealand Road is not maintained in winter. GPS Coordinates: 44.2221 N, 71.4780 W

Contact: White Mountain National Forest Headquarters, 71 White Mountain Drive, Campton, NH 03246, 603/536-6100, TDD for hearing impaired 603/536-3665, www.fs.fed.us/r9/white. Appalachian Mountain Club Pinkham Notch Visitor Center, P.O.

Box 298, Gorham, NH 03581, 603/466-2721, www.outdoors.org.

35 ZEALAND NOTCH/ TWINS LOOP

16.1 mi one-way/2 days   👣 4   🔺 9

in the White Mountain National Forest south of Twin Mountain

It does require shuttling cars between trailheads, but with superb views, lots of relatively easy terrain, and a reasonable distance to cover in two days, this moderately difficult 16-mile trek is a fairly popular weekend loop for backpackers. Taking you high above Zealand Notch to the summits of Zealand Mountain (4,260 ft.), Mount Guyot (4,580 ft.), South Twin Mountain (4,902 ft.), and North Twin Mountain (4,761 ft.), this hike nets an elevation gain of approximately 3,500 feet; portions of the route coincide with the Appalachian Trail.

From the Zealand Road parking lot, follow the relatively easy Zealand Trail south for 2.5 miles to its junction with the Ethan Pond Trail and the Twinway. Turn right onto the Twinway, which coincides with the white-blazed Appalachian Trail (AT), climbing 0.2 mile to the Appalachian Mountain Club's Zealand Falls hut. Beyond the hut, the AT/Twinway passes nice cascades and the Lend-a-Hand Trail junction and cliimbs high above Zealand Notch. Where the trail takes a right turn at 3.9 miles into this trip, a short side path loops out to the Zeacliff overlook, with a spectacular view of Zealand Notch and mountains—from Carrigain to the south to Mount Washington and the Presidential Range to the northeast.

Just 0.1 mile farther up the AT/Twinway, the Zeacliff Trail departs to the left, descending steeply into the notch. This hike continues along the AT/Twinway, which traverses more level terrain on Zealand Mountain, passing a spur trail to Zeacliff Pond at 4.4 miles. After a short climb above the pond, the trail passes a side path at 5.6 miles that leads right on a flat 0.1-mile spur to the summit of 4,260-foot Zealand Mountain. The AT/Twinway then dips and climbs again to the flat, open summit of Mount Guyot, with views in every direction. Passing over the summit, the AT/ Twinway reaches another junction at 8.1 miles. The AT/Twinway bears right and the Bondcliff Trail diverges left (south); the Guyot campsite, a logical stop for the night, is 0.8 mile away along the Bondcliff Trail. (The 1.6 miles round-trip to the campsite is figured into this hike's total distance.)

Back on the AT/Twinway heading northwest, the trail traverses easy terrain, then climbs more steeply on the final short stretch up South Twin Mountain, 8.9 miles into this trek and, at 4,902 feet, the highest point on this trip and the eighth-highest mountain in New Hampshire. The views span much of the Pemigewasset Wilderness and stretch to the Presidential Range. Turn north off the AT/Twinway onto the North Twin Spur, descending into a saddle, then climbing to the wooded and viewless summit of North Twin Mountain (4,761 ft.), 1.3 miles from South Twin's summit and 10.2 miles into this trek. Turn right onto the North Twin Trail, soon emerging from the trees onto open ledges with one of the best views of the White Mountains on this trip. The trail descends, quite steeply for long stretches, for two miles to the Little River; it then swings left and follows an old railroad bed along the river for more than two miles to the parking area where your second vehicle awaits.

The Appalachian Mountain Club (AMC) operates the Zealand Falls hut year-round; it is on the Twinway, 0.2 mile from the junction of the Zealand, Twinway, and Ethan Pond Trails and 2.7 miles from the end of Zealand Road.

The AMC also operates the first-come, first-served Guyot campsite, with a shelter and several tent platforms, located just off the Bondcliff Trail 0.8 mile from the Twinway on Mount Guyot. A caretaker collects the $8 per person nightly fee late spring–fall.

User Groups: Hikers and dogs. No bikes, horses, or wheelchair facilities.

Permits: No backcountry permit is needed, but a permit is required for day use or overnight parking at any White Mountain National Forest trailhead. Permits are available at several area stores and from the national forest at a cost of $5 for seven consecutive days or $20 per year. A $3 one-day permit can be purchased at self-service stations at national forest trailheads, but the pass is good only for the trailhead at which it's purchased.

Maps: A waterproof area trail map is available from the Appalachian Mountain Club (Franconia–Pemigewasset Range, $9.95). For topographic area maps, request Mount Washington, Bethlehem, South Twin Mountain, and Crawford Notch from the USGS.

Directions: You will need to shuttle two vehicles for this trip. To reach this hike's endpoint from the junction of U.S. 302 and U.S. 3 in Twin Mountain, drive south on U.S. 3 for 2.5 miles and turn left onto Haystack Road (Fire Road 304). Or from I-93 north of Franconia Notch State Park, take Exit 35 for U.S. 3 north and continue about 7.5 miles, then turn right onto Fire Road 304. Follow Fire Road 304 to its end and a parking area at the trailhead. Leave one vehicle there. To reach the start of this hike from the junction of U.S. 3 and U.S. 302 in Twin Mountain, drive east on U.S. 302 for 2.3 miles and turn right onto Zealand Road. Continue 3.5 miles to a parking lot at the end of the road. The AMC-run hiker shuttle bus also provides service in this area and may be able to provide transportation for the return trip.

Zealand Road is not maintained in winter; the winter parking lot is on U.S. 302 immediately east of Zealand Road.

GPS Coordinates: 44.2221 N, 71.4780 W

Contact: White Mountain National Forest Headquarters, 71 White Mountain Drive, Campton, NH 03246, 603/536-6100, TDD for hearing impaired 603/536-3665, www.fs.fed.us/r9/white. Appalachian Mountain Club Pinkham Notch Visitor Center, P.O. Box 298, Gorham, NH 03581, 603/466-2721, www.outdoors.org. For route information and to make reservations for the AMC-run hiker shuttle bus, call 603/466-2727.

36 NORTH TWIN MOUNTAIN
8.6 mi/6 hr 🏃4 ⛰9

in the White Mountain National Forest south of Twin Mountain

Although it is the 12th-highest mountain in New Hampshire at 4,761 feet, North Twin lies sufficiently out of the way and attracts far fewer hikers than nearby Franconia Ridge and Zealand Notch. But the climb is worth it for both the solitude and the scenery. From open ledges just below the summit, nice views are had south to the Pemigewasset Wilderness, east toward the Presidential Range, and west to Franconia. The vertical ascent is about 2,800 feet.

Leaving from the parking area at the end of Fire Road 304, the North Twin Trail heads southeast on an old railroad bed for its first two miles. The trail then turns sharply west (right), crosses the Little River—a daunting ford when the water is high—and makes a steep and sustained ascent of the mountain's east side. A little more than four miles from the trailhead, the trail abruptly breaks from the scrub forest to finally reach the summit ledges. Just a few hundred feet farther lies the true summit, which is wooded. Hike back the same way. For a scenic ridge walk to a summit with somewhat better views, from the top of North Twin, follow the North Twin Spur Trail to the 4,902-foot summit of South Twin Mountain, adding 2.6 miles round-trip to this hike's distance.

User Groups: Hikers and dogs. No bikes, horses, or wheelchair facilities.

Permits: No backcountry permit is needed, but a permit is required for day use or overnight parking at any White Mountain National Forest trailhead. Permits are available

at several area stores and from the national forest at a cost of $5 for seven consecutive days or $20 per year. A $3 one-day permit can be purchased at self-service stations at national forest trailheads, but the pass is good only for the trailhead at which it's purchased.

Maps: A waterproof trail map is available from the Appalachian Mountain Club (Franconia–Pemigewasset Range, $9.95). For topographic area maps, request Bethlehem and South Twin Mountain from the USGS.

Directions: From the junction of U.S. 302 and U.S. 3 in Twin Mountain, drive south on U.S. 3 for 2.5 miles and turn left onto Haystack Road/Fire Road 304, which may be marked only by a faded post reading "USFS 304." Or from I-93 north of Franconia Notch State Park, take Exit 35 for U.S. 3 north and continue about 7.5 miles; then turn right onto Fire Road 304. Follow Fire Road 304 to its end and a parking area at the trailhead for the North Twin Trail.

GPS Coordinates: 44.2394 N, 71.5493 W

Contact: White Mountain National Forest Headquarters, 71 White Mountain Drive, Campton, NH 03246, 603/536-6100, TDD for hearing impaired 603/536-3665, www.fs.fed.us/r9/white.

37 GALEHEAD MOUNTAIN
10.2 mi/5 hr   👫3 ⛰7

in the White Mountain National Forest south of Twin Mountain

Galehead Mountain, despite being an official 4,000-footer, attracts few hikers because trees cover its 4,024-foot summit, blocking any views. There is a good view of the tight valley of Twin Brook and a ridge of South Twin Mountain, however, from an overlook on the Frost Trail halfway between the Galehead hut and the summit. For visitors to the Galehead hut, the summit demands no more than a fairly easy one-mile hike—one that promises an opportunity for some quiet. This

hike's elevation gain is about 2,400 feet; portions of the route coincide with the Appalachian Trail.

From the parking area, follow the Gale River Trail, a wide and relatively flat path, until right before it crosses the north branch of the Gale River—over a wooden footbridge—at about 1.5 miles. For more than a mile beyond that bridge, the trail parallels the river, one of this 10-mile hike's most appealing stretches. It then makes a second river crossing on rocks, which could be difficult in high water. Four miles from the trailhead, the Gale River Trail ends at a junction with the Garfield Ridge Trail, which coincides with the Appalachian Trail (AT). Bear left on the white-blazed AT/Garfield Ridge Trail and follow it another 0.6 mile to its junction with the Twinway. Turn right onto the Twinway for the Galehead hut (the Appalachian Trail also turns to coincide with the Twinway). Behind the hut, pick up the Frost Trail, which leads 0.5 mile to the Galehead's wooded summit; stop about halfway up and take the short side path to the scenic overlook. Descend the same way you came. For a longer hike combining Galehead and Mount Garfield, see the *Mount Garfield* listing in this chapter.

The Appalachian Mountain Club operates the Galehead hut, where a crew prepares meals and guests share bunkrooms and bathrooms. The hut lies at the western end of the trail called the Twinway, about 100 feet from the junction of the Twinway and the Garfield Ridge Trail.

User Groups: Hikers and dogs. No bikes, horses, or wheelchair facilities.

Permits: No backcountry permit is needed, but a permit is required for day use or overnight parking at any White Mountain National Forest trailhead. Permits are available at several area stores and from the national forest at a cost of $5 for seven consecutive days or $20 per year. A $3 one-day permit can be purchased at self-service stations at national forest trailheads, but the pass is good only for the trailhead at which it's purchased.

Maps: A waterproof area trail map is available from the Appalachian Mountain Club (Franconia–Pemigewasset Range, $9.95). For topographic area maps, request South Twin Mountain and Bethlehem from the USGS.

Directions: From I-93 north of Franconia Notch State Park, take Exit 35 for U.S. 3 north. Drive about 4.8 miles and then turn right onto the dirt Fire Road 25 at a sign for the Gale River Trail. Or from the junction of U.S. 3 and U.S. 302 in Twin Mountain, drive south on U.S. 3 for 5.3 miles and turn left on Fire Road 25. Follow Fire Road 25 for 1.3 miles and turn right onto Fire Road 92. Continue 0.3 mile to a parking area on the left for the Gale River Trail.

GPS Coordinates: 44.2347 N, 71.6085 W

Contact: White Mountain National Forest Headquarters, 71 White Mountain Drive, Campton, NH 03246, 603/536-6100, TDD for hearing impaired 603/536-3665, www.fs.fed.us/r9/white. Appalachian Mountain Club Pinkham Notch Visitor Center, P.O. Box 298, Gorham, NH 03581, 603/466-2721, www.outdoors.org.

38 MOUNT GARFIELD
10 mi/5 hr   ₃ ⛰₉

in the White Mountain National Forest south of Twin Mountain

Holding down the northwest corner of the Pemigewasset Wilderness in the White Mountains, the craggy, 4,500-foot summit of Garfield offers views in all directions, taking in Franconia Ridge to the southwest, the wooded mound of Owl's Head directly south, the Bonds and Mount Carrigain to the southeast, the valley of the Ammonoosuc River to the north, and Galehead Mountain, as well as the long ridge comprising North and South Twin Mountains, due east. When weather permits, you will see the peaks of the Presidential Range poking above the Twins. The hike up the Garfield Trail, while fairly

long and gaining nearly 3,000 feet in elevation, never gets very steep or exposed, portions of the route coincide with the Appalachian Trail.

From the parking area, follow the Garfield Trail, which for a short time parallels Spruce Brook on its steady ascent through the woods. The path is wide and obvious. At 4.8 miles, the trail terminates at a junction with the Garfield Ridge Trail, which is part of the white-blazed Appalachian Trail (AT). To the left (east) on the AT/Garfield Ridge Trail, it's 0.2 mile to the spur trail to the Garfield Ridge campsite. The summit lies 0.2 mile to the right (west), where you'll find the foundation of an old fire tower. Descend the same way you came.

Special note: Mount Garfield and Galehead Mountain (see the *Galehead Mountain* listing in this chapter) can be combined on a loop of 13.5 miles, in which they are linked by hiking 2.7 miles along the Garfield Ridge Trail between the Garfield Trail and the Gale River Trail. The best way to do the loop is to begin on the Gale River Trail and descend the Garfield Trail; that way you will ascend, rather than descend, the often slick, steep, and rocky stretch of the Garfield Ridge Trail east of Mount Garfield. The Gale River Trail and Garfield Trail both begin on Fire Road 92, 1.6 miles apart (a distance not figured into the 13.5-mile loop).

The Appalachian Mountain Club operates the Garfield Ridge campsite (a shelter and seven tent platforms), reached via a 200-yard spur trail off the Garfield Ridge Trail, 0.2 mile east of its junction with the Garfield Trail. A caretaker collects the $8 per person nightly fee late spring–fall.

User Groups: Hikers and dogs. No bikes, horses, or wheelchair facilities.

Permits: No backcountry permit is needed, but a permit is required for day use or overnight parking at any White Mountain National Forest trailhead. Permits are available at several area stores and from the national forest at a cost of $5 for seven consecutive days or $20 per year. A $3 one-day permit can be

purchased at self-service stations at national forest trailheads, but the pass is good only for the trailhead at which it's purchased.

Maps: A waterproof area trail map is available from the Appalachian Mountain Club (Franconia–Pemigewasset Range, $9.95). For topographic area maps, request South Twin Mountain and Bethlehem from the USGS.

Directions: From I-93 north of Franconia Notch State Park, take Exit 35 for U.S. 3 north, continue about 4.5 miles, and then turn right on the dirt Fire Road 92. Or from the junction of U.S. 3 and U.S. 302 in Twin Mountain, drive south on U.S. 3 for 5.6 miles and turn left on Fire Road 92. Follow Fire Road 92 for 1.3 miles to a parking area on the right for the Garfield Trail.

GPS Coordinates: 44.2283 N, 71.6342 W

Contact: White Mountain National Forest Headquarters, 71 White Mountain Drive, Campton, NH 03246, 603/536-6100, TDD for hearing impaired 603/536-3665, www.fs.fed.us/r9/white. Appalachian Mountain Club Pinkham Notch Visitor Center, P.O. Box 298, Gorham, NH 03581, 603/466-2721, www.outdoors.org.

39 ETHAN POND/ THOREAU FALLS

10.4 mi/5.5 hr   🏃3 ⛰9

in the White Mountain National Forest between Zealand Notch and Crawford Notch

BEST (

This moderate day hike—much of it following a flat section of the Appalachian Trail—begins at one of New Hampshire's most spectacular notches and takes in a popular backcountry pond and towering waterfall. With a short, easy detour off this route, you can also take in a second notch. The total elevation gained on this hike is about 1,200 feet.

From the parking area in Crawford Notch State Park, follow the white blazes of the Appalachian Trail, which coincides here with the Ethan Pond Trail. After crossing railroad

tracks, the trail begins a steady climb. At 0.2 mile, in a stand of tall birch trees, the trail passes a junction with the Ripley Falls Trail on the left (a worthwhile side trip of 0.2 mile; see the *Ripley Falls* listing in this chapter). At 1.6 miles, a junction is reached with the Willey Range Trail; turn left (west) with the white blazes to stay on the AT/Ethan Pond Trail, which soon flattens out. A mile farther, turn right onto the side path leading about 0.1 mile to scenic Ethan Pond and the Appalachian Mountain Club's Ethan Pond shelter. Back on the AT/Ethan Pond Trail, continue west on flat ground for another 2.5 miles, then turn left onto the Thoreau Falls Trail for the 0.1-mile walk to the waterfall. Hike back along the same route.

The Appalachian Mountain Club operates the Ethan Pond shelter, located just off the Ethan Pond Trail, 2.6 miles from U.S. 302 in Crawford Notch. A caretaker collects the $6 per person nightly fee late spring–fall.

User Groups: Hikers and dogs. No bikes, horses, or wheelchair facilities.

Permits: No backcountry permit is needed, but a permit is required for day use or overnight parking at any White Mountain National Forest trailhead. Permits are available at several area stores and from the national forest at a cost of $5 for seven consecutive days or $20 per year. A $3 one-day permit can be purchased at self-service stations at national forest trailheads, but the pass is good only for the trailhead at which it's purchased.

Maps: Two waterproof area trail maps available from the Appalachian Mountain Club cover this hike (Franconia–Pemigewasset Range map and Crawford Notch–Sandwich Range/ Moosilauke–Kinsman map, $9.95 each). For a topographic area map, request Crawford Notch from the USGS.

Directions: From the Crawford Notch Appalachian Mountain Club Highland Center, continue south on U.S. 302 for approximately 3.9 miles. At a sign for Ripley Falls, turn right onto a paved road. Drive 0.3 mile and park at the end of the road.

NEW HAMPSHIRE

GPS Coordinates: 44.1670 N, 71.3860 W
Contact: White Mountain National Forest Headquarters, 71 White Mountain Drive, Campton, NH 03246, 603/536-6100, TDD for hearing impaired 603/536-3665, www.fs.fed.us/r9/white. Appalachian Mountain Club Pinkham Notch Visitor Center, P.O. Box 298, Gorham, NH 03581, 603/466-2721, www.outdoors.org.

40 MOUNT AVALON
3.6 mi/1.5 hr   👥2 ⛰9

in the White Mountain National Forest and Crawford Notch State Park north of Bartlett and south of Twin Mountain

Named for a rugged hill it was thought to resemble in the Avalon region of Newfoundland, Canada, from various spots on Mount Avalon's 3,442-foot-high summit, you'll get views of the Whites in virtually every direction. A good summit climb for beginners and families, this hike has a moderate 1,400 feet net elevation gain.

From the parking area, cross the railroad tracks behind the visitors center and pick up the Avalon Trail heading southwest. At about 0.2 mile, turn left onto the Cascade Loop Trail, which passes scenic Beecher and Pearl cascades and rejoins the Avalon Trail about a half mile from the parking lot. (The cascades are a worthy destination for an easy hike of a mile; Beecher, an impressive flumelike cascade above a gorge, lies just 0.3 mile from the trailhead and Pearl is a short distance farther.) Turning left to rejoin the Avalon Trail, follow it another 0.8 mile to a junction with the A-Z Trail; bear left, staying on the Avalon, which grows very steep and rocky for the next half mile. Then turn left onto a spur trail that climbs 100 yards to Avalon's craggy summit. Follow the same route back.

User Groups: Hikers and leashed dogs. No bikes, horses, or wheelchair facilities.

Permits: Parking and access are free.

Maps: Two waterproof area trail maps are available from the Appalachian Mountain Club (Franconia–Pemigewasset Range map and the Crawford Notch–Sandwich Range/Moosilauke–Kinsman map, $9.95 each). For a topographic area map, request Crawford Notch from the USGS.

Directions: To reach the Appalachian Mountain Club Highland Center at Crawford Notch, from Twin Mountain, follow U.S. 302 for approximately 10 miles to the Highland Center, located on the right. Ample parking is available.

GPS Coordinates: 44.2178 N, 71.4110 W
Contact: White Mountain National Forest Headquarters, 71 White Mountain Drive, Campton, NH 03246, 603/536-6100, TDD for hearing impaired 603/536-3665, www.fs.fed.us/r9/white.

41 MOUNT WILLARD
2.8 mi/2 hr   👥1 ⛰9

in Crawford Notch State Park north of Bartlett and south of Twin Mountain

BEST (

The view from the cliffs of Mount Willard (2,865 ft.) is widely considered one of the best in the White Mountains for the relatively minor effort—a gradual ascent of less than 900 feet—required to reach it. Nestled at the top of Crawford Notch and not far from the bustling Appalachian Mountain Club Highland Center, scenic Mount Willard is one of the most popular hikes in the region. Come in late September for a bit more solitude and the chance to have a front row seat for a vivid show of fall color. Crawford Notch may be off-the-beaten path for most leaf peepers, but heavy deciduous forest cover along the lower elevations here yields gorgeous autumn foliage.

From the parking area, cross the railroad tracks behind the visitors center and pick up the Avalon Trail. Within 100 yards, turn left onto the Mount Willard Trail, which ascends at a moderate grade. At 1.2 miles, a side path on the left leads 0.2 mile downhill to the Hitchcock Flume, a dramatic gorge worn into the mountainside by erosion. From that trail junction, it's just another 0.2 mile of flat walking on the Mount Willard Trail to Willard's wide summit. Open ledges afford excellent views from high above the notch, with the Webster Cliffs to the east (left) and the Willey Slide directly south (straight ahead). As you take time to explore, look closely at the ground for the unmistakable prints of the snowshoe hare. Like people, these animals flock to Mount Willard's summit. Hike back the same way.

User Groups: Hikers and leashed dogs. No bikes, horses, or wheelchair facilities.

Permits: Parking and access are free.

Maps: Three waterproof area trail maps available from the Appalachian Mountain Club show this hike (Franconia–Pemigewasset Range map, Presidential Range map, and Crawford Notch–Sandwich Range/Moosilauke–Kinsman map, $9.95 each). For a topographic area map, request Crawford Notch from the USGS.

Directions: To reach the Appalachian Mountain Club Highland Center at Crawford Notch, from Twin Mountain, follow U.S. 302 for approximately 10 miles to the Highland Center, located on the right. Ample parking is available.

GPS Coordinates: 44.2178 N, 71.4110 W

Contact: White Mountain National Forest Headquarters, 71 White Mountain Drive, Campton, NH 03246, 603/536-6100, TDD for hearing impaired 603/536-3665, www.fs.fed.us/r9/white.

42 MOUNTS PIERCE AND EISENHOWER
10.8 mi/6 hr   👫4 ⛰10

in the White Mountain National Forest and Crawford Notch State Park

The Crawford Path is reputedly the oldest continuously maintained footpath in the country, dating back to 1819, when Abel Crawford and his son Ethan Allen Crawford cut the first section. It's also the easiest route onto the high ridge of the Presidential Range—the road sits at 2,000 feet, and the trail breaks out above the trees in less than three miles. Once on the ridge, you'll have sweeping views of the Whites; the 4,760-foot Mount Eisenhower itself is one of the more distinctive summits in the southern Presidentials. This can, however, be a difficult trail to follow down in foul weather, particularly when it comes to finding your way back into the woods on Mount Pierce. The vertical ascent is more than 2,700 feet.

From the parking lot, the Crawford Connector spur leads 0.2 mile to the Crawford Path. Less than a half mile up the Crawford Path, watch for a short side trail to Gibbs Falls, a pleasant detour if you have the time. After emerging from the woods nearly three miles from the trailhead, the Crawford Path joins the Webster Cliffs Trail and together the trails head south 0.1 mile to the summit of 4,312-foot Mount Pierce. Turning back down the Crawford Path from Pierce makes a six-mile round-trip. This hike follows the Crawford Path—which from here coincides with the Appalachian Trail—north another two miles to the Eisenhower Loop Trail, then 0.4 mile up the loop trail to the Eisenhower summit, which has excellent views in every direction. To the north rises the Northeast's tallest peak, 6,288-foot Mount Washington. Stretching northwest from Washington are the northern Presidentials. The distinct hump in the ridge between Eisenhower and Washington is Mount Monroe. To the east you can see the Montalban Ridge running south from Washington—which includes Mount Isolation, a rocky high point about midway along the ridge—and beyond the ridge into western Maine. To the southwest are the peaks and valleys of the Pemigewasset Wilderness, with Mount Carrigain tallest among them. And in the distance, more west than south, rises Franconia Ridge, including Mounts Lincoln and Lafayette, as well as Flume and Liberty. Hike back along the same route.

User Groups: Hikers and dogs. No bikes, horses, or wheelchair facilities. This trail should not be attempted in winter except by hikers experienced in mountaineering and prepared for severe winter weather, and is not suitable for skis.

Permits: No backcountry permit is needed, but a permit is required for day use or overnight parking at any White Mountain National Forest trailhead. Permits are available at several area stores and from the national forest at a cost of $5 for seven consecutive days or $20 per year. A $3 one-day permit can be purchased at self-service stations at national forest trailheads, but the pass is good only for the trailhead at which it's purchased.

Maps: A waterproof area trail map showing this hike is available from the Appalachian Mountain Club (Presidential Range, $9.95). For topographic area maps, request Crawford Notch and Stairs Mountain from the USGS.

Directions: From the Appalachian Mountain Club Highland Center on U.S. 302 in Crawford Notch, turn left onto U.S. 302 and drive north for less than 0.1 mile to a right turn for Mount Clinton Road. Follow the road only a short distance to the trailhead parking area.

GPS Coordinates: 44.2200 N, 71.4100 W

Contact: White Mountain National Forest Headquarters, 71 White Mountain Drive, Campton, NH 03246, 603/536-6100, TDD for hearing impaired 603/536-3665, www.fs.fed.us/r9/white. The Appalachian Mountain Club Pinkham Notch Visitor Center has up-to-date weather and trail information about the Whites; call 603/466-2725.

43 ELEPHANT HEAD
0.6 mi/0.5 hr 🏃1 ⛰8

in Crawford Notch State Park

From the north end of Saco Lake in Crawford Notch, gaze south toward the short but prominent cliff at the far end of the pond. The mass of gray rock striped with white quartzite bears an uncanny resemblance to the head and trunk of an elephant. A short, easy hike along the Webster-Jackson Trail takes you to this natural marvel.

Leaving the parking area just south of the Appalachian Mountain Club Highland Center, cross U.S. 302 to the Webster-Jackson Trail (leaving from the east side of the road). The blue-blazed trail quickly enters the woods and after just 0.1 mile, comes to the side path for the Elephant Head Trail. Turn right onto the spur and continue 0.2 mile to the top of the cliff, with fine views over the notch. Return the way you came.

User Groups: Hikers and leashed dogs. No bikes, horses, or wheelchair facilities.

Permits: Parking and access are free.

Maps: Two waterproof area trail maps from the Appalachian Mountain Club cover this hike (Presidential Range map and Franconia–Pemigewasset Range map, $9.95 each). For a topographic area map, request Crawford Notch from the USGS.

Directions: From the Appalachian Mountain Club Highland Center in Crawford Notch, drive south on U.S. 302, 0.3 to the parking turnout on the left.

GPS Coordinates: 44.2151 N, 71.4080 W

Contact: White Mountain National Forest Headquarters, 71 White Mountain Drive, Campton, NH 03246, 603/536-6100, TDD for hearing impaired 603/536-3665, www.fs.fed.us/r9/white.

44 WEBSTER CLIFFS
9.4 mi/5.5 hr 🏃4 ⛰10

in the White Mountain National Forest and
Crawford Notch State Park north of Bartlett
and south of Twin Mountain

This rugged, 9.4-mile hike along a particularly
scenic stretch of the Appalachian Trail (AT) follows the brink of the Webster Cliffs high above
Crawford Notch before eventually reaching the
summits of Mount Webster (3,910 ft.) and the
show stopping Mount Jackson (4,052 ft.), an
open summit with fine views in every direction.
The elevation gain is about 2,700 feet.

From the parking area, cross U.S. 302 to
find a sign for the Appalachian Trail/Webster
Cliffs Trail. The white-blazed trail ascends
steadily with good footing at first, then grows
steeper and rockier. The first good view comes
within two miles, from a wide, flat ledge overlooking the notch and White Mountains to
the south and west.

For a round-trip hike of just four miles,
this ledge makes a worthwhile destination.
But from there, you can see the next open
ledge, just 0.2 mile farther and a little higher
along the ridge, beckoning you onward. The
trail continues past several outlooks along
the cliffs with sweeping views of the Whites,
including the Willey Range across Crawford
Notch and Mount Chocorua, the prominent
horned peak to the southeast. At 3.3 miles, the
AT passes over Mount Webster's 3,910-foot
partly wooded but craggy summit, with excellent views of the notch and mountains from
Chocorua to Mount Carrigain and the Saco
River Valley. Descending slightly off Webster, the trail crosses relatively flat and boggy
terrain, then slabs up to the open summit of
Jackson, 4.7 miles from the trailhead. Head
back the same way.

User Groups: Hikers and dogs. No bikes, horses, or wheelchair facilities. This trail should
not be attempted in winter except by hikers
experienced in mountaineering and prepared
for severe winter weather.

Permits: Parking and access are free.
Maps: Three waterproof area trail maps from
the Appalachian Mountain Club cover this
hike (Franconia–Pemigewasset Range map,
Presidential Range map, and the Crawford
Notch–Sandwich Range/Moosilauke–Kinsman map, $9.95 each). For a topographic
area map, request Crawford Notch from the
USGS.
Directions: From the Crawford Notch Appalachian Mountain Club Highland Center,
continue south on U.S. 302 for approximately
3.9 miles. At a sign for Ripley Falls, turn right
onto a paved road. Drive 0.3 mile and park at
the end of the road.
GPS Coordinates: 44.1670 N, 71.3860 W
Contact: White Mountain National Forest
Headquarters, 71 White Mountain Drive,
Campton, NH 03246, 603/536-6100, TDD
for hearing impaired 603/536-3665, www.
fs.fed.us/r9/white. New Hampshire Division
of Parks and Recreation, Bureau of Trails,
P.O. Box 1856, Concord, NH 03302-1856,
603/271-3254.

45 MOUNT ISOLATION TRAVERSE
20 mi one-way/2 days 🏃4 ⛰9

in the White Mountain National Forest north of
Jackson and east of Crawford Notch State Park

In the heart of the Dry River Wilderness,
south of Mount Washington, Mount Isolation's baldpate lies too far from any road for
most day hikers—which translates into a true
sense of isolation. If you have the urge to get
away from it all, but with a rugged backpack
trek to a scenic 4,000-footer that requires shuttling cars between trailheads, this two-day traverse could be for you. The total elevation gain
to Isolation's summit is about 3,000 feet.

From the parking area off Route 16, follow
the Rocky Branch Trail west for 3.7 miles to
the Rocky Branch, an aptly named tributary
of the Saco River. Cross the stream and turn

NEW HAMPSHIRE

right (north) on the Isolation Trail, passing a shelter and eventually swinging west in a climb onto the Montalban Ridge. Approximately 2.6 miles out from the Rocky Branch, the trail comes to a junction with the Davis Path. Turn left (south) on the Davis Path and find a place to camp that is well off the trail. Leave your backpack behind for the one-mile hike south on the Davis Path to the short but steep spur trail to Mount Isolation's barren summit (4,005 ft.). You'll have terrific views west and north to the southern Presidentials and Mount Washington, and to the southwest and south of the sprawling Whites. Return to your campsite.

On day two, hike north 0.3 mile on the Davis Path to where the Isolation Trail turns west (left) toward the valley of the Dry River; be careful, because this trail junction is easily overlooked. In about 2.5 miles, turn left (south) on the Dry River Trail, paralleling the broad, boulder-choked river and crossing countless mountain brooks feeding into it. When the trees are bare, you get some fine views of Mount Washington directly upriver. It's nearly five miles from the Isolation Trail junction to U.S. 302.

There is a lean-to shelter (Rocky Branch shelter 2) at the junction of the Rocky Branch Trail and Isolation Trail that is slated to be dismantled as soon as it needs major maintenance.

User Groups: Hikers and dogs. No bikes, horses, or wheelchair facilities. This trail should not be attempted in winter except by hikers experienced in mountaineering and prepared for severe winter weather.

Permits: No backcountry permit is needed, but a permit is required for day use or overnight parking at any White Mountain National Forest trailhead. Permits are available at several area stores and from the national forest at a cost of $5 for seven consecutive days or $20 per year. A $3 one-day permit can be purchased at self-service stations at national forest trailheads, but the pass is good only for the trailhead at which it's purchased.

Maps: A waterproof area trail map is available from the Appalachian Mountain Club (Presidential Range, $9.95). For topographic area maps, request Jackson and Stairs Mountain from the USGS.

Directions: You will need to shuttle two vehicles. Leave one at the roadside turnout at the Dry River Trailhead on U.S. 302, 0.3 mile north of the Dry River Campground and 4.5 miles south of the Appalachian Mountain Club Highland Center in Crawford Notch. Then drive south on U.S. 302 to Glen, turn left onto Route 16 north, and drive 8.1 miles to a large parking lot on the left for the Rocky Branch Trail.

GPS Coordinates: 44.2038 N, 71.2408 W

Contact: White Mountain National Forest Headquarters, 71 White Mountain Drive, Campton, NH 03246, 603/536-6100, TDD for hearing impaired 603/536-3665, www.fs.fed.us/r9/white. The Appalachian Mountain Club Pinkham Notch Visitor Center has up-to-date weather and trail information about the Whites; call 603/466-2725.

46 THE BALDIES LOOP

9.7 mi/7 hr   🏃5 ⛰10

in the White Mountain National Forest near North Chatham

BEST (

As their names suggest, the pair of 3,500-foot peaks called the Baldies mimic higher mountains with their craggy summits, four miles of open ridge, and some of the best views east of Mount Washington. This rugged hike is not to be underestimated. Besides its length of almost 10 miles and some 3,300 feet of vertical ascent, it climbs steep exposed ledges on the way up South Baldface that may make some hikers uncomfortable. The Baldies can also attract harsh conditions—winds encountered here are often strong enough to make standing difficult. Although it's probably the most popular hike in the Evans Notch area, this loop still sees less boot traffic than other parts of the Whites.

From the parking area, walk 50 yards north on Route 113 and cross the road to the start of the Baldface Circle Trail. It's a wide, easy trail for 0.7 mile to Circle Junction, where a side trail leads right 0.1 mile to Emerald Pool, a highly worthwhile detour that adds 0.2 mile to this hike (see the *Emerald Pool* listing in this chapter). From Circle Junction, this hike bears left at a sign for South Baldface and, climbing steadily, the trail reaches the South Baldface shelter 2.5 miles from the road. Beyond the lean-to, the trail hits all the prominent ledges visible from the road and for nearly a half mile winds up them, requiring steep scrambling. A bit more than three miles from the road, the trail reaches the level shoulder of South Baldface, where the Baldface Knob Trail leads left (south) to Baldface Knob and Eastman Mountain. Stay on the Circle Trail; from here, you'll get your first view into the broad glacial cirque, or ravine, bounded by North and South Baldface and the Bicknell Ridge. The Circle Trail then continues a half mile west—and 500 feet up—to the 3,569-foot summit of South Baldface. The summit views extend to much of the White Mountains to the west and south, including Mounts Washington, Carrigain, and Chocorua. To the north rise the Mahoosuc Range and a long chain of mountains reaching far into Maine. To the east lies a landscape of lakes and low hills, most prominently the long, low ridge of Pleasant Mountain.

Continue northwest on the Circle Trail another 1.2 miles, dropping into the woods and then ascending to the 3,591-foot summit of North Baldface, where the views are equally awesome. Descend north off North Baldy via the Circle Trail, and continue nearly a mile to the signed junction with the Bicknell Ridge Trail. Turn right (east) on Bicknell, a scenic alternative to completing the Circle Trail loop. The Bicknell descends an open ridge for about a mile before entering the forest and reaching its lower junction with the Circle Trail

in 2.5 miles, at a stream crossing. Follow the Circle Trail another 0.7 mile to Circle Junction. Turn left and the trail returns 0.7 mile back to the road.

User Groups: Hikers and dogs. No bikes, horses, or wheelchair facilities.

Permits: No backcountry permit is needed, but a permit is required for day use or overnight parking at any White Mountain National Forest trailhead. Permits are available at several area stores and from the national forest at a cost of $5 for seven consecutive days or $20 per year. A $3 one-day permit can be purchased at self-service stations at national forest trailheads, but the pass is good only for the trailhead at which it's purchased.

Maps: A trail map is available from the Chatham Trails Association (Map of Cold River Valley and Evans Notch, $6). This hike is also covered on a waterproof area trail map available from the Appalachian Mountain Club (Carter Range–Evans Notch/North Country–Mahoosuc, $9.95). For a topographic area map, request Chatham from the USGS.

Directions: The trail begins near a large parking lot on the east side of Route 113, 2.7 miles north of the northern junction of Routes 113 and 113B in North Chatham.

GPS Coordinates: 44.2385 N, 71.0169 W

Contact: White Mountain National Forest Headquarters, 71 White Mountain Drive, Campton, NH 03246, 603/536-6100, TDD for hearing impaired 603/536-3665, www. fs.fed.us/r9/white. Chatham Trails Association, P.O. Box 605, Center Conway, NH 03813, http://chathamtrails.org.

47 EMERALD POOL
1.6 mi/1 hr   🏃1 ⛰9

in the White Mountain National Forest near North Chatham

The aptly named and gorgeous Emerald Pool is a deep hole of verdant water just below the narrow gorge and falls along Charles Brook.

It's a flat, easy walk to the pool, making this a good hike for young children.

From the parking area, walk 50 yards north on Route 113 and cross the road to the start of the Baldface Circle Trail. Follow the wide, easy trail for 0.7 mile to Circle Junction, where a side trail leads right 0.1 mile to Emerald Pool. As pretty as it is to look at, it's even better to take a dip in the inviting water, a popular local swimming hole in the summer months. Return the same way.

User Groups: Hikers and dogs. No bikes, horses, or wheelchair facilities.

Permits: No backcountry permit is needed, but a permit is required for day use or overnight parking at any White Mountain National Forest trailhead. Permits are available at several area stores and from the national forest at a cost of $5 for seven consecutive days or $20 per year. A $3 one-day permit can be purchased at self-service stations at national forest trailheads, but the permit is good only for the trailhead at which it's purchased.

Maps: A trail map is available from the Chatham Trails Association (Map of Cold River Valley and Evans Notch, $6). A waterproof area trail map showing this hike is available from the Appalachian Mountain Club (Carter Range–Evans Notch/North Country–Mahoosuc, $9.95). For a topographic area map, request Chatham from the USGS.

Directions: The trail begins near a large parking lot on the east side of Route 113, 2.7 miles north of the northern junction of Routes 113 and 113B in North Chatham. GPS Coordinates: 44.2385 N, 71.0169 W

Contact: White Mountain National Forest Headquarters, 71 White Mountain Drive, Campton, NH 03246, 603/536-6100, TDD for hearing impaired 603/536-3665, www. fs.fed.us/r9/white. Chatham Trails Association, P.O. Box 605, Center Conway, NH 03813, http://chathamtrails.org.

48 MOUNT LAFAYETTE: SKOOKUMCHUCK TRAIL
10 mi/6 hr 4 10

in the White Mountain National Forest north of Franconia Notch State Park

Compared to other routes up popular Mount Lafayette (5,260 ft.), the Skookumchuck is less traveled, a bit longer than some, and ascends more gradually. Still, it's 10 miles round-trip, and you will gain more than 3,500 feet in elevation. Views from the top of the Lafayette summit, part of the Franconia Ridge, make the long trek worth it. At the summit you are rewarded with a panorama spanning the peaks and valleys of the Pemigewasset Wilderness all the way to the Presidential Range, Vermont's Green Mountains, and, on a very clear day, New York's Adirondacks. This trail offers a nice winter outing on snowshoes, but turn around before reaching the Garfield Ridge Trail if you're not prepared for severe cold and wind. This is also a great hike for seeing woodland wildflowers in May.

From the parking lot, pick up the Skookumchuck Trail, which is sporadically marked with blue blazes (the trail corridor is fairly obvious). It contours southward around the west slope of a hill called Big Bickford Mountain, crossing an overgrown logging road a few times. Upon reaching Skookumchuck Brook at a little over a mile (Skookumchuck means "rapid water" in some Native American dialects), the trail turns east to climb steadily along the brook for more than a half mile. It then leaves the brook at 1.8 miles and begins to ascend a steep mountainside, passing through beautiful birch forest. Ascending into subalpine forest, you get your first views through the trees of the upper slopes of Lafayette. Shortly after breaking out of the forest, the Skookumchuck terminates at the Garfield Ridge Trail at 4.3 miles. Turn right (south) and follow the Garfield Ridge Trail another 0.7 mile along the exposed ridge to the summit of Lafayette. Return the way you came.

User Groups: Hikers and dogs. No bikes, horses, or wheelchair facilities. This trail should not be attempted in winter except by hikers experienced in mountaineering and prepared for severe winter weather.

Permits: No backcountry permit is needed, but a permit is required for day use or overnight parking at any White Mountain National Forest trailhead. Permits are available at several area stores and from the national forest at a cost of $5 for seven consecutive days or $20 per year. A $3 one-day permit can be purchased at self-service stations at national forest trailheads, but the pass is good only for the trailhead at which it's purchased.

Maps: Two waterproof area trail maps available from the Appalachian Mountain Club show this hike (Franconia–Pemigewasset Range map and Crawford Notch–Sandwich Range/Moosilauke–Kinsman map, $9.95 each). For a topographic area map, request Franconia from the USGS.

Directions: In Franconia Notch, the Skookumchuck Trail begins at a parking lot on U.S. 3, about 0.6 mile north of Exit 35 off I-93. GPS Coordinates: 44.1944 N, 71.6807 W

Contact: White Mountain National Forest Headquarters, 71 White Mountain Drive, Campton, NH 03246, 603/536-6100, TDD for hearing impaired 603/536-3665, www.fs.fed.us/r9/white.

49 CANNON MOUNTAIN: KINSMAN RIDGE TRAIL

4.4 mi/3 hr   🏃3 ⛰7

in Franconia Notch State Park north of Lincoln and south of Franconia

Cannon Mountain (4,077 ft.) stands out at the north end of spectacular Franconia Notch because of the 1,000-foot cliff on its east face. That cliff was once the home of the Old Man of the Mountain, the famous stone profile that suddenly gave way to gravity in 2003. The "Great Stone Face" may be gone from the mountain, but this moderate hike of 4.4 miles round-trip, climbing 2,100 feet in elevation, still leads to the excellent views from Cannon's scenic summit.

From the tramway parking lot, follow the Kinsman Ridge Trail through a picnic area and briefly along a ski area trail before entering the woods. The trail ascends at a moderate grade, passing a short side path at 1.5 miles that leads to open ledges and a nice view across the notch to Franconia Ridge. The Kinsman Ridge Trail swings right, soon climbing more steeply to the summit, where there is an observation platform and the summit tramway station. To the east, the views extend to Mounts Lafayette and Lincoln. To the west, you can see Vermont's Green Mountains and New York's Adirondacks on a clear day. Head back along the same route.

User Groups: Hikers and leashed dogs. No bikes, horses, or wheelchair facilities. This trail should not be attempted in winter except by hikers prepared for severe winter weather, and is not suitable for skis.

Permits: Parking and access are free.

Maps: Two waterproof area trail maps available from the Appalachian Mountain Club show this hike (Franconia–Pemigewasset Range map and Crawford Notch–Sandwich Range/Moosilauke–Kinsman map, $9.95 each). For a topographic area map, request Franconia from the USGS.

Directions: From Lincoln, follow I-93 north for about 10 miles to Franconia Notch. The hike begins from the tramway parking lot at Exit 34B off I-93, at the north end of the notch. Look for a sign for the Kinsman Ridge Trail.

GPS Coordinates: 44.1684 N, 71.6861 W

Contact: White Mountain National Forest Headquarters, 71 White Mountain Drive, Campton, NH 03246, 603/536-6100, TDD for hearing impaired 603/536-3665, www.fs.fed.us/r9/white. Franconia Notch State Park, Franconia, NH 03580, 603/745-8391, www.franconianotchstatepark.com.

NEW HAMPSHIRE

50 CANNON MOUNTAIN: HI-CANNON TRAIL
5.6 mi/3.5 hr   👣4 ⛰9

in Franconia Notch State Park north of Lincoln
and south of Franconia

The most rigorous trail on Cannon Mountain (4,077 ft.), the Hi-Cannon's route is so steep in sections that hikers are required to climb a 15-foot tall ladder just to stay on trail. A net climb of 2,300 feet, the views from open ledges along the way and the panoramic tableau that awaits at Canonn's summit make this calf burner worth the effort.

From the Lafayette Campground parking lot, pick up the Lonesome Lake Trail at the trail marker and follow it through the campground, ascending steadily toward Lonesome Lake. At 0.4 mile, turn right onto the Hi-Cannon Trail (look for the trail marker at the well-defined trail junction). Hi-Cannon at first climbs steadily through a series of switchbacks, but at 1.2 miles from the campground, the trail suddenly becomes increasingly vertical and rugged on its way up a ridge. Pass a fine overlook with views towards Franconia Notch at 1.6 miles and, a few yards later, climb up a ladder to negotiate a cliff-like rock slab. Tall hikers and those carrying tall frame packs should be mindful of a rock overhang hovering overhead at the top of the ladder. Continuing on, still on rocky, somewhat open terrain, at 2.4 miles from the campground, turn right on the Kinsman Ridge Trail and follow it 0.4 mile to Cannon's summit, with good views in every direction, most spectacularly toward Franconia Ridge (see the *Cannon Mountain: Kinsman Ridge Trail* listing in this chapter for more information). Return the way you came.

User Groups: Hikers and leashed dogs. No bikes, horses, or wheelchair facilities. This trail should not be attempted in winter and is not suitable for skis.

Permits: Parking and access are free.

Maps: Two waterproof trail maps showing this hike are available from the Appalachian Mountain Club (Franconia–Pemigewasset Range map and Crawford Notch–Sandwich Range/Moosilauke–Kinsman map, $9.95 each). For a topographic area map, request Franconia from the USGS Map.

Directions: From Lincoln, follow I-93 north for approximately 10 miles to enter Franconia Notch. At signs for the Lafayette Place Campground, park in one of the large parking lots on the east side of I-93 (for southbound vehicles, another parking lot is on the west side of the highway). From the east side parking lot, hikers can cross under the highway to the Lafayette Place Campground on the west side, where the trail begins.

GPS Coordinates: 44.1419 N, 71.6860 W

Contact: Franconia Notch State Park, Franconia, NH 03580, 603/745-8391, www.franconianotchstatepark.com. White Mountain National Forest Headquarters, 71 White Mountain Drive, Campton, NH 03246, 603/536-6100, TDD for hearing impaired 603/536-3665, www.fs.fed.us/r9/white.

51 LONESOME LAKE
3.2 mi/2 hr   👣2 ⛰10

in Franconia Notch State Park north of Lincoln
and south of Franconia

Lonesome Lake's name gives a newcomer to Franconia Notch no forewarning of the crowds that flock to this scenic mountain tarn. Nonetheless, if you accept the likelihood of sharing this beautiful spot with dozens of other visitors, the view from the lake's southwest corner across its crystal waters to Mounts Lafayette and Lincoln on Franconia Ridge has no comparison. The trail to Lonesome Lake passes through extensive boggy areas, which, combined with heavy foot traffic, can make for a muddy hike. It ascends about 1,000 feet in elevation.

From the parking lot, pick up the Lonesome Lake Trail, which crosses Lafayette Place Campground and ascends at a moderate grade for 1.2 miles to the northeast corner of the lake. Turn left (south) on the Cascade Brook Trail, following it nearly 0.3 mile to the south end of the lake. Turn right on the Fishin' Jimmy Trail, crossing the lake's outlet and reaching a small beach area where people often swim. The Appalachian Mountain Club hut lies a short distance off the lake, in the woods. Bear right off the Fishin' Jimmy Trail onto the Around-Lonesome-Lake Trail, which heads north along the lake's west shore, crossing boggy areas on boardwalks. In 0.3 mile, turn right (east) on the Lonesome Lake Trail and follow it 1.4 miles back to the campground.

The Appalachian Mountain Club (AMC) operates the Lonesome Lake hut on the Fishin' Jimmy Trail near Lonesome Lake; contact the AMC for reservation and rate information.

User Groups: Hikers and leashed dogs. No bikes, horses, or wheelchair facilities.

Permits: Parking and access are free.

Maps: Two waterproof area trail maps available from the Appalachian Mountain Club show this hike (Franconia–Pemigewasset Range map and Crawford Notch–Sandwich Range/Moosilauke–Kinsman map, $9.95 each). For a topographic area map, request Franconia from the USGS.

Directions: From Lincoln, follow I-93 north for approximately 10 miles to reach Franconia Notch. At signs for the Lafayette Place Campground, park in one of the large parking lots on the east side of I-93 (for southbound vehicles, another parking lot is on the west side of the highway). From the east side parking lot, hikers can cross under the highway to the Lafayette Place Campground on the west side, where the trail begins.

GPS Coordinates: 44.1419 N, 71.6860 W

Contact: White Mountain National Forest Headquarters, 71 White Mountain Drive, Campton, NH 03246, 603/536-6100, TDD for hearing impaired 603/536-3665, www.fs.fed.us/r9/white. Franconia Notch State Park, Franconia, NH 03580, 603/745-8391, www.franconianotchstatepark.com. Appalachian Mountain Club Pinkham Notch Visitor Center, P.O. Box 298, Gorham, NH 03581, 603/466-2721, www.outdoors.org.

52 NORTH AND SOUTH KINSMAN

11.1 mi/8 hr 🏃4 ⛰9

in the White Mountain National Forest and Franconia Notch State Park north of Lincoln and south of Franconia

Rising high above Franconia Notch, opposite the 5,000-foot peaks of Lafayette and Lincoln, Kinsman Mountain's two distinct peaks offer good views of the notch. But the more popular attractions on this 11.1-mile hike are the 1.5 miles of falls and cascades along Cascade Brook and the views across Lonesome Lake to Franconia Ridge. Many hikers, especially families with young children, explore only as far as the brook—a refreshing place on a hot summer day. Most of the stream crossings on this hike utilize rocks or downed trees, and can be difficult at times of high water. Also, heavily used trails in the area are often wet and muddy, making rocks and exposed roots slick and footing difficult. This hike ascends about 2,500 feet in elevation; portions of the route coincide with the Appalachian Trail.

You can begin this hike on either side of I-93. From the parking lot on the northbound side of I-93, follow the signs to the Basin, passing beneath I-93 and crossing a footbridge over the Pemigewasset River. Beyond the bridge, the trail bends right; within 100 feet, bear left at a sign for the Basin-Cascades Trail. From the parking lot on the southbound side, follow the walkway south to the Basin. Turn right on the bridge over the Pemigewasset and watch for the Basin-Cascades Trail branching left. Hikers from either parking lot will converge at this trailhead near the Basin, a natural stone bowl carved out by the Pemigewasset River and a popular spot for tourists. Follow the Basin-Cascades Trail just 0.1 mile before the Basin-Cascades Trail meets the Cascade Brook Trail.

From this junction to the summit of 4,356-foot South Kinsman, the hike coincides with the white-blazed Appalachian Trail (AT). Turn right (northwest) on the AT/Cascade Brook Trail, immediately crossing the brook on stones or a downed tree. A half mile farther, the Kinsman Pond Trail bears left and crosses Cascade Brook; however, you should bear right and continue roughly north on the AT/Cascade Brook Trail another mile to a junction with the Fishin' Jimmy Trail at the south end of Lonesome Lake. Turn left (west) with the AT onto the Fishin' Jimmy Trail, crossing a log bridge over the lake's outlet to a beachlike area popular for swimming. There's an outstanding view across Lonesome Lake to Franconia Ridge and Mounts Lafayette and Lincoln and Little Haystack (from left to right). Stay on the AT/Fishin' Jimmy Trail, passing the Appalachian Mountain Club's Lonesome Lake hut, which sits back in the woods just above the beach area. The trail rises and falls, passing over the hump separating Lonesome Lake from the upper flanks of Kinsman Mountain. After crossing a feeder stream to Cascade Brook, the trail ascends steeply, often up rock slabs into which wooden steps have been drilled in places. Two miles from Lonesome Lake, the Fishin' Jimmy Trail terminates at Kinsman Junction.

From the junction, follow the AT straight (west) onto the Kinsman Ridge Trail, climbing steep rock. Reach the wooded summit of 4,293-foot North Kinsman 0.4 mile from the junction; a side path leads 20 feet from the summit cairn to an open ledge with a sweeping view eastward. Continue south on the AT/Kinsman Ridge Trail, descending past two open areas with good views. The trail drops into the saddle between the two peaks, then ascends steadily to the broad, flat summit of South Kinsman, nearly a mile from North Kinsman's summit. From various spots on South Kinsman's summit, you have views toward Franconia Ridge, North Kinsman, and Moosilauke to the south.

Backtrack to North Kinsman and descend to Kinsman Junction. Turn right (south) on the Kinsman Pond Trail, reaching the Appalachian Mountain Club shelter at Kinsman Pond in 0.1 mile. The trail follows the eastern shore of this scenic mountain tarn, below the summit cone of North Kinsman. It then hooks southeast into the forest, leading steadily downhill and making four stream crossings; this stretch of trail may be poorly marked, wet, and difficult to follow. It reaches the AT/Cascade Brook Trail 2.5 miles from Kinsman Junction, right after crossing Cascade Brook. Bear right (southeast) onto the AT/Cascade Brook Trail, following it a half mile. Immediately after crossing Cascade Brook again, turn left onto the Basin-Cascades Trail, which leads a mile back to the Basin.

The Appalachian Mountain Club (AMC) operates the Kinsman Pond campsite, with a shelter and three tent platforms, located along the Kinsman Pond Trail, 0.1 mile from Kinsman Junction and 4.5 miles from the Basin. A caretaker collects the $8 per person nightly fee during the warmer months. The AMC also operates the Lonesome Lake hut, where a crew prepares meals and guests share bunkrooms and bathrooms; contact the AMC for reservation and rate information.

User Groups: Hikers and dogs. No bikes, horses, or wheelchair facilities. This trail should not be attempted in winter except by hikers experienced in mountaineering and prepared for severe winter weather.

Permits: Parking and access are free.

Maps: Two waterproof area trail maps available from the Appalachian Mountain Club show this hike (Franconia–Pemigewasset Range map and Crawford Notch–Sandwich Range/Moosilauke–Kinsman map, $9.95 each). For topographic area maps, request Franconia and Lincoln from the USGS.

Directions: From Lincoln, follow I-93 north for 10 miles into Franconia Notch; take the exit at the sign for the Basin. Park in one of the large parking lots on the east side of I-93 (for southbound vehicles, another parking lot is on the west side of the highway). From the east side parking lot, hikers can cross under the highway to the west side, where the trail begins. This hike begins in Franconia Notch State Park, but much of it lies within the White Mountain National Forest.

GPS Coordinates: 44.1199 N, 71.6826 W

Contact: White Mountain National Forest Headquarters, 71 White Mountain Drive, Campton, NH 03246, 603/536-6100, TDD for hearing impaired 603/536-3665, www.fs.fed.us/r9/white. Franconia Notch State Park, Franconia, NH 03580, 603/745-8391, www.franconianotchstatepark.com. Appalachian Mountain Club Pinkham Notch Visitor Center, P.O. Box 298, Gorham, NH 03581, 603/466-2721, www.outdoors.org.

53 FRANCONIA NOTCH: PEMI TRAIL

5.5 mi one-way/2.5 hr   👫2 ⛰8

in Franconia Notch State Park north of Lincoln and south of Franconia

The Pemi Trail offers an easy and scenic 5.5-mile, one-way walk (a shuttling of cars is suggested) through Franconia Notch, with periodic views of the cliffs and peaks flanking the notch.

From the parking area, the trail follows the west shore of Profile Lake, with excellent views across the water to Eagle Cliff on Mount Lafayette. When the light is right, you can distinguish a free-standing rock pinnacle in a gully separating two major cliffs on this shoulder of Lafayette. Known as the Eaglet, this pinnacle is a destination for rock climbers and has been a nesting site in spring for peregrine falcons, which you might see flying around in spring. After crossing the paved bike path through the notch just south of Profile Lake and a second time just north of Lafayette Place Campground, the Pemi Trail follows a campground road along the west bank of the Pemigewasset River, then

leaves the campground and parallels the river all the way to the water-sculpted rock at the Basin. It crosses the Basin-Cascades Trail, meets the Cascade Brook Trail, crosses east beneath I-93, and finishes at the parking lot immediately north of the Flume. Return the way you came or find the second car you left earlier waiting in the lot.

User Groups: Hikers and leashed dogs. No bikes, horses, or wheelchair facilities.

Permits: Parking and access are free.

Maps: Obtain the free map of Franconia Notch State Park, available at the state park or from the New Hampshire Division of Parks and Recreation. Two waterproof area trail maps available from the Appalachian Mountain Club show this hike (Franconia–Pemigewasset Range map and Crawford Notch–Sandwich Range/Moosilauke–Kinsman map, $9.95 each). For topographic area maps, request Franconia and Lincoln from the USGS.

Directions: This one-way trail requires a shuttling of cars. From Lincoln, follow I-93 north for about 10 miles to Franconia Notch. Leave one car at the parking area off I-93, immediately north of the Flume (the end of the Pemi Trail). The hike begins from the tramway parking lot at Exit 34B off I-93, at the northern end of the notch.

GPS Coordinates: 44.1003 N, 71.6827 W

Contact: Franconia Notch State Park, Franconia, NH 03580, 603/745-8391, www.franconianotchstatepark.com.

54 MOUNT LAFAYETTE: OLD BRIDLE PATH

8 mi/6 hr   👫5 ⛰10

in the White Mountain National Forest and Franconia Notch State Park north of Lincoln and south of Franconia

This eight-mile hike provides the most direct and popular route to the 5,260-foot summit of Mount Lafayette, the sixth-highest peak in the White Mountains. The elevation gain is about 3,500 feet, ranking this hike among the most difficult in New England, though it does not present the exposure of hikes like Mount Washington's Huntington Ravine. It is also a fairly well-traveled route in winter, often with a packed snow trough that makes footing a bit easier. The Appalachian Mountain Club's Greenleaf hut offers a scenic location for making this hike a two-day trip and a way to catch the sunset high up the mountain. (See the *Mounts Lincoln and Lafayette* listing in this chapter for more description of the views from the Old Bridle Path, Greenleaf Trail, and Lafayette's summit.)

From the parking lot on the east side of I-93, follow the Falling Waters Trail and Old Bridle Path for 0.2 mile. Where the Falling Waters Trail turns sharply right, continue straight ahead on the Old Bridle Path. It climbs fairly easily at first through mostly deciduous forest, then grows steeper as it ascends the prominent west ridge of Lafayette. Once on the crest of that ridge, you'll get great views from a few open ledges of the summits of Lafayette to the left and Mount Lincoln (5,089 ft.) to the right of Lafayette. At 2.9 miles from the trailhead, the Old Bridle Path terminates at the Greenleaf Trail and Greenleaf hut. From there, follow the Greenleaf Trail as it dips down into a shallow basin, passes through subalpine forest, and soon emerges onto the rocky, open west slope of Lafayette, climbing another 1.1 miles and 1,000 feet in elevation to Lafayette's summit. The views from the summit take in most of the White Mountains and the North Country as well as Vermont's Green Mountains to the west. Return the way you came.

The Appalachian Mountain Club (AMC) operates the Greenleaf hut at the junction of the Greenleaf Trail and Old Bridle Path; contact the AMC for reservation and rate information.

User Groups: Hikers and leashed dogs. No bikes, horses, or wheelchair facilities. This trail should not be attempted in winter except by hikers experienced in mountaineering and prepared for severe winter weather.

Permits: Parking and access are free.

Maps: Two waterproof area trail maps available from the Appalachian Mountain Club show this hike (Franconia–Pemigewasset Range map and Crawford Notch–Sandwich Range/Moosilauke–Kinsman map, $9.95 each). For a topographic area map, request Franconia from the USGS.

Directions: From Lincoln, follow I-93 north for approximately 10 miles to reach Franconia Notch. At the signs for the Lafayette Place Campground, park in the large parking lot on the east side of I-93, where the trail begins. For southbound vehicles, another parking lot is located on the west side of the highway. From the west side parking lot, hikers can walk under the highway to the east lot and trailhead.

GPS Coordinates: 44.1411 N, 71.6818 W

Contact: White Mountain National Forest Headquarters, 71 White Mountain Drive, Campton, NH 03246, 603/536-6100, TDD for hearing impaired 603/536-3665, www.fs.fed.us/r9/white. Franconia Notch State Park, Franconia, NH 03580, 603/745-8391, www.franconianotchstatepark.com. Appalachian Mountain Club Pinkham Notch Visitor Center, P.O. Box 298, Gorham, NH 03581, 603/466-2721, www.outdoors.org.

55 MOUNTS LINCOLN AND LAFAYETTE
8.8 mi/6.5 hr   🏃5 ⛰10

in the White Mountain National Forest and Franconia Notch State Park north of Lincoln and south of Franconia

BEST (

For many New England hikers, this 8.8-mile loop over the sixth- and seventh-highest peaks in New Hampshire becomes a favorite hike revisited many times over the years. With nearly two miles of continuous, exposed ridgeline high above the forest connecting Mounts Lincoln (5,089 ft.) and Lafayette (5,260 ft.), this hike lures hundreds of people on warm weekends in summer and fall. The views from Franconia Ridge encompass most of the White Mountains, spanning the peaks and valleys of the Pemigewasset Wilderness all the way to the Presidential Range, Vermont's Green Mountains, and, on a very clear day, New York's Adirondacks. The Falling Waters Trail passes several waterfalls and cascades and the Old Bridle Path follows a long shoulder of Mount Lafayette over some open ledges that offer excellent views of Lincoln and Lafayette. This rugged climb offers a net elevation gain of 3,600 feet; portions of the route coincide with the Appalachian Trail (AT).

From the parking lot on the east side of I-93, follow the Falling Waters Trail, which coincides for 0.2 mile with the Old Bridle Path, then turns sharply right and crosses Walker Brook on a bridge. The trail climbs steadily and steeply, crossing Dry Brook at 0.7 mile, which could be difficult in high water. Over the ensuing mile, it passes several cascades and waterfalls, including Cloudland Falls, with a sheer drop of 80 feet, and makes two more crossings of the brook.

Continue up the Falling Waters Trail, emerging above the trees about 0.1 mile before reaching the Appalachian Trail/Franconia Ridge Trail at the summit of Little Haystack Mountain, 3.2 miles from the trailhead. Turn left (north) on the open ridge, following the cairns and white blazes of the AT/Franconia Ridge Trail. Briefly following easy ground, the trail then climbs steeply to the summit of Lincoln, 0.7 mile from Haystack. It then passes over a subsidiary summit of Lincoln immediately to the north, dropping into a saddle before making the long ascent of Mount Lafayette, 0.9 mile from Lincoln's summit. This highest point on the ridge, predictably, tends to be the windiest and coldest spot as well, although there are sheltered places in the rocks on the summit's north side. Turn left (west) and descend the Greenleaf Trail, much of it over open terrain, for 1.1 miles to the Appalachian Mountain Club's Greenleaf hut. Just beyond the hut, bear left onto the

Old Bridle Path, descending southwest over the crest of a long ridge before reentering the woods and eventually reaching the parking lot, 2.9 miles from the hut.

Special note: Under most conditions, it's desirable to hike this loop in the direction described here because the steep sections of the Falling Waters Trail are easier to ascend than descend, especially when the trail is wet. But if you're doing the hike on a day with cold wind, consider reversing the direction; the wind generally comes from the northwest, and reversing this hike's direction would put it at your back while atop Franconia Ridge, rather than in your face.

The Appalachian Mountain Club (AMC) operates the Greenleaf hut at the junction of the Greenleaf Trail and Old Bridle Path; contact the AMC for reservation and rate information.

User Groups: Hikers and leashed dogs. No bikes, horses, or wheelchair facilities. This trail should not be attempted in winter except by hikers experienced in mountaineering and prepared for severe winter weather.

Permits: Parking and access are free.

Maps: Two waterproof area trail maps showing this hike are available from the Appalachian Mountain Club (Franconia–Pemigewasset Range map and Crawford Notch–Sandwich Range/Moosilauke–Kinsman map, $9.95 each). For a topographic area map, request Franconia from the USGS.

Directions: From Lincoln, follow I-93 north for approximately 10 miles to reach Franconia Notch. At the signs for the Lafayette Place Campground, park in the large parking lot on the east side of I-93, where the trail begins. For southbound vehicles, another parking lot is located on the west side of the highway. From the west side parking lot, hikers can walk under the highway to the east lot and trailhead.

GPS Coordinates: 44.1411 N, 71.6818 W

Contact: White Mountain National Forest Headquarters, 71 White Mountain Drive, Campton, NH 03246, 603/536-6100, TDD for hearing impaired 603/536-3665, www. fs.fed.us/r9/white. Franconia Notch State Park, Franconia, NH 03580, 603/745-8391, www.franconianotchstatepark.com. Appalachian Mountain Club Pinkham Notch Visitor Center, P.O. Box 298, Gorham, NH 03581, 603/466-2721, www.outdoors.org.

56 FRANCONIA NOTCH LOOP
14 mi/9 hr or 1-2 days 🥾5 ⛰10

in the White Mountain National Forest and Franconia Notch State Park north of Lincoln and south of Franconia

Making the most of the skywalk effect atop Franconia Ridge, this 14-mile loop heads south on the ridge to bag Mount Lafayette (5,260 ft.), Mount Lincoln (5,089 ft.), Little Haystack Mountain (4,760 ft.), and Mount Liberty (4,459 ft.). While this loop can be done in a day by fit hikers, you might want to make an overnight trip of it, staying either in the Greenleaf hut or at the Liberty Springs campsite. Either place gives you a great high-elevation base from which to catch the sunset and then get back up to the ridge the next morning to see the sun burst majestically over the White's eastern peaks. The cumulative elevation gained on this hike is about 4,700 feet; portions of the route coincide with the Appalachian Trail.

From the parking lot on the east side of I-93, follow the Falling Waters Trail and the Old Bridle Path for 0.2 mile to where the trails split; then continue straight ahead on the Old Bridle Path. An easy climb at first, the trail pushes steeply for 2.9 miles to reach a junction with the Greenleaf Trail at the Greenleaf hut. From the hut, continue east on the Greenleaf Trail as it dips down into a shallow basin, passes through subalpine forest, and soon emerges onto the rocky, open west slope of Lafayette, climbing another 1.1 miles and more than 1,000 feet in elevation to Lafayette's summit, with open views in all directions.

Turn right (south) on the Franconia Ridge Trail, which coincides with the Appalachian Trail (AT), and hike the rugged, open, and in places narrow Franconia Ridge for only one mile before reaching the 5,089-foot summit of Mount Lincoln. It's then another 0.7 mile to the summit of Little Haystack (4,760 ft.).

Continuing south on the AT/Franconia Ridge Trail, the path soon drops into subalpine forest—although the forest cover is thin and the ridge narrow enough that you can see through the trees and know how abruptly the earth drops off to either side. At 1.8 miles past Little Haystack, the AT departs the Franconia Ridge Trail, turning right (west) to follow the Liberty Spring Trail. Continue south on the Franconia Ridge Trail another 0.3 mile, climbing less than 300 feet to the rocky summit of Mount Liberty for excellent, 360-degree views encompassing the Whites, the Pemigewasset Wilderness, the Green Mountains to the west, and on a clear day, as far west as New York's Adirondacks.

From Liberty's summit, backtrack 0.3 mile to the Liberty Spring Trail and descend it. Within 0.3 mile you'll reach the Liberty Spring campsite, where you can spend the night if backpacking. From the campsite, descend the Liberty Spring Trail another 2.6 miles to the blue-blazed Whitehouse Trail (it coincides with the Franconia Notch Bike Path). Cross the Pemigewasset River on a bridge, and just beyond the bridge turn right onto the Pemi Trail. Walk under the highway, then stay to the right (north) on the Pemi Trail and follow it nearly a mile to the Basin, where the Pemigewasset River has carved impressive natural bowls and cascades into the granite bedrock. From the Basin, you can stay on the Pemi Trail, or follow the paved bike path, about two miles farther to the parking lot on the west side of the highway at Lafayette Place Campground. If you parked on the east side of the highway, you can walk under the highway to that parking lot.

The Appalachian Mountain Club (AMC) operates the Greenleaf hut at the junction of the Greenleaf Trail and Old Bridle Path; contact the AMC for current reservation and rate information. The AMC also manages the Liberty Spring campsite, with 12 tent platforms, located along the Liberty Spring Trail, 2.6 miles from the Whitehouse Trail and 0.3 mile from the Franconia Ridge Trail. A caretaker collects the $8 per person nightly fee during the warmer months.

User Groups: Hikers and leashed dogs. No bikes, horses, or wheelchair facilities. This trail should not be attempted in winter except by hikers experienced in mountaineering and prepared for severe winter weather.

Permits: Parking and access are free.

Maps: Two waterproof area trail maps showing this hike are available from the Appalachian Mountain Club (Franconia–Pemigewasset Range map and Crawford Notch–Sandwich Range/Moosilauke–Kinsman map, $9.95 each). For a topographic area map, request Franconia from the USGS.

Directions: From Lincoln, follow I-93 north for approximately 10 miles to reach Franconia Notch. At the signs for the Lafayette Place Campground, park in the large parking lot on the east side of I-93, where the trail begins. For southbound vehicles, another parking lot is located on the west side of the highway. From the west side parking lot, hikers can walk under the highway to the east lot and trailhead.

GPS Coordinates: 44.1411 N, 71.6818 W

Contact: White Mountain National Forest Headquarters, 71 White Mountain Drive, Campton, NH 03246, 603/536-6100, TDD for hearing impaired 603/536-3665, www.fs.fed.us/r9/white. Franconia Notch State Park, Franconia, NH 03580, 603/745-8391, www.franconianotchstatepark.com. Appalachian Mountain Club Pinkham Notch Visitor Center, P.O. Box 298, Gorham, NH 03581, 603/466-2721, www.outdoors.org.

57 FRANCONIA NOTCH BIKE PATH

8.5 mi one-way/3.5 hr

in the White Mountain National Forest and Franconia Notch State Park north of Lincoln and south of Franconia

The Franconia Notch Bike Path runs like a stream, north/south for about 8.5 miles through Franconia Notch, providing a paved route for exploring one of the most spectacular notches in New England. Popular with families, it's great for cycling, walking, wheelchair hiking, running, snowshoeing, and cross-country skiing. With several access points, you can do as much of the path as you like. Much of it is in the forest, but there are numerous views of the surrounding peaks from the path. The path is accessible for wheelchairs provided the user can manage the few short, but somewhat steep, hills that mark the route.

The elevation begins at about 1,700 feet at the Skookumchuck trailhead, rises to around 2,000 feet at the base of Cannon Mountain and Profile Lake, then drops to about 1,100 feet at the Flume; going north to south on the path is easier, especially from anywhere south of Profile Lake. Scenic points along the path include the Flume, a natural cleavage in the mountainside; the Basin, where the still-small Pemigewasset River pours through natural bowls in the bedrock; a view of Cannon Cliff from a spot immediately north of Profile Lake; and the truck-sized boulder, estimated to weigh between 20 and 30 tons, lying right beside the paved path north of Lafayette Place campground, deposited there by a rockslide off Cannon Cliff in 1997.

User Groups: Hikers, leashed dogs, bikes, horses, and wheelchairs. In-line skating is prohibited.

Permits: Parking and access are free within Franconia Notch State Park, but the Skookumchuck Trail parking lot lies within the White Mountain National Forest, and a permit is required for day use or overnight

NEW HAMPSHIRE

parking. Permits are available at several area stores and from the national forest at a cost of $5 for seven consecutive days or $20 per year. A $3 one-day permit can be purchased at self-service stations at national forest trailheads, but the pass is good only for the trailhead at which it's purchased.

Maps: A waterproof area trail map is available from the Appalachian Mountain Club (Franconia–Pemigewasset Range, $9.95). For topographic area maps, request Franconia and Lincoln from the USGS.

Directions: The bike path can be accessed from several points. Its northern end is at the parking lot for the Skookumchuck Trail, on U.S. 3 about 0.6 mile north of Exit 35 off I-93 in Franconia. Its southern end is at the Flume, reached via the exit for the Flume off I-93 in Franconia Notch. Other access points in Franconia Notch include the Cannon Mountain parking lot at Exit 2, the Profile Lake parking lot, the Lafayette Place Campground, and the Basin parking lot.

GPS Coordinates: 44.1003 N, 71.6827 W

Contact: White Mountain National Forest Headquarters, 71 White Mountain Drive, Campton, NH 03246, 603/536-6100, TDD for hearing impaired 603/536-3665, www.fs.fed.us/r9/white. Franconia Notch State Park, Franconia, NH 03580, 603/745-8391, www.franconianotchstatepark.com.

58 MOUNTS FLUME AND LIBERTY

9.8 mi/7 hr

in the White Mountain National Forest and Franconia Notch State Park north of Lincoln and south of Franconia

If these two summits were located almost anywhere else in the region, this loop hike would enjoy enormous popularity. But the 5,000-footers to the north, Lafayette and Lincoln, are what captures the attention of most hikers venturing onto the sweeping Franconia Ridge. Many people who call the Lafayette-Lincoln Loop (see the *Mounts Lincoln and Lafayette* listing in this chapter) their favorite hike in the Whites have never enjoyed the uninterrupted views from the rocky summits of 4,325-foot Flume or 4,459-foot Liberty: Franconia Notch, west to Mount Moosilauke and the Green Mountains, and a grand sweep of peaks to the east all the way to the Presidential Range. This hike's cumulative elevation gain is nearly 2,500 feet.

From the parking lot, take the blue-blazed Whitehouse Trail north for nearly a mile (it coincides briefly with the Franconia Notch Bike Path). Pick up the white-blazed Liberty Spring Trail—a part of the Appalachian Trail—heading east. Within a half mile, signs mark where the Flume Slide Trail branches right. From that junction to the slide, the trail is somewhat overgrown, marked very sporadically with light-blue blazes and can be hard to follow. It grows steep on the upper part of the slide, and you will scramble over rocks that can be very slick when wet. (For a less exposed route to the summit of Mount Liberty, go up and down the Liberty Spring Trail.)

At 3.3 miles from where the Flume Slide Trail left the Liberty Spring Trail, it hits the ridge crest and reaches a junction. Turn left onto the Osseo Trail, which leads a short distance to Mount Flume's open summit. Continue north over the summit on the Franconia Ridge Trail (look for the marker), dipping into the saddle between the peaks, then climbing to Liberty's summit a mile past the top of Flume. Another 0.3 mile beyond the summit, turn left onto the Liberty Spring Trail and descend for 2.9 miles to the Whitehouse Trail, following it back to the parking lot.

The Appalachian Mountain Club operates the Liberty Spring campsite, with 12 tent platforms, located along the Liberty Spring Trail, 2.6 miles from the Whitehouse Trail and 0.3 mile from the Franconia Ridge Trail. A caretaker collects the $8 per person nightly fee during the warmer months.

User Groups: Hikers and leashed dogs. No

bikes, horses, or wheelchair facilities. This trail should not be attempted in winter except by hikers experienced in mountaineering and prepared for severe winter weather and is not suitable for skis.

Permits: Parking and access are free. This hike begins in Franconia Notch State Park, but much of it lies within the White Mountain National Forest.

Maps: Two waterproof area trail maps available from the Appalachian Mountain Club show this hike (Franconia–Pemigewasset Range map and Crawford Notch–Sandwich Range/Moosilauke–Kinsman map, $9.95 each). For topographic area maps, request Franconia and Lincoln from the USGS.

Directions: From Lincoln, follow I-93 north for approximately 10 miles into Franconia Notch. Follow the signs for the Flume exit and then follow signs leading to ample trailhead parking for the Whitehouse Trail and the Appalachian Trail.

GPS Coordinates: 44.1114 N, 71.6821 W

Contact: Franconia Notch State Park, Franconia, NH 03580, 603/745-8391, www.franconianotchstatepark.com. White Mountain National Forest Headquarters, 71 White Mountain Drive, Campton, NH 03246, 603/536-6100, TDD for hearing impaired 603/536-3665, www.fs.fed.us/r9/white. Appalachian Mountain Club Pinkham Notch Visitor Center, P.O. Box 298, Gorham, NH 03581, 603/466-2721, www.outdoors.org.

59 PEMIGEWASSET WILDERNESS TRAVERSE

19.5 mi one-way/10-12 hr or 1-2 days

🥾3 ⛰️10

in the White Mountain National Forest between U.S. 302 near Twin Mountain and Route 112 east of Lincoln

BEST (

The Pemigewasset Wilderness is the sprawling roadless area of mountains and wide valleys in the heart of the White Mountains. A federally designated wilderness area, the Pemi harbors

spectacular big-mountain hikes such as Mount Carrigain (see *Mount Carrigain* listing in this chapter), but this traverse follows the wooded valleys of the Pemi. Much of it is relatively easy hiking along routes once followed by the railroads of 19th-century logging companies. A climb of only about 1,000 feet in elevation, this hike is best broken up into a two-day backpacking trip.

From the summer parking lot at the end of Zealand Road, pick up the blue-blazed Zealand Trail, a winding walk through the forest on fairly flat ground, with some short, steep steps. At 2.5 miles, the trail comes to a junction. To the right, the Twinway leads 0.2 mile uphill to the Appalachian Mountain Club's Zealand Falls hut. This hike continues straight ahead onto the Ethan Pond Trail, which coincides with the Appalachian Trail (AT). The Ethan Pond Trail contours along the west slope of Whitewall Mountain.

About 1.3 miles past the Zealand Trail, the AT/Ethan Pond Trail emerges from the forest onto the open scar of an old rockslide on Whitewall, in the middle of Zealand Notch. Above loom the towering cliffs of the mountain; below, the rockslide's fallout, a broad boulder field. Across the notch rises Zealand Mountain, and straight ahead, to the south, stands Carrigain. The trail crosses the rockslide for about 0.2 mile, then reenters the woods. At 2.1 miles past the Zealand Trail, bear right onto the Thoreau Falls Trail, following easy terrain for 0.1 mile to Thoreau Falls, which tumbles more than 100 feet and forms an impressive cascade of ice in winter. The trail crosses the stream immediately above the brink of the falls. Be careful here in any season, but especially in winter, and do not assume that any snow or ice bridge is safe.

Once across the stream, the trail climbs steeply, angling across a wooded hillside, then dropping just as steeply down the other side. At 4.7 miles from the Ethan Pond Trail, the trail crosses a bridge over the east branch of the Pemigewasset River. Just 0.4 mile past the bridge, turn right (west) onto the Wilderness

Trail, which is the easiest trail on this route. The Wilderness Trail crosses the river again in 0.9 mile, on a 180-foot suspension bridge, then parallels the river for the remaining 5.4 flat miles to the Lincoln Woods parking lot on the Kancamangus Highway (the last three miles of the trail are also called the Lincoln Woods Trail).

The Appalachian Mountain Club (AMC) operates the Zealand Falls hut year-round; it is on the Twinway, 0.2 mile from the junction of the Zealand, Twinway, and Ethan Pond Trails and 2.7 miles from the end of Zealand Road. Contact the AMC for information on cost and reservations. The Franconia Brook campsite (16 tent platforms), operated by the White Mountain National Forest, costs $8 per person and is open only during summer and fall; the campsite is reached by hiking the trail known as East Branch Road for three miles from the Lincoln Woods trailhead. On this hike, you would reach this campsite by turning left (south) from the Wilderness Trail onto the Cedar Brook Trail right before the second bridge crossing of the east branch of the Pemigewasset River; following the Cedar Brook Trail west for a little more than a half mile; then turning right onto the East Branch Road, which is overgrown and may be easily overlooked. Camping in the forest is legal, provided you remain at least 200 feet from a trail and a quarter mile from established camping areas such as Guyot campsite.

User Groups: Hikers and dogs. No bikes, horses, or wheelchair facilities. This trail should not be attempted in winter except by hikers experienced in mountaineering and prepared for severe winter weather.

Permits: No backcountry permit is needed, but a permit is required for day use or overnight parking at any White Mountain National Forest trailhead. Permits are available at several area stores and from the national forest at a cost of $5 for seven consecutive days or $20 per year. A $3 one-day permit can be purchased at self-service stations at national forest trailheads, but the pass is good only for the trailhead at which it's purchased.

Maps: A waterproof area trail map is available from the Appalachian Mountain Club (Franconia–Pemigewasset Range, $9.95). For topographic area maps, request Bethlehem, Mount Washington, South Twin Mountain, Crawford Notch, Mount Osceola, and Mount Carrigain from the USGS.

Directions: You need to shuttle two vehicles for this one-way traverse. To go north to south, as described here, leave one vehicle in the Lincoln Woods parking lot, where there is a White Mountain National Forest ranger station. The lot is off the Kancamangus Highway (Route 112), five miles east of the McDonald's in Lincoln and just east of the bridge where the Kancamagus crosses the east branch of the Pemigewasset River. The Wilderness Trail—also known for its initial three miles as the Lincoln Woods Trail—begins here. To reach the start of this hike, from the junction of U.S. 3 and U.S. 302 in Twin Mountain, drive east on U.S. 302 for 2.3 miles and turn right onto Zealand Road, then continue 3.5 miles to a parking lot at the end of the road. Zealand Road is not maintained in winter.

GPS Coordinates: 44.2221 N, 71.4780 W

Contact: White Mountain National Forest Headquarters, 71 White Mountain Drive, Campton, NH 03246, 603/536-6100, TDD for hearing impaired 603/536-3665, www.fs.fed.us/r9/white. Appalachian Mountain Club Pinkham Notch Visitor Center, P.O. Box 298, Gorham, NH 03581, 603/466-2721, www.outdoors.org.

60 ARETHUSA FALLS

2.8 mi/1.5 hr

in Crawford Notch State Park north of Bartlett and south of Twin Mountain

With a thundering drop of nearly 200 feet, Arethusa Falls is the tallest waterfall in New

Hampshire. It's unusual name comes from a poem by Percy Bysshe Shelley that tells the tale of the beautiful Arethusa, a nymph who is transformed into a fountain. A climb of approximately 900 feet, this fairly easy hike and its watery, scenic payoff rank the falls as among the region's most frequently visited natural wonders.

From the far end of the lower parking lot, you can pick up a connector trail to the upper lot. There, follow the Arethusa Falls Trail (marked) for 0.1 mile to a left turn onto the Bemis Brook Trail, which parallels the Arethusa Trail for a half mile and eventually rejoins it. Bemis Brook Trail is more interesting for the short cascades it passes—Bemis Falls and Coliseum Falls—as well as Fawn Pool. After reaching the Arethusa Trail again, turn left and continue uphill another 0.8 mile to the base of the magnificent falls. Taking in the powerful cascade, you will probably notice the views would be even better on the other side of Bemis Brook. Crossing the brook can be very difficult under high water conditions and should not be attempted by children. Return the way you came.

User Groups: Hikers and leashed dogs. No bikes, horses, or wheelchair facilities.

Permits: Parking and access are free.

Maps: Two waterproof area trail maps available from the Appalachian Mountain Club cover this hike (Franconia–Pemigewasset Range map and Crawford Notch–Sandwich Range/Moosilauke–Kinsman map, $9.95 each). For topographic area maps, request Crawford Notch and Stairs Mountain from the USGS.

Directions: From the Appalachian Mountain Club Highland Center in Crawford Depot, follow U.S. 302 south for 5.2 miles to a sign for Arethusa Falls. Turn right onto the paved road and park in the lower lot immediately on the right, or drive 0.2 mile and park at the end of the road.

GPS Coordinates: 44.1478 N, 71.3693 W

Contact: White Mountain National Forest Headquarters, 71 White Mountain Drive, Campton, NH 03246, 603/536-6100, TDD for hearing impaired 603/536-3665, www.fs.fed.us/r9/white.

61 RIPLEY FALLS
1 mi/0.75 hr

in Crawford Notch State Park north of Bartlett and south of Twin Mountain

As Avalanche Brook races out of the Pemigewasset Wilderness towards the lowland of Crawford Notch, it stops long enough to tumble down an impressive 100-foot sheer granite face known as Ripley Falls. An easy walk from the trailhead at any time of year, the falls tend to be at their picturesque best in late spring and early summer when the brook swells with runoff.

From the railroad tracks at the end of the access road and parking area, pick up the Ethan Pond Trail, which coincides here with the white-blazed Appalachian Trail (AT). As the easy, wide trail climbs steadily uphill, it passes through an area of tall birch trees at 0.2 mile and then reaches a fork. The Ethan Pond Trail/AT bears right, but go left onto the Ripley Falls Trail. Continue 0.3 mile to the cascading falls and then return the way you came.

Special note: It is possible to reach soaring Arethusa Falls (see the *Arethusa Falls* listing in this chapter) from Ripley Falls by continuing on the Arethusa-Ripley Falls Trail for another 2.3 miles (adding 4.6 miles round-trip and 400 feet in elevation gain to this hike).

User Groups: Hikers and dogs. No bikes, horses, or wheelchair facilities.

Permits: Parking and access are free.

Maps: Two waterproof area trail maps available from the Appalachian Mountain Club cover this hike (Franconia–Pemigewasset Range map and Crawford Notch–Sandwich Range/Moosilauke–Kinsman map, $9.95 each). For a topographic area map, request Crawford Notch from the USGS.

NEW HAMPSHIRE

Directions: From the Appalachian Mountain Club Highland Center in Crawford Depot, drive south on U.S. 302 for 3.9 miles to a sign for Ripley Falls. Turn right and drive 0.3 mile to parking at the end of the road.

GPS Coordinates: 44.1669 N, 71.3863 W

Contact: White Mountain National Forest Headquarters, 71 White Mountain Drive, Campton, NH 03246, 603/536-6100, TDD for hearing impaired 603/536-3665, www. fs.fed.us/r9/white. New Hampshire Division of Parks and Recreation, Bureau of Trails, P.O. Box 1856, Concord, NH 03302-1856, 603/271-3254.

62 STAIRS MOUNTAIN
9.2 mi/5 hr   🏃4 ⛰8

in the White Mountain National Forest north of Bartlett

Stairs Mountain is so named because of its Giant Stairs, a pair of steplike ledges on the 3,463-foot mountain's south end. From the cliffs atop the Giant Stairs, you get wide views of the wild backcountry of the Saco River valley. A net climb of approximately 2,100 feet, this hike can be done in a day or can be split up over two days with a stay on one of the shelters near this route.

From the end of Jericho Road, follow the Rocky Branch Trail north a flat two miles to the Rocky Branch Shelter 1, where there is a lean-to and a tent site. Just beyond it, the Stairs Col Trail turns left (west) and ascends steadily for nearly two miles, passing below the Giant Stairs and through Stairs Col to the Davis Path. Turn right (north) on the Davis Path and follow it for less than a half mile to a side path leading right for about 0.2 mile to the summit cliffs above the Giant Stairs. Return the way you came. To spend the night before heading back, retrace your steps on the Davis Path and pass the junction with the Stairs Col Trail, staying south on the Davis Path for another 0.3 mile to the Resolution Shelter.

User Groups: Hikers and dogs. No bikes, horses, or wheelchair facilities.

Permits: No backcountry permit is needed, but a permit is required for day use or overnight parking at any White Mountain National Forest trailhead. Permits are available at several area stores and from the national forest at a cost of $5 for seven consecutive days or $20 per year. A $3 one-day permit can be purchased at self-service stations at national forest trailheads, but the pass is good only for the trailhead at which it's purchased.

Maps: A waterproof area trail map showing this hike is available from the Appalachian Mountain Club (Crawford Notch–Sandwich Range/Moosilauke–Kinsman, $9.95). For topographic area maps, request North Conway West, Bartlett, and Stairs Mountain from the USGS.

Directions: From the junction of Route 16 and U.S. 302 in Glen, drive west on U.S. 302 for one mile and turn right onto Jericho Road/Rocky Branch Road. Follow the road, which is paved for about a mile and then becomes gravel for the remaining five miles. At the end of the road is a parking area and the Rocky Branch trailhead.

GPS Coordinates: 44.1388 N, 71.2664 W

Contact: White Mountain National Forest Headquarters, 71 White Mountain Drive, Campton, NH 03246, 603/536-6100, TDD for hearing impaired 603/536-3665, www. fs.fed.us/r9/white. The Appalachian Mountain Club Pinkham Notch Visitor Center has up-to-date weather and trail information about the Whites; call 603/466-2725.

63 THE WILDERNESS/ LINCOLN WOODS TRAIL
10.8 mi/5 hr   🏃2 ⛰8

in the White Mountain National Forest, east of Lincoln

This scenic hike along the east branch of the Pemigewasset River is virtually flat for its entire distance—making it a pleasant walk in the wilderness, rather than a grueling climb. Some visitors only go the nearly three miles out to the first bridge, over Franconia Brook, and return. This description covers the 5.4 miles out to the suspension bridge over the east branch of the Pemi at the junction with the Thoreau Falls Trail.

From the visitors center parking lot, take the bridge over the east branch of the Pemigewasset River, then turn right onto the Lincoln Woods Trail—the name given in recent years to the first three miles of what was formerly known entirely as the Wilderness Trail. Following an old railroad grade, the trail is wide, level, and shady as it runs parallel to the river (Pemigewasset is Abenaki for "swiftly moving," an apt name for this river, especially in late spring/early summer). At 2.6 miles, pass a side path leading 0.8 mile to Black Pond Trail and at 2.7 miles, reach a side path on the left leading 0.4 mile to Franconia Falls, a worthwhile detour (no wheelchair facilities). Staying on the Lincoln Woods, the trail crosses a footbridge over Franconia Brook and at 2.9 miles, officially enters the Pemigewasset Wilderness. Now called the Wilderness Trail and still following the river, the trail continues straight ahead, passing a junction with the Bondcliff Trail at 4.7 miles. The trail soon crosses Black Brook on a bridge near an old logging railroad bridge and from there, it's just another 0.7 mile to the suspension bridge over the Pemi's east branch (at the junction with the Thoreau Falls Trail). Return the way you came.

Special note: You can make a loop of about the same distance from the Lincoln Woods trailhead by starting out on the Pemi East Side Trail, also leaving from the visitors center parking lot, but staying on the east side of the river. Within four miles, you'll turn left (east) onto the Cedar Brook Trail; follow it about a half mile, cross the bridge over the east branch of the Pemi River, then turn left (west) and follow the Wilderness Trail back to the trailhead.

The Franconia Brook campsite (16 tent platforms), operated by the White Mountain National Forest, costs $8 per person and is open only during summer and fall. The campsite is reached by hiking the trail known as East Branch Road for three miles from the Lincoln Woods trailhead. On this hike, you would reach this campsite from the Wilderness Trail by crossing the bridge over the east branch of the Pemigewasset River and turning right (west) onto the Cedar Brook Trail. From there, follow the Cedar Brook Trail west for a little more than a half mile before turning right onto the East Branch Road, which is overgrown and may be easily overlooked. Follow East Branch Road to the campground.

User Groups: Hikers and dogs. The Lincoln Woods Trail is accessible for wheelchairs for approximately the first half mile; as the wide path continues, old railroad ties surface and the route becomes uneven. No bikes or horses.

Permits: No backcountry permit is needed, but a permit is required for day use or overnight parking at any White Mountain National Forest trailhead. Permits are available at several area stores and from the national forest at a cost of $5 for seven consecutive days or $20 per year. A $3 one-day permit can be purchased at self-service stations at national forest trailheads, but the pass is good only for the trailhead at which it's purchased.

Maps: Two waterproof area trail maps available from the Appalachian Mountain Club show this hike (Franconia–Pemigewasset Range map and Crawford Notch–Sandwich Range/Moosilauke–Kinsman map, $9.95 each). For a topographic area map, request the Mount Osceola map from the USGS.

Directions: Drive to the large parking lot at Lincoln Woods along the Kancamagus Highway/Route 112, five miles east of the McDonald's in Lincoln, and just east of the bridge where the Kancamagus crosses the east branch of the Pemigewasset River. The Wilderness Trail—also known for its initial three miles as the Lincoln Woods Trail—begins here.

GPS Coordinates: 44.0643 N, 71.5904 W

NEW HAMPSHIRE

Contact: White Mountain National Forest Headquarters, 71 White Mountain Drive, Campton, NH 03246, 603/536-6100, TDD for hearing impaired 603/536-3665, www. fs.fed.us/r9/white.

64 MOUNT CARRIGAIN
10 mi/7 hr ⊞4 ◭10

in the White Mountain National Forest southwest of Crawford Notch State Park

The tallest peak in this corner of the Whites, 4,700-foot Carrigain offers one of the finest—and unquestionably unique—views in these mountains from the observation tower on its summit. On a clear day, the panorama takes in Mount Washington and the Presidential Range, the vast sweep of peaks across the Pemigewasset Wilderness to Franconia Ridge, Moosilauke to the west, and the peaks above Waterville Valley and the distinctive horn of Chocorua to the south. Although 10 miles round-trip, with a vertical ascent of about 3,300 feet, this hike grows steep only for the ascent to the crest of Signal Ridge, which itself has spectacular views, including one toward the cliffs of Mount Lowell to the east.

From the parking area, pick up the marked Signal Ridge Trail. At first following Whiteface Brook as it tumbles along in a series of picturesque cascades, at 0.6 mile, the trail veers away from the brook and at 1.7 miles from the road, passes a junction with the Carrigain Notch Trail (just before a crossing of the Carrigain Brook). From here, the trail grows increasingly steep and changes direction several times; most of the hike's elevation is gained in the final 1.5-mile push to the summit. Finally reaching the open terrain of Signal Ridge at about 4.5 miles out, enjoy the many excellent views, particularly east across Carrigain Notch to Mount Lowell's cliffs. The ridge ascends easily to the summit observation tower. Return the same way you came.

User Groups: Hikers and dogs. No bikes, horses, or wheelchair facilities.
Permits: No backcountry permit is needed, but a permit is required for day use or overnight parking at any White Mountain National Forest trailhead. Permits are available at several area stores and from the national forest at a cost of $5 for seven consecutive days or $20 per year. A $3 one-day permit can be purchased at self-service stations at national forest trailheads, but the pass is good only for the trailhead at which it's purchased.
Maps: Two waterproof area trail maps available from the Appalachian Mountain Club show this hike (Franconia–Pemigewasset Range map and Crawford Notch–Sandwich Range/Moosilauke–Kinsman map, $9.95 each). For topographic area maps, request Mount Carrigain and Bartlett from the USGS.
Directions: From U.S. 302, 10.7 miles south of the visitor information center in Crawford Notch and 10.3 miles north of the junction of U.S. 302 and Route 16 in Glen, turn south onto Sawyer River Road/Fire Road 34. Follow it for two miles to the Signal Ridge Trail on the right, just before a bridge over Whiteface Brook. There is parking on the left, just past the brook. Sawyer River Road/Fire Road 34 is usually closed to vehicles once snow arrives. GPS Coordinates: 44.0704 N, 71.3841 W
Contact: White Mountain National Forest Headquarters, 71 White Mountain Drive, Campton, NH 03246, 603/536-6100, TDD for hearing impaired 603/536-3665, www. fs.fed.us/r9/white.

65 MOUNT STANTON
3 mi/2 hr ⊞2 ◭8

in the White Mountain National Forest between Bartlett and Glen

At just 1,716 feet above sea level, Mount Stanton offers open ledges with good views and the feel of a big mountain climb for relatively little work—just three miles and 1,000 feet of elevation gain. These factors make it a good hike for children or for a day when bad weather keeps you off the big mountains. The trail does have a few moderately steep stretches, but they are neither sustained nor very difficult; fit people could easily run up the path for a quick workout.

From the roadside trailhead marker, the moderately ascending trail curves in an almost serpentine-shaped route, heading west, north, east, north, and then west again all within its first mile. As the trail nears the Mount Stanton summit, you will see the open ledges to the left (south). Venture out on the ledges and you are on the brink of a 500-foot sheer drop, atop a cliff called White's Ledge (a wonderful technical rock climb for those with experience). You might see rock climbers reaching the top at this popular climbing area; be careful not to kick stones over the edge. The ledges offer broad views of the Saco River Valley. Follow the same route back.

User Groups: Hikers and dogs. No bikes, horses, or wheelchair facilities.

Permits: Parking and access are free.

Maps: A waterproof area trail map is available from the Appalachian Mountain Club (Crawford Notch–Sandwich Range/Moosilauke–Kinsman, $9.95). For a topographic area map, request North Conway West from the USGS.

Directions: From the junction of U.S. 302 and Highway 16 in Glen, drive on U.S. 302 west toward Bartlett for about two miles. Just before the covered bridge, turn right onto Covered Bridge Lane (there is a small sign high on a tree). Follow the paved road 0.2 mile and bear right onto Oak Ridge Drive. Almost immediately, make a sharp right turn onto Hemlock Drive, which is a dirt road for a short distance before becoming paved, and continue for 0.3 mile. Park by the trail sign on the road. The trail begins just uphill on the left side of the driveway near the trail sign.

GPS Coordinates: 44.0960 N, 71.2120 W

Contact: White Mountain National Forest Headquarters, 71 White Mountain Drive, Campton, NH 03246, 603/536-6100, TDD for hearing impaired 603/536-3665, www.fs.fed.us/r9/white.

66 MOUNT MOOSILAUKE: BEAVER BROOK TRAIL

7.6 mi/5.5 hr

in the White Mountain National Forest west of North Woodstock

A 4,802-foot massif in the southwest corner of the White Mountains, Mount Moosilauke is the western most of the range's 4,000-footers. Passing numerous cascades and scaling rough terrain on its way to an alpine summit with views spanning much of the White Mountains and west to the Green Mountains in Vermont and New York's Adirondacks, the Beaver Brook Trail is a steep, scenic trek to Moosilauke's top with a net climb of approximately 3,000 feet. The Beaver Brook Trail coincides with the Appalachian Trail (AT) for its entire length.

Leaving from the parking area on Route 112, the white-blazed AT/Beaver Brook Trail immediately pushes southwest in a sharp, sustained uphill climb as it runs parallel to the tumbling cascades of Beaver Brook; rock and wood steps, and iron rings help with the ascent. Leaving the brook near the one-mile mark, the trail levels out somewhat, passing a Dartmouth Outing Club shelter at 1.5 miles. And then at 1.9 miles, the relentless climb begins again as the trail skirts the edge of Jobildunk Ravine and runs just below the wooded shoulder known as Mount Blue (4,529 ft.). Emerging from the trees, the AT/Beaver Brook Trail comes to a junction with the Benton Trail. Here the AT/Beaver Brook Trail turns left, coinciding with the southbound Benton Trail for a nearly flat 0.4-mile walk to the summit. Hike back the way you came.

Special note: By shuttling two vehicles to the trailheads, this hike can be combined with the Glencliff Trail for a traverse of

Moosilauke via the Appalachian Trail (see the *Mount Moosilauke: Glencliff Trail* listing in this chapter). **User Groups:** Hikers and dogs. No bikes, horses, or wheelchair facilities. **Permits:** No backcountry permit is needed, but a permit is required for day use or overnight parking at any White Mountain National Forest trailhead. Permits are available at several area stores and from the national forest at a cost of $5 for seven consecutive days or $20 per year. A $3 one-day permit can be purchased at self-service stations at national forest trailheads, but the pass is good only for the trailhead at which it's purchased. **Maps:** A waterproof area trail map is available from the Appalachian Mountain Club (Crawford Notch–Sandwich Range/Moosilauke–Kinsman, $9.95). For a topographic area map, request Mount Moosilauke from the USGS. **Directions:** The Beaver Brook Trail, which coincides with the Appalachian Trail, begins from a parking lot along Route 112 at the height of land in Kinsman Notch, 6.2 miles west of North Woodstock and 4.8 miles south of the junction of Routes 112 and 116. GPS Coordinates: 44.0394 N, 71.7921 W **Contact:** White Mountain National Forest Headquarters, 71 White Mountain Drive, Campton, NH 03246, 603/536-6100, TDD for hearing impaired 603/536-3665, www.fs.fed.us/r9/white.

67 MOUNT MOOSILAUKE: GLENCLIFF TRAIL
7.8 mi/5.5 hr 🥾5 ⛰10

in the White Mountain National Forest north of Warren

The Glencliff Trail, a section of the white-blazed Appalachian Trail, offers a scenic, but steep route to the 4,802-foot summit of Mount Moosilauke, where an extensive alpine area offers panoramic views stretching across much of the White Mountains and west to

Vermont's Green Mountains and New York's Adirondacks. Leaving from Benton State Forest and taking a northeasterly approach to the pinnacle of the Moosilauke massif, this hike gains about 3,300 feet in elevation.

From the parking lot, follow the white blazes of the Appalachian Trail (AT) past a gate and along an old farm road. Entering the woods at 0.4 mile, immediately pass a small side path leading left to a Dartmouth College cabin (not open to the public) and a junction with the Hurricane Trail to the right. The AT/Glencliff Trail ascends steadily but at a moderate grade for the next two miles, then grows very steep as it rises into the mountain's krummholtz, the scrub conifers that grow in the subalpine zone. At three miles, a spur path leads right (south) 0.2 mile to Moosilauke's craggy south peak, a worthwhile detour. This hike continues, meeting up almost immediately with the Moosilauke Carriage Road. Here, the AT/Glencliff Trail turns left (north) and follows the wide carriage road over easy ground along the open ridge—with great views—on its gentle ascent to the summit at 3.9 miles. Return the way you came. (For a full traverse of Moosilauke via the Appalachian Trail, see the *Mount Moosilauke: Beaver Brook Trail* listing.) **User Groups:** Hikers and dogs. No bikes, horses, or wheelchair facilities. This trail should not be attempted in winter except by hikers experienced in mountaineering and prepared for severe winter weather, and is not suitable for skis. **Permits:** No backcountry permit is needed, but a permit is required for day use or overnight parking at any White Mountain National Forest trailhead. Permits are available at several area stores and from the national forest at a cost of $5 for seven consecutive days or $20 per year. A $3 one-day permit can be purchased at self-service stations at national forest trailheads, but the pass is good only for the trailhead at which it's purchased. **Maps:** A waterproof area trail map is available from the Appalachian Mountain Club (Crawford Notch–Sandwich Range/

Moosilauke–Kinsman, \$9.95). For a topographic area map, request Mount Moosilauke from the USGS.

Directions: From Route 25 in Glencliff Village, turn onto High Street, just past the sign for the Glencliff Home for the Elderly. Drive 1.2 miles to a dirt parking lot on the right. GPS Coordinates: 43.9980 N, 71.8820 W

Contact: White Mountain National Forest Headquarters, 71 White Mountain Drive, Campton, NH 03246, 603/536-6100, TDD for hearing impaired 603/536-3665, www.fs.fed.us/r9/white.

68 MOUNT OSCEOLA
6.4 mi/4 hr 　　　　🏃3 ⛰9

in the White Mountain National Forest north of Waterville Valley and east of Lincoln

One of the easiest 4,000-footers in New Hampshire to hike—with a vertical ascent of only about 2,000 feet—Osceola's summit ledges, rising 4,340 feet above sea level, give a sweeping view to the south and southeast of Waterville Valley and Mount Tripyramid, and northeast to the Pemigewasset Wilderness and the Presidential Range.

From the parking area on Tripoli Road, follow the Mount Osceola Trail as it ascends the mountain's Breadtray Ridge over somewhat rocky footing. A moderate climb with numerous switchbacks, the trail reaches a ledge overlook with a view of Sandwich Mountain at 2.1 miles and crosses a small brook at 2.3 miles. The switchbacks continue for the next mile as the trail ascends the ridge and reaches the summit ledges at 3.2 miles. To reach 4,156-foot East Osceola, follow the trail for one more mile, adding two miles and approximately 1.5 hours to this hike's distance and time. This hike returns along the same route.

User Groups: Hikers and dogs. No bikes, horses, or wheelchair facilities.

Permits: No backcountry permit is needed, but a permit is required for day use or overnight parking at any White Mountain National Forest trailhead. Permits are available at several area stores and from the national forest at a cost of \$5 for seven consecutive days or \$20 per year. A \$3 one-day permit can be

NEW HAMPSHIRE

© JACQUELINE TOURVILLE

Mount Osceola

purchased at self-service stations at national forest trailheads, but the pass is good only for the trailhead at which it's purchased.

Maps: Two waterproof area trail maps available from the Appalachian Mountain Club show this hike (Franconia–Pemigewasset Range map and Crawford Notch–Sandwich Range/Moosilauke–Kinsman map, $9.95 each). For topographic area maps, request Mount Osceola and Waterville Valley from the USGS.

Directions: From I-93, take Exit 31 for Tripoli Road. Drive east on Tripoli Road for seven miles to a parking lot on the left for the Mount Osceola Trail. Tripoli Road is generally not maintained in winter.

GPS Coordinates: 43.9834 N, 71.5588 W

Contact: White Mountain National Forest Headquarters, 71 White Mountain Drive, Campton, NH 03246, 603/536-6100, TDD for hearing impaired 603/536-3665, www.fs.fed.us/r9/white.

69 GREELEY PONDS NORTH
4.4 mi/2 hr   🏃2 ⛰8

in the White Mountain National Forest on the Kancamagus Highway/Route 112 between Lincoln and Conway

This fairly flat 4.4-mile hike offers the shortest and easiest route to the Greeley Ponds, two pool-like bodies of water nestled at the bottom of Mad River Notch. With an elevation gain of only a few hundred feet, this is a pleasant hike for beginners and a fun one for kids—especially if you spot a moose or two taking a dip at these favorite watering holes.

From the parking area along the Kancamagus Highway, follow the Greeley Ponds Trail as it winds southward through a mixed deciduous and conifer forest. At 1.3 miles, the Mount Osceola Trail diverges to the right (east), soon to climb steeply up East Osceola and Osceola, a worthwhile side trip. This

hike continues south on the Greeley Ponds Trail for nearly another half mile to the upper Greeley Pond, which sits in a scenic basin below the dramatic cliffs of East Osceola. Continuing another half mile on the trail brings you to the lower pond. Return the way you came.

Camping and fires are prohibited within the Greeley Ponds Scenic Area, the boundary of which is marked by a sign along the trail.

User Groups: Hikers and dogs. No bikes, horses, or wheelchair facilities.

Permits: No backcountry permit is needed, but a permit is required for day use or overnight parking at any White Mountain National Forest trailhead. Permits are available at several area stores and from the national forest at a cost of $5 for seven consecutive days or $20 per year. A $3 one-day permit can be purchased at self-service stations at national forest trailheads, but the pass is good only for the trailhead at which it's purchased.

Maps: Two waterproof area trail maps from the Appalachian Mountain Club show this hike (Franconia–Pemigewasset Range map and Crawford Notch–Sandwich Range/Moosilauke–Kinsman map, $9.95 each). For topographic area maps, request the Mount Osceola, Mount Carrigain, Mount Tripyramid, and Waterville Valley maps from the USGS.

Directions: The hike begins at a small parking area along the Kancamagus Highway/Route 112, 9.9 miles east of the McDonald's on Route 112 in Lincoln (Exit 32 off I-93), 3.4 miles west of the sign at Kancamagus Pass and 25.6 miles west of the junction of Routes 112 and 16 in Conway.

GPS Coordinates: 44.0317 N, 71.5168 W

Contact: White Mountain National Forest Headquarters, 71 White Mountain Drive, Campton, NH 03246, 603/536-6100, TDD for hearing impaired 603/536-3665, www.fs.fed.us/r9/white.

70 GREELEY PONDS SOUTH
7.4 mi/4 hr   👥2 △8

in Waterville Valley in the White Mountain National Forest

This popular 7.4-mile round-tripper from Waterville Valley leads to the two scenic Greeley Ponds on a route that is longer and with a bit more climb to it than the approach to the ponds from the north (see the *Greeley Ponds North* listing in the chapter). The total vertical ascent on this hike is about 700 feet.

From the parking lot on West Branch Road, follow the Livermore Trail for 0.25 mile, turning left at the sign for the Greeley Ponds Trail. (If you are here in winter, the trail is not groomed but is often packed and tracked by snowshoers and skiers, making it a good destination for a cold weather trek.) Flat at first and running parallel to the Mad River, the wide, well worn path passes a number of trail junctions in its first two miles as it makes its way into the notch. With the cliffs of Mount Osceola towering to the left and Mount Kancamagus looming to the right, the trail grows considerably steeper in the last 0.1 mile before reaching the lower Greeley Pond. After passing a short path that leads to different viewing points along the pond (a worthwhile detour), the trail crosses over the Mad River to its left bank. From here, it's another 0.5 mile to the upper pond. Return the way you came.

Camping and fires are prohibited within the Greeley Ponds Scenic Area, the boundary of which is marked by a sign along the trail.
User Groups: Hikers and dogs. No bikes, horses, or wheelchair facilities.
Permits: No backcountry permit is needed, but a permit is required for day use or overnight parking at any White Mountain National Forest trailhead. Permits are available at several area stores and from the national forest at a cost of $5 for seven consecutive days or $20 per year. A $3 one-day permit can be purchased at self-service stations at national forest trailheads, but the pass is good only for the trailhead at which it's purchased.
Maps: Two waterproof area trail maps from the Appalachian Mountain Club show this hike (Franconia–Pemigewasset Range map and Crawford Notch–Sandwich Range/Moosilauke–Kinsman map, $9.95 each). For topographic area maps, request the Mount Osceola, Mount Carrigain, Mount Tripyramid, and Waterville Valley maps from the USGS.
Directions: From I-93 in Campton, take Exit 28 onto Route 49 east. Drive about 11.4 miles into Waterville Valley and turn right onto Valley Road, which is still Route 49. Just 0.4 mile farther, turn left onto West Branch Road, in front of the Osceola Library. Drive another 0.7 mile and turn right into the parking lot, just before the bridge.
GPS Coordinates: 43.9654 N, 71.5138 W
Contact: White Mountain National Forest Headquarters, 71 White Mountain Drive, Campton, NH 03246, 603/536-6100, TDD for hearing impaired 603/536-3665, www.fs.fed.us/r9/white.

71 CATHEDRAL LEDGE
0.1 mi/0.25 hr   👥1 △8

in Echo Lake State Park west of North Conway

This is less of a hike than it is an easy, five-minute walk to the top of Cathedral Ledge, a sheer, 400-foot cliff with breathtaking views of North Conway and the surrounding mountains. Popular with tourists when the access road is open late spring–autumn, the lookout is protected by a fence to keep visitors from wandering too close to the brink. Cathedral is one of New Hampshire's most popular rock-climbing areas, so you're likely to see climbers pulling over the top of the cliff right in front of you. Obviously, you should not throw anything off the cliff, given the likelihood of there being people below.

From the parking circle at the end of the access road, look for the Cathedral Ledge sign

NEW HAMPSHIRE

NEW HAMPSHIRE

© JASON D. BROWN

Cathedral Ledge

marker and follow the wide, obvious path as it leads a short distance through the woods to the top of the cliff. From this perch high above Echo Lake State Park, views take in Echo Lake almost directly below, the town of North Conway, and due east to the ski slopes of Cranmore Mountain and surrounding hills. Return the same way.

User Groups: Hikers and leashed dogs. No bikes, horses, or wheelchair facilities.

Permits: Parking and access are free.

Maps: Although no map is necessary for this hike, it is shown on the Crawford Notch–Sandwich Range/Moosilauke–Kinsman map, available from the Appalachian Mountain Club ($9.95, waterproof). For a topographic map of the area, request North Conway West from the USGS.

Directions: From Route 16 in North Conway in front of the Eastern Slope Inn, turn west at traffic lights onto River Road. Continue 1.5 miles and turn left at a sign for Cathedral Ledge. Follow the road for more than a mile

to its end at a circle near the cliff top. The access road is not maintained in winter and is blocked by a gate.

GPS Coordinates: 44.0628 N, 71.1672 W

Contact: New Hampshire Division of Parks and Recreation, P.O. Box 1856, 172 Pembroke Rd., Concord, NH 03302, 603/271-3556, camping reservations 603/271-3628, www. nhstateparks.org.

72 DIANA'S BATH

1.6 mi/1 hr 🏃1 ⛰9

in the White Mountain National Forest west of North Conway

BEST (

A bathtub fit for a goddess, Diana's Bath is a series of crashing cascades and swirling potholes formed by the rushing water of Lucy Brook. In spring, the water roars through in a can't-miss spectacle. But when levels drop somewhat in the heat of summer, the curiously circular potholes—the result of glacial erosion—transform into a number of surprisingly warm and very popular swimming holes. The trail to Diana's Bath is flat and accessible, making this a good destination for wheelchair hikers and others in need of a level walking surface.

From the fully accessible parking area, follow the level walkway 0.8 mile to Diana's Bath. Reaching the bath, different viewing points along the path lead to a 20-foot waterfall (definitely at its best in spring) as well as close-up looks at the cascades, naturally forming waterspouts, and the potholes. Future Forest Service plans for this path include the installation of an all-access vault style toilet at the trailhead and an extension of the walkway to more viewing points.

User Groups: Hikers, dogs, and wheelchairs. No bikes or horses.

Permits: No backcountry permit is needed, but a permit is required for day use or overnight parking at any White Mountain National Forest trailhead. Permits are available at several area stores and from the national forest at a cost of $5 for seven consecutive days or $20 per year. A $3 one-day permit can be purchased at self-service stations at national forest trailheads, but the pass is good only for the trailhead at which it's purchased.

Maps: A waterproof trail map is available from the Appalachian Mountain Club (Crawford Notch–Sandwich Range/Moosilauke–Kinsman, $9.95). For a topographic area map, request North Conway West from the USGS.

Directions: From Route 16 in North Conway, turn west at the traffic lights in front of the Eastern Slope Inn onto River Road. Continue about 2.2 miles to a large parking area on the left for Diana's Bath.

GPS Coordinates: 44.0716 N, 71.1701 W

Contact: White Mountain National Forest Headquarters, 71 White Mountain Drive, Campton, NH 03246, 603/536-6100, TDD for hearing impaired 603/536-3665, www.fs.fed.us/r9/white.

73 NORTH MOAT MOUNTAIN
8.4 mi/6 hr   🥾3 ⛰9

in the White Mountain National Forest west of North Conway

North Moat (3,196 ft.) is one of the finest summit hikes you can make in the White Mountains without going up a big peak. From North Moat on a clear day, the views extend due north as far as Mount Washington. A popular climb for visitors to the resort town of North Conway, this 8.4-mile round-trip nets an elevation gain of nearly 2,700 feet.

From the parking area for Diana's Bath on the left (west) side of the road, strike out on the North Moat Trail heading almost due west. A flat, well-trod path running parallel to Lucy Brook, at 1.5 miles, the trail takes a sharp left to begin the climb to the North Moat summit (the Attitash Trail continues straight ahead). It's a steady climb under forest cover for much of the way. The trail grows truly steep only in its last 0.5-mile push to

the rocky summit. Enjoy views east to the village of North Conway and north to the Saco River valley, Wildcat Mountain, and the soaring Mount Washington. Return the way you came.

User Groups: Hikers and dogs. No bikes, horses, or wheelchair facilities.

Permits: No backcountry permit is needed, but a permit is required for day use or overnight parking at any White Mountain National Forest trailhead. Permits are available at several area stores and from the national forest at a cost of $5 for seven consecutive days or $20 per year. A $3 one-day permit can be purchased at self-service stations at national forest trailheads, but the pass is good only for the trailhead at which it's purchased.

Maps: A waterproof trail map is available from the Appalachian Mountain Club (Crawford Notch–Sandwich Range/Moosilauke–Kinsman map, $9.95). For a topographic area map, request North Conway West from the USGS.

Directions: From Route 16 in North Conway, turn west at the traffic lights in front of the Eastern Slope Inn onto River Road. Continue about 2.2 miles to a large parking area on the left for Diana's Baths. The trail begins on the west side of the parking area.

GPS Coordinates: 44.0716 N, 71.1701 W

Contact: White Mountain National Forest Headquarters, 71 White Mountain Drive, Campton, NH 03246, 603/536-6100, TDD for hearing impaired 603/536-3665, www.fs.fed.us/r9/white.

74 ROCKY GORGE
0.5 mi/0.5 hr   🥾1 ⛰8

in the White Mountain National Forest on the Kancamagus Highway

This wheelchair-accessible trail leads to a dramatic gorge and picturesque pond formed by the aptly named Swift River. Rocky Gorge scenic area is also a popular picnic area and rest stop for travelers on the Kancamagus Highway. From the parking area, follow the paved path to a bridge just below the Swift River gorge. Across the bridge, the path narrows as it winds along the edge of the gorge to another viewing area (depending on ability, this may not be suitable for all wheelchair hikers). The path continues up a small ridge at an 8 percent grade to the top, where it crosses the Nanamocomuck Trail, then descends in a short section of 14 percent grade before arriving at Falls Pond and a hardened viewing area near the water's edge. There are benches for resting along the trail from the parking area to the pond. The total distance of the trail to Falls Pond is approximately 1,300 feet. Return the way you came.

Note: A second choice is to proceed from the parking lot and, instead of crossing the bridge, continuing on the hardened gravel trail as it follows the river. The level trail runs for approximately 1,000 feet before ending at a widened area with a beautiful view upstream back to the bridge. Return the way you came.

User Groups: Hikers, dogs, and wheelchairs. No bikes or horses.

Permits: No backcountry permit is needed, but a permit is required for day use or overnight parking at any White Mountain National Forest trailhead. Permits are available at several area stores and from the national forest at a cost of $5 for seven consecutive days or $20 per year. A $3 one-day permit can be purchased at self-service stations at national forest trailheads, but the pass is good only for the trailhead at which it's purchased.

Maps: Two waterproof area trail maps available from the Appalachian Mountain Club show this hike (Franconia–Pemigewasset Range map and Crawford Notch–Sandwich Range/Moosilauke–Kinsman map, $9.95 each). For a topographic area map, request Mount Tripyramid from the USGS.

Directions: The hike begins at the Rocky Gorge Scenic Area parking lot along the Kancamagus Highway/Route 112, 26 miles east of Lincoln and approximately 10 miles west of the junction of Routes 16 and 112 (Kancamangus Highway) in Conway.

GPS Coordinates: 44.0072 N, 71.2753 W

Contact: White Mountain National Forest Headquarters, 71 White Mountain Drive, Campton, NH 03246, 603/536-6100, TDD for hearing impaired 603/536-3665, www.fs.fed.us/r9/white.

75 SABBADAY FALLS
0.8 mi/0.75 hr   🏃1 ⛰10

in the White Mountain National Forest on the Kancamagus Highway

BEST (

The early explorers of the Passaconaway Valley reached Sabbaday Falls on a Sunday, and thereafter the spectacular falls became a popular destination on the Sabbath. Formed by the gouging action of rocks and sand released by glacial melt-off 10,000 years ago, the roaring falls drop twice through a narrow gorge so perfect in its geometry it seems the work of engineers. Below the gorge, Sabbaday Brook settles quietly, if briefly, in a clear pool. This easy hike is a great one for young children.

From the picnic area, follow the wide gravel and dirt Sabbaday Brook Trail, which parallels the rocky brook. The trail ascends very little over its first 0.3 mile to where a side path to the falls leads left. With the sound of rushing water growing thunderous, the path loops past the lower pool and above the gorge, crossing a bridge with nice views of the falls and back down to the pool; a handrail is located all along this stretch of the trail. Ascending a series of steps as it turns away from the gorge, the path rejoins the Sabbaday Brook Trail. Turn right to return to the parking area.

User Groups: Hikers and dogs. No bikes, horses, or wheelchair facilities.

Permits: No backcountry permit is needed, but a permit is required for day use or overnight parking at any White Mountain

National Forest trailhead. Permits are available at several area stores and from the national forest at a cost of $5 for seven consecutive days or $20 per year. A $3 one-day permit can be purchased at self-service stations at national forest trailheads, but the pass is good only for the trailhead at which it's purchased.

Maps: Two waterproof area trail maps available from the Appalachian Mountain Club show this hike (Franconia–Pemigewasset Range map and Crawford Notch–Sandwich Range/ Moosilauke–Kinsman map, $9.95 each). For a topographic area map, request Mount Tripyramid from the USGS.

Directions: The hike begins at the Sabbaday Falls parking area along the Kancamagus Highway/Route 112, 19.9 miles east of the McDonald's on Route 112 in Lincoln, 6.6 miles east of the sign at Kancamagus Pass, and 15.6 miles west of the junction of Routes 112 and 16 in Conway.
GPS Coordinates: 43.9973 N, 71.3925 W

Contact: White Mountain National Forest Headquarters, 71 White Mountain Drive, Campton, NH 03246, 603/536-6100, TDD for hearing impaired 603/536-3665, www. fs.fed.us/r9/white.

76 MOUNT TRIPYRAMID
11 mi/7 hr

in the White Mountain National Forest east of Waterville Valley

Tripyramid's three wooded summits offer little in the way of compelling views, but the challenging scramble up and down Tripyramid's two rockslides and the fact that North Tripyramid (4,180 ft.) and Middle Tripyramid (4,140 ft.) are both official 4,000-footers are enough to make this a popular draw for hikers on the lookout for a more rugged mountain experience. The loop hike to all three summits ascends about 3,000 feet over its length and involves some exposed scrambling, especially

going up the north slide; it is not for the faint of heart or anyone not in good shape.

From the parking area, walk around the gate onto Livermore Road (also called the Livermore Trail), an old logging road that rises steadily 2.6 miles to the south end of the Mount Tripyramid Trail. To add extra flavor to this hike, mountain bike this stretch and stash your bike in the woods near the Mount Tripyramid trailhead. Turning right onto the Mount Tripyramid Trail from Livermore Road, the path begins its ascent up the mountain's exposed and steep north side. At 0.5 mile out from Livermore Road, the trail reaches the bottom of the slide and the real climb begins. Gaining 1,200 feet in elevation over the next 0.5 mile, the trail becomes almost vertical as it traverses the rock slabs; footing here can be treacherous when the rocks are wet or icy. Leveling out somewhat after such a strenuous push, the trail reaches North Tripyramid at 1.2 miles, with limited views. Stay on the narrow path as it leaves the summit, passing a junction with the Sabbaday Brook Trail 0.5 mile past the north peak and reaching Middle Tripyramid (4,140 ft.) 0.3 mile farther. A pair of outlooks just off the trail offer decent views. The trail continues to South Peak (4,090 ft.), which is wooded. Just beyond that peak, bear right to descend the steep south slide. Rocks here are loose and footing can be tricky. At the end of the slide, the trail enters the woods again and follows Slide Brook past nice pools to the Livermore Trail, 2.5 miles from South Peak. Turn right and hike (or bike) 3.6 miles back to the parking area.

User Groups: Hikers and dogs on the Mount Tripyramid Trail; hikers, dogs, and bikes on the Livermore Trail. No horses or wheelchair facilities. The Mount Tripyramid Trail should not be attempted in winter except by hikers experienced in mountaineering and prepared for severe winter weather.

Permits: No backcountry permit is needed, but a permit is required for day use or overnight parking at any White Mountain National Forest trailhead. Permits are available

at several area stores and from the national forest at a cost of $5 for seven consecutive days or $20 per year. A $3 one-day permit can be purchased at self-service stations at national forest trailheads, but the pass is good only for the trailhead at which it's purchased.

Maps: Two waterproof area trail maps available from the Appalachian Mountain Club show this hike (Franconia–Pemigewasset Range map and Crawford Notch–Sandwich Range/Moosilauke–Kinsman map, $9.95 each). For topographic area maps, request Mount Tripyramid and Waterville Valley from the USGS.

Directions: From I-93 in Campton, take Exit 28 onto Route 49 east. Drive about 11.4 miles into Waterville Valley and turn right onto Valley Road, which is still Route 49 east. Just 0.4 mile farther, turn left onto West Branch Road, in front of the Osceola Library. Drive another 0.7 mile and turn right (before the bridge) into the parking lot at the start of the Livermore Trail (also called the Livermore Road). In the winter months, you can ski or snowshoe up Livermore Trail, which is groomed and tracked for skating or diagonal skiing, without having to pay the trail fee for the cross-country ski touring center in Waterville Valley because Livermore Trail is within the national forest.

GPS Coordinates: 43.9834 N, 71.5588 W

Contact: White Mountain National Forest Headquarters, 71 White Mountain Drive, Campton, NH 03246, 603/536-6100, TDD for hearing impaired 603/536-3665, www.fs.fed.us/r9/white.

🔢 WELCH AND DICKEY
4.5 mi/3.5 hr   🥾3 ⛰10

in the White Mountain National Forest southwest of Waterville Valley

BEST (

A delightful hike in July and August, this 4.5-mile loop over Welch (2,605 ft.) and Dickey (2,736 ft.) may best be saved for September or October when views from the mountains' many open ledges simply burst with autumn color. Relatively easy, with just a few brief, steep stretches, it's a good hike for children, entailing only about 1,700 feet of uphill over 4.5 miles.

From the parking area, pick up the Welch Mountain Trail (views are best when hiking this loop counterclockwise). Within a mile, the trail emerges onto open ledges just below the summit of Welch Mountain, with a wide view across the Mad River Valley to Sandwich Mountain. During peak fall foliage season, the vista here will be ablaze with yellow, orange, and red. The trail turns left and ascends another mile to the summit, with broad views in every direction, including Dickey Mountain to the north. Continuing on the trail, you drop steeply into a shallow saddle, then climb up onto Dickey, a half mile from Welch. Watch for a sign pointing to nearby ledges, where there is a good view toward Franconia Notch. From Dickey's summit, follow an arrow onto an obvious trail north, which soon descends steeply to slab ledges above the cliffs of Dickey Mountain, overlooking a beautiful, narrow valley between Welch and Dickey that lights up with color in the fall. The Dickey Mountain Trail continues descending the ridge, re-entering the woods, then reaching the parking area, two miles from Dickey's summit.

User Groups: Hikers and dogs. No bikes, horses, or wheelchair facilities.

Permits: No backcountry permit is needed, but a permit is required for day use or overnight parking at any White Mountain National Forest trailhead. Permits are available at several area stores and from the national forest at a cost of $5 for seven consecutive days or $20 per year. A $3 one-day permit can be purchased at self-service stations at national forest trailheads, but the pass is good only for the trailhead at which it's purchased.

Maps: Two waterproof area trail maps from the Appalachian Mountain Club show this hike (Franconia–Pemigewasset Range map and Crawford Notch–Sandwich Range/

Moosilauke–Kinsman map, $9.95 each). For a topographic area map, request Waterville Valley from the USGS.

Directions: From I-93 in Campton, take Exit 28 onto Route 49 north, toward Waterville Valley. After passing through the traffic lights in Campton, drive another 4.4 miles on Route 49, then turn left onto Upper Mad River Road, immediately crossing the Mad River on Six Mile Bridge. Continue 0.7 mile from Route 49, then turn right onto Orris Road at a small sign reading Welch Mountain Trail. Drive another 0.7 mile to a parking area on the right.

GPS Coordinates: 43.9038 N, 71.5886 W

Contact: White Mountain National Forest Headquarters, 71 White Mountain Drive, Campton, NH 03246, 603/536-6100, TDD for hearing impaired 603/536-3665, www.fs.fed.us/r9/white.

78 SANDWICH MOUNTAIN
8.3 mi/5.5 hr

in Waterville Valley in the White Mountain National Forest

At 3,993 feet, Sandwich Mountain is a tad short to attract the same attention among hikers as many of the 4,000-footers in the White Mountains. But from the small area of rocks jutting just above the forest at its summit, you get a wide view from the northwest to the east of most of the White Mountains—certainly more peaks are visible from here than from many of the smaller 4,000-footers in the Whites. This loop over Sandwich Mountain can be done in either direction—the hike in this description follows a clockwise route and nets 2,500 feet in elevation gain.

From the north end of the parking lot, pick up the Drake's Brook Trail. Follow the old logging road for 0.4 mile, bearing right to stay on the trail where a junction is reached with a bike path. The trail then crosses Drake's Brook (difficult during times of high water) and runs parallel to the brook for the next 2.5 miles before finally swinging to the right and climbing a steep 0.3 mile to a junction with the Sandwich Mountain Trail (SMT). Turn left on the SMT and continue on 1.1 miles to the summit, breaking out of the spruce forest to spectacular views of Waterville Valley in the near foreground, including the peaks surrounding it (from left to right): Tecumseh, Osceola, and Tripyramid, with its south slide visible. To the east, the view encompasses the broad ridge connecting Whiteface, Passaconaway, and Chocorua's bald knob beyond. Massive Mount Moosilauke dominates the horizon to the west. The high Franconia Ridge rises above everything else in the distant northwest. And to the northeast, the biggest peaks in the Whites, Mount Washington and the Presidential Range, are clearly visible. Behind you, look for a somewhat hidden footpath through scrub trees that leads a few feet to a view south toward the Lakes Region. Descend the Sandwich Mountain Trail for 3.9 miles back to the parking area.

User Groups: Hikers and dogs. No bikes, horses, or wheelchair facilities.

Permits: No backcountry permit is needed, but a permit is required for day use or overnight parking at any White Mountain National Forest trailhead. Permits are available at several area stores and from the national forest at a cost of $5 for seven consecutive days or $20 per year. A $3 one-day permit can be purchased at self-service stations at national forest trailheads, but the pass is good only for the trailhead at which it's purchased.

Maps: Two waterproof area trail maps from the Appalachian Mountain Club show this hike (Franconia–Pemigewasset Range map and Crawford Notch–Sandwich Range/Moosilauke–Kinsman map, $9.95 each). For topographic area maps, request the Waterville Valley and Mount Tripyramid maps from the USGS.

Directions: From Exit 28 off I-93 in Campton, take Route 49 north for about 10.2 miles and turn right into a parking lot for the Drake's Brook and Sandwich Mountain Trails.

NEW HAMPSHIRE

GPS Coordinates: 43.9379 N, 71.5116 W
Contact: White Mountain National Forest Headquarters, 71 White Mountain Drive, Campton, NH 03246, 603/536-6100, TDD for hearing impaired 603/536-3665, www. fs.fed.us/r9/white.

79 MOUNT WHITEFACE
8.2 mi/5.5 hr

in the southern White Mountain National Forest north of Wonalancet

Whiteface, at 4,010 feet, is not among the best-known 4,000-footers in the Whites, but the cliffs just below its summit offer dramatic views of the southern Whites, Mount Washington, and the Lakes Region to the south. Come here in September and early October to see the surrounding woods lit with color. This climb's vertical ascent is approximately 3,800 feet. (For a longer loop linking Whiteface with Passaconaway, see the *Mount Passaconaway* listing in this chapter.)

From the parking lot, walk back to the road and turn right, following the road for 0.3 mile to the Blueberry Ledge trailhead (marked). At first following a single-lane dirt road, the trail crosses a bridge over Wonalancet Brook and continues on to where it enters the woods. Now a footpath, the Blueberry Ledge Trail remains a fairly level trek until reaching slab ledges at 1.5 miles from the parking lot. For the next two miles, the route grows increasingly steep. Good views south to the lakes region begin at 3.6 miles, where the Blueberry Ledge Trail turns sharply right at a slab and the brink of a cliff. This can be a hazardous spot when wet or icy; on a winter hike, you might want the security of roping up and belaying this section. Continue up the Blueberry Ledge Trail for another 0.3 mile; you will pass ledges with terrific views down into the broad glacial cirque known as the Bowl (which is framed by Whiteface and neighboring Mount Passaconaway), east to Mount Chocorua, and

north to Mount Washington. At 3.9 miles, rear right at a trail junction onto the Rollins Trail, following it 0.2 mile to the wooded summit of Whiteface. Descend along the same route.
User Groups: Hikers and dogs. No bikes, horses, or wheelchair facilities.
Permits: No backcountry permit is needed, but a permit is required for day use or overnight parking at any White Mountain National Forest trailhead. Permits are available at several area stores and from the national forest at a cost of $5 for seven consecutive days or $20 per year. A $3 one-day permit can be purchased at self-service stations at national forest trailheads, but the pass is good only for the trailhead at which it's purchased.
Maps: A waterproof area trail map is available from the Appalachian Mountain Club (Crawford Notch–Sandwich Range/Moosilauke–Kinsman, $9.95). For topographic area maps, request Mount Chocorua and Mount Tripyramid from the USGS.
Directions: From Route 113A in Wonalancet, turn north onto Ferncroft Road. Follow it for a half mile and bear right at a sign into the hiker parking lot. Trails in this part of the national forest are accessed through private land; be sure to stay on trails.
GPS Coordinates: 43.9128 N, 71.3653 W
Contact: Wonalancet Out Door Club, HCR 64 Box 248, Wonalancet, NH 03897, www. wodc.org. White Mountain National Forest Headquarters, 71 White Mountain Drive, Campton, NH 03246, 603/536-6100, TDD for hearing impaired 603/536-3665, www. fs.fed.us/r9/white.

80 MOUNT PASSACONAWAY
9.5 mi/6.5 hr   ⛹5 ⛰8

in the southern White Mountain National Forest north of Wonalancet

Mount Passaconaway (4,060 ft.) is wooded, with no views (unless you're here in winter and standing on several feet of snow to see over the low spruce trees). But there are two nice views near the summit that make this mountain, named for the famed Penacook leader, Chief Passaconaway, worth the effort. The trails are marked with blue blazes and the vertical ascent is about 3,800 feet.

From the parking lot, walk back to the road and turn right, following the road for 0.8 mile straight onto the Dicey's Mill Trail. Soon after entering the woods, the trail crosses into the national forest. It parallels and eventually crosses Wonalancet Brook at 2.3 miles (0.4 mile beyond the Wiggin Trail junction), then begins ascending more steeply. The trail passes the junction with the Rollins Trail, which comes in from the left (west) at 3.7 miles, and then passes the East Loop Trail at 3.9 miles. At around 4.5 miles, you'll get a view toward the peaks above Waterville Valley to the northwest. The junction with the Walden Trail is reached at 4.6 miles; from there, a spur path leads to the right about 50 yards to Passaconaway's summit. Follow the Walden Trail around the summit cone about 100 yards to the best view on this hike, from a ledge overlooking Mount Chocorua to the east and Mount Washington to the north. Continue descending the Walden Trail, dropping steeply to the East Loop, 0.6 mile from the summit spur path. Turn right (west) on the East Loop, which leads 0.2 mile back to the Dicey's Mill Trail. Turn left (south) and follow that trail 3.9 miles back to the Ferncroft Road parking area.

Special note: You can combine Passaconaway and Mount Whiteface on a rugged loop of nearly 12 miles, with more than 4,600 feet of climbing. Hike the Blueberry Ledge Trail up Whiteface, then the Rollins Trail for 2.3 miles over the high ridge connecting the two peaks; there are some views along the Rollins, though much of it is within the subalpine conifer forest. Turn left (north) on the Dicey's Mill Trail and then complete the Passaconaway hike described in this listing.

Camping is permitted on the hardened ground at the former site of the Camp Rich shelter, near the junction of the Rollins and Dicey's Mill Trails. See the Wonalancet Out Door Club website (www.wodc.org) for current information.

User Groups: Hikers and dogs. No bikes, horses, or wheelchair facilities.

Permits: No backcountry permit is needed, but a permit is required for day use or overnight parking at any White Mountain National Forest trailhead. Permits are available at several area stores and from the national forest at a cost of $5 for seven consecutive days or $20 per year. A $3 one-day permit can be purchased at self-service stations at national forest trailheads, but the pass is good only for the trailhead at which it's purchased.

Maps: A waterproof trail map is available from the Appalachian Mountain Club (Crawford Notch–Sandwich Range/Moosilauke–Kinsman, $9.95). For topographic area maps, request Mount Chocorua and Mount Tripyramid from the USGS.

Directions: From Route 113A in Wonalancet, turn north onto Ferncroft Road. Follow it for a half mile and bear right at a sign into the hiker parking lot. Trails in this part of the national forest are accessed through private land; be sure to stay on the path.

GPS Coordinates: 43.9147 N, 71.3659 W

Contact: Wonalancet Out Door Club, HCR 64 Box 248, Wonalancet, NH 03897, www.wodc.org. White Mountain National Forest Headquarters, 71 White Mountain Drive, Campton, NH 03246, 603/536-6100, TDD for hearing impaired 603/536-3665, www.fs.fed.us/r9/white.

81 MOUNT CHOCORUA: BROOK-LIBERTY LOOP

7.4 mi/5 hr   🏃4 ⛰10

in the White Mountain National Forest north of Tamworth and east of Wonalancet

The eye-catching eastern end of the Sandwich Range, Chocorua's distinctive horn-shaped

© MATT SINGER

the great horn of Mount Chocorua

summit cone makes this 3,500-foot peak a natural draw for visitors. Some come just to stand in the parking lot and snap photos of this "mini Alp," but during peak hiking season, Chocorua is one of the most traveled mountains in New Hampshire. The intent of this loop is to get away from the crowds (as much as possible) for a more solitary experience of Chocorua's splendor. This hike climbs about 2,600 feet in elevation.

This hike ascends via the Brook Trail, which is steep, and descends via the Liberty Trail, known as the easiest route on Chocorua. (Hikers looking for a less demanding route could opt to go up and down the Liberty Trail.) From the parking area, walk past the gate and follow the gravel woods road, which the Brook Trail leaves within a half mile. The trail passes a small waterfall along Claybank Brook less than two miles up and after some easy to moderately-difficult hiking, emerges from the woods onto the bare rock of Chocorua's summit cone at three miles. The trail's final 0.6 mile ascends steep slabs and ledges; the Liberty Trail coincides with the Brook Trail for the last 0.2 mile to the top. Open summit views stretch north to Mount Washington, west across the White Mountains, south to the lakes region, and east over the hills and lakes of western Maine. To descend, follow the two trails down for that 0.2 mile, and then bear left onto the Liberty Trail. It traverses somewhat rocky ground high on the mountain, passing the U.S. Forest Service's Jim Liberty cabin within a half mile. The descent grows more moderate, eventually following an old bridle path back to the parking area, 3.8 miles from the summit.

The U.S. Forest Service maintains the Jim Liberty cabin (which has a capacity of nine) on the Liberty Trail, a half mile below Chocorua's summit; a fee is charged and the water source is unreliable in dry seasons. Contact the White Mountain National Forest for rate and reservation information.

User Groups: Hikers and dogs. No bikes, horses, or wheelchair facilities.

Permits: No backcountry permit is needed, but a permit is required for day use or overnight parking at any White Mountain National Forest trailhead. Permits are available

at several area stores and from the national forest at a cost of $5 for seven consecutive days or $20 per year. A $3 one-day permit can be purchased at self-service stations at national forest trailheads, but the pass is good only for the trailhead at which it's purchased.

Maps: A waterproof area trail map is available from the Appalachian Mountain Club (Crawford Notch–Sandwich Range/Moosilauke–Kinsman, $9.95). For topographic area maps, request Mount Chocorua and Silver Lake from the USGS.

Directions: From the junction of Routes 113 and 113A in Tamworth, drive west on Route 113A for 3.4 miles and turn right onto the dirt Howler's Mill Road. Continue for 1.2 miles and turn left (at trail signs) onto Paugus Road/Fire Road 68. The parking area and trailhead lie 0.8 mile up the road.

GPS Coordinates: 43.9174 N, 71.2932 W

Contact: White Mountain National Forest Headquarters, 71 White Mountain Drive, Campton, NH 03246, 603/536-6100, TDD for hearing impaired 603/536-3665, www.fs.fed.us/r9/white.

82 MOUNT CHOCORUA: PIPER TRAIL

9 mi/6.5 hr

in the White Mountain National Forest north of Chocorua and west of Conway

This is the most heavily used route up the popular, 3,500-foot Mount Chocorua, though at nine miles for the round-trip, it is not the shortest. The trail suffers from erosion due to overuse, which can make the footing difficult in places. This hike nets an elevation gain of 2,700 feet.

From the parking area, the trail starts out on easy ground, entering the woods. About two miles out, it crosses the Chocorua River and ascends in switchbacks up the mountainside. At 3.1 miles, a short side path leads to the Camp Penacook shelter and tent sites. The

final half mile of trail passes over open ledges with sweeping views and on to the summit, where the panoramic views take in Mount Washington to the north, New Hampshire's Lakes Region to the south, the hills and lakes of western Maine to the east, and the grand sweep of the White Mountains to the west and northwest. Views here are especially pleasing in early fall. Descend the same trail.

The national forest maintains Camp Penacook, which consists of a lean-to shelter and four tent platforms, 3.1 miles up the Piper Trail and 1.4 miles below Chocorua's summit; there is no fee.

User Groups: Hikers and dogs. No bikes, horses, or wheelchair facilities.

Permits: No backcountry permit is needed, but a permit is required for day use or overnight parking at any White Mountain National Forest trailhead. Permits are available at several area stores and from the national forest at a cost of $5 for seven consecutive days or $20 per year. A $3 one-day permit can be purchased at self-service stations at national forest trailheads, but the pass is good only for the trailhead at which it's purchased.

Maps: A waterproof area trail map is available from the Appalachian Mountain Club (Crawford Notch–Sandwich Range/Moosilauke–Kinsman, $9.95). For topographic area maps, request Mount Chocorua and Silver Lake from the USGS.

Directions: The Piper Trail begins behind the Piper Trail Restaurant and Cabins on Route 16 between the towns of Chocorua and Conway, six miles south of the junction of Route 16 and Route 112/Kancamagus Highway. Follow the dirt road to the right of the store for a quarter mile to the trailhead parking area.

GPS Coordinates: 43.9312 N, 71.2243 W

Contact: White Mountain National Forest Headquarters, 71 White Mountain Drive, Campton, NH 03246, 603/536-6100, TDD for hearing impaired 603/536-3665, www.fs.fed.us/r9/white.

83 MOUNT ISRAEL
4.2 mi/2.5 hr

in the southern White Mountain National Forest northwest of Center Sandwich

Just 2,630 feet high, Mount Israel's summit ledges have nice views of the entire Sandwich Range to the north and Mount Moosilauke to the west. Considering the hike's relatively easy access and the ascent of just 1,600 feet, this should be one of the most popular climbs in the area. But Mount Israel is one scenic summit that is definitely overlooked; you may share the mountain with only a few other hikers, even in peak season.

From the Mead Base Camp parking area, pass to the left of the main Mead Base building and pick up the Wentworth Trail, which is marked by a sign. The trail climbs steadily up the mountain's southern slope, keeping the grade reduced by a number of sweeping switchbacks. At 1.5 miles, the trail reaches a good overlook south to the Lakes Region. Approximately two miles from the start of this hike, the trail emerges at the summit ledges and a wide view of the Sandwich Range (from left to right): Sandwich Mountain, Tripyramid, Whiteface with a cliff near its summit, Passaconaway immediately behind and to the right of Whiteface, and Chocorua far to the right, barely within sight. From a nearby ledge, you can look west to Moosilauke. Descend the way you came.

User Groups: Hikers and dogs. No bikes, horses, or wheelchair facilities.

Permits: No backcountry permit is needed, but a permit is required for day use or overnight parking at any White Mountain National Forest trailhead. Permits are available at several area stores and from the national forest at a cost of $5 for seven consecutive days or $20 per year. A $3 one-day permit can be purchased at self-service stations at national forest trailheads, but the pass is good only for the trailhead at which it's purchased.

Maps: A waterproof trail map is available from the Appalachian Mountain Club (Crawford Notch–Sandwich Range/Moosilauke–Kinsman, $9.95). For topographic area maps, request Squam Mountains and Center Sandwich from the USGS.

Directions: From Route 113 in Center Sandwich, turn onto Grove Street at a sign for Sandwich Notch. At 0.4 mile, bear left on Diamond Ledge Road (don't be deceived by the name of the road bearing right—Mount Israel Road). At 2.5 miles from Route 113, bear right at a sign for Mead Base Camp. Follow that road another mile to its end at Mead Base Camp and parking on the right.

GPS Coordinates: 43.8257 N, 71.4838 W

Contact: White Mountain National Forest Headquarters, 71 White Mountain Drive, Campton, NH 03246, 603/536-6100, TDD for hearing impaired 603/536-3665, www.fs.fed.us/r9/white. Squam Lakes Association, P.O. Box 204, Holderness, NH 03245, 603/968-7336, www.squamlakes.org.

84 STINSON MOUNTAIN
3.6 mi/2.5 hr

north of Rumney in the White Mountain National Forest

Tucked away in the very southwestern corner of the White Mountain National Forest is little Stinson Mountain (2,900 ft.), a small mountain with a great summit view of the valley of the Baker River, the state college town of Plymouth, and the surrounding hills. It's a nice spot to catch the sunrise or foliage at its peak. This hike ascends 1,400 feet in a 1.8-mile uphill jaunt.

Follow the Stinson Mountain Trail, which begins quite easily, then grows moderately steep but never very difficult. Within a quarter mile the trail crosses an old logging road and in a half mile it bears right where an old wooden footbridge leads left on a former trail. Although the trail is generally an easy, wide, and obvious path, be careful not to be fooled into these wrong turns. Within a hundred yards of the summit, or 1.8 miles from the trailhead, the trail forks, with both branches leading to the summit ledges. Trees block the view somewhat from the summit, but immediately north of the summit ledges, a side path leads 200 feet to good views of Stinson Lake and the Moosilauke massif. Return the way you came.

User Groups: Hikers and dogs. No bikes, horses, or wheelchair facilities.

Permits: No backcountry permit is needed, but a permit is required for day use or overnight parking at any White Mountain National Forest trailhead. Permits are available at several area stores and from the national forest at a cost of $5 for seven consecutive days or $20 per year. A $3 one-day permit can be purchased at self-service stations at national forest trailheads, but the pass is good only for the trailhead at which it's purchased.

Maps: A waterproof area trail map is available from the Appalachian Mountain Club

(Crawford Notch–Sandwich Range/Moosilauke–Kinsman, $9.95). For a topographic area map, request Rumney from the USGS.

Directions: From Route 25 in Rumney Village (3.5 miles north of the traffic circle at Routes 25 and 3A, 2.1 miles north of the Polar Caves Park, 7.7 miles west of I-93 Exit 26, and 4.2 miles south of the junction of Routes 25 and 118), turn at a blinking yellow light onto Main Street. In a mile, the street becomes Stinson Lake Road. At 5.1 miles from Route 25, bear right on Cross Road at a sign for Hawthorne Village. In 0.3 mile, bear right onto a gravel road, then drive another half mile and turn right at a sign for the Stinson Mountain Trail. Drive 0.3 mile farther to parking on the left and a trail sign.

GPS Coordinates: 43.8528 N, 71.7991 W

Contact: White Mountain National Forest Headquarters, 71 White Mountain Drive, Campton, NH 03246, 603/536-6100, TDD for hearing impaired 603/536-3665, www.fs.fed.us/r9/white.

NEW HAMPSHIRE

THE
LAKES REGION
AND SOUTH

BEST HIKES

◖ Bird-Watching
Great Bay National Estuarine Research Reserve,
   page 241.

◖ Fall Foliage
Mount Monadnock: White Dot Trail, page 246.

◖ Summit Hikes
Mount Cardigan: West Side Loop, page 235.

The sky-high peaks of the northern White Mountains may stand out as the Granite State's star attraction, but for smaller summits in the lower half of New Hampshire – regional favorites such as Monadnock, Cardigan, Kearsarge, Sunapee, Major, and Smarts – the beauty is in the details. This is the land of rolling countryside, lakeside cliffs, and proudly isolated summits. Leaving behind the predominant conifer cover found in the northern part of the state, the deciduous forest of maples, beech, oaks, and birch found so abundantly here provide treks with a backdrop of ever-changing color. Lime green in June and lush blue in summer, the landscape gradually heats up to an autumn fire of red, orange, and golden yellow.

Southern New Hampshire is also home to the state's 18-mile-long seacoast (the shortest stretch of seaboard located within the boundaries of one state). Shoehorned between Massachusetts and Maine, New Hampshire's coastal area offers sandy beaches and rocky shoreline, but the heart of this region is found in the tidal estuaries that form a great inland bay. Hikes around aptly named Great Bay take you to a unique marine environment where fertile fields and freshwater rivers meet salt marshes and coastal tides.

Along the coast, as well as in the rest of the southern and central portions of the state – from hills along the Appalachian Trail in the Upper Connecticut Valley and the scenic Lakes Region to magnificent Mount Monadnock and wooded rambles along the Massachusetts border – access to the outdoors is easy to come by. Almost 85 percent of New Hampshire is forest-covered and state parks, town forests, and private reserves liberally scattered throughout the region offer countless miles of hiking trails, reclaimed railroad tracks, and old logging roads. Two long-distance trails in southern New Hampshire – the 21-mile Wapack Trail and the 50-mile Monadnock-Sunapee Greenway – offer scenic hiking over hills that see far fewer boots than popular corners of the Whites.

Along the Appalachian Trail in New Hampshire (Moose Mountain, Smarts Mountain, and Holt's Ledge in this chapter), dogs must be under verbal or physical restraint at all times. Hikers should carry a leash not longer than 6 feet and be prepared to leash a dog quickly if conditions warrant. Horses, bikes, hunting, and firearms are prohibited. Cross-country skiing and showshoeing are allowed on the Appalachian Trail, though the trail is often too rugged for skiing.

In most state parks and forests, dogs are allowed, but must remain leashed; private reserves and land conservancies often prohibit pets. The woods throughout much of the region are populated by an assortment of deer, beaver, fox, fisher cats, wild turkey, water fowl, and even a few reclusive brown bears and moose. Most state parks and forests allow certain types of hunting in season and hikers will need to take appropriate precautions in the woods at these times. The prime, snow-free hiking season in southern New Hampshire generally runs from April or May through mid-November.

NEW HAMPSHIRE

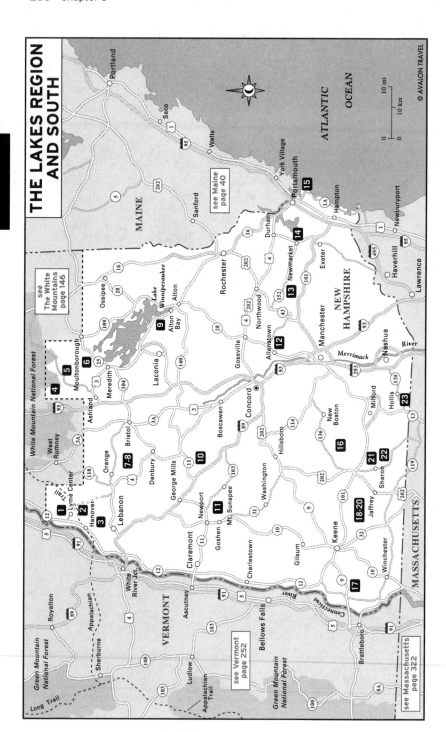

THE LAKES REGION AND SOUTH

© AVALON TRAVEL

see Maine
page 40

see
The White
Mountains
page 146

see Vermont
page 252

see Massachusetts
page 322

ATLANTIC OCEAN

MAINE

NEW HAMPSHIRE

VERMONT

MASSACHUSETTS

White Mountain National Forest

Green Mountain National Forest

Appalachian Trail

Long Trail

Connecticut River

Merrimack River

⊓ SMARTS MOUNTAIN

8.2 mi/3.5 hr 🏃3 ⛰8

in Lyme

A popular hike for students from nearby Dartmouth College and one of the first summits encountered along the New Hampshire stretch of the northbound Appalachian Trail, Smarts (3,240 ft.) blends a walk in the woods and along the rocky crest of a ridge with a rigorous push to the summit. Though mostly wooded at the top, an abandoned fire tower can still be climbed and is what makes the finish of this hike so spectacular. On a clear day, panoramic views take in the upper Connecticut Valley, the nearby Green Mountains, and north to more rugged peaks (Smarts is actually an isolated southern summit of the White Mountains). From the trailhead, this hike offers a net elevation gain of about 2,100 feet.

Near the entrance to the parking area, pick up the white-blazed Lambert Ridge Trail at the large trail marker (this is also the Appalachian Trail). An unmarked wide path seen at the end of the lot is the Ranger Trail, your route of descent. The hike starts as a slightly steep trek through mixed woods, with several switchbacks helping to reduce the grade. At 0.3 mile, the trail begins the ascent up rocky Lambert Ridge—itself a nice destination for a short hike. For the next 1.3 miles, tree cover thins and views become frequent. The trail then drops slightly, changes direction a few times—watch for white blazes—and ascends the relentlessly steep west slope of Smarts, passing an unmarked junction with the Ranger Trail at 3.5 miles from the parking lot. Here, you will also notice the beech and maple trees giving way to a boreal forest of firs and evergreen (the only boreal forest found this far south in New Hampshire). A half-mile more and you've reached the mountain's flat, wooded summit. Continue on for another 0.1 mile, watching on the left for a spur trail to the fire tower. Another summit spur trail leads to a tent camping site. Return to the parking area by backtracking 0.6 mile to the trail junction and bearing left for the 3.5-mile descent along the more moderately graded Ranger Trail.

NEW HAMPSHIRE

© KD TALBOT/WWW.GHOSTFLOWERS.COM

A hiker takes in the view from Smarts Mountain.

User Groups: Hikers and dogs. No horses, mountain bikes, or wheelchair facilities.

Permits: Parking and access are free.

Maps: Local trail maps are available from the Dartmouth Outing Club (including a three-color, double-sided map covering a 75-mile section of the AT from Route 12 in Woodstock, VT, to Route 112 in Woodstock, NH, $2). For a topographic map, request Smarts Mountain from the USGS.

Directions: From Route 10 on the Green in Lyme, take Dorchester Road (at the white church), following signs for the Dartmouth Skiway. Two miles from the Green, you'll pass through the village of Lyme Center. Continue for another 1.3 miles and then bear left onto the gravel Lyme-Dorchester Road. Follow for 1.8 miles. Just before an iron bridge over Grant Brook, park in a small lot on the left, at the trailhead.

GPS Coordinates: 43.7971 N, 72.0719 W

Contact: Appalachian Trail Conference, 799 Washington St., P.O. Box 807, Harpers Ferry, WV 25425-0807, 304/535-6331, www.appalachiantrail.org. Dartmouth Outdoor Programs Office, 119 Robinson Hall, Dartmouth College, Hanover, NH 03755, 603/646-2834, www.dartmouth.edu/~doc.

2 HOLT'S LEDGE
2.4 mi/1.5 hr ���2 ▲8

in Lyme

Holt's Ledge, at the top of a tall, rugged cliff, lies at the end of a fairly short and easy walk along the Appalachian Trail. On a clear day, the views from this high perch (2,100 ft.) are expansive: Smarts Mountain, Mount Cube, and Mounts Cardigan and Kearsarge are seen to the north and east; to the south, Vermont's Ascutney rises in the distance. The total elevation gain for this hike is 1,000 feet.

To pick up this stretch of the Appalachian Trail (AT), leave the Dartmouth Skiway parking area and walk 0.1 mile back towards Dorchester Road. Find the white-blazed AT on the left (west) side of the road. Beginning as a gentle ascent south through mixed woods, the trail crosses over a stone wall and a double-rut access road before reaching a trail junction at 0.6 mile. Here, a blue-blazed spur trail leads to the Trapper John shelter, an AT lean-to named for the character on the TV Show *MASH* (Dr. John McIntyre supposedly went to Dartmouth College). Continue on the AT and as the climb becomes a steeper ascent up the hillside, another junction is reached at 1.1 miles. To reach the open ledges, leave the AT and turn left onto an orange-black-orange-blazed side trail leading 0.1 mile to the cliff's scenic overlook. Descend along the same route.

Special Note: Hikers on the ledge will notice a weathered fence at the edge of the cliff. There not only to keep people away from a rather precipitous drop, the fence also protects the privacy of peregrine falcons nesting just below. In the 1970s, pesticide contamination ravaged populations of the majestic bird in New England (exposure to DDT caused falcon eggs to thin and break). Holt's Ledge was one of the first sites in the state where peregrines were successfully reintroduced and today remains one of the region's most popular nesting grounds.

User Groups: Hikers and dogs. No bikes, horses, or wheelchair facilities.

Permits: Parking and access are free.

Maps: Local trail maps are available from the Dartmouth Outing Club (including a three-color, double-sided map covering a 75-mile section of the AT from Route 12 in Woodstock, VT, to Route 112 in Woodstock, NH, $2). For a topographic map, request Smarts Mountain from the USGS.

Directions: From Route 10 on the Green in Lyme, take Dorchester Road (at the white church), following signs for the Dartmouth Skiway. Two miles from the Green, you'll pass through the village of Lyme Center. In another 1.3 miles, bear right at the fork in the road and drive 0.1 mile to the Dartmouth Skiway parking area.

GPS Coordinates: 43.7924 N, 72.1031 W
Contact: Dartmouth Outdoor Programs Office, 119 Robinson Hall, Dartmouth College, Hanover, NH 03755, 603/646-2834, www.dartmouth.edu/~doc.

3 MOOSE MOUNTAIN
4.1 mi/2 hr 👣2 ⛰6

in Hanover

Twin-peaked Moose Mountain rises 2,290 feet along the northeastern edge of Hanover, a quaint Upper Valley town and, most notably, the home of Dartmouth College. Passing over the higher of Moose's two summits (south summit), this loop hike uses the Appalachian Trail (AT) for its ascent. For not much effort, surprisingly open views can be had to the east and southeast, taking in Goose Pond (in the foreground) and Clark Pond (in the distance) in the town of Canaan, and Mounts Cardigan and Kearsarge even farther in the distance. The hike to south summit climbs just under 1,000 feet.

From the parking area along Three Mile Road, cross the road heading east and pick up the white-blazed AT at the large sign marker. The trail fords a brook and then crosses the wide, two-track Harris Trail (at 0.4 mile). The AT then begins the ascent of Moose Mountain, climbing at a moderate angle at first, leveling somewhat, then climbing again to the south summit at 1.8 miles. The lack of forest cover here is the result of a plane crash that happened on the mountain over 40 years ago (during the crash recovery effort, bulldozers cleared the summit for use as a helicopter landing). Continue on the trail north across the clearing, following the white blazes another 0.5 mile to a junction with the Clark Pond Loop. Straight ahead the AT continues on to the north summit of Moose Mountain. For this hike, turn left (west) onto the Clark Loop and descend 0.7 mile to reach a gravel road. Take a left and follow the road for about 50

feet. At another junction, turn left (south) onto the Harris Trail and after 0.7 mile reach the junction with the AT. Turn right and follow the AT's white blazes 0.4 mile back to Three Mile Road.

User Groups: Hikers and dogs. No bikes, horses, or wheelchair facilities. This trail is not suitable for skis.

Permits: Parking and access are free.

Maps: Local trail maps are available from the Dartmouth Outing Club (including a three-color, double-sided map covering a 75-mile section of the AT from Route 12 in Woodstock, VT, to Route 112 in Woodstock, NH $2). For topographic area maps, request Hanover and Canaan from the USGS.

Directions: From the center of Hanover, drive straight through the traffic lights (the Dartmouth College Green is to your left) onto East Wheelock Street and follow it 4.3 miles into the Hanover village of Etna. Turn left onto Etna Road, proceed 0.8 mile, and then turn right onto Ruddsboro Road. Continue 1.5 miles and then turn left onto Three Mile Road. Drive another 1.3 miles to a turnout on the left, where the white-blazed Appalachian Trail crosses the road.

The Moose Mountain AT shelter is located 0.2 mile off this loop, as the AT continues to the north summit (2.3 miles from the AT trailhead at Three Mile Road).

GPS Coordinates: 43.7187 N, 72.1752 W

Contact: Dartmouth Outdoor Programs Office, 119 Robinson Hall, Dartmouth College, Hanover, NH 03755, 603/646-2834, www.dartmouth.edu/~doc.

4 SQUAM MOUNTAINS
5.1 mi/3 hr 👣5 ⛰9

between Holderness and Center Sandwich

In late summer and early fall, this low mountain range suddenly lights up as its mainly mixed deciduous forest transforms into a colorful palette of reds, oranges, and yellows.

NEW HAMPSHIRE

NEW HAMPSHIRE

The contrast of fall foliage is especially vivid against the blue backdrop of Sqaum Lake and Lake Winnipesaukee and leaf peepers come from far and wide to take in the sights; peak foliage season typically runs from late September through the third weekend of October. This popular and fairly easy hike takes you to Squam's Mount Morgan (2,200 ft.) and Mount Percival (2,212 ft.) and includes only one short, difficult section—the cliffs on the Mount Morgan Trail—which can be avoided. The vertical ascent is about 1,400 feet.

From the parking area on Route 113, walk around the gate to pick up the yellow-blazed Mount Morgan Trail. Ascend gently along the trail for more than a mile. At 1.5 miles, the climb becomes somewhat steeper and at 1.7 miles, watch for the Crawford-Ridgepole Trail to enter from the left; it then coincides with the Mount Morgan Trail for the next 0.2 mile. Where the two trails split again, the Crawford-Ridgepole bears right for an easier route up Mount Morgan. This hike, however, turns left and continues on the Mount Morgan Trail, immediately scaling low cliffs on a wooden ladder, after which you crawl through a cavelike rock passage and emerge atop the cliffs with an excellent view of the big lakes to the south. Follow the blazes up the slabs to Morgan's open, rocky summit and again enjoy extensive views south. From the summit, follow the marked Crawford-Ridgepole Trail eastward along the Squam Mountains Ridge, a pleasant, relatively level walk filled with blueberry bushes for a quick summer snack. After 0.8 mile, reach the open summit of Mount Percival, which has equally excellent views of Squam and Winnipesaukee Lakes. Descend using the Mount Percival Trail to the southeast (look for a small trail sign nailed to a tree at the base of the summit slabs). Initially very steep, the trail quickly turns into a relatively easy descent of 1.9 miles back to Route 113. Once you reach the road, turn right and walk for 0.3 mile to the parking area.

Special note: Some hikers will find that hiking this loop in the opposite direction, going up the steep section just below the summit of Mount Percival, rather than down it, is much easier on the knees.

User Groups: Hikers and dogs. No bikes, horses, or wheelchair facilities.

Permits: Parking and access are free.

Maps: Squam Lakes trail map is available from the Squam Lakes Association for a modest fee. A waterproof trail map is available from the Appalachian Mountain Club (Crawford Notch–Sandwich Range/Moosilauke–Kinsman, $7.95). For a topographic area map, request Squam Mountains from the USGS.

Directions: From Route 3 in Holderness, follow Route 113 east for 5.5 miles to the marked parking turnout.

GPS Coordinates: 43.7892 N, 71.5486 W

Contact: Squam Lakes Association, P.O. Box 204, Holderness, NH 03245, 603/968-7336, www.squamlakes.org.

5 WEST RATTLESNAKE
1.8 mi/1 hr 🧍2 ⛰9

between Holderness and Center Sandwich

The classic movie *On Golden Pond* was filmed along the shores of Squam Lake and this easy hike to a cliff top above the lake offers cinematic views of Squam and the surrounding landscape (net elevation gain 450 feet). From the parking area for the Mount Morgan Trail, cross Route 113 and walk west about 100 feet to the sign marker for the Old Bridle Path. Follow the well-worn, gently-inclining path for almost a mile through the birch-filled woods. At 0.9 mile, where the main trail turns left, follow a side path to the right about 100 feet to the cliffs. At the summit, you may notice rock barriers surrounding Douglas' Knotweed, an endangered plant; avoid walking on the vegetation. Return the way you came.

User Groups: Hikers and dogs. No bikes, horses, or wheelchair facilities.

Permits: Parking and access are free.

Maps: Local trail guide and map are sold by

the Squam Lakes Association for a modest fee. A waterproof trail map is available from the Appalachian Mountain Club (Crawford Notch–Sandwich Range/Moosilauke–Kinsman, $7.95). For a topographic area map, request Squam Mountains Quad from the USGS.

Directions: From Route 3 in Holderness, follow Route 113 east for 5.6 miles to the marked parking turnout.

GPS Coordinates: 43.7892 N, 71.5486 W

Contact: Squam Lakes Association, P.O. Box 204, Holderness, NH 03245, 603/968-7336, www.squamlakes.org.

6 EAGLE CLIFF
1.2 mi/45 min

north of Center Harbor

The open ledges of Eagle Cliff rise 800 vertical feet over Squam Lake, providing hikers with a perfect bird's-eye view of this picturesque body of water. A short trek, the climbing is easy until a sharp ascent at the very end forces a steep scramble to the top of the cliff.

From the parking turnout on Bean Road, cross the road to what looks like an unmarked trailhead. Just a few steps down the path (and out of sight from the road) is a small sign reading Eagle Cliff Trail. A pleasant, moderate rise through mixed forest for the first 0.4 mile, the trail suddenly grows into a somewhat steep rock scramble for much of the final 0.2-mile push to Eagle Cliff. Finally reaching the open ledges, the views are dramatic. Sweeping out almost right underneath you is the lake, with the low ridge of the Squam Mountains visible in the distance. Look to the north for views of the southern White Mountains; the most readily identifiable is the horn of Mount Chocorua to the northeast. Hike back along the same route or descend north from the cliff along the much more gently inclined Teedie Trail. The recommended route for this hike (both up and down) when the ground is wet

or icy, Teedie Trail brings you back to Bean Road, next to a private tennis court at the Sandwich-Moltonborough town line, 0.4 mile north from where you parked.

User Groups: Hikers and dogs. Trail is not suitable for bikes or horses. No wheelchair facilities.

Permits: Parking and access are free.

Maps: Local trail guide and map are sold by the Squam Lakes Association for a modest fee. A waterproof trail map is available from the Appalachian Mountain Club (Crawford Notch–Sandwich Range/Moosilauke–Kinsman, $7.95). For a topographic area map, request Squam Mountains Quad from the USGS.

Directions: In Center Harbor, immediately east of the junction of Routes 25 and 25B, turn north off Route 25 onto Bean Road. Follow for five miles, crossing the Sandwich-Moultonborough town line. At 0.4 mile beyond the town line—where the road becomes Squam Lakes Road—look for roadside parking in the southbound turnout. The trail marker is a small sign located downhill from the roadside and is not visible until you start down the path.

GPS: 43.7695 N, 71.4807 W

Contact: Squam Lakes Association, P.O. Box 204, Holderness, NH 03245, 603/968-7336, www.squamlakes.org.

7 MOUNT CARDIGAN: WEST SIDE LOOP
3.5 mi/2 hr   🏃2 △10

in Cardigan State Park east of Canaan

BEST (

Left bare by a fire in 1855, the 3,121-foot crown of Mount Cardigan, "Old Baldy," affords a 360-degree panoramic view of the Green and White Mountains and of prominent hills to the south, such as Sunapee and Vermont's Mount Ascutney. It's a popular hike: Hundreds of people, many of them children, will climb Cardigan on sunny weekends during the warm months. This easy loop on the west side of the mountain sees the most foot traffic of any of the Cardigan summit routes and offers a vertical gain of about 1,200 feet.

From the parking area, the orange blazes of the West Ridge Trail lead immediately uphill, climbing steadily on a wide and somewhat rocky footpath. At the half-mile mark, the South Ridge Trail enters from the right. Stay to the left on the West Ridge Trail, crossing a small brook on a wooden footbridge and passing by another trail junction. More than a mile from the trailhead, the West Ridge Trail emerges onto the nearly barren upper cone of Mount Cardigan, climbing steep slabs to the summit. The views here are long and unobstructed, but a fire tower at the summit offers even longer views. For the return trip, turn back for about 100 feet on the West Ridge Trail and take a left at a marked junction to follow the white blazes of the Clark Trail. The trail becomes briefly quite steep on slabs that can be a bit hazardous when wet, reaching the tiny ranger's cabin 0.2 mile past Cardigan's summit. Here, turn right and follow the orange blazes of the South Ridge Trail past the cabin, moving in and out of low trees for 0.3 mile to South Peak, with good views to the south and west of the hills of central and western New Hampshire. The South Ridge Trail enters the forest and continues descending, very steeply in spots, for another mile to the West Ridge Trail. Turn left and descend another half mile to the parking lot.

User Groups: Hikers and leashed dogs. No bikes, horses, or wheelchair facilities. Snowshoeing is possible at lower elevations but may be difficult above the tree line due to ice and harsh weather.

Permits: Parking and access are free.

Maps: Free, basic trail maps are available at the trailhead parking lot. A waterproof trail map is available from the Appalachian Mountain Club (Monadnock/Cardigan, $7.95). For a topographic area map, request Mount Cardigan from the USGS.

Directions: From the junction of Routes 4

and 118 in Canaan, drive north on Route 118 for 0.6 mile and then turn right at a sign for Cardigan State Park. Follow that road for 4.1 miles to a large dirt parking lot. The trail begins beside the parking lot. The access road is maintained in winter only to a parking area about 0.6 mile before the summer parking lot.

GPS Coordinates: 43.6515 N, 71.9514 W

Contact: New Hampshire Division of Parks and Recreation, P.O. Box 1856, Concord, NH 03302, 603/271-3254, www.nhstateparks.org. Trails on Mount Cardigan are maintained by the Cardigan Highlanders, P.O. Box 104, Enfield Center, NH 03749, 603/632-5640.

8 MOUNT CARDIGAN: EAST SIDE LOOP

5.2 mi/3.5 hr   🏃3 ⛰10

in Cardigan State Park west of Alexandria

This relatively steep hike up the east side of Cardigan provides experienced hikers with a more rigorous climb to the mountain's summit (3,121 ft.). But even the most adept mountaineers should pay attention to weather conditions before starting out on this route: The upper portion of the trail requires scrambling over exposed slabs that quickly become dangerous when wet or icy. On a sunny summer or early fall day, however, when other routes on Cardigan are choked with visitors, choosing the mountain's eastside trails is often the best way to experience Cardigan without the crowds. The loop's vertical gain is about 1,800 feet.

From the parking area at the Appalachian Mountain Club's Cardigan Lodge, pick up the Holt Trail heading west (look for the sign marker). The trail follows a wide, nearly flat woods road for almost a mile. At 1.1 miles, the trail crosses Bailey Brook and then turns slightly to run parallel to the brook. Growing steeper, the trail leaves the brook and begins a very sharp ascent. Crossing exposed rock slabs for the final 0.3 mile, the trail reaches the summit 2.2 miles from the parking area. After stopping to take in the expansive views or taking a turn climbing the fire tower, turn right (north) onto the white-blazed and cairn-marked Mowglis Trail. Follow it off the summit, dropping sharply into the saddle between the main summit and Firescrew Mountain, a shoulder of Cardigan. The Mowglis Trail then climbs to the open top of Firescrew, with more long views, 0.6 mile from Cardigan's summit. Turn right (east) and follow the Manning Trail, descending steadily with good views for about 0.2 mile. Reentering the woods, walk for 2.2 more miles before reaching the Holt Trail. Turn left and walk the short distance back to the parking lot.

User Groups: Hikers and leashed dogs. No bikes, horses, or wheelchair facilities.

Permits: Parking and access are free.

Maps: A waterproof trail map is available from the Appalachian Mountain Club (Monadnock/Cardigan, $7.95). For topographic maps, request Mount Cardigan and Newfound Lake from the USGS.

Directions: From the junction of Routes 3A and 104 in Bristol, drive north on Route 3A for 2.1 miles. At a stone church near the south end of Newfound Lake, turn left onto West Shore Road. Continue 1.9 miles and proceed straight through a crossroads. Reaching a fork in 1.2 miles, bear right onto Fowler River Road, and then turn left 3.2 miles farther onto Brook Road. Continue another 1.1 miles and turn right onto the dirt Shem Valley Road. Just 0.1 mile farther, bear right at a red schoolhouse. Drive 1.4 miles to the end of that road, where parking is available near the Appalachian Mountain Club's Cardigan Lodge. (At intersections along these roads, there are signs indicating the direction to the Cardigan Lodge.) The access road is maintained in winter.

GPS Coordinates: 43.6495 N, 71.8775 W

Contact: New Hampshire Division of Parks and Recreation, P.O. Box 1856, Concord, NH 03302, 603/271-3254, www.nhstateparks.org. Trails on Mount Cardigan are maintained by the Cardigan Highlanders, P.O. Box 104, Enfield Center, NH 03749, 603/632-5640.

🗐 MOUNT MAJOR
3 mi/1.5 hr

between West Alton and Alton Bay

Located not far from the southern end of Lake Winnipesaukee, this low-lying mountain is perhaps the most popular hike in the lakes region, especially among families with young children. It's an easy climb to Major's 1,000-foot summit and the views of Lake Winnipesaukee and the high peaks of the White Mountains in the distance are nothing short of stunning.

From the parking area along Route 11, follow a gravel-strewn jeep trail 0.1 mile until you reach a fork in the road. Here bear right for the Mount Major Trail and follow the gradually ascending slope. At 1.3 miles from the parking area, rocky slabs just off the trail offer a scenic lake overlook and a perfect spot for a picnic. Push on to reach the summit, 1.5 miles from the start of the hike. Descend the same way.

User Groups: Hikers and leashed dogs. No bikes, horses, or wheelchair facilities.

Permits: Parking and access are free.

Maps: For a topographic area map, request Squam Mountains from the USGS.

Directions: From the junction of Routes 11 and 28A in Alton Bay, follow Route 11 north to a large parking area on the left (west) side of the road. The state owns the summit area and maintains the parking lot, but the trail crosses private property.

GPS Coordinates: 43.5192 N, 71.2738 W

Contact: New Hampshire Division of Parks and Recreation, P.O. Box 1856, Concord, NH 03302, 603/271-3556, www.nhstateparks.org.

NEW HAMPSHIRE

❿ MOUNT KEARSARGE
2.9 mi/2 hr   🏃3 ⛰9

in Winslow State Park in Wilmot

The climb to the bald, 2,937-foot summit of Mount Kearsarge, with its views of the White Mountains, Green Mountains, and southern New Hampshire, is one of the finest short hikes in New England and, while steep, a great adventure for children. Netting an elevation gain of about 1,100 feet, this loop uses the Winslow Trail to reach the summit and the Barlow Trail, a gentler route that's easy on the knees, for the descent.

From the upper end of the parking lot in Winslow State Park, pick up the red-blazed Winslow Trail. The wide, well-beaten path rises quite steeply and relentlessly and grows even more rugged the higher you go. At 0.8 mile, scramble a large boulder on the left for a good view north. A short distance farther, the trail breaks out of the trees and onto the bald summit, with views in every direction, including nearby Sunapee, Ragged, and Cardigan mountains and more distant Mount Monadnock and Ascutney. On very clear days, views extend to the White Mountains, the Green Mountains of Vermont, the Atlantic Ocean, and Boston. This is a wonderful hike during the height of the fall foliage colors (and because of this, Kearsarge's trails are usually packed during peak fall weekends). A fire tower stands at the summit, and nearby are a pair of picnic tables, along with a very large and very out-of-place-looking communications tower—the one drawback to Kearsarge's otherwise impeccable mountaintop. For the return trip, pick up the yellow-blazed Barlow Trail off the eastern edge of the summit. Follow the blazes and cairns, soon descending into scrubby pine. Follow the trail for 1.8 miles back to the parking area.

User Groups: Hikers and leashed dogs. No bikes, horses, or wheelchair facilities.

Permits: Park admission is $4 for adults; $2 for children ages 6–11; free for children ages 5 and under and New Hampshire residents age 65 and over.

Maps: A basic trail map of Winslow State Park is available at the park or from the New Hampshire Division of Parks and Recreation. For topographic area maps, request New London, Andover, Bradford, and Warner from the USGS.

Directions: Take I-89 to Exit 10 and follow the signs to Winslow State Park. From the tollbooth at the state park entrance, drive to the dirt parking lot at the end of the road.

Winslow State Park is open 9 A.M.–8 P.M. May 1–mid-November. The last 0.6 mile of the entrance road (beyond the fork at the dead end sign) is not maintained in winter.

GPS Coordinates: 43.3895 N, 71.8672 W

Contact: Winslow State Park, P.O. Box 295, Newbury, NH 03255, 603/526-6168. New Hampshire Division of Parks and Recreation, P.O. Box 1856, 172 Pembroke Rd., Concord, NH 03302, 603/271-3556, camping reservations 603/271-3628, www.nhstateparks.org.

⓫ MOUNT SUNAPEE
12.4 mi/7 hr   🏃5 ⛰8

in Mount Sunapee State Park in Newbury

The Summit Trail up central New Hampshire's popular Mount Sunapee offers a fairly easy, four-mile round-trip route from the ski area parking lot to the 2,743-foot summit. Many hikers will be satisfied with that. But this description also covers a section of the Monadnock-Sunapee Greenway Trail from Sunapee's summit to Lucia's Lookout on Sunapee's long southern ridge. Views along the ridge, particularly overlooking Lake Solitude, make this ambitious trek well worth the time and effort. The climb to Sunapee's summit is about 1,300 feet.

From the Sunapee ski area parking lot, walk behind the North Peak Lodge about 100 feet to where two ski trails merge; look to the right for a sign for the red-blazed Summit Trail.

Ascending steadily through the woods for approximately two miles, the trail emerges onto an open meadow, where to the right (south) you get a view toward Mount Monadnock. Turn left and walk to the summit lodge a short distance ahead. Some of the best views on the mountain are from the decks at the lodge, with Mount Ascutney and the Green Mountains visible to the west, and Mounts Cardigan and Moosilauke and Franconia Ridge to the north. To complete this four-mile hike, return the way you came. To lengthen it with a walk along the somewhat rugged Sunapee Ridge, head across the summit approximately 50 feet to the left (east) of the ski lift, looking for the sign and white blazes marking the Monadnock-Sunapee Greenway Trail.

Reentering the woods, the greenway heads east and slightly south to reach the open White Ledges 0.9 mile from the summit. The trail then swings left, but walking to the right will lead you to an open ledge with an excellent view of Lake Solitude, a small tarn tucked into the mountain's shoulder (a large arrow painted on a rock tells you where to find the lookout). Continuing on the greenway, the trail passes over an open ledge 2.7 miles from the Sunapee summit before reaching Lucia's Lookout, 4.2 miles from the summit. Here, the views take in Mount Monadnock and Lovewell Mountain to the south, the Green Mountains to the west, and Mount Kearsarge and the White Mountains to the north. Hike back the way you came.

User Groups: Hikers and leashed dogs. No bikes, horses, or wheelchair facilities.

Permits: Parking and access are free.

Maps: A free map of the trails is available at the state park or from the New Hampshire Division of Parks and Recreation. A trail guide and waterproof map of the entire Monadnock-Sunapee Greenway, a trail stretching 50 miles from Mount Monadnock to Mount Sunapee, can be purchased from the Monadnock-Sunapee Greenway Trail Club ($14). For a topographic area map, request Newport from the USGS.

Directions: From Sunapee Village, head south on Route 103B until reaching a roundabout. Go halfway around the traffic circle and bear right at a sign for the state park. Continue to the end of the road and a large parking area at the base of the ski area.

GPS Coordinates: 43.3324 N, 72.0795 W

Contact: New Hampshire Division of Parks and Recreation, P.O. Box 1856, Concord, NH 03302, 603/271-3556, www.nhstateparks.org. Monadnock-Sunapee Greenway Trail Club (MSGTC), P.O. Box 164, Marlow, NH 03456, www.msgtc.org.

12 CATAMOUNT HILL
2.2 mi/1 hr   🏃2 ⛰3

in Bear Brook State Park in Allenstown

Located in the southeast region of the state, Bear Brook, with over 10,000 acres, is the largest developed state park in New Hampshire. Forty miles of trails wind through thick forest, traveling to an almost countless number of marshes, bogs, ponds, and hilly summits. This 2.2-mile hike ascends a few hundred feet to one of the park's highest points, 721-foot Catamount Hill, where a mostly wooded ridge offers limited views of the state park's rambling forest.

From the parking lot near the toll booth, cross Deerfield Road and follow it briefly back toward Route 28. About 100 feet past the toll booth, a trail marked One Mile Road enters the woods. Follow it for 0.2 mile, bearing left where another dirt road enters from the right. In 0.1 mile from that junction, turn right onto the Catamount Hill Trail, which is marked by a sign. The trail climbs steadily, reaching the first lookout about 0.6 mile past the dirt road, just below the summit. Continue another 0.2 mile to the summit ridge, where another view is partially obscured by low trees. Return the way you came. At the bottom of the Catamount Hill Trail, turn left on One Mile Road; do not take the first trail on the right, which leads to a footbridge over Bear Brook. At the

NEW HAMPSHIRE

second junction, bear right to return to the toll booth area.

Special Note: Bear Brook State Park is also home to an assortment of museums dedicated to outdoor pursuits. Located 0.5 mile from the toll booth are the New Hampshire Antique Snowmobile Museum, Museum of Family Camping, Old Allenstown Meeting House, and the Richard Diehl Civilian Conservation Corps (CCC) Museum. Most of the museums are housed in historic CCC buildings. Contact park for seasonal hours.

User Groups: Hikers and leashed dogs. No bikes, horses, or wheelchair facilities on this trail (access varies along other trails in the park).

Permits: During the summer recreation season, an entrance fee of $4 per adult and $2 per child (ages 6–11) is collected at the state park entrance. Children under 5 and New Hampshire residents 65 and older enter for free.

Maps: A free trail map is available at the park entrance. For topographic area maps, request Suncook and Gossville from the USGS.

Directions: From the junction of U.S. 3 and Route 28 in Allenstown, bear right on Route 28 and follow it to the entrance of Bear Brook State Park at Deerfield Road (look for the large state park sign). Turn left into a parking lot just past the entrance toll booth.

GPS Coordinates: 43.1621 N, 71.3889 W

Contact: Bear Brook State Park, 157 Deerfield Rd., Allenstown, NH 03275, 603/485-9874. New Hampshire Division of Parks and Recreation, P.O. Box 1856, 172 Pembroke Rd., Concord, NH 03302, 603/271-3556, camping reservations 603/271-3628, www.nhstateparks.org.

13 PAWTUCKAWAY STATE PARK

7 mi/3.5 hr 5 8

in Raymond

Home to a lake and sandy swimming beach, marshland, fields, forest, and upland hills, Pawtuckaway is far and away the most diverse natural area in southeastern New Hampshire. Many of its trails are ideal for hiking, mountain biking, or cross-country skiing, and you might be surprised by the extensive views from the ledges and fire tower atop South Mountain, rising less than 1,000 feet above sea level. Besides this hike, there are numerous trails to explore—try stretching this hike into a 12-mile loop by combining Tower Road with the Shaw and Fundy Trails. Fun to spot at Pawtuckaway are the numerous glacial erratics dotting the landscape; some of these giant boulders dumped by the retreating glaciers of the last Ice Age soar to over 20 feet in height.

From the parking lot near the entrance to the park, follow the paved road north for about 0.25 mile. After passing a pond on your left, a sign marker on the left indicates the beginning of the Mountain Trail. Head in a northeasterly direction along the trail, staying to the right when a junction is reached with the round Pond Trail. Approximately three miles from the hike's starting point, you will reach junction 5 (marked by a sign); turn right and ascend the trail to the summit of South Mountain. Check out the views from the ledges to the left and right of the trail just below the summit; the east-facing trails to the right will be warmer on a sunny day when the breeze is cool. Climb the fire tower for even longer views of the surrounding countryside.

User Groups: Hikers and bikes (though trails are closed to bikes during mud season, usually the month of April). No wheelchair facilities. Dogs and horses are prohibited.

Permits: During mid-June–Labor Day, an entrance fee of $4 per adult and $2 per child (ages 6–11) is collected at the state park entrance. Children under 5 and New Hampshire residents 65 and older enter for free. There is no fee the rest of the year.

Maps: A free, noncontour map of park trails is available at the park's main entrance. For a topographic area map, request Mount Pawtuckaway from the USGS.

Directions: From Route 101 in Raymond, take Exit 5 (there is a sign for Pawtuckaway). Follow Route 156 north and turn left onto Mountain Road at the sign for Pawtuckaway State Park. Follow the road two miles to the state park entrance; the parking lot is on the left.

The parking lot opens at 10 A.M. Monday–Thursday and at 9 A.M. Friday–Sunday. GPS Coordinates: 43.0780 N, 71.1727 W

Contact: Pawtuckaway State Park, 128 Mountain Rd., Nottingham, NH 03290, 603/895-3031. New Hampshire Division of Parks and Recreation, P.O. Box 1856, 172 Pembroke Rd., Concord, NH 03302, 603/271-3556, camping reservations 603/271-3628, www.nhstateparks.org.

14 GREAT BAY NATIONAL ESTUARINE RESEARCH RESERVE

1 mi/0.75 hr   🕺1 ▲6

in Stratham

BEST (

Hands down the state's most ecologically diverse area, the 4,500-acre tidal estuary and 800 acres of coastal land at Great Bay National Estuarine Research Reserve provide refuge for 23 species of endangered or threatened plant and animal species. Bald eagles winter here, osprey nest, and cormorants and great blue heron are readily seen. Sandy Point Trail is a universally accessible interpretive trail and boardwalk that allows visitors to experience the vast diversity of the estuarine ecosystem.

From the Great Bay Discovery Center parking lot, a short path zigzags down the slope to the trailhead. From here, the graded, gravel trail enters a mature, upland forest of oak, hickory, elm, and beech. The trail becomes a boardwalk just before reaching the wetter ground of the red maple–sensitive fern swamp ecosystem. Here, look for jack-in-the-pulpit, spotted touch-me-not-fern, royal fern, and cinnamon fern. Continuing on, the boardwalk reaches a junction. The Woodland Trail enters the forest to the left, but this route takes the boardwalk to the right, entering the salt marsh. Almost immediately to your right, take note of the almost pure stand of feather-tufted common reed, a threatened plant species in North America (this is the last known example of the plant in the state). As the boardwalk bends to the left, Great Bay comes into view. A series of mudflats at low tide, the estuary at high tide becomes a vivid blue lake. This is a good spot for bird-watching: Blue heron, egret, osprey, kingfisher, and waterfowl all frequent this part of Great Bay. Follow the boardwalk as it forms a loop through the marsh and retrace your steps back to the Great Bay Discovery Center. Stop by the center for lots of fun, hands-on learning about the estuary.

User Groups: Hikers and wheelchairs only. No bikes, dogs, or horses.

Permits: Parking and access are free.

Maps: An interpretive trail pamphlet available at the Great Bay Discovery Center guides visitors along the boardwalk at the estuary's edge and offers information about natural history and the local environment. For topographic area maps, request Newmarket and Portsmouth from the USGS.

Directions: From the Stratham traffic circle at the junction of Routes 108 and 33, drive 1.4 miles north on Route 33 and turn left onto Depot Road at a sign for the Great Bay Discovery Center. At the end of Depot Road, turn left on Tidewater Farm Road. The Discovery Center is at the end of the road and the trail begins behind the center.

Great Bay Discovery Center is open to the public 10 A.M.–4 P.M. Wednesday–Sunday May 1–September 30 and on weekends in October. The grounds are open during daylight hours throughout the year. GPS Coordinates: 43.0546 N, 70.8964 W

Contact: Great Bay National Estuarine Research Reserve, 89 Depot Rd., Greenland, NH 03840, 603/778-0015, www.greatbay.org/sandypoint.

NEW HAMPSHIRE

© JACQUELINE TOURVILLE

Odiorne Point State Park

15 ODIORNE POINT STATE PARK

1.9 mi/1 hr

in Rye

Just down the road from Portsmouth's bustling downtown and not far from Hampton's crowded beaches, rocky Odiorne Point is the largest tract of undeveloped land left along New Hampshire's tiny 18-mile shoreline. Nestled within a 330-acre state park overlooking both the Atlantic Ocean and Portsmouth's Little Harbor, Odiorne's most notable use was as the site of Fort Dearborn, a U.S. Military installation built during World War II. With long-abandoned bunkers looking more like grassy dunes than strategic defense points, Odiorne today offers visitors the chance to ramble along a rugged shore with unfettered ocean views. Portions of this hike are wheelchair accessible.

From the eastern end of the parking lot, the paved, handicap-accessible walkway quickly comes to a view of the ocean, taking you past a small grove of low trees known as the Sunken Forest and continuing out to the Odiorne Point promontory and picnic area. Scramble down to the rocky beach to explore the tidal pools at low tide or simply stop to take in the vast ocean views; on a clear day you can see the Isles of Shoals, a small chain of low-lying offshore islands. To the north, closer to shore, spot the hardworking Whaleback Lighthouse in Kittery, Maine. The paved walkway leads through the picnic area to form a loop leading back to the parking lot. To continue on a longer walk, follow the shoreline's well-worn path. The trail takes you first to the Seacoast Science Center—if you have kids in tow, the center's marine touch tank and many aquariums are a must-see. The path then takes you past long-abandoned bunkers, a salt marsh, and boat launch, before skirting the edge of Little Harbor and eventually leading all the way out to the jetty at Frost Point (about a mile from your starting point). Circle back from the end of the jetty and bear left at a fork just off Frost Point to return to the science center and parking lot.

User Groups: Hikers and wheelchairs (the paved portion on this route is wheelchair accessible). Separate bike paths are located elsewhere in the park. Dogs and horses are prohibited.

Permits: The park is open daily year-round. In early May–mid-October, admission is $4 for adults; $2 for children, ages 6–11; children ages 5 and under and New Hampshire residents age 65 and over enter for free. The Seacoast Science Center charges separate admissions fees.

Maps: For a map with historical and natural information about Odiorne, contact the New Hampshire Division of Parks and Recreation. For a topographic area map, request Kittery from the USGS.

Directions: From Portsmouth, follow Route 1A south for three miles to Odiorne State Park's main entrance (on the left). The parking area is just past the gatehouse to the right. GPS Coordinates: 43.0442 N, 70.7149 W

Contact: Odiorne State Park, Rte. 1A, Rye, NH 03870, 603/436-7406. New Hampshire Division of Parks and Recreation, P.O. Box 1856, Concord, NH 03302, 603/271-3556, www.nhstateparks.org. Seacoast Science Center, 570 Ocean Blvd., Rye, NH 03870, 603/436-8043, www.seacoastsciencecenter.org.

16 NORTH PACK MONADNOCK
3.2 mi/2 hr   🥾3 ⛰7

in Greenfield

This fairly easy 3.2-mile hike ascends less than 1,000 feet in elevation to the top of North Pack Monadnock. Not to be confused with nearby Grand Monadnock, North Pack is the northern terminus of the 21-mile Wapack Trail and is located in a national wildlife refuge of almost 2,000 acres of timbered uplands. Steep in some places, the consistently ascending Wapack Trail takes you under pine trees and birches, offers nice views and places to rest

along the way, and culminates with a rewarding summit experience.

From the parking area, walk south into the woods, following the yellow triangle blazes of the Wapack Trail. For more than a mile, the trail ascends at an easy grade through forest cover, then climbs steep ledges and passes over one open ledge before reaching the summit at 1.6 miles. From the 2,276-foot summit, the views of southern New Hampshire's wooded hills and valleys are very good, especially to the west and north. Return the way you came.

Camping is allowed only at designated sites along the entire 21-mile Wapack Trail, but not along this hike. Fires are prohibited.

User Groups: Hikers, snowshoers, and dogs. No wheelchair facilities. This trail is not suitable for bikes, horses, or skis.

Permits: Parking and access are free.

Maps: A Wapack Trail map and guide is available for $11 from Friends of the Wapack. For topographic area maps, request Peterborough South, Peterborough North, Greenfield, and Greenville from the USGS.

Directions: From the intersection of Routes 101 and 202 in Peterborough, head north on Route 202. Follow for 1.1 miles and then bear right onto Sand Hill Road. Proceed 3.9 miles, including a sharp left curve (at about 2.6 miles) and a sharp right curve (at about 3 miles), until you see the trail markers on the south (right) side of the road. GPS Coordinates: 42.9001 N, 71.8707 W

Contact: Friends of the Wapack, Box 115, West Peterborough, NH 03468, www.wapack.org.

17 MOUNT PISGAH/ PISGAH LEDGES
5 mi/3 hr   🥾5 ⛰7

in Pisgah State Park between Chesterfield and Hinsdale

Tucked away in the state's rural southwest corner, New Hampshire's largest state park includes this big hill called Mount Pisgah, where open summit ledges afford nice views of rolling countryside and Mount Monadnock to the east and Massachusetts and Vermont to the southwest. Key trail junctions are marked with signs and there's just a few hundred feet of uphill. A pleasant hike in spring or summer hike, the trail really comes to life in early autumn when the surrounding deciduous forest blazes with fall colors.

From the park entrance and parking area at Kilburn Road, follow the marked Kilburn Road Trail, bearing left at marked junctions with the Kilburn Loop Trail, and eventually turning onto the Pisgah Mountain Trail (at 1.2 miles from the trailhead). Follow the Pisgah Ridge Trail 0.2 mile to reach the hill's open ledges. Follow 0.2 mile to reach the hill's open ledges. To bag the wooded summit (which unfortunately lacks any kind of view), double back to the trail junction and ascend a short distance to the mountaintop. From the summit or ledges, head back down along the same trails, this time bearing right at junctions with the Kilburn Loop Trail.

User Groups: Hikers and leashed dogs. No wheelchair facilities. The trail is not suitable for bikes or horses. Hunting is allowed in season.

Permits: During the summer recreation season, park admission is $4 for adults; $2 for children, ages 6–11; children ages 5 and under and New Hampshire residents age 65 and over enter for free.

Maps: For a map of park trails, contact the New Hampshire Division of Parks and Recreation. For topographic area maps, request Winchester and Keene from the USGS.

Directions: From Keene, follow Route 9 west for approximately nine miles. At an intersection with Route 63, turn left (south), pass through Chesterfield, and continue three more miles to an entrance and parking area for Kilburn Road in Pisgah State Park.

GPS Coordinates: 42.8346 N, 72.4834 W

Contact: Pisgah State Park, P.O. Box 242, Winchester, NH 03470-0242, 603/239-8153.

New Hampshire Division of Parks and Recreation, P.O. Box 1856, Concord, NH 03302, 603/271-3556, www.nhstateparks.org.

18 MOUNT MONADNOCK: MARLBORO TRAIL
4.2 mi/3.5 hr   🚶5   ▲10

in Monadnock State Park in Marlborough

If there is a trail less traveled leading to the summit of Mount Monadnock (3,165 ft.), it's the Marlboro Trail, an uphill walk to the summit past interesting boulder formations. Leaving from a small trailhead along a dirt road almost due west of the mountain peak, this route to the summit sees only a fraction of the foot traffic experienced by popular trailheads clustered around the state park entrance to the southeast of Monadnock (see the *Mount Monadnock: White Arrow Trail* listing in this chapter). The Marlboro Trail's net elevation gain is approximately 1,800 feet.

From the parking area along Shaker Road, find the trail marker and begin walking east on the gently graded trail (look for white blazes). Enjoy the solitude on this pleasant walk through the woods. And with fewer fellow hikers to watch out for, take time to examine the mountain's diverse flora and fauna. In spring and early summer, the forest floor blooms with such delicate beauty as trilliums and pink lady slipper; mountain turtles may crawl along as you pass, and deer, wild turkeys, and even a reclusive moose may make themselves known along this stretch of the trail. As the one-mile mark approaches, the second half of the trail begins a sharp and steep ascent, leveling out somewhat (here you will notice a set of granite boulders named Rock House for their shelter-like appearance) and then pushing above the tree line to intersect with the Dublin, 0.3 mile below the summit. Together the two trails combine as a single route, bearing right to ascend Monadnock's slabs and ledges from the south. Enjoy an unparalleled scenic vista extending to all six New England states. Return along the same route to the parking area at the trailhead.

User Groups: Hikers only. No bikes, dogs, horses, or wheelchair facilities.

Permits: Parking and access are free.

Maps: A free map of trails is available from the state park or the New Hampshire Division of Parks and Recreation. A waterproof trail map is available from the Appalachian Mountain Club (Monadnock/Cardigan, $7.95). For topographic area maps, request Monadnock Mountain and Marlborough from the USGS.

Directions: From the center of Marlborough, follow Route 124 south for 4.2 miles to a left hand turn onto Shaker Farms Road. Follow for approximately 0.7 mile to the parking area on the right.

GPS Coordinates: 42.8588 N, 72.1383 W

Contact: Monadnock State Park, P.O. Box 181, Jaffrey, NH 03452, 603/532-8862, www.nhstateparks.org. New Hampshire Division of Parks and Recreation, P.O. Box 1856, Concord, NH 03302, 603/271-3556, www.nhstateparks.org.

19 MOUNT MONADNOCK: WHITE ARROW TRAIL

4.6 mi/3 hr   🏃5 ⛰10

in Monadnock State Park in Jaffrey

At 3,165 feet high, majestic Mount Monadnock (also called Grand Monadnock) rises high above the surrounding countryside of southern New Hampshire, making it prominently visible from many other lower peaks in the region. The mountain's name comes from an Abenaki phrase likely meaning "place of an unexcelled mountain." Borrowing from the Abenaki, modern geologists use the term "monadnock" to mean an isolated peak in an otherwise eroded plain (there are actually several of these monadnocks in both New Hampshire and Vermont). With its large, rocky

summit and unhindered view encompassing all six New England states, Grand Monadnock is the region's most popular peak. It's often claimed that Monadnock is hiked more than any mountain in the world except Japan's Mount Fuji—although any ranger in the state park would tell you that's impossible to prove. This hike, a vertical ascent of 1,600 feet, is one of the most commonly used Monadnock summit routes and can be a very crowded place in the spring, summer, and fall.

From the parking lot on the north side of Route 124, walk past the gate onto the old toll road and immediately bear left at the sign marker for the Old Halfway House Trail. A moderate ascent of 1.2 miles, the trail ends at a meadow known as the Halfway House site, the former grounds of a hotel built in the late 19th century for mountain tourists (and located at the midway point to the summit). Cross the meadow to the White Arrow Trail, which ascends a rock-strewn but wide path for another 1.1 miles to the summit of Mount Monadnock. The final quarter mile is above the mountain's tree line and very exposed to harsh weather. White blazes are painted on the rocks above the trees. Just below the summit, the trail makes a sharp right turn, then ascends slabs to the summit. Hike back the same way.

User Groups: Hikers only. No bikes, dogs, horses, or wheelchair facilities.

Permits: During April–November, an entrance fee of $4 per adult and $2 per child (ages 6–11) is collected at the state park entrance. Children under 5 and New Hampshire residents 65 and older enter state parks for free.

Maps: A free map of trails is available from the state park or the New Hampshire Division of Parks and Recreation. A waterproof trail map is available from the Appalachian Mountain Club (Monadnock/Cardigan, $7.95). For topographic area maps, request Monadnock Mountain and Marlborough from the USGS.

Directions: This hike begins from a parking lot on the north side of Route 124, 7.1 miles east of the junction of Routes 101 and 124 in Marlborough and 5.4 miles west of the junction of Route 124, Route 137, and U.S. 202 in Jaffrey.

GPS Coordinates: 42.8348 N, 72.1140 W
Contact: Monadnock State Park, P.O. Box 181, Jaffrey, NH 03452, 603/532-8862, www.nhstateparks.org. New Hampshire Division of Parks and Recreation, P.O. Box 1856, Concord, NH 03302, 603/271-3556, www.nhstateparks.org.

20 MOUNT MONADNOCK: WHITE DOT TRAIL
4.2 mi/3 hr   🚶5 ⛰10

in Monadnock State Park in Jaffrey

BEST (

While on a trek through the Monadnock region, literary luminary Mark Twain noted, "In these October days Monadnock and the valley and its framing hills make an inspiring picture." On a sunny autumn day, a hike to the summit along the White Dot Trail is a leaf peeper's paradise, with views as inspiring now as they were in Twain's day. Passing through a mixed forest of beech, maple, birch, and evergreen and then out onto open ledges, this moderately steep climb is also the shortest, most direct route to the Monadnock summit (3,165 ft.).

From the parking lot, walk up the road to find the marked trailhead for the very well-trod White Dot Trail, just past the state park headquarters. The wide path dips slightly, crosses a brook, and then begins a gradual ascent. At 0.5 mile, the Spruce Link bears left, leading in 0.3 mile to the White Cross Trail, but stay to the right on the White Dot. At 0.7 mile, a marked spur trail turns left, leading a short distance to Falcon Spring, a burbling water source that's a big hit with kids. This hike, though, continues straight ahead on the White Dot. The trail climbs steeply for the next 0.4 mile, with some limited views, until emerging onto open ledges at 1.1 miles. It then follows more level terrain, enters a forest of

low evergreens, and ascends again to its upper junction with the White Cross Trail at 1.7 miles. The trail climbs the open, rocky terrain of the upper mountain for the final 0.3 mile to the summit. On clear days, Boston skyscrapers and even the Atlantic Ocean can be seen in the distance. Descend along the same route.

User Groups: Hikers only. No bikes, dogs, horses, or wheelchair facilities. This trail may be difficult to snowshoe, in part because of severe winter weather.

Permits: During April–November, an entrance fee of $4 per adult and $2 per child (ages 6–11) is collected at the state park entrance. Children under 5 and New Hampshire residents 65 and older enter state parks for free.

Maps: A free map of trails is available from the state park or the New Hampshire Division of Parks and Recreation. A waterproof trail map is available from the Appalachian Mountain Club (Monadnock/Cardigan, $7.95). For topographic area maps, request Mount Monadnock and Marlborough from the USGS.

Directions: From Route 101 west in Peterborough, turn left for U.S. 202 west to Jaffrey. Follow for 6.2 miles and then turn right onto Route 124 west. In 4.3 miles, follow signs leading to Monadnock State Park (on the right). Park in the large lot near the park's main entrance.

GPS Coordinates: 42.845 N, -72.088 W
Contact: Monadnock State Park, P.O. Box 181, Jaffrey, NH 03452-0181, 603/532-8862, www.nhstateparks.org. New Hampshire Division of Parks and Recreation, P.O. Box 1856, 172 Pembroke Rd., Concord, NH 03302, 603/271-3556, camping reservations 603/271-3628, www.nhstateparks.org.

21 WAPACK TRAIL: TEMPLE MOUNTAIN LEDGES
5.8 mi/3.5 hr   🚶5 ⛰7

in Sharon

One of the more scenic stretches of the Wapack Ridge Trail, a 21-mile interstate footpath

© JACQUELINE TOURVILLE

view from the Temple Mountain Ledges

stretching from Mount Watatic in Ashburnham, Massachusetts to North Pack Monadnock, this hike traverses the long ridge of Temple Mountain all the way to the Temple Mountain Ledges, a 5.8-mile round-trip with, all told, more than 1,200 feet of climbing. For those seeking a slightly shorter trek along the Wapack, several nice views along the way make for worthwhile out-and-back destinations. The wild blueberry bushes found in abundance along the trail are one of this hike's special treats. Berries ripen by mid-July and usually last through early September.

From the parking area, cross Temple Road and follow the yellow triangle blazes of the Wapack Trail into the woods, soon passing a dilapidated old house. At 0.3 mile, the trail reaches an open area at the start of the Sharon Ledges, with views of Mount Monadnock. A sign marker points to an overlook 75 feet to the right with a view toward Mount Watatic (the "Wa" in Wapack and the 21-mile trail's southern terminus). Continuing northeast,

the Wapack follows the Sharon Ledges for 0.75 mile, with a series of views eastward toward the hills and woods of southern New Hampshire. The trail enters the woods again and, at 1.4 miles from the trailhead, passes over the wooded subsidiary summit known as Burton Peak. In another 0.5 mile, a side path leads right to the top of cliffs and an unobstructed view to the east; on a clear day, the Boston skyline can be distinguished on the horizon. A short distance farther north on the Wapack lies an open ledge with a great view west to Monadnock—one of the nicest on this hike. The trail continues north 0.7 mile to the wooded summit of Holt Peak, another significant bump on the ridge. A short distance beyond Holt, watch through the trees on the left for a glimpse of an unusually tall rock cairn, then a side path leading to a flat, broad rock ledge with several tall cairns and good views in almost every direction. These are the Temple Mountain Ledges. The Wapack continues over Temple Mountain to Route 101, but this hike heads back the same way you came.

Camping is allowed only at designated sites along the entire 21-mile Wapack Trail; there are no designated sites along this hike. Fires are illegal without landowner permission and a permit from the town forest-fire warden.

User Groups: Hikers and dogs. No wheelchair facilities. This trail is fairly difficult to ski and is not suitable for bikes or horses.

Permits: Parking and access are free.

Maps: A Wapack Trail map and guide is available for $11 from Friends of the Wapack. For topographic area maps, request Peterborough South and Greenville from the USGS.

Directions: From the intersection of Routes 101 and 123 in Peterborough (west of the Temple Mountain Ski Area), drive south four miles on Route 123 and then turn left on Temple Road. Continue another 0.7 mile to a small dirt parking area on the right. GPS: 42.8035 N, 71.9092 W

Contact: Friends of the Wapack, Box 115, West Peterborough, NH 03468, www.wapack. org. New Hampshire Division of Parks and

Recreation, Bureau of Trails, P.O. Box 1856, Concord, NH 03302-1856, 603/271-3254.

22 KIDDER MOUNTAIN
3 mi/2 hr

in New Ipswich

This gentle, three-mile hike gains less than 400 feet in elevation, yet the views from the open meadow atop 1,800-foot Kidder Mountain take in a grand sweep of this rural corner of southern New Hampshire. To the south, the Wapack Range extends to Mount Watatic in Massachusetts; behind Watatic rises the popular Massachusetts ski mountain, Mount Wachusett. It's a great family hike, an easy way to introduce both young and old to the pleasures of hiking, and is a scenic side trip as you hike the Wapack through New Ipswich. Even Benton MacKaye, the creator of the Appalachian Trail, named Kidder Mountain as one of his favorites. MacKaye helped blaze the first Kidder Mountain Trail in 1926 while working as a school teacher in Massachusetts.

From the parking area on the north side of Route 123, follow the yellow triangle blazes of the Wapack Trail into the woods, heading north. At 0.3 mile, the trail enters a clearing and ascends a small hillside to the woods. At 0.6 mile from the road, the Wapack crosses a power line right-of-way. Walk a short distance more and turn right (east) at a sign for the Kidder Mountain Trail. The trail at first follows a jeep road under the power line corridor for 0.1 mile, then turns left, crossing under the lines and entering the woods. It gradually ascends Kidder, reaching the open summit meadow nearly a mile from the Wapack Trail junction. Feast on the blueberries that grow wild here in the summer and take in the views of surrounding hills and rolling countryside. Follow the same route back.

Camping is allowed only at designated sites along the entire 21-mile Wapack Trail; there are no designated sites along this hike. Fires are illegal without landowner permission and a permit from the town forest-fire warden.

User Groups: Hikers and dogs. No bikes, horses, or wheelchair facilities.

Permits: Parking and access are free.

Maps: A Wapack Trail map and guide is available for $11 from Friends of the Wapack. For topographic area maps, request Peterborough South and Greenville from the USGS.

Directions: The trailhead parking area is on the north side of Routes 123/124 in New Ipswich, 2.9 miles west of the junction with Route 123A and 0.7 mile east of where Routes 123 and 124 split.

GPS Coordinates: 42.7734 N, 71.8996 W

Contact: Friends of the Wapack, Box 115, West Peterborough, NH 03468, www.wapack.org.

23 BEAVER BROOK ASSOCIATION
2.5 mi/1.5 hr

in Hollis

Tucked away along the edge of sleepy Hollis, a small, rural community known for its centuries-old old apple orchards and quaint village center, Beaver Brook Association is a sprawling 2,000-acre nature conservancy comprised of forest, fields, and wetlands. With over 35 miles of trails, this local jewel attracts hikers, snowshoers, cross-country skiers, and mountain bikers from as far away as Boston (a 90-minute drive from Beaver Brook). The terrain varies from ponds and marshes dotted with beaver dams and duck nests to rolling meadows, thick forest, and gentle hills. Many of the trails are ideal for beginning hikers and children; some are appropriate for people with intermediate skills. This short hike helps first-time visitors explore the area's natural diversity.

From the office and parking area, follow the wide woods road called Cow Lane less than 0.1 mile to a turn-off on the left for the Porcupine Trail. The forested path is a gentle downhill incline leading to Beaver Brook's extensive wetlands. Chipmunks, garter snakes, and tree frogs are readily spotted here, but the trail's namesake is somewhat elusive (though a sign marker about halfway down the trail helps hikers identify a porcupine habitat). At the end of the trail, turn right at the sign for the Beaver Brook Trail, a relatively flat stretch running parallel to a broad marsh. Soon reaching a boardwalk to the left, cross over the marsh and continue straight until you reach the Eastman Meadow Trail (look for the sign). Here, take a right and follow briefly before turning right again onto the wide forest road called Elkins Road. Follow the road about 0.5 mile until it ends at a trail junction. Turn right onto another woods road, cross a bridge back over Beaver Brook, and continue onto the Brown Lane barn. Walk Brown Lane a short distance and turn right onto the Tepee Trail. At first passing through a lush meadow dotted with bird nesting boxes, the Tepee Trail re-enters the forest and, in another 0.2 mile, ends at Cow Lane. Turn left to return to your car.

User Groups: Hikers and leashed dogs. No wheelchair facilities. Bikes and horses allowed on certain trails (look for sign markers).

Permits: Parking and access are free.

Maps: A trail map is available at the Beaver Brook Association office for a small fee. For a topographic area map, request Pepperell from the USGS.

Directions: From the junction of Routes 130 and 122 in Hollis, drive south on Route 122 for 0.9 mile and turn right onto Ridge Road. Follow Ridge Road to the Maple Hill Farm and the office of the Beaver Brook Association. The parking lot is just past the office to the right.

GPS Coordinates: 42.7224 N, 71.6067 W

Contact: Beaver Brook Association, 117 Ridge Rd., Hollis, NH 03049, 603/465-7787, www.beaverbrook.org, office hours are 9 A.M.–4 P.M. Monday–Friday.

Vermont

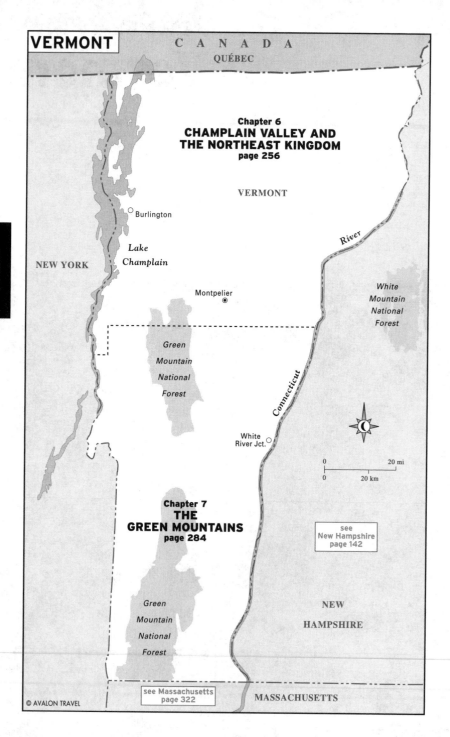

VERMONT

CANADA
QUÉBEC

Chapter 6
CHAMPLAIN VALLEY AND
THE NORTHEAST KINGDOM
page 256

VERMONT

○ Burlington

NEW YORK

Lake
Champlain

Montpelier
◉

River

White
Mountain
National
Forest

Green
Mountain
National
Forest

Connecticut

White ○
River Jct.

0   20 mi
0   20 km

Chapter 7
THE
GREEN MOUNTAINS
page 284

see
New Hampshire
page 142

Green
Mountain
National
Forest

NEW

HAMPSHIRE

© AVALON TRAVEL

see Massachusetts
page 322

MASSACHUSETTS

CHAMPLAIN VALLEY AND THE NORTHEAST KINGDOM

© STEPHEN DEMARS

BEST HIKES

❰ Backpacking
The Long Trail: Appalachian Gap to the Winooski
   River, page 276.
The Monroe Skyline, page 278.

❰ Coastal or Island Hikes
Burton Island, page 257.
Burlington Waterfront Bike Path, page 261.
Button Bay State Park, page 275.

❰ Fall Foliage
Smuggler's Notch, page 262.
Mount Mansfield: Long Trail, page 266.
Mount Hunger, page 268.

❰ Kids
Burton Island, page 257.
Stowe Pinnacle, page 267.

❰ Lakes and Swimming Holes
Burton Island, page 257.
Button Bay State Park, page 275.

❰ Sunsets
Burlington Waterfront Bike Path, page 261.
Mount Mansfield: Sunset Ridge and Laura Cowles
   Trails, page 263.
Mount Philo, page 270.
Button Bay State Park, page 275.

❰ Wheelchair Access
Burlington Waterfront Bike Path, page 261.

From the New York State side of Lake Champlain,

the peaks of the Green Mountains form an almost unbroken chain rising in the distance beyond the lake's glinting waters. The lofty heights of such peaks as Camel's Hump and Mount Mansfield, the state's highest summit, seem to have little to do with the murky depths of Lake Champlain. But it was the lake – or rather the sea it once was – that led to the mountains' formation. Over 500 million years ago, the Atlantic Ocean flowed into the Lake Champlain Basin creating a vast inland sea known as the Iapetus Ocean. Geologists believe that eventually this outlet of the Atlantic closed and the sedimentary rocks of the shoreline and continental shelf folded and faulted to create the Green Mountains. As proof of the mountains' watery past, it is not uncommon to find trilobite and other marine fossils at elevations that would seemingly defy explanation.

The Northeast Kingdom formed at the same time as the Green Mountains. Only in this more inland area, geological pressure led to the formation and eruption of several massive volcanoes, the probable cause of the region's rich granite deposits. And then the glaciers came. The other major land-shaping force in Vermont, glaciers scoured mountain flanks into cliff faces and dug deep valleys to form a network of long lakes and kettle-shaped ponds. The retreating ice sheets also dumped tons of rocks in the area, still seen lying about in farm pastures and on forest floors.

Roughly half of the 24 hikes in this chapter are along the northern portion of the 270-mile Long Trail (LT), the ridge-line footpath that runs the length of the Green Mountains' spine, stretching from Massachusetts to the Canadian border. Some of Vermont's highest, most rugged, and most challenging and enjoyable peaks – including Camel's Hump and Mount Mansfield – are here on the LT. Camel's Hump and several other summits lie along the famed Monroe Skyline, the LT's most spectacular stretch. Other hikes in the chapter include short, easy, and scenic walks along Lake Champlain and on lower hills with views of the Green Mountains, as well as a few hikes in the rural forests of "The Kingdom," as locals call this special place. Vermont hikes are popular destinations, but the northernmost trails in this chapter – Jay Peak, Mounts Pisgah and Hor, Laraway Lookout, and Prospect Rock – are among the most remote and least-traveled trails in New England and good places to escape the crowds.

The Green Mountain Club (GMC) maintains the Long Trail and the numerous shelters and camping areas along it, including lean-to shelters with one open side, similar to those found along the Appalachian Trail, and the enclosed cabins, or lodges, most of which are on the trail's northern half. On-site GMC caretakers collect a nominal overnight fee for staying in its shelters. The water sources at most shelters and camping areas are usually reliable, though water is never guaranteed in a dry season. In the Green Mountain National Forest, no-trace camping is permitted, dogs must be leashed, and hunting is allowed in season, but not near trails.

The prime hiking season begins in late spring, when higher-elevation snows have melted away and lower-elevation mud has dried up, and lasts until the leaves hit the ground, usually in early October (though all of October can provide some great cool-weather hiking with a small chance of snow). To prevent erosion, parts of the Long Trail are closed to hiking during mud season, roughly mid-April-Memorial Day. Where the Long Trail crosses private land, camping is prohibited except at the GMC cabins and shelters. Winters are long and cold throughout Vermont – although there's great ski touring and snowshoeing to be had – and road access through the mountain passes is never assured (the Lincoln-Warren Highway through Lincoln Gap is not maintained in winter).

VERMONT

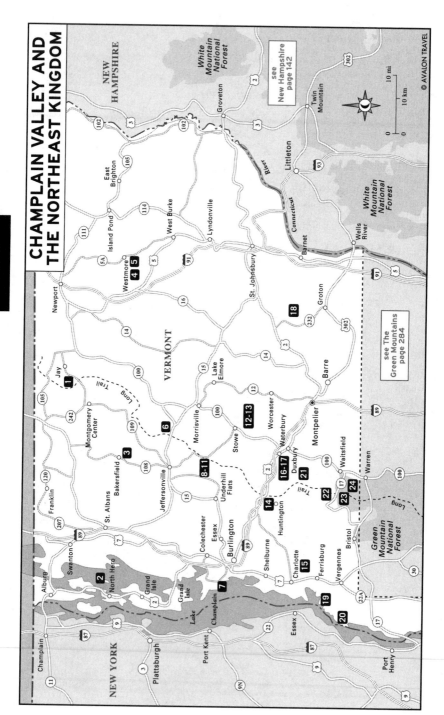

CHAMPLAIN VALLEY AND THE NORTHEAST KINGDOM

VERMONT

© AVALON TRAVEL

see New Hampshire page 142

see The Green Mountains page 284

1 JAY PEAK

3.4 mi/2.5 hr   🏃4 ⛰9

between Jay and Montgomery Center

At 3,861 feet in elevation and just 10 trail miles from the Canadian border, Jay Peak is one of the more remote large mountains along the entire 270-mile length of the Long Trail. The views from the summit—where there are buildings belonging to the Jay Peak Ski Area—are of a vast North Country of mountains, forest, and few roads. And just about half of what you see lies in Canada. Remember that winter arrives earlier here than on peaks farther south; the downhill ski season typically begins at the end of November. This hike climbs almost 1,700 feet.

From the turnout, cross the highway and follow the white blazes of the Long Trail northbound. You immediately pass the small lean-to known as Atlas Valley shelter (not designed for overnight use). In 0.1 mile, the Jay Loop Trail, also a part of the Catamount ski trail, branches left, leading 0.2 mile to the Jay Camp cabin. Just 0.3 mile farther up the LT, you pass the north end of the Jay Loop. The LT ascends steadily onto the mountain's southeast ridge. Just over a mile from the road, you start getting obstructed views to the south and west through the subalpine forest. The wooded peak to the west, connected to Jay by a high ridge, is Big Jay Mountain, at 3,800 feet one of New England's 100 highest summits and a destination for hikers seeking to tick off that list. At 1.5 miles from the highway, the LT crosses a ski resort trail and then climbs over open, rocky terrain the final 0.2 mile to the summit. Descend the way you came.

This Long Trail section is on private land. Camping is prohibited except at the Green Mountain Club cabins and shelters. The Jay Camp cabin is located 0.3 mile north of Route 242 and 1.6 miles south of the Jay Peak summit, 0.2 mile off the Long Trail. The Laura Woodward shelter lies 1.5 miles north of Jay Peak, on the LT. The Atlas Valley shelter is a small lean-to a few steps north of Route 242 on the LT; exposed to winds, it does not provide good overnight shelter.

User Groups: Hikers and leashed dogs. No bikes, horses, or wheelchair facilities. This trail should not be attempted in winter except by hikers prepared for severe winter weather.

Permits: Parking and access are free.

Maps: The waterproof End-to-End Map of the Long Trail is available for $9.95 from the Green Mountain Club. For a topographic area map, request Jay Peak from the USGS.

Directions: Park in a large turnout where the Long Trail crosses Route 242, 6.5 miles east of the junction of Routes 242 and 118 in Montgomery Center and 6.5 miles west of the junction of Routes 242 and 101 in Jay. GPS Coordinates: 44.9299 N, 72.5002 W

Contact: Green Mountain Club Inc., 4711 Waterbury-Stowe Rd., Waterbury Center, VT 05677, 802/244-7037, www.greenmountainclub.org.

2 BURTON ISLAND

3 mi/1.5 hr   🏃1 ⛰10

in St. Albans Bay

BEST (

Accessible only by boat, Burton Island in Lake Champlain is a 253-acre state park just off the southwestern tip of St. Albans Point. A seasonal ferry service for passengers makes the 10-minute trip from Kill Kare State Park several times a day. (No cars are allowed on the island.) Starting in the 1700s, Burton Island was used primarily as pasture and farmland; through the early 1900s, cows, pigs, sheep, and chickens roamed the island's windswept fields. Though forest cover has taken back much of the landscape, remnants of the island's agricultural past, such as fence lines and stone piles, rusted farm implements, and the foundation of the old barn, are still visible. Kids will love exploring this place. Campsites on the island are popular (especially among families) and tend to fill up quickly. This

VERMONT

kid-friendly hike connects three of the state park's interpretive nature trails, creating a scenic and educational island circuit.

From the ferry dock, first stop at the park office for the map and interpretive brochure, and then follow the signs to the Burton Island Nature Center; the half-mile long Island Farm Nature Trail begins next to the building. Skirting St. Albans Bay, the trail takes you past a glacial erratic strewn beach, evidence of the last Ice Age's major role in shaping the Champlain Valley. Turning inland, enter an upland grove of sumac, pass the remains of an old barn foundation, and cross a bridge over a marsh. Just before the return to the nature center, look for a dirt path leading left. Follow the path to reach a dirt road and then turn left on the road; you'll soon see a sign for the Southern Tip Trail. Within 15 minutes, the forested Southern Tip Trail breaks out into wide views of Lake Champlain, the Adirondacks to the south and southwest, and nearby Ball Island. A mowed patch right at the water's edge makes a pleasant spot for a lakeside picnic. The trail then continues on, moving clockwise along the island's shore, with alternate patches of forest cover and lake views. Reaching Eagle Point at the northern end of the island, look for a large outcropping of boulders and a trail sign for the North Shore Trail. This short return leg brings you back to the marina and ferry dock.

User Groups: Hikers and leashed dogs. Mountain bikers and wheelchair users can access the dirt road system crisscrossing the island. Dogs are not allowed in day-use areas such as picnic areas, but are not restricted on trails. No horses.

Permits: No permits required. Ferry service runs between Kill Kare State Park and Burton Island, Memorial Day–Columbus Day 8:30 A.M.–6:30 P.M. Round-trip fare is $8 per person, with kids under 3 years old riding for free; bikes are an extra $4 round-trip.

Maps: A free, basic map is available at the entrance gate. For a topographic area map, request Saint Albans Bay from the USGS.

Directions: To reach the ferry dock at Kill Kare State Park, from Main Street/Route 7 in St. Albans, head west on Lake Street for 2.9 miles to a right turn at Lake Road. Reaching a rotary in 0.4 mile, take the first exit to stay on Lake Road. Continue for another 2.6 miles to a right turn onto Hathaway Road. Follow 0.2 mile to the state park. GPS Coordinates: 44.4635 N, 73.1228 W

Contact: Burton Island State Park, Box 123, St. Albans Bay, VT 05481, 802/524-6353, www.vtstateparks.com/htm/burton.cfm. Kill Kare State Park, Hathaway Point Rd., St Albans, VT, 05478, 802/524-6021 (for ferry schedule), www.vtstateparks.com/htm/killkare.cfm. Vermont Department of Forests, Parks, and Recreation Commissioner's Office, 103 South Main St., Waterbury, VT 05671-0601, 802/241-3655, www.vtfpr.org.

🖪 LARAWAY LOOKOUT
3.6 mi/2.0 hr   🏃3 ⛰9

between Waterville and Belvidere Junction

A rocky outcropping on the side of Laraway Mountain, Laraway Lookout provides long views to the southwest and west, taking in the vast waters of Lake Champlain and beyond to the brooding purple peaks of the Adirondack Mountains in New York State. A short, rugged route that may be difficult for those with knee problems, this hike climbs about 1,500 feet.

From the parking area, follow the white-blazed Long Trail (LT) northbound. The wide path crosses a brook in 0.1 mile and then follows its opposite bank for about 200 yards, turning sharply left near picturesque cascades. The LT ascends gradually through woods and then grows increasingly steep. In its final 0.3 mile, the trail passes beneath dramatically overhanging cliffs and then climbs a narrow, rocky gully to reach the open ledge at Laraway Lookout. The wooded summit of Laraway Mountain lies just 0.4 mile farther up the Long Trail, but this hike returns the way you came.

This Long Trail section is on private land. Camping is prohibited except at the Green Mountain Club cabins and shelters. The Corliss Camp is three miles north of Laraway Lookout on the Long Trail.

User Groups: Hikers and leashed dogs. No bikes, horses, or wheelchair facilities.

Permits: Parking and access are free.

Maps: The waterproof End-to-End Map of the Long Trail is available for $9.95 from the Green Mountain Club. For a topographic area map, request Johnson from the USGS.

Directions: From Route 109, 1.8 miles north of the Waterville Market in the town center and 8.8 miles south of the junction of Routes 109 and 118 in Belvidere Corners, turn east onto Codding Hollow Road. Drive 1.4 miles and bear left at a fork and a sign for Long Trail parking. A mile farther, the road narrows to a two-track that may not be passable in mud season. Follow that two-track for 0.2 mile to a dirt parking lot on the left. GPS Coordinates: 44.7007 N, 72.7045 W

Contact: Green Mountain Club Inc., 4711 Waterbury-Stowe Rd., Waterbury Center, VT 05677, 802/244-7037, www.greenmountainclub.org.

◢ MOUNT HOR
2.8 mi/1.5 hr

in Willoughby State Forest in Barton

Lake Willoughby is a long finger of water embraced on both sides by the sheer cliffs of Mount Hor to the west and Mount Pisgah to the east. Tucked away in Vermont's remote Northeast Kingdom, Willoughby's topography inspires images of a Norwegian fjord more than it does the bucolic farmland and forests surrounding Willoughby State Forest. This is a great hike for viewing the fall foliage, which normally peaks by late September this far north. Although the views from 2,656-foot Mount Hor are not as spectacular as they are from Mount Pisgah, Hor's views are still

beautiful and the mountain comes with the added bonus of being much easier to hike than Mount Pisgah. After driving the CCC Road to the trailhead, the actual hike climbs less than 500 feet.

From the parking area, walk 40 feet farther up the road and turn right onto the Herbert Hawkes Trail. In another 30 feet, turn right with the trail onto an old logging road. The hike is easy and nearly flat for the first 0.4 mile, passing through several wet, muddy areas. The road eventually narrows to a trail, then swings left, and ascends the mountainside. At 0.7 mile you reach a trail junction marked by signs. To the left it is 0.3 mile to the wooded, viewless summit of Mount Hor (not included in this hike's distance). For this hike, turn right and follow the fairly easy trail another half mile to the first overlook of Lake Willoughby and Mount Pisgah and 0.1 mile beyond that to the second overlook. After you've taken in the views, hike back along the same route to the parking area.

User Groups: Hikers and dogs. No bikes, horses, or wheelchair facilities. Dogs are not allowed in day-use areas such as picnic areas, but are not restricted on trails.

Permits: Parking and access are free.

Maps: The Northern Vermont Hiking Trail Map, which covers Mount Mansfield, Camel's Hump, Lake Willoughby (including Mounts Hor and Pisgah), Cotton Brook, Little River, the Worcester Range (including Stowe Pinnacle and Mount Hunger), and Mount Elmore, is available from the Green Mountain Club for $5.95. For a free, basic map of hiking trails, contact the Vermont Department of Forests, Parks, and Recreation. For topographic area maps, request Sutton and Westmore from the USGS.

Directions: Take I-91 to Exit 25 for Barton. Turn right off the ramp onto Route 16 east. Drive one mile into Barton and turn right, then go 0.2 mile and turn left, staying on Route 16 east. Follow Route 16 for another 7.2 miles to the north end of Lake Willoughby and turn right onto Route 5A south. Drive 5.7

VERMONT

VERMONT

miles, beyond the foot of the lake, and turn right onto the gravel CCC Road beside a dirt parking lot. Follow that road for 1.8 miles to a parking area on the right. Trails are closed during the spring mud season, usually mid-April–mid-May, and are posted when closed for peregrine falcon nesting in spring.
GPS Coordinates: 44.7099 N, 72.0244 W
Contact: Green Mountain Club Inc., 4711 Waterbury-Stowe Rd., Waterbury Center, VT 05677, 802/244-7037, www.greenmountainclub.org. Vermont Department of Forests, Parks, and Recreation, 103 South Main St., Waterbury, VT 05671-0601, 802/241-3655, www.vtfpr.org.

5 MOUNT PISGAH
3.8 mi/2.5 hr

in Willoughby State Forest in Westmore

The cliffs of Mount Pisgah (2,751 ft.), rising abruptly to tower over the eastern shore of Willoughby Lake, offer breathtaking views of the bucolic Northeast Kingdom. Designated a State Fragile Area and a National Natural Landmark, the sheer drop of granite is home to a number of rare and tenacious alpine plants; the mountain's upper ledges are also nesting grounds for peregrine falcons. It's a steep, challenging route to the top of Pisgah. Get maximum payback for so much effort by saving this hike for late September or early October when the surrounding countryside blazes with fall color. In winter, Pisgah's west-facing cliff face transforms into one of New England's best ice climbing venues. This hike up Mount Pisgah climbs about 1,500 feet.

From the parking area, cross the highway to the South Trail, which begins at a sign labeled Willoughby State Forest Trailhead. The trail soon crosses a swampy, flooded area on a boardwalk and then starts climbing a wide path well marked with blue blazes. After about 0.7 mile, you pass the first of three successive lookouts on the left with partly obstructed

views of Lake Willoughby and Mount Hor; the third lookout is the best among them. At one mile, you reach a short side path leading left to Pulpit Rock, with an excellent view of the lake. Some hikers may choose to turn back from here for a round-trip of two miles.

Continue up the trail, scrambling up rock slabs a half mile beyond Pulpit Rock, and then watch for a side path leading to the right about 100 feet to a view southeast to New Hampshire's White Mountains. Return to the South Trail, turn right, and continue to Mount Pisgah's 2,751-foot summit, 1.9 miles from the road. Three side paths around the wooded summit lead left to ledges atop tall cliffs with sweeping views west. A sign points to the last side path, the north overlook. Head back the way you came.

User Groups: Hikers and dogs. No bikes, horses, or wheelchair facilities. Dogs are not allowed in day-use areas such as picnic areas, but are not restricted on trails.
Permits: Parking and access are free.
Maps: The Northern Vermont Hiking Trail Map, which covers Mount Mansfield, Camel's Hump, Lake Willoughby (including Mounts Hor and Pisgah), Cotton Brook, Little River, the Worcester Range, and Mount Elmore, is available from the Green Mountain Club for $5.95. For a free, basic map of hiking trails, contact the Vermont Department of Forests, Parks, and Recreation. For topographic area maps, request Sutton and Westmore from the USGS.
Directions: Take I-91 to Exit 25 for Barton. Turn right off the ramp onto Route 16 east. Drive one mile into Barton and turn right, drive 0.2 mile, and turn left, staying on Route 16 east. Follow Route 16 for another 7.2 miles to the north end of Lake Willoughby and turn right onto Route 5A south. Drive 5.7 miles, beyond the foot of the lake, to a dirt parking lot on the right. Trails are closed during the spring mud season, usually mid-April–mid-May, and are posted when closed for peregrine falcon nesting in spring.
GPS Coordinates: 44.7099 N, 72.0244 W

Contact: Vermont Department of Forests, Parks, and Recreation, 103 South Main St., Waterbury, VT 05671-0601, 802/241-3655, www.vtfpr.org.

6 PROSPECT ROCK
1.6 mi/1 hr

in Johnson

Leaving Jeffersonville and traveling east on Route 15 towards Johnson, look to your left, and you will see the steep cliffs of Prospect Rock (1,040 ft.), a nice side trip for those staying at Smuggler's Notch. Climbing about 500 feet in less than a mile, this relatively easy hike winds along a more remote Long Trail stretch, leading to Prospect's scenic lookout point and nice views south to the Lamoille River Valley and the Sterling Range (the mountains that make up Smuggler's Notch). You may want to pack lunch before setting out on this trek—the large flat area atop these ledges is a peaceful setting for an upland picnic.

From the turnout, follow the Long Trail (LT) white blazes northbound up the dirt road for about 0.1 mile and then turn left with the trail into the woods. The LT at first follows an old woods road and then swings right onto a footpath winding uphill, steeply at times, to reach Prospect Rock, 0.8 mile from the parking area. Follow the same route back.

This Long Trail section is on private land. Camping is prohibited except at the Green Mountain Club cabins and shelters. The Roundtop shelter is located 1.8 miles north of Prospect Rock on the Long Trail.

User Groups: Hikers and leashed dogs. No bikes, horses, or wheelchair facilities.

Permits: Parking and access are free.

Maps: The waterproof End-to-End Map of the Long Trail is available for $9.95 from the Green Mountain Club. For a topographic area map, request Johnson from the USGS.

Directions: From Route 15, two miles west of the junction of Routes 15 and 100C in Johnson and immediately east of the Lamoille River bridge, turn north onto a secondary road at signs for the Long Trail and Waterville. Continue 0.9 mile to a turnout on the right, across the road from the Ithiel Falls Camp Meeting Ground. You see the LT's white blazes on rocks at the turnout. Do not block the dirt road with your vehicle.

GPS Coordinates: 44.6479 N, 72.7123 W

Contact: Green Mountain Club Inc., 4711 Waterbury-Stowe Rd., Waterbury Center, VT 05677, 802/244-7037, www.greenmountainclub.org.

7 BURLINGTON WATERFRONT BIKE PATH
7.5 mi one-way/3 hr

in Burlington

BEST (

Stretching from Colchester Point Road in the north to a southern terminus at Oakledge Park, the paved, flat recreation path hugs the shore of Lake Champlain for its entire distance, offering incredible views west over the sailboat-dotted lake waters to the purple peaks of the Adirondacks. The bike path links six major waterfront parks, along with Burlington High School and the central Burlington Waterfront district. The bike path is a former railroad line, and while there's enough room here for bikers, hikers, wheelchair users, and in-line skaters, the path tends to become crowded during the peak tourist season. During peak daytime hours, the busiest parts of the trail are found near the ferry dock and waterfront park; heading north towards Colchester to the trail's terminus at Airport Park, foot and bike traffic tend to trail off. Hold off on hitting the bike path until late afternoon/early evening, not only for a bit more solitude, but also for the chance to take in the majestic sunset over the Adirondacks of New York State. If you are on foot, you will want to shuffle cars or use access points on the path to cut this into

VERMONT

a less blister-inducing trek. Bike rentals are found near the ferry dock. If you are visiting Burlington, consider renting a bike to take in as much of this scenic locale as possible. Plus, on a hot summer day, there's no more instant relief from the heat than tooling down the bike path with the cool lake breeze in your hair.

User Groups: Hikers, leashed dogs, bikes, and wheelchairs. No horses.

Permits: Trail access is free. A parking fee of $3 is applied to cars left at Oakledge Park. Metered and lot parking is available in the city of Burlington.

Maps: A free map is available from Local Motion's Trailside Center. For topographic area maps, request Burlington from the USGS.

Directions: To reach Airport Park in Colchester from downtown Burlington, follow Pearl Street to a right on North Champlain Street. At the end of North Champlain Street, bear left onto Route 127. Follow for 7 miles to a left turn on Porters Point Road. Follow for a half mile to a left turn on Colchester Point Road. Airport Park, where the path begins, is a short distance down this road. To reach Oakledge Park, from the corner of Church Street and Main Street, drive two blocks south on Main Street to a left turn onto Pine Street. Follow Pine Street for several blocks to a right turn at Flynn Avenue. Follow Flynn Avenue to the entrance of Oakledge Park. Other access points include (mileage given from Oakledge Park): Union Station (1 King Street; 2.1 miles), North Beach (9 Institute Road; 3.4 miles), and Leddy Park (290 Leddy Park Road; 5.1 miles).

GPS Coordinates (Oakledge Park): 44.4558 N, 73.2243 W

Contact: Local Motion's Trailside Center On the Burlington Bike Path, 1 Steele St. #103, Burlington, VT 05401, 802/652-2453, www.localmotion.org.

🎱 SMUGGLER'S NOTCH
0.2 mi/0.25 hr 🏃1 ⛰9

in Smuggler's Notch State Park between Stowe and Jeffersonville

BEST (

Smuggler's Notch separates Mount Mansfield, the highest summit in the Green Mountains, from Spruce Peak and the Sterling Range. The place is as rich in history as it is in picturesque scenery: The notch served as the route for illegal trade with Canada after President Thomas Jefferson's 1807 embargo forbade American trade with Great Britain and Canada. It also was used as an escape route to Canada for fugitive slaves, and, once an improved road was built through the notch in 1922, served as a route for smuggling liquor from Canada during Prohibition.

During the warm months, this hike is an easy walk around the height of land in Smuggler's Notch, where massive boulders line the narrow, winding roadway and lie strewn throughout the woods. Tall cliffs flank the notch to either side, making it look more like the White Mountains than the usually more tame Green Mountains. During the fall foliage season, however, the notch becomes quintessentially "autumn in Vermont" as maples, oaks, and elms burn bright with color and leaf peepers from far and wide come to take in the show.

From the south end of the parking turnout, follow a short but obvious path about 200 feet back into the jumble of garage-sized boulders known as Smuggler's Cave, reputedly a stash for contraband during the War of 1812. Then wander around the notch; you'll see the white blazes of the Long Trail enter the woods across the road, a short distance uphill from the turnout. In winter, this hike transforms into a more involved outing, not to mention one typically accompanied by a frigid wind. With Route 108 not maintained through the notch, you have to hike or cross-country ski up to the height of land—about a mile at an easy to moderate grade from the Jeffersonville side and about 2.3 miles from the Stowe side, which is much steeper. But the notch makes for a scenic ski tour and a fun descent.

User Groups: Hikers and dogs. In winter, cross-country skiers and snowshoers. No bikes, horses, or wheelchair facilities. Dogs are not allowed in day-use areas such as picnic areas, but are not restricted on trails.

Permits: Parking and access are free.

Maps: The Northern Vermont Hiking Trail Map, which covers Mount Mansfield, Camel's Hump, Lake Willoughby, Cotton Brook, Little River, the Worcester Range, and Mount Elmore, is available from the Green Mountain Club for $5.95. For a topographic area map, request Mount Mansfield from the USGS.

Directions: Drive to the turnout immediately north of the height of land on Route 108 in Smuggler's Notch, south of Jeffersonville and north of Stowe. Trails are closed during the spring mud season, usually mid-April–mid-May. Route 108 is not maintained through Smuggler's Notch once the snow falls. But the road often has a packed-snow surface in winter, making it possible to drive up from the Jeffersonville side with a four-wheel-drive vehicle or ski or hike up from either side. GPS Coordinates: 44.5524 N, 72.7974

Contact: Vermont Department of Forests, Parks, and Recreation, 103 South Main St., Waterbury, VT 05671-0601, 802/241-3655, www.vtfpr.org. Green Mountain Club Inc., 4711 Waterbury-Stowe Rd., Waterbury Center, VT 05677, 802/244-7037, www.greenmountainclub.org.

9 MOUNT MANSFIELD: SUNSET RIDGE AND LAURA COWLES TRAILS
6.2 mi/4.5 hr   🏃5 ⛰10

in Underhill State Park and Mount Mansfield State Forest in Underhill Center

BEST (

This 6.2-mile loop hike up Vermont's highest peak ascends the spectacular Sunset Ridge, much of it above the trees, with long views and rugged alpine terrain of the kind rarely found in the Green Mountains. About half of the two-mile ridge ascent is over exposed ground. This hike passes over the Chin, Mansfield's true summit at 4,393 feet, with a 360-degree view encompassing the entire sweep of Vermont, west to Lake Champlain and the Adirondacks, and east to New Hampshire's White Mountains. As with virtually any trail up Mansfield, this is a popular hike in summer and fall, and even attracts winter climbers (who should have the proper gear and skills). And yes, it is a beautiful place to watch the sunset. The trail gains about 2,100 feet in elevation from the state park to the summit.

From the parking lot at the ranger station, hike up the dirt CCC Road for about a mile; just beyond a sharp right bend in the road, the blue-blazed Sunset Ridge Trail, marked by a sign, enters the woods. Follow the trail over two wooden footbridges spanning brooks to a junction with the Laura Cowles Trail just 0.1 mile from the road, branching right; you will descend that trail. Continue up the Sunset Ridge Trail, ascending moderately, and you'll see the first views through breaks in the forest within a half mile from the road. At 0.7 mile, turn left onto the Cantilever Rock Trail and follow it 0.1 mile to its namesake rock, a needlelike formation projecting horizontally about 40 feet from high up a cliff face. Backtrack to the Sunset Ridge Trail and continue climbing up through forest marked by occasional large boulders. About one mile from the road, the trail makes a short step up exposed rocks and emerges above the tree line for the first broad views south and west.

The trail then follows the ridge upward, over rocky terrain where scrub spruce grow close to the ground in places, to a junction at about two miles with the Laura Cowles Trail, branching right—this hike's descent route. Continue another 0.2 mile up the Sunset Ridge Trail to its terminus at the Long Trail, on Mansfield's exposed summit ridge. Turn left (north) and follow the LT 0.2 mile to the

VERMONT

Chin. Backtrack on the LT and Sunset Ridge Trail to the Laura Cowles Trail, and descend the Laura Cowles, reentering the woods within a half mile of the Sunset Ridge Trail. The Cowles Trail drops steadily for another 0.9 mile to its lower junction with the Sunset Ridge Trail. Turn left and walk 0.1 mile back to the CCC Road.

Camping is prohibited except at the Green Mountain Club cabins and shelters.

near the summit of Mount Mansfield

© BRIAN WHITE

User Groups: Hikers and leashed dogs. No bikes, horses, or wheelchair facilities. This trail should not be attempted in winter except by hikers experienced in mountaineering and prepared for severe winter weather.

Permits: An entrance fee of $3 per person ages 14 and older, and $2 for children ages 4–13, is collected at the ranger station, Memorial Day–Columbus Day.

Maps: The waterproof End-to-End Map of the Long Trail is available for $9.95 from the Green Mountain Club, as is the Northern Vermont Hiking Trail Map, which covers Mount Mansfield, Camel's Hump, Lake Willoughby, Cotton Brook, Little River, the Worcester Range, and Mount Elmore, for $5.95. For a topographic area map, request Mount Mansfield from the USGS.

Directions: From Route 15 in Underhill Flats, drive east on the road to Underhill Center. In Underhill Center, three miles from Route 15, continue straight past the Underhill Country Store for one mile and turn right (at a sign for Underhill State Park) onto Mountain Road/TH2. Drive approximately two miles farther to a large parking lot at the ranger station. Once the snow falls, the CCC Road is maintained only to a point about a half mile before the start of this hike, where winter visitors can park.

GPS Coordinates: 44.5269 N, 72.8428 W

Contact: Underhill State Park, P.O. Box 249, Underhill Center, VT 05490, 802/899-3022 in summer, 802/879-5674 in winter, or 800/252-2363. Vermont Department of Forests, Parks, and Recreation, Essex Junction District, 111 West St., Essex Junction, VT 05452, 802/879-6565. Vermont Department of Forests, Parks, and Recreation Commissioner's Office, 103 South Main St., Waterbury, VT 05671-0601, 802/241-3655, www.state.vt.us/anr/fpr. Green Mountain Club Inc., 4711 Waterbury-Stowe Rd., Waterbury Center, VT 05677, 802/244-7037, www.greenmountainclub.org.

⑩ MOUNT MANSFIELD: HELL BROOK TRAIL

5.8 mi/6 hr   🏃5 ⛰10

in Smuggler's Notch State Park and Mount Mansfield State Forest in Stowe

Linking some of the steepest, most rugged trails on Mount Mansfield (Vermont's highest peak), this 5.8-mile hike may be one of the most difficult mountain hikes in all of New England. Because of the scrambling involved on parts of the trail and the potential for harsh weather at higher elevations (freezing fog and rime ice can be experienced here as early as September), even fit hikers typically need six hours to complete the trek. Most trail junctions are marked by signs and the Long Trail is marked by white blazes. This hike ascends more than 2,500 feet in elevation.

From the Big Spring parking area, cross the road and walk uphill 150 feet to the Hell Brook Trail. The Hell Brook Trailhead is well-beaten and almost impossible to miss, but you may not find a trail sign as it seems to be a popular one to steal. It climbs very steeply, through dense and often wet forest where you find yourself grabbing roots and tree branches for aid in places. At 0.9 mile, the Hell Brook Cutoff branches left, but stay to the right on the Hell Brook Trail. At 1.3 miles, a junction appears with the Adam's Apple Trail on the left. The Bear Pond Trail heading north from this junction is closed, although you may still be able to access scenic Lake of the Clouds on a short spur trail a very short distance down the former Bear Pond Trail. Climb the Adam's Apple Trail 0.1 mile to the rocky secondary summit of Mount Mansfield (known as the Adam's Apple) for excellent views of the true summit lying a stone's throw to the south. Descend over the Adam's Apple another 0.1 mile to rejoin the Hell Brook Trail and reach the Long Trail (LT) at Eagle Pass. Hikers looking to cut this loop short can descend the LT by turning left and hiking for two miles to Route 108; once reaching the road, turn left and walk a half mile to Big Spring.

This hike bears right at Eagle Pass onto the LT southbound, climbing the steep cliffs of Mansfield's summit for 0.3 mile onto the Chin, Mansfield's true summit at 4,393 feet. The Green Mountains reach to the north and south horizons; to the west is Lake Champlain and New York's Adirondack Mountains; and to the east you can see New Hampshire's White Mountains on a clear day. The LT continues south over Mansfield's long, exposed summit ridge, the most extensive of Vermont's few alpine areas, with fragile and rare vegetation; stay on the trail or walk on bare rock.

Stay on the LT southbound along the ridge for 0.4 mile, then turn left onto the Cliff Trail. Within 0.1 mile, a spur trail leads right 50 feet to the Cave of the Winds, a deep joint in the cliff. Continue along the Cliff Trail, descending over very rocky terrain below the imposing cliffs of the summit ridge to your right and overlooking Smuggler's Notch and the ski area below on your left. After 0.3 mile down the trail, a path to the left leads 0.1 mile downhill to the top of the ski area gondola. Hikers uncomfortable with the difficulty of the Cliff Trail can bail out here and hike down a ski trail, bearing in mind that the Cliff Trail's greatest challenges lie ahead.

Continuing on the Cliff Trail, in another 0.1 mile you'll reach Wall Street, where the trail squeezes through a claustrophobia-inducing gap between towering rock walls. For the next 0.7 mile, the Cliff Trail climbs up and down over rock and through dense subalpine forest, leading hikers up wooden ladders bolted into sheer rock. At trail's end, turn left onto the summit road and follow it downhill for nearly a half mile, then turn left onto the Haselton Trail, which coincides here with a ski trail called Nose Dive. This descends at a steep grade that is hard on the knees. Watch for where the Haselton Trail reenters the woods, within 0.3 mile, on the left. It's two miles from the Cliff Trail to the ski area parking lot via the Haselton Trail.

Camping is prohibited except at the Green Mountain Club cabins and shelters. The Taft Lodge cabin is located on the Long Trail, 1.7 miles south of Route 108.

User Groups: Hikers and leashed dogs. No bikes, horses, or wheelchair facilities. This trail should not be attempted in winter except by hikers experienced in mountaineering and prepared for severe winter weather.

Permits: Parking and access are free.

Maps: The waterproof End-to-End Map of the Long Trail is available for $9.95 from the Green Mountain Club, as is the Northern Vermont Hiking Trail Map, which covers Mount Mansfield, Camel's Hump, Lake Willoughby, Cotton Brook, Little River, the Worcester Range, and Mount Elmore, for $5.95. For a topographic area map, request Mount Mansfield from the USGS.

VERMONT

Directions: You will need to either shuttle two vehicles for this hike or hike an extra 1.6 miles along Route 108 between the ski area and the Hell Brook Trailhead. Another option is to shorten this hike by descending the Long Trail, which would require walking a half mile on Route 108 back to this hike's start. From the junction of Routes 108 and 100 in Stowe, drive 7.4 miles west on Route 108 and turn left into the gondola base station parking lot for the Mount Mansfield Ski Area; leave one vehicle there, turn back onto Route 108 west, and continue another 1.6 miles to the small dirt lot on the right at Big Spring, which is 1.2 miles east of the Route 108 height of land in Smuggler's Notch. Route 108 is not maintained through Smuggler's Notch once the snow falls, only to a point about a mile east of this hike's start.

GPS Coordinates: 44.5481 N, 72.7939 W

Contact: Vermont Department of Forests, Parks, and Recreation Region III-Northwest Vermont, 111 West St., Essex Junction, VT 05452, 802/879-5666. Vermont Department of Forests, Parks, and Recreation Commissioner's Office, 103 South Main St., Waterbury, VT 05671-0601, 802/241-3655, www.vtfpr.org. Green Mountain Club Inc., 4711 Waterbury-Stowe Rd., Waterbury Center, VT 05677, 802/244-7037, www.greenmountainclub.org.

11 MOUNT MANSFIELD: LONG TRAIL

4.6 mi/3.5 hr   🏃4 ⛰10

in Smuggler's Notch State Park in Stowe

BEST (

Probably the most commonly hiked route up Vermont's highest peak, 4,393-foot Mount Mansfield, the Long Trail is a good trail of only moderate difficulty. And just 2.3 miles from the road in Smuggler's Notch—after an elevation gain of nearly 2,800 feet—you are standing atop the Chin, Mansfield's true summit, with a 360-degree view taking in

all of northern Vermont, including much of the Green Mountains, and stretching to New Hampshire's White Mountains, New York's Adirondacks, and Quebec. Predictably, this is a very popular hike that sees many boots on nice weekends in summer and fall.

Numerous features on Mansfield's long, completely exposed ridge bear names that derive from the mountain's resemblance, especially from the east, to a man's profile: the Chin, the Nose, the Forehead, the Upper and Lower Lip, and the Adam's Apple. Mansfield is one of just two peaks in Vermont—the other being Camel's Hump (see the two Camel's Hump listings in this chapter)—with a significant alpine area, or area above the tree line. The rare plants that grow in this tundra-like terrain are fragile, so take care to walk only on the trail or rocks. Be aware also that alpine terrain signals frequent harsh weather: Mansfield can attract wintry weather in any month of the year, so come here prepared for the worst and be willing to turn back whenever conditions turn threatening. A Green Mountain Club caretaker is on duty during the prime hiking season to assist hikers and ensure the protection of the alpine area. There are also TV and radio stations at the summit, a toll road up the mountain, and a ski area operating on its east side.

From the parking area, walk a short distance south on Route 108 and turn right (southbound) onto the white-blazed Long Trail (LT). The trail climbs steadily, crossing a brook and changing direction a few times before reaching Taft Lodge at 1.7 miles. From the clearing at the lodge, you can see the imposing cliffs below the summit. Continue up the LT. The trail emerges from the trees within 0.3 mile of the lodge and then climbs steeply another 0.3 mile to the summit. Return the way you came.

Camping is prohibited except at the Green Mountain Club cabins and shelters. The Taft Lodge cabin is located on the Long Trail, 1.7 miles south of Route 108.

User Groups: Hikers and leashed dogs. No

bikes, horses, or wheelchair facilities. This trail should not be attempted in winter except by hikers experienced in mountaineering and prepared for severe winter weather.

Permits: Parking and access are free.

Maps: The waterproof End-to-End Map of the Long Trail is available for $9.95 from the Green Mountain Club, as is the Northern Vermont Hiking Trail Map, which covers Mount Mansfield, Camel's Hump, Lake Willoughby, Cotton Brook, Little River, the Worcester Range, and Mount Elmore, for $5.95. For a topographic area map, request Mount Mansfield from the USGS.

Directions: Drive to the roadside parking area immediately north of where the northbound Long Trail from Mount Mansfield reaches Route 108, 8.5 miles west of the junction of Routes 108 and 100 in Stowe, and 1.7 miles east of the height of land in Smuggler's Notch. Route 108 is not maintained through Smuggler's Notch once the snow falls, only to a point about a half mile east of this hike's start. GPS Coordinates: 44.5393 N, 72.7914 W

Contact: Vermont Department of Forests, Parks, and Recreation Commissioner's Office, 103 South Main St., Waterbury, VT 05671-0601, 802/241-3655, www.vtfpr.org. Green Mountain Club Inc., 4711 Waterbury-Stowe Rd., Waterbury Center, VT 05677, 802/244-7037, www.greenmountainclub.org.

12 STOWE PINNACLE
2.3 mi/1.5 hr   👣2   ⛰10

in Putnam State Forest near Stowe

BEST (

This fairly easy round-trip hike of 2.3 miles leads to the open, craggy summit of Stowe Pinnacle, which is visible from the parking area. A great hike for young children and quite popular with families, its summit offers excellent views, especially in a wide sweep from the northwest to the southwest, including Camel's Hump to the southwest, Mount Mansfield to the west, and the ski town of

Stowe in the valley separating the pinnacle from Mansfield.

The trail begins at the rear of the parking area. Following easy terrain at first, the blue-blazed path traverses areas that are often muddy. It ascends moderately through the woods to a junction with the Skyline Trail (marked by a sign) just over a mile from the parking lot. Turn right and hike uphill another 0.1 mile to the Stowe Pinnacle summit. Return the way you came. (See the *Mount Hunger* listing in this chapter for a way to link the two hikes on a nice ridge walk.)

User Groups: Hikers and leashed dogs. Dogs are not allowed in day-use areas such as picnic areas, but are not restricted on trails. No bikes, horses, or wheelchair facilities.

Permits: Parking and access are free.

Maps: The Northern Vermont Hiking Trail Map, which covers Mount Mansfield, Camel's Hump, Lake Willoughby (including Mounts Hor and Pisgah), Cotton Brook, Little River, the Worcester Range (including Stowe Pinnacle and Mount Hunger), and Mount Elmore, is available from the Green Mountain Club for $5.95. For a topographic area map, request Stowe from the USGS.

Directions: Take I-89 to Exit 10 and turn north onto Route 100. Continue about 10 miles and turn right onto School Street. Drive 0.3 mile and bear right onto Stowe Hollow Road. In another 1.5 miles, drive straight onto Upper Hollow Road and continue 0.7 mile to a parking area for the Pinnacle Trail on the left. Trails are closed during the spring mud season, usually mid-April–mid-May. GPS Coordinates: 44.4391 N, 72.6677 W

Contact: Vermont Department of Forests, Parks, and Recreation, Barre District, 324 North Main St., Barre, VT 05641, 802/476-0170. Vermont Department of Forests, Parks, and Recreation Commissioner's Office, 103 South Main St., Waterbury, VT 05671, 802/241-3655, www.vtfpr.org. Green Mountain Club Inc., 4711 Waterbury-Stowe Rd., Waterbury Center, VT 05677, 802/244-7037, www.greenmountainclub.org.

VERMONT

🔟🔟 MOUNT HUNGER

4 mi/3 hr   🚶🚶3 △10

in Putnam State Forest near Stowe

BEST (

One of the nicest hikes in Vermont and one requiring less effort than higher Green Mountain peaks, Mount Hunger offers long views in virtually every direction from its 3,539-foot summit of bare rock. Dominating the western horizon is the long chain of the Green Mountains, with Camel's Hump the prominent peak to the southwest and Mount Mansfield, Vermont's highest, rising due west. Between Hunger and Mansfield lies a pastoral valley of open fields interspersed with sprawling forest; in fall, this scene transforms into a breathtakingly vibrant tableau of crimson, orange, and gold. For leaf peeping hikers, this is one view not to be missed. To the east, on a clear day, you can make out the White Mountains, particularly the towering wall of Franconia Ridge, and farther off, Mount Washington. Hike up here in late fall or winter and you may see the Whites capped in white. The ascent of Hunger is more than 2,200 feet. A longer loop takes you over Hunger and Stowe Pinnacle, a particularly nice trek during autumn foliage season.

From the parking lot, the blue-blazed Waterbury Trail makes a moderately difficult ascent as it weaves back and forth for two miles, crossing and re-crossing a tumbling stream bed before emerging above the tree line about 100 yards below the summit. After reaching the summit, head back the way you came.

Special note: A ridge trail links the Mount Hunger summit with Stowe Pinnacle (see *Stowe Pinnacle* listing in this chapter). By shuttling cars to the parking lots at each trailhead, you can make this Worcester Range ridge walk of about seven miles a 4–5 hour hike. From the Hunger summit, look for the cairns and blazes of the Skyline Trail heading north. The trail dips back into the woods and remains in the trees, but it's an interesting, if somewhat rugged, walk through a lush subalpine

forest on a trail that experiences a fraction of the foot traffic seen on the primary trails up Hunger and Stowe Pinnacle. Three miles out from the top of Hunger, after the Skyline Trail passes over the wooded, 3,440-foot bump of Hogback Mountain, it descends, steeply in places, to a junction with the Pinnacle Trail. Bear left, reaching the top of Stowe Pinnacle in 0.1 mile. Descend the Pinnacle Trail 1.1 miles to the trailhead parking lot.

User Groups: Hikers and dogs. No bikes, horses, or wheelchair facilities. Dogs are not allowed in day-use areas such as picnic areas, but are not restricted on trails.

Permits: Parking and access are free.

Maps: The Northern Vermont Hiking Trail Map, which covers Mount Mansfield, Camel's Hump, Lake Willoughby (including Mounts Hor and Pisgah), Cotton Brook, Little River, the Worcester Range (including Stowe Pinnacle and Mount Hunger), and Mount Elmore, is available from the Green Mountain Club for $5.95. For a topographic area map, request Stowe from the USGS.

Directions: Take I-89 to Exit 10 and turn north onto Route 100 in Stowe. Drive about three miles and turn right onto Howard Avenue. Continue 0.4 mile and turn left onto Maple Street. In 0.1 mile, turn right onto Loomis Hill, then drive two miles to the junction with Sweet and Ripley Roads. Continue left onto Sweet Road. The parking entrance is roughly 1.4 miles farther on the right. There is a sign on the right. Trails are closed during the spring mud season, usually mid-April–mid-May.

GPS Coordinates: 44.4071 N, 72.6758 N

Contact: Vermont Department of Forests, Parks, and Recreation, Barre District, 324 North Main St., Barre, VT 05641, 802/476-0170. Vermont Department of Forests, Parks, and Recreation Commissioner's Office, 103 South Main St., Waterbury, VT 05671, 802/241-3655, www.vtfpr.org. Green Mountain Club Inc., 4711 Waterbury-Stowe Rd., Waterbury Center, VT 05677, 802/244-7037, www.greenmountainclub.org.

14 GREEN MOUNTAIN AUDUBON NATURE CENTER

3 mi /1.5 hr 2 9

in Huntington

Nestled in the foothills of the Green Mountains, the 255-acre Green Mountain Audubon Center's trail system winds its way through a northern hardwood forest (including a sugar bush), hemlock swamp, and the Huntington River flood plain. A stunning spot in a state known for its natural beauty, the landscape is almost secondary to the center's abundant diversity of flora and fauna. Over 100 species of birds breed or winter in the area, including the hermit thrush, blackburnian warbler, red-eyed vireo, and rose-breasted grosbeak. Wetlands offer critical breeding areas for amphibians such as spotted salamanders and wood frogs, as well as year round residence for sizeable populations of beaver, deer, rabbit, fox, squirrel, and bats. During the spring, the forest floor bursts forth in early wildflower color; while in the fall, the forest canopy puts on its own showing of brilliant foliage. This four-mile loop through the property takes you to the center's showcase features, with Lookout Rock providing nice views of the center and surrounding countryside.

From the parking lot next to the center's barn and office, cross Sherman Hollow Road and pick up the wide, obvious White Pine Trail. Following it less than 0.2 mile and at the second trail junction you reach, bear right to cross through Hemlock Swamp; parts of the trail take you onto a boardwalk. Emerging from the swamp in another 0.2 mile, the trail rises, leaving behind the hemlocks to emerge into a working sugarbush. Come here in March to see the annual tree tapping; the trail bears to the right to bring you to the sugarhouse, open in spring for maple syrup production. From here, pick up the River Trail, bearing left past the sugarhouse. In the next half mile, the trail hugs the banks of the Huntington River. Where the trail ends, pick up the Brook Trail, following the Sherman Hollow Brook for another half mile back to the road. Cross the road and continue on the Brook Trail, which ends at the Hires Trail in another 0.1 mile. Bear right and head uphill, soon reaching nice views from Lookout Rock. Continue on the Hires Trail until it ends at the Sensory Trail. Follow this 0.7-mile loop, equipped with rope lines and braille interpretative panels for blind visitors. The loop ends back at the parking area and barn.

User Groups: Hikers and leashed dogs. Some trails below Sherman Hollow Road restrict pet access; check with the office upon arrival. No bikes or horses. Trails around the sugarbush and sugarhouse are flattened by tractor use and may be accessible for some wheelchair uses; call Vermont Audubon for details.

Permits: Parking and trail access are free; donations welcome.

Maps: A trail map is available from the Green Mountain Audubon Center. For topographic area maps, request Huntington and Richmond from the USGS.

Directions: From I-89, take exit 11 to Richmond. Driving two miles into Richmond, turn right at the stoplight onto Bridge Street. Continue on, and after passing Round Church, bear right, now on Huntington Road. Follow signs for Huntington; in approximately five miles, take a right onto Sherman Hollow Road. Parking and the Vermont Audubon Center Office and Education Barn are 0.25 mile up the road on the left.

GPS Coordinates: 44.3564 N, 72.9967 W

Contact: Green Mountain Audubon Center, 255 Sherman Hollow Rd., Huntington, VT 05462, 802/434-3068, http://vt.audubon.org.

VERMONT

15 MOUNT PHILO

2.2 mi/1.5 hr

in Mount Philo State Park between North
Ferrisburgh and Charlotte

BEST (

The view from atop the cliffs of 968-foot
Mount Philo far exceeds the expectations you
may have while driving toward this tiny hill.
The bucolic Champlain Valley sprawls before
you, flanked by the Green Mountains chain
stretching far southward and the brooding
Adirondack Mountains rising to west across
Lake Champlain. This 2.2-mile loop over the
summit is somewhat steep in places, although
not difficult. When the road is open, you can
drive to the top of Philo and walk about 0.1
mile to the cliff overlooks, a magical spot to
watch a glowing Lake Champlain sunset.

The blue-blazed trail begins just past the
gate, on the left. The trail—which tends to
be muddy and slippery in spring—winds up
Mount Philo, crossing the summit road once,
to the overlooks. After taking in the views,
continue past the summit overlooks on a dirt
road for 0.1 mile to a large parking lot and
descend the paved park road 1.2 miles back
to the hike's start.

User Groups: Hikers, cross-country skiers, and
leashed dogs. No horses or wheelchair facilities
on trail. Also, no bikes on the trail, but bikes
are allowed on the summit road.

Permits: An entrance fee of $3 per person ages
14 and older and $2 for children ages 4–13 is
charged Memorial Day–Columbus Day.

Maps: While no map is necessary for this
hike, a free, basic map is available at park
entrances for virtually all state parks. For a
topographic area map, request Mount Philo
from the USGS.

Directions: From U.S. 7, about 1.2 miles north
of North Ferrisburg and 2.5 miles south of
the junction of U.S. 7 and Route F5 in Charlotte, turn east onto State Park Road. Drive
a half mile to a parking lot at the base of the
mountain, just outside the gate. Trails are
closed during the spring mud season, usually

mid-April–mid-May. The park road is not
maintained in winter, making it a strenuous
cross-country skiing route up the mountain.
GPS Coordinates: 44.2776 N, 73.2226 W
Contact: Mount Philo State Park, 5425 Mount
Philo Rd., Charlotte, VT 05445; or RD 1
Box 1049, North Ferrisburgh, VT 05473,
802/425-2390 in summer, 802/483-2001 in
winter. Vermont Department of Forests, Parks,
and Recreation Commissioner's Office, 103
South Main St., Waterbury, VT 05671-0601,
802/241-3655, www.vtfpr.org.

16 CAMEL'S HUMP: FOREST CITY/ BURROWS TRAILS LOOP

6.4 mi/4.5 hr   🏕5 ⛰10

in Camel's Hump State Park in Huntington
Center

With the only undeveloped alpine area in the
Green Mountain State and a skyline that sets
itself apart from everything else for miles,
4,083-foot Camel's Hump may be Vermont's
finest peak. The views from its distinctive
summit are among the best in New England.
To the west are the Adirondacks and Lake
Champlain; to the south the Green Mountains
stretch out in a long chain; to the southeast
rises the prominent mound of Mount Ascutney; to the northeast lie Mount Hunger and
Stowe Pinnacle in the Worcester Range; far
to the northeast, on a clear day, the White
Mountains are visible; and to the north, when
not smothered in clouds, are Bolton Mountain
and Mount Mansfield.

You can hike this loop in either direction,
but this ascent, beginning on the Forest City
Trail, takes you up Camel's Hump's southern
ridge, a wonderful climb that builds excite-
ment for the summit. The vertical ascent
on the loop is about 2,700 feet. The Forest
City and Burrows Trails are well-worn paths
and well marked with blue blazes; the Long
Trail is blazed white. Trail junctions have

© STEPHEN DEMARS

from the summit, looking back at the Camel's Hump ridge

cabins—Montclair Glen Lodge, near the Burrows and Long Trails junction, and Bamforth Ridge shelter 5.4 miles north of Montclair Glen Lodge on the Long Trail—and at the Hump Brook tenting area, just off the Dean Trail. A Green Mountain Club caretaker is on duty Memorial Day weekend–Columbus Day and a per-person nightly fee is collected to stay at either cabin.

User Groups: Hikers and dogs. Dogs must be leashed above the tree line. No bikes, horses, or wheelchair facilities. This trail should not be attempted in winter except by hikers experienced in mountaineering and prepared for severe winter weather.

Permits: Parking and access are free.

Maps: A basic trail map with state park information is sometimes available at the trailhead hiker register. The Northern Vermont Hiking Trail Map, which covers Mount Mansfield, Camel's Hump, Lake Willoughby (including Mounts Hor and Pisgah), Cotton Brook, Little River, the Worcester Range (including Stowe Pinnacle and Mount Hunger), and Mount Elmore, is available from the Green Mountain Club and costs $5.95. For topographic area maps, request Huntington and Waterbury from the USGS.

Directions: In Huntington Center, 2.5 miles south of the post office in Huntington Village, turn onto Camel's Hump Road at the signs for Camel's Hump State Park. Follow the dirt road, bearing right at forks (state park signs point the way). At 2.8 miles from Huntington Center, there is a small parking area on the right at the Forest City Trailhead; you can start this loop from there (adding 1.5 miles to this hike's distance) or continue up the road another 0.7 mile to a larger parking area at the Burrows Trailhead. The trails are closed to hikers during mud season, mid-April–Memorial Day.

GPS Coordinates: 44.2983 N, 72.9189 W

Contact: Vermont Department of Forests, Parks, and Recreation Region III-Northwest Vermont, 111 West St., Essex Junction, VT 05452, 802/879-5666. Vermont Department

been marked with signs in the past, but don't count on them.

From the Burrows Trailhead, turn right onto the connector trail leading 0.1 mile to the Forest City Trail and then turn left onto it, hiking east. The trail ascends at a moderate grade, reaching the Long Trail (LT) about 1.6 miles from the Burrows Trailhead. Turn left (north) on the LT and follow it for nearly two miles to the summit, climbing below and around spectacular cliffs. Beyond the summit, stay on the LT for another 0.3 mile to the Camel's Hump hut clearing and then turn left (west) on the Burrows Trail, which leads 2.4 miles back to the trailhead.

Left intentionally as a place to be forever wild, the mountain is also Vermont's least developed state park, with backwoods camping the norm and few services. Be sure to sign in at one of the logbooks located at all Camel's Hump trailheads, noting the time you left and your destination. Camping is prohibited except at the two Green Mountain Club

of Forests, Parks, and Recreation Commissioner's Office, 103 South Main St., Waterbury, VT 05671, 802/241-3655, www.vtfpr.org. Green Mountain Club Inc., 4711 Waterbury-Stowe Rd., Waterbury Center, VT 05677, 802/244-7037, www.greenmountainclub.org.

🔟 CAMEL'S HUMP: MONROE/ALPINE TRAILS LOOP
6.6 mi/4.5 hr   🏃5 ⛰10

in Camel's Hump State Park in North Duxbury

Waubanaukee Indians first named the mountain *Tah-wak-be-dee-ee-wadso* (Saddle Mountain). Samuel de Champlain's explorers in the 1600s called it *lion couchant* (resting lion). The name Camel's Rump was used on a historical map by Ira Allen in 1798; this became Camel's Hump in 1830. Another name derivation: a large portion of this hike takes place on the Monroe Trail—named for Professor Will Monroe, father of the Monroe Skyline (see *The Monroe Skyline* listing in this chapter). This rugged, but popular route up this very popular Green Mountains peak offers a vertical gain of 2,583 feet.

At the west end of the parking lot, the trail begins at a signpost; sign the hiker registry before heading out. Immediately entering a hardwood forest of birch and maple, the blue-blazed Monroe Trail ascends at a moderate grade at first but grows steeper as you climb higher. Trail sections are often wet, even into autumn. At 2.5 miles, turn left onto the yellow-blazed Alpine Trail, which is wooded and fairly rugged along this stretch. Within a half mile, you pass near the wing of a WWII bomber that crashed into the mountain during a wartime training flight at night.

Just beyond the wreckage, the Alpine Trail meets the Long Trail (LT). Turn right (north) on the white-blazed LT, quickly emerging from the trees for your first sweeping views from below the towering cliffs on the Camel's

Hump south face. The LT swings left below the cliffs and ascends the mountain's west face to its open, 4,083-foot summit, 0.2 mile from the Alpine Trail. Continue on the LT north over the summit, descending rocky terrain for 0.3 mile to the Camel's Hump hut clearing. Turn right onto the Monroe Trail, which takes you down 3.1 miles to the parking area.

Left intentionally as a place to be forever wild, the mountain is also Vermont's least developed state park, with backwoods camping the norm and few services. Be sure to sign in at one of the logbooks located at all Camel's Hump trailheads, noting the time you left and your destination. Camping is prohibited except at the two Green Mountain Club cabins—Montclair Glen Lodge, near the Burrows and Long Trails junction, and Bamforth Ridge shelter 5.4 miles north of Montclair Glen Lodge on the Long Trail—and at the Hump Brook tenting area, just off the Dean Trail. A Green Mountain Club caretaker is on duty Memorial Day weekend–Columbus Day and a per-person nightly fee is collected to stay at either cabin.

User Groups: Hikers and dogs. Dogs must be leashed above the tree line. No bikes, horses, or wheelchair facilities. This trail should not be attempted in winter except by hikers experienced in mountaineering and prepared for severe winter weather.

Permits: Parking and access are free.

Maps: A basic trail map with state park information is sometimes available at the trailhead hiker register. The waterproof End-to-End Map of the Long Trail is available for $9.95 from the Green Mountain Club, as is the Northern Vermont Hiking Trail Map, which covers Mount Mansfield, Camel's Hump, Lake Willoughby, Cotton Brook, Little River, the Worcester Range, and Mount Elmore, for $5.95. For topographic area maps, request Huntington and Waterbury from the USGS.

Directions: From the south, take I-89 to Exit 10. Turn south, drive about a half mile to the end of the road, and turn left onto U.S. 2

east. Continue 1.3 miles and then turn right onto Route 100 south. Proceed just 0.2 mile and turn right onto Duxbury Road; continue six miles down that road, then turn left at a sign for Camel's Hump trails. Drive 1.2 miles and bear left over a bridge. Continue another 2.4 miles to the parking lot at the end of the road, at the so-called Couching Lion site. The trails are closed to hiking during mud season, roughly mid-April–Memorial Day. Winter parking is in the lot for Camel's Hump View, a half mile before the Couching Lion site.

From the north, take I-89 to Exit 11 for U.S. 2 east. Drive about five miles into Jonesville, and just beyond the post office (on the left), turn right, crossing the bridge over the Winooski River. In 0.2 mile, turn left onto Duxbury Road and continue six miles to the sign for Camel's Hump trails. Turn right, cross the bridge at 1.2 miles, and continue 2.4 miles to the Couching Lion site. GPS Coordinates: 44.3392 N, 72.9173 W

Contact: Vermont Department of Forests, Parks, and Recreation Region III-Northwest Vermont, 111 West St., Essex Junction, VT 05452, 802/879-5666. Vermont Department of Forests, Parks, and Recreation Commissioner's Office, 103 South Main St., Waterbury, VT 05671, 802/241-3655, www.vtfpr.org. Green Mountain Club Inc., 4711 Waterbury-Stowe Rd., Waterbury Center, VT 05677, 802/244-7037, www.greenmountainclub.org.

18 BIG DEER MOUNTAIN
4.2 mi/3 hr   🏃4 ⛰️8

in Groton State Forest

Rising above Osmore Pond in the Northeast Kingdom's remote Groton State Forest, Big Deer Mountain offers good views for a hill not even 2,000 feet high. This hike begins from different parking areas, depending upon whether the road into the New Discovery

Campground is open. The elevation gain is about 300 feet.

In winter, parking at the gate, walk 0.1 mile past the gate to a field; in summer, backtrack the road from the Osmore Pond picnic area to the field. Facing that field, turn left onto an obvious dirt forest road and follow it 0.3 mile and turn right onto the Big Deer Mountain Trail (marked by a sign). Follow the blue blazes through the woods on a trail that's mostly flat for 1.1 miles. Then, at a trail junction, continue straight ahead, climbing about 200 feet in elevation over 0.6 mile of rocky trail onto Big Deer Mountain. The trail ends at open ledges with a view to the south, overlooking Lake Groton. Just before the trail's end, a side path leads left a short distance to another open ledge with a view east from high above Peacham Bog. On a clear day, you can see the White Mountains. Backtrack 0.6 mile to the junction and turn left onto the Big Deer Mountain Trail toward Osmore Pond. It descends gently, crosses a marshy area, passes over a slight rise, and then descends more steeply to a trail junction near the south end of Osmore Pond, 0.9 mile from the last junction. Turn right onto the Osmore Pond Hiking Loop, a rock-strewn but flat trail that parallels the pond's east shore and loops around its north end. In winter, about 0.7 mile from the trail junction at the pond's south end, turn right again onto a connector trail leading back to the New Discovery Campground. In summer, follow the loop trail around the pond to the picnic area.

Beyond Big Deer, take time to explore Groton State Forest. This Northeast Kingdom gem, with over 26,000 acres, is the second largest landholding administered by the Department of Forests, Parks, and Recreation. It has over 17 miles of hiking trails and over 20 miles of gravel roads and multi-use trails suitable for mountain biking and horseback riding.

User Groups: Hikers and dogs. No bikes, horses, or wheelchair facilities. Dogs are not

VERMONT

allowed in day-use areas such as picnic areas, but are not restricted on trails.

Permits: An entrance fee of $3 per person ages 14 and older, and $2 for children ages 4–13, is charged from a week before Memorial Day–Labor Day.

Maps: A free, basic map is available at park entrances for virtually all state parks. For a topographic area map, request Marshfield from the USGS.

Directions: From I-91, take Exit 17 onto U.S. 302 west. Drive about 8.8 miles and turn right onto Route 232 north. Drive 9.4 miles and turn right into the New Discovery Campground. On Memorial Day weekend–Labor Day, continue 0.1 mile past the open gate to a field, turn right, and drive to the picnic shelter on Osmore Pond to park. In winter, park at the gate without blocking it. Trails are closed during the spring mud season, usually mid-April–mid-May. The road into the New Discovery Campground is closed and blocked by a gate when the park is closed, Labor Day–Memorial Day weekend.

GPS Coordinates: 44.1920 N, 72.1732 W

Contact: New Discovery Campground, 802/426-3042. Vermont Department of Forests, Parks, and Recreation Commissioner's Office, 103 South Main St., Waterbury, VT 05671-0601, 802/241-3655, www.vtfpr.org.

19 KINGSLAND BAY STATE PARK
1 mi/0.75 hr

in Ferrisburg

On the picturesque shores of Lake Champlain, the land occupied by 264-acre Kingsland Bay State Park dates back to the first settlers in Ferrisburg. The property was once a working farm and then run as an exclusive girls camp until the late 1960s. This hike, on an unmarked but obvious trail, begins behind the tennis courts and soon forks, creating a loop through the conifer woods on a point

that juts into Lake Champlain; the loop can be done in either direction. Much of the one-mile, easy trail remains in the woods, with limited lake views. One clearing offers nice views northeast toward Camel's Hump and the Green Mountains.

User Groups: Hikers and leashed dogs. No bikes, horses, or wheelchair facilities. Dogs are not allowed in day-use areas such as picnic areas, but are not restricted on trails.

Permits: An entrance fee of $3 for persons 14 and older and $2 for children ages 4–13 is charged Memorial Day–Labor Day.

Maps: While no map is necessary for this hike, a free, basic map is available at the park entrance. For a topographic area map, request Westport from the USGS.

Directions: From the junction of U.S. 7 and Route 22A north of Vergennes, drive north on U.S. 7 for a half mile and then turn left (west) onto Tuppers Crossing Road. Proceed 0.4 mile and bear right onto Bottsford Road. Drive 0.8 mile and continue straight through a crossroads onto Hawkins Road. Or from North Ferrisburg, drive south on U.S. 7 for about four miles and turn right (west) onto Little Chicago Road. Continue a mile and turn right onto Hawkins. Follow Hawkins Road for 3.4 miles and then turn right at a sign into Kingsland Bay State Park. Follow the dirt park road about a half mile and park at the roadside near the tennis courts. Trails are closed during the spring mud season, usually mid-April–mid-May. The park road is closed to traffic in the off-season, but you can walk the road, adding a mile round-trip to this hike's distance.

GPS Coordinates: 44.1357 N, 73.1665 W

Contact: Kingsland Bay State Park, RR 1, Box 245, 787 Kingsland Bay State Park Rd., Ferrisburg, VT 05456, 802/877-3445 in summer, 802/483-2001 in winter, or 800/658-1622. Vermont Department of Forests, Parks, and Recreation Commissioner's Office, 103 South Main St., Waterbury, VT 05671-0601, 802/241-3655, www.vtfpr.org.

20 BUTTON BAY STATE PARK
1 mi/0.75 hr 👫₁ ▲₈

in Ferrisburg

BEST (

Located on the sparkling waters of Lake Champlain, Button Bay is named for the buttonlike concretions formed by clay deposits found along the shore. As part of the lake's rich history, Button Bay was visited by such famous persons as Samuel De Champlain, Ethan Allen, Ben Franklin, and Benedict Arnold. This flat walk of a mile round-trip along a wide gravel road leads to Button Point, a rocky bluff thrust far out into the lake with views encompassing a wide sweep from Camel's Hump and the Green Mountains to the east, to the Adirondacks across the lake. From the parking lot, walk the gravel road a half mile to its end at Button Point. This is a beautiful spot to watch the sunset. Return the same way.

User Groups: Hikers, bikers, leashed dogs, and wheelchairs. Wheelchair users can drive the dirt road beyond the public parking lots to wheelchair-accessible parking just 100 yards before the point on Lake Champlain. This trail is not suitable for horses. Dogs are not allowed in day-use areas such as picnic areas, but are not restricted on trails.

Permits: An entrance fee of $3 per person ages 14 and older and $2 for children ages 4–13 is charged Memorial Day–Columbus Day.

Maps: While no map is necessary for this hike, a free, basic map is available at the entrance gate. For a topographic area map, request Westport from the USGS.

Directions: From the green in the center of Vergennes, drive south on Route 22A for a half mile and turn right onto Panton Road. Proceed 1.4 miles and turn right onto Basin Harbor Road. Continue 4.5 miles, turn left onto Button Bay Road and follow it 0.6 mile to the entrance on the right to Button Bay State Park. Drive about a half mile down the park road to two gravel parking lots on the left, across from the pavilion. Trails are closed during the spring mud season, usually mid-April–Memorial Day. The park road is closed to traffic in the off-season, but you can walk the road, adding a mile round-trip to this hike's distance.

GPS Coordinates: 44.1083 N, 73.2153 W

VERMONT

© J. D. BROWN

Button Bay on Lake Champlain

Contact: Button Bay State Park, RD 3, Box 4075, 5 Button Bay State Park Rd., Vergennes, VT 05491, 802/475-2377 in summer, 802/483-2001 in winter, or 800/658-1622. Vermont Department of Forests, Parks, and Recreation Commissioner's Office, 103 South Main St., Waterbury, VT 05671-0601, 802/241-3655, www.vtfpr.org.

21 THE LONG TRAIL: APPALACHIAN GAP TO THE WINOOSKI RIVER

18.4 mi one-way/2-3 days 🏃5 ⛺10

between Appalachian Gap and North Duxbury

BEST (

This 18.4-mile leg of the Long Trail is arguably its most spectacular stretch. The hike's centerpiece is 4,083-foot Camel's Hump, but less well-known Burnt Rock Mountain offers one of the best views on the Long Trail; Molly Stark's Balcony is another choice spot; and the trail harbors some gems in the woods like Ladder Ravine. This is the northern section of the fabled Monroe Skyline (see *The Monroe Skyline* listing in this chapter). The one-way traverse covers rugged terrain and involves more than 3,500 feet of climbing and much more descending (the descent from the summit of Camel's Hump to the Winooski River alone is about 3,700 feet); it can easily take three days.

This hike, especially the Camel's Hump area, is popular in summer and fall, and the shelters tend to fill up quickly on weekends. When above tree line, remember that the fragile alpine vegetation suffers under boots, so stay on the marked trail or rocks. Also be advised that water sources are few along the ridge and generally found only at the shelters.

From Route 17, the Long Trail (LT) northbound climbs steeply out of Appalachian Gap for 0.4 mile, descends steeply, and then climbs again to the top of Molly Stark Mountain at one mile from the road. At 1.3 miles, the trail passes over Molly Stark's Balcony,

a rock outcropping atop a cliff rising above the trees, where you get a long view north toward Camel's Hump and northeast to the Worcester Range, which includes Mount Hunger and Stowe Pinnacle. Descending more easily, the LT reaches the Beane Trail at 2.6 miles, which leads left (west) to the Birch Glen Camp (about 100 feet from the junction) and to a road that travels 1.5 miles to Hanksville (0.9 mile from the junction). The LT follows easier ground from here, ascending gradually to Cowles Cove shelter at 5.5 miles. Climbing slightly, the trail passes the Hedgehog Brook Trail at 6.4 miles, which descends right (east) 2.5 miles to a road two miles outside North Fayston. Then the Long Trail quickly grows more rugged, climbing to the open, rocky Burnt Rock Mountain summit seven miles into this hike. At 3,168 feet, the summit offers long views of the Green Mountains arcing southward, the Worcester Range to the east and the White Mountains beyond, the Lake Champlain southern tip to the southwest, and New York's Adirondacks brooding darkly behind the lake.

Follow the blazes and cairns carefully as the trail makes numerous turns over Burnt Rock's bare crown. The LT reenters the lush, wild forest, reaching Ladder Ravine at 7.4 miles, a perpetually wet place where a wooden ladder is employed to descend a short cliff. Continuing over rough terrain, the trail climbs over the wooded humps of Ira Allen (at 8.5 miles) and Ethan Allen's two peaks (at 9.5 and 9.6 miles) and then descends past the Allis Trail at 10.4 miles; that trail leads straight ahead to Allis Lookout, where there is a view of the mountains to the north, and terminates at the Long Trail in 0.3 mile. The LT, meanwhile, swings left and descends to Montclair Glen Lodge at 10.6 miles. Just downhill from the cabin on the LT, the Forest City Trail departs left (west), dropping gradually for 2.2 miles to a road outside Huntington Center.

The LT then begins the ascent of Camel's Hump, passing the Dean Trail in Wind Gap (at 10.8 miles), which leads right (east) 2.3 miles to the Couching Lion site. Traversing open ledges on the east side of the Hump's southern ridge, the LT affords excellent views south along the Green Mountains and east in a wide sweep from Mount Ascutney to the Worcester Range. It then reenters the woods again briefly, climbing steeply to a junction at 12.3 miles with the Alpine Trail, which departs right (east) and provides an alternate route around the summit in bad weather, swinging north and reaching the Bamforth Ridge Trail/Long Trail in 1.7 miles. There is 0.2 mile more of steep, exposed hiking, with the trail swinging left around tall cliffs and ascending the west face up the rocky summit cone of Camel's Hump. (For a more detailed summit description, see the *Camel's Hump: Forest City/Burrows Trails Loop* listing in this chapter.)

Dropping north off the summit, the LT reaches the Camel's Hump hut clearing at 12.8 miles, where the Monroe Trail leaves right (east), descending 3.1 miles to the Couching Lion site, and the Burrows Trail leaves left (west), descending 2.6 miles to a road outside Huntington Center. Reentering the woods, the LT—since being re-routed in 1996—follows the old Bamforth Ridge Trail north. The descent is rugged, dipping and climbing repeatedly, and often steeply, and traversing some boggy terrain. But open ledges at many points along the ridge offer the best views of any trail on Camel's Hump. The LT reaches the parking lot on River Road at 18.4 miles.

Camping is prohibited except at the Green Mountain Club shelters and campsites: the Birch Glen Camp, 2.6 miles north of Route 17 and 100 feet off the LT on the Beane Trail; the Cowles Cove shelter, 5.5 miles north of Route 17; the Montclair Glen Lodge near the Forest City and Long Trails junction, 10.6 miles north of Route 17; and the Bamforth Ridge shelter 16 miles north of Route 17. A Green Mountain Club caretaker is on duty Memorial Day weekend–Columbus Day and a per-person nightly fee is collected to stay at a cabin.

User Groups: Hikers and dogs. Dogs must be leashed above tree line. No bikes, horses, or wheelchair facilities. This trail should not be attempted in winter except by hikers experienced in mountaineering and prepared for severe winter weather.

Permits: Parking and access are free.

Maps: A basic trail map is available at trailheads in Camel's Hump State Park. The waterproof End-to-End Map of the Long Trail is available for $9.95 from the Green Mountain Club, as is the Northern Vermont Hiking Trail Map, which covers Mount Mansfield, Camel's Hump, Lake Willoughby, Cotton Brook, Little River, the Worcester Range, and Mount Elmore, for $5.95. For topographic area maps, request Mount Ellen, Huntington, and Waterbury from the USGS.

Directions: You need to shuttle two vehicles for this one-way traverse. To hike south to north, as described here, leave one vehicle in the Long Trail/Banforth Ridge trailhead parking lot in North Duxbury. To reach the trailhead, take I-89 to Exit 11 for Route 2 east. Drive about five miles into Jonesville, and just beyond the post office (on the left), turn right, crossing the bridge over the Winooski River. At 0.2 mile from Route 2, turn left onto Duxbury Road and continue 3.3 miles to the Long Trail/Banforth Ridge parking area on the right (you will see a green Long Trail sign).

The Long Trail is closed from Appalachian Gap to the Winooski River mid-April–Memorial Day. Much of this Long Trail section is in Camel's Hump State Park; the remainder is on private land.

GPS Coordinates: 44.2080 N, 72.9244 W

Contact: Vermont Department of Forests, Parks, and Recreation Commissioner's Office, 103 South Main St., Waterbury, VT 05671, 802/241-3655, www.vtfpr.org. Green Mountain Club Inc., 4711 Waterbury-Stowe Rd., Waterbury Center, VT 05677, 802/244-7037, www.greenmountainclub.org.

VERMONT

22 MOLLY STARK'S BALCONY

2.6 mi/2 hr 👥5 ⛰8

north of Appalachian Gap

From Molly Stark's Balcony, a rocky ledge atop a cliff jutting above the woods, you get a long view north toward Camel's Hump and northeast to the Worcester Range, which includes Mount Hunger and Stowe Pinnacle. Though just a 2.6-mile round-trip climbing several hundred feet, this hike has very steep uphill stretches and descents.

From the parking turnout, the Long Trail (LT) northbound climbs steeply out of Appalachian Gap for 0.4 mile. Follow the white blazes as it drops steeply, then climbs again to Molly Stark Mountain's highest point at one mile from the road. Continue north on the LT for 0.3 mile to the balcony, a small ledge on the right side of the trail immediately before another steep downhill. Return the way you came.

This stretch of the Long Trail passes through Camel's Hump State Park, where camping is prohibited except at the Green Mountain Club shelters. The Birch Glen Camp is 1.3 miles north of Molly Stark's Balcony and 100 feet off the LT on the Beane Trail.

User Groups: Hikers and leashed dogs. No bikes, horses, or wheelchair facilities.

Permits: Parking and access are free.

Maps: The waterproof End-to-End Map of the Long Trail is available for $9.95 from the Green Mountain Club, as is the Northern Vermont Hiking Trail Map, which covers Mount Mansfield, Camel's Hump, Lake Willoughby, Cotton Brook, Little River, the Worcester Range, and Mount Elmore, for $5.95. For a topographic area map, request Mount Ellen from the USGS.

Directions: Drive to where the Long Trail crosses Route 17 in Appalachian Gap, three miles east of the Huntington Road and six miles west of Route 100 in Irasville. The Long Trail is closed from Appalachian Gap to the Winooski River mid-April–Memorial Day.

GPS Coordinates: 44.2080 N, 72.9244 W

Contact: Vermont Department of Forests, Parks, and Recreation Commissioner's Office, 103 South Main St., Waterbury, VT 05671-0601, 802/241-3655, www.vtfpr.org. Green Mountain Club Inc., 4711 Waterbury-Stowe Rd., Waterbury Center, VT 05677, 802/244-7037, www.greenmountainclub.org.

23 THE MONROE SKYLINE

47.4 mi one-way/5–6 days 👥5 ⛰10

between Middlebury Gap and North Duxbury

BEST (

When the nation's first long-distance hiking trail was in its formative years, this stretch of nearly 50 miles was not along the high mountain ridges it now traverses. It was mired down in the woods, where the state forestry officials who did much of the early trail work wanted it to be so they could access forest fires. Then along came Professor Will Monroe, a respected botanist and author, who over several years beginning in 1916 became the catalyst behind the Green Mountain Club's effort to move the Long Trail up onto the rugged chain of peaks between Middlebury Gap and the Winooski River. Now dubbed the Monroe Skyline, this 47.4-mile section is widely considered the soul of the Long Trail, and is a much-sought-after multiday trek. For backpackers who want to sample the best of the Long Trail and have a week or less, this is the trip to take.

The Monroe Skyline links three sections of the Long Trail. For details, see the descriptions for the following two hikes in this chapter: *Lincoln Mountain Traverse* and *The Long Trail: Appalachian Gap to the Winooski River*.

User Groups: Hikers and leashed dogs. No wheelchair facilities. This trail should not be attempted in winter except by hikers experienced in mountaineering and prepared for severe winter weather, and is not suitable for bikes, horses, or skis. Hunting is allowed in season, but not near trails.

Permits: Parking and access are free. See specific access information for the Long Trail sections covered separately.

Maps: The waterproof End-to-End Map of the Long Trail is available for $9.95 from the Green Mountain Club, as is the Northern Vermont Hiking Trail Map, which covers Mount Mansfield, Camel's Hump, Lake Willoughby, Cotton Brook, Little River, the Worcester Range, and Mount Elmore, for $5.95. For topographic area maps, request Bread Loaf, Lincoln, Mount Ellen, Huntington, and Waterbury from the USGS.

Directions: You need to shuttle two vehicles for this one-way traverse. To hike south to north, leave one vehicle in the trailhead parking lot on Duxbury Road in North Duxbury. To reach, take I-89 to Exit 11 for Route 2 east. Drive about five miles into Jonesville, and just beyond the post office (on the left), turn right, crossing the bridge over the Winooski River. At 0.2 mile from Route 2, turn left onto Duxbury Road and continue 3.3 miles to the Long Trail/Banforth Ridge parking area on the right (you will see a green Long Trail sign). GPS Coordinates: 43.9444 N, 72.9499 W

Contact: Vermont Department of Forests, Parks, and Recreation Commissioner's Office, 103 South Main St., Waterbury, VT 05671-0601, 802/241-3655, www.vtfpr.org. Green Mountain Club Inc., 4711 Waterbury-Stowe Rd., Waterbury Center, VT 05677, 802/244-7037, www.greenmountainclub.org.

24 LINCOLN MOUNTAIN TRAVERSE

11.6 mi one-way/8.5 hr   👣 5   ⛰ 10

between Lincoln Gap and Appalachian Gap

Lincoln Mountain is made up of five peaks, all at more than 3,800 feet. This 11.6-mile traverse of the high, narrow ridge of Lincoln Mountain passes over all of the summits, including the spectacular 4,006-foot Mount Abraham; the last few miles of the hike lead to General Stark Mountain, a separate peak. Skirting parts of the Sugarbush Valley Ski Area, the route is one of the premier sections of the Long Trail (LT) and also the middle portion of the fabled Monroe Skyline (see *The Monroe Skyline* listing in this chapter). Although this hike can be done in a long day, many people make a two-day backpacking trip of it or hike it as a link in a longer outing on the LT. The scenic route is a popular destination and shelters tend to fill up quickly on weekends in summer and fall. Also be advised that water sources are few along the ridge and generally found only at the shelters (although the spring at the Theron Dean shelter is not reliable in dry seasons). The cumulative elevation gain is nearly 2,500 feet.

From the Lincoln-Warren Highway, follow the Long Trail white blazes northbound, gradually beginning the ascent of Mount Abraham. At 1.2 miles, the trail passes a pair of huge boulders named the Carpenters, after two trail workers. At 1.7 miles, the LT passes a junction with the Battell Trail and 0.1 mile farther, reaches the Battell shelter. The trail then climbs more steeply, over rocky terrain and exposed slabs, until it emerges from the trees into the alpine zone atop Abraham, 2.6 miles from the road. The views stretch far down the Green Mountain chain to the south, east to the White Mountains, west to Lake Champlain and the Adirondacks, and north to Lincoln Mountain's other peaks. When exploring the summit, remember that when above the tree line, fragile alpine vegetation suffers under boots, so stay on the marked trail or rocks.

Continuing on, at 3.3 miles, a sign indicates you've reached the wooded summit of Little Abe and 0.1 mile farther the LT crosses Lincoln Peak, at 3,975 feet, where an observation deck to the trail's right offers good views. Just past the observation deck, the LT passes through a cleared area above the Sugarbush Valley Ski Area, bears left, and reenters the forest. The hiking is fairly easy along the ridge, with little elevation shift. At four miles, the

VERMONT

LT traverses the wooded summit of Nancy Hanks Peak, passes a Sugarbush chairlift at 4.7 miles, then climbs about 250 feet in elevation to the 4,022-foot Cutts Peak summit, which has good views, at 5.9 miles. Just 0.4 mile farther, the trail passes over the wooded and viewless Mount Ellen summit, at 4,083 feet tied with Camel's Hump for third-highest of Vermont's five official 4,000-footers. (Cutts Peak does not qualify because there is not enough elevation gain and loss between it and Mount Ellen.) The LT almost immediately passes a chairlift for the Sugarbush North Ski Area, bears left along a ski trail for 100 feet, and reenters the woods, descending very rocky ground where footing is difficult.

At 6.7 miles, the LT leaves the national forest and at 8.1 miles reaches a junction with the Jerusalem Trail, which departs left (west) and continues 2.5 miles to a road. Just 0.1 mile farther, the LT reaches the Barton Trail, which leads to the right (east) 0.2 mile to the Glen Ellen Lodge. The LT then climbs steeply for a short distance to the height of General Stark Mountain (3,662 ft.), at 8.5 miles, and reaches the Stark's Nest shelter at 9.1 miles. The LT follows a ski trail briefly, turns left into the woods, crosses a cross-country skiing trail, and then descends steeply to the Theron Dean shelter at 9.8 miles. A path leads a short distance past the shelter to a good view of the mountains to the north. From the shelter, the LT drops steeply, passes another chairlift station at 10 miles, and reaches Route 17 at 11.6 miles.

No-trace camping is permitted within the Green Mountain National Forest. North of the national forest boundary the Long Trail passes through private land and camping is prohibited except at the Green Mountain Club's Glen Ellen Lodge cabin, located on the Barton Trail, 0.3 mile east of the Long Trail and 8.2 miles north of Lincoln Gap. A Green Mountain Club caretaker is on duty Memorial Day weekend–Columbus Day and a per person nightly fee is collected at the Battell shelter on the LT, 1.8 miles north of Lincoln Gap. The Theron Dean shelter is on the LT, 9.8 miles north of Lincoln Gap and 1.8 miles south of Appalachian Gap.

User Groups: Hikers and leashed dogs. No bikes, horses, or wheelchair facilities. This trail should not be attempted in winter except by hikers experienced in mountaineering and prepared for severe winter weather.

Permits: Parking and access are free.

Maps: The waterproof End-to-End Map of the Long Trail is available for $9.95 from the Green Mountain Club. For topographic area maps, request Lincoln and Mount Ellen from the USGS.

Directions: You need to shuttle two vehicles for this one-way traverse. To hike south to north, as described here, leave one vehicle where the Long Trail crosses Route 17 in Appalachian Gap, three miles east of the Huntington Road and six miles west of Route 100 in Irasville. Then drive to where the Long Trail crosses the Lincoln-Warren Highway in Lincoln Gap, 4.7 miles east of Lincoln and 4.1 miles west of Route 100 in Warren. There is parking 0.2 mile west of Lincoln Gap, as well as along the road near the trail crossing. The Long Trail is closed from Lincoln Gap to Appalachian Gap mid-April–Memorial Day. The road through Lincoln Gap is not maintained during winter.

GPS Coordinates: 44.0960 N, 72.9274 W

Contact: Green Mountain National Forest Supervisor, 231 North Main St., Rutland, VT 05701, 802/747-6700, fax 802/747-6766, www.fs.fed.us/r9/forests/greenmountain. Green Mountain Club Inc., 4711 Waterbury-Stowe Rd., Waterbury Center, VT 05677, 802/244-7037, www.greenmountainclub. org.

THE GREEN MOUNTAINS

© CLAIRE BROWN

BEST HIKES

VERMONT

In the southern half of the Green Mountains

State, the land creates its own unique blend of rolling hills, gentle valleys, and somewhat isolated tall peaks. It's often viewed as the Green Mountains version of Vermont Lite and, for this reason, the area is often bypassed in favor of the many superstar hikes to the north. But don't miss it. From the Massachusetts border to the dividing line near I-89, the upland contours of this pastoral region offer unmatched rewards to those who stop by long enough to seek them out. Local destinations, including such standouts as Equinox Mountain, the forest at Marsh-Billings-Rockefeller National Historical Park, Skylight Pond, and Killington provide peaceful walks, gorgeous wooded rambles, and no shortage of scenic views and highly scalable summits.

Also in this region are enduringly popular peaks such as Ascutney Mountain (along the New Hampshire border) and secluded places such as Silent Cliff, Shrewsbury Peak, and Rattlesnake Cliffs. For those starting out – or winding down – a trek along the Long Trail, Glastenbury Mountain, Stratton Mountain, and Bromley Mountain has summit towers offering incredibly long 360-degree views. Several of the Long Trail (LT) hikes described in this chapter are long-distance hikes that may require an overnight stay in the woods. If you aren't an expert backpacker, these routes are lower in elevation than LT treks in the north and are an ideal way to hone your backwoods skills. Follow these longer hikes end-to-end or break into sections to suit your comfort level.

The Appalachian National Scenic Trail (AT) coincides with the Long Trail for more than 100 miles throughout the uplands of southern Vermont, from the Massachusetts line to just north of U.S. 4 in Sherburne Pass. Along both the AT and LT, dogs must be kept under control and bikes, horses, hunting, and firearms are prohibited.

With maple, elm, oak, hickory, and birch the dominant forest cover over so much of this region, the southern portion of the state is the clear winner for vivid fall foliage. Try Mount Tom in Woodstock or the fire tower at Giles Mountain in Norwich for postcard perfect views of the blazing countryside.

VERMONT

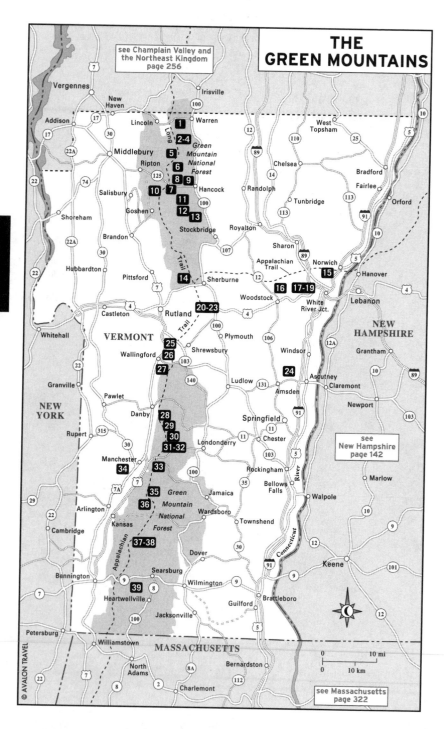

1 MOUNT ABRAHAM

5.2 mi/4 hr   🏃5 ⛰10

in the Green Mountain National Forest north of
Lincoln Gap

BEST (

At 4,006 feet in elevation, Mount Abraham
is one of just five Vermont summits that rise
above 4,000 feet—and one of just four that
thrust a rocky crown above the trees. The
360-degree views from the top of Abraham
stretch south along the Green Mountain chain
to Killington, west to the Champlain Valley
and the Adirondacks, east to the White Mountains, and north along the high ridge of the
five-peaked Lincoln Mountain, anchored by
Abraham, at its south end. The hike ascends
a rugged 1,600 feet.

From the Lincoln-Warren Highway, follow
the Long Trail (LT) white blazes northbound,
gradually beginning the ascent of Mount
Abraham. At 1.2 miles, the trail passes a pair
of huge boulders known as the Carpenters,
named after two trail workers. At 1.7 miles,
the LT reaches a junction with the Battell
Trail, which veers left (west) to the Battell
Shelter in 0.2 mile. Stay on the LT, and continue on the now much more steep and rocky
trail. As you begin to near the tree line, the
krummholz forest appears (at two miles), finally giving way to rocky slabs as you ascend
the summit. As you explore the alpine area,
look for cairns and stay on the trail to protect
the fragile alpine vegetation. For a total trip
of 5.2 miles, return the way you came. From
Abraham's summit, you can continue north
along the level, high ridge of Lincoln Mountain to 3,975-foot Lincoln Peak (making this
hike's round-trip distance 6.8 miles), where an
observation deck just to the trail's right offers
views in every direction.

Still feeling strong? Keep hiking north to
Cutts Peak, which has good views, and then an
easy 0.4 mile beyond Cutts to the wooded and
viewless summit of another Vermont 4,000-
footer (4,083-foot Mount Ellen), making this
marathon hike a 12.6-mile round-trip from

descending from the summit of Mount
Abraham

Lincoln Gap. Turn around and descend the
way you came.

No-trace camping is permitted within the
Green Mountain National Forest. A Green
Mountain Club caretaker is on duty Memorial
Day weekend–Columbus Day and a nightly
fee is collected to stay at the Battell shelter,
which is on the Long Trail 1.8 miles north
of Lincoln Gap.

User Groups: Hikers and leashed dogs. No
bikes, horses, or wheelchair facilities. This trail
should not be attempted in winter except by
hikers experienced in mountaineering and
prepared for severe winter weather.

Permits: Parking and access are free.

Maps: The waterproof End-to-End Map of
the Long Trail is available for $9.95 from the
Green Mountain Club. For topographic area
maps, request Lincoln and Mount Ellen from
the USGS.

Directions: From the Sugarbush Ski Area in
Warren, drive south on Route 100 for 2.1 miles
to a slight right onto Lincoln Gap Road (called

the Lincoln-Warren Highway on some maps). Follow for 4.1 miles to where the Long Trail crosses Lincoln Gap. Park along the road near the trail crossing. This point is also 4.7 miles east of Lincoln. The road through Lincoln Gap is not maintained during winter. The Long Trail is closed from Lincoln Gap to Appalachian Gap mid-April–Memorial Day. GPS Coordinates: 44.0984 N, 72.9303 W **Contact:** Green Mountain National Forest Supervisor, 231 North Main St., Rutland, VT 05701, 802/747-6700, www.fs.fed.us/ r9/forests/greenmountain/. Green Mountain Club Inc., 4711 Waterbury-Stowe Rd., Waterbury Center, VT 05677, 802/244-7037, www. greenmountainclub.org.

❷ EASTWOOD'S RISE AND MOUNT GRANT
7.8 mi/5 hr

in the Green Mountain National Forest south of Lincoln Gap

This one hike really presents the possibility of two different hikes, one a fairly easy round-trip of just 0.8 mile to Eastwood's Rise, a wide, flat ledge looking west all the way to New York's Adirondacks and a nice place to watch the sun sink over these majestic purple peaks. Hikers seeking a longer outing can continue on to the Mount Grant summit (3,623 ft.), with its view south to the Green Mountains' Bread Loaf Wilderness, for a 7.8-mile round-trip. This entire hike ascends about 1,500 feet.

From Lincoln Gap, follow the white blazes of the Long Trail (LT) southbound. A steady uphill climb, the trail passes Eastwood's Rise at 0.4 mile and then another scenic overlook, Sunset Ledge, at 1.1 miles. But don't let the name fool you. Exposed tree roots and rocky terrain in sections of the trail around Sunset Ledge would make it difficult to safely descend in the gloaming darkness. Leaving the ledges, the LT climbs steadily under forest cover to Mount Grant at 3.9 miles. A somewhat open

summit provides nice views south. Hike back to the parking area along the same route.

No-trace camping is permitted within the Green Mountain National Forest. The Cooley Glen shelter is 0.8 mile south of Mount Grant on the Long Trail.

User Groups: Hikers and leashed dogs. No bikes, horses, or wheelchair facilities.

Permits: Parking and access are free.

Maps: The waterproof End-to-End Map of the Long Trail is available for $9.95 from the Green Mountain Club. For a topographic area map, request Lincoln from the USGS.

Directions: From the Sugarbush Ski Area in Warren, drive south on Route 100 for 2.1 miles to a slight right onto Lincoln Gap Road (called the Lincoln-Warren Highway on some maps). Follow for 4.1 miles to where the Long Trail crosses Lincoln Gap. Park along the road near the trail crossing. This point is also 4.7 miles east of Lincoln. The road through Lincoln Gap is not maintained during winter.

GPS Coordinates: 44.0984 N, 72.9303 W

Contact: Green Mountain National Forest Supervisor, 231 North Main St., Rutland, VT 05701, 802/747-6700, www.fs.fed.us/ r9/forests/greenmountain/. Green Mountain Club Inc., 4711 Waterbury-Stowe Rd., Waterbury Center, VT 05677, 802/244-7037, www. greenmountainclub.org.

❸ MOUNT WILSON/BREAD LOAF MOUNTAIN
8.6 mi/6 hr

in the Green Mountain National Forest near South Lincoln

One of the finest views to be had along the lower half of the Long Trail is the one from the ledges near the top of Mount Wilson (3,745 ft.). Looking south, the long, bumpy chain of the Green Mountains is the back of a mythical serpent snaking its way towards the far off hills of Massachusetts. But to reach this view, you must first endure a rugged climb of approximately 2,000 feet in elevation gain.

From the trailhead signpost in the parking area, the hike follows the Emily Proctor Trail as it begins its ascent on an old logging road. In the first two miles, the trail crosses a tributary of the New Haven River three times, once on rocks. The crossings can be tricky in high water; be careful here in spring or after severe rain. Climbing moderately for much of its distance, the trail becomes steeper just before reaching the Long Trail (LT) at the Emily Proctor shelter, 3.5 miles from the parking area. At the shelter, turn left and follow the LT northbound for a rugged 0.8 mile to the summit of Mount Wilson. An obvious footpath leads a short distance to the overlook. Return the way you came.

On the return, you might consider making the worthwhile side trip to 3,835-foot Bread Loaf Mountain for a sweeping view south and west of the Green Mountains, the Champlain Valley, and the Adirondack Mountains. From the LT junction with the Emily Proctor Trail, hike southbound on the LT for 0.7 mile to the wooded top of Bread Loaf Mountain. Here, the LT swings left and a side path leads right for 0.1 mile to the overlook. Bagging Bread Loaf Mountain makes this hike's round-trip distance 10 miles.

No-trace camping is permitted within the Green Mountain National Forest. The Emily Proctor shelter is located at the Long Trail and Emily Proctor Trail junction, 3.5 miles into this hike. The Skyline Lodge cabin is 0.1 mile east of the Long Trail via the Skylight Pond Trail and 1.2 miles south of the Bread Loaf Mountain summit.

User Groups: Hikers and leashed dogs. No bikes, horses, or wheelchair facilities.

Permits: Parking and access are free.

Maps: The waterproof End-to-End Map of the Long Trail is available for $9.95 from the Green Mountain Club. For topographic area maps, request Bread Loaf and Lincoln from the USGS.

Directions: From the general store in the center of Lincoln, follow the South River Road to South Lincoln for one mile and turn right at a sign for the Emily Proctor Trail onto South Lincoln Road. Drive 1.9 miles (it becomes a dirt road) and continue straight on South Lincoln Road for another two miles. Turn left onto USFS Road 201 and proceed 0.3 mile to parking on the left.

GPS Coordinates: 44.0296 N, 72.9634 W

Contact: Green Mountain National Forest Supervisor, 231 North Main St., Rutland, VT 05701, 802/747-6700, www.fs.fed.us/r9/forests/greenmountain/. Green Mountain Club Inc., 4711 Waterbury-Stowe Rd., Waterbury Center, VT 05677, 802/244-7037, www.greenmountainclub.org.

⁴ COOLEY GLEN TRAIL/ EMILY PROCTOR TRAIL LOOP

12.5 mi/8.5 hr

in the Green Mountain National Forest near South Lincoln

Vermont, like its New Hampshire neighbor, likes to name its mountains after former U.S. presidents. This 12.5-mile loop traverses three of the named 3,000-footers, Mounts Cleveland, Roosevelt, and Wilson, the last two of which have good views. The cumulative elevation gain is about 2,500 feet. From the parking area, take the Cooley Glen Trail, which climbs at a moderate grade east, then northeast, paralleling and crossing a stream before reaching the Long Trail (LT) at 3.4 miles. The Cooley Glen shelter lies at this trail junction. Turn right (south) on the white-blazed LT, climbing a half mile, steeply at times, to the wooded summit of 3,482-foot Mount Cleveland. The Long Trail follows a ridge through several short dips and climbs for 3.1 miles to the Mount Roosevelt summit, at 3,528 feet, and a spot known as Killington View, with a good outlook south and west of the mountains.

Descending briefly off Roosevelt, the LT

reaches the Clark Brook Trail in another 0.4 mile; that trail branches left (east), leading three miles to a road. The LT then ascends 0.8 mile to Mount Wilson (3,745 ft.) and the best view on this hike; follow the obvious side path about 100 feet to the left to an open ledge with a long view south down the backbone of the Green Mountains. Just 0.8 mile farther south on the LT, turn right (north) onto the Emily Proctor Trail, near the shelter of the same name, and descend steadily for 3.5 miles to the parking area.

No-trace camping is permitted within the Green Mountain National Forest. The Cooley Glen shelter is at the Long Trail and the Cooley Glen Trail junction is 3.4 miles into this hike. The Emily Proctor shelter is located at the Long Trail and Emily Proctor Trail junction, 5.6 miles south of the Cooley Glen shelter.

User Groups: Hikers and leashed dogs. No bikes, horses, or wheelchair facilities.

Permits: Parking and access are free.

Maps: The waterproof End-to-End Map of the Long Trail is available for $9.95 from the Green Mountain Club. For topographic area maps, request Bread Loaf and Lincoln from the USGS.

Directions: From the general store in the center of Lincoln, follow the South River Road to South Lincoln for one mile and turn right at a sign for the Emily Proctor Trail onto South Lincoln Road. Drive 1.9 miles (it becomes a dirt road) and continue straight on South Lincoln Road for another two miles. Turn left onto USFS Road 201 and proceed 0.3 mile to parking on the left. The access road is not maintained for winter access to the trailhead parking lot.

GPS Coordinates: 44.0296 N, 72.9634 W

Contact: Green Mountain National Forest Supervisor, 231 North Main St., Rutland, VT 05701, 802/747-6700, www.fs.fed.us/r9/forests/greenmountain/. Green Mountain Club Inc., 4711 Waterbury-Stowe Rd., Waterbury Center, VT 05677, 802/244-7037, www.greenmountainclub.org.

5 THE LONG TRAIL: MIDDLEBURY GAP TO LINCOLN GAP

17.4 mi one-way/2 days

in the Green Mountain National Forest between Middlebury Gap and Lincoln Gap

This initial leg and fairly rugged stretch of the Long Trail passes over nine named 3,000-foot peaks in 17.4 miles. Although most of this ridge walk is wooded, there are several good, long views of the Green Mountains. This is also the southern section of the famous Monroe Skyline. Typical of New England's mountains, the Long Trail here takes you on a roller coaster ride up and down these peaks in a series of short, often steep steps that can seem endless. While no climb is more than 500 feet, over the course of this traverse you'll walk some 4,500 feet uphill.

From Route 125, the Long Trail (LT) northbound climbs steeply for 0.4 mile to a junction with a blue-blazed trail branching right and leading 0.4 mile to Silent Cliff. This easy detour (figured into this hike's distance) takes only about 20–30 minutes round-trip and leads to a ledge jutting out over thin air atop Silent Cliff, with a view of Middlebury Gap and the Middlebury Snow Bowl Ski Area and west to the Champlain Valley and the Adirondacks on a clear day. Immediately before the cliff, a footpath veers right a few steps to Silent Cave, a passage beneath a massive boulder perched against the mountainside.

From the Silent Cliff Trail junction, the Long Trail swings left and ascends more moderately over 3,040-foot Burnt Hill at 2.1 miles from Route 125, passes the Burnt Hill Trail (which leads west 2.2 miles to a road), and then traverses up and down several summits along the ridge: Kirby Peak (3,140 ft.) at 2.7 miles, Mount Boyce (3,323 ft.) at 3.6 miles, and Battell Mountain (3,482 ft.) at 5 miles from Route 125. Between Kirby and Boyce, the trail passes Boyce shelter at 3.2 miles. There are a few limited views of surrounding mountains and valleys from along this part of the ridge. At 5.3 miles, the LT is crossed by the Skylight Pond Trail, which leads left (west) 2.3 miles to a road and right (east) 0.1 mile to Skyline Lodge and Skylight Pond, one of the most picturesque spots on this hike. This is a good place to stop for the night.

From the Skylight Pond Trail, the LT climbs about 400 feet in elevation to Bread Loaf Mountain, where at 6.4 miles a side path leads 0.1 mile to a good overlook south to the long Green Mountains chain and west to the Champlain Valley and Adirondack Mountains. At 7.1 miles, the LT passes the Emily Proctor shelter and the Emily Proctor Trail, which leads north 3.5 miles to a road outside South Lincoln. The LT then ascends about 300 feet to Mount Wilson at 7.9 miles. Do not pass up the obvious path that leads about 100 feet off the trail to ledges where you get a view south down the long backbone of the Greens. The LT descends to a junction with the Clark Brook Trail at 8.7 miles, which leads east 3 miles to a road; the LT then climbs less than 200 feet to reach the top of 3,528-foot Mount Roosevelt at 9.1 miles and a spot called Killington View, with a good prospect south and west toward the mountains.

After several more short climbs and descents, the trail passes over the wooded Mount Cleveland summit (3,482 ft.) at 12.2 miles and descends to the Cooley Glen shelter at 12.7 miles. From the shelter, the LT swings west and climbs 500 feet over 0.8 mile to the Mount Grant summit (3,623 ft.) at 13.5 miles, where you get a view of the Green Mountains' Bread Loaf Wilderness to the south. The LT continues north along the ridge, passing through an interesting birch forest to Eastwood's Rise, an open ledge at 17 miles offering a broad view west all the way to the Adirondacks. The trail drops fairly easily to the Lincoln-Warren Highway in Lincoln Gap.

No-trace camping is permitted within the Green Mountain National Forest. North from Route 125 on the Long Trail, it is 5.1 miles to the Skylight Pond Trail, which leads east 0.1

mile to the Skyline Lodge cabin; 6.9 miles to the Emily Proctor shelter; and 12.6 miles to the Cooley Glen shelter (the last is 4.7 miles south of the Lincoln-Warren Highway).

User Groups: Hikers and leashed dogs. No bikes, horses, or wheelchair facilities.

Permits: Parking and access are free.

Maps: The waterproof End-to-End Map of the Long Trail is available for $9.95 from the Green Mountain Club. For topographic area maps, request Bread Loaf and Lincoln from the USGS.

Directions: You need to shuttle two vehicles for this one-way traverse. To hike south to north, as described here, leave one vehicle where the Long Trail crosses the Lincoln-Warren Highway in Lincoln Gap, 4.7 miles east of Lincoln and 4.1 miles west of Route 100 in Warren. There is parking 0.2 mile west of Lincoln Gap, as well as along the road near the trail crossing. Then drive to the large turnout on Route 125's south side, immediately west of where the Long Trail crosses the road in Middlebury Gap, 5.6 miles east of Ripton and 6.4 miles west of Route 100 in Hancock. The road through Lincoln Gap is not maintained during winter.

GPS Coordinates: 43.9382 N, 72.9492 W

Contact: Green Mountain National Forest Supervisor, 231 North Main St., Rutland, VT 05701, 802/747-6700, www.fs.fed.us/r9/forests/greenmountain/. Green Mountain Club Inc., 4711 Waterbury-Stowe Rd., Waterbury Center, VT 05677, 802/244-7037, www.greenmountainclub.org.

6 SKYLIGHT POND
4.8 mi/3.2 hr

in the Green Mountain National Forest between Middlebury Gap and Lincoln Gap

South of Bread Loaf Mountain, the still waters of Skylight Pond are a luminous, atmospheric mirror. On sunny days, the pond is bright blue with flecks of white and yellow; in less

VERMONT

favorable weather, the pond is an unbroken sheet of slate gray. Its showiest moment may be at dawn, when a spectacularly glowing sunrise comes to life on the distant eastern horizon, with mountain ridges and fog-filled valleys in the middle distance and the whole fiery scene reflected in Skylight Pond. This 4.8-mile round-trip hike can easily be done in a half day, but you just might be tempted to spend the night at the Skylight Pond Lodge to catch the unparalleled magnificence of the rising sun.

From the parking area, follow the Skylight Pond Trail, which ascends moderately for 2.3 miles to the Long Trail (LT). It crosses the LT and continues 0.1 mile to the lodge and pond, completing a climb of about 1,400 feet. Return the way you came.

Special note: Want to make a longer adventure of it? By shuttling two vehicles, you could combine this hike and Mount Wilson (see *Mount Wilson/Bread Loaf Mountain* listing in this chapter) by taking the Skylight Pond Trail to the pond, the Long Trail north over Bread Loaf Mountain to Mount Wilson, then backtracking on the LT and descending the Emily Proctor Trail, a 9.4-mile trek. From the Skylight Pond Trail parking area, continue driving north on USFS Road 59, bear right onto USFS Road 54, and then turn right onto USFS Road 201 to reach the Emily Proctor Trail parking area.

No-trace camping is permitted within the Green Mountain National Forest. The Skyline Lodge cabin is 0.1 mile off the Long Trail, 2.4 miles into this hike, at the Skylight Pond Trail's end.

User Groups: Hikers and leashed dogs. No bikes, horses, or wheelchair facilities.

Permits: Parking and access are free.

Maps: The waterproof End-to-End Map of the Long Trail is available for $9.95 from the Green Mountain Club. For topographic area maps, request Bread Loaf and Lincoln from the USGS.

Directions: From Route 125, 9 miles west of the junction of Routes 125 and 100 in Hancock and 2.8 miles east of Ripton (or 0.8 mile east of the Robert Frost Interpretive Trail parking lot), turn north onto USFS Road 59 and drive about 3.5 miles to parking for the Skylight Pond Trail. USFS Road 59 is not maintained in winter.

GPS Coordinates: 43.9702 N, 72.9987 W

Contact: Green Mountain National Forest Supervisor, 231 North Main St., Rutland, VT 05701, 802/747-6700, www.fs.fed.us/r9/forests/greenmountain/. Green Mountain Club Inc., 4711 Waterbury-Stowe Rd., Waterbury Center, VT 05677, 802/244-7037, www.greenmountainclub.org.

▇ ROBERT FROST INTERPRETIVE TRAIL
1 mi/0.75 hr   🏃1 ⚠7

in the Green Mountain National Forest between Ripton and Hancock

When he was 44 years old, Robert Frost moved from New Hampshire to Vermont to "seek a better place to farm and especially grow apples." For the next four decades, Frost lived in the Green Mountains State, becoming Vermont's official poet laureate. Frost wrote much of his verse in a log cabin in Ripton. And now, close by to his old stomping grounds, is the Robert Frost Interpretive Trail, a flat, one-mile loop through various microenvironments, including forest, marsh, brooks, and an open meadow with lovely Green Mountains views. Along the trail are information boards identifying vegetation and offering relevant snippets from Frost's many poems. The trail is an easy walk and the first 0.3 mile—across a beaver pond boardwalk out to the South Branch of the Middlebury River—is accessible and suitable for wheelchairs.

User Groups: Hikers and leashed dogs. No bikes or horses. A portion of this trail is wheelchair accessible.

Permits: Parking and access are free.

Maps: No map is necessary for this hike. A

thistle growing near the Robert Frost Interpretive Trail

brochure with information about this trail is available from the Green Mountain National Forest Supervisor. For a topographic area map, request Bread Loaf from the USGS.

Directions: Drive to the parking area on the south side of Route 125, 9.8 miles west of the junction of Routes 125 and 100 in Hancock and 2 miles east of Ripton (also 0.1 mile west of the Robert Frost Wayside Area on Route 125).

GPS Coordinates: 43.9692 N, 73.0125 W

Contact: Green Mountain National Forest Supervisor, 231 North Main St., Rutland, VT 05701, 802/747-6700, www.fs.fed.us/r9/forests/greenmountain/.

8 SILENT CLIFF
1.6 mi/1 hr

in the Green Mountain National Forest at Middlebury Gap

The view from atop Silent Cliff, where a ledge juts out into thin air like a defiant chin,

takes in a wide sweep of Middlebury Gap, the Middlebury Snow Bowl Ski Area across the gap, and west to the Champlain Valley and the Adirondacks on a clear day. While half the hike is steep, it's just 1.6 miles round-trip and about 400 feet uphill and is an exciting adventure for young children.

From the parking area on Route 125, cross the road and follow the Long Trail northbound, climbing steeply for 0.4 mile. Turn right onto the blue-blazed Silent Cliff Trail, which leads 0.4 mile over much easier terrain to the cliff. If you do have kids in tow, keep a reasonable distance back from the edge. Immediately before the cliff is Silent Cave, a steep and tight cavelike passage beneath a massive boulder perched against the mountainside—another attraction guaranteed to fascinate young hikers and not-so-young ones, too. Return the way you came. You might combine this with the much longer Middlebury Gap hike (see *Middlebury Gap* listing in this chapter).

No-trace camping is permitted within the Green Mountain National Forest. The Boyce shelter is on the Long Trail, 3.1 miles north of Route 125 and 2.7 miles beyond the junction of the Long and Silent Cliff trails.

User Groups: Hikers and leashed dogs. No bikes, horses, or wheelchair facilities.

Permits: Parking and access are free.

Maps: The waterproof End-to-End Map of the Long Trail is available for $9.95 from the Green Mountain Club. For a topographic area map, request Bread Loaf from the USGS.

Directions: Drive to the large turnout on the south side of Route 125, immediately west of where the Long Trail crosses the road in Middlebury Gap, 5.6 miles east of Ripton and 6.4 miles west of Route 100 in Hancock.

GPS Coordinates: 43.9382 N, 72.9492 W

Contact: Green Mountain National Forest Supervisor, 231 North Main St., Rutland, VT 05701, 802/747-6700, www.fs.fed.us/r9/forests/greenmountain/. Green Mountain Club Inc., 4711 Waterbury-Stowe Rd., Waterbury Center, VT 05677, 802/244-7037, www.greenmountainclub.org.

VERMONT

© JAROSLAW TRAPSZO

VERMONT

⁹ TEXAS FALLS NATURE TRAIL
1 mi/0.5 hr   🏃2 ⛰8

in the Green Mountain National Forest between Ripton and Hancock

Cross USFS Road 39 from the parking turnout, walk down a few steps, and you are at Texas Falls, where Texas Brook charges through a narrow, spectacular gorge. Cross the brook on a wooden bridge—with an excellent view of the gorge—to the start of the one-mile nature trail loop. Bearing left, the trail follows the brook upstream along a well-graded, easy path. Within a half mile, the trail swings right, ascends the hillside briefly, then swings right again, looping back to the start. It's a good hike for introducing young children to the national forest.

User Groups: Hikers and leashed dogs. Trail is not suitable for bikes or horses; no wheelchair facilities.

Permits: Parking and access are free.

Maps: No map is necessary for this hike. A brochure with information about this trail is available from the Green Mountain National Forest Supervisor. For a topographic area map, request Bread Loaf from the USGS.

Directions: From Route 125, 3.1 miles west of the junction of Routes 125 and 100 in Hancock and 8.7 miles east of Ripton, turn north onto USFS Road 39 at a sign for Texas Falls. Drive a half mile to a turnout on the left.

The Texas Falls Recreation Area is closed 10 P.M.–6 A.M. From late fall into spring, USFS Road 39 can be hazardous due to snow and ice.

GPS Coordinates: 43.942 N, 72.9026 W

Contact: Green Mountain National Forest Supervisor, 231 North Main St., Rutland, VT 05701, 802/747-6700, www.fs.fed.us/r9/forests/greenmountain/.

🔟 FALLS OF LANA AND RATTLESNAKE CLIFFS
4.8 mi/3 hr   🏃3 ⛰9

in the Green Mountain National Forest and Branbury State Park south of Middlebury

BEST (

This hike leads to two worthwhile scenic locales. First up is the Falls of Lana, a horsetail of water shooting down through a tight gorge to form a deep and surprisingly calm pool of water. With minimal tree coverage overhead, the pool is kept just warm enough to make Lana one of the area's favorite swimming holes. And then it's on to Rattlesnake Cliffs for long views stretching to New York's Adirondack Mountains. This moderate hike begins in Branbury State Park and enters the Green Mountain National Forest, ascending about 1,000 feet to Rattlesnake Cliffs. Try to time your hike to make it to the cliffs just before dusk to take in the almost other-worldly sight of a burnt orange sunset over the Adirondacks' dark purple peaks.

From the parking area, follow the wide woods road a half mile to the Falls of Lana. Be sure to look for faint side paths leading left to various viewpoints above the falls, which tumble well over 100 feet through several picturesque cascades and pools. Many hikers turn back from the Falls of Lana for a round-trip of just one mile, but this hike continues past the falls, crossing Sucker Brook in another 0.1 mile. (To the right of the bridge is the Falls picnic area.) Beyond the bridge, walk straight ahead onto the North Branch Trail and then bear right within 100 feet at signs for Rattlesnake Cliffs and the North Branch Trail. Follow that trail for 0.1 mile, then turn left at a sign onto the Aunt Jennie Trail. The trail ascends, steeply in some places, about one mile until you reach the junction with the Rattlesnake Cliffs Trail. Turn left and follow that trail 0.1 mile to another junction. Bear left and hike 0.2 mile to the trail's end atop cliffs with a sweeping view that encompasses tiny Silver Lake, the bigger Lake Dunmore, and the Adirondacks in the distance. Backtrack up the trail about 50 yards to a side path branching to the right. Continue on the path downhill for 0.1 mile to another sweeping view, this one to the south. Backtrack again all the way to the Rattlesnake Cliffs Trail and descend to the parking area the same way you came.

User Groups: Hikers and leashed dogs. Trail is not suitable for bikes or horses; no wheelchair facilities.

Permits: Parking and access are free.

Maps: A basic trail map with state park information is available from the Vermont Department of Forests, Parks, and Recreation and Branbury State Park. A similar basic trail map with information about this hike is available from the Green Mountain National Forest Supervisor. For a topographic area map, request East Middlebury from the USGS.

Directions: Drive to the parking area on the east side of Route 53, 5.3 miles north of the junction of Routes 53 and 73 in Forest Dale and 0.4 mile south of the Branbury State Park entrance.

GPS Coordinates: 43.9000 N, 73.0634 W

Contact: Branbury State Park, 3570 Lake Dunmore Rd., Route 53, Salisbury, VT 05733, 802/247-5925 in summer, 802/483-2001 in winter, or 800/658-1622. Vermont Department of Forests, Parks, and Recreation Commissioner's Office, 103 South Main St., Waterbury, VT 05671-0601, 802/241-3655, www.vtfpr.org. Green Mountain National Forest Supervisor, 231 North Main St., Rutland, VT 05701, 802/747-6700, www.fs.fed. us/r9/forests/greenmountain/.

11 MIDDLEBURY GAP

6.4 mi/4.5 hr   🏃3 ⛰7

in the Green Mountain National Forest at Middlebury Gap

Hiking the Long Trail south from Middlebury Gap will bring you past a series of views, which, while neither sweeping nor grand, make for a pleasant jaunt on a relatively quiet section of the trail. The cumulative elevation gained hiking out and back approaches 2,000 feet.

From the road, the trail climbs slightly for 0.4 mile to a side path on the right that leads 0.1 mile to Lake Pleiad and the site of a former shelter. Continuing south on the white-blazed Long Trail (LT), you cross a pair of ski area trails and soon reach the first viewpoint, Robert Frost Lookout. The LT goes through some short ups and downs to Monastery Lookout, 2.6 miles from Middlebury Gap. The wooded Worth Mountain summit lies just 0.1 mile farther and then the trail descends for a half mile past other limited views to South Worth Lookout, 3.2 miles from the highway. Head back the way you came.

No-trace camping is permitted within the Green Mountain National Forest. The Sucker Brook shelter is on the Long Trail, 4.4 miles south of Route 125 and 1.2 miles beyond the turnaround point for this hike.

User Groups: Hikers and leashed dogs. Trail is not suitable for bikes or horses; no wheelchair facilities.

Permits: Parking and access are free.

Maps: The waterproof End-to-End Map of the Long Trail is available for $9.95 from the Green Mountain Club. For a topographic area map, request Bread Loaf from the USGS.

Directions: Drive to the large turnout on the south side of Route 125, immediately west of where the Long Trail crosses the road in Middlebury Gap, 5.6 miles east of Ripton and 6.4 miles west of Route 100 in Hancock.

GPS Coordinates: 43.9382 N, 72.9492 W

Contact: Green Mountain National Forest Supervisor, 231 North Main St., Rutland, VT 05701, 802/747-6700, www.fs.fed.us/ r9/forests/greenmountain/. Green Mountain Club Inc., 4711 Waterbury-Stowe Rd., Waterbury Center, VT 05677, 802/244-7037, www. greenmountainclub.org.

VERMONT

VERMONT

12 THE LONG TRAIL: MOUNT HORRID TO LAKE PLEIAD
9.8 mi one-way/7.5 hr 🚶5 ⛰8

in the Green Mountain National Forest between Brandon Gap and Middlebury Gap

The most spectacular natural feature along this 9.8-mile stretch of the Long Trail is the Great Cliff of Mount Horrid, but there are also views from points on the mostly wooded ridge north of Worth Mountain. The trail continues to grow more rugged, with repeated short but fairly steep climbs and descents and significant elevation gains and losses—the biggest being the climb of about 1,200 feet from the road in Brandon Gap to the 3,366-foot Gillespie Peak summit. The cumulative elevation gain on this hike approaches 2,500 feet.

From Route 73, follow the white blazes of the Long Trail (LT) northbound. The trail makes quick left and right turns, enters the woods, and begins a steep ascent of 0.6 mile to a junction with a blue-blazed side path leading right 0.1 mile to the view of the gap from the Great Cliff at Mount Horrid (see *Great Cliff of Mount Horrid* listing in this chapter for details). From that junction, the LT ascends more moderately, passing over the wooded Mount Horrid summit (3,216 ft.) at 1.2 miles. It then follows the forested ridge, with steep and rocky rises and dips, over Cape Lookoff Mountain at 1.7 miles, Gillespie Peak at 3.2 miles, and Romance Mountain's east summit (3,125 ft.) at 4 miles, before descending to the Sucker Brook shelter at 5.4 miles. The trail then ascends, steeply at times, reaching Worth Mountain at 7.1 miles and follows the ridge north of the mountain past some views to the east and west.

Gradually descending, the LT passes a chairlift station for the Middlebury Snow Bowl, crosses a pair of ski trails, and then reaches a side path on the left at 9.4 miles that leads 0.1 mile to Lake Pleiad and the former site of a shelter. The trail then descends slightly to Route 125 at 9.8 miles.

No-trace camping is permitted within the Green Mountain National Forest. The Sucker Brook shelter is on the Long Trail, 5.4 miles north of Route 73.

User Groups: Hikers and leashed dogs. No bikes, horses, or wheelchair facilities.

Permits: Parking and access are free.

Maps: The waterproof End-to-End Map of the Long Trail is available for $9.95 from the Green Mountain Club. For topographic area maps, request Mount Carmel and Bread Loaf from the USGS.

Directions: You need to shuttle two vehicles for this one-way traverse. To hike south to north, as described here, leave one vehicle in the large turnout on the south side of Route 125, immediately west of where the LT crosses the road in Middlebury Gap, 5.6 miles east of Ripton and 6.4 miles west of Route 100 in Hancock. Then drive to the parking area immediately west of where the LT crosses Route 73 in Brandon Gap, 5.2 miles east of Forest Dale and 9.7 miles west of the Route 100 junction south of Rochester.

GPS Coordinates: 43.8429 N, 72.9628 W

Contact: Green Mountain National Forest Supervisor, 231 North Main St., Rutland, VT 05701, 802/747-6700, www.fs.fed.us/r9/forests/greenmountain/. Green Mountain Club Inc., 4711 Waterbury-Stowe Rd., Waterbury Center, VT 05677, 802/244-7037, www.greenmountainclub.org.

13 GREAT CLIFF OF MOUNT HORRID
1.2 mi/1 hr 🚶2 ⛰8

in the Green Mountain National Forest at Brandon Gap

The Great Cliff of Mount Horrid scowls high above the highway in Brandon Gap, its scarred and crumbling face something of an anomaly in the rounded, generally heavily wooded Green Mountains. This hike, while just 1.2 miles round-trip, climbs quite steeply for about

600 feet to the excellent view of the gap and mountains from the cliff.

From Route 73, follow the white blazes of the Long Trail northbound. The trail turns left and right, enters the woods, and climbs for 0.6 mile to a junction with a blue-blazed side path on the right. Follow that side trail 0.1 mile to the view from the cliff. Hike back the same way.

No-trace camping is permitted within the Green Mountain National Forest. The Sucker Brook shelter is on the Long Trail, 5.4 miles north of Route 73.

User Groups: Hikers and leashed dogs. No bikes, horses, or wheelchair facilities.

Permits: Parking and access are free.

Maps: The waterproof End-to-End Map of the Long Trail is available for $9.95 from the Green Mountain Club. For a topographic area map, request Mount Carmel from the USGS.

Directions: Drive to the parking area immediately west of where the Long Trail crosses Route 73 in Brandon Gap, 5.2 miles east of Forest Dale and 9.7 miles west of the Route 100 junction south of Rochester.

GPS Coordinates: 43.8429 N, 72.9628 W

Contact: Green Mountain National Forest Supervisor, 231 North Main St., Rutland, VT 05701, 802/747-6700, www.fs.fed.us/r9/forests/greenmountain/. Green Mountain Club Inc., 4711 Waterbury-Stowe Rd., Waterbury Center, VT 05677, 802/244-7037, www.greenmountainclub.org.

14 DEER LEAP MOUNTAIN
3.1 mi/2 hr   👣2 ⛰8

in Sherburne

Although steep for more than half its course, this 3.1-mile round-trip to Deer Leap Mountain's open ledges meets the criteria for an excellent hike for very young hikers: It feels like a big mountain to them, both in relative difficulty and the views which reward them. From the lookout, you peer way down on Sherburne Pass and across to the ski slopes of Pico Peak. On a clear day, views extend west to New York's Adirondack Mountains. The hike climbs about 600 feet in elevation.

VERMONT

© KD TALBOT/WWW.GHOSTFLOWERS.COM

From Deer Leap Mountain, the popular ski mountain Pico Peak is visible just beyond Sherburne Pass.

From the parking area, cross U.S. 4 and pick up the blue-blazed Sherburne Pass Trail (formerly the Long Trail northbound), entering the woods just east of the Inn at Long Trail. The trail immediately begins a steep, rocky, half-mile climb to a junction with the Appalachian Trail (AT). Turn onto the AT southbound (actually walking north briefly), and within moments you'll reach the Deer Leap Trail, marked by blue blazes. Follow it up onto a small ridge and through birch forest for 0.9 mile, then turn left onto the Deer Leap Overlook Trail and follow it a quarter mile to the open ledges overlooking the Coolidge Range and Sherburne Pass.

Backtrack to the Deer Leap Trail. To complete a loop hike, turn north, descending steeply to a brook, then climbing over wooded Big Deer Leap Mountain. The trail will return you to the AT. Turn right, following the AT northbound (though walking southward) back to the Sherburne Pass Trail, then follow the latter back to the trailhead.

User Groups: Hikers and dogs. No bikes, horses, or wheelchair facilities.

Permits: Parking and access are free.

Maps: The waterproof End-to-End Map of the Long Trail is available for $9.95 from the Green Mountain Club. For a topographic area map, request Pico Peak from the USGS.

Directions: From Route 7/Main Street in Rutland, turn right on Woodstock Avenue. Follow U.S. 4 for 8.2 miles to the Inn at Long Trail. The parking area is on the left, across the street from the Inn at the height of land in Sherburne Pass.

GPS Coordinates: 43.6660 N, 72.8285 W

Contact: Green Mountain Club Inc., 4711 Waterbury-Stowe Rd., Waterbury Center, VT 05677, 802/244-7037, www.greenmountain-club.org. Appalachian Trail Conservancy, 799 Washington St., P.O. Box 807, Harpers Ferry, WV 25425-0807, 304/535-6331, www.appalachiantrail.org.

🔟 GILE MOUNTAIN
1.4 mi/1 hr

in Norwich

A popular hike for students at nearby Dartmouth College, this hike up Gile Mountain (1,872 ft.) is a short, easy uphill climb to excellent views, courtesy of Gile's firetower lookout. From atop the tower, enjoy a sweeping panorama extending south to Mount Ascutney, west to Killington and Abraham, northwest to Camel's Hump, northeast to Mount Moosilauke and Franconia Ridge in the White Mountains, and east across the Connecticut River to the ridge that connects, from north to south, Mount Cube, Smarts Mountain, Holt's Ledge, and Moose Mountain. This climb of only a few hundred feet is a great place to catch a sunset or to take in the spectacle of fall foliage season.

From the turnout, follow the Tower Trail, climbing steadily for 0.4 mile and then crossing under power lines. At 0.7 mile, the trail reaches an abandoned fire ranger's cabin. Follow the trail a short distance beyond the cabin to the fire tower. Return the same way you came.

User Groups: Hikers and dogs. No wheelchair facilities. The last half of this trail is not suitable for bikes or horses.

Permits: Parking and access are free.

Maps: For a topographic area map, request Hanover from the USGS.

Directions: From I-91, take Exit 13 and follow the signs into Norwich. Reaching the town center, continue straight through town on Main Street for 0.6 mile and turn left onto Turnpike Road. Drive 0.9 mile and bear left at a fork. In another 1.7 miles, drive straight onto the dirt Lower Turnpike Road. Drive 2.6 miles farther to a turnout on the left for the Gile Mountain Trail.

GPS Coordinates: 43.7916 N, 72.3435 W

Contact: Dartmouth Outing Club, 113 Robinson Hall, Dartmouth College, Hanover, NH 03755, 603/646-2429, www.dartmouth.edu/~doc.

16 SKYLINE TRAIL TRAVERSE

6.3 mi one-way/3.5 hr   🏃3 ⛰8

in Pomfret

The Skyline Trail was conceived in the 1960s by Richard Brett, a local resident who wanted to build a ski trail connecting his homes in Barnard and Woodstock. By gaining the permission of landowners, Brett was able to cut a trail connecting abandoned woods roads, logging roads, and pastures along a woodland ridge between Amity Pond and the Suicide Six Ski Area. Although efforts to complete the route to Woodstock have never succeeded, this trail offers a classic portrait of the Vermont countryside, ranging from dense, quiet woods to farm pastures with long views of green hills. It's a pleasant hike any time of year and especially beautiful in autumn. This trail has fairly short uphill sections, but actually drops about 1,000 feet in elevation over its course.

From the turnout at the start of the Skyline Trail, follow the trail toward Amity Pond. Where the trail branches left toward the lean-to, take the right fork. The trail soon crosses a broad meadow with long views of the mountains. Beyond the meadow, avoid the local side trails and follow the blue-blazed Skyline Trail. It can be difficult to detect in spots, but is generally fairly obvious. The trail crosses several roads and descends one woods road near its end, before traversing an open hillside, then dropping steeply to reach the Suicide Six Ski Area.

The entire trail lies on private land. Access could change, so stay on the trail and obey any no trespassing signs. Camping is allowed only in the lean-to shelter at Amity Pond. The trail is generally well marked, but not maintained.

User Groups: Hikers and dogs. No bikes, horses, or wheelchair facilities.

Permits: Parking and access are free.

Maps: A pamphlet with a sketch map and route description is available from the Woodstock Nordic Ski Center. For a topographic area map, request Woodstock North from the USGS.

Directions: You need to shuttle two vehicles for this one-way traverse. To do it north to south, as described here, drive U.S. 4 into Woodstock. Just east of the village center, turn onto Route 12 north, turning right where Route 12 makes a dogleg within 0.2 mile. At 1.3 miles from U.S. 4, bear right, following signs for the Suicide Six Ski Area, and leave a vehicle in the parking lot. Turn right out of the parking lot, back onto Route 12 south, and drive a quarter mile to South Pomfret. Turn left onto County Road. Continue another five miles to Hewitt's Corner and take a left at a sign for Sharon. Within a quarter mile, turn left onto a gravel road. Follow it for roughly two miles; after it bends right and climbs a hill, park in the turnout on the right. The trail begins across the road and is marked by blue trail markers and a sign for the Amity Pond Natural Area.

GPS Coordinates: 43.7300 N, 72.5327 W

Contact: Woodstock Nordic Center, Rte. 106, Woodstock, VT 05091, 802/457-6674, www.woodstockinn.com.

17 MOUNT TOM

2 mi/1 hr   🏃2 ⛰9

in Woodstock

Visitors to the popular tourist town of Woodstock will have no problem finding this hike: Mount Tom (1,340 ft.) is the tall hill towering almost directly over the village center. The one-mile jaunt to the top of Tom yields postcard perfect views of Woodstock, the nearby Billings Farm, and Ottauquechee River. Mount Tom is adjacent to the Marsh-Billings-Rockefeller National Historical Park, another destination worth exploring. This hike climbs approximately 500 feet.

Leaving from Woodstock's town center on foot, cross the Mountain Avenue covered bridge

VERMONT

VERMONT

© J. D. BROWN

stone bridge crossing on Woodstock's Mount Tom

Directions: From I-89, take Exit 1. At the end of the exit, follow U.S. 4 west, continuing on the road for approximately 13.5 miles to the covered footbridge. On-street parking is available.

GPS Coordinates: 43.6247 N, 72.5198 W

Contact: Woodstock Chamber of Commerce. P.O. Box 486, Woodstock, VT 05091, 802/457-3555, www.woodstockvt.com.

18 MARSH-BILLINGS-ROCKEFELLER NATIONAL HISTORICAL PARK
2.5 mi/1.5 hr

in Woodstock

A mansion, carriage house, and sprawling forest, Marsh-Billings-Rockefeller National Historical Park is the only national park to interpret for visitors the evolving land conservation movement in the U.S. The boyhood home of George Perkins Marsh, one of America's first conservationists, and later the home of Frederick Billings, the property was donated for use as a park by its most recent owners, Laurance S. and Mary F. Rockefeller; the grounds were officially taken over by the National Park Service in 1992. Within the park, 20 miles of scenic carriage roads and trails crisscross the gentle northern slope of Mount Tom, one of the oldest professionally managed woodlands in America. This loop through the park takes you under the cool canopy of centuries-old hemlocks and beech and sugar maples to visit the Pogue, a 14-acre pond perched on Mount Tom.

past River Street. Follow around a left curve to the prominent rock wall; look for the opening and turn left up a paved path that leads to the trail head at Faulkner Park. The trail starts up the mountain, a well-worn and very wide path. As it climbs, the Faulkner Trail undergoes a series of switchbacks to reduce grade. Some have bushwhacked a beeline to the top, but it's easy to tell the difference between these fainter footpaths and the main trail. In the final 100 yards before the summit, the easy walk suddenly turns steep and precipitous. Use the guardrails to steady yourself; stone stairs cut into the trail also provide for a bit surer footing. Still, young children who may have run up the mountain to this point, will need a bit more guidance in this final section. At the summit, enjoy the views and then return the way you came.

User Groups: Hikers and leashed dogs. No bikes, horses, or wheelchair facilities.

Permits: Parking and access are free.

Maps: No map is needed for this hike. For topographic area maps, request Woodstock South and Woodstock North quads from the USGS.

From the Billings Farm Visitor Center, pick up the Mountain Road, a double-rutted carriage road. The grassy lanes wind through a dense forest of maple and white pine, first planted in 1911. In a little over a mile, the Mountain Road comes to a fork. Bear left, edging the summer pasture on your right and a maple grove on your left. Reaching the Pogue, the property's artificially-made pond, the maples give way to majestic elms. Circling around the pond—a former bog that was dammed to create this pleasant puddle of water—the Mountain Road returns to the fork. Bear left and return the way you came. Other side paths branching off the carriage road are worth inspecting, taking you even deeper into the lush forest. All trails are clearly marked and most connect back up to the carriage roads; consult the NPS-provided map.

User Groups: Hikers, leashed dogs, and horses. No bikes on the property. The visitors center and mansion are wheelchair accessible.

Permits: Parking and trail access are free. Admission is charged for mansion tours, available late-May–October.

Maps: A trail map of the property, including carriage roads and footpaths, is available at the visitors center. For topographic area maps, request Woodstock South and Woodstock North quads from the USGS.

Directions: From I-89, take Exit 1. Follow U.S. 4 west about 13 miles, through Quechee and Taftsville to Woodstock. Turn right onto Route 12 north and bear right after the iron bridge, continuing for a quarter mile to the Billings Farm and Museum parking lot. Begin your visit at the Billings Farm and Museum Visitor Center, where park rangers are also stationed. Carriage roads and hiking trails on the property are open dawn–dusk in spring, summer, and fall. In winter, the trails are groomed for cross-country skiing only.

GPS Coordinates: 43.6303 N, 72.5171 W

Contact: Marsh-Billings-Rockefeller National Historical Park, 54 Elm St., Woodstock, VT 05091, 802/457-3368, www.nps.gov./mabi/index.htm.

19 QUECHEE GORGE
2.2 mi/1 hr   🏃2 ⛰8

in Quechee Gorge State Park

West of Quechee Village, the Ottauquechee River flows eastward within a broad and

Quechee Gorge

shallow valley. At Dewey's Mills, just east of Quechee Village, the river turns abruptly southward and plunges into the narrow, rocky cleft of Quechee Gorge, over a mile in length and Vermont's deepest gorge at a depth of 165 feet. Also one of the state's top tourist attractions, the gorge allows visitors to look down at the Ottauquechee River from a bridge spanning U.S. 4. But this hike goes beyond the crowds, dropping closer to the bottom of Ottauquechee and trailing the river through the gorge for most of its distance.

From the parking area, walk down the steps in front of the gift shop to the gorge trail and turn left (south), passing under the highway bridge. Follow the well-graded trail above the gorge downhill about a half mile to a bend in the river, where there is a bench. Turn left, continue about 0.2 mile along the river, walk up a small hill with good views of the river, and cross a small footbridge. Turn left onto the Beaver Dam Trail, marked by red wooden blocks on trees, which winds up through the

VERMONT

© J. D. BROWN

state park, leaving the park boundaries briefly and crossing private property. The trail leads a mile to U.S. 4, at the state park campground entrance and a half mile east of the bridge. You can walk along the road back to the start of this hike or, especially if on skis, cross the highway and walk behind the Wildflowers Restaurant to an easy ski trail. Turn left and follow it a half mile back to the gorge trail. Turn left and continue a short distance back to the start of this hike.

Most of this hike is within Quechee Gorge State Park, but the Beaver Dam Trail briefly exits the state park onto private property; take care not to wander off the trail.

User Groups: Hikers and dogs. No bikes, horses, or wheelchair facilities.

Permits: Parking and access are free.

Maps: A basic trail map is available at the state park entrance. For a topographic area map, request Quechee from the USGS.

Directions: From I-89 southbound, take Exit 1 onto U.S. 4 west and drive 2.5 miles to the east side of the U.S. 4 bridge over Quechee Gorge. From I-89 northbound, take Exit 1 and drive 3.2 miles to the gorge. Park at the gift shop or information booth on the bridge's east side. GPS Coordinates: 43.6370 N, 72.4072 W

Contact: Quechee Gorge State Park, 190 Dewey Mills Rd., White River Junction, VT 05001, 802/295-2990 in summer, 802/885-8891 in winter, or 800/299-3071. Vermont Department of Forests, Parks, and Recreation Commissioner's Office, 103 South Main St., Waterbury, VT 05671-0601, 802/241-3655, www.vtfpr.org. Friends of the Quechee Gorge, P.O. Box Q, Quechee, VT 05059.

20 KILLINGTON PEAK: BUCKLIN TRAIL

7.4 mi/6 hr   🏃5 ⛰️10

in Mendon and Sherburne

This 7.4-mile hike provides a route of moderate distance and difficulty up Vermont's second-highest peak, 4,241-foot Killington, where the barren, rocky summit boasts one of the finest panoramas in the state. From the summit, where there are radio transmission facilities and a fire tower, the views extend to Mount Mansfield to the north, numerous other Green Mountains peaks to the north and south, Lake Champlain and the Adirondack Mountains to the west, Mount Ascutney to the southeast, and the White Mountains to the northeast. The vertical ascent is about 2,400 feet.

From the parking area, take the blue-blazed Bucklin Trail. It follows an abandoned logging road, first on the north bank of Brewers Brook, then the south bank, for nearly two miles. It grows steeper beyond the logging road, reaching the white-blazed Long Trail/Appalachian Trail at 3.3 miles. Continue uphill on the Long Trail (LT) southbound, reaching the Cooper Lodge in 0.2 mile; just beyond it, the LT swings right, and the spur trail to Killington's summit continues straight ahead. Hike up the very steep and rocky spur trail for 0.2 mile to the summit. Hike back along the same route.

Most of this hike takes place on private land. Camping is prohibited except at the Green Mountain Club cabins and shelters. The Cooper Lodge cabin is located on the Long Trail, 0.1 mile south of the Bucklin Trail junction.

User Groups: Hikers and dogs. No bikes, horses, or wheelchair facilities. This trail should not be attempted in winter except by hikers experienced in mountaineering and prepared for severe winter weather.

Permits: Parking and access are free.

Maps: For a map of hiking trails, get the waterproof End-to-End Map of the Long Trail, available for $9.95 from the Green Mountain Club. For a topographic area map, request Killington Peak from the USGS.

Directions: From U.S. 4, 5.1 miles east of the northern junction of U.S. 4 and U.S. 7 in Rutland and 4.1 miles west of the Inn at Long Trail in Sherburne Pass, turn south onto

Wheelerville Road. Follow it for 4.1 miles to a turnout on the left.

GPS Coordinates: 43.6242 N, 72.8768 W

Contact: Green Mountain Club Inc., 4711 Waterbury-Stowe Rd., Waterbury Center, VT 05677, 802/244-7037, www.greenmountain-club.org.

21 KILLINGTON PEAK: SHERBURNE PASS TRAIL

11.4 mi/8 hr   🏃5 ⛰10

in Sherburne

Although a fairly challenging hike of more than 11 miles, the Sherburne Pass Trail from Sherburne Pass presents a good route to the crown of Vermont's second-highest peak, 4,241-foot Killington. With the trailhead at 2,150 feet, the vertical ascent is about 2,100 feet, less than taking the Bucklin Trail up Killington (see the *Killington Peak: Bucklin Trail* listing in this chapter). And this hike also offers the option of bagging Pico Peak. On the craggy Killington summit, where there are radio transmission facilities and a fire tower, the 360-degree views encompass Mount Mansfield to the north, numerous other Green Mountains peaks to the north and south, Lake Champlain and the Adirondack Mountains to the west, Mount Ascutney to the southeast, and the White Mountains to the northeast.

From the parking area at Sherburne Pass, follow a short spur trail to the Sherburne Pass Trail southbound. The blue-blazed trail climbs gradually for 0.6 mile to a side path that leads 0.1 mile right to a view from the top of a chairlift and an alpine slide at the Pico Ski Area. Continuing its steady ascent, the Sherburne Pass Trail reaches a ski trail at two miles and follows it for 300 yards before reentering the woods. At 2.5 miles from the pass, the Sherburne Pass Trail reaches Pico Camp. A side path, Pico Link, leads 0.4 mile up steep and rocky ground from behind Pico Camp to the 3,957-foot Pico Mountain summit, where there are good views (adding 0.8 mile to this hike's distance). Continue on the Sherburne Pass Trail southbound, mostly contouring along the rugged ridge to Killington Peak. About a half mile south of Pico Camp, you reach a junction with the white-blazed Long Trail/Appalachian Trail. Walk southbound on it. At about 5.5 miles from Sherburne Pass, the trail reaches Cooper Lodge and the junction with the spur trail to Killington's summit. Turn left and climb the very steep and rocky spur for 0.2 mile to the open summit. Return the way you came.

Parts of this hike are on private land. Camping is prohibited except at the Green Mountain Club cabins and shelters. The Pico Camp cabin is at the junction of the Sherburne Pass Trail and Pico Link, 2.5 miles south of Sherburne Pass and a half mile north of the junction of the Long Trail/Appalachian Trail and the Sherburne Pass Trail. The Cooper Lodge cabin is located on the Long Trail, 0.1 mile south of the Bucklin Trail junction and 2.5 miles south of the junction of the Sherburne Pass and Long Trails; from Cooper Lodge, it is 5.5 miles to Sherburne Pass and U.S. 4 via the Sherburne Pass Trail and 6.3 miles to U.S. 4 via the Long Trail.

User Groups: Hikers and dogs. No bikes, horses, or wheelchair facilities. This trail should not be attempted in winter except by hikers experienced in mountaineering and prepared for severe winter weather.

Permits: Parking and access are free.

Maps: For a map of hiking trails, get the waterproof End-to-End Map of the Long Trail, available for $9.95 from the Green Mountain Club. For topographic area maps, request Killington Peak and Pico Peak from the USGS.

Directions: From Route 7/Main Street in Rutland, turn right on Woodstock Avenue. Follow U.S. 4 for 8.2 miles to the Inn at Long Trail. The parking area is on the left, across the street from the Inn at the height of land in Sherburne Pass.

GPS Coordinates: 43.6660 N, 72.8285 W

VERMONT

VERMONT

Contact: Green Mountain Club Inc., 4711 Waterbury-Stowe Rd., Waterbury Center, VT 05677, 802/244-7037, www.greenmountainclub.org.

22 THE LONG TRAIL: ROUTE 103 TO U.S. 4

17.9 mi one-way/2 days   👣5 ⛰9

between Shrewsbury and Sherburne

BEST (

For someone hiking the entire Long Trail from south to north, this stretch is where the trail begins to metamorphose from a casual walk in the woods with occasional views to a more serious and rugged tromp through the mountains. The difference in elevation from Route 103 to the summit of Killington Peak—Vermont's second-tallest mountain at 4,241 feet—is about 3,400 feet. The views in every direction from the rocky, open Killington summit, where there are radio transmission facilities and a fire tower, encompass Mount Mansfield to the north, numerous other Green Mountains peaks to the north and south, Lake Champlain and the Adirondack Mountains to the west, Mount Ascutney to the southeast, and the White Mountains to the northeast. Remember that weather at the higher elevations can turn wintry in any month.

From the parking area on Route 103, the white-blazed Long Trail (LT), which coincides here with the Appalachian Trail (AT), crosses the highway and employs wooden stepladders to get over barbed wire fencing enclosing a field. Crossing the field into the woods, the trail follows a woods road and climbs steeply through a narrow, boulder-strewn ravine. Above the ravine, the LT passes a view to the south and west (0.4 mile from Route 103) and then descends to another woods road a mile from Route 103. To the right, a short distance down the road, is the Clarendon shelter. The LT crosses the road and a brook and ascends Beacon Hill at 1.5 miles, where there is a view south from an open area at the summit. The

trail descends again, crossing Lottery Road at 1.9 miles and the dirt Keiffer Road at 3.6 miles. After following Northam Brook, it turns right onto Cold River Road (also called Lower Road), at 3.9 miles. The LT soon reenters the woods, following a ridge high above the Cold River, and descends steeply to cross the river's east branch on rocks, which could be tricky in times of high water. After paralleling the river's west branch, the trail crosses Upper Cold River Road at 5.4 miles.

At six miles, turn left onto a dirt road, walk over a bridge, and then turn immediately right into the woods. The trail crosses one more road before reaching the Governor Clement shelter at 6.9 miles from Route 103. Passing the shelter, the trail follows a flat woods road for less than a half mile and then starts the long climb up Little Killington and Killington Peak, becoming increasingly rockier, with difficult footing, as the trail narrows through a dense spruce forest. You gain nearly 2,400 feet in elevation. At nine miles, the LT crosses two small brooks, passes through a ski area trail on Killington, and then reaches a junction at 9.8 miles with the Shrewsbury Peak Trail (see *Shrewsbury Peak* listing in this chapter). At the junction, swing left to stay with the LT.

After crossing another ski trail, the hiking grows easier, contouring around the south and west slopes of Killington Peak. At 10.9 miles, a side path bears right and climbs very steeply, over rocky terrain, 0.2 mile to the Killington summit (included in this hike's mileage). Leave your pack behind for the climb up the summit. Back on the LT, the trail passes the Cooper Lodge and descends for 0.2 mile before swinging north again. At 13.3 miles, the blue-blazed Sherburne Pass Trail diverges right, following the former route of the LT for a half mile to Pico Camp (there, a blue-blazed side trail, the Pico Link, leads steeply uphill for 0.4 mile to the Pico summit, where there are views and a chairlift station), and, beyond the Pico Camp, continues three more miles to U.S. 4 at Sherburne Pass.

Descending through a birch glade, the

trail crosses a stream and a bridge across a brook. At 4.4 miles beyond Cooper Lodge, a spur trail leads 0.1 mile to the Churchill Scott shelter, which sleeps 10 and has a tent platform nearby. It's another 2.4 miles on the LT/AT from Churchill Scott shelter to where the trail crosses U.S. 4 about a mile west of Sherburne Pass.

Except for a patch of state-owned land on Killington Peak, this hike is on private land; camping is prohibited except at the Green Mountain Club shelters. From Route 103, it is one mile north to the Clarendon shelter, reached via a short walk down a woods road from the Long Trail; 6.8 miles to the Governor Clement shelter; 11.1 miles to the Cooper Lodge cabin; and 15.5 miles to Churchill Scott shelter. The Pico Camp cabin is on the Sherburne Pass Trail, a half mile north of its junction with the LT and three miles south of U.S. 4.

User Groups: Hikers and dogs. No bikes, horses, or wheelchair facilities. This trail should not be attempted in winter except by hikers prepared for severe winter weather.

Permits: Parking and access are free.

Maps: For a map of hiking trails, refer to the waterproof End-to-End Map of the Long Trail available for $9.95 from the Green Mountain Club. For topographic area maps, request Rutland, Killington Peak, and Pico Peak from the USGS.

Directions: You need to shuttle two vehicles for this one-way traverse. To hike south to north, as described here, leave one vehicle where the Long Trail/Appalachian Trail crosses U.S. 4, one mile west of Sherburne Pass. Then drive to the parking area where the trail crosses Route 103, two miles east of U.S. 7 in Clarendon and three miles west of Cuttingsville.

GPS Coordinates: 43.5284 N, 72.9293 W

Contact: Green Mountain Club Inc., 4711 Waterbury-Stowe Rd., Waterbury Center, VT 05677, 802/244-7037, www.greenmountainclub.org.

23 SHREWSBURY PEAK
3.6 mi/2.5 hr

in Coolidge State Forest outside North Shrewsbury

Part of the Coolidge Range, Shrewsbury Peak (3,710 ft.) is flanked to the northwest by Little Killington (3,917 ft.) and to the south by a small ring of lower-lying hills. For not much effort to reach the top, wonderfully long views await in a wide sweep to the northeast, east, and south. On a clear day, you may see all the way to Franconia Ridge in the White Mountains, Mount Ascutney to the east, Mount Monadnock to the southeast, and a long chain of the Green Mountains trailing off to the south. Through openings in the trees looking north, you might even catch a glimpse of Killington (which can be reached via the Shrewsbury Peak Trail for a scenic if quite rugged round-trip hike of 10.2 miles). This hike climbs about 1,400 feet.

The Shrewsbury Peak Trail is unmarked but obvious and begins from the stone wall at the rear of the parking lot. Within 0.2 mile, it passes in front of a lean-to. Follow the blue blazes over moderate terrain, which grows steeper as the trail ascends into the subalpine hemlock and spruce forest. At 1.8 miles, you emerge at an open area at the summit. To complete this hike, return the way you came. To continue to Killington Peak, follow the Shrewsbury Peak Trail northward. In two miles, turn right (north) on the white-blazed Long Trail and follow it 1.1 miles to the Killington Peak Spur Trail. Turn right and climb very steeply 0.2 mile to the Killington summit.

User Groups: Hikers and leashed dogs. No bikes, horses, or wheelchair facilities.

Permits: Parking and access are free.

Maps: The waterproof End-to-End Map of the Long Trail is available for $9.95 from the Green Mountain Club. For a topographic area map, request Killington Peak from the USGS.

VERMONT

Directions: From Route 100, 3.1 miles south of its junction with U.S. 4 in West Bridgewater and 2.2 miles north of its junction with Route 100A in Plymouth Union, turn west onto the dirt CCC Road at a sign for Meadowsweet Herb Farm. Drive 3.4 miles to a parking area on the right at a sign for the Coolidge State Forest. Or from the center of North Shrewsbury, pick up the CCC Road (marked by a sign) heading east, which begins as pavement and turns to dirt. At 1.1 miles, bear right at a fork and continue 1.6 miles farther to the parking area on the left. The CCC Road can be difficult to drive, especially from the east, in muddy or icy conditions.

GPS Coordinates: 43.5615 N, 72.8013 W

Contact: Vermont Department of Forests, Parks, and Recreation Commissioner's Office, 103 South Main St., Waterbury, VT 05671-0601, 802/241-3655, www.vtfpr.org. Green Mountain Club Inc., 4711 Waterbury-Stowe Rd., Waterbury Center, VT 05677, 802/244-7037, www.greenmountainclub.org.

24 MOUNT ASCUTNEY
6.8 mi/4.5 hr   4 9

in Ascutney State Park in Windsor

Mount Ascutney, at 3,150 feet, belongs to a class of small New England mountains that rise much higher than any piece of earth surrounding them—much like famous Mount Monadnock does in southern New Hampshire. The eroded core of an ancient volcano that once rose to 20,000 feet, Ascutney soars above the Connecticut River Valley. Its observation tower offers excellent views of the Green Mountains to the west, Monadnock to the southeast, Mounts Sunapee and Cardigan to the northeast, and the White Mountains beyond. The first trail up Ascutney was cut in 1825; today, several paths run up the mountain. This loop hike climbs about 2,400 feet in elevation.

Follow the Brownsville Trail's white blazes,

climbing steadily along a wide woods path. At 1.1 miles, the trail passes by the Norcross Quarry remains on the right, where granite was mined until 1910. The trail continues upward, passing a short side path at 1.3 miles leading to an overlook. A second lookout is reached at two miles, offering a view eastward. At 2.3 miles, the trail crosses a grassy area atop wooded North Peak (2,660 ft.). After reaching the Windsor Trail junction (on the left) at 2.9 miles, bear right for the summit. Just 0.1 mile beyond that junction, you reach the remains of the Stone Hut, a former shelter. An unmarked trail leads left 0.7 mile to the Ascutney auto road, and to the right, a short path leads to Brownsville Rock, which offers good views north.

Continue up the Windsor Trail 0.2 mile to the summit observation tower. Descend the same route for 0.3 mile and then turn right to follow the white-blazed Windsor Trail down. The trail crosses the two branches of Mountain Brook and then parallels the brook on a wide, old woods road through a wild drainage. At 2.6 miles below the summit, you reach Route 44A and the parking area for the Windsor Trail. If you have no vehicle here, turn left and follow 44A onto Route 44 west for 0.9 mile to the start of this hike.

User Groups: Hikers and dogs. No bikes, horses, or wheelchair facilities. Dogs are not allowed in day-use areas such as picnic areas, but are not restricted on trails.

Permits: Parking and access are free.

Maps: The Ascutney Trails Association publishes an Ascutney guidebook and map, available from the association for $7. A free, basic map is available at the park entrance. For a topographic area map, request Mount Ascutney from the USGS.

Directions: If you have two vehicles, drive one to the Windsor Trail parking area at the end of this hike, reducing this hike's distance by the 0.9 mile of paved road separating the trailheads; otherwise, just note the location of the Windsor Trail on your way to the start of the Brownsville Trail. From the north, take I-91 to Exit 9 and then U.S. 5 south into the center of Windsor; from the south, take I-91 to Exit 8 and then U.S. 5 north into Windsor. At the junction of U.S. 5 and Route 44 in Windsor, turn west onto Route 44 and follow it for 3.3 miles to its junction with Route 44A. The Windsor Trail parking area is just 100 yards down Route 44A, on the right. Continue west on Route 44 for 0.9 mile to parking on the left side of the road for the Brownsville Trail. Trails are closed during the spring mud season, usually mid-April–mid-May.

GPS Coordinates: 43.4407 N, 72.4088 W

Contact: Ascutney State Park, Box 186, HCR 71, 1826 Black Mountain Rd., Windsor, VT 05089, 802/674-2060 in summer, 802/885-8891 in winter, or 800/299-3071. Vermont Department of Forests, Parks, and Recreation Commissioner's Office, 103 South Main St., Waterbury, VT 05671-0601, 802/241-3655, www.vtfpr.org. Ascutney Trails Association, P.O. Box 147, Windsor, Vermont 05089, www.ascutneytrails.org.

25 CLARENDON GORGE AND AIRPORT LOOKOUT

1.8 mi/1 hr   👥2 ⛰7

between Shrewsbury and Clarendon

For the view down into Clarendon Gorge, you need only walk southbound on the white-blazed Long Trail/Appalachian Trail for 0.1 mile to the suspension bridge spanning the dramatic chasm. But the added uphill climb of less than a mile and several hundred feet to Airport Lookout is worth the effort. Its open ledges atop low cliffs afford a view west to the Rutland Airport, the valley that U.S. 7 runs through, and the southern Adirondacks. Be careful scrambling around on these ledges; it can be a treacherously slippery spot, even when not very wet. From Airport Lookout, backtrack the way you came.

User Groups: Hikers and dogs. No bikes, horses, or wheelchair facilities.

Permits: Parking and access are free.

Maps: No map is necessary for this hike, but for a map of hiking trails, refer to map 6 in the Map and Guide to the Appalachian Trail in New Hampshire/Vermont, an eight-map set available for $14.95 from the Appalachian Trail Conservancy. Or get the waterproof End-to-End Map of the Long Trail, available for $9.95 from the Green Mountain Club. For a topographic area map, request Rutland from the USGS.

Directions: Drive to the parking area on Route 103, three miles west of Cuttingsville and two miles east of U.S. 7 in Clarendon.

GPS Coordinates: 43.5258 N, 72.9277 W

Contact: Green Mountain Club Inc., 4711 Waterbury-Stowe Rd., Waterbury Center, VT 05677, 802/244-7037, www.greenmountainclub.org. Appalachian Trail Conservancy, 799 Washington St., P.O. Box 807, Harpers Ferry, WV 25425-0807, 304/535-6331, www.appalachiantrail.org.

26 LONG TRAIL: BEAR MOUNTAIN AND CLARENDON GORGE TRAVERSE

6.3 mi one-way/3.5 hr   👥3 ⛰7

between Shrewsbury and Clarendon

Beginning with an ascent of the south ridge of 2,262-foot Bear Mountain and finishing at the steep-walled Clarendon Gorge, this long, 6.3-mile stretch of trail is still safe and moderate enough of a route for a beginner backpacking trek or a first-time long distance traverse. The cumulative elevation gain is just under 1,200 feet.

From Route 140, follow the Long Trail (LT) northbound up Bear Mountain. Rocky, but not so steep, the short spur trail to an open ledge overlooking the Otter Creek Valley to the south (at approximately one mile) should not be missed. The LT continues north, contouring just below the ridgeline, descends the steep north side of Bear Mountain, crosses a beaver meadow, and then follows a woods road to rejoin the old route of the LT just south of Minerva Hinchey shelter. At about 2.6 miles into this hike, a side path leads to the shelter. Beyond it, the LT climbs over a low, wooded hill and descends and passes through Spring Lake Clearing, 3.2 miles from Route 140. It follows a wooded ridge to Airport Lookout at 4.5 miles, where open ledges atop low cliffs offer a view west of the Rutland Airport, the valley that U.S. 7 runs through, and the southern Adirondacks. Descending, the trail reaches Clarendon Gorge, crossing the gorge on a suspension bridge that offers a dramatic view down into the chasm. Just 0.1 mile farther, you reach Route 103.

Except for a patch of state-owned land at Clarendon Gorge, this hike is on private land. Camping is prohibited except at the Green Mountain Club Minerva Hinchey shelter, reached via a short side path off the Long Trail, 2.6 miles north of Route 140.

User Groups: Hikers and dogs. No bikes, horses, or wheelchair facilities.

Permits: Parking and access are free.

Maps: For a map of hiking trails, refer to map 6 in the Map and Guide to the Appalachian Trail in New Hampshire/Vermont, an eight-map set available for $14.95 from the Appalachian Trail Conservancy. Or get the waterproof End-to-End Map of the Long Trail, available for $9.95 from the Green Mountain Club. For topographic area maps, request Wallingford and Rutland from the USGS.

Directions: You need to shuttle two vehicles for this one-way traverse. To hike south to north, as described here, leave one vehicle in the parking area on Route 103, two miles east of U.S. 7 in Clarendon and three miles west of Cuttingsville. Then drive to where the Long Trail/Appalachian Trail crosses Route 140, about 2.8 miles east of U.S. 7 in Wallingford and about 3.7 miles west of the junction of Routes 140, 155, and 103 in East Wallingford.

GPS Coordinates: 43.4589 N, 72.9454 W

Contact: Green Mountain Club Inc., 4711 Waterbury-Stowe Rd., Waterbury Center, VT 05677, 802/244-7037, www.greenmountainclub.org. Appalachian Trail Conservancy, 799 Washington St., P.O. Box 807, Harpers Ferry, WV 25425-0807, 304/535-6331, www.appalachiantrail.org.

27 WHITE ROCKS CLIFF
2.6 mi/2 hr   🏃3 ⛰8

in the Green Mountain National Forest east of Wallingford

During the last Ice Age, glaciers exposed and scoured the hillside, revealing the White Rocks' distinct cliff face of white quartzite. Native Americans once quarried this stone for tools; early Vermont settlers cleared the surrounding forest, leaving the cliffs in the middle of farmland and upland pasture. Now once again surrounded by forest, the White Rocks Cliffs have been set aside as part of a National Recreation Area for backcountry recreation. This moderately difficult climb nets an elevation gain of 1,500 feet.

From the White Rocks Recreation Area, follow the Keewaydin Trail steeply uphill. It soon passes a newly rerouted stretch of the northbound Long Trail bearing left; continue up the Keewaydin, and at 0.8 mile from the trailhead you'll reach a junction with the Greenwall Spur, a trail leading left a half mile to the Greenwall shelter. Turn right (south) on the Long Trail, hike 0.3 mile, and then turn right (west) on the White Rocks Cliff Trail. This trail descends steeply for 0.2 mile and ends at the top of the cliffs, with good views of the valley south of Wallingford. There are numerous footpaths around the cliffs, but take care because the rock is loose and footing can be dangerous. Return the way you came.

Camping is prohibited except at the Green Mountain Club cabins and shelters. The Greenwall shelter is located on the Greenwall

Spur, a half mile north of the Keewaydin Trail and Long Trail junction.

User Groups: Hikers and leashed dogs. No bikes, horses, or wheelchair facilities.

Permits: Parking and access are free.

Maps: For a map of hiking trails, refer to map 6 in the Map and Guide to the Appalachian Trail in New Hampshire/Vermont, an eight-map set available for $14.95 from the Appalachian Trail Conservancy. Or get the waterproof End-to-End Map of the Long Trail, available for $9.95 from the Green Mountain Club. For a topographic area map, request Wallingford from the USGS.

Directions: From Route 140, 4.1 miles west of the junction of Routes 140 and 155 in East Wallingford and 2.1 miles east of the junction of 140 and U.S. 7 in Wallingford, turn south onto the dirt Sugar Hill Road. Drive 0.1 mile and turn right onto the dirt USFS Road 52 at a sign for the White Rocks Picnic Area. Continue a half mile to the White Rocks Recreation Area.

GPS Coordinates: 43.4579 N, 72.9439 W

Contact: Green Mountain National Forest Supervisor, 231 North Main St., Rutland, VT 05701, 802/747-6700, www.fs.fed.us/r9/forests/greenmountain/. Green Mountain Club Inc., 4711 Waterbury-Stowe Rd., Waterbury Center, VT 05677, 802/244-7037, www.greenmountainclub.org. Appalachian Trail Conservancy, 799 Washington St., P.O. Box 807, Harpers Ferry, WV 25425-0807, 304/535-6331, www.appalachiantrail.org.

28 GRIFFITH LAKE AND BAKER PEAK

8.5 mi/6 hr

in the Green Mountain National Forest southeast of Danby

Baker Peak, though just 2,850 feet high, thrusts a rocky spine above the trees for great views of the valley around the little town of Danby. And Griffith Lake is one of several scenic ponds and lakes along the Long Trail. This 8.5-mile loop incorporates both places and involves about 2,000 feet of climbing.

From the parking area, follow the Lake Trail. It ascends very gently at first, then steeply for two miles. Where the Baker Peak Trail bears left, stay to the right on the Lake Trail. It nearly levels off again before reaching the Long Trail (LT)—which coincides here with the Appalachian Trail—at 3.5 miles from the trailhead. Turning right (south), walk the LT for 0.1 mile to the Griffith Lake camping area and enjoy views of the lake. Spin around and hike north on the LT for 1.8 relatively easy miles to the Baker Peak Trail junction. Here, turn right with the LT and scramble up the long rock ridge protruding from the earth for 0.1 mile to the open Baker Peak summit. Then backtrack, descending the Baker Peak Trail, past the Quarry View overlook, for a mile to the Lake Trail. Turn right (west) and descend another two miles to the parking area.

Camping is prohibited except at the Green Mountain Club cabins and shelters. The Griffith Lake camping area, with tent sites, is located 0.1 mile south of the Lake and Long Trails junction. A Green Mountain Club caretaker is on duty and collects a nightly fee Memorial Day weekend–Labor Day.

User Groups: Hikers and leashed dogs. No bikes, horses, or wheelchair facilities.

Permits: Parking and access are free.

Maps: For a map of hiking trails, refer to map 7 in the Map and Guide to the Appalachian Trail in New Hampshire/Vermont, an eight-map set available for $14.95 from the Appalachian Trail Conservancy. Or get the waterproof End-to-End Map of the Long Trail available for $9.95 from the Green Mountain Club. For a topographic area map, request Danby from the USGS.

Directions: From the crossroads in Danby, drive south on U.S. 7 for 2.1 miles and turn left onto Town Route 5. Drive a half mile to parking on the left for the Lake Trail.

GPS Coordinates: 43.3202 N, 72.9919 W

Contact: Green Mountain National Forest

Supervisor, 231 North Main St., Rutland, VT 05701, 802/747-6700, www.fs.fed.us/ r9/forests/greenmountain/. Green Mountain Club Inc., 4711 Waterbury-Stowe Rd., Waterbury Center, VT 05677, 802/244-7037, www.greenmountainclub.org. Appalachian Trail Conservancy, 799 Washington St., P.O. Box 807, Harpers Ferry, WV 25425-0807, 304/535-6331, www.appalachiantrail.org.

29 THE LONG TRAIL: ROUTE 11/30 TO USFS ROAD 10

17.3 mi one-way/2 days 👣 4 ⛰ 9

in the Green Mountain National Forest east of Danby

Imagine standing solo on Styles Peak (3,394 ft.) at sunset or sitting alone on big rocks beside the roaring, clear waters of the Big Branch River. If you like hikes that come with good views and a sense of solitude and peaceful isolation, this fairly scenic, though quiet stretch of the Long Trail may quickly become your favorite. The 17.3-mile traverse makes for a moderate, two-day backpacking trip. The cumulative elevation gain is nearly 3,000 feet, but spread over more than 17 miles, is not steep.

From the parking lot on Route 11/30, follow the white blazes of the Long Trail (LT) northbound, which here coincides with the Appalachian Trail. Watch closely for the blazes; many unmarked trails cross the LT on this side of Bromley. At 0.8 mile into this hike, a spur trail leads 150 feet to the right to the Bromley tenting area. Two miles from the road, the LT grows steeper and at 2.6 miles it emerges from the woods onto a wide ski trail. Hike up the ski trail 0.2 mile to the mountain's summit, where there are ski area buildings. To the right are an observation deck—which offers views in every direction—and the warming hut. The LT swings left from the ski trail just before a chairlift and descends a steep, rocky section. At 3.3 miles (a half mile beyond the summit),

the LT climbs over the rugged, wooded north summit of Bromley and then descends to cross USFS Road 21 in Mad Tom Notch at 5.3 miles. There is a water pump at the roadside that may not be working. Continuing north, the LT makes a steady, though not difficult, ascent of nearly 1,000 feet in elevation to the 3,394-foot Styles Peak summit, at 6.7 miles.

Following the ridge north, the LT dips slightly and then ascends slightly to the wooded Peru Peak summit (3,429 ft.) at 8.4 miles, where a side path leads 75 feet right to a largely obscured view eastward. Descending steeply, the trail reaches the Peru Peak shelter at 9.8 miles, with a good stream nearby. The LT crosses the stream on a wooden bridge and continues a flat 0.7 mile to Griffith Lake at 10.4 miles, where there are tent sites. The Old Job Trail leaves right (east), swinging north to loop 5.3 miles back to the Long Trail at a point 0.1 mile east of the Big Branch suspension bridge. The Lake Trail departs left (west) at 10.5 miles, descending 3.5 miles to Town Route 5 in Danby (a half mile from U.S. 7).

The Long Trail continues north over easy terrain and then climbs to a junction, at 12.2 miles, with the Baker Peak Trail (which descends west for 2.9 miles to Town Route 5 via the Lake Trail). Turn right with the LT and scramble up a spine of exposed rock for 0.1 mile to the open summit of 2,850-foot Baker Peak, with great views of the valley around the little town of Danby. The trail then reenters the forest and traverses fairly easy terrain, reaching and following an old woods road to a junction, at 14.3 miles, with a short side path leading left to the Lost Pond shelter.

Continuing on the woods road, the LT reaches the Big Branch River at 15.8 miles, swings left along it for 0.1 mile, and then crosses the river on a suspension bridge. The trail swings left again, following the boulder-choked river to the Big Branch shelter at 16.2 miles. Easy hiking for another 1.2 miles brings you to USFS Road 10. Turn left and walk the road for 0.1 mile to the parking lot at this hike's north end.

No-trace camping is permitted within the Green Mountain National Forest, except at Griffith Lake, where camping within 200 feet of shore is restricted to designated sites. Backpackers can stay overnight in the warming hut on Bromley Mountain's summit, beside the observation deck; there is no water source. The Bromley tenting area is 0.7 mile north of Route 11/30, reached via a short spur trail off the Long Trail. The Peru Peak shelter sits beside the LT at 9.8 miles, the Griffith Lake campsite at 10.4 miles, the Lost Pond shelter at 14.3 miles, and the Big Branch shelter at 16.2 miles (the last 1.3 miles south of the parking lot on USFS Road 10). A Green Mountain Club caretaker is on duty Memorial Day weekend–Labor Day and a nightly fee is collected to stay at the Peru Peak shelter and the Griffith Lake campsite.

User Groups: Hikers and leashed dogs. No bikes, horses, or wheelchair facilities.

Permits: Parking and access are free.

Maps: For a map of hiking trails, refer to map 7 in the Map and Guide to the Appalachian Trail in New Hampshire/Vermont, an eight-map set for $14.95 from the Appalachian Trail Conservancy. Or get the waterproof End-to-End Map of the Long Trail, available for $9.95 from the Green Mountain Club. For topographic area maps, request Peru and Danby from the USGS.

Directions: You need to shuttle two vehicles for this one-way traverse. To hike south to north, as described here, leave one vehicle in the parking lot on USFS Road 10 at Big Black Branch, 3.5 miles west of U.S. 7 in Danby and 13.6 miles north of Route 11 in Peru. Drive to the parking lot on the north side of Route 11/30, 6 miles east of Manchester Center and 4.4 miles west of Peru. USFS Road 10 is not maintained during the winter.

GPS Coordinates: 43.2112 N, 72.9657 W

Contact: Green Mountain National Forest Supervisor, 231 North Main St., Rutland, VT 05701, 802/747-6700, www.fs.fed.us/ r9/forests/greenmountain/. Green Mountain Club Inc., 4711 Waterbury-Stowe Rd., Waterbury Center, VT 05677, 802/244-7037, www.greenmountainclub.org. Appalachian Trail Conservancy, 799 Washington St., P.O. Box 807, Harpers Ferry, WV 25425-0807, 304/535-6331, www.appalachiantrail.org.

30 STYLES PEAK

2.8 mi/2 hr

in the Peru Peak Wilderness in the Green Mountain National Forest west of Peru

Styles Peak, 3,394 feet high, has a small crag of a summit that affords views to the east and south of the southern Green Mountains and the rumpled landscape of southeastern Vermont and southwestern New Hampshire. This quiet spot is a great place to catch the sunrise and with just 1.4 miles to hike nearly 1,000 feet uphill to reach the summit, getting here before dawn to watch the sunrise is a reasonable objective.

From the parking area, walk east a few steps on the road to the junction with the Long Trail (LT) and turn left (north). After passing a water pump (which may not be working), follow the white-blazed Long Trail, which coincides here with the Appalachian Trail, as it climbs steadily and then steeply to the open rocks atop Styles Peak. Return the way you came.

No-trace camping is permitted within the Green Mountain National Forest. The Peru Peak shelter is on the Long Trail, 4.4 miles north of USFS Road 21 and 3 miles north of the Styles Peak summit. A Green Mountain Club caretaker is on duty and collects a nightly fee Memorial Day weekend–Labor Day.

User Groups: Hikers and leashed dogs. No bikes, horses, or wheelchair facilities.

Permits: Parking and access are free.

Maps: For a trail map, see map 7 in the Map and Guide to the Appalachian Trail in New Hampshire/Vermont, an eight-map set and guidebook available for $14.95 from the Appalachian Trail Conservancy. Or get the waterproof End-to-End Map of the Long Trail, available for $9.95 from the Green Mountain

Club. For a topographic area map, request Peru from the USGS.

Directions: Drive to the parking area on USFS Road 21, immediately west of the height of land in Mad Tom Notch and the Long Trail crossing and 4.3 miles west of Route 11 in Peru. USFS Road 21 is maintained in winter only to a point about 2.5 miles from the Long Trail.

GPS Coordinates: 43.2125 N, 72.9709 W

Contact: Green Mountain National Forest Supervisor, 231 North Main St., Rutland, VT 05701, 802/747-6700, www.fs.fed.us/r9/forests/greenmountain/. Green Mountain Club Inc., 4711 Waterbury-Stowe Rd., Waterbury Center, VT 05677, 802/244-7037, www.greenmountainclub.org. Appalachian Trail Conservancy, 799 Washington St., P.O. Box 807, Harpers Ferry, WV 25425-0807, 304/535-6331, www.appalachiantrail.org.

31 BROMLEY MOUNTAIN FROM MAD TOM NOTCH
5 mi/3.5 hr   👫2 ⛰9

in the Green Mountain National Forest west of Peru

This round-trip route from the north to the top of 3,260-foot Bromley Mountain is a bit more wild and less trammeled than taking the Long Trail from the south (see *Bromley Mountain from Route 11/30* listing in this chapter). A ski area in winter, Bromley offers some of the better views along the southern Long Trail from its summit observation deck. This hike climbs about 800 feet.

From the parking lot, walk east on the road for a short stretch, then turn right and follow the white blazes of the Long Trail southbound, which here coincides with the Appalachian Trail. The trail ascends easily at first and then climbs more steeply, over rocky terrain, to Bromley's wooded north summit at two miles. After dipping slightly, it climbs to the open summit of Bromley Mountain, 2.5 miles from the road. Cross the clearing

to the observation deck and warming hut. Descend the same way you came.

No-trace camping is permitted within the Green Mountain National Forest. Backpackers can stay overnight in the warming hut on Bromley's summit, beside the observation deck; there is no water source.

User Groups: Hikers and leashed dogs. No bikes, horses, or wheelchair facilities.

Permits: Parking and access are free.

Maps: For a map of hiking trails, refer to map 7 in the Map and Guide to the Appalachian Trail in New Hampshire/Vermont, an eight-map set available for $14.95 from the Appalachian Trail Conservancy. Or get the waterproof End-to-End Map of the Long Trail, available for $9.95 from the Green Mountain Club. For a topographic area map, request Peru from the USGS.

Directions: Drive to the parking area on USFS Road 21, immediately west of the height of land in Mad Tom Notch and the Long Trail crossing and 4.3 miles west of Route 11 in Peru. USFS Road 21 is maintained in winter only to a point about 2.5 miles from the Long Trail.

GPS Coordinates: 43.2125 N, 72.9709 W

Contact: Green Mountain National Forest Supervisor, 231 North Main St., Rutland, VT 05701, 802/747-6700, www.fs.fed.us/r9/forests/greenmountain/. Green Mountain Club Inc., 4711 Waterbury-Stowe Rd., Waterbury Center, VT 05677, 802/244-7037, www.greenmountainclub.org. Appalachian Trail Conservancy, 799 Washington St., P.O. Box 807, Harpers Ferry, WV 25425-0807, 304/535-6331, www.appalachiantrail.org.

32 BROMLEY MOUNTAIN FROM ROUTE 11/30
5.6 mi/3.5 hr   👫3 ⛰9

in the Green Mountain National Forest between Peru and Manchester Center

Bromley Mountain, a ski area in winter, offers some of the better views along the southern

Long Trail from the observation deck on its 3,260-foot summit. This 5.6-mile route up Bromley is a popular hike and, due to this heavy boot traffic, suffers from erosion and muddy ground in some spots. Stick to the trail and avoid the mountain when trail conditions are wet to help prevent further erosion. This hike ascends 1,460 feet.

From the parking lot, follow the white blazes of the Long Trail (LT) northbound, which here coincides with the Appalachian Trail. Watch closely for the blazes; numerous unmarked trails cross the LT on this side of Bromley. At two miles into this hike you reach the Bromley shelter, where there's a lean-to that sleeps 12 and four tent platforms. Beyond it, the LT grows steeper, and at 2.6 miles it emerges from the woods onto a wide ski trail. Hike up the ski trail 0.2 mile to the mountain's summit, where there are ski area buildings. Turn right and walk 100 feet to the observation deck. The views extend in every direction. Stratton Mountain looms prominently to the south. Beside the tower is the warming hut. Descend the way you came.

No-trace camping is permitted within the Green Mountain National Forest. The Bromley shelter and tent platforms are two miles north of Route 11/30. Backpackers can stay overnight in the warming hut on Bromley's summit, beside the observation deck; there is no water source.

User Groups: Hikers and leashed dogs. No bikes, horses, or wheelchair facilities.

Permits: Parking and access are free.

Maps: For a map of hiking trails, refer to map 7 in the Map and Guide to the Appalachian Trail in New Hampshire/Vermont, an eight-map set available for $14.95 from the Appalachian Trail Conservancy. Or get the waterproof End-to-End Map of the Long Trail, available for $9.95 from the Green Mountain Club. For a topographic area map, request Peru from the USGS.

Directions: Drive to the parking lot on the north side of Route 11/30, 6 miles east of Manchester Center and 4.4 miles west of Peru.

GPS Coordinates: 43.2087 N, 72.9698 W

Contact: Green Mountain National Forest Supervisor, 231 North Main St., Rutland, VT 05701, 802/747-6700, www.fs.fed.us/r9/forests/greenmountain/. Green Mountain Club Inc., 4711 Waterbury-Stowe Rd., Waterbury Center, VT 05677, 802/244-7037, www.greenmountainclub.org. Appalachian Trail Conservancy, 799 Washington St., P.O. Box 807, Harpers Ferry, WV 25425-0807, 304/535-6331, www.appalachiantrail.org.

🟥 SPRUCE PEAK
4.4 mi/2.5 hr   🚶3 ⛰8

in the Green Mountain National Forest south of Peru

This fairly easy hike of 4.4 miles takes you up to Spruce Peak, at 2,040 feet no more than a small bump along a wooded Green Mountain ridge, but a spot with a couple of good views west to the valley at Manchester Center and out to the Taconic Range. Come here on a cloudless Indian summer day in October and take in the peak foliage fanning out across the valley below.

From the parking area, cross Route 11/30 and follow the white blazes of the Long Trail (LT) southbound into the woods. The hiking is mostly easy, climbing only a few hundred feet in elevation, with the trail passing through an area of moss-covered boulders and rocks. At 2.2 miles from the road, turn right (west) onto a side path that leads about 300 feet to the Spruce Peak summit. There is a limited view west at the actual summit, but just below the summit, a few steps off the path, is a better view. Return the way you came.

No-trace camping is permitted within the Green Mountain National Forest. The Spruce Peak shelter is 0.1 mile down a side path off the LT, 2.7 miles south of Route 11/30 and a half mile south of the side path to Spruce Peak.

User Groups: Hikers and leashed dogs. No bikes, horses, or wheelchair facilities.

VERMONT

Permits: Parking and access are free.

Maps: For a map of hiking trails, refer to map 7 in the Map and Guide to the Appalachian Trail in New Hampshire/Vermont, an eight-map set available for $14.95 from the Appalachian Trail Conservancy. Or get the waterproof End-to-End Map of the Long Trail, available for $9.95 from the Green Mountain Club. For a topographic area map, request Peru from the USGS.

Directions: Drive to the parking lot on the north side of Route 11/30, 6 miles east of Manchester Center and 4.4 miles west of Peru.

GPS Coordinates: 43.2087 N, 72.9698 W

Contact: Green Mountain National Forest Supervisor, 231 North Main St., Rutland, VT 05701, 802/747-6700, www.fs.fed.us/r9/forests/greenmountain/. Green Mountain Club Inc., 4711 Waterbury-Stowe Rd., Waterbury Center, VT 05677, 802/244-7037, www.greenmountainclub.org. Appalachian Trail Conservancy, 799 Washington St., P.O. Box 807, Harpers Ferry, WV 25425-0807, 304/535-6331, www.appalachiantrail.org.

③④ EQUINOX MOUNTAIN
5.2 mi/2.5 hr

in Manchester

At 3,850 feet, Equinox towers above the surrounding landscape of southernmost Vermont and holds the distinction as the highest summit in the Taconic Range, of which Mount Greylock (3,491 ft.) and Connecticut's Mount Frissell (2,454 ft.) are also a part. The largest rich northern hardwood forest in New England—over 2,000 acres—is located on Mount Equinox; the mountain's deep humus soil supports lush woodlands of paper birch, balsam fir, pin cherry, yellow birch, and red spruce. This hike to the top of Equinox leads to the Inn at the Equinox (accessed by a summit road) and then out to Lookout Rock for long views

stretching across the rolling countryside. The summit hike climbs more than 2,700 feet. The Inn at Equinox sits at the summit of Equinox Mountain, accessible by car via the Equinox Sky Line Drive, a private toll road on the other side of the mountain from the hiking trail.

From the parking area, follow the Red Gate Trail a few feet to the Blue Summit Trail. Beginning its ascent as a rather steep woods road, the blue-blazed Blue Summit Trail passes the Trillium Trail junction at 0.4 mile and the Maidenhair Trail junction at 0.6 mile, continuing on until reaching a junction with the Upper Spring Trail at 2 miles. Here, the wide road then narrows to a footpath, climbing steadily through high elevation forest and eventually reaching the Red/Yellow trail. Follow the spur a short distance to views from Lookout Rock. Take in the sights north and east to the Manchester Valley, White Mountains, Mount Ascutney, and Mount Monadnock.

User Groups: Hikers and dogs. No horses or wheelchair facilities. Bikes are allowed on the old woods road portion of the trail before Upper Spring Trail junction.

Permits: Parking and trail access are free.

Maps: A trail map is available from the Equinox Preservation Trust. Informational kiosks are located at both entrances to the Preserve. An enlarged trail map is on display along with copies of the pocket guide and trail map. A third kiosk is located near the trail connector at the rear of the Equinox Hotel parking area. For a topographic area map, request Manchester from the USGS.

Directions: From Manchester Center, drive south on U.S. 7A for 1.7 miles to a right turn onto Seminary Avenue. Follow 0.3 mile to West Union Street. Park at the end of the road next to the Red Gate Trailhead.

GPS Coordinates: 43.1620 N, 73.0838 W

Contact: Equinox Preservation Trust and Vermont Institute of Natural Science, Box 46, Manchester, VT 05254, 802/362-4374, www.equinoxpreservationtrust.org.

35 THE LONG TRAIL: ARLINGTON-WEST WARDSBORO ROAD TO ROUTE 11/30

16.3 mi one-way/11 hr or 1-2 days
🥾4 ⛰9

in the Green Mountain National Forest
between Stratton and Peru

The highlights of this 16.3-mile traverse of the Long Trail's southern stretch are the 360-degree view from the observation tower on 3,936-foot Stratton Mountain and beautiful Stratton Pond. But you also get a view from Spruce Peak and the northern part of this trek offers seclusion and a sense of isolation not found at popular Stratton Mountain. The cumulative elevation gain is more than 2,500 feet, most of that involved in the 1,800-foot climb up Stratton Mountain.

From the parking area, head north on the white-blazed Long Trail (LT; which coincides here with the Appalachian Trail). It rises gently through muddy areas, growing progressively steeper—and passing one outlook south—over the 3.4-mile climb to Stratton's summit. A Green Mountain Club caretaker cabin is located on the edge of the summit clearing and a caretaker is on duty during the late spring–fall hiking season to answer questions and assist hikers. After climbing up the observation tower, take in wide views south to Somerset Reservoir and Mount Greylock, the Taconic Range to the west, Mount Ascutney to the northeast, and Mount Monadnock to the southeast.

Continue north on the LT, descending for 2.6 miles to Willis Ross Clearing on the east shore of Stratton Pond, the largest water body and one of the busiest spots on the Long Trail. The Lye Brook Trail leads left while the LT swings right, passing a junction with the North Shore Trail within 0.1 mile. The LT contours, for easy hiking, to the Winhall River at 7.9 miles into this hike; the river is crossed on a bridge and the trail enters the Lye Brook Wilderness.

At 10.3 miles, the Branch Pond Trail leads left (west) into the Lye Brook Wilderness to the William B. Douglas shelter. Crossing a brook, the LT turns left and follows a wide logging road. At 11.4 miles, an unmarked side path leads about 200 feet to Prospect Rock, with a good view of Downer Glen. The LT turns right (northeast) off the road and climbs steadily before descending again to a side path, at 13.6 miles, leading 0.1 mile to the Spruce Peak cabin. After more easy hiking, at 14.1 miles, a side path leads about 300 feet left to the Spruce Peak summit, where there is a limited view west. But just below the summit is a better view of the valley and the Taconic Mountains. Continuing north, the LT crosses easy ground for 2.2 miles, passing through an area of interesting, moss-covered boulders, to reach Route 11/30 at 16.3 miles. Cross the highway to the parking lot.

No-trace camping is permitted within the Green Mountain National Forest, except at Stratton Pond, where camping is restricted to the North Shore tenting area, which lies a half mile down the North Shore Trail from its junction with the Long Trail, 0.1 mile north of Willis Ross Clearing; and the new Stratton Pond shelter, located 100 yards down the Stratton Pond Trail from its junction with the LT/AT. A Green Mountain Club caretaker is on duty and a nightly fee is collected to stay at the Stratton Pond shelter and the North Shore tenting area Memorial Day weekend–Columbus Day. Two Green Mountain Club shelters on Stratton Pond—Vondell shelter and Bigelow shelter—were removed in 2000 and 1997, respectively. Camping is prohibited on the upper slopes of Stratton Mountain, which is privately owned. The Williams B. Douglas shelter lies a half mile south of the LT on the Branch Pond Trail, 10.3 miles north of the Arlington–West Wardsboro Road. The Spruce Peak shelter lies 0.1 mile down a side path off the LT, at 13.6 miles into this hike.

User Groups: Hikers and leashed dogs. No bike, horses, or wheelchair facilities.

Permits: Parking and access are free.

VERMONT

Maps: For a map of hiking trails, refer to map 7 in the Map and Guide to the Appalachian Trail in New Hampshire/Vermont, an eight-map set available for $14.95 from the Appalachian Trail Conservancy. Or get the waterproof End-to-End Map of the Long Trail, available for $9.95 from the Green Mountain Club. For topographic area maps, request Stratton Mountain, Manchester, and Peru from the USGS.

Directions: You need to shuttle two vehicles for this one-way traverse. To hike south to north, as described here, leave one vehicle in the parking lot on the north side of Route 11/30, 6 miles east of Manchester Center and 4.4 miles west of Peru. Then drive to the large parking area on the Arlington–West Wardsboro Road, 13.3 miles east of U.S. 7 in Arlington and 8 miles west of Route 100 in West Wardsboro. The Arlington–West Wardsboro Road is not maintained in winter.

GPS Coordinates: 43.0651 N, 72.9889 W

Contact: Green Mountain National Forest Supervisor, 231 North Main St., Rutland, VT 05701, 802/747-6700, www.fs.fed.us/r9/forests/greenmountain/. Green Mountain Club Inc., 4711 Waterbury-Stowe Rd., Waterbury Center, VT 05677, 802/244-7037, www.greenmountainclub.org. Appalachian Trail Conservancy, 799 Washington St., P.O. Box 807, Harpers Ferry, WV 25425-0807, 304/535-6331, www.appalachiantrail.org.

36 STRATTON MOUNTAIN AND STRATTON POND

11 mi/7 hr   🥾4 ⛰️10

in the Green Mountain National Forest between Arlington and West Wardsboro

BEST (

From the observation tower atop Stratton Mountain, you get one of the most sweeping panoramas on the Long Trail, a particularly dazzling sight in fall when the surrounding deciduous forest cover bursts with autumn color, especially the views south into Massachusetts. And merely climbing the tower will be an adventure for children, as well as adults not accustomed to heights. This 11-mile hike climbs about 1,500 feet. For a shorter hike—though with just as much climbing—you can make a 6.8-mile round-trip on the Long Trail to the 3,936-foot Stratton summit and return the same way.

From the parking area, follow the white-blazed Long Trail (LT) north (which coincides here with the Appalachian Trail). It rises steadily, through muddy areas at the lower elevations, and passes one outlook south (around two miles), before growing steep just before the summit. On top of 3,936-foot Stratton is the Green Mountain Club's caretaker cabin and a caretaker is on duty during the late spring–fall hiking season to answer questions and assist hikers. Climb the fire tower, where the views take in Somerset Reservoir and Mount Greylock to the south, the Taconic Range to the west, Mount Ascutney to the northeast, and Mount Monadnock to the southeast.

Return the same way, or make an 11-mile loop by continuing north on the LT, descending for 2.6 miles to beautiful Stratton Pond, the largest body of water and one of the busiest areas on the Long Trail. The Long Trail reaches the east shore of Stratton Pond at Willis Ross Clearing. From here, a loop of about 1.5 miles around the pond is possible, taking the Lye Brook Trail along the south shore, and the North Shore Trail back to the Long Trail, 0.1 mile north of Willis Ross Clearing (this distance is not included in this hike's mileage). From the clearing, backtrack 0.1 mile south on the LT, turn right onto the Stratton Pond Trail, and follow it for an easy 3.8 miles back to the Arlington–West Wardsboro Road. Turn left (east) and walk the road 1.1 miles back to the parking area.

No-trace camping is permitted within the Green Mountain National Forest, except at Stratton Pond, where camping is restricted to the North Shore tenting area, which lies a half mile down the North Shore Trail from its junction with the Long Trail, 0.1 mile north of Willis Ross Clearing; and the new Stratton Pond shelter, located 100 yards down the Stratton Pond Trail from its junction with the LT/AT. A Green Mountain Club caretaker is on duty and a nightly fee is collected to stay at the Stratton shelter and the North Shore tenting area Memorial Day weekend–Columbus Day. Two Green Mountain Club shelters on Stratton Pond—Vondell shelter and Bigelow shelter—were removed in 2000 and 1997, respectively. Camping is prohibited on the upper slopes of Stratton Mountain, which is privately owned.

User Groups: Hikers and leashed dogs. No bikes, horses, or wheelchair facilities.

Permits: Parking and access are free.

Maps: For a map of hiking trails, refer to map 7 in the Map and Guide to the Appalachian Trail in New Hampshire/Vermont, an eight-map set available for $14.95 from the Appalachian Trail Conservancy. Or get the waterproof End-to-End Map of the Long Trail, available for $9.95 from the Green Mountain Club. For a topographic area map, request Stratton Mountain from the USGS.

Directions: The hike begins from a large parking area on the Arlington–West Wardsboro Road, 13.3 miles east of U.S. 7 in Arlington and 8 miles west of Route 100 in West Wardsboro. The Arlington–West Wardsboro Road is not maintained in winter.

GPS Coordinates: 43.0667 N, 72.9933 W

Contact: Green Mountain National Forest Supervisor, 231 North Main St., Rutland, VT 05701, 802/747-6700, www.fs.fed. us/r9/forests/greenmountain/. Green Mountain Club Inc., 4711 Waterbury-Stowe Rd., Waterbury Center, VT 05677, 802/244-7037, www.greenmountainclub. org. Appalachian Trail Conservancy, 799 Washington St., P.O. Box 807, Harpers Ferry, WV 25425-0807, 304/535-6331, www.appalachiantrail.org.

37 THE LONG TRAIL: ROUTE 9 TO ARLINGTON–WEST WARDSBORO ROAD

22.3 mi one-way/2-3 days 🏃5 ⛰8

in the Green Mountain National Forest between Woodford and Stratton

While much of this 22.3-mile stretch of the Long Trail/Appalachian Trail remains in the woods, it makes for a nice walk along a wooded ridge, on a relatively easy backpacking trip that can be done in two days without extreme effort. And there are a few breathtaking views, most particularly from the fire tower on the 3,748-foot Glastenbury Mountain summit, which offers one of the finest panoramas seen on the Long Trail. The cumulative elevation gain over the course of this hike exceeds 4,000 feet.

From the parking lot, follow the white blazes of the Long Trail (LT) northbound. The trail parallels City Stream briefly and then crosses it on a wooden bridge. Climbing steadily, the trail crosses an old woods road 0.2 mile from the highway and then passes between the twin halves of Split Rock, formerly one giant boulder, at 0.6 mile. At 1.6 miles, a side path leads right a short distance to the Melville Nauheim shelter. Ascending north from the shelter, the trail crosses a power line atop Maple Hill at two miles, which affords a view toward Bennington. The trail then traverses the more level terrain of a wooded ridge and crosses Hell Hollow Brook, a reliable water source, on a bridge at three miles.

Passing through a stand of beech trees, the LT reaches Little Pond Lookout at 5.7 miles, with a good view east, then Glastenbury Lookout at 7.4 miles, with its view of Glastenbury Mountain. The trail then ascends about 600 feet at a moderate angle to Goddard shelter, at 10.1 miles. From the shelter, it's a not-too-rigorous, 0.3-mile walk uphill on the LT to the Glastenbury summit. From the fire tower, the 360-degree view encompasses the Berkshires—most prominently Mount

VERMONT

Greylock—to the south, the Taconic Range to the west, Stratton Mountain to the north, and Somerset Reservoir to the east. Continuing north, the LT descends about 500 feet in elevation and then follows a wooded ridge, with slight rises and dips, for about 4 miles, finally descending at a moderate angle to a side path on the right at 14.2 miles, which leads 0.1 mile to the Kid Gore shelter. About 0.1 mile farther north on the LT, the other end of that side loop reaches the LT near the Caughnawaga tent site. The LT then goes through more slight ups and downs before reaching the Story Spring shelter, 19 miles north of Route 9 and 3.6 miles south of the Arlington–West Wardsboro Road. The LT crosses USFS Road 71 at 20.3 miles, passes beaver ponds, traverses an area often wet and muddy, and then crosses Black Brook, a reliable water source, on a wooden bridge at 21.3 miles. Paralleling the east branch of the Deerfield River, the trail reaches the Arlington–West Wardsboro Road at 22.3 miles. Turn right (east) and walk 200 feet to the parking area.

No-trace camping is permitted within the Green Mountain National Forest. The Green Mountain Club Melville Nauheim shelter is located 1.6 miles north of Route 9 on the Long Trail, the Goddard shelter at 10.1 miles, the Kid Gore shelter at 14.2 miles, the Caughnawaga tent site (a former shelter, now dismantled) at 14.4 miles, and the Story Spring shelter at 19 miles (or 3.6 miles south of the Arlington–West Wardsboro Road).

User Groups: Hikers and leashed dogs. No bikes, horses, or wheelchair facilities.

Permits: Parking and access are free.

Maps: For a map of hiking trails, refer to map 8 in the Map and Guide to the Appalachian Trail in New Hampshire/Vermont, an eight-map set and guidebook available for $14.95 from the Appalachian Trail Conservancy. Or get the waterproof End-to-End Map of the Long Trail, available for $9.95 from the Green Mountain Club. For topographic area maps, request Woodford, Sunderland, and Stratton Mountain from the USGS.

Directions: You need to shuttle two vehicles for this one-way traverse. To hike south to north, as described here, leave one vehicle in the roadside parking area where the Long Trail/Appalachian Trail crosses the Arlington–West Wardsboro Road, 13.3 miles east of U.S. 7 in Arlington and 8 miles west of Route 100 in West Wardsboro. Then drive to the large parking lot at the Long Trail/Appalachian Trail crossing of Route 9, 5.2 miles east of Bennington and 2.8 miles west of Woodford. The Arlington–West Wardsboro Road is not maintained in winter.

GPS Coordinates: 42.8843 N, 73.1157 W

Contact: Green Mountain National Forest Supervisor, 231 North Main St., Rutland, VT 05701, 802/747-6700, www.fs.fed.us/r9/forests/greenmountain/. Green Mountain Club Inc., 4711 Waterbury-Stowe Rd., Waterbury Center, VT 05677, 802/244-7037, www.greenmountainclub.org. Appalachian Trail Conservancy, 799 Washington St., P.O. Box 807, Harpers Ferry, WV 25425-0807, 304/535-6331, www.appalachiantrail.org.

38 GLASTENBURY MOUNTAIN

20.2 mi/2 days 🏃5 ⛰9

in the Green Mountain National Forest between Bennington and Woodford

BEST (

While much of the southern third of the Long Trail, which coincides with the Appalachian Trail, remains in the woods, the fire tower on the 3,748-foot Glastenbury Mountain summit offers a superb panorama of the gently rolling, southern Green Mountains wilderness. Other views include the Berkshires, particularly Mount Greylock, due south, the Taconic Range to the west, Stratton Mountain to the north, and Somerset Reservoir to the east.

This 20.2-mile round-trip—which involves nearly 4,000 feet of uphill—is best spread over two days, with an overnight stay at the spacious Goddard shelter (or tenting in the area). Goddard, which has a nice view south to Greylock, can be a popular place on temperate weekends in summer and fall. See the trail notes for *The Long Trail: Route 9 to Arlington–West Wardsboro Road* listing for the description of this hike from Route 9 to the Goddard shelter. At the shelter, leave your packs behind for the 0.3-mile walk uphill on the LT to the Glastenbury summit and the fire tower. On the second day, you can return the same way you came. Or to avoid backtracking, hike the West Ridge Trail from Goddard shelter, a fairly easy route that leads 7.7 miles to the Bald Mountain summit and a junction at 7.8 miles with the Bald Mountain Trail. Turn left on that trail and descend 1.9 miles to a public road. Turning right on the road, you reach Route 9 in 0.8 mile, 1.2 miles west of the parking lot where you began this hike.

No-trace camping is permitted within the Green Mountain National Forest. The Green Mountain Club Melville Nauheim shelter is located 1.6 miles north of Route 9 on the Long Trail, and the Goddard shelter 10.1 miles north of the highway.

User Groups: Hikers and leashed dogs. No bikes, horses, or wheelchair facilities.

Permits: Parking and access are free.

Maps: For a map of hiking trails, refer to map 8 in the Map and Guide to the Appalachian Trail in New Hampshire/Vermont, an eight-map set for $14.95 from the Appalachian Trail Conservancy. Or get the waterproof End-to-End Map of the Long Trail, available for $9.95 from the Green Mountain Club. For a topographic area map, request Woodford from the USGS.

Directions: Drive to the large parking lot at the Long Trail/Appalachian Trail crossing of Route 9, 5.2 miles east of Bennington and 2.8 miles west of Woodford.

GPS Coordinates: 42.8843 N, 73.1157 W

Contact: Green Mountain National Forest Supervisor, 231 North Main St., Rutland, VT 05701, 802/747-6700, www.fs.fed.us/r9/forests/greenmountain/. Green Mountain Club Inc., 4711 Waterbury-Stowe Rd.,

Waterbury Center, VT 05677, 802/244-7037, www.greenmountainclub.org. Appalachian Trail Conservancy, 799 Washington St., P.O. Box 807, Harpers Ferry, WV 25425-0807, 304/535-6331, www.appalachiantrail.org.

39 THE LONG TRAIL: MASSACHUSETTS LINE TO ROUTE 9

14.2 mi one-way/2 days   🏃3 ▲7

in the Green Mountain National Forest between Clarksburg, Massachusetts, and Woodford

BEST (

This southernmost stretch of the Long Trail—here coinciding with the Appalachian Trail—is for the most part an easy hike along a mostly flat, wooded ridge. The cumulative elevation gain is well under 1,000 feet per day. The southern Green Mountains are not known for spectacular views, although there are a few on this hike. This would be a good overnight backpacking trip for hikers who prefer a woods walk or for a beginner backpacker. Because the Long Trail's southern terminus lies in the forest on the Vermont-Massachusetts border, you have to access this hike via one of two trails, adding either 3.6 miles or 4 miles to this hike's distance.

The Pine Cobble Trail, the more interesting and slightly shorter of the two access trails, reaches the LT in 3.6 miles; from the parking area, walk east on Brooks Road for 0.2 mile and turn left on Pine Cobble Road. The trail begins 0.1 mile up the road on the right and is marked by a sign. Follow the trail's blue blazes to the Pine Cobble summit, looking for blazes to guide the way on a sharp left-hand hook in the trail at 1.5 miles out from the trailhead. After reaching the summit at 1.6 miles, continue north on the trail for the remaining two miles to the Appalachian Trail crossing. At the junction, turn left onto the white-blazed AT. It's a pleasant and easy uphill climb to the state line and the beginning of the Long Trail.

VERMONT

near the southern terminus of Vermont's Long Trail

The white-blazed Appalachian Trail takes four miles to reach the border of the two states, passing a view south to Mount Greylock from an old rock slide 2.4 miles from Route 2. From the state border, the Long Trail (LT) begins at a signpost. In its first miles, the LT follows level, wooded terrain, crossing several old logging roads. At 2.6 miles, the LT passes a junction with the Broad Brook Trail, which branches left (west) and leads four miles to a road outside Williamstown. At 2.8 miles, another junction is reached with the Seth Warner Trail. This short spur leads left (west) 0.2 mile to the Seth Warner shelter. Continuing north, the LT crosses the dirt County Road at 3.1 miles, which connects Pownal and Stamford and may be passable by motor vehicle as far as the Long Trail. The LT ascends several hundred feet over a 3,000-foot hill, drops down the other side, and then makes an easier climb over Consultation Peak (2,810 ft.) before reaching Congdon Camp at 10 miles. At 10.5 miles, the LT crosses the Dunville Hollow Trail, which leads left (west) 0.7 mile to a rough woods road (turning right onto that road leads 1.8 miles to houses on Burgess Road

and 4 miles to Route 9, a mile east of Bennington). The LT follows more easy terrain before climbing slightly to the top of Harmon Hill (2,325 ft.) at 12.5 miles, from which there are some views west toward Bennington and north toward Glastenbury Mountain. Continuing north, the trail descends at an easy grade for a mile, then drops steeply over the final half mile to Route 9.

No-trace camping is permitted within the Green Mountain National Forest. The Seth Warner shelter is 300 yards west of the Long Trail, reached via a side path off the LT, 2.8 miles north of the Massachusetts border. The Congdon Camp shelter is on the Long Trail, 10 miles north of the Massachusetts border and 4.3 miles south of Route 9.

User Groups: Hikers and leashed dogs. No bikes, horses, or wheelchair facilities.

Permits: Parking and access are free.

Maps: For a map of hiking trails, refer to map 8 in the Map and Guide to the Appalachian Trail in New Hampshire/Vermont, an eight-map set available for $14.95 from the Appalachian Trail Conservancy. Or get the waterproof End-to-End Map of the Long

Trail, available for $9.95 from the Green Mountain Club. For topographic area maps, request Pownal, Stamford, Bennington, and Woodford from the USGS.

Directions: You need to shuttle two vehicles for this one-way traverse. To hike south to north, as described here, leave one vehicle in the large parking lot at the Long Trail/Appalachian Trail crossing of Route 9, 5.2 miles east of Bennington and 2.8 miles west of Woodford. Then drive to one of two possible starts for this hike, both in Massachusetts. For the Pine Cobble start, from U.S. 7 in Williamstown, a mile south of the Vermont line and 0.3 mile north of the Hoosic River bridge, turn east on North Housac Road. Drive a half mile and turn right on Brooks Road. Drive 0.7 mile and park in a dirt lot on the left marked by a sign reading, Parking for Pine Cobble Trail. For the Appalachian Trail start, drive to the AT footbridge over the Hoosic River (where there is no convenient parking) on Route 2, 2.9 miles east of Williamstown center and 2.5 miles west of North Adams center. With prior permission only, cars may be parked at Scarafonis Ford dealership on Route 2, 0.8 miles east of the AT crossing, or at the Greylock Community Club, 100 yards east of the AT crossing on Route 2.

GPS Coordinates (Pine Cobble): 42.7161 N, 73.1765 W

GPS Coordinates (Appalachian Trail): 42.6983 N, 73.1479 W

Contact: Green Mountain National Forest Supervisor, 231 North Main St., Rutland, VT 05701, 802/747-6700, www.fs.fed.us/r9/forests/greenmountain/. Green Mountain Club Inc., 4711 Waterbury-Stowe Rd., Waterbury Center, VT 05677, 802/244-7037, www.greenmountainclub.org. Appalachian Trail Conservancy, 799 Washington St., P.O. Box 807, Harpers Ferry, WV 25425-0807, 304/535-6331, www.appalachiantrail.org.

VERMONT

Massachusetts

MASSACHUSETTS

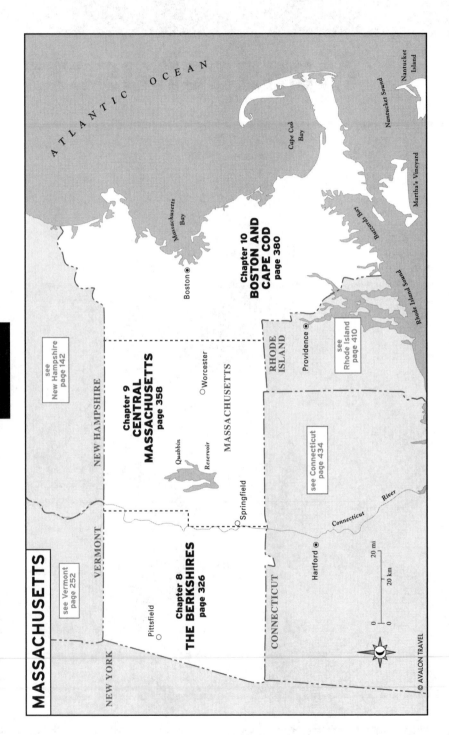

MASSACHUSETTS

ATLANTIC OCEAN

Nantucket Island

Nantucket Sound

Cape Cod Bay

Martha's Vineyard

Buzzards Bay

Massachusetts Bay

see New Hampshire page 142

NEW HAMPSHIRE

Chapter 10
BOSTON AND CAPE COD
page 380

⊙ Boston

○ Worcester

Chapter 9
CENTRAL MASSACHUSETTS
page 358

MASSACHUSETTS

RHODE ISLAND

Rhode Island Sound

Providence ⊙

see Rhode Island page 410

Quabbin Reservoir

see Vermont page 252

VERMONT

○ Springfield

see Connecticut page 434

Connecticut River

Chapter 8
THE BERKSHIRES
page 326

Pittsfield ○

Hartford ⊙

CONNECTICUT

NEW YORK

20 mi
20 km

0
0

© AVALON TRAVEL

THE BERKSHIRES

© JAROSLAW TRAPSZO

BEST HIKES

Less than a three-hour drive from both Boston

and New York City, the rural hills and pastoral landscape of western Massachusetts offer little evidence that such large urban centers are so close by. This is a place where summit views miraculously still yield rolling farmland, quaint village skylines, and unbroken acres of forest; and where traffic jams often come in the form of wild turkeys slowly strutting across a backwoods trail.

The Berkshires region harbors the Bay State's highest peak, 3,491-foot Mount Greylock (technically a part of the Taconic Range), as well as other rugged mountains, including Monument Mountain and Mount Everett. The Appalachian Trail runs for 89 miles through the Berkshires, with such highlights as Mount Greylock and the beautiful Riga Plateau; both are popular destinations for day hiking and backpacking, especially July–September, when camping areas tend to fill up quickly on weekends. But both are also far enough south and low enough that the prime hiking season often begins by mid-spring and lasts through late autumn.

Fall color in the mixed hardwood forests of the Berkshires is spectacular. Foliage usually peaks around Columbus Day weekend, the perfect opportunity for a long weekend in the mountains. (Leaf peepers often use Stockbridge or Lenox as a homebase for outings – each is close to many of the area's most scenic trailheads.) Winters are typically cold and see plenty of snow in the hills. Several of the hikes included in this chapter make excellent, easy-to-moderate outings on snowshoes or cross-country skis.

Though the Appalachian Trail does tend to draw the heaviest hiker traffic, there's plenty of other fine hiking in western Massachusetts, from state forests with hidden gems like Alander Mountain and the Hubbard River Gorge to one of New England's most beautiful waterfalls, Bash Bish Falls. Lining the Connecticut River Valley is the much-loved Mount Tom and the multi-use Norwottuck rail trail, a bike path located near many of the area's colleges. Many of the trails in this rural region simply ramble through the woods and make for great wildlife viewing: hawks, owls, frogs, fish, beaver, otter, fox, gray squirrel, muskrats, white-tailed deer, snowshoe hares, and even the reclusive black bear all call this region home.

Along the Appalachian Trail, dogs must be kept under control, and bikes, horses, hunting, and firearms are prohibited. In state parks and forests, dogs must be leashed; horses are allowed in most state forests and parks, as is hunting in season.

MASSACHUSETTS

MASSACHUSETTS

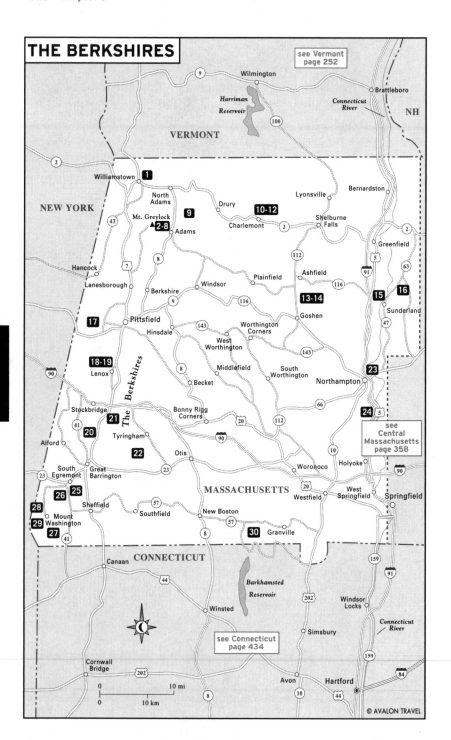

THE BERKSHIRES

see Vermont
page 252

VERMONT

Harriman
Reservoir

Connecticut
River

NH

Wilmington

Brattleboro

NEW YORK

Williamstown **1**

North
Adams

Mt. Greylock

2-8

Adams

Drury

Lyonsville

Bernardston

9

10-12

Charlemont

Shelburne
Falls

Greenfield

Hancock

Lanesborough

Berkshire

Windsor

Plainfield

Ashfield

13-14

Goshen

Sunderland

15

16

Pittsfield

Hinsdale

West
Worthington

Worthington
Corners

Northampton

23

17

18-19

Lenox

Middlefield

South
Worthington

Becket

24

see
Central
Massachusetts
page 358

Stockbridge

21

Bonny Rigg
Corners

20

Tyringham

22

Otis

Woronoco

Holyoke

Alford

South
Egremont

Great
Barrington

MASSACHUSETTS

West
Springfield

Springfield

26 **25**

Sheffield

Southfield

New Boston

Westfield

28

Mount
Washington

30

Granville

29

27

CONNECTICUT

Canaan

Barkhamsted
Reservoir

Windsor
Locks

Connecticut
River

Winsted

see Connecticut
page 434

Simsbury

Cornwall
Bridge

0   10 mi

0   10 km

Avon

Hartford

© AVALON TRAVEL

1 PINE COBBLE

3.2 mi/2 hr

in Williamstown

Tucked away in the Bay State's northwest corner, the extensive quartzite ledges atop 1,894-foot Pine Cobble offer excellent views of the Hoosic Valley, including the low, green hills flanking the Hoosic River and towering Mount Greylock. Ascending at an easy to moderate grade, this 3.2-mile round-trip trek is popular with students at nearby Williams College and—like so many of the hikes in the Berkshire region—is an adventurous outing for young children. Passing through an unusual forest mix of oak and white pine, this hike nets an elevation gain of about 900 feet.

From the parking area, walk across Pine Cobble Road to the Pine Cobble Trail. Follow the trail's blue blazes and well-worn path. In less than a mile, pass a side path on the right leading 350 feet downhill to Bear Spring, a worthwhile detour. Continuing along the Pine Cobble Trail, at 1.5 miles from the parking area, the blue blazes hook sharply left and a spur path leads to the right 0.1 mile to Pine Cobble's summit. Take the spur path, soon reaching a ledge with views west to the Taconic Range. About 100 feet farther uphill is the summit. The best views are from the open ledges about 30 feet beyond the summit. Looking south (right) you see Mount Greylock; east lie the Clarksburg State Forest's woods and hills; and to the north extends an array of hills traversed by Appalachian Trail hikers on their way into Vermont. Return the same way you came.

Special note: Hikers interested in a longer outing can continue north on the Pine Cobble Trail 0.5 mile to the Appalachian Trail, turn left (north), and hike another 0.5 mile to a view south of Mount Greylock from Eph's Lookout. The added distance makes the entire round-trip 5.2 miles.

User Groups: Hikers and dogs. This trail is not suitable for bikes or horses; no wheelchair facilities.

Permits: Parking and access are free.

Maps: A map of area trails is available from the Appalachian Mountain Club (Northern Berkshires/Southwestern Massachusetts/Wachusett Mountain, $5.95). For a topographic area map, request North Adams from the USGS.

Directions: From the junction of U.S. 7 and Route 2 in Williamstown, drive east on Route 2 for 0.6 mile, then turn left on Cole Avenue at the first traffic light. Drive another 0.8 mile, crossing a bridge over the Hoosic River and railroad tracks and then turn right on North Housac Road. Follow it 0.4 mile to a left turn onto Pine Cobble Road and continue to the parking area 0.2 mile up on the left, across the street from the trailhead.

GPS Coordinates: 42.7157 N, 73.1849 W

Contact: Williamstown Rural Lands Foundation, 671 Cold Spring Rd., Williamstown, MA 01267, 413/458-2494, www.wrlf.org.

2 MOUNT GREYLOCK: MONEY BROOK FALLS

5 mi/3 hr

in Mount Greylock State Reservation in Williamstown, North Adams, Adams, and Lanesborough

Money Brook Falls tumbles from an impressive height of 40 feet into a ravine choked with trees that haven't survived the steep, erosive terrain. Despite being one of the most spectacular natural features on the biggest hill in the Bay State, it is also among Massachusetts's best-kept secrets. Keeping foot traffic light could be the trail's several stream crossings, some of which can be difficult in high water, especially in late spring when the falls are at their viewing peak.

From the parking area, walk past the gate onto the Hopper Trail and follow a flat, grassy lane for 0.2 mile. Where the Hopper Trail diverges right, continue straight ahead on the

© JAROSLAW TRAPSZO

Money Brook Falls on Mount Greylock

Money Brook Trail (look for the trail marker). The trail ascends gently at first, but after passing the Mount Prospect Trail junction at 1.5 miles, it goes through some short, steep stretches. At 2.4 miles, turn right onto a side path that leads 0.1 mile to the falls. Hike back the way you came.

There is a lean-to and a dispersed backcountry camping zone along the Money Brook Trail.

User Groups: Hikers and leashed dogs. No horses, bikes, or wheelchair facilities.

Permits: A daily fee of $2 is collected mid-May–mid-October at some parking areas.

Maps: Find free, basic trail maps of Mount Greylock State Reservation at the park visitors center or online at the Massachusetts Division of State Parks and Recreation website. A map of area trails is available from the Appalachian Mountain Club (Northern Berkshires/Southwestern Massachusetts/Wachusett Mountain, $5.95). For topographic area maps,

request North Adams and Cheshire from the USGS.

Directions: From Route 43 in Williamstown, 2.5 miles south of the junction of Routes 43 and 2 and 2.3 miles north of the junction of Route 43 and U.S. 7, turn east onto Hopper Road at a sign for Mount Hope Park. Drive 1.4 miles and bear left onto a dirt road. Continue 0.7 mile to the parking area on the right.

From the mid-December close of hunting season through mid-May, roads within the state reservation are closed to vehicles (and groomed for snowmobiles), but Hopper Road is maintained to this trailhead.

GPS Coordinates: 42.6546 N, 73.1986 W

Contact: Mount Greylock State Reservation, P.O. Box 138, Rockwell Rd., Lanesborough, MA 01237, 413/499-4262 or 413/499-4263. Massachusetts Division of State Parks and Recreation, 251 Causeway St., Suite 600, Boston, MA 02114-2104, 617/626-1250, www.mass.gov/dcr/parks/mtGreylock.

❸ MOUNT GREYLOCK CIRCUIT

12 mi/8 hr

in Mount Greylock State Reservation in Williamstown, North Adams, Adams, and Lanesborough

A long, scenic loop around the highest peak in Massachusetts, 3,491-foot Mount Greylock, this 12-mile circuit takes in as many of the mountain's best features as possible on a day hike. Climb through and around the spectacular glacial cirque known as the Hopper, pass two waterfalls, travel over the summit, follow a stretch of the Appalachian Trail, and then descend through the rugged ravine of beautiful Money Brook. You can shave the distance by two miles by skipping the side trail to March Cataract Falls, and another mile by skipping Robinson Point. This entire hike gains more than 2,500 feet in elevation.

From the parking area, walk past the gate

MASSACHUSETTS

onto the Hopper Trail and follow a flat, grassy lane 0.2 mile to a junction with the Money Brook Trail. Bear right with the Hopper Trail, ascending an old, and sometimes steep logging road, another two miles until you reach Sperry Road. Turn left and walk the road 0.1 mile; just before the parking area on the right, turn left on a dirt campground road. Walk about 200 feet, past the Chimney Group Camping Area, and turn left at a sign for the March Cataract Falls Trail. It leads a mile, descending through switchbacks, to March Cataract Falls, a 30-foot falls that usually maintains a flow even during dry seasons.

Backtrack to Sperry Road, turn left, walk about 100 yards past the parking area, and then turn left at a sign onto the Hopper Trail. The wide path climbs at a moderate grade past a short falls. Where the Deer Hill Trail diverges right, bear left to stay on the Hopper Trail. Within a mile of Sperry Road, where the Hopper Trail makes a sharp right, turn left onto the Overlook Trail. You reach the first view of the Hopper within minutes, though trees partially obstruct it. A half mile down the Overlook Trail lies the second view, which is better; Stony Ledge is visible across the Hopper to the west. Continue on the Overlook Trail to the paved Notch Road, 1.2 miles from the Hopper Trail junction. Turn left and walk the road downhill 0.1 mile, past a day-use parking turnout, then turn left onto a trail marked by blue blazes. It descends steeply 0.2 mile to Robinson Point and a view of the Hopper superior to anything on the Overlook Trail. Double back to the Overlook Trail, cross Notch Road, and follow the Overlook Trail uphill for 0.4 mile to the white-blazed Appalachian Trail (AT). Turn left on the AT, following it across the parking lot to the summit, where you find the War Memorial Tower and the Bascom Lodge. The best views are to the east from the meadow beyond the tower; there are also good views to the west.

From the tower, follow the AT north. About a mile from the summit is a good eastern view. About 2.4 miles from the summit, a side trail

War Memorial Tower at the summit of Mount Greylock

© JAROSLAW TRAPSZO

MASSACHUSETTS

leads left to Notch Road, but continue 0.2 mile straight ahead on the AT over Mount Williams, one of Greylock's secondary summits. The AT swings left here, descending easily 0.9 mile to Notch Road. Cross the road and, after 0.1 mile in the woods, turn left onto the Money Brook Trail; in 0.2 mile, pass a short side path leading to the Wilbur's Clearing shelter. The trail reaches a side path 0.7 mile beyond the shelter that leads a short distance to rugged Money Brook Falls. Backtrack from the falls on the side path and continue on the Money Brook Trail, following the brook through a wild, narrow valley, with a few crossings that could be tricky in high water. Nearly a mile past the falls, the Mount Prospect Trail branches right; stay on the Money Brook Trail another 1.5 miles to the Hopper Trail; continue straight ahead on the Hopper Trail 0.2 mile back to the parking area.

There is a lean-to and a dispersed backcountry camping zone along the Money Brook Trail.

User Groups: Hikers and leashed dogs. This trail should not be attempted in winter except by hikers prepared for severe winter weather. No bikes, horses, or wheelchair facilities.

Permits: A daily fee of $2 is collected mid-May–mid-October at some parking areas.

Maps: Find free, basic trail maps of Mount Greylock State Reservation at the park visitors center or online at the Massachusetts Division of State Parks and Recreation website. A map of area trails is available from the Appalachian Mountain Club (Northern Berkshires/Southwestern Massachusetts/Wachusett Mountain, $5.95). For topographic area maps, request North Adams and Cheshire from the USGS.

Directions: From Route 43 in Williamstown, 2.5 miles south of the junction of Routes 43 and 2 in Williamstown and 2.3 miles north of the junction of Route 43 and U.S. 7, turn east onto Hopper Road at a sign for Mount Hope Park. Drive 1.4 miles and bear left onto a dirt road. Continue 0.7 mile to the parking area on the right.

From the mid-December close of hunting season through mid-May, roads within the state reservation are closed to vehicles (and groomed for snowmobiles), but Hopper Road is maintained to this trailhead.

GPS Coordinates: 42.6546 N, 73.1986 W

Contact: Mount Greylock State Reservation, P.O. Box 138, Rockwell Rd., Lanesborough, MA 01237, 413/499-4262 or 413/499-4263. Massachusetts Division of State Parks and Recreation, 251 Causeway St., Suite 600, Boston, MA 02114-2104, 617/626-1250, www.mass.gov/dcr/parks/mtGreylock.

◼ MOUNT GREYLOCK: ROBINSON POINT
0.4 mi/0.5 hr

in Mount Greylock State Reservation in Williamstown, North Adams, Adams, and Lanesborough

The high ledge at Robinson Point offers one of the best views of the Hopper, the huge glacial cirque carved into Mount Greylock's northwest flank. Visible from the ledge are Stony Ledge, at the end of the ridge forming the Hopper's western wall; Williamstown, in the valley beyond the Hopper's mouth; and the Taconic Range on the horizon. This very short trek is not too easy: the trail's steep descent could be a bit too hard on the knees for some hikers.

From the parking turnout on Notch Road, walk downhill just a few steps and then turn left onto a trail marked by blue blazes. It descends a very steep 0.2 mile to Robinson Point. Return the same way.

User Groups: Hikers and leashed dogs. This trail is not suitable for horses. Bikes are prohibited; no wheelchair facilities.

Permits: A daily fee of $2 is collected mid-May–mid-October at some parking areas.

Maps: Find free, basic trail maps of Mount Greylock State Reservation at the park visitors center or online at the Massachusetts Division of State Parks and Recreation website. A map of area trails is available from the Appalachian Mountain Club (Northern Berkshires/Southwestern Massachusetts/Wachusett Mountain, $5.95). For topographic area maps, request North Adams and Cheshire from the USGS.

Directions: From Route 2 in Williamstown, 3.7 miles east of the junction of Routes 2 and 43, turn south onto Notch Road. Follow Notch Road up the mountain for 7.4 miles to a turnout for day-use parking on the right. From U.S. 7 in Lanesborough, 1.3 miles north of town center and 4.2 miles south of the Lanesborough/New Ashford line, turn east onto North Main Street. Drive 0.7 mile and turn right onto Quarry Road. Continue 0.6 mile and bear left at a sign reading Rockwell Road to Greylock. The Greylock Visitor Center is 0.6 mile farther up that road. From the visitors center, follow Rockwell Road up the mountain for 7.2 miles, turn left onto Notch Road, and continue 0.9 mile to the day-use parking turnout on the left.

From the mid-December close of hunting

season through mid-May, roads within the state reservation are closed to vehicles (and groomed for snowmobiles). This trailhead is not accessible by car in the winter months. GPS Coordinates: 42.6416 N, 73.1660 W
Contact: Mount Greylock State Reservation, P.O. Box 138, Rockwell Rd., Lanesborough, MA 01237, 413/499-4262 or 413/499-4263. Massachusetts Division of State Parks and Recreation, 251 Causeway St., Suite 600, Boston, MA 02114-2104, 617/626-1250, www.mass.gov/dcr/parks/mtGreylock.

5 MOUNT GREYLOCK: DEER HILL TRAIL

2.6 mi/1.5 hr

in Mount Greylock State Reservation in Williamstown, North Adams, Adams, and Lanesborough

Passing through a deep, dark grove of hemlock, this fairly easy two-mile loop leads to Deer Hill Falls, a feathering cascade of water on the upper reaches of Roaring Brook. If you have time, walk the mile from the parking area on this hike to the end of Sperry Road for excellent views from Stony Ledge of the huge glacial cirque on Greylock known as the Hopper.

From the parking area, walk or bike 0.2 mile up Sperry Road to the trailhead; stash your bike in the woods near the trailhead. the Campground Trail/Deer Hill Trail will be on the left (east). Within 0.4 mile of the trailhead, the flat, wide path crosses a brook and then comes to a right turn, descending past a grove of tall hemlocks. Just beyond, a lean-to is reached at the one-mile mark. Here, the trail descends abruptly, crosses over a stream on a wooden bridge, and then climbs steeply up to Deer Hill Falls. Another 0.2 mile above the falls, make a right turn onto the Roaring Brook Trail, which leads back to Sperry Road. Walk back 0.6 mile to the parking area at Rockwell Road.

on Deer Hill Trail

© JAROSLAW TRAPSZO

There is a lean-to for overnight camping along the Deer Hill Trail.
User Groups: Hiker and leashed dogs. This trail is not suitable for horses; no wheelchair facilities. Bikes are prohibited.
Permits: A daily fee of $2 is collected mid-May–mid-October at some parking areas.
Maps: Find free, basic trail maps of Mount Greylock State Reservation at the park visitors center or online at the Massachusetts Division of State Parks and Recreation website. A map of area trails is available from the Appalachian Mountain Club (Northern Berkshires/Southwestern Massachusetts/Wachusett Mountain, $5.95). For topographic area maps, request North Adams and Cheshire from the USGS.
Directions: From Route 2 in Williamstown, 3.7 miles east of the junction of Routes 2 and 43, turn south onto Notch Road. Follow Notch Road up the mountain for 8.3 miles and turn right onto Rockwell Road. Continue 1.7 miles to the parking area at Sperry Road

(Sperry Road was closed to vehicle traffic in 2008). Walk or bike the road 0.2 mile to the trailhead.

From the mid-December close of hunting season through mid-May, roads within the state reservation are closed to vehicles (and groomed for snowmobiles). This trailhead is not accessible by car in winter.

GPS Coordinates: 42.6242 N, 73.1899 W

Contact: Mount Greylock State Reservation, P.O. Box 138, Rockwell Rd., Lanesborough, MA 01237, 413/499-4262 or 413/499-4263. Massachusetts Division of State Parks and Recreation, 251 Causeway St., Suite 600, Boston, MA 02114-2104, 617/626-1250, www.mass.gov/dcr/parks/mtGreylock.

6 MOUNT GREYLOCK: MARCH CATARACT FALLS/ STONY LEDGE

3.2 mi/1.5 hr

in Mount Greylock State Reservation in Williamstown, North Adams, Adams, and Lanesborough

A short, somewhat steep walk downhill from the Sperry Road Campground leads to March Cataract Falls, a 30-foot-high water curtain tumbling down the western slope of Mount Greylock. The falls are at their most magnificent in late spring and early summer; by mid-summer, it's likely that all you could find here is a gentle trickle of water.

From the parking area, walk or bike 0.6 mile to the dirt campground access road, a short half-circle that takes you to the March Cataract Falls Trail, marked by a sign. Heading east, the trail starts out on easy ground and then descends through switchbacks, reaching March Cataract Falls a mile from the campground. Though steep in sections, the trail is still suitable for kids. Head back along the same route.

Note: If the falls are just too dried up to be of any scenic value, head back to Sperry Road and walk or bike 0.5 mile north to the end of the road. Here, find Stony Ledge and matchless views of the huge glacial cirque on Greylock known as the Hopper. This detour adds an additional one mile to the round-trip, but is an easy walk on relatively flat road.

User Groups: Hikers and leashed dogs. The trail to the falls is not suitable for horses or bikes; no wheelchair facilities.

Permits: A daily fee of $2 is collected mid-May–mid-October at some parking areas.

Maps: Find free, basic trail maps of Mount Greylock State Reservation at the park visitors center or online at the Massachusetts Division of State Parks and Recreation website. A map of area trails is available from the Appalachian Mountain Club (Northern Berkshires/Southwestern Massachusetts/Wachusett Mountain, $5.95). For topographic area maps, request North Adams and Cheshire from the USGS.

Directions: From Route 2, 3.7 miles east of the junction of Routes 2 and 43 in Williamstown and 1.3 miles west of the junction of Routes 2 and 8A in North Adams, turn south onto Notch Road. Follow Notch Road up the mountain for 8.3 miles and turn right onto Rockwell Road. Continue 1.7 miles to the parking area at Sperry Road (Sperry Road closed to vehicle traffic in 2008). Walk or bike the road 0.6 mile to the dirt campground road and trailhead. Bike racks are available at the campground entrance. (This hike leaves from a trailhead only steps away from the walk-in campground off Sperry Road.)

From the mid-December close of hunting season through mid-May, roads in the state reservation are closed to vehicles (and groomed for snowmobiles). This trailhead is not accessible by car in winter.

GPS Coordinates: 42.6242 N, 73.1899 W

Contact: Mount Greylock State Reservation, P.O. Box 138, Rockwell Rd., Lanesborough, MA 01237, 413/499-4262 or 413/499-4263. Massachusetts Division of State Parks and Recreation, 251 Causeway St., Suite 600, Boston, MA 02114-2104, 617/626-1250, www.mass.gov/dcr/parks/mtGreylock.

⑦ MOUNT GREYLOCK: JONES NOSE

1 mi/0.75 hr   👫2 ⛰8

in Mount Greylock State Reservation in
Williamstown, North Adams, Adams, and
Lanesborough

Jones Nose (2,552 ft.) is an open ledge on
Greylock's southern ridge with broad views to
the south and west all the way to the Catskill
Mountains of New York State. Once an upland farm pasture and still relatively clear of
forest growth, Jones Nose is a good place to
catch a sunset or bring your binoculars for a
fun afternoon of bird-watching. From the aery
perch, you are almost certain to see hawks circling and swooping overhead, but keep an eye
out for some of the northern forest dwelling
birds that breed on the mountain, including
swainson's thrush, yellow-rumped warbler,
and dark-eyed junco.

From the parking area, walk north on the
Jones Nose Trail (look for the trail marker).
A well-beaten path, the trail passes through
woods, crosses a meadow, and then ascends
steeply to a side path on the left, a half mile
from the parking lot. Follow that path 40 feet
to the viewpoint. Return the way you came.

User Groups: Hikers and leashed dogs. This
trail is not suitable for horses; no wheelchair
facilities. Bikes are prohibited.

Permits: A daily fee of $2 is collected mid-
May–mid-October at some parking areas.

Maps: Find free, basic trail maps of Mount
Greylock State Reservation at the park visitors
center or online at the Massachusetts Division of State Parks and Recreation website.
A map of area trails is available from the Appalachian Mountain Club (Northern Berk-
shires/Southwestern Massachusetts/Wachusett
Mountain, $5.95). For topographic area maps,
request North Adams and Cheshire from the
USGS.

Directions: From Route 2 in Williamstown,
3.7 miles east of the junction of Routes 2
and 43, turn south onto Notch Road. Follow
Notch Road up the mountain for 8.3 miles
and turn right onto Rockwell Road. Continue
3.5 miles to the Jones Nose parking lot on
the left.

From the mid-December close of hunting
season through mid-May, roads in the state
reservation are closed to vehicles (and groomed
for snowmobiles). This trailhead is not accessible by car in winter.

GPS Coordinates: 42.6014 N, 73.2007 W

Contact: Mount Greylock State Reservation,
P.O. Box 138, Rockwell Rd., Lanesborough,
MA 01237, 413/499-4262 or 413/499-4263.
Massachusetts Division of State Parks and
Recreation, 251 Causeway St., Suite 600, Bos-
ton, MA 02114-2104, 617/626-1250, www.
mass.gov/dcr/parks/mtGreylock.

⑧ MOUNT GREYLOCK: ROUNDS ROCK

1 mi/0.75 hr   👫1 ⛰9

in Mount Greylock State Reservation in
Williamstown, North Adams, Adams, and
Lanesborough

This easy one-mile loop to a pair of knobby
ledges offers some of the most dramatic views
to be had on Mount Greylock—and for little
effort. Passing through former 1800s farmland
now reforested with northern hardwoods, the
short ramble through the woods leads to a
sweeping vista extending south and west across
the Berkshires and the Catskill Mountains. A
terrific introductory hike for young children
and an easy way to catch a spectacular sunset,
this hike is at its best in early fall when the
views burst with colorful foliage.

From the turnout, cross the road to the
Rounds Rock Trail. Follow it through woods
and across blueberry patches about a half mile
to where a side path (at a sign that reads Scenic
Vista) leads left about 75 yards to a sweeping
view south from atop a low cliff. Backtrack
and turn left on the main trail, following it
0.1 mile to another, shorter side path and a

MASSACHUSETTS

© JAROSLAW TRAPSZO

a dog's eye view from the Mount Greylock summit

view south and west. Complete the loop on the Rounds Rock Trail by following it out to Rockwell Road. Turn right and walk along the road about 150 yards back to the turnout.

User Groups: Hikers and leashed dogs. This trail is not suitable for horses or skis; no wheelchair facilities. Bikes are prohibited.

Permits: A daily fee of $2 is collected mid-May–mid-October at some parking areas.

Maps: Find free, basic trail maps of Mount Greylock State Reservation at the park visitors center or online at the Massachusetts Division of State Parks and Recreation website. A map of area trails is available from the Appalachian Mountain Club (Northern Berkshires/Southwestern Massachusetts/Wachusett Mountain, $5.95). For topographic area maps, request North Adams and Cheshire from the USGS.

Directions: From Route 2 in Williamstown, 3.7 miles east of the junction of Routes 2 and 43, turn south onto Notch Road. Follow Notch Road up the mountain for 8.3 miles and turn right onto Rockwell Road. Continue 4.2 miles to a turnout on the left, across from the Rounds Rock Trail.

From the mid-December close of hunting season through mid-May, roads in the state reservation are closed to vehicles (and groomed for snowmobiles). This trailhead is not accessible by car in winter.

GPS Coordinates: 42.6014 N, 73.2007 W

Contact: Mount Greylock State Reservation, P.O. Box 138, Rockwell Rd., Lanesborough, MA 01237, 413/499-4262 or 413/499-4263. Massachusetts Division of State Parks and Recreation, 251 Causeway St., Suite 600, Boston, MA 02114-2104, 617/626-1250, www.mass.gov/dcr/parks/mtGreylock.

9 SPRUCE HILL
3 mi/1.5 hr   🚶🚶3 ⛰8

in Savoy Mountain State Forest near North Adams and Adams

BEST (

Overshadowed by Mount Greylock to the west and the Mohawk Trail State Forest to the east, Savoy Mountain State Forest—the fourth-largest piece of Bay State public land—is also one of the state's least-known preserves. Even with 48 miles of hiking, mountain biking, and snowshoeing trails, visitor traffic is relatively low and the forest retains a rustic backwoods feel. This easy, three-mile hike provides some of the most attractive views in the region for such minimal effort; only the last stretch turns somewhat steep, and only briefly at that. Spruce Hill's summit is at 2,566 feet. The total elevation gained is about 1,200 feet.

From the parking turnout, continue for 100 feet up the forest road and turn right onto a trail signed for Spruce Hill, Hawk Lookout. Within 150 yards, the trail crosses a power line easement. About a quarter mile farther, it crosses a second set of power lines; just beyond those lines, continue straight onto the Busby Trail (marked by a sign), going uphill and following blue blazes. In a quarter mile or so, the trail crosses an old stone wall. Then, within the span of about a quarter mile, you cross a small brook, pass an old stone foundation on your right, and then pass over a stone wall. On the other side of the wall, another trail branches left, but continue straight ahead, still following the blue blazes. About 0.1 mile farther, the trail forks; both forks go to the summit, but the right option is easier and more direct, reaching the bare top of Spruce Hill within a quarter mile.

Though a few low trees grow in isolated groves on the hilltop, the summit's several open areas provide excellent views in all directions. To the west lies the Hoosic River Valley, where Route 8 runs through the towns of Adams and North Adams. Farther northwest you can see Williamstown. Across the valley rises the highest peak in Massachusetts, 3,491-foot Mount Greylock, with a prominent war memorial tower on its summit. And yes, you will see hawks. The counting station at Spruce Hill documents up to 500 birds each year, mostly seen in pairs or solitary flight. Other birds in the area include chickadees, warblers, and thrushes. Descend the way you came.

User Groups: Hikers and leashed dogs. This trail is not suitable for horses or bikes; no wheelchair facilities.

Permits: A daily parking fee of $5 is collected mid-May–mid-October.

Maps: A map of area trails is available from the Appalachian Mountain Club (Northern Berkshires/Southwestern Massachusetts/Wachusett Mountain, $5.95). For topographic area maps, request North Adams, Cheshire, and Ashfield from the USGS.

Directions: From Route 2 in Florida, 6.9 miles west of the Florida/Savoy town line and 0.4 mile east of the Florida/North Adams line, turn south onto Central Shaft Road. Continue 2.9 miles, following signs for the Savoy Mountain State Forest, to the headquarters on the right (where maps are available). Less than 0.1 mile beyond the headquarters, leave your car at the parking turnout at the start of Old Florida Road, an unmaintained woods road.

GPS Coordinates: 42.6580 N, 73.0556 W

Contact: Savoy Mountain State Forest, 260 Central Shaft Rd., Florida, MA, 01247, 413/663-8469. Massachusetts Division of State Parks and Recreation, 251 Causeway St., Suite 600, Boston, MA 02114-2104, 617/626-1250, www.mass.gov/dcr/parks/western/svym.htm.

🔟 MOHAWK TRAIL

5 mi/3.5 hr   🚶2   ⛰7

in Mohawk Trail State Forest in Charlemont

BEST (

This mostly wooded ridge walk follows a historical route: the original Mohawk Trail, used for hundreds of years by the area's Native Americans as a connector path between the Connecticut and Hudson River Valleys. With such a storied past and still-rustic feel (parts of the route pass through a towering old-growth forest), the Mohawk Trail is a great way to bring history alive for kids. The hike ascends about 700 feet.

From the visitors center parking area, continue up the paved road, bearing left toward the camping area where the road forks, then bearing right at a sign for the Indian Trail

a birch-lined trail in the Mohawk Trail State Forest, Charlemont

at 0.7 mile. The trail remains flat for only about 200 feet, then turns right, and begins the steep and relentless ascent for a half mile to the ridge. This trail is not well marked and can be easy to lose in a few places. Once atop the ridge, the walking grows much easier and you will quickly reach a well-marked trail junction. Here, turn right onto the Todd Mountain Trail, following it a half mile to an open ledge with a good view overlooking the Cold River Valley. Double back to the trail junction and this time, continue straight ahead on the Clark Mountain Trail; you will see disks on trees indicating that this is the old Mohawk Trail. The easy, wide path predates European settlement here by hundreds of years. About 0.8 mile past the trail junction, the Clark Mountain/Mohawk Trail swings right and begins descending; double back from here to the junction and descend the Indian Trail back to the start.

User Groups: Hikers and leashed dogs. This trail is not suitable for bikes or horses; no wheelchair facilities.

Permits: A daily parking fee of $5 is collected mid-May–mid-October.

Maps: A free, basic trail and contour map of Mohawk Trail State Forest is available at the state forest headquarters or at the Massachusetts Division of State Parks and Recreation website. For a topographic area map, request Rowe from the USGS.

Directions: From the junction of Routes 2 and 8A in Charlemont, follow Route 2 west for 3.7 miles to the state forest entrance road on the right. Drive the state forest road for 0.2 mile, through a gate, and park just beyond the gate on the left, behind the headquarters building.

GPS Coordinates: 42.6430 N, 72.9464 W

Contact: Mohawk Trail State Forest, P.O. Box 7, Rte. 2, Charlemont, MA 01339, 413/339-5504. Massachusetts Division of State Parks and Recreation, 251 Causeway St., Suite 600, Boston, MA 02114-2104, 617/626-1250, www.mass.gov/dcr/parks/western/mhwk.htm.

11 GIANT TREES OF CLARK RIDGE

1.5 mi/1 hr 🏃4 ⛰8

in Mohawk Trail State Forest in Charlemont

The steep, rugged terrain you encounter on the north flank of Clark Ridge is probably a big part of the reason loggers left so many giant trees untouched here over the past few centuries—a time period during which most of New England was deforested. Within an area of about 75 acres are an uncounted number of sugar maple, red oak, white ash, beech, and other hardwoods reaching more than 120 feet into the sky, and aged 200–300 years. One respected regional expert has identified a 160-foot white pine here as the tallest living thing in New England. Walking around in this cathedral of bark is a rare and stirring experience. And unlike other hikes in this book, this one doesn't follow an established trail. It begins on an abandoned, somewhat overgrown logging road and becomes a bushwhack through the woods.

From either parking area near the Zoar picnic area, walk across the bridge and immediately turn left, following a faint footpath down across a wash and a cleared area and onto a distinct trail—actually an abandoned logging road. The road dissipates within about a half mile, but you need only to continue walking a quarter mile, then turn right, and bushwhack uphill on the ridge to find the tall trees—there is no mistaking it when you get there. Other bushwhackers before you may have already carved out a pretty recognizable trail, but this is still off-grid hiking; bring a compass, be sure to remember how to find your way back to the logging road, and allow extra time for taking in the wild beauty of this ancient forest.

User Groups: Hikers and leashed dogs. This trail is not suitable for bikes or horses; no wheelchair facilities.

Permits: A daily parking fee of $5 is collected mid-May–mid-October.

Maps: There is no trail map for this hike, but a free, basic map of the Mohawk Trail State Forest is available at the state forest headquarters or at the Massachusetts Division of State Parks and Recreation website. For a topographic area map, request Rowe from the USGS.

Directions: From the junction of Routes 2 and 8A in Charlemont, follow Route 2 for 1.6 miles to a right turn at the Rowe/Monroe sign. Proceed 2.2 miles, bear left, and continue another 0.8 mile to the Zoar picnic area on the left, where there is parking, or to parking 0.1 mile farther on the right, immediately before the bridge over Deerfield River.

GPS Coordinates: 42.6523 N, 72.9514 W

Contact: Mohawk Trail State Forest, P.O. Box 7, Rte. 2, Charlemont, MA 01339, 413/339-5504. Massachusetts Division of State Parks and Recreation, 251 Causeway St., Suite 600, Boston, MA 02114-2104, 617/626-1250, www.mass.gov/dcr/parks/western/mhwk.htm.

⓬ THE LOOKOUT
2.2 mi/1.5 hr

in Mohawk Trail State Forest in Charlemont

Here's an easy 2.2-mile walk through the tranquil woods of Mohawk Trail State Forest to a lookout with a good view east toward the pastoral Deerfield River Valley and Charlemont. Without any real rugged footing to be weary of, it's a great opportunity to spot squirrels, rabbits, and deer darting to and fro along the trail. Even ruffled grouse are seen in the area, but stay quiet when you spot one—the woodland birds often explode into flight and beat their wings very loudly when surprised.

From the parking turnout and picnic area, cross the road to the Totem Trail, which begins behind a stone marker for the state forest. The trail is obvious and well marked, crossing a small brook and reaching the overlook in 1.1 miles. Hike back along the same route. This hike climbs about 600 feet.

User Groups: Hikers and leashed dogs. The trail is not suitable for bikes or horses; no wheelchair facilities.

Permits: A daily parking fee of $5 is collected mid-May–mid-October.

Maps: A free, basic trail and contour map of Mohawk Trail State Forest is available at the state forest headquarters or at the Massachusetts Division of State Parks and Recreation website. For a topographic area map, request Rowe from the USGS.

Directions: From the junction of Routes 2 and 8A in Charlemont, follow Route 2 west for 4.6 miles to a parking turnout and picnic area (0.9 mile west of the Mohawk Trail State Forest's main entrance).

GPS Coordinates: 42.6420 N, 72.9476 W

Contact: Mohawk Trail State Forest, P.O. Box 7, Rte. 2, Charlemont, MA 01339, 413/339-5504. Massachusetts Division of State Parks and Recreation, 251 Causeway St., Suite 600, Boston, MA 02114-2104, 617/626-1250, www.mass.gov/dcr/parks/western/mhwk.htm.

MASSACHUSETTS

13 FIRE TOWER HIKE
3 mi/1.5 hr   👫2 △7

in D.A.R. State Forest in Goshen

A winding walk through the 1,800-acre D.A.R. State Forest, a tract of former farmland donated to the state by the Daughters of the American Revolution (D.A.R.), this hike passes through lush woodlands on the way to panoramic views from the state forest's fire tower. Out and back, the total elevation gain on this trek is a modest 250 feet.

From the parking area at Moore Hill Road, this hike begins between the boat launch and the night registration office and follows the Long Trail (not to be confused with the trail running the length of Vermont). The path is well marked as it twists and turns its way 1.5 miles through the forest to reach the fire tower atop Moore's Hill (1,697 ft.). Climbing the tower's steps, views of the surrounding countryside stretch all the way northeast to New Hampshire's Mount Monadnock, southeast to the Holyoke Range and Mount Tom, and northwest to Mount Greylock. Descend the same way you hiked up.

User Groups: Hikers and leashed dogs. This trail is not suitable for bikes or horses; no wheelchair facilities.

Permits: A daily parking fee of $5 is collected mid-May–mid-October.

Maps: A free trail map is available at the state forest or at the Massachusetts Division of State Parks and Recreation website. For topographic area maps, request Holyoke from the USGS.

Directions: From North Main Street in Northampton, follow Route 9 west for 12 miles to Goshen. Turn right onto Cape Street/Route 112 north and continue for 0.7 mile. The park entrance is on the right at Moore Hill Road. In summer, park in the second lot along Moore Hill Road, located just past the left turn for the boat launch and nature center. In winter, park in the first lot, near the restrooms and warming hut (Moore Hill Road is not maintained beyond that point).

GPS Coordinates: 42.4569 N, 72.7917 W
Contact: D.A.R. State Forest, Rte. 112, Goshen, MA, 413/268-7098; or mail to 555 East St., RFD 1, Williamsburg, MA 01096. Massachusetts Division of State Parks and Recreation, 251 Causeway St., Suite 600, Boston, MA 02114-2104, 617/626-1250, www.mass.gov/dcr/parks/western/darf.htm.

14 BALANCING ROCK
1 mi/0.75 hr   👫2 △7

in D.A.R. State Forest in Goshen

Here is a hike of about one mile that is both worthwhile and easy—even for young children—leading to the "balancing rock," a gravity defying glacial erratic set in the middle of a beautiful deciduous forest (a blazing sight for the eyes in autumn). Other erratics are tucked away along the trail, all dumped here thousands of years ago by melting Ice Age glaciers.

From the summer parking lot along Moore Hill Road, cross the road to head south along the blue-blazed woods road. At the intersection of several trails, turn left onto the trail with orange blazes and follow it all the way to Balancing Rock, a truck-size boulder in the woods. Continue on the orange-blazed trail past Balancing Rock, paralleling a stone wall at one point and then ducking into deep woods for a short loop back to the multi-trail junction. Reaching the junction, turn left on the blue-blazed trail and return to the parking lot.

User Groups: Hikers and leashed dogs. No horses, bikes, or wheelchair facilities.

Permits: A daily parking fee of $5 is collected mid-May–mid-October.

Maps: A free trail map is available at the state forest or at the Massachusetts Division of State Parks and Recreation website.

Directions: From North Main Street in Northampton, follow Route 9 west for 12 miles to Goshen. Turn right onto Cape Street/

Route 112 north and continue for 0.7 mile. The park entrance is on the right at Moore Hill Road. In summer, park in the second lot along Moore Hill Road, located just past the left turn for the boat launch and nature center. In winter, park in the first lot, near the restrooms and warming hut (Moore Hill Road is not maintained beyond that point). GPS Coordinates: 42.4569 N, 72.7917 W

Contact: D.A.R. State Forest, Rte. 112, Goshen, MA, 413/268-7098; or mail to 555 East St., RFD 1, Williamsburg, MA 01096. Massachusetts Division of State Parks and Recreation, 251 Causeway St., Suite 600, Boston, MA 02114-2104, 617/626-1250, www.mass.gov/dcr/parks/western/darf.htm.

15 SOUTH SUGARLOAF MOUNTAIN
1.5 mi/1 hr

in Mount Sugarloaf State Reservation in South Deerfield

At just 652 feet above sea level, South Sugarloaf is barely a hill. But as it rises abruptly from the flat valley, its cliffs loom surprisingly high over the wide Connecticut River and surrounding landscape of town, farmland, and forest. Reached via a short but steep hike, the South Sugarloaf summit offers some of the Bay State's best views of the Connecticut Valley's quaint tableau. The vertical ascent of the hike is about 300 feet.

From the parking lot, the wide (though unmarked) West Side Trail leads into the woods. Take the West Side Trail only a very short distance before leaving on the side trail branching to the right. This trail leads across the Summit Road to the start of the Pocumtuck Ridge Trail, marked by a wooden post without a sign. (The Pocumtuck Ridge Trail can also be reached by walking up the Summit Road about 100 feet inside the gate.) Follow the Pocumtuck's blue blazes straight up the steep hillside under power lines; the trail finally makes several switchbacks just below the summit ledges. As the sweeping vista comes in to view from atop the cliffs, continue on to the summit's observation tower for even longer views of the surrounding countryside. Return the same way.

User Groups: Hikers and leashed dogs. This trail is not suitable for bikes or horses; no wheelchair facilities.

© JAROSLAW TRAPSZO

view from South Sugarloaf Mountain

Permits: A daily parking fee of $2 is collected mid-May–mid-October.

Maps: For a free, basic map of hiking trails, contact the Mount Sugarloaf State Reservation or see the Massachusetts Division of State Parks and Recreation website. For a topographic area map, request Williamsburg from the USGS.

Directions: From the junction of Routes 47 and 116 in Sunderland, drive 0.7 mile west on Route 116 and turn right onto Sugarloaf Road. The Mount Sugarloaf State Reservation Summit Road begins immediately on the right; park in the dirt lot along Sugarloaf Road just beyond the turn for the Summit Road.

GPS Coordinates: 42.4675 N, 72.5945 W

Contact: Mount Sugarloaf State Reservation, Sugarloaf St./Rte. 116, South Deerfield, MA 01373, 413/545-5993. Massachusetts Division of State Parks and Recreation, 251 Causeway St., Suite 600, Boston, MA 02114-2104, 617/626-1250, www.mass.gov/dcr/parks/central/msug.htm.

16 MOUNT TOBY
5 mi/3.5 hr

in Sunderland

Mount Toby's 1,269-foot summit is wooded, but a fire tower open to the public offers panoramic views stretching up to 50 miles across five states when the weather is clear. The well-maintained Summit Road provides a route to the top that can be hiked easily—or biked or skied by anyone seeking a fairly challenging climb and a fast descent. The hike described here ascends the Summit Road but descends the steeper Telephone Line Trail, a net climb of 800 feet.

The Summit Road begins behind the Mount Toby Forest sign, with frequent white blazes on the route beginning a short distance down the road. After less than a mile, the Telephone Line Trail (which you'll follow on the descent) diverges right. Approaching

the summit at almost two miles, the road coincides with the orange-blazed Robert Frost Trail to reach the top. From the fire tower at the top, follow the marked Telephone Line Trail for the descent off Mount Toby. The Telephone Line Trail eventually reaches the Summit Road near the start of the hike; turn left and follow the Summit Road back to the trailhead. Another option for the return trip is to pick up the Robert Frost Trail, which diverges left about halfway down the Telephone Line Trail and also leads back to the Summit Road start.

User Groups: Hikers and leashed dogs. The Summit Road is suitable for bikes and horses; no wheelchair facilities.

Permits: Mount Toby Reservation is owned by the University of Massachusetts, but is open for public use. Parking and access are free.

Maps: The Mount Toby Reservation Trail Map is $3.95 from New England Cartographics, 413/549-4124 or toll-free 888/995-6277, www.necartographics.com. For topographic area maps, request Greenfield and Williamsburg from the USGS.

Directions: From the junction of Routes 47 and 63 in Sunderland, follow Route 47 south for 0.9 mile to a left turn onto Reservation Road. Follow the road for a half mile and park in a dirt lot on the right, just past the sign for the Mount Toby Forest.

GPS Coordinates: 42.5037 N, 72.5311 W

Contact: University of Massachusetts, Natural Resources Conservation, 160 Holdsworth Way, Amherst, MA 01003-9285, 413/545-2665.

17 PITTSFIELD STATE FOREST: TRANQUILITY TRAIL
1.5 mi/1 hr

in Pittsfield

BEST (

Sitting almost directly on the Taconic Range ridgeline, Pittsfield State Forest is a sprawling

MASSACHUSETTS

10,000-acre tract of woods, hills, ponds, streams, and over 65 acres of azaleas—a big tourist draw in June when the flowering shrubs burst into bloom. The paved three-quarter mile long Tranquility Trail is popular with wheelchair hikers and other visitors who favor a smooth walking surface. A quiet woodland ramble right in the middle of one of the Berkshire's most popular recreation areas, this satisfying hike really lives up to its name. Other universal access amenities in the state forest include a wheelchair-accessible picnic and restroom, both located very close to the trailhead.

The well-marked Tranquility Trail begins next to the ski area parking lot. Crossing a wheelchair-accessible bridge just steps from the trailhead, the paved path then winds along under a canopy of mixed forest cover to reach its end at a picturesque pond. Along the route, you will probably spot some of the region's more common animal inhabitants—salamanders, turtles, and garter snakes are often fellow travelers along the path and wild turkey, fox, deer, porcupines, and weasel can sometimes be seen lurking among the trees. To learn more about the flora and fauna of the Tranquility Trail, interpretive audio tapes are available from the forest headquarters (near the entrance gate). Return the way you came.

User Groups: Hikers, wheelchairs, bikes, horses, and leashed dogs.

Permits: A $5 day-use fee per vehicle is charged early-May–mid-October. Parking is free for ParksPass holders, vehicles with Handicapped, POW, and disabled veteran plates/placard, and seniors 62 and above with the Massachusetts Senior Pass.

Maps: A basic trail map for Pittsfield State Forest is available at the park entrance. For a topographic map of area trails, request the Pittsfield quad from the USGS.

Directions: From downtown Pittsfield, head south on North Street to a right turn on U.S. 20 west. Follow U.S. 20 for 2.2 miles and then take a right turn onto Hungerford Avenue;

continue for 0.2 mile, then bear left onto Fort Hill Avenue and continue for 1 mile. Turn left onto West Street. Continue for 0.2 mile, and turn right onto Churchill Street and continue for 1.7 miles to Cascade Street. Turn left and follow the brown lead-in signs to the park. From the park entrance, follow the access road a short distance to the ski area. The Tranquility Trail begins at the handicap-accessible parking lot on the left. The forest is open sunrise–8 P.M. year-round.

GPS Coordinates: 42.4895 N, 73.2995 W

Contact: Pittsfield State Forest, 1041 Cascade St., Pittsfield, MA 01201, 413/442-8992, www.mass.gov/dcr/parks/western/pitt.htm. Universal Access Program, Massachusetts Department of Conservation and Recreation, P.O. Box 484, Amherst, MA 01004, 413/545-5353 (voice), 413/577-2200 (TTY), www.mass.gov/dcr/universal_access.

18 PLEASANT VALLEY WILDLIFE SANCTUARY: BEAVER LOOP

1.6 mi/1 hr   🚶1 ⛰8

in Lenox

The Berkshires' outpost of the Massachusetts Audubon Society, Pleasant Valley Wildlife Sanctuary is a network of ponds, meadows, marshes, and upland forest at the foot of Lenox Mountain. Known for its enormous beaver population, the sanctuary is also home to a variety or waterfowl and wood warblers and is a nesting ground for the common yellowthroat. This easy loop takes you through the variety of ecosystems found within the sanctuary and offers the best chance for wildlife-viewing. Trails within the sanctuary are clearly signed and marked with two sets of blazes: blue blazes on the trail indicate you are moving away from the office and nature center; yellow blazes mean you are returning to the office.

From the parking area near the sanctuary office, follow the gravel path to the nature center, passing a bee balm and wildflower garden filled with fluttering hummingbirds and butterflies. At the center, pick up the Blue Bird Trail and follow briefly to a trail junction. Here, turn right on the Alexander Trail and enter a hardwood forest of linden, black birch, and ash. At 0.3 mile from the office, reach another trail junction. Turn right on the Yokun Trail and then turn left on a short loop path that edges along a marshy beaver pond. Turn left again once you return to the Yokun Trail and follow 0.5 mile to a left turn onto the Old Woods Road. Crossing over two brooks, the wide, forest-covered path ambles along to a junction with the Beaver Trail. Turn left on the Beaver Trail and wander along the edge of Beaver Pond, taking in what can only be described as a beaver's version of urban sprawl: Dams are everywhere. Also living here are muskrats, similar in appearance to beavers, except for their rat-like tails. At one mile, leave the pond and turn left on the Bluebird Trail, a downhill jaunt through hemlock woods. At 1.3 miles, turn right on the Yokun Trail, skirting two shallow ponds, a favorite haunt of local waterfowl, including heron, mallards, and Canada geese. At 1.6 miles, the trail circles back to the office, crossing a broad swamp before returning to the parking area.

User Groups: Hikers only. No bikes, dogs, or horses. There are no wheelchair facilities on this hike; the sanctuary's All People Trail, nature center, and all restroom facilities do offer universal access.

Permits: Trails open dawn–dusk on the days the Pleasant Valley nature center is open. Access costs are $4 for nonmember adults and $3 for nonmember children (ages 2–12) and seniors.

Maps: A sanctuary trail map is available at the Pleasant Valley nature center.

Directions: From the center of Lenox, follow U.S. 7A north to an intersection with U.S. 7/U.S. 20; turn left and continue approximately one mile to a left turn onto West Dugway Road. The sanctuary and parking area are 1.6 miles ahead on the right. Nature center hours: Tuesday–Friday 9 A.M.–5 P.M.; Saturday, Sunday, and Monday holidays, 10 A.M.–4 P.M. GPS Coordinates: 42.3852 N, 73.2969 W

Contact: Pleasant Valley Audubon Wildlife Sanctuary, 472 West Mountain Rd., Lenox, MA 01240, 413/637-0320, www.massaudubon.org/Nature_Connection/Sanctuaries/Pleasant_Valley.

19 PLEASANT VALLEY WILDLIFE SANCTUARY: LENOX MOUNTAIN
2 mi/1.5 hr   🏃3 ⛰8

in Lenox

Lenox Mountain is a popular hike for summer visitors to Lenox. A few hikers (with either super human hearing or a very good imagination) claim music from nearby Tanglewood can be heard from the mountain's lofty heights. Whether you hear nature sounds or a few stray notes of Mozart as you make your way up the short, moderately strenuous trek to the top of 2,126-foot Lenox Mountain, the fire tower lookout at the summit offers a symphony of views extending to the surrounding Berkshire hills and even west into New York State. This out-and-back hike starts and finishes at the Massachusetts Audubon Society's Pleasant Valley Wildlife Sanctuary, a refuge nestled at the foot of Lenox Mountain that is known for its large beaver populations. The Overlook Trail climb nets an elevation gain of 800 feet.

From the parking area near the sanctuary office, follow the gravel path to the nature center. At the center, pick up the Blue Bird Trail and follow briefly, crossing through a field and over a brook before reaching a well-marked trail junction. Here, turn left on the Overlook Trail and follow the blue blazes up the rapidly steepening trail. (Blue blazes mark the trail up and indicate you are moving away from the office; on the descent, yellow blazes on the other side of the trees indicate you are headed towards the office.) In about one mile, the mountain's open summit is reached. Enhance your views by climbing the fire tower. Take in the breathtaking landscape or look to the sky to spot hawks and even the occasional bald eagle. Return the way you came, following the yellow blazes back to the parking area.

User Groups: Hikers only. No bikes, dogs, or horses. There are no wheelchair facilities on this hike; the sanctuary's All People Trail, nature center, and all restroom facilities do offer universal access.

Permits: Trails open dawn–dusk on the days the Pleasant Valley nature center is open. Access costs are $4 for nonmember adults and $3 for nonmember children (ages 2–12) and seniors.

Maps: A sanctuary trail map is available at the Pleasant Valley nature center.

Directions: From the center of Lenox, follow U.S. 7A north to an intersection with U.S. 7/U.S. 20; turn left and continue approximately one mile to a left turn onto West Dugway Road. The sanctuary and parking area are 1.6 miles ahead on the right. Nature center hours: Tuesday–Friday 9 A.M.–5 P.M.; Saturday, Sunday, and Monday holidays, 10 A.M.–4 P.M. GPS Coordinates: 42.3852 N, 73.2969 W

Contact: Pleasant Valley Audubon Wildlife Sanctuary, 472 West Mountain Rd., Lenox, MA 01240, 413/637-0320, www.massaudubon.org/Nature_Connection/Sanctuaries/Pleasant_Valley.

20 MONUMENT MOUNTAIN
1.6 mi/1 hr   🏃2 ⛰10

in Great Barrington

BEST **(**

A fine trek that rivals even the Mount Greylock region for the best hiking in southern New England, Monument Mountain is an unmistakable gray-white quartzite ridge thrust high above the surrounding landscape. Its summit, Squaw Peak, rises to 1,640 feet and offers three-state views in all directions. Arguably even more dramatic, though, are the cliffs south of Squaw Peak and the detached rock pinnacle known as Devil's Pulpit. A good time to come here is mid-June, when the mountain laurel blooms, or late September when the surrounding hills turn crimson and gold. This unique hill has been popular since at least the 19th century: In 1850, so legend goes, Nathaniel Hawthorne, Oliver Wendell Holmes, and Herman Melville picnicked together on Monument's summit. And William Cullen Bryant wrote a poem titled "Monument Mountain" relating the tale of a Mahican maiden who, spurned in love, leapt to her death from the cliffs. Your hike may be less historic and less traumatic than either of those, but Monument Mountain is one not to miss.

This fairly easy, 1.6-mile hike ascends and descends the Hickey Trail, but you may enjoy making a loop hike, going up the Hickey and coming down the 1.3-mile Indian Monument Trail, which joins up with the Hickey below the summit. At the picnic area, a sign describes the trail heading south, the Indian Monument Trail, as easier, and the Hickey Trail, which heads north, as steeper. The Hickey actually grows steep for only a short section below the summit and is otherwise a well-graded and well-maintained trail. Following the Hickey's white blazes, you parallel a brook with a small waterfall. Nearing the summit ridge, watch for a trail entering on the right; that's the Indian Monument Trail, and you want to be able to distinguish it from the Hickey on your way back down. From the summit, continue following the white blazes south about a quarter mile, passing a pile of rocks, until you reach the cliffs. Devil's Pulpit is the obvious pinnacle at the far end of the cliffs. Return the way you came or take the Indian Monument Trail.

User Groups: Hikers and leashed dogs. No wheelchair facilities. Bikes and horses are prohibited.

Permits: Parking and access are free. On-site donations welcome.

Maps: A map of trails is posted on an information board at the picnic area and a paper map is available at the trailhead. A map is also available from The Trustees of Reservations. For topographic area maps, request Great Barrington and Stockbridge from the USGS.

Directions: From intersection of U.S 7 and Route 102 at the Red Lion Inn in Stockbridge center, take U.S. 7 south and follow for three miles; entrance and parking are on the right. From Great Barrington, take U.S. 7 north for four miles to entrance and parking (room for 56 cars) on left. Monument Mountain is open to the public sunrise–sunset year-round. GPS Coordinates: 42.2468 N, 73.3325 W

Contact: The Trustees of Reservations Western Management Region, Mission House, P.O. Box 792, Sergeant St., Stockbridge, MA 01262-0792, 413/298-3239, www.thetrustees.org.

21 ICE GLEN AND LAURA'S TOWER LOOP

3.3 mi/2 hr 🏃2 ⛰8

in Stockbridge

Not far from Stockbridge's quaint village center is the Ice Glen, a boulder strewn ravine popular with hikers in spring when meltwaters refreeze on the rocks to form a sparkling fairyland of temporary ice sculptures. For summer visitors to Stockbridge, the moss-covered glen provides a cool escape from the heat and from the area's tourist crowds. This easy loop hike takes you first on a gentle climb to Laura's Tower, a picturesque overlook with excellent views of Stockbridge. Expect an elevation gain of approximately 650 feet on this pleasant trek.

From the parking circle, pick up the white-blazed Ice Glen Trail at a large marker and trail map. Only a few steps into this hike, a suspension bridge takes you over the Housatonic River; the trail then crosses railroad tracks, passes under power lines, and enters the woods within the first 0.25 mile. Next, when you reach a trail junction, bear left onto the orange-blazed Laura's Tower Trail. Follow the path 0.7 mile to an observation tower; climbing up on the open platform reveals postcard perfect views of Stockbridge's historic village center. Retracing your steps back to the trail junction, take a left on the Ice Glen Trail and in another 0.3 mile, enter the ravine's rocky maze. Pay attention to footing as the trail picks its way along often slippery moss-covered boulders. After 0.4 mile, the trail leaves the ravine and reenters the woods (look here for a very tall pine tree, reportedly the tallest one in Massachusetts). In 0.1 mile, the trail passes a private driveway and continues straight to reach Ice Glen Road. Turn right and follow the road 0.5 mile back to U.S. 7. Turn right again and follow U.S. 7 for 0.3 mile to a right turn onto Park Street. From here, it's only a short distance to the parking circle.

User Groups: Hikers only. This trail is not suitable for bikes, dogs, or horses; no wheelchair facilities.

Permits: Parking and access are free.

Maps: A free trail map is available from the Laurel Hill Association, the village improvement society in charge of maintaining the trails. For a topographic area map, request Stockbridge from the USGS.

Directions: From the center of Stockbridge, drive south 0.2 mile on U.S. 7 to a left turn onto Park Street. Drive 0.3 mile to the road's end and parking circle. GPS Coordinates: 42.2782 N, 73.3076 W

Contact: Laurel Hill Association - Trails, P.O. Box 24, Stockbridge, MA 01262.

22 BENEDICT POND AND THE LEDGES

2.5 mi/1.5 hr 🏃2 ⛰8

in Beartown State Forest in Monterey

BEST(

An easy loop around pristine Benedict Pond, this hike takes you to a place simply teaming with critters: hear the tap, tap, tapping of woodpeckers; see beavers hard at work; watch mallards and Canada geese take flight across the water; and catch sight of frogs and toads patiently awaiting their next meal. The loop also leads to the Ledges, a stop on the Appalachian Trail with excellent views west towards East Mountain and Mount Everett. Kids love this nature trek, a net climb of only a few hundred feet.

From the parking area, follow the blue-blazed Pond Loop Trail as it edges along the water to the pond's eastern end. Here, the trail merges with the white-blazed Appalachian Trail (AT). Turn left. The coinciding trails soon reach a woods road and split again. Turn right onto the AT, ascending a low hillside. Where the AT hooks right and crosses a brook, continue straight ahead on a short side path to an impressive beaver dam that has flooded a swamp. Backtrack, cross the brook on the AT, and within several minutes you reach the Ledges, with a view west toward East Mountain and Mount Everett. Backtrack on the AT to the woods road and turn right onto the Pond Loop Trail. Watch for where the trail bears left off the woods road (at a sign and blue blazes). The trail passes through the state forest campground on the way back to the parking area.

User Groups: Hikers and leashed dogs. Bikes and horses are prohibited; no wheelchair facilities.

Permits: A daily parking fee of $5 is collected mid-May–mid-October.

Maps: A contour map of trails (designating uses allowed on each trail) is available in boxes at the state forest headquarters, at the trailhead parking area, at a trail information kiosk at the swimming area and restrooms, and at the campground. You can also find one at the Massachusetts Division of State Parks and Recreation website. A map of area trails is available from the Appalachian Mountain Club (Blue Hills, Mount Tom, Mount Holyoke, $6.95). For topographic area maps, request Great Barrington and Otis from the USGS.

Directions: From the Monterey General Store

in Monterey, follow Route 23 for 2.4 miles west to a left turn on Blue Hill (signs are posted for Beartown State Forest). Follow Blue Hill Road 0.7 mile to the forest headquarters on the left. Continuing north on Blue Hill Road, you pass the Appalachian Trail crossing 1.3 miles from the headquarters; at 1.5 miles, turn right onto Benedict Pond Road (shown as Beartown Road on the park map). Follow signs to the Pond Loop Trail; the trailhead leaves from a dirt parking area. A short distance farther up the road are public restrooms and a state forest campground. Beartown State Forest is closed from dusk to a half hour before sunrise year-round.

GPS Coordinates: 42.2023 N, 73.2889 W

Contact: Beartown State Forest, Blue Hill Rd., P.O. Box 97, Monterey, MA 01245-0097, 413/528-0904. Massachusetts Division of State Parks and Recreation, 251 Causeway St., Suite 600, Boston, MA 02114-2104, 617/626-1250, www.mass.gov/dcr/parks/western/bear.htm.

23 NORWOTTUCK TRAIL
10.1 mi one-way/5 hr   🏃‍‍1 ⛰7

in Northampton

The 10.1-mile-long Norwottuck Trail is a paved bike path that follows a former railroad bed from Northampton, crossing over the Connecticut River and passing through Hadley and Amherst, on its way into Belchertown. The trail's flat course provides a linear, universally accessible recreation area for walkers, runners, bicyclists, in-line skaters, and wheelchairs. Historians believe that the Native Americans who lived here before the European settlers were called the Norwottucks. Translated, norwottuck means "in the midst of the river," the Native American term for the entire Connecticut River Valley. As with any bike or pedestrian path, the Norwottuck is popular with families because it provides a refuge from traffic. The place from which many users access the trail is the large parking lot at its western end; this lot is often full, so it's wise to try one of the other access points listed in the directions.

User Groups: Hikers, bikers, dogs, and wheelchair users. Dogs must be leashed. Horses are prohibited.

Permits: Parking and access are free.

Maps: A brochure/map is available at both trailheads. The Western Massachusetts Bicycle Map, a detailed bicycling map covering the state from the New York border to the Quabbin Reservoir, including the Norwottuck Trail, is available for $4.25 from Rubel BikeMaps (P.O. Box 401035, Cambridge, MA 02140, 617/776-6567, www.bikemaps.com) and from area stores listed at the website. For topographic area maps, request Easthampton and Holyoke from the USGS.

Directions: To reach the trail's western end from the south, take I-91 to Exit 19 in Northampton. Down the off-ramp, drive straight through the intersection and turn right into the Connecticut River Greenway State Park/Elwell Recreation Area. From the north, take I-91 to Exit 20 in Northampton. Turn left at the traffic lights and drive 1.5 miles to the Elwell Recreation Area on the left. The trail can also be accessed from four other parking areas: behind the Whole Foods store in the Mountain Farms Mall on Route 9 in Hadley, 3.7 miles from the Elwell Recreation Area parking lot; near the junction of Mill Lane and Southeast Street, off Route 9 in Amherst; on Station Road in Amherst (reached via Southeast Street off Route 9), 1.6 miles from the trail's eastern terminus; and on Warren Wright Road in Belchertown, the trail's eastern terminus. Public restrooms are available at the parking area at Elwell Recreation Area. GPS Coordinates: 42.3350 N, 72.6220 W

Contact: Connecticut River Greenway State Park/Elwell Recreation Area, 136 Damon Rd., Northampton, MA 01060, 413/586-8706, ext. 12. Massachusetts Division of State Parks and Recreation, 251 Causeway St., Suite 600, Boston, MA 02114-2104, 617/626-1250, www.mass.gov/dcr/parks/central/nwrt.htm.

24 MOUNT TOM
5.4 mi/2.5 hr   🏃4 △8

in Mount Tom State Reservation in Holyoke

BEST (

One of the most popular stretches of the 98-mile Metacomet-Monadnock Trail is this traverse of the Mount Tom Ridge. A steep mountainside capped by tall basalt cliffs defines Mount Tom's west face and the trail follows the brink of that precipice for nearly two miles, treating hikers to commanding views west as far as the Berkshires on a clear day. Mount Tom is also one of New England's premier sites for spotting migrating hawks. Each fall, thousands of hawks and other birds fly past the mountain on their way south. For all the incredible scenery, this hike climbs less than 500 feet.

From the parking area, walk up the paved Smiths Ferry Road for about 75 yards to reach the reservation's interpretative center (located in a stone house). Turn right at the house and enter the woods; the trail is marked by white rectangular blazes and a triangular marker for the Metacomet-Monadnock Trail. Within minutes, the trail veers right and climbs steeply toward Goat Peak. Pass a good view westward and then reach the open clearing of Goat Peak, where the lookout tower offers pleasing panoramic views. Double back to Smiths Ferry Road, turn right, walk about 75 yards, and then enter the woods on the left, following the white blazes of the Metacomet-Monadnock Trail. It crosses the Quarry Trail and then ascends the ridge. Numerous side paths lead to the right to great views from the cliffs, with each view better than the last, until you reach the Mount Tom summit, where there are radio and television transmission stations. Take in the sights again as you retrace your steps on the Metacomet-Monadnock Trail to your car.

User Groups: Hikers and leashed dogs. Bikes and horses are prohibited; no wheelchair facilities.

Permits: A daily parking fee of $2 is collected mid-May–mid-October.

Maps: A free map of hiking trails is available at the reservation headquarters and the stone house, or at the Massachusetts Division of State Parks and Recreation website. A map of area trails is available from the Appalachian Mountain Club (Blue Hills Reservation/ Mount Tom/Holyoke Range, $6.95). For topographic area maps, request Mount Tom, Easthampton, Mount Holyoke, and Spring-field North from the USGS.

Directions: From I-91, take Exit 18 (East-hampton/Holyoke)to U.S. 5 south. Follow U.S. 5 south for roughly 3.3 miles to a right turn onto Smiths Ferry Road, at the entrance to Mount Tom State Reservation. Follow the road for nearly a mile, passing under I-91 to a horseshoe-shaped parking area on the right. The parking area is about 0.2 mile before the reservation's interpretive center.

GPS Coordinates: 42.2680 N, 72.6320 W

Contact: Mount Tom State Reservation, 125 Reservation Rd., U.S. 5, Holyoke, MA 01040, 413/534-1186. Massachusetts Division of State Parks and Recreation, 251 Causeway St., Suite 600, Boston, MA 02114-2104, 617/626-1250, www.mass.gov/dcr/parks/central/mtom. htm.

25 JUG END
2.2 mi/1 hr

in Egremont

No, the summit of Jug End (1,770 ft.) looks nothing like a handle, base, or spout of a jug. The name comes from a rather poor English translation of the Dutch and German word for youth, *jugend,* as early Dutch settlers in the area were called. However you pronounce it, the views from the cliffs and open ledges on Jug End are well worth the short, if steep, hike of more than 500 feet uphill.

From the turnout, follow the white blazes of the Appalachian Trail in an instantly steep uphill trudge. Within 0.3 mile, the trail as-cends the ridge, reaching the first open views

at about 0.7 mile from the road. Continuing on, Jug End's summit is soon reached at 1.1 miles from the road. Good views northward toward the pastoral valley and the surrounding hills of the southern Berkshires are especially spectacular in early autumn. After you've taken in the views, head back to the parking area the same way you hiked up. This is a sharp descent that can be hard on the knees.

User Groups: Hikers and leashed dogs. Trail is not suitable for bikes or horses; no wheelchair facilities.

Permits: Parking and access are free.

Maps: A free map of hiking trails is available from the reservation headquarters or at the Massachusetts Division of State Parks and Recreation website. For topographic area maps, request Ashley Falls and Great Bar-rington from the USGS.

Directions: From the junction of Routes 23 and 41 in Egremont, drive south on Route 41 for 0.1 mile and turn right onto Mount Washington Road. Continue 0.8 mile and turn left on Avenue Road. After a half mile, bear left onto Jug End Road and continue 0.3 mile to a turnout on the right where the Ap-palachian Trail emerges from the woods. Park in the turnout.

GPS Coordinates: 42.1444 N, 73.4316 W

Contact: Jug End State Reservation and Wild-life Management Area, RD East St., Mount Washington, MA 01258, 413/528-0330. Mas-sachusetts Division of State Parks and Recre-ation, 251 Causeway St., Suite 600, Boston, MA 02114-2104, 617/626-1250, www.mass. gov/dcr/parks/western/juge.htm.

26 MOUNT EVERETT
5.4 mi/3.5 hr

in the town of Mount Washington

BEST (

Mount Everett, at 2,602 feet, is among the taller of those little hills in southwestern Massachusetts with the green, rounded tops and steep flanks that seem close enough for

MASSACHUSETTS

swamp at the base of Mount Everett

someone standing in the valley to reach out and touch. Long views east from atop Everett make it a good place to catch sun rising across the charming landscape of rolling hills and countryside. As a bonus, you pass several waterfalls on the way to Mount Everett's peak. This hike climbs about 1,900 feet.

From the kiosk, follow the Race Brook Trail. Not far up the trail, a sign marks a side path leading right to a view of the lower falls along Race Brook. The main trail bears left and grows steeper just before crossing the brook below upper Race Brook Falls, some 80 feet high—an impressive sight at times of high runoff, most common in the spring. Above the falls, you reach a ledge with a view east. The trail then descends slightly to a third crossing of the brook.

At the Appalachian Trail (AT), marked by signs, turn right (north) for the remaining 0.7 mile to Everett's summit. You are now walking on bare rock exposed by the footsteps of the many hikers who have come before you—thousands of whom were backpacking the entire white-blazed AT from Georgia to Maine. Notice how thin and worn the soil is

on the path, a good lesson in how hiker traffic erodes even the most well-cared for of trails. The views eastward begin before the summit, where only stunted trees and vegetation grow. In this rural southwest corner of Massachusetts, the valley and expanse of wooded hills show amazingly few signs of human presence. An abandoned fire tower (unsafe to climb) marks the summit; walk close to it for views toward the Catskills. Hike down along the same route.

User Groups: Hikers and leashed dogs. This trail is not suitable for bikes or horses; no wheelchair facilities.

Permits: Parking and access are free.

Maps: A free trail map of Mount Washington State Forest, which covers Mount Everett, is available at the state forest headquarters or at the Massachusetts Division of State Parks and Recreation website. A map of area trails is available from the Appalachian Mountain Club (Northern Berkshires/Southwestern Massachusetts/Wachusett Mountain, $5.95). For a topographic area map, request Ashley Falls from the USGS.

Directions: From the junction where Routes

23 and 41 split in Egremont, follow Route 41 south for 5.2 miles to a turnout on the right. A kiosk and blue blazes mark the start of the Race Brook Trail.

GPS Coordinates: 42.0861 N, 73.4144 W

Contact: Mount Washington State Forest, RD 3 East St., Mount Washington, MA 01258, 413/528-0330. Massachusetts Division of State Parks and Recreation, 251 Causeway St., Suite 600, Boston, MA 02114-2104, 617/626-1250, www.mass.gov/dcr/parks/western/meve.htm.

27 THE RIGA PLATEAU
17 mi/2 days 👥5 🏕9

between Egremont, Massachusetts, and Salisbury, Connecticut

BEST (

This very popular Appalachian Trail stretch offers easy hiking along a low ridge with numerous long views of the green hills and rural countryside that so beautifully mark this quiet corner of New England. Expect to see lots of day hikers and backpackers on warm weekends here, with shelters and camping areas tending to fill to overflowing; midweek, however, the campsite and trail are sparsely populated. Or try coming here in May, after the trails and woods have dried out, but before the summer crowds, high temperatures, and swarms of mosquitoes arrive. The cumulative elevation gained over the course of this hike is about 3,500 feet.

From the turnout on Jug End Road, follow the white blazes of the Appalachian Trail (AT) southbound. The trail ascends gently, then steeply, through the woods to Jug End at 1.1 miles, the northern tip of the so-called Riga Plateau, with wide views northward to the Berkshire Mountains. On a clear day, Mount Greylock, the highest peak in Massachusetts, is visible in the distance. Now you're on the ridge, with only fairly easy climbs and dips ahead. The trail passes several open ledges on the Mount Bushnell ascent, reaching its 1,834-foot summit at 2.3 miles. Easy woods walking leads you into the Mount Everett State Reservation, crossing a road at 3.9 miles; a short distance to the right is serene Guilder Pond, a worthwhile detour. Continuing on the AT, the trail steepens a bit to a fire tower at 4.3 miles and Everett's summit (2,602 ft.) at 4.6 miles, with breathtaking views in all directions.

The AT descends off Everett at an easy slope and heads back into the woods, then climbs slightly to the open, rocky Race Mountain crown, 6.4 miles into this hike and 2,365 feet above the ocean. The trail follows the crest of cliffs with wide views northeast to southeast of the Housatonic Valley. At 8.1 miles, you pass near Bear Rock Falls (on the left) and its namesake camping area. Beyond here, the trail descends steadily, then a bit more steeply into the dark defile of Sages Ravine, another camping area at 9.6 miles, as the AT enters Connecticut.

The AT follows the ravine, then leaves it for the most strenuous part of this hike, the 1.4-mile climb to the 2,316-foot Bear Mountain summit, the highest peak in Connecticut. From the top of Bear, at 10.9 miles, the trail descends steadily, if easily, over open terrain with long views of Connecticut's northwestern corner before reentering the woods. The Undermountain Trail turns sharply left at 11.8 miles; continue straight ahead on the AT, soon passing the Brassie Brook, Ball Brook, and Riga camping areas. The forest along here is bright and, although trees block the views, you're on the ridge and it feels high.

Stay southbound on the AT, soon climbing more steeply to reach the open ledges of the Lion's Head at 14.2 miles, with some of the hike's best views of a bucolic countryside, including the town of Salisbury, CT, and Prospect Mountain straight ahead. Double back a short distance from the Lion's Head ledges and descend on the AT, passing a junction with the Lion's Head Trail. The trail now descends at a steady grade through quiet woods, reaching the parking lot on Route 41 at 17 miles from Jug End Road.

Camping is permitted only at designated

shelters and campsites along this section of the Appalachian Trail. From north to south, they are: Glen Brook shelter, reached via a short side trail off the AT, 3.4 miles into this hike; a campsite 0.4 mile off the AT down the Race Brook Falls Trail, 5.3 miles into this hike; the Bear Rock Falls campsite, beside the AT at 8.1 miles; Sages Ravine at 9.6 miles; the Brassie Brook shelter and campsites at 12.3 miles; the Ball Brook campsite at 12.9 miles; the Riga camping area at 13.5 miles; and the Plateau campsite at 13.7 miles, a short distance from the hike's end. Campfires are prohibited from Bear Rock Falls campsite south to the Plateau campsite. Campers must cook with portable camp stoves.

User Groups: Hikers and dogs. Bikes and horses are prohibited; no wheelchair facilities.

Permits: Parking and access are free.

Maps: See maps 3 and 4 in the Map and Guide to the Appalachian Trail in Massachusetts and Connecticut, a five-map set and guidebook available for $19.95 ($14.95 for the maps alone) from the Appalachian Trail Conservancy. For topographic area maps, request Great Barrington, Ashley Falls, and Sharon from the USGS.

Directions: You need to shuttle two vehicles to make this one-way traverse. To hike north to south, as described here, leave one vehicle in the Appalachian Trail parking lot on Route 41 in Salisbury, CT, 0.8 mile north of the junction of Routes 44 and 41. To reach this hike's start, drive your second vehicle north on Route 41 to Egremont. Just before reaching Route 23, turn left onto Mount Washington Road. Continue 0.8 mile and turn left on Avenue Road. At a half mile, bear to the left onto Jug End Road and continue 0.3 mile to a turnout on the right where the Appalachian Trail emerges from the woods. Park in the turnout.

GPS Coordinates: 42.1445 N, 73.4314 W

Contact: Appalachian Trail Conservancy, 799 Washington St., P.O. Box 807, Harpers Ferry, WV 25425-0807, 304/535-6331, www.appalachiantrail.org.

28 BASH BISH FALLS
0.5 mi/0.75 hr   🚶🏼2 ⛰10

in Bash Bish Falls State Park in Mount Washington

BEST (

After driving along what has to be one of the most winding roads in Massachusetts, you hike this extremely short trail to what may be the state's most spectacular waterfall. As the Bash Bish Brook tumbles through a vertical stack of giant boulders, it splits into twin columns of water on either side of a huge, triangular block; then settles briefly in a clear, deep pool at the base of the falls before dropping in a foaming torrent through the water-carved rock walls of Bash Bish Gorge. The falls are, predictably, enhanced by spring rains and snowmelt and are much thinner in fall. The Bash Bish Falls Trail is well marked with blue triangles and only a quarter-mile walk downhill from the roadside turnout leads to the falls.

User Groups: Hikers and leashed dogs. This trail is not suitable for bikes or horses; no wheelchair facilities.

Permits: Parking and access are free.

Maps: Although no map is needed for this hike, a free area trail map is available at the Mount Washington State Forest headquarters or at the Massachusetts Division of State Parks and Recreation website. This area is covered in the Northern Berkshires/Southwestern Massachusetts/Wachusett Mountain map, $5.95 in paper, available from the Appalachian Mountain Club. For a topographic area map, request Ashley Falls from the USGS.

Directions: From the junction of Routes 23 and 41 in Egremont, drive south on Route 41 for 0.1 mile and turn right onto Mount Washington Road, which becomes East Street. Follow the signs several miles to Bash Bish Falls State Park and a turnout on the left. To reach the Mount Washington State Forest headquarters, follow the signs from East Street.

GPS Coordinates: 42.1152 N, 73.4917 W

Contact: Mount Washington State Forest, RD 3 East St., Mount Washington, MA 01258,

413/528-0330. Massachusetts Division of State Parks and Recreation, 251 Causeway St., Suite 600, Boston, MA 02114-2104, 617/626-1250, www.mass.gov/dcr/parks/western/mwas. htm.

29 ALANDER MOUNTAIN
5.6 mi/3 hr   🥾4 ⚠️9

in Mount Washington State Forest in Mount Washington

Less than a mile from the New York border and a few miles from Connecticut, Alander Mountain (2,240 ft.) has two broad, flat summits. The westernmost summit has the best views of the southern Berkshires and of the hills and farmland of eastern New York, all the way to the Catskill Mountains. An open ridge running south from the summit offers even more sweeping views. A fun adventure for hikers of all levels, this fairly easy climb nets an elevation gain of 500 feet.

From the kiosk behind the headquarters, the Alander Mountain Trail gradually ascends a woods road for much of its distance, then narrows to a trail and grows steeper. Just past the first-come, first-served state forest cabin site, a sign points left to the east summit loop and right to the west summit loop; both loops take just minutes to walk. The west loop offers great views to the north, east, and south. At the mountain's true summit are three old concrete blocks, probably the foundation of a former fire tower. Continue over the summit on the white-blazed South Taconic Trail for views westward into New York. Turn back and descend the way you came.

Special note: By hiking northbound from Alander's summit on the scenic South Taconic Trail, you can reach Bash Bish Falls (see *Bash Bish Falls* listing in this chapter) and then return to Alander, adding four miles round-trip to this hike's distance.

Backcountry camping is available in the Mount Washington State Forest at 15 wilderness campsites, 1.5 miles from the trailhead, and in a cabin that sleeps six just below Alander's summit. The cabin (which has a wood-burning stove) and the campsites are filled on a first-come, first-served basis.

User Groups: Hikers, bikers, leashed dogs, and horses; no wheelchair facilities. During the winter watch out for snowmobiles on this trail.

Permits: Parking and access are free.

Maps: An area trail map is available from the Appalachian Mountain Club (Northern Berkshires/Southwestern Massachusetts/Wachusett Mountain, $5.95). A free map of Mount Washington State Forest is available at the state forest headquarters or at the Massachusetts Division of State Parks and Recreation website. For a topographic area map, request Ashley Falls from the USGS.

Directions: From the junction of Routes 23 and 41 in Egremont, drive south on Route 41 for 0.1 mile and turn right onto Mount Washington Road, which becomes East Street. Follow the signs about nine miles to the Mount Washington State Forest headquarters on the right. The blue-blazed Alander Mountain Trail begins behind the headquarters.

GPS Coordinates: 42.0842 N, 73.4665 W

Contact: Mount Washington State Forest, RD 3 East St., Mount Washington, MA 01258, 413/528-0330. Massachusetts Division of State Parks and Recreation, 251 Causeway St., Suite 600, Boston, MA 02114-2104, 617/626-1250, www.mass.gov/dcr/parks/western/mwas. htm.

30 GRANVILLE STATE FOREST: HUBBARD RIVER GORGE
6 mi/2.5 hr   🥾2 ⚠️9

in Granville State Forest in Granville

Located along the southern border of Massachusetts in the towns of Granville and Tolland, Granville State Forest borders with

Hubbard River Gorge, Granville State Forest

Connecticut's Tunxis State Forest to create a true sense of tranquil remoteness. Formerly the hunting and fishing grounds of the Tunxis tribe, later open farmland and pastures, and now slowly reverting back into a northern hardwood-conifer forest, this out-and-back hike features the highlight of this out-of-the-way state forest: Hubbard River Gorge, a stunning, 2.5-mile long series of cascades and waterfalls.

From the dirt parking lot, backtrack over the bridge and turn right onto a paved road leading a half mile to the now-closed Hubbard River Campground. The Hubbard River Trail begins at the road's end. Follow the trail, an old woods road marked by blue triangles bearing a hiker symbol, southeast along the Hubbard River. After turning briefly away from the river, the road hugs the rim of the spectacular gorge, passing many spots that afford views of the river and cascades. Follow the trail as far as you like, then turn around and return the same way. If you go all the way to an old woods road marked on the map as Hartland Hollow Road before turning back, the round-trip is six miles. If you'd like to see another area similar to the Hubbard River Gorge, turn left and hike upstream (north) along Hartland Hollow Road. Watch for the stream through the trees to your right; you'll discover a small gorge and pools in there within less than a half mile from the Hubbard River Trail.

Special note: This quiet corner of Massachusetts is a wonderfully charming area to drive through or, better yet, bicycle. The quaint rural villages of Granville and West Granville are both on the National Register of Historic Districts.

User Groups: Hikers, bikers, leashed dogs, and

horses. No wheelchair facilities. Swimming in the Hubbard River is prohibited under penalty of fine.

Permits: Parking and access are free.

Maps: A free map of hiking trails is available at the sate forest headquarters or at the Massachusetts Division of State Parks and Recreation website. For a topographic area map, request Southwick from the USGS.

Directions: From the junction of Routes 189 and 57 in Granville, drive six miles west on Route 57 and turn left onto West Hartland Road. In another 0.6 mile, you pass a sign for the Granville State Forest; the rough dirt road heading left from that point is where this loop hike will emerge. Continue another 0.3 mile, cross the bridge over the Hubbard River, and park in the dirt lot on the left. The state forest headquarters is on West Hartland Road, 0.6 mile beyond the bridge.

GPS Coordinates: 42.0576 N, 72.9635 W

Contact: Granville State Forest, 323 West Hartland Rd., Granville, MA 01034, 413/357-6611. Massachusetts Division of State Parks and Recreation, 251 Causeway St., Suite 600, Boston, MA 02114-2104, 617/626-1250, www.mass.gov/dcr/parks/western/gran.htm.

CENTRAL
MASSACHUSETTS

Massachusetts at its midsection is a rumpled

blanket of rolling hills, thick forest, and a string of low but craggy summits that rise above the trees to give long views of the surrounding landscape. Far enough away from Boston, but without the same tourist crowds as the Berkshire region, trails to the top of such notable peaks as Mount Holyoke, Wachusett Mountain, and Mount Wataic tend to be quiet, uncrowded, and easy to reach. These are hikes that are great for beginners and kids as well as serious hikers and backpackers trying to get their legs in shape for more strenuous trips elsewhere. Beyond these hills, you will mostly find pleasant woods walks that are easy to moderately difficult and a number of shorter treks leading to gorges, caves, and lush mountain meadows.

Central Massachusetts is also home to two long-distance trails, both of which are largely used by day hikers. The white-blazed Metacomet-Monadnock Trail (Crag Mountain, Mount Holyoke) bounces along the Holyoke Range and through the hills of north-central Massachusetts on its 117-mile course from the Massachusetts/Connecticut line near Agawam and Southwick to the summit of Mount Monadnock in Jaffrey, New Hampshire. In 2009, the federal government designated the Metacomet-Monadnock Trail as part of the new New England National Scenic

Trail, a 200-mile trail route comprised of the Metacomet-Monadnock Trail and the Mattabesett Trail in Connecticut. The blue-blazed Midstate Trail extends 92 miles from Douglas (on the Rhode Island border) to the New Hampshire line at Ashburnham, crossing through woods and over small hills. Significant stretches of both trails are on private land, so be aware of and respect any closures.

This area is snow country in Massachusetts, with the hilly terrain near Worcester and Leominster usually racking up the highest annual snowfall totals in the state. Trails in mid-Massachusetts usually become free of snow sometime between mid-March and mid-April, though they often will be muddy for a few weeks after the snow melts (New England's infamous mud season).

Many of the hikes in this chapter are in state parks and forests, where dogs must be leashed; horses are allowed in most state forests and parks, as is hunting in season. Trails leading to the Quabbin Reservoir, one of the largest artificially-made public water supplies in the United States, have special access rules: dogs are prohibited and hikers and mountain bikers should be aware that trails may be closed or rerouted and public access suspended at any time in order to maintain water supply safety.

MASSACHUSETTS

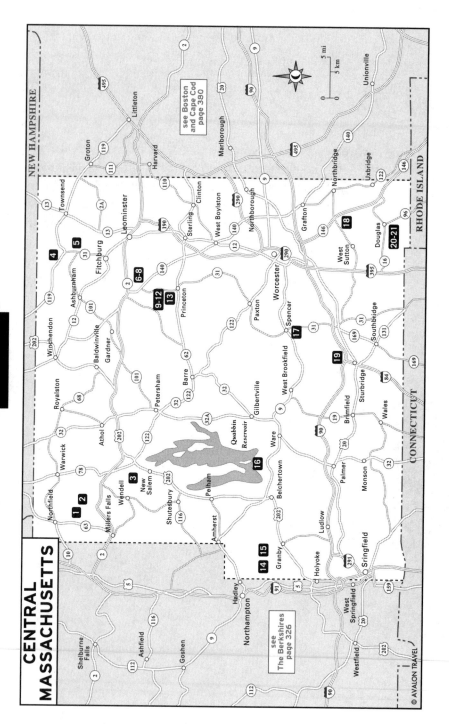

CENTRAL MASSACHUSETTS

MASSACHUSETTS

NEW HAMPSHIRE

RHODE ISLAND

CONNECTICUT

see Boston and Cape Cod page 380

The Berkshires page 326

© AVALON TRAVEL

5 mi
5 km

1 NORTHFIELD MOUNTAIN: ROSE LEDGE

4.2 mi/2.5 hr   🏃3 ⛰8

in Northfield

The Northfield Mountain Recreation and Environmental Center's 25 miles of hiking and multi-use trails comprise one of the best trail systems open year-round in Massachusetts. The Metacomet-Monadnock Trail is not far from this system and can be reached via a marked trail off the 10th Mountain Trail, near Bugaboo Pass on Northfield Mountain. Other activities, including orienteering, canoeing on the nearby Connecticut River, and educational programs, are conducted through the center. This hike takes in some of the mountain's best features—including the Rose Ledge cliffs and a view of the reservoir at the 1,100-foot summit—but many other loop options are possible here. The route described here climbs about 600–700 feet in elevation.

From the parking lot and visitors center, follow the wide carriage road of the 10th Mountain Trail to the right. Reaching a trail sign 0.1 mile from the parking lot, turn left onto the Rose Ledge Trail footpath, marked here by blue diamonds. Follow the trail 0.2 mile across a carriage road and then turn right with the trail (note the trail is now orange-blazed). In the next 0.8 mile, the trail crosses two carriage roads, Hemlock Hill and Jug End, and then bears left at the fork to traverse above the cliffs, with some views of nearby wooded hills. Just before reaching the wide carriage road called Rock Oak Ramble, turn right at an easily overlooked connector trail leading downhill a short distance to the Lower Ledge Trail. Turn left on the Lower Ledge and you're soon walking below the cliffs and may see rock climbers on them; be careful of loose rock falling from above if you venture near the cliff base. At 1.4 miles, the Lower Ledge Trail rejoins the Rose Ledge Trail. Continuing on as a

steady uphill climb through the woods, in another 0.6 mile, the Summit Trail enters on the left and coincides with the Rose Ledge Trail for the final 0.2 mile uphill push to the summit. From the viewing platform, enjoy the watery vista of Northfield Reservoir. On the return trip, follow the Reservoir Road off the summit, staying on the road for about 0.1 mile until reaching a junction with the Bobcat Trail. Turn left on the trail and follow downhill a little less than two miles back to the parking area, passing the Chocolate Pot shelter a little more than halfway down.

User Groups: Hikers and leashed dogs. No bikes, horses, or wheelchair facilities. Bikes and horses are allowed on multi-use trails (not included in this hike), but bikers must register once per season at the visitors center and horseback riders must check in for parking and trail information; helmets are required for both biking and horseback riding. Trails are often closed to bikes and horses during mud season, usually until late April.

Permits: Northfield Mountain is a pumped storage hydroelectric facility owned and operated by FirstLight Power Resources. No fee is charged for parking or trail use.

Maps: A trail map is available at the visitors center and online from Northfield Mountain Recreation and Environmental Center. For topographic area maps, request Northfield and Orange from the USGS.

Directions: From the junction of the Routes 63 and 10 in Northfield, drive south on Route 63 to a left turn for the Northfield Mountain visitors center and recreation parking area. The visitors center is open 9 A.M.–5 P.M. Wednesday–Sunday, spring–fall. The cross-country center is open 9 A.M.–5 P.M. daily during the ski season.

GPS Coordinates: 42.6110 N, 72.4720 W

Contact: Northfield Mountain Recreation and Environmental Center, 99 Millers Falls Rd./Rte. 63, Northfield, MA 01360, 413/659-3714, www.firstlightpower.com/northfield.

MASSACHUSETTS

2 CRAG MOUNTAIN
3.4 mi/2 hr

in Northfield

One of the rocky outcroppings of Northfield's Bald Hills region, this easy hike—ascending only a few hundred feet—leads to Crag Mountain (1,503 ft.) and expansive views from its open, knife-edge summit. From the mountain's center-of-New England locale, take in the Berkshires and the southern Green Mountains of Vermont to the west and northwest, New Hampshire's Mount Monadnock to the northeast, the central hills of Massachusetts to the east, and the nearby Northfield Mountain Reservoir, Mount Toby, and South Sugarloaf Mountain to the south.

From the parking turnout, follow the white blazes of the Metacomet-Monadnock Trail as it heads south into the woods. Not far from the trailhead, the path crosses one wet area and then begins its gentle rise through a mixed deciduous and conifer forest. Breaking out of the woods and crossing on rockier terrain just yards from the top, the trail reaches Crag's open summit ridge 1.7 miles from the road. Enjoy the scenery and hike back along the same route.

User Groups: Hikers and dogs. No bikes, horses, or wheelchair facilities.

Permits: Parking and access are free.

Maps: A map of this trail is included with The Metacomet-Monadnock Trail Guide, available for $14.95 from the AMC Berkshire Chapter. For a topographic area map, request Northfield from the USGS.

Directions: From Route 10/63 in Northfield, about 0.2 mile south of the town center and 0.3 mile north of the southern junction of Routes 10 and 63, turn west onto Maple Street, which becomes Gulf Road. Drive 3.1 miles to a turnout on the right, where the white blazes of the Metacomet-Monadnock Trail enter the woods.

GPS Coordinates: 42.6603 N, 72.4182 W

Contact: AMC Berkshire Chapter, P.O. Box 9369, North Amherst, MA 01059. (The Appalachian Mountain Club's Berkshire's chapter is charged with maintaining portions of the Metacomet-Monadnock Trail crossing private land.)

3 BEAR'S DEN
0.2 mi/0.5 hr

in New Salem

This compact but dramatic gorge along the Middle Branch of the Swift River is a beautiful spot hidden away just steps from the road. From the parking area, follow the left fork of the trail to reach the gorge rim, which, in just a few feet, places you at the brink of a precipitous drop to the river. Double back and follow the trail downhill to the banks of the river, where the foundations of an old grist mill still stand. A sign near the trail's beginning relates some of this spot's history: how a settler killed a black bear here, thus explaining the name Bear's Den, and how the Wampanoag chief King Phillip supposedly met with other chiefs here in 1675 during their wars with European settlers in the Connecticut Valley.

User Groups: Hikers and dogs. No wheelchair facilities. This trail is not suitable for bikes, horses, or skis.

Permits: Parking and access are free.

Maps: No map is necessary for this short and easy walk.

Directions: From the junction of Routes 202 and 122 in New Salem, follow Route 202 south for 0.4 mile. Turn right onto Elm Street, drive 0.7 mile, and then turn left onto Neilson Road. Drive a half mile and park at the roadside. The entrance is on the right, where a short trail leads to the gorge. The reservation is open to the public sunrise–sunset year-round.

GPS Coordinates: 42.5438 N, 72.3206 W

Contact: The Trustees of Reservations Central Region Office, Doyle Reservation, 325 Lindell Ave., Leominster, MA 01453-5414, 978/840-4446, www.thetrustees.org.

❹ MOUNT WATATIC AND NUTTING HILL
2.8 mi/1.5 hr

👫2 ⛰9

in Ashburnham

The scenic southern terminus of the long-distance Wapack footpath, 1,832-foot Mount Watatic's pair of barren, rocky summit ledges offer excellent views of nearby peaks such as Wachusett Mountain and Kidder and Temples Mountains. The views extend north into North Hampshire and, on a clear day, to landmarks as distant as Mount Greylock, the White Mountains, and even the Boston skyline. The Midstate Trail was rerouted in recent years to coincide with the Wapack Trail over Watatic's summit; both are well blazed with yellow triangles. This hike leads first to Watatic's scenic outcropping, Nutting Hill.

From the parking area, follow an old woods road north, ascending gradually. At 0.3 mile, the Wapack/Midstate Trail turns right (east), but this hike continues straight ahead on the blue-blazed State Line Trail to reach Nutting Hill. A half mile farther, you reach a junction where the State Line Trail forks left; continue straight ahead on the Midstate Trail (yellow-blazed), which is rejoined by the Wapack Trail within another 0.2 mile. It is nearly a mile to Watatic's summit from this point. Soon passing over Nutting Hill's open top and veering to the right, watch for the cairns marking the way. Reentering the woods, you climb Watatic's northwest slope, passing by the somewhat overgrown trails of the former Mount Watatic ski area. Just below the summit stands an abandoned fire tower, now closed and unsafe. From the summit, an unmarked path leads to the lower, southeast summit. Double back to the fire tower, turn left, and follow the Wapack, passing an open ledge with views and, farther down, an enormous split boulder. At the Midstate Trail junction, turn left for the parking area.

User Groups: Hikers and dogs. This trail is not suitable for bikes or horses; no wheelchair facilities.

Permits: Parking and access are free.

Maps: A map and guide to the Wapack Trail, including this hike, is available for $11 from the Friends of the Wapack. For a topographic area map, request Ashburnham from the USGS.

Directions: The trailhead parking area is on the north side of Route 119 in Ashburnham, 1.4 miles west of its junction with Route 101.

GPS Coordinates: 42.6870 N, 71.8901 W

Contact: Friends of the Wapack, P.O. Box 115, West Peterborough, NH 03468, www.wapack.org.

❺ WILLARD BROOK
2 mi/1 hr

👫1 ⛰7

in Willard Brook State Forest in Ashby

A good, gentle hike for introducing very young children to the woods, this easy walk hugs the rock-strewn Willard Brook through its tight valley, winding through hemlock groves and among huge boulders. The trail begins from either side of the stone bridge over Willard Brook, just below Damon Pond. Toward the other (northeast) end of the trail, it ascends a hillside and reaches a forest road; turning left brings you shortly to the state forest headquarters. Most people just double back to the start for a nice two-mile stroll. There are several miles of woods roads in the state forest open to other activities, such as mountain biking or horseback riding.

User Groups: Hikers and leashed dogs. No bikes, horses, or wheelchair facilities.

Permits: A daily parking fee of $5 is collected mid-May–mid-October.

Maps: A free, basic trail map of the state forest is available at the headquarters on Route 119 in West Townsend, just before the Ashby town line, or at the Massachusetts Division of State Parks and Recreation website. For a

MASSACHUSETTS

covered bridge crossing of Willard Brook, Ashby

topographic area map, request Ashburnham from the USGS.

Directions: From the junction of Routes 119 and 31 in Ashby, drive 0.2 mile east on Route 119 to the Damon Pond entrance and parking area.

GPS Coordinates: 42.6870 N, 71.8901 W

Contact: Willard Brook State Forest, Rte. 119, West Townsend, MA 01474, 978/597-8802. Massachusetts Division of State Parks and Recreation, 251 Causeway St., Suite 600, Boston, MA 02114-2104, 617/626-1250, www.state.ma.us/dem/forparks.htm.

⑥ CROW HILLS
0.7 mi/0.75 hr

in Leominster State Forest in Westminster

The hike up Crow Hills, at the western edge of the more than 4,000-acre Leominster State Forest, is a short loop that can be done with young children, though the trail does grow steep and rocky in a few small sections. Despite its brevity and the climb of just a few hundred feet, it is one of the most dramatic walks in central Massachusetts, traversing the top of tall cliffs with commanding views of the wooded hills and ponds of the state forest and nearby Wachusett Mountain. Climb the hills in early autumn and the vivid crimson-colored woods may convince you to make this trek an annual event.

From the parking lot, cross Route 31 to a wide, well-marked trail entering the woods. Within 100 feet, the trail turns sharply left, then swings right and climbs steeply to the base of cliffs, 100 feet high in places. The trail then diverges right and left, with both branches looping up to the cliff tops. You can hike the loop in either direction; this description leads to the right (counterclockwise). Walk below the cliff to where stones arranged in steps lead steeply uphill to a junction with the Midstate Trail, marked by yellow triangular blazes. Turn left, carefully following the trail atop the cliffs past several spots that offer sweeping views; the best views are at the far end of the cliffs. Wachusett Mountain, with its ski slopes, is visible to the southwest. Take care not to kick any loose stones or wander near the cliff's edge as there are often rock climbers and hikers below. From the last open ledges, the Midstate Trail swings right, entering the woods again and continuing about 75 yards, then turning left and descending a steep, rocky gully. At its bottom, turn left again and, diverging from the Midstate, walk the trail around the base of the cliffs to this loop's beginning. Turn right and descend to the parking lot.

User Groups: Hikers and leashed dogs. This trail is not suitable for bikes or horses; no wheelchair facilities.

Permits: A $5 parking fee is collected May–October; a season pass costs $35. The parking lot may not always be plowed in winter; call the state forest headquarters for more information.

Maps: A free, basic trail map of Leominster State Forest is available at the state forest headquarters or at the Massachusetts Division of State Parks and Recreation website. The Mount Wachusett and Leominster State Forest Trail Map costs $3.95 from New England Cartographics (413/549-4124 or toll-free 888/995-6277, www.necartographics.com). For a topographic area map, request Fitchburg from the USGS.

Directions: The hike begins from a large parking lot at the Crow Hills Pond Picnic Area along Route 31 on the Westminster/Princeton line, 2.2 miles south of the junction of Routes 31 and 2 and 1.5 miles north of the junction of Routes 31 and 140.

GPS Coordinates: 42.5351 N, 71.8541 W

Contact: Leominster State Forest, Rte. 31, Princeton, MA 01541, 978/874-2303. Massachusetts Division of State Parks and Recreation, 251 Causeway St., Suite 600, Boston, MA 02114-2104, 617/626-1250, www.state.ma.us/dem/forparks.htm.

7 BALL HILL LOOP
3.5 mi/2.5 hr

in Leominster State Forest in Westminster, Princeton, and Leominster

Leominster State Forest has a network of marked trails and less-distinct footpaths weaving throughout, most in its northern half, north of Rocky Pond Road/Parmenter Road. (South of that dirt road, which is open to bikes but not motor vehicles, the state forest is crossed mainly by old woods roads.) This hike ascends one of the low, wooded hills in the state forest into an area where even frequent visitors to Leominster find it easy to stumble across trails they don't recognize. There are myriad trails through here and it's easy to get lost once you venture over Ball Hill. Nonetheless, the woodlands are quiet and fun to explore. This hike ascends small hills but never climbs more than a few hundred feet.

From the parking area, walk across the earthen dike between the two halves of Crow Hills Pond and then turn right, following a blazed trail south along the shore of the pond. Within a half mile, turn left (east) onto the Rocky Pond Trail, which climbs Ball Hill, steeply for short stretches. Near the hilltop, about one mile from the hike's start, is a spot where the trees thin enough to allow a partially obstructed view of the hills to the west. Anyone concerned about getting lost might want to turn back from here. Otherwise, continue over the hill, through quiet woods crossed by the occasional stone wall.

Descending the back side of the hill, ignore the trails branching off to the right. Turn left at the first opportunity: about 2.5 miles from the parking area, where you see a landfill through the trees at the state forest edge. The trail swings north, then west; continue bearing left at trail junctions. On your way back, you pass through a wet area, over a low hillock, and eventually reach the paved parking lot at the public beach at the Crow Hills Pond's north end. Cross the parking lot to the south (left),

MASSACHUSETTS

a Medusa-like tree growing in Leominster State Forest

picking up the trail again for the short walk back to the dike across the pond.

User Groups: Hikers and leashed dogs. This trail is not suitable for bikes or horses; no wheelchair facilities.

Permits: A $5 parking fee is collected May–October; a season pass costs $35. The parking lot may not always be plowed in winter; call the state forest headquarters for more information.

Maps: A free, basic trail map of Leominster State Forest is available at the state forest headquarters or at the Massachusetts Division of State Parks and Recreation website. The Mount Wachusett and Leominster State Forest Trail Map costs $3.95 from New England Cartographics (413/549-4124 or toll-free 888/995-6277, www.necartographics.com). For a topographic area map, request Fitchburg from the USGS.

Directions: The hike begins from a large parking lot at the Crow Hills Pond Picnic Area along Route 31 on the Westminster-Princeton line, 2.2 miles south of the junction of Routes 31 and 2 and 1.5 miles north of the junction of Routes 31 and 140.

GPS Coordinates: 42.5351 N, 71.8541 W

Contact: Leominster State Forest, Rte. 31, Princeton, MA 01541, 978/874-2303. Massachusetts Division of State Parks and Recreation, 251 Causeway St., Suite 600, Boston, MA 02114-2104, 617/626-1250, www.state. ma.us/dem/forparks.htm.

8 LEOMINSTER FOREST ROADS LOOP

5.5 mi/2.5 hr   3 7

in Leominster State Forest in Westminster, Princeton, and Leominster

This loop of approximately 5.5 miles largely follows old forest roads through the southern half of Leominster State Forest, making it particularly fun on a mountain bike or cross-country skis—Leominster is in the Bay State's "snow belt" and regularly sees several feet of snow cover each winter. There are small hills along these roads—nothing that is difficult to hike, but which can make skiing or mountain biking moderately difficult.

From the parking lot, cross the picnic area and the earthen dike dividing the two halves of Crow Hills Pond. Across the dike, turn right (south), following the trail along the pond and past it about 0.7 mile to the dirt Rocky Pond Road (which is not open to motor vehicles). Cross Rocky Pond Road onto Wolf Rock Road and continue about a half mile. Where the road forks, bear right and then watch for an unmarked footpath diverging left within 0.2 mile (if you reach the state forest boundary near private homes, you've gone too far). Follow that winding, narrow path through the woods less than a half mile to Wolf Rock Road and turn right. You descend a steep hill on the road, turn left onto Center Road, and follow it about 1.2 miles to Parmenter Road. Turn left (west), climbing a hill and crossing from Leominster into Princeton, where the road becomes Rocky Pond Road. From the road's high point, continue west for less than a mile to the junction of Rocky Pond Road, Wolf Rock Road, and the trail from Crow Hills Pond; turn right on the trail to return to this hike's start.

Special note: Short sections of this loop follow hiking trails that would be difficult on a bike. Cyclists might instead begin this loop from the dirt parking area and gate where Rocky Pond Road crosses Route 31, 0.6 mile south of the main parking area. Pedal east on Rocky Pond Road for about 0.4 mile and then turn right onto the wide Wolf Rock Road. A half mile farther, where the road forks, bear left, staying on Wolf Rock Road, which leads to Center Road and the continuation of this hike.

User Groups: Hikers, bikers, and leashed dogs. No horses or wheelchair facilities.

Permits: A $5 parking fee is collected May–October; a season pass costs $35. The parking lot may not always be plowed in winter; call the state forest headquarters for more information.

Maps: A free, basic trail map of Leominster State Forest is available at the state forest headquarters or at the Massachusetts Division

fallen autumn leaves, Leominster State Forest

of State Parks and Recreation website. The Mount Wachusett and Leominster State Forest Trail Map costs $3.95 from New England Cartographics (413/549-4124 or toll-free 888/995-6277, www.necartographics.com). For a topographic area map, request Fitchburg from the USGS.

Directions: The hike begins from a large parking lot at the Crow Hills Pond Picnic Area along Route 31 on the Westminster/Princeton line, 2.2 miles south of the junction of Routes 31 and 2 and 1.5 miles north of the junction of Routes 31 and 140.

GPS Coordinates: 42.5351 N, 71.8541 W

Contact: Leominster State Forest, Rte. 31, Princeton, MA 01541, 978/874-2303. Massachusetts Division of State Parks and Recreation, 251 Causeway St., Suite 600, Boston, MA 02114-2104, 617/626-1250, www.state.ma.us/dem/forparks.htm.

© JACQUELINE TOURVILLE

MASSACHUSETTS

☰ WACHUSETT MOUNTAIN: BALANCED ROCK

0.6 mi/0.5 hr 🏃2 △7

in Wachusett Mountain State Reservation in Princeton

Balanced Rock is a glacial-erratic boulder that well lives up to its name. Pick up the Midstate Trail's yellow triangular blazes from the parking lot, behind and to the right of the lodge. Here the trail is also known as the Balanced Rock Trail. Follow it, climbing gently, for 0.3 mile to Balanced Rock. To finish this hike, return the way you came. Hikers looking for a bit more of an outing can continue on the Midstate Trail to the Wachusett summit via the Semuhenna and Harrington Trails and then descend the Old Indian Trail back to the Midstate Trail to return for a loop of several miles. Consult the map and inquire at the visitors center for specific distances.

User Groups: Hikers and leashed dogs. Bikes and horses are prohibited; no wheelchair facilities.

Permits: A daily parking fee of $2 is collected mid-May–mid-October.

Maps: A free contour map of hiking trails is available at the visitors center or at the Massachusetts Division of State Parks and Recreation website. The Mount Wachusett and Leominster State Forest Trail Map costs $3.95 from New England Cartographics (413/549-4124 or toll-free 888/995-6277, www.necartographics.com). For topographic area maps, request Sterling and Fitchburg from the USGS.

Directions: From Route 140, 2.2 miles south of the junction of Routes 140 and 2 in Westminster and 1.8 miles north of the junction of Routes 140 and 31, turn onto Mile Hill Road, following signs to the Wachusett Mountain Ski Area. Drive a mile, turn right into the ski area parking lot, and then cross to the rear of the lot, behind the lodge. The Wachusett Mountain State Reservation Visitor Center is farther up Mile Hill Road.

GPS Coordinates: 42.5114 N, 71.8866 W

Contact: Wachusett Mountain State Reservation, Mountain Rd., P.O. Box 248, Princeton, MA 01541, 978/464-2987. Massachusetts Division of State Parks and Recreation, 251 Causeway St., Suite 600, Boston, MA 02114-2104, 617/626-1250, www.state.ma.us/dem/forparks.htm.

☷ WACHUSETT MOUNTAIN: PINE HILL TRAIL

2 mi/1.5 hr 🏃4 △8

in Wachusett Mountain State Reservation in Princeton

At 2,006 feet and the biggest hill in central Massachusetts, Wachusett may be better known for its downhill ski area. But the state reservation has a fairly extensive network of fine hiking trails, including a section of the Midstate Trail that passes over the summit. The summit offers views in all directions: on a clear day, you can see New Hampshire's Mount Monadnock to the north and the Boston skyline 40 miles to the east. Trail junctions are marked with signs. The Pine Hill Trail is a steep, rocky climb that could be dangerous in snowy or icy conditions.

From the visitors center parking lot, follow the Bicentennial Trail about 0.1 mile to the first trail branching off to the right, the Pine Hill Trail—actually an old ski trail and the most direct route to the summit, about a half mile. The trail ascends at a moderate grade over fairly rocky terrain. After checking out the views from various spots on the broad summit, cross to its southwest corner and look for the Harrington Trail sign. Descending the Harrington, you soon cross the paved summit road; after reentering the woods, take a short side path left off the Harrington to enjoy a long view west over the sparsely populated hills and valleys of central Massachusetts. Backtrack and descend the Harrington to the Link Trail, turning left. Turn right onto the Mountain House Trail, descend briefly, and then bear left onto the Loop Trail, which descends to the Bicentennial Trail. Turn left for the visitors center.

User Groups: Hikers and leashed dogs. Bikes and horses are prohibited; no wheelchair facilities.

Permits: A daily parking fee of $2 is collected mid-May–mid-October.

Maps: A free contour map of hiking trails is available at the visitors center at the Massachusetts Division of State Parks and Recreation website. The Mount Wachusett and Leominster State Forest Trail Map costs $3.95 from New England Cartographics (413/549-4124 or toll-free 888/995-6277, www.necartographics.com). For topographic area maps, request Sterling and Fitchburg from the USGS.

Directions: From Route 140, 2.2 miles south of the junction of Routes 140 and 2 in Westminster and 1.8 miles north of the junction of Routes 140 and 31, turn onto Mile Hill Road, following signs to the Wachusett Mountain State Reservation Visitor Center.

GPS Coordinates: 42.5114 N, 71.8866 W

Contact: Wachusett Mountain State Reservation, Mountain Rd., P.O. Box 248, Princeton, MA 01541, 978/464-2987. Massachusetts Division of State Parks and Recreation, 251 Causeway St., Suite 600, Boston, MA 02114-2104, 617/626-1250, www.state.ma.us/dem/forparks.htm.

⓫ WACHUSETT MOUNTAIN LOOP
5 mi/3 hr

in Wachusett Mountain State Reservation in Princeton

This hike to the summit of Wachusett (2,006 ft.) follows a circuitous, but enjoyable route up the largest mountain in central Massachusetts, taking advantage of the extensive trail network here. Although sections of the trail are somewhat rocky and steep for brief stretches, it's not very difficult, ascending about 700

feet in elevation. You can easily shorten or lengthen this hike as well; check out the trail map and improvise from this description. A scenic alternative is the Jack Frost Trail, which passes through dense hemlock forest.

From the visitors center parking lot, follow the Bicentennial Trail for about a mile as it contours around the mountain's base, passing three trail junctions, then bear left onto the High Meadow Trail. Follow it across an open meadow and then back into the woods again before reaching Echo Lake. Stay to the left on the gravel road beside the lake for about 0.1 mile, turn left on the Echo Lake Trail, and follow it less than a half mile to a parking lot. Crossing the small lot, pick up the Stage Coach Trail, climbing steadily up an old carriage road, which narrows to a footpath. After more than a half mile, bear right on the Harrington Trail. It crosses West Road, then the Administration Road, before suddenly growing much steeper as it makes a direct line for the summit. But right before that steep part begins, turn left on the Semuhenna Trail, staying on it for about a half mile. Cross the paved summit road, reenter the woods, and then immediately turn right on the West Side Trail. You're on that path for less than a half mile before turning right again on the Old Indian Trail, the steepest part of this hike. As you climb to the summit, you'll pass a ski area chairlift station right before reaching the top. Cross the summit to the paved road that heads down, follow it about 100 feet, and then bear right into the woods on the Mountain House Trail. Descend about a quarter mile, turn left, continue another quarter mile or less, and turn left again on the Loop Trail, descending over rocks to the Bicentennial Trail. Turn left for the visitors center.

User Groups: Hikers and leashed dogs. No bikes, horses, or wheelchair facilities.

Permits: A daily parking fee of $2 is collected mid-May–mid-October.

Maps: A free contour map of hiking trails is available at the visitors center or at the

Massachusetts Division of State Parks and Recreation website. The Mount Wachusett and Leominster State Forest Trail Map costs $3.95 from New England Cartographics (413/549-4124 or toll-free 888/995-6277, www.necartographics.com). For topographic area maps, request Sterling and Fitchburg from the USGS.

Directions: From Route 140, 2.2 miles south of the junction of Routes 140 and 2 in Westminster and 1.8 miles north of the junction of Routes 140 and 31, turn onto Mile Hill Road, following signs to the Wachusett Mountain State Reservation Visitor Center.

GPS Coordinates: 42.5114 N, 71.8866 W

Contact: Wachusett Mountain State Reservation, Mountain Rd., P.O. Box 248, Princeton, MA 01541, 978/464-2987. Massachusetts Division of State Parks and Recreation, 251 Causeway St., Suite 600, Boston, MA 02114-2104, 617/626-1250, www.state.ma.us/dem/forparks.htm.

12 REDEMPTION ROCK TO WACHUSETT MOUNTAIN
1.8 mi/1 hr

in Princeton

Legend has it that a Concord settler named John Hoar sat atop this massive, flat-topped boulder with members of a band of Wampanoags in 1676 to negotiate the release of Mary Rowlandson, wife of the minister in the nearby town of Lancaster, whom the Wampanoags had abducted and held captive for 11 weeks. A fun spot to explore with kids, Redemption Rock is just off the roadside. This hike continues past the rock through the woods for a short distance to the base of Wachusett Mountain and back, following a fairly quiet Midstate Trail stretch where you might see a deer or grouse.

After exploring Redemption Rock, which sits beside the parking area, follow the Midstate Trail's yellow triangular blazes into the woods. Watch closely for the blazes; several side trails branch off the Midstate Trail. It proceeds generally westward through the woods, climbing slightly and traversing some rocky trail stretches and some wet areas, reaching Mountain Road and the parking lot for the Wachusett Mountain Ski Area in 0.9 mile. Turn around and return the way you came or combine this with the Wachusett Mountain: Balanced Rock hike, which begins across the ski area parking lot.

User Groups: Hikers and dogs. The trail is not suitable for bikes or horses; no wheelchair facilities.

Permits: Parking and access are free.

Maps: The Mount Wachusett and Leominster State Forest Trail Map costs $3.95 from New England Cartographics (413/549-4124 or toll-free 888/995-6277, www.necartographics.com). For topographic area maps, request Fitchburg and Sterling from the USGS.

Directions: The hike begins from the small parking lot at Redemption Rock along Route 140 in Princeton, 3.1 miles south of the junction of Routes 140 and 2 in Westminster and 0.9 mile north of the junction of Routes 140 and 31 in Princeton. Redemption Rock is open to the public sunrise–sunset year-round.

GPS Coordinates: 42.4817 N, 71.8475 W

Contact: The Trustees of Reservations Central Region Office, Doyle Reservation, 325 Lindell Ave., Leominster, MA 01453-5414, 978/840-4446, www.thetrustees.org.

13 WACHUSETT MEADOW TO WACHUSETT MOUNTAIN
6.2 mi/3.5 hr

in Princeton in the Wachusett Meadow Wildlife Sanctuary

Beginning from Wachusett Meadow, the picturesque 977-acre Audubon wildlife refuge, much of this Midstate Trail stretch is relatively easy, ascending less than 1,000 feet in elevation, much of that over the steep final 0.3-mile climb to the Wachusett Mountain summit, where there are long views in every direction. Visitors to Wachusett Meadow shouldn't miss the 300-year-old Crocker maple, one of the largest sugar maples in the country, with a trunk circumference of more than 15 feet. It sits on the west edge of the meadow, a very short detour off this hike's route, and it is guaranteed to awe children and adults alike.

From the wildlife sanctuary parking area, walk north into the meadow on the Mountain Trail and then turn left in the middle of the meadow at post six, heading for the woods and reaching a junction with the Midstate Trail about 0.2 mile from the parking lot. Turn right (north), following the Midstate over easy terrain through the woods. The trail crosses a dirt road about a mile from the hike's start, passes over a small hill, and then crosses paved Westminster Road at 1.8 miles. After crossing a field, the trail enters the woods again, ascending a low hill and passing just below the summit. After crossing paved Administration Road, the Midstate Trail (here also called the Harrington Trail) reaches a junction with the Semuhenna Trail one mile from Westminster Road. The Semuhenna/Midstate turns left, but this hike continues straight up the Harrington another 0.3 mile to the Wachusett Mountain summit. Hike back the way you came.

Special note: To avoid backtracking, and for a somewhat shorter hike, shuttle vehicles to Wachusett Meadow and the Wachusett Mountain State Reservation Visitor Center and do this hike one-way. From the summit descend the Pine Hill Trail and Bicentennial Trail to the Wachusett Mountain Visitor Center, as described in the *Redemption Rock to Wachusett Mountain* listing in this chapter.

User Groups: Hikers only. This trail is not suitable for horses; no wheelchair facilities. Bikes and dogs are prohibited.

Permits: A fee of $4 per adult and $3 per child ages 3–12 and seniors is charged at Wachusett Meadow to nonmembers of the Massachusetts Audubon Society. A daily parking fee of $2 is

collected mid-May–mid-October at Wachusett Mountain State Reservation.

Maps: A map of Wachusett Meadow is available at an information board beside the parking lot. A free contour map of hiking trails in the Wachusett Mountain State Reservation is available at the state reservation or at the Massachusetts Division of State Parks and Recreation website The Mount Wachusett and Leominster State Forest Trail Map costs $3.95 from New England Cartographics (413/549-4124 or toll-free 888/995-6277, www.necartographics.com). For a topographic area map, request Sterling from the USGS.

Directions: From the junction of Routes 62 and 31 in Princeton center, drive west on Route 62 for a half mile and turn right onto Goodnow Road at a sign for the Wachusett Meadow Sanctuary. Continue a mile to the end of the paved road and park at the sanctuary visitors center.

The Wachusett Meadow Visitor Center trails are open dawn–dusk Tuesday–Sunday and on Monday holidays. The Nature Center is open Tuesday–Saturday 10 A.M.–2 P.M. GPS Coordinates: 42.4521 N, 71.8922 W

Contact: Massachusetts Audubon Society Wachusett Meadow Wildlife Sanctuary, 113 Goodnow Rd., Princeton, MA 01541, 978/464-2712, wachusett@massaudubon. org. Massachusetts Division of State Parks and Recreation, 251 Causeway St., Suite 600, Boston, MA 02114-2104, 617/626-1250, www.state.ma.us/dem/forparks.htm.

14 MOUNT HOLYOKE
3.2 mi/2 hr 🏃3 ⛰8

in Skinner State Park in Hadley

Along the up-and-down ridge of 878-foot Mount Holyoke, the Summit House stands out prominently, easily visible to I-91 motorists several miles to the west. Although mostly wooded, the rugged Holyoke ridgeline has several overlooks that afford splendid views west to the Connecticut Valley and the Berkshires, and some views southward. This hike climbs about 700 feet in elevation, with much of the route along open ridge.

Follow the Metacomet-Monadnock Trail east from the road, immediately climbing a steep hillside; the trail soon swings north and ascends the ridge, reaching the first views in just over a half mile. At 1.6 miles, the trail passes by the historic Summit House, once a fashionable mountaintop hotel and now part of the state park; it's open weekends Memorial Day–Columbus Day for tours and programs. Picnic grounds also mark the top of Holyoke and numerous observation points offer unmatched views of the Connecticut Valley. You can return the way you came or continue over the summit, crossing the paved Mountain Road and turning right (south) in Taylor's Notch onto the red-blazed Dry Brook Trail. Follow it down the small valley, trending to the southwest and finally to the west and back to your vehicle.

User Groups: Hikers and leashed dogs. This trail is not suitable for bikes or horses; no wheelchair facilities.

Permits: Parking and access are free.

Maps: A free trail map of Skinner State Park is available at the Halfway House on Mountain Road (off Route 47) when a staff person is there; at the Notch Visitor Center on Route 116, where the Metacomet-Monadnock Trail crosses the road and enters Holyoke Range State Park in Amherst; or at the Massachusetts Division of State Parks and Recreation website. The Holyoke Range/Skinner State Park Trail Map (Western Section) costs $3.95 from New England Cartographics (413/549-4124 or toll-free 888/995-6277, www.necartographics.com). For a topographic area map, request Mount Holyoke from the USGS.

Directions: From the junction of Routes 47 and 9 in Hadley, drive south on Route 47 for 4.9 miles (you'll see the Summit House on the Mount Holyoke ridge straight ahead). Across from the Hockanum Cemetery, turn left, continue 0.1 mile, and park at the roadside where

the white blazes of the Metacomet-Monadnock Trail enter the woods on the right. Or from the junction of Routes 47 and 116 in South Hadley, drive north on Route 47 for 2.7 miles, turn right at Hockanum Cemetery, and then continue 0.1 mile to the trailhead.

GPS Coordinates: 42.3084 N, 72.5896 W

Contact: Skinner State Park, Rte. 47, Box 91, Hadley, MA 01035, 413/586-0350 or 413/253-2883. Massachusetts Division of State Parks and Recreation, 251 Causeway St., Suite 600, Boston, MA 02114-2104, 617/626-1250, www.state.ma.us/dem/forparks.htm.

15 RATTLESNAKE KNOB AND THE HORSE CAVES
4.5 mi/2.5 hr   🏃2 ⛰7

in Granby

The highest point on the saddle between Mounts Long and Norwottock, at an elevation of 813 feet, Rattlesnake Knob's relatively easy climb and excellent views make it a worthy destination along the ridgy Holyoke Range's eastern end. This hike also takes you to the Horse Caves, a large cleft in the rocks near the base of Mount Norwottuck. The caves are an interesting geological formation to explore, but are most well-known for the supposed role they played as the hideout for Daniel Shays and his followers after their raid on the Springfield Arsenal in 1786, part of the tax revolt known as Shay's Rebellion. This is a great hike for bringing history class alive for kids and only comes with a modest few hundred feet in elevation gain.

From the parking area, reach the trailhead at a brown metal gate marked Main Entrance. On the other side of the gate, follow the well-worn path to a junction at 0.2 mile. Here, bear right on the Upper Access Trail. For the next mile, the trail passes through a pleasant forest of oaks and hickory, stands of birch, and pine. Listen for the sound of woodpeckers and note their telltale drill holes in the bark of many of the trees along the route. At 0.9 mile, pass a rusted out old car (and make a guess as to how it ended up here) and then at 1.6 miles, bear right onto the red-blazed Cliffside Trail. From here it's only a few feet to a left turn onto the combined Robert Frost Trail (orange-blazed) and Metacomet-Monadnock Trail (white-blazed). At 1.7 miles, bear left again to stay with the orange and white blazes and begin to climb the rocky hillside. Reaching Rattlesnake Knob in another 0.1 mile, follow the sign marked To Viewpoint. From the open ledge of Rattlesnake, Mount Long rises in a green mound to the east and to the north lies the village of Amherst and surrounding Pioneer Valley countryside.

Backtracking from the viewing area, follow the orange and white blazes again as they pass over the knob and drop quickly to reach a sign for the Horse Caves (at 2.1 miles). Bear right and follow the Horse Cave trail less than a half mile to the caves; once you are done exploring, retrace your steps to the orange and white blazes and continue downhill. At the next junction, bear left onto the blue blazes of the Swamp Trail and follow 0.4 mile to a right turn onto the Southside Trail. At 3.2 miles, turn onto the trail marked Lower Access Trails to B-Street Gate. Follow past a large beaver dam and then bear right at the last trail junction before returning to your car.

User Groups: Hikers, dogs, bikes, and horses. No wheelchair facilities. The upper portions of this trail are unsuitable for bikes and horses.

Permits: Parking and access are free.

Maps: A free trail map and informational brochure are available at the park entrance at the Notch Visitor Center. For a topographic area map, request Holyoke from the USGS.

Directions: From Springfield, take I-91 north to Exit 19. From the exit, follow Route 9 east, soon crossing the Connecticut River. At 0.5 mile, turn right onto Bay Road, follow signs for Route 47 south. At 2.3 miles from the highway, turn left to remain on Bay Road and leave Route 47. At 5.2 miles, reach Atkins Farms Country Market and turn right onto

Route 116 south. At 6.4 miles, turn left into the Notch Visitor Center for free maps and an interesting natural history center. Reach the trailhead by continuing south on Route 116, turning left onto Amherst Street at 7.5 miles (at a sign for Route 202 and Granby). At 7.9 miles, turn left onto Bachelor Street. Finally, at 8.6 miles, park on either shoulder of the road when you reach a brown metal gate on your left.

GPS Coordinates: 42.2811 N, 72.4938 W

Contact: Mount Holyoke State Park, Rte. 116, Amherst, MA 01002, 413/586-0350. Massachusetts Division of State Parks and Recreation, 251 Causeway St., Suite 600, Boston, MA 02114-2104, 617/626-1250, www.state.ma.us/dem/forparks.htm.

16 QUABBIN RESERVOIR
4 mi/2 hr　　　　　🏃1 ⛰9

in Belchertown

Created in the 1930s by the construction of two huge earthen dams along the Swift River, the vast Quabbin Reservoir covers 39 square miles and is the main public water supply for the metro Boston area. Though artificial, the Quabbin still qualifies as the largest body of water in Massachusetts. Surrounding the reservoir is Quabbin Park, managed by the state as a recreational area, with hiking and bike trails crisscrossing acres of woods and many low, rolling hills. This easy hike takes you from Quabbin Hill to the scenic Enfield Lookout for expansive views of the reservoir and surrounding Swift River Valley.

From the parking area near the top of Quabbin Hill, walk a few more feet uphill to the stone observation tower and views north towards the water. Backtracking to the parking area, the yellow-blazed trailhead is located on the eastern end of the lot. Follow the trail on a gentle descent through pleasant woods; frequent breaks in the tress offer glimpses of the reservoir off in the distance. After a mile of walking, cross through a grassy area (follow the yellow markers) to a right turn onto a dirt jeep road. After only a few yards, arrive at an intersection with a paved road. Turn right on the paved road to reach the Enfield Lookout, an upland bluff not far from the shoreline and a popular perch for bird-watching—soaring bald eagles are frequently spotted here. To reach the water's edge, retrace your steps to the dirt road and take a right, descending another 0.75 mile through thick stands of pine (known as the Pine Plantation) before reaching the shore. For the two-mile return trip to your car, follow the dirt road back to the hiking trail, climbing uphill to the parking lot.

User Groups: Hikers only. Bikes are allowed on the dirt jeep road only (this can be picked up near the parking area). No dogs, horses, or wheelchair facilities.

Permits: Parking and access are free.

Maps: A free trail map is available at the Quabbin Visitor Center. For a topographic area map, request Holyoke from the USGS.

Directions: From the corner of West Street and Route 9/Main Street in downtown Ware, turn left on Main Street and follow for 4.7 miles to a right turn at a sign for the Quabbin Reservoir (as Route 9 leaves Ware, it is also called Belchertown Road). Follow the park access road for 0.3 mile to the parking area (almost at the top of Quabbin Hill).

State regulations require visitors to enter and exit through gates or other designated areas only; no off trail hiking or biking. Anything that could pollute the water supply system, such as litter or refuse of any sort, is prohibited. Direct water contact activities, such as swimming and wading, are strictly prohibited by regulation. Dogs, horses, and pets are not allowed on any property associated with Quabbin Reservoir.

GPS Coordinates: 42.2160 N, 71.9999 W

Contact: Quabbin Visitor Center, 485 Ware Rd. (Rte. 9), Belchertown, MA 01007, 413/323-7221. Massachusetts Division of State Parks and Recreation, 251 Causeway St., Suite 600, Boston, MA 02114-2104, 617/626-1250, www.state.ma.us/dem/forparks.htm.

🔟 SPENCER STATE FOREST
1 mi/0.5 hr   🏃1 ⛰7

in Spencer

At almost 1,000 acres, Spencer State Forest is a landscape of hilly terrain, creeks, wetlands, and a beautiful transitional forest of oak, hickory, ash, and birch. The forest's most notable feature is the Howe Pond parcel, an estate formerly belonging to Elias Howe, the inventor of the sewing machine. Though the remains of the estate are limited to a mill pond and dam constructed by the inventor, their peaceful setting in the Spencer woods still makes for a pleasant, and relatively flat, forest ramble.

From the parking area, first take in the beauty of the woods by crossing the road and heading north along the old bridle trail. A loop of about a half mile, the trail takes you by the upper reaches of the Cranberry River, an especially pleasing stroll in autumn, when the wetlands here are a little less mosquito infested. Crossing over the river, the trail brings you back to the parking area. Next, head past the picnic area to reach the Howe Pond. The trail passes over the dam and then hugs the shore of the Mill Pond, a popular swimming hole in summer. There is no loop around the pond. Walk to the end of the trail about halfway around the water's edge, then turn around and walk back to your car.

User Groups: Hikers and leashed dogs. Bike and horses are allowed on the bridle path. Wheelchair users can get good views of the dam and pond from the wheelchair accessible picnic area.

Permits: Parking and access are free.

Maps: A free trail map is available near the picnic/parking area or online from the Massachusetts Division of State Parks and Recreation.

For a topographic area map, request Leicester from the USGS.

Directions: From the center of Spencer, head east on Main Street toward Maple Street. Take the first right onto Maple Street and follow for one mile to a right turn onto Howe Road. Follow Howe Road for one mile to the forest entrance; keep following the road a short distance to the parking and picnic area.

GPS Coordinates: 42.2158 N, 71.9990 W

Contact: Spencer State Forest, Howe Rd., Spencer, MA, 01562, 508/886-6333. Massachusetts Division of State Parks and Recreation, 251 Causeway St., Suite 600, Boston, MA 02114-2104, 617/626-1250, www.state.ma.us/dem/forparks.htm.

18 PURGATORY CHASM
0.5 mi/0.5 hr   🚶1 ⛰8

in Purgatory Chasm State Reservation in Sutton

Short and sweet, this little adventure will have you scrambling over rocks and into the mouth of a chasm stretching a quarter mile before you, its floor littered with huge boulders. Rock walls rise as high as 70 feet on either side of this narrow defile, which geologists theorize was created by catastrophic force after melting glacial ice suddenly released torrents of flood water that shattered this gap through the granite bedrock. As if clinging to its prehistoric roots, Purgatory Chasm today is known to harbor pockets of ice into May and June. A nice escape on a hot summer day, the air is often at least 10 degrees cooler than in the parking lot you've just left behind. Although the scrambling can be difficult for people who are uncomfortable moving over rocks, this half-mile loop is mostly flat and a good one for children.

From the information kiosk, walk toward the pavilion, but before reaching it turn right where the blue-blazed Chasm Loop Trail leads down through the chasm; you may see rock climbers on the walls. At the chasm's far end, poke your head inside the aptly named Coffin, a tight space among the boulders to the trail's right. Then turn left and follow the Chasm Loop Trail's blue blazes uphill onto the rim above the chasm, past deep cracks that have been given such names as Fat Man's Misery and the Corn Crib. The trail leads back to the parking lot.

User Groups: Hikers and leashed dogs. No wheelchair facilities. The trail is not suitable for bikes, horses, or skis.

Permits: Parking and access are free.

Maps: A free map of hiking trails is available at the information kiosk and online from the Massachusetts Division of State Parks and Recreation. For topographic area maps, request Milford and Worcester South from the USGS.

Directions: From Route 146 in Northbridge, take the exit for Purgatory Road. Turn west on Purgatory Road and drive 0.6 mile to parking on the left, beside a pavilion and information kiosk. Purgatory Chasm State Reservation is open sunrise–sunset daily, year-round.

GPS Coordinates: 42.1260 N, 71.7010 W

Contact: Purgatory Chasm State Reservation, Purgatory Rd., Sutton, MA 01590, 508/234-3733. Massachusetts Division of State Parks and Recreation, 251 Causeway St., Suite 600, Boston, MA 02114-2104, 617/626-1250, www.state.ma.us/dem/forparks.htm.

19 CARPENTER ROCKS
2.5 mi/1.5 hr   🚶2 ⛰7

in Wells State Park in Sturbridge

More than 10 miles of hiking trails crisscross this 1,400-acre woodland park, but the most popular route leads to the grand metamorphic cliff face at Carpenter Rocks. A low-elevation walk in the woods until a final scramble to the top of the cliffs, this trail also takes you to Mill Pond, a picturesque wetland that's a favorite hangout for local waterfowl.

MASSACHUSETTS

From the parking area, follow the markers for the Mill Pond Trail. A little more than a quarter mile in length, this wheelchair accessible path hugs the shore of Mill Pond, a serene little pool of water that's home to ducks, Canada geese, and beaver. At the end of the trail, continue straight ahead onto the North Trail. In a very short distance, North Trail crosses a stream and reaches a trail junction. Here, turn left on the smaller footpath, this is the trail that will lead you to Carpenter Rocks. Continue on for another half mile through a mix of hardwood forest and wetland. As you come upon the cliff, the trail suddenly grows much more rugged and steep and, almost without knowing it, you are on the cliff tops taking in a sweeping vista of nearby Walker Pond and the surrounding wooded valley. Return the way you came.

User Groups: Hikers and leashed dogs. This hike is suitable for wheelchair users along the Mill Pond portion of the route. At the end of the Mill Pond Trail, wheelchair users can turn onto the park access road to return to the parking area. Bike and horses are allowed on certain park trails; the path to the Carpenter Rocks is for hikers and dogs only.

Permits: Parking and access are free.

Maps: A free trail map is available at the park entrance. For a topographic area map, request Southbridge from the USGS.

Directions: Follow the Massachusetts Turnpike (I-90) to Exit 9 (Sturbridge). After the toll booths, follow Route 20 east less than a mile to the intersection with Route 49. Turn left onto Route 49 North. The Park entrance is the third left off Route 49.

GPS Coordinates: 42.1425 N, 72.0408 W

Contact: Wells State Park, Rte. 49, Sturbridge, MA 01518 508/347-9257. Massachusetts Division of State Parks and Recreation, 251 Causeway St., Suite 600, Boston, MA 02114-2104, 617/626-1250, www.state.ma.us/dem/forparks.htm.

20 MIDSTATE TRAIL LOOP
6.5 mi/3.5 hr   🏃5 ⛰7

in Douglas State Forest in Douglas

This loop, mostly on forest roads, uses the Midstate Trail to explore the big piece of Douglas State Forest that lies south of Route 16. The loop sections that employ forest roads are easy or moderately difficult for mountain bikers; however, the stretches that follow a rougher trail are more difficult. The Midstate Trail is fairly flat but crosses some streams and gets rocky in places. It's a well-blazed trail with yellow triangles, yet most other forest roads are not marked; use the map.

The Midstate Trail is accessed via the Coffeehouse Loop's southern arm, a forest road beginning at the south end of the parking lot. When you reach the Midstate Trail, turn right (north) onto it. The Midstate makes several turns and, three miles out, reaches a T intersection at a forest road; you'll probably hear traffic on Route 16 to the left. This loop turns right, following the forest road south. At a fork, bear right and cross the dirt Southwest Main Street (where, if you turned left, you would shortly reach the intersection of Cedar Road and Wallum Street). The next intersection reconnects you with the Midstate Trail; backtrack on the Midstate southbound to return.

User Groups: Hikers, bikers, leashed dogs, and horses. No wheelchair facilities.

Permits: A daily parking fee of $5 is collected mid-May–mid-October. The fee can be avoided by accessing the state forest at other roadside parking areas. Consult the map for other access points.

Maps: A free trail map and informational brochure are available at the park entrance or online from the Massachusetts Division of State Parks and Recreation. For a topographic area map, request Webster from the USGS.

Directions: From I-395, take Exit 2 for Route 16 east. Drive 5.1 miles and turn right onto Cedar Road (there may be no street sign) at the sign for Douglas State Forest. Drive 1.8 miles to a crossroads at Southwest Main Street and proceed straight through onto Wallum Street. At 0.9 mile farther, turn right into the state forest and drive 0.7 mile to an information panel where a box contains maps. Bear right and continue a short distance to a parking lot.

GPS Coordinates: 42.0413 N, 71.7627 W

Contact: Douglas State Forest, 107 Wallum Lake Rd., Douglas, MA 01516, 508/476-7872. Massachusetts Division of State Parks and Recreation, 251 Causeway St., Suite 600, Boston, MA 02114-2104, 617/626-1250, www.state.ma.us/dem/forparks.htm.

21 COFFEEHOUSE LOOP
2.2 mi/1.5 hr   🏃1 ⛰7

in Douglas State Forest in Douglas

This relatively flat trail makes a gentle loop through peaceful woods, with the terrain growing slightly rocky in only a few places. Easy to follow, with trail junctions clearly signed, this hike also offers access to a longer outing on the Midstate Trail for those with extra time and energy. The loop begins at the parking lot's north end, eventually reaches and coincides for a short distance with the Midstate Trail southbound, then diverges left from the Midstate Trail and returns to the parking lot via a forest road.

User Groups: Hikers, dogs, skiers, and snowshoers. Dogs must be leashed. No wheelchair facilities. Bikes and horses are prohibited on part of this loop. Hunting is allowed in season.

Permits: A daily parking fee of $5 is collected mid-May–mid-October. The fee can be avoided by accessing the state forest at other roadside parking areas. Consult the map for other access points.

Maps: A free trail map and informational brochure are available at the park entrance or online from the Massachusetts Division of State Parks and Recreation. For a topographic area map, request Webster from the USGS.

Directions: From I-395, take Exit 2 for Route 16 east. Drive 5.1 miles and turn right onto Cedar Road (there may be no street sign) at the sign for Douglas State Forest. Drive 1.8 miles to a crossroads at Southwest Main Street and proceed straight through onto Wallum Street. At 0.9 mile farther, turn right into the state forest and drive 0.7 mile to an information panel where a box contains maps. Bear right and continue a short distance to a parking lot.

GPS Coordinates: 42.0413 N, 71.7627 W

Contact: Douglas State Forest, 107 Wallum Lake Rd., Douglas, MA 01516, 508/476-7872. Massachusetts Division of State Parks and Recreation, 251 Causeway St., Suite 600, Boston, MA 02114-2104, 617/626-1250, www.state.ma.us/dem/forparks.htm.

BOSTON AND CAPE COD

© JACQUELINE TOURVILLE

BEST HIKES

Even in the midst of New England's largest urban

area – and its premier natural tourist attraction – the landscape of eastern Massachusetts provides hikers with a surprisingly varied mix of trails. From the rocky and scenic Blue Hills and Middlesex Fells, two oases of quiet, wooded hills just minutes from downtown Boston, to such rare and cherished recreation areas as Walden Pond and the coastal dunes of the Cape Cod National Seashore, hikes in Greater Boston lead to unusual microenvironments, history-drenched waypoints, and much-needed breathing room from the urban hustle and bustle.

Trails closest to Boston occupy compact acreage, but elsewhere in the region, lands such as Bradley Palmer State Park and Myles Standish State Forest offer sprawling, four-season recreation centers for thousands of local residents. Likewise, the Trustees of Reservations properties – Noanet Woodlands, Rocky Woods, and World's End – provide valuable local places to walk, exercise, and sightsee. Maudslay State Park, Walden Pond State Park Reservation, and the Minuteman National Historical Park are not only great places to walk, but preserve invaluable pieces of local history. And Great Meadows, Plum Island, Caratunk, and Mass Audubon's Drumlin Farm Wildlife Sanctuary are on the must-see destinations list of many bird-watchers.

On the Cape Cod peninsula, the Cape Cod National Seashore occupies over forty miles of pristine sandy beach, marshes, ponds, and forested uplands. A true glimpse of Cape Cod's past and continuing ways of life, boardwalk covered trails lead through terrain with a windswept, still-wild feel. Highlights here include the Great Island Trail, an unforgettable place to watch the sunset over Cape Cod Bay, and the Province Lands Trail, taking you all the way to Race Point beach at the very tip of Cape Cod.

Winter weather is erratic in the Boston area, but generally milder in this area than much of New England, opening up opportunities for visiting many of these places year-round without having to deal with snow or extreme cold. More commonly, visitors must deal with wind and, in certain seasons, biting insects and traffic. Cape Cod sees more rain than snow in winter; if the weather is dry, and the winds calm, hiking here often extends into early December and starts again in early spring. No matter what time of year you take to the trails, your best bet is to dress in layers for changing conditions.

It's also a good idea to contact the land preserve or park you are visiting before setting out on your trip. Hiker regulations vary widely under different land-management agencies (including the National Parks Service and Massachusetts Audubon Society); be aware of pet restrictions and changing trail-use constraints.

MASSACHUSETTS

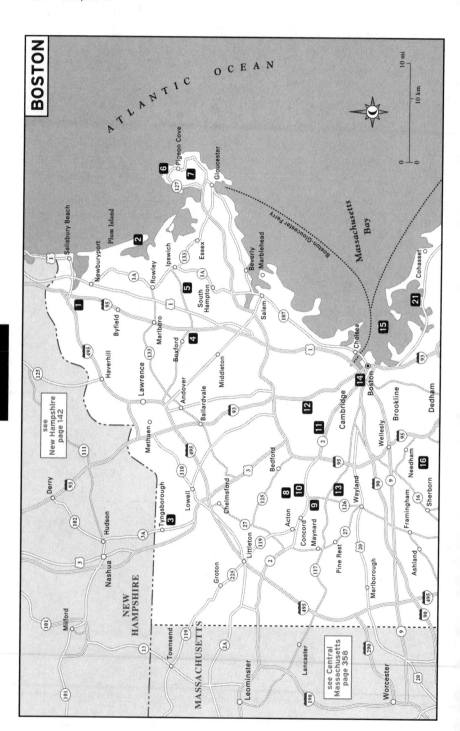

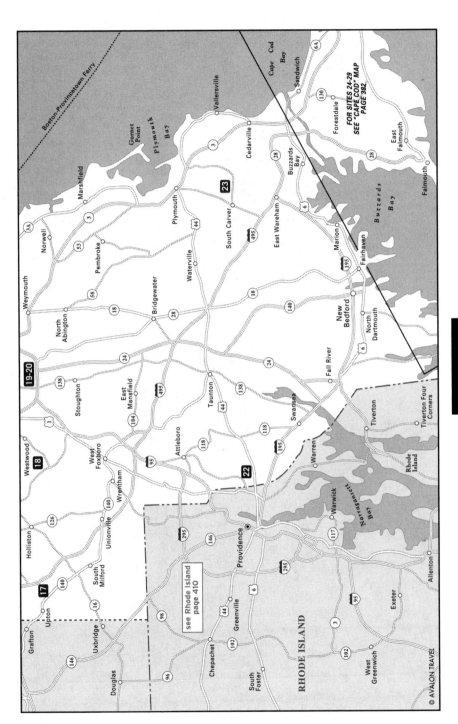

MASSACHUSETTS

MASSACHUSETTS

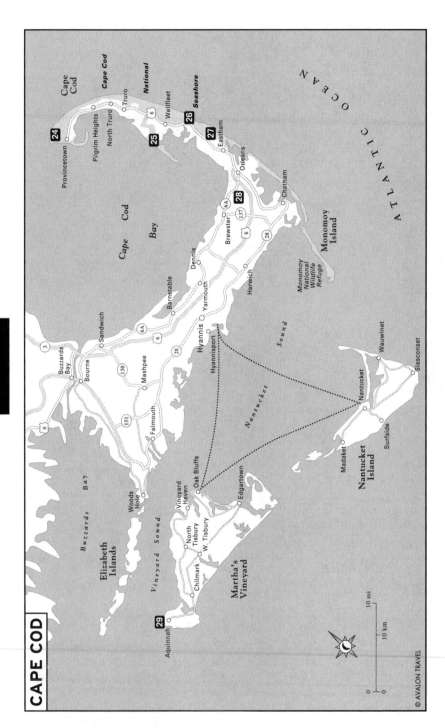

CAPE COD

© AVALON TRAVEL

◼ MAUDSLAY STATE PARK

2.5 mi/1.5 hr   🏃1 ⛰8

in Newburyport

This 480-acre park on the Merrimack River was the 19th-century estate of the Moseleys, one of New England's wealthiest families. George Washington visited this area in 1789, and a regular ferry crossed the river here in the 17th century. Today you can hike trails through its many gardens and one of the largest naturally occurring mountain laurel stands in eastern Massachusetts, and stroll grounds where more flowers and plants bloom than you probably even knew existed. Mid-June is the time to catch the brilliant white flowers of the mountain laurel.

From the parking lot, walk past the headquarters to Curzon Mill Road, following it a short distance to a right turn onto Main Drive, a dirt road. Passing the beautiful Italian Gardens on the right and the pastoral Main House on the left, the trail ends at the Merrimack River Trail, which is marked by blue, white, and green blazes. Straight ahead is the Merrimack River. Turn right onto the Merrimack River Trail, following it along the hilltop and down into woods. After crossing two brooks on wooden bridges, the trail bears left onto another road and crosses over a dam at the end of the Flowering Pond. At the hike's halfway point, you reach the Laurel Walk, where the Merrimack River Trail branches right and left. The area to the left is closed November 1–March 31; take the right branch during these months. Otherwise, turn left and follow the Merrimack River Trail as it winds between the riverbank and the edge of the grove. Where the trail meets the Castle Hill Trail for the first time, bear left and stay with the Merrimack River Trail. Next, reach the end of a tree-lined road, another outlet of the Castle Hill Trail. Turn right to follow the Castle Hill Trail as it quickly crests Castle Hill, with views of the state park and this corner of the Merrimack Valley. Over the hilltop, turn right onto one road, quickly left onto another, and then right onto Line Road. It leads straight onto the Main Road (backtracking over the Merrimack River Trail's right branch). Take the stone bridge over the Flowering Pond, turn left onto the Pasture Trail, and follow it back to the parking lot. Picnickers are welcome.

User Groups: Hikers, bikers, leashed dogs, and horses. No wheelchair facilities.

Permits: A daily parking fee of $2 is collected year-round. A special-use permit is required for weddings, family reunions, and school groups.

Maps: A free, good trail map, including historical information and the seasons for viewing various park flora in bloom, is available at park headquarters. A basic map is also available at online from the Massachusetts Division of State Parks and Recreation website. For a topographic area map, request Newburyport from the USGS.

GPS Coordinates: 42.8224 N, 70.9218 W

Directions: From I-95, take Exit 57 in Newburyport for Route 113 west. Drive a half mile and then turn right onto Hoyt's Lane/Gypsy Lane. At the road's end, turn right (in front of the park headquarters) onto Pine Hill Road and right again into the parking lot. The park is open 8 A.M.–sunset year-round.

Contact: Maudslay State Park, Curzon's Mill Rd., Newburyport, MA 01950, 978/465-7223. Massachusetts Division of State Parks and Recreation, 251 Causeway St., Suite 600, Boston, MA 02114-2104, 617/626-1250, www.state.ma.us/dem/forparks.htm.

◼ BAR HEAD DRUMLIN/ PLUM ISLAND

3 mi/1.5 hr   🏃2 ⛰7

in Sandy Point State Reservation in Ipswich

BEST (

This easy hike combines a walk along a sandy beach and a rocky shoreline with a hike onto the glacial drumlin, an oval mound of earth deposited by a receding glacier 10,000 years

MASSACHUSETTS

ago. Today several plant and animal species rarely found near a sandy beach thrive on Bar Head Drumlin. Fifty feet high and covering 15 acres, the drumlin is shrinking under constant erosion by the ocean. Nearby, the sprawling Parker River National Wildlife Refuge is home to numerous bird species in summer, including cormorants, herons, kingfishers, and ducks. Nearly across from the parking area for this hike is an observation tower with a view of the refuge's marshlands. Bring bug repellent in summer—there are lots of biting insects, especially on the overgrown road along the refuge boundary. Inspect your skin and clothing afterward for ticks.

From the parking lot, pass through a gate onto the beach boardwalk and turn right. The trail—a rock-strewn stretch that eventually gives way to sandy beach—begins below the eroded cliffs of the Bar Head Drumlin. Follow the waterline around to the right until you reach a fence at the wildlife refuge boundary. Turn right and follow an overgrown road along the refuge boundary to a parking lot for the state reservation. Cross the lot to an unmarked, overgrown trail leading up onto Bar Head.

Although the trees and brush atop the drumlin are too dense and high to afford views, a few side trails to the cliffs permit beach and ocean views, good perches to watch the sun rise majestically over the open ocean waters. (Visiting in the early morning hours also helps you avoid the crowds that typically plague Bar Head in summer.) The trail leads over Bar Head and back to the beach near the boardwalk where you started.

User Groups: Hikers only. Bicycles are permitted only on the refuge road and in designated parking areas. No horses, dogs, or wheelchair facilities.

Permits: The fee for entering the Parker River National Wildlife Refuge is $5 per vehicle or $2 for anyone entering on foot or bike, year-round. During the warmer months, the refuge often fills to capacity and the entrance closes temporarily, even to visitors on foot. Arrive early to avoid this inconvenience.

Maps: No map is really needed for this hike, but two different maps are available at the refuge's website. For topographic area maps, request Ipswich and Newburyport from the USGS.

Directions: From I-95 take Exit 57 and travel east on Route 113, then continue straight onto U.S. 1A South to the intersection with Rolfe's Lane for a total of 3.5 miles. Turn left onto Rolfe's Lane and travel 0.5 mile to its end. Turn right onto the Plum Island Turnpike and travel two miles crossing the Sgt. Donald Wilkinson Bridge to Plum Island. Take your first right onto Sunset Drive and travel 0.5 mile to the refuge entrance. From the entrance, drive 6.5 miles to a dirt lot at the end of the road and park. Refuge headquarters is located at the north end of Plum Island near the Newburyport Harbor Lighthouse and is open Monday–Friday 8 A.M.–4:30 P.M., except on federal holidays.

The reservation is open daily sunrise–sunset. Walk only on trails, boardwalks, roads, parking areas, observation areas, and the beach; all other areas, including the dunes, are closed to the public. The beach is closed April 1 through at least July 1, portions possibly through late August, to protect nesting areas for the threatened piping plover.

GPS Coordinates: 42.718 N, 70.7812 W

Contact: Parker River National Wildlife Refuge, 6 Plum Island Turnpike, Newburyport, MA 01950, 978/465-5753 or 800/877-8339 for the hearing impaired, http://parkerriver. fws.gov. U.S. Fish and Wildlife Service, 800/344-9453, www.fws.gov.

◳ LOWELL-DRACUT-TYNGSBORO STATE FOREST

2 mi/1 hr

in Tyngsboro and Lowell

Archaeologists believe the Lowell-Dracut-Tyngsboro State Forest, a collection of 1,140 acres dominated by ponds, swamps, wetlands, and mixed forest, was once the site of a precolonial Native American village. The backwoods oasis today stands in welcome contrast to busy city life, offering a kind of quiet and solitude that is often in short supply around these parts. The Family Loop Trail is a flat, easy loop that takes you into the heart of the Spruce Swamp, a marshy wetlands that is home to ducks, osprey, eagles, geese, owls, and even great blue heron.

From the parking area, pick up the marked Family Loop/Healthy Heart Trail. Following this loop clockwise, bear left. At first under heavy tree cover, the landscape opens up as the trail reaches the swamplands to views of marshy ponds, cattails, and jutting poles of deadened trees. Unique swamp-loving plant species are fun to spot here, including white water lily, yellowdock, and pickerel weed. Frogs leap and salamanders scamper off the trail, the call of ducks is constant, and mosquitoes buzz about in great quantity, especially in July and August. Finally reaching drier land, the loop dips back into the forest before returning to the parking area.

User Groups: Hikers and leashed dogs; no wheelchair facilities. This trail is not suitable for horses or bikes.

Permits: Parking and access are free.

Maps: A free map is available at the park entrance. The map can also be obtained online from the Massachusetts Division of State Parks and Recreation. For a topographic area map, request Nashua South from the USGS.

Directions: From the Drum Hill Rotary in Chelmsford, take the Drum Hill Road spoke. Follow the road, passing through five sets of lights and then crossing over the Merrimack River on the Rourk Bridge. Turn left at the lights on the other side of the bridge. In another 500 yards, turn right onto Old Ferry Road and then left onto Varnum Avenue. Follow for a half mile to a right turn onto Trotting Park Road. Parking lot is at the gate.

GPS Coordinates: 42.6498 N, 71.3708 W

Contact: Lowell-Dracut-Tyngsboro State Forest, Trotting Park Rd., Lowell, MA 01854, 978/369-6312. Massachusetts Division of State Parks and Recreation, 251 Causeway St., Suite 600, Boston, MA 02114-2104, 617/626-1250, www.state.ma.us/dem/forparks.htm.

◢ BALD HILL
3 mi/2 hr

in Boxford State Forest

Here is yet another sizable chunk of state land on the North Shore with a wealth of trails ideal for many activities. This loop takes you through the forest's southeast corner and over Bald Hill, but there's a lot more to this place worth checking out. You may stumble across old gravestones or home foundations from when this was farmland. This loop largely follows forest roads, is hilly, and the terrain can be rocky and rugged—a challenge if you take to the trails on a mountain bike. Many trail intersections have numbered markers that correspond to numbers on the trail map. The forest tends toward the soggy, meaning a plague of mosquitoes in spring and early summer.

From the turnout, head past the gate onto the dirt Bald Hill Road. Past Crooked Pond, bear left at Intersection 14, and left again at Intersection 13. Farther along, turn right, climbing fairly steeply up Bald Hill. On its open summit, cross the field to the left and pick up a forest road heading back down. Bear right and you'll pass a stone foundation at the former Russell-Hooper farmhouse site (marked by a small sign). Just beyond it, to the right of the trail, is the Russell-Hooper barn site. Follow the trail around to the right. At Intersection 8A, turn right; eventually you follow white blazes. At Intersection 26, turn right again and follow this trail back to Intersection 13.

User Groups: Hikers, bikers, leashed dogs, and horses. No wheelchair facilities.

Permits: Parking and access are free.

Maps: A trail map is available online from the Massachusetts Division of State Parks and Recreation.

Directions: From I-95 in Boxford, take Exit 51 for Endicott Road. Drive west and turn right onto Middleton Road. After passing Fuller Lane on the right, continue on Middleton Road another 0.8 mile. Park at a roadside turnout on the left.

GPS Coordinates: 42.6475 N, 70.9990 W

Contact: Boxford State Forest, c/o Harold Parker State Forest, 1951 Turnpike Rd., North Andover, MA 01845-6326, 978/686-3391. Massachusetts Division of State Parks and Recreation, 251 Causeway St., Suite 600, Boston, MA 02114-2104, 617/626-1250, www.state.ma.us/dem/forparks.htm.

5 BRADLEY PALMER STATE PARK

2.5 mi/1.5 hr   🥾2 ⛰7

in Topsfield

Wild tansy grows along the trail in Bradley Palmer State Park.

One of Topsfield's more famous former residents, Bradley Palmer, was a noted attorney in the early 1900s who represented Sinclair Oil in the Teapot Dome Scandal and President Wilson at the Versailles Peace Conference after World War I. Palmer's 732-acre estate is now a multi-use recreation area marked by moderately sloping hills, wide forest roads, and rugged trails offering varied opportunities for mountain biking and hiking. This hike merely introduces you to this park; use it as a jumping off point for further exploration of this North Shore hidden gem.

From the parking area, cross the paved road and head onto a broad forest road. Bear left and start climbing Blueberry Hill (a rigorous climb on a bike). Take the third right onto another forest road and then the second left to reach the open hilltop. If you imagine entering the hilltop meadow at six o'clock, cross the hilltop and turn right, toward a road entering the woods at about three o'clock. Watch for a narrower trail exiting left off that road and follow it down a steep hill. Bear right onto another trail, which leads down to the Ipswich River and land in the Essex County Greenbelt. Turn left along a trail paralleling the river; you'll begin seeing the blue blazes, with a paw print on them, of the Discover Hamilton Trail. Where a footbridge leads right over the river, turn left up a forest road. At a long, wide meadow, turn right and continue onto a forest road back to the park headquarters.

User Groups: Hikers, bikers, leashed dogs, and horses. No wheelchair facilities.

Permits: A daily parking fee of $5 is collected mid-May–mid-October.

Maps: A free trail map is available at the park headquarters or online from the Massachusetts Division of State Parks and Recreation. For a topographic area map, request Georgetown from the USGS.

Directions: From U.S. 1 in Topsfield, turn east onto Ipswich Road (at a traffic light). Drive 1.2 miles and turn right onto Asbury Street.

The state park entrance is on the left, a short distance down the road. Park in a dirt area just before the state park headquarters.

GPS Coordinates: 42.6551 N, 70.9123 W

Contact: Bradley Palmer State Park, Asbury St., Topsfield, MA 01983, 978/887-5931. Massachusetts Division of State Parks and Recreation, 251 Causeway St., Suite 600, Boston, MA 02114-2104, 617/626-1250, www.state.ma.us/dem/forparks.htm.

6 HALIBUT POINT
0.5 mi/0.5 hr

in Halibut Point State Park and Reservation in Rockport

Halibut Point consists of Halibut Point Reservation and Halibut Point State Park and is jointly managed by The Trustees of Reservations and the state. The state park surrounds the site of the former Babson Farm granite quarry, a small pond now filled with water and ringed by the sheer cliffs of the quarry walls. The park's name derives from "Haul About Point," the name given to the 50-foot granite cliff at the ocean's edge by sailors tacking around the point to approach Cape Ann.

From the parking lot, cross Gott Avenue, following signs to the park entrance. A short trail through trees leads to the quarry. The park headquarters is to the left. Take the trail that goes around the quarry to the right. You pass a mooring stone—an enormous granite slab sunk underwater that anchors an oak post used as a mooring for fishermen's boats. Turn onto a trail branching to the right, toward the ocean, to reach The Trustees of Reservations property. The shore here is very rocky, an extremely wild place when the surf is high; be sure not to get too close to the water because the riptide is powerful. Walk to the left along the shore and then follow a trail back up toward the quarry. To return, walk around the quarry to the left, which takes you back to the entrance trail.

User Groups: Hikers and leashed dogs. No wheelchair facilities. This trail is not suitable for bikes or horses.

Permits: No permits required. A $2 fee is charged for parking mid-May–mid-October. For the rest of the year, the park is open at no charge during the daylight hours. The Trustees of Reservations members park for free.

Maps: A free trail map is available at the park. A map is also available online from the Massachusetts Division of State Parks and Recreation.

Directions: From the junction of Routes 128 and 127, follow Route 127 north (on Eastern Avenue) toward Rockport. After three miles, turn left onto Railroad Avenue, which is still Route 127. After another 2.4 miles, turn right onto Gott Avenue. The parking lot is on the right a short distance up the road.

The park is open daily 8 A.M.–8 P.M. Memorial Day–Labor Day; a parking fee is charged. From Labor Day to Memorial Day the park is open sunrise–sunset.

GPS Coordinates: 42.6868 N, 70.6311 W

Contact: Halibut Point State Park, Gott Ave., Rockport, MA 01966, 978/546-2997. The Trustees of Reservations, Long Hill, 572 Essex St., Beverly, MA 01915-1530, 978/921-1944, www.thetrustees.org. Massachusetts Division of State Parks and Recreation, 251 Causeway St., Suite 600, Boston, MA 02114-2104, 617/626-1250, www.state.ma.us/dem/forparks.htm.

7 DOGTOWN
8.8 mi/4 hr

in Gloucester and Rockport

This patch of untamed woods in the heart of Cape Ann has become a favorite among local hikers and mountain bikers for its rugged trails, glacial-erratic boulders scattered through the forest, and the legacy of a wealthy financier named Roger Babson. Earlier in this century, Babson hired stonecutters to carve sayings into rocks here like Get a Job and Never Try Never Win. The old woods roads along this hike carry names but are not maintained thoroughfares for motor vehicles; many are very difficult to negotiate, even for experienced mountain bikers. This rolling, nearly nine-mile route through Dogtown could take five hours hiking, three to four hours on bikes.

From the parking area, go around the gate and follow the rough dirt Dogtown Road for 1.2 miles, passing old cellar holes on the left, to Dogtown Square, a junction of trails where a rock is inscribed D.T. SQ. From Dogtown Square, turn right onto a rock-strewn dirt road and follow it for 0.1 mile, then turn right again (where the red blazes of the Beaver Dam Trail branch left) onto the Tent Rock Trail, sometimes called the Boulder Trail. It continues for a mile to Babson Reservoir, along the way passing the large boulders inscribed with messages such as Truth, Industry, and Help Mother. From the view of the reservoir, the trail turns left, crosses railroad tracks, and reaches the rough dirt Old Rockport Road behind Blackburn Industrial Park, 1.4 miles from Dogtown Square. Turn left and follow the road 1.2 miles to the Babson Museum on Eastern Avenue/Route 127. Behind the museum, turn left onto the red-blazed Beaver Dam Trail. Crossing the railroad tracks, then skipping back and forth across a brook, the trail passes over a small hill, takes a sharp right, and reaches Dogtown Square, 1.4 miles from the museum. Turn right onto Wharf Road and follow it 0.4 mile to Common Road. Turn right onto the Whale's Jaw Trail, pass a huge boulder called Peter's Pulpit at about 0.3 mile, and reach the Whale's Jaw, another massive boulder, at 0.8 mile. Backtrack the same way to Dogtown Square and follow Dogtown Road back to the parking area.

User Groups: Hikers, bikes, and dogs. No wheelchair facilities. This trail is not suitable for horses.

Permits: Parking and access are free.

Maps: A free trail map of Dogtown is available

from the Gloucester Chamber of Commerce. For a topographic area map, request Rockport from the USGS.

Directions: From the Grant Circle Rotary on Route 128 in Gloucester, take Route 127/Washington Street north for 0.9 mile and turn right onto Reynard Street. Follow Reynard Street to a left onto Cherry Street. Then turn right onto the access road to Dogtown, 1.5 miles from Grant Circle Rotary. Drive less than a half mile to a parking area and a gate.

GPS Coordinates: 42.6338 N, 70.6681 W

Contact: Cape Ann Chamber of Commerce, 33 Commercial St., Gloucester, MA 01930, 978/283-1601, www.capeannvacations.com.

◻ GREAT MEADOWS NATIONAL WILDLIFE REFUGE
2 mi/1.5 hr   🚶1 ▲9

in Concord

BEST (

Although most visitors here are bird-watchers, even the casual walker can't help but be impressed by the profusion of winged creatures on this 3,000-acre refuge, stretching along 12 miles of the Concord River. From great blue herons and osprey to songbirds and wood ducks, 221 bird species have been observed here. On this hike, binoculars are a must—the Dike Trail around the broad wetlands is considered one of the best birding sites in the state. Besides birds, animals such as deer, muskrats, foxes, raccoons, cottontail rabbits, and weasels call the refuge home. With all the standing water here, you can bet there are lots of bugs too, especially in spring. Interestingly, relics of human habitation here date back to 5500 B.C.

Before you begin your hike, check out the view from the observation tower beside the parking lot. Then pick up the Dike Trail, to the right of the tower, which traverses the meadows between Upper Pool and Lower

© JACQUELINE TOURVILLE

bird-watchers at Great Meadows National Wildlife Refuge

MASSACHUSETTS

Pool. On the other side, the trail reaches the Concord River banks (where canoeists pull ashore to walk the trail). Turn left, following the trail along the Upper Pool about a quarter mile to the refuge boundary, marked by signs. Turn back and follow the trail around the Lower Pool. You can either double back or, where the Lower Pool ends, take the Edge Trail through the woods back to the entrance road. Turn right on the road to return to the parking lot.

Special note: You can canoe the gentle Sudbury and Concord Rivers through the refuge and put ashore here to walk this trail. Depending on how long a day trip you want, put in along either Route 27, Route 117, or Route 62 and take out along Route 225 on the Carlisle/Bedford line.

User Groups: Hikers, leashed dogs, and wheelchair users. No bikes or horses.

Permits: Parking and access are free.

Maps: A map of hiking trails and a number of brochures about Great Meadows, including a list of bird species sighted here, are available at the trailhead. For a topographic area map, request Maynard from the USGS.

Directions: From Main Street/Route 62 in Concord Center, drive 0.7 mile east towards Monument Square. Bear left onto Lowell Road at the square and then take a quick right onto Bedford Street, staying on Route 62. Follow Bedford Street for 1.3 miles, then turn left onto Monsen Road, a dead end street (You will see a small brown sign for Great Meadows just before the turn). Stay on Monsen Road until it ends in the Great Meadows parking area, next to the observation tower. GPS Coordinates: 42.4746 N, 71.3277 W

Contact: Great Meadows National Wildlife Refuge, Refuge Manager, 73 Weir Hill Rd., Sudbury, MA 01776, 978/443-4661, http://greatmeadows.fws.gov.

🖪 WALDEN POND

1.7 mi/1 hr

in Walden Pond State Park Reservation in Concord

In 1845, a 27-year-old former schoolteacher named Henry David Thoreau came to Walden

© JACQUELINE TOURVILLE

Walden Pond

Pond to live on 14 acres owned by his friend, Ralph Waldo Emerson. Thoreau built a small one-room cabin and began his "experiment in simplicity," living a sustenance lifestyle on the pond. At the time, much of Concord was already deforested and the land converted to farms, but the woods around Walden Pond had remained untouched because the sandy soil was not very fertile. Two years, two months, and two days later, Thoreau closed up his house and returned to village life in Concord. Emerson sold the cabin to his gardener. (The cabin no longer stands, but a replica can be seen beside the parking lot.) In 1854, Thoreau published *Walden, or Life in the Woods*, still considered a classic of American literature. Ever since, Walden Pond has stood as a symbol of the American conservation movement.

Today, Walden Pond sits in the middle of a small patch of woods within earshot of busy state routes and a railroad line, yet it remains popular with hikers and cross-country skiers, as well as anglers and canoeists (a boat launch is on the right side of Route 126, just beyond the parking area). Songbirds, Canada geese, and ducks are commonly seen here.

From the parking lot, cross Route 126 and walk downhill to the pond. From either end of the beach, the Pond Path circles the pond, usually staying just above the shoreline but offering almost constant pond views. It's a wide, mostly flat trail under the canopy of tall pines. A short side trail, marked by a sign along the Pond Path, leads to Thoreau's house site. Stay on the trails—erosion is a problem here.

User Groups: Hikers only. Wheelchair users can access the beginning of this trail above the beach on Walden Pond. Bikes, dogs, and horses are prohibited.

Permits: A daily parking fee of $5 is collected year-round.

Maps: A free map and an informational brochure about Walden Pond are available outside the Shop at Walden Pond, next to the park office at the parking lot's south end. The map can also be obtained online from the Massachusetts Division of State Parks and Recreation. For a topographic area map, request Maynard from the USGS.

Directions: From the junction of Routes 2 and 126 in Concord, drive south on Route 126 for

0.3 mile to the Walden Pond State Reservation entrance and parking lot on the left.

Park officials may close the entrance if the park reaches capacity. The park is open to the public 5 A.M.–sunset; check for the closing time posted in the parking lot.

GPS Coordinates: 42.4415 N, 71.3363 W

Contact: Walden Pond State Park Reservation, 915 Walden St./Rte. 126, Concord, MA 01742, 978/369-3254. Massachusetts Division of State Parks and Recreation, 251 Causeway St., Suite 600, Boston, MA 02114-2104, 617/626-1250, www.state.ma.us/dem/forparks.htm. The Shop at Walden Pond, 508/287-5477.

🔟 MINUTE MAN NATIONAL HISTORICAL PARK

11 mi/6 hr   🏃🏃 3 ⛰️ 10

in Concord

BEST (

Like an American history textbook come to life, this hike, retracing the route of the American Revolution's opening moments, is a Bay State gem and can't-miss national treasure. After the fateful "shot heard round the world" was fired on Lexington Green in the early morning hours of April 19, 1775, British soldiers continued their march to Concord on orders to seize a rebel cache of weapons. Turned back at North Bridge in Concord by farmers and villagers turned Minute Men soldiers overnight, British redcoats were unmercifully chased back to Boston by the rapidly growing ranks of rebel fighters. Much of the trail follows original remnants of the Battle Road; other sections leave the historic road to follow the route of the Minute Men, traversing the fields, wetlands, and forests that provided cover and the element of surprise for their guerrilla-style tactics. The flat, easy terrain and opportunity to bring history alive for kids makes this a great hike for families.

From the parking area at Meriam's Corner, the Battle Road begins near the Meriam House, site of the first rebel attacks on the Red Coats. Visit the house if you like, but the flat, wheelchair accessible path quickly veers into the adjacent farmland, notable as remaining in the same configuration as it was in 1775; it's easy to imagine the stealthily advancing Minute Men creeping across the freshly tilled earth. The trail then continues, passing historic homes of noted Patriot figures, preserved wayside taverns and inns, sites of intense fighting, and the Paul Revere capture site. Interpretative panels are frequent along the Battle Road path and original buildings still standing are open for visits during the summer tourist season. The path ends at Fisk Hill and the Ebenezer Fiske house site. Retrace your steps or loop back via a walking trail through historic pastureland.

Special Note: If an 11-mile round trip is not feasible, a walk to the Hartwell Tavern (at this hike's halfway point) creates a round-trip of about 5 history-rich miles. For even shorter walks to points along the trail, other parking areas off Lexington Road take you within steps of the Josiah Brooks House and Brooks Tavern (mile 1.5 of this hike), Hartwell Tavern (mile 2.5 of this hike), the Paul Revere capture site (mile 3.2 of this hike), and the Thomas Nelson House site (mile 4 of this hike).

User Groups: Hikers, leashed dogs, wheelchair hikers, and horses. Because the Battle Road Trail is primarily an educational trail, it is not suitable for high speed bicycling. If you do bring your bike, be aware that you will be sharing the trail with many others.

Permits: Parking and access are free.

Maps: A free map is available at Minute Man Visitor Center. For a topographic area map, request Concord from the USGS.

Directions: From Lexington, follow Route 2 west for approximately 6.5 miles to a right turn onto Bypass Road/Route 2A. At the end of the road, take a left onto Lexington Road. Follow brown signs for Minute Man National Historical Park/Meriam's Corner, taking a right about a half mile down the road into the

MASSACHUSETTS

parking area for Meriam House. The Battle Road trail starts here.

GPS Coordinates: 42.4593 N, 71.3229 W

Contact: Minute Man Visitor Center, 250 North Great Rd., Lincoln MA, 01773, 978/369-6993, www.nps.gov/mima/index. htm.

11 MINUTEMAN BIKEWAY
11 mi/5.5 hr   🏃₁ ⛰₈

in Somerville, Cambridge, Arlington, Lexington, and Bedford

This paved bikeway follows a former railroad bed and is popular with walkers, runners, bicyclists, families, in-line skaters, and—when there's snow—cross-country skiers. Many people, particularly students, use the bikeway to commute to work and classes. The bikeway passes mainly through forest in Bedford and Lexington, and through a wetland in Lexington as well. From Arlington into Cambridge and Somerville, the bikeway becomes increasingly an urban recreation path. It is flat and can be done in sections of short lengths, which is why this receives an easy difficulty rating despite its 11-mile total length.

User Groups: Hikers, bikers, dogs, and wheelchair hikers. No horses.

Permits: Parking and access are free.

Maps: A brochure and map of the bikeway is available from the Arlington Planning Department. Boston's Bikemap, a detailed bicycling map of the metropolitan area, which includes the Minuteman Bikeway, is available for $4.25 from Rubel BikeMaps (P.O. Box 401035, Cambridge, MA 02140, www.bikemaps.com) and from area stores listed at the website. For topographic area maps, request Boston South, Boston North, and Maynard from the USGS.

Directions: The Minuteman Bikeway can be accessed from numerous points for walks or rides of virtually any distance. Its endpoints are behind the T station in Davis Square, between Holland Street and Meacham Road in Somerville; and at the junction of Railroad Avenue and Loomis Street in Bedford. Access points include Massachusetts Avenue in Cambridge at Cameron Avenue and Harvey Street, 0.4 mile south of Route 16; the Alewife T station at the junction of Routes 2 and 16; a parking lot on Lake Street in Arlington, just west of the Brooks Avenue traffic lights; Swan Place and Mystic Street in Arlington center, near the junction of Routes 2A and 60 (where the bikeway crosses Massachusetts Avenue); Park Avenue in Arlington (via a stairway), just north of Massachusetts Avenue; Maple Street (Route 2A) in Lexington; Woburn Street in Lexington, just west of Massachusetts Avenue; Hancock and Meriam Streets (at a large parking lot), off Bedford Street (Route 4 and Route 225) and the Lexington Battle Green; and Bedford Street (Route 4 and Route 225) between North Hancock and Revere Streets in Lexington.

GPS Coordinates to Bedford Trailhead: 42.4858 N, 71.2772 W

Contact: The Friends of the Minuteman Bikeway, www.minutemanbikeway.org. Rails to Trails Conservancy, 1100 17th St. Northwest, 10th floor, Washington, DC 20036, 202/331-9696, www.railtrails.org.

12 MIDDLESEX FELLS SKYLINE TRAIL
7 mi/4 hr   🏃₅ ⛰₈

in Middlesex Fells Reservation in Medford, Malden, Winchester, Melrose, and Stoneham

Even in the midst of some of Boston's busiest suburbs, you can still find quiet and solitude hiking the Fells, a 2,500-acre chunk of woods and hills located a few miles north of the city off I-93. ("Fells" is a Saxon word for rocky hills.) The Skyline Trail—the premier hiking circuit in the Fells—loops around the Winchester Reservoirs, passing through forest and traversing countless rocky ledges, some with good views of the surrounding hills and, occasionally, the Boston skyline. Perhaps the best view is from atop Pine Hill and the stone Wright's Tower lookout, near the start of this loop, which overlooks Boston's skyline and the Blue Hills to the south. The trail dries out fairly quickly after the snow melts—it's a glorious hike on the first warm day of spring. Bikes are prohibited from this trail, but there are many forest roads and trails forming a network through the Fells that offer good mountain biking opportunities.

From the parking lot, walk along the right side of Bellevue Pond and onto a wide forest road at the opposite end of the pond. Look for the white-blazed Skyline Trail leading to the right, up Pine Hill. The trail is generally easy to follow, but it crosses many other paths and forest roads, which can cause confusion; be sure to look for the white blazes. The loop eventually brings you back to this intersection.

User Groups: Hikers and leashed dogs. No wheelchair facilities or horses. Bikes are prohibited from the Skyline Trail. Mountain biking in groups of five or fewer is permitted on fire roads and the designated Mountain Bike Loop mid-April–mid-December. Mountain biking is not permitted on single-track (hiking) trails and is prohibited in all parts of the reservation January 1–April 15 to protect trails and fire roads from erosion damage during this often-muddy season.

Permits: Parking and access are free.

Maps: A trail map of the Middlesex Fells Reservation is available for $6 via mail (with SASE) from The Friends of Middlesex Fells Reservation. For a topographic map of area trails, request Boston North from the USGS.

Directions: Take I-93 to Exit 33 in Medford. From the traffic circle, turn onto South Border Road. Drive 0.2 mile and turn into a parking area on the right, at Bellevue Pond. The reservation is open year-round sunrise–sunset. GPS Coodinates: 42.4317 N, 71.1074 W

Contact: Middlesex Fells Reservation, 781/322-2851 or 781/662-5230. Massachusetts Division of Urban Parks and Recreation, Commissioner's Office, 20 Somerset St., Boston, MA 02108, 617/722-5000, www.state.ma.us/mdc/mdc_home. The Friends of the Middlesex Fells Reservation, 4 Woodland Rd., Stoneham, MA 02180, 781/662-2340, www.fells.org.

13 DRUMLIN FARM WILDLIFE SANCTUARY
2 mi/1 hr 🏃1 ⛰7

in Lincoln

BEST (

A working farm and 232-acre Audubon sanctuary on the fringes of suburban Boston, Drumlin Farm maintains a variety of habitats for visitors to explore: grasslands, agricultural fields, shrubs and thickets, mature forests, and small ponds and swamps. This easy, ambling loop hike brings you to many of the farm's best features, including the sanctuary's namesake, a whale-shaped drumlin hill created long ago by glaciers and now one of the highest points in the greater Boston area. On a clear day, views from the top offer glimpses of Mount Wachusett to the west and New Hampshire's Mount Monadnock almost due north.

From behind the Drumlin Farm Nature Center, pick up the Drumlin Loop at the trail marker. Bear left onto the loop, soon passing though mixed woods as the trail sweeps in a gentle curve to bring you to the top of the drumlin. Take in nice landscape views and be sure to look skyward: goshawks, red tail hawks, and turkey vultures are a common sight circling overhead. Continuing over the drumlin, pass the first junction with the Hayfield Loop Trail. A little farther, the trail reaches a split. To return almost immediately to the nature center, turn right to stay on the Drumlin Loop Trail (a completed loop of about just over a half mile). This hike, however, continues straight ahead on the marked Hayfield Loop Trail. Edging along fields, shrubs, thickets, and more trees, birds spotted in this area include field sparrows, yellow-bellied eastern meadowlarks, and indigo buntings. After passing a junction with

MASSACHUSETTS

the Town Trail, the Hayfield Loop sweeps left and soon reaches the Bobolink Trail. Turn left on the Bobolink Trail and skirt the dedicated bird conservation area. This is a good place to whip out the binoculars: More than 100 different species of birds call this area home. At the end of the Bobolink, turn left on the Field Trail and follow as it curves by fields and a sheep pasture and then passes a vernal pond. Now reaching the working farm itself, bear right to crest Bird Hill. At the bottom of the hill are the Farm Life Center and a variety of barns, stables, and farm animals awaiting your visit. From the Farm Life Center, bear right to return to the visitors center and parking area.

User Groups: Hikers only. No bikes, dogs, horses, or wheelchair facilities.

Permits: Admission is free for Massachusetts Audubon Society members. Nonmember adults, $6; nonmember children (ages 2–12) and seniors, $4.

Maps: A trail map is available at the visitors center. For a topographic map of area trails, request Concord from the USGS.

Directions: From Route 2 in Concord (east or west), turn onto Route 126 south (at the sign for Walden Pond, Framingham) and follow for 2.5 miles to the intersection of Route 126 and Route 117. Take a left onto Route 117 east and the sanctuary is one mile ahead on the right. GPS Coordinates: 42.4086 N, 71.3284 W

Contact: Massachusetts Audubon Society Drumlin Farm Wildlife Sanctuary, 208 South Great Rd., Lincoln, MA 01773, 781/259-2200, www.massaudubon.org.

14 CHARLES RIVER BIKE PATH: HARVARD UNIVERSITY

14 mi/6 hr   🏃1 ⚠8

in the Charles River Reservation, Boston, Cambridge, and Watertown

The paved Paul Dudley White Bike Path along both banks of the Charles River teems with activity weekday evenings and weekends: walkers, runners, in-line skaters, bicyclists, wheelchair users, skateboarders, people of all ages out getting exercise in the middle of the city. It is easily reached from such colleges as MIT, Boston University, and Harvard, and accesses such riverside attractions as the Esplanade and Hatch Shell, the sight of the famous Fourth of July Boston Pops Concert and fireworks. The bike path provides a more convenient, more pleasant, and often faster means of getting around the city than driving or using public transportation. Some sections of the path are quite wide, others no wider than a pair of bikes; likewise, some stretches see much heavier use than others. The entire path forms a 14-mile loop between the Museum of Science and Watertown Square and can be traveled in either direction and done in smaller sections, which is why this trail receives such an easy difficulty rating. The Cambridge side of the trail where it winds between the Charles River and Harvard University is arguably the most scenic stretch of the entire trail and the most recommendable for a walk.

From the end of Hawthorn Street, cross Memorial Drive and walk toward the river. Turn left (east) at the path, a paved strip running parallel to Memorial Drive and the river. As you walk, take in incomparable views across the river to Boston and, to the left, the historic red brick skyline of Harvard University. It's a leafy and shady walk thanks to lindens and maackias, as well as maples and stands of ancient oaks. Continue over JFK Street, passing the Harvard University Crew building. (Crew teams from both Harvard and Boston University can often be seen sculling the waters of the Charles.) Where Memorial Drive reaches an intersection with Flagg Street, you have reached the edge of the Harvard campus. Turn around and retrace your steps—this reverse vantage point is equal in its lovely Cambridge, Boston, and Charles River views. You can also cross the bridge and walk back along the Boston side of the river, but there the path is close to traffic and not as enjoyable.

User Groups: Hikers, bikers, leashed dogs, and wheelchair users. No horses.

Permits: Parking and access are free.

Maps: Boston's Bikemap, a detailed bicycling map of the metropolitan area, which covers the Paul Dudley White Charles River Bike Path, is available for $4.25 from Rubel BikeMaps (P.O. Box 401035, Cambridge, MA 02140, www.bikemaps.com) and from area stores listed at the website. For a topographic area map, request Boston South from the USGS.

Directions: The bike path runs for seven miles along both sides of the Charles River, from the Boston Museum of Science on the O'Brien Route/Route 28 to Watertown Square in Watertown (the junction of Routes 16 and 20), forming a 14-mile loop. It is accessible from numerous points in Boston, Cambridge, and Watertown, including the footbridges over Storrow Drive in Boston, although not from the Longfellow and Boston University bridges on the Boston side. For this portion of the bike path, leave your car in metered parking or one of the public parking lots near Harvard Square. From Harvard Square, follow Brattle Street to Hawthorn Street (a five-block walk). Turn left on Hawthorn Street and follow a few blocks to the intersection with Memorial Drive.

GPS Coordinates: 42.3762 N, 71.1200 W

Contact: Massachusetts Division of Urban Parks and Recreation, Commissioner's Office, 20 Somerset St., Boston, MA 02108, 617/722-5000, www.state.ma.us/mdc/mdc_home.

15 BOSTON HARBOR: SPECTACLE ISLAND AND GEORGES ISLAND
6 mi/3 hr 〽️1 ⛰8

in Boston Harbor

A bit of the rustic wild in full view of sleek, modern Boston, this fun hike—and quick and easy city escape—takes you on a day trip to Spectacle and Georges Islands, the two most popular destinations in the Boston Harbor island chain; both are maintained by the National Parks Service. Access to the islands is seasonal, with ferries running May–September. When planning for this trip, factor in a little more than an hour total for ferry boarding and the ride through Boston Harbor. How much time you spend exploring the islands is up to you (and the ferry schedule). Try leaving on an early morning ferry to give your trip a more leisurely pace.

Only a 10-minute boat ride from downtown Boston, tiny 105-acre Spectacle Island offers an incredible five miles of walking trails. From the ferry dock, wander out on the island's twisting footpaths. As you follow the windswept shore, turn inland to crest the island's 157 foot-high hill, with panoramic views of the harbor and the city. Tree cover here is sparse and there is really no way to get lost. (Low-lying cover is as much due to wind as it is to the island's once bleak past as a garbage dump for the city of Boston.) Spectacle's visitors center offers exhibits about island history and nature, restrooms, and a cafe; jazz concerts are held at the visitors center every Sunday afternoon in summer.

Twenty-five minutes from the hustle and bustle of Boston is Georges Island, a 39-acre pinpoint of land that manages to squeeze in a large dock, picnic grounds, open fields, paved walkways, a parade ground, gravel beach, and the remains of Fort Warren, a National Historic Landmark. Built in 1847, Fort Warren served as a training area, patrol point, and prison during the Civil War, gaining a favorable reputation for the humane treatment of its Confederate prisoners. National Park rangers offer guided tours of the fort several times each day during the summer (you can also explore on your own); on weekdays in the spring, the island is a popular destination for school field trips. For a little extra room to roam on what can be a very crowded piece of real estate, visit Georges Island at low tide. The island actually grows to 53 acres, perfect for a meandering stroll along the sandy shore.

User Groups: Hikers only. No bikes, dogs, or horses. The visitors center, beach, and portions of trail at Spectacle Island are wheelchair accessible. For wheelchair users and others interested in visiting Spectacle Island only, a separate ferry ticket is available.

Permits: Trail, beach, and Fort Warren access are free.

Maps: Maps of the islands are available at the Spectacle Island visitors center. For a topographic map of area trails, request Hull from the USGS.

Directions: Boston's Long Wharf is next to the Marriott Long Wharf hotel and across the street from Faneuil Hall Marketplace, a short walk from the MBTA's Blue Line/Aquarium stop and from both the Green and Orange Lines at Haymarket. Inexpensive parking is available at nearby Fan Pier.

Round-Trip ferry tickets from Boston to stops at Spectacle and Georges Islands are $14 for adults and $8 for children ages 3–11. Ferries depart Long Wharf for Georges and Spectacle Islands every hour on the hour 9 A.M.–4 P.M. Monday–Thursday, June 21–September 1. Return trips from Georges Island are every hour on the half-hour. On Fridays and weekends during the summer, ferries depart Long Wharf daily every half-hour 9 A.M.–5 P.M. Return trips from both Spectacle and Georges run hourly.

GPS Coordinates: 42.3601 N, 71.0496 W

Contact: Boston Harbor Islands Ferry, 408 Atlantic Ave., Boston, MA 02110, 617/223-8666, www.bostonislands.com. Boston Harbor Islands Partnership, 408 Atlantic Ave., Suite 228, Boston, MA 02110, 617/223-8666, www.nps.gov/boha/index.htm.

16 NOANET WOODLANDS
4 mi/2 hr   🏃3 △8

in Dover

The 695-acre Noanet Woodlands is a surprisingly quiet and secluded-feeling forest patch plunked down in the middle of suburbia. It might come as a shock to many first-time hikers of 387-foot Noanet Peak to find that virtually the only sign of civilization visible from this rocky knob is the Boston skyline 20 miles away, floating on the horizon like the Emerald City. You have to scan the unbroken forest and rolling hills for a glimpse of another building. And you may hear no other sounds than the breeze and singing of birds.

The yellow-blazed Caryl Trail begins at one end of the parking lot. Follow it to Junction 6 (trail junction signs are on trees) and turn left onto an unmarked trail. Pass a trail entering on the right. At the next junction, turn right and then left up a hill. You soon reach the open ledge atop Noanet Peak. After enjoying the view, walk to your right a short distance onto a trail that follows a wooded ridge crest, slowly descending to the Caryl Trail; turn left (you'll almost immediately recross the trail leading to Noanet's summit, but do not turn onto it). Follow the Caryl Trail to Junction 18 and walk straight onto the blue-blazed Peabody Trail. Pass ponds and the site of an old mill on the right. (From 1815 to 1840, Noanet Brook powered the Dover Union Iron Company. A flood breached the huge dam at Noanet Falls in 1876. In 1954, then-owner Amelia Peabody rebuilt the dam.) Bear left through Junction 4 and turn right onto the Caryl Trail again, which leads back to the parking lot.

User Groups: Hikers and horses. No wheelchair facilities. Bikes are allowed by permit only; the price of the permit is discounted for Trustees of Reservations members. Dogs are prohibited at Caryl Park, but visitors who walk to Noanet Woodlands can bring their dogs.

Permits: Parking and access are free. A biking permit can be obtained at the Noanet Woodlands ranger station at the Caryl Park entrance on weekends and holidays, or from the Southeast Region office of The Trustees of Reservations.

Maps: A trail map is posted on an information board at the trailhead, and one is available free from The Trustees of Reservations, either at the trailhead or through The Trustees headquarters. Major trail junctions in Noanet are marked with numbered signs that correspond to markings on the map. For topographic area maps, request Boston South, Framingham, Medfield, and Norwood from the USGS.

Directions: From I-95/Route 128, take Exit 17 onto Route 135 west. Drive about 0.6 mile and turn left at the traffic lights onto South Street. Drive 0.7 mile and bear left at a fork. After another 0.4 mile, turn left onto Chestnut Street. Cross the Charles River and enter Dover; turn right onto Dedham Street. Two miles past the river, turn left into Caryl Park; the sign is hard to see, but the parking lot is next to tennis courts. Noanet Woodlands is open to the public sunrise–sunset year-round.

GPS Coordinates: 42.2483 N, 71.2712 W

Contact: The Trustees of Reservations Southeast/Cape Cod Regional Office, The Bradley Estate, 2468B Washington St., Canton, MA 02021-1124, 781/821-2977, www.thetrustees. org.

🔟 WHISTLING CAVE
3 mi/1.5 hr

in Upton State Forest in Upton

Whistling Cave is not a cave but two large boulders, one leaning against the other, with a small passageway beneath them. It's located in an interesting little wooded stream valley littered with such boulders. Trails are well blazed, the forest road intersections are marked by signs, and the state forest has many more miles of both trails and roads. This hike has some hills but is relatively easy.

From the parking lot, head past the gate on a dirt forest road to the junction of Loop Road and Park Road. Bear right on Park Road, passing one blue-blazed trail on the left (which may not appear on the map). Continue up a gentle hill to a pullout on the left. The Whistling Cave Trail, marked by a sign and blazed with blue triangles, begins there. It soon drops over ledges and down a steep embankment, then levels out. You cross a couple of small brooks and then enter the area of boulders. Whistling Cave is right on the trail at this area's far end, shortly after you start up a hillside. Just beyond it, the trail ends at the junction of Middle Road and Loop Road. (To reach Whistling Cave on bikes, horses, or skis, take Loop Road to this intersection, walk or attempt to ski to the boulders, and double back.) You can return on either Loop Road or Middle Road; the former remains a forest road, while the latter eventually narrows to an easy trail marked by blue triangles.

User Groups: Hikers and leashed dogs. No bikes, horses, or wheelchair facilities.

Permits: Parking and access are free.

Maps: A free map is available at the state forest entrance or online from the Massachusetts Division of State Parks and Recreation. For a topographic area map, request Milford from the USGS.

Directions: From I-495, take Exit 21B for West Main Street, Upton, and drive 3.7 miles south to the junction of High Street, Hopkinton Road, and Westboro Road; there is a pond to the left. (The junction can be reached in the other direction from Route 140 in Upton center by taking North Main Street for a half mile.) Turn north onto Westboro Road, drive two miles, and then turn right at the sign for Upton State Forest. Bear right onto a dirt road and stop at the map box. Continue down that dirt road a short distance to a parking lot at a gate.

GPS Coordinates: 42.1971 N, 71.6107 W

Contact: Upton State Forest, 205 Westboro Rd., Upton, MA 01568, 508/278-6486. Massachusetts Division of State Parks and Recreation, 251 Causeway St., Suite 600, Boston, MA 02114-2104, 617/626-1250, www.state. ma.us/dem/forparks.htm.

🔟 ROCKY WOODS
2.3 mi/1.5 hr

in Medfield

This 491-acre patch of woodlands boasts more than 12 miles of cart paths and foot trails and is popular with locals for activities such as walking, cross-country skiing, and fishing (catch-and-release only). There are many more loop possibilities besides the one described here.

Walk down the entrance road to the Quarry Trail and follow it 0.1 mile along the shore of Chickering Pond. Bear left at Junction 2, continue 0.1 mile, and then continue straight through Junction 3. At Junction 4, a half mile from Junction 3, cross the Harwood Notch Trail diagonally, staying on the Quarry Trail. A quarter mile farther, at Junction 7, turn right on the Ridge Trail and walk 0.7 mile. Bear right at Junction 6, turn left immediately after that at Junction 5, and follow the cart path more than a half mile back to Junction 2. The pond and parking area lie straight ahead.

User Groups: Hikers, leashed dogs, bikes, and horses. No wheelchair facilities.

Permits: Admission is free for Trustees members. Nonmember adults $4; nonmember children (ages 12 and under) free. Fees collected by ranger on weekends and holidays; honor system applies at all other times.

Maps: A free trail map is available from the ranger on duty weekends and holidays. Trail intersections numbered on the map correspond to numbered trail signs. For topographic area maps, request Medfield and Norwood from the USGS.

Directions: From I-95/Route 128 in Westwood, take Exit 16B onto Route 109, driving west for 5.7 miles. Take a sharp right onto Hartford Street and continue 0.6 mile to the reservation entrance on the left. Or from the junction of Routes 27 and 109 in Medfield, drive 1.7 miles east on Route 109 and bear left on Hartford Street and park along that street. The reservation is open daily sunrise–sunset year-round.

GPS Coordinates: 42.2011 N, 71.2794 W

Contact: The Trustees of Reservations Southeast/Cape Cod Regional Office, The Bradley Estate, 2468B Washington St., Canton, MA 02021-1124, 781/821-2977, www.thetrustees. org.

🔟 BLUE HILLS: SKYLINE TRAIL LOOP
4.5 mi/2.5 hr

in the Blue Hills Reservation in Canton

With 5,800 forest acres spread over 20 hilltops, the Blue Hills Reservation in Quincy, Braintree, Randolph, Canton, and Milton comprises the largest tract of open space in Greater Boston. It hosts a broad diversity of flora and fauna, including the timber rattlesnake, which you are extremely unlikely to encounter given the snake's fear of people. The reservation harbors an extensive network of trails and carriage roads. But be aware that some are unmarked and confusing, and many are rocky and surprisingly rugged. At 635 feet, Great Blue Hill, near the reservation's western end, is the park's highest point and probably its most popular hike.

This 4.5-mile loop on the north and south branches of the Skyline Trail passes over Great Blue and four other hills, climbing a cumulative total of about 1,200 feet. It incorporates several good views—the best being the panorama from the stone tower on Great Blue, reached near this hike's end. In fact, while the native granite tower is less than 50 years old, it symbolizes this high point's long history. Patriots used Great Blue as a lookout during the Revolutionary War, lighting beacons up here to warn of any British attack. For several hundred years, fires have been lit on Great Blue to celebrate historic occurrences, beginning with the repeal of the Stamp Act and including the signing of the Declaration of Independence.

From the parking lot, walk back on Route 138 in the direction you came, watching for blue blazes that cross the road within 100 feet. Enter the woods at a granite post inscribed with the words Skyline Trail. The trail ascends steeply for a half mile, reaching open ledges and the carriage road just below the summit. Turn right on the carriage road, where blue blazes are often marked on stones. Pass the path leading to the summit (there aren't any views, and the weather observatory here is private property) and within 0.1 mile turn right with the blue blazes onto a footpath marked by a post inscribed South Skyline Trail. It descends ledges with good views of the Boston skyline and Houghton Pond, enters the woods, and, within a mile of Great Blue, reaches wooded Houghton Hill. Descend a short distance to Hillside Street, cross it, turn left, and follow the blue blazes about 150 feet to where the blazes direct you back across the street toward the reservation headquarters (passing a post marked North Skyline Trail). Walk up the driveway and left of the headquarters onto a carriage path. In about 75 feet, turn right at a sign onto the North Skyline Trail. In minutes you reach an open ledge on Hancock Hill with a view of Great Blue Hill.

Continuing over Hemenway Hill and Wolcott Hill in the next mile, watch for side paths leading right to views of Boston. The Skyline Trail drops downhill, crosses a carriage path, and then climbs the north side of Great Blue to the stone tower. Climb the stairs to the tower for a sweeping view of woods, city, and ocean. From the tower's observation deck looking west (out over the stone building beside the tower), you may see Mount Wachusett. Standing on the side of the tower facing Boston, look left: On a clear day, you'll spy Mount Monadnock between two tall radio towers in the distance. Descend the stone tower and turn right on the Skyline Trail, circling around Great Blue, past the posts marking the south and north Skyline Trail branches. Make a left turn at the third Skyline Trail post and descend a half mile to Route 138, where you began this hike.

User Groups: Hikers and leashed dogs. No wheelchair facilities. Bikes and horses are prohibited on this hike, but are permitted on some other specifically marked trails in the Blue Hills.

Permits: Parking and access are free.

Maps: A trail map of the Blue Hills is available at the reservation headquarters or the Massachusetts Audubon Society Blue Hills Trailside Museum. For a topographic area map, request Norwood from the USGS.

Directions: From I-93, take Exit 2B onto Route 138 north. Continue for nearly a half mile to a commuter parking lot on the left—park here for this hike. The Blue Hills Reservation Headquarters is located at 695 Hillside Street in Milton, 0.25 mile north of Houghton's Pond, beside the State Police Station. GPS Coordinates: 42.2141 N, 71.1200W

Contact: Blue Hills Reservation Headquarters, 695 Hillside St., Milton, MA 02186, 617/698-1802, www.mass.gov/dcr/parks/metroboston/blue.htm. Friends of the Blue Hills, P.O. Box 416, Milton, MA 02186, 781/828-1805, www.friendsofthebluehills.org. Massachusetts Audubon Society Blue Hills Trailside Museum, 1904 Canton Ave./Route 138, Milton, MA 02186, 781/333-0690, www.massaudubon.org/Nature_Connection/Sanctuaries/Blue_Hills.

20 BLUE HILLS: RATTLESNAKE AND WAMPATUCK HILLS
2.2 mi/1.5 hr   🏃2 ⛰8

in the Blue Hills Reservation in Braintree

While many hikers flock to the west side of the reservation and to Great Blue Hill, the east side of the reservation remains a fairly well-kept secret—and the views from there are arguably better than those from Great Blue Hill. Standing in a warm summer breeze on Rattlesnake Hill, gazing out over an expanse of woods to the Boston skyline in the distance, many who visit here are amazed to hear only the breeze and the singing of birds, despite having left the interstate behind just a half hour earlier and hiking merely a half mile.

From the roadside parking area, follow the Skyline Trail, which quickly ascends a short but steep hillside to a view of the thickly forested, rolling hills of the reservation and the Boston skyline beyond. The trail bends around an old quarry now filled with water, and about a half mile from the road reaches the rocky top of Rattlesnake Hill, with excellent views of the hills and skyline. Wampatuck Hill, with more good views, lies less than a half mile farther. There is a short, rocky scramble along the trail between Rattlesnake and Wampatuck that may be intimidating for some inexperienced hikers. Return the same way.

User Groups: Hikers and leashed dogs. No wheelchair facilities. Bikes and horses are prohibited on this hike, but are permitted on some other specifically marked trails in the Blue Hills.

Permits: Parking and access are free.

Maps: A trail map of the Blue Hills is available at the reservation headquarters or the Massachusetts Audubon Society Blue Hills Trailside Museum. For a topographic area map, request Norwood from the USGS.

Directions: From I-93 in Braintree, take Exit 6 and follow signs to Willard Street. About a mile from I-93, watch for the ice rink on the left. Drive 0.2 mile beyond the rink, turn left on Hayden Street, and then immediately left again on Wampatuck Road. Drive another 0.2 mile and park at the roadside on the right, where a post marks the Skyline Trail. The reservation headquarters is at 695 Hillside Street in Milton, reached via the reservation entrance on Route 138 or from Randolph Avenue (I-93 Exit 5). This trail is open dawn–8 P.M.

GPS Coordinates: 42.2368 N, 71.0321 W

Contact: Blue Hills Reservation Headquarters, 695 Hillside St., Milton, MA 02186, 617/698-1802, www.state.ma.us/mdc/blue. htm. Friends of the Blue Hills, P.O. Box 416, Milton, MA 02186, 781/828-1805, www.

friendsofthebluehills.org. Massachusetts Audubon Society Blue Hills Trailside Museum, 1904 Canton Ave./Route 138, Milton, MA 02186, 781/333-0690, www.massaudubon.org/Nature_Connection/ Sanctuaries/ Blue_Hills.

21 WORLD'S END
2.9 mi/1.5 hr   🏃2 ⛰8

in Hingham

BEST (

This 251-acre peninsula in Hingham nearly became a community of 163 homes in the late 1800s, when then-landowner John Brewer hired none other than the famous landscape architect Frederick Law Olmsted to design a landscape of carriage paths lined by English oaks and native hardwoods. That much was accomplished, but the Brewer family continued to farm the land rather than develop it. Today, thanks to The Trustees of Reservations, this string of four low hills rising above Hingham Harbor provides local people with a wonderful recreation area for walking, running, or cross-country skiing. Bird-watchers flock here, particularly in spring and fall, to observe migratory species. From various spots, you'll enjoy views of the Boston skyline, Hingham Harbor, and across the Weir River to Hull. This hike loops around the property's perimeter, but four miles of carriage paths and three miles of foot trails, all interconnected, offer many other possible routes for exploration.

From the entrance, walk straight (northwest) along the flat carriage path for a quarter mile and then bear left around the west flank of Planter's Hill. A quarter mile past Planter's, cross the narrow land bar between the harbor and river, and turn left onto another carriage road. This follows a half-mile curve around a hillside; turn left at the next junction of carriage paths. After another half mile, bear left again, reaching the land bar a quarter mile farther. Bear left, continue 0.3 mile, then turn right and walk nearly 0.4 mile back to the entrance.

User Groups: Hikers and leashed dogs. Horses are allowed by permit only from the Trustees of Reservations. No wheelchair facilities or bikes.

Permits: There is an entrance fee of $4.50 per person ages 12 and older, except for members of The Trustees of Reservations, who enter for free. Horse permits are free but must be obtained in advance by contacting the Trustees of Reservations Southeast/Cape Cod Regional Office.

Maps: A map of the carriage paths and trails is available free at the entrance. For a topographic area map, request Hull from the USGS.

Directions: From the junction of Routes 228 and 3A, drive north on Route 3A for 0.6 mile. Turn right on Summer Street, drive 0.3 mile, proceed straight through the traffic lights, and then continue another 0.8 mile to the World's End entrance. The reservation is open daily 8 A.M.–sunset year-round.

GPS Coordinates: 42.2480 N, 70.8727 W

Contact: The Trustees of Reservations Southeast/Cape Cod Regional Office, The Bradley Estate, 2468B Washington St., Canton, MA 02021-1124, 781/821-2977, www.thetrustees.org.

22 CARATUNK WILDLIFE REFUGE
2 mi/1 hr   🏃1 ⛰7

in Seekonk

BEST (

Bird-watchers will want to visit here during April and May or late August–October to catch the migratory birds, but this easy, two-mile walk mostly through woods is a satisfying outing any time of year. There are a few trail options in the refuge, all of them well blazed; this loop, mostly on the blue trail, is the longest, winding through much of the property, past open fields, wetlands, and two small ponds.

From the parking lot, walk to the right of the building, past the information kiosk

and along the field's right edge. Soon a short side path loops into the woods to the right, bringing you along a bog, then back out to the field. Walk a short distance farther along the field, then turn right onto the red trail. After passing through a pine grove and skirting the far edge of the same field where you began, turn right onto the yellow trail and then bear left onto the blue trail. At the edge of Muskrat Pond, turn right, staying on the blue trail past Ice Pond, crossing power lines, passing another pond, and continuing through the beech woods and a hemlock stand; you'll pass several trail junctions and loop back to the bog, where you begin backtracking on the blue trail. After crossing the power lines and passing Ice Pond in the other direction, stay on the blue trail past one junction with the yellow trail and then bear left onto the yellow trail at the next junction. Upon reaching the field, turn right on the red trail and follow it around the field back to the refuge office and parking lot.

User Groups: Hikers only. No bikes, dogs, horses, or wheelchair facilities.

Permits: A donation of $1 is requested for nonmembers of the Audubon Society.

Maps: A map is available at the refuge. For a topographic area map, request Providence from the USGS.

Directions: From I-95 in Attleboro, take Exit 2 onto Newport Avenue southbound/Route 1A. Drive 1.8 miles from the interstate, turn left onto Armistice Boulevard/Route 15, and follow it 1.2 miles to its end. Turn right onto Route 152 south, continue 0.6 mile, and then turn left at a church onto Brown Avenue. Proceed 0.8 mile farther to the refuge entrance on the right. The refuge is open daily sunrise–sunset. Visitors should stay on trails.

GPS Coordinates: 41.8743 N, 71.3179 W

Contact: Caratunk Wildlife Refuge, 301 Brown Ave., Seekonk, MA 02771, 508/761-8230. The Audubon Society of Rhode Island, 12 Sanderson Rd., Smithfield, RI 02917, 401/949-5454, www.asri.org.

23 MYLES STANDISH STATE FOREST LOOP

11 mi/6 hr

in Carver

Myles Standish State Forest sprawls over more than 14,000 acres, making it one of the largest public lands in Massachusetts. A grid work of old woods roads cuts through this pine barrens, along with a hiking trail and a paved bicycle path. This loop from the forest headquarters connects several dirt woods roads. The grid pattern of roads and the signs at many intersections makes navigating through this vast landscape easier than it might be otherwise, but bring a map. Although the pine-covered terrain is mostly flat, there are slight rises and dips that can make the workout a little harder if you take to the trail on a bike or cross-country skis.

From the parking lot, head back out onto Cranberry Road, turn right, and then immediately right again past the headquarters building onto paved Lower College Pond Road into the state forest. Within a half mile, bicyclists can turn left onto the paved bike path, which leads to the dirt Halfway Pond Road; others will continue a quarter mile on Lower College Pond Road to the Halfway Pond Road intersection. Turn left onto Halfway Pond Road, follow it a half mile to a crossroads, and turn right onto Jessup Road. Continue about 0.7 mile and bear right at a sign reading Ebeeme Road, which is shown as Jessup Road on the state map. A half mile farther, turn right at a crossroads onto Federal Pond Road. Follow it a mile, crossing the bridle trail, a gas line right-of-way, and Kamesit Way, and then turn right onto Sabbatia Road. Continue a mile and then turn left onto Three Cornered Pond Road. Reaching the paved Lower College Pond Road within a quarter mile, turn right, then bear left immediately and proceed straight onto the bridle path (don't turn left onto another bridle path branch),

marked by a horse symbol. In a quarter mile, at the next intersection, turn left onto Negas Road, continue a half mile, and then turn left onto paved Upper College Pond Road. Proceed nearly a half mile and turn right onto Three Cornered Pond Road. Three-quarters of a mile farther, turn right again onto Cobb Road and follow it 0.75 mile to its end. Turn right onto Halfway Pond Road, go about 0.2 mile, and then take the first left. In about 0.3 mile, turn left again onto Doctor's Pond Road, go a half mile, and then turn right onto Webster Springs Road. Follow it nearly a mile, crossing paved Circuit Drive, a dirt road, the bike path, and the bridle path before reaching Upper College Pond Road. Turn left, following the paved road nearly a half mile to its end. Turn right on paved Fearing Pond Road and continue a half mile back to the forest headquarters.

User Groups: Hikers, bikers, and leashed dogs. The paved bike path is wheelchair accessible. Horses are prohibited.

Permits: A daily parking fee of $5 is collected mid-May–mid-October.

Maps: A free, basic trail map of Myles Standish State Forest is available at the state forest headquarters or online from the Massachusetts Division of State Parks and Recreation. For topographic area maps, request Plymouth and Wareham from the USGS.

Directions: From I-495, take Exit 2 on the Middleborough-Wareham line onto Route 58 north. Drive 2.5 miles to where Route 58 turns left, but continue straight ahead, following signs for the state forest. Proceed another 0.8 mile, turn right onto Cranberry Road, and then drive 2.8 miles to the state forest headquarters and a parking lot on the left. GPS Coordinates: 41.8389 N, 70.6941 W

Contact: Myles Standish State Forest, Cranberry Rd., P.O. Box 66, South Carver, MA 02366, 508/866-2526. Massachusetts Division of State Parks and Recreation, 251 Causeway St., Suite 600, Boston, MA 02114-2104, 617/626-1250, www.state.ma.us/dem/forparks.htm.

24 PROVINCE LANDS TRAIL
6 mi/3 hr   🏃1 ⛰8

in the Cape Cod National Seashore in
Provincetown

BEST (

This paved path is popular with bikers, hikers, runners, in-line skaters, and others, and it's good for wheelchairs, too. Making a circuitous loop through forest, past ponds, and over sprawling sand dunes, this multi-use trail is the region's most geographically diverse. Be sure to take the spur path a half mile out to Race Point (included in the mileage), which is near the very tip of Massachusetts and a great place for whale-watching during the seasonal migrations, when the whales often swim close to shore. Heed the center dividing line on this path, especially around its many blind corners. Pick up the bike path from the Beech Forest parking lot; the loop returns here.

User Groups: Hikers, leashed dogs, bikes, and wheelchair users. Horses are prohibited.

Permits: Parking and access are free.

Maps: A guide to national seashore bike trails is available at the Province Lands and Salt Pond Visitor Centers in Eastham. The Cape Cod & North Shore Bicycle Map, a detailed map of roads and bike paths on Cape Cod and the Islands and Cape Ann and the North Shore, is available for $4.25 from Rubel BikeMaps (P.O. Box 401035, Cambridge, MA 02140, www.bikemaps.com) and from area stores listed at the website. Or get the waterproof Cape Cod National Seashore Map #250 for $11.95 from Trails Illustrated (800/962-1643, www.natgeomaps.com/ti_massachusetts.html). For a topographic area map, request Provincetown from the USGS.

Directions: Drive U.S. 6 east to Provincetown. At the traffic lights on U.S. 6, turn right onto Race Point Road. Continue to the Beech Forest parking area on the left; the Province Lands Visitor Center is a short distance farther on the right.

Trails are open to the public 6 A.M.–midnight. The Province Lands Visitor Center on Race Point Road is open daily 9 A.M.–4:30 P.M.

GPS Coordinates: 42.0600 N, 70.1906 W

Contact: Cape Cod National Seashore, 99 Marconi Station Site Rd., Wellfleet, MA 02667, 508/349-3785, www.nps.gov/caco/index.htm. Salt Pond Visitor Center (corner of Nauset Road and U.S. 6, Eastham), 508/255-3421. Province Lands Visitor Center (on Race Point Road, off U.S. 6, at the northern end of Cape Cod National Seashore and approximately one mile from Provincetown), 508/487-1256.

25 GREAT ISLAND TRAIL
6 mi/3.5 hr   🏃5 ⛰10

in the Cape Cod National Seashore in Wellfleet

BEST (

As the sinking sun ignites the dunes a vivid yellow, tiny crabs scatter in the growing shadows, and the shoreline takes on a bluish hue as the wet sand blends with the purple-indigo of Cape Cod Bay. This west-facing vantage point is simply the best place to take in the sunset on Cape Cod, both for the majestic views as well as the sense of solitude. Even in the middle of a crowded Cape Cod summer, come here towards dusk and your only company may be a lone sea kayaker paddling the glassy waters of the bay far offshore.

From the parking lot, the trail enters the woods, following a wide forest road. An optional side loop (adding two miles to the hike) leads to the Tavern Site, so named because fragments of a 17th-century tavern were excavated there; nothing remains today, however. The main trail leads over Great Beach Hill (which has no views) and out to the grasslands separating the beach from the forest. Follow that old road around to Jeremy Point overlook, where the dunes end abruptly and you reach the beach on Cape Cod Bay. At low tide, the long spit out to Jeremy Point may be walkable, but be aware that it disappears

MASSACHUSETTS

sunset over Cape Cod Bay

ti_massachusetts.html). For a topographic area map, request Wellfleet from the USGS.

Directions: From the Salt Pond Visitor Center at the Doane Road Exit in Eastham, drive U.S. 6 east for 8.2 miles. Turn left at the sign for Wellfleet Center and Harbor. Drive 0.4 mile and turn left at the sign for Blue Harbor. In another 0.6 mile you reach the marina; turn right, following the road (with the water on your left) for 2.5 miles to the Great Island parking lot on the left.

Trails are open to the public 6 A.M.–midnight. The Salt Pond Visitor Center is open daily 9 A.M.–4:30 P.M.

GPS Coordinates: 41.9351 N, 70.0682 W

Contact: Cape Cod National Seashore, 99 Marconi Station Site Rd., Wellfleet, MA 02667, 508/349-3785, www.nps.gov/caco/index.htm. Salt Pond Visitor Center (corner of Nauset Road and U.S. 6, Eastham), 508/255-3421. Province Lands Visitor Center, 508/487-1256.

26 ATLANTIC WHITE CEDAR SWAMP
1 mi/0.75 hr   🥾1 ⛰10

in the Cape Cod National Seashore in South Wellfleet

This is one of the true highlights of the national seashore, as much for the site's historic significance as for the short, but uniquely beautiful walk through a swamp. It was from this spot, on January 18, 1903, that the Italian Guglielmo Marconi transmitted the first two-way transoceanic communication and first wireless telegram between America and Europe. The four huge towers that once stood here are long gone; in fact, more than half the land where they stood has since eroded into the sea. Considering the way the ocean and wind continually batter this narrowest section of Cape Cod—the peninsula is barely a mile across here—one has to wonder how many years will elapse before

under the ocean when the tide rises. Return the way you came.

User Groups: Hikers only. No wheelchair facilities. Bikes, dogs, and horses are prohibited.

Permits: Parking and access are free.

Maps: An information board is at the trailhead, and trail information is available at the Salt Pond Visitor Center. The Cape Cod & North Shore Bicycle Map, a detailed map of roads and bike paths on Cape Cod and the Islands and Cape Ann and the North Shore, is available for $4.25 from Rubel BikeMaps (P.O. Box 401035, Cambridge, MA 02140, 617/776-6567, www.bikemaps.com) and from area stores listed at the website. Or get the waterproof Cape Cod National Seashore Map #250 for $11.95 from Trails Illustrated (800/962-1643, www.natgeomaps.com/

the sea cuts the outer cape off completely from the mainland.

From the parking lot, the Atlantic White Cedar Swamp Trail begins among stunted oak and pine trees. But as you descend at a very gentle grade, the trees grow taller; they are more protected from the harsh ocean climate in this hollow of sorts. Pitch pine, black and white oak, golden beach-heather, and broom crowberry thrive here, though many are still twisted in the manner characteristic of a place buffeted by almost constant winds. The swamp itself is an eerie depression formed, like other kettles on the cape, by a melting glacial ice block. Crossing on a boardwalk, cedars crowd in from both sides, some leaning over it, creating an almost overwhelming sense of intimacy in this odd little forest. The trail emerges abruptly from the swamp onto an old sand road that leads back to the parking lot.

User Groups: Hikers only. The Marconi station is wheelchair accessible. Bikes, dogs, and horses are prohibited.

Permits: Parking and access are free.

Maps: A trail guide is available at the trailhead. Maps and information about the national seashore are available at the Salt Pond Visitor Center. The Cape Cod & North Shore Bicycle Map, a detailed map of roads and bike paths on Cape Cod and the Islands and Cape Ann and the North Shore, is available for $4.25 from Rubel BikeMaps (P.O. Box 401035, Cambridge, MA 02140, www.bikemaps.com) and from area stores listed at the website. Or get the waterproof Cape Cod National Seashore Map #250 for $11.95 from Trails Illustrated (800/962-1643, www.natgeomaps.com/ti_massachusetts.html). For a topographic area map, request Wellfleet from the USGS.

Directions: Drive U.S. 6 east to Eastham. Five miles beyond the Doane Road exit for the Salt Pond Visitor Center, turn right at signs for the Marconi station and continue to the parking lot. The Marconi station, which has historical displays, is between the lot and the beach. The trail begins at the parking lot.

Trails are open to the public 6 A.M.– midnight. The Salt Pond Visitor Center is open daily 9 A.M.–4:30 P.M.

GPS Coordinates: 41.9044 N, 69.9843 W

Contact: Cape Cod National Seashore, 99 Marconi Station Site Rd., Wellfleet, MA 02667, 508/349-3785, www.nps.gov/caco/index.htm. Salt Pond Visitor Center (corner of Nauset Road and U.S. 6, Eastham), 508/255-3421. Province Lands Visitor Center, 508/487-1256.

27 NAUSET MARSH
1.2 mi/0.75 hr

in the Cape Cod National Seashore in Eastham

This easy-to-follow trail has numerous interpretive signs with information about its abundant flora and a good view of Nauset Marsh. From the visitors center parking lot, start out on the Buttonbush Trail for the Blind, which leads shortly to the Nauset Marsh Trail. The Marsh Trail passes through pitch pine, black cherry, and eastern red cedar trees, then follows the edge of Salt Pond. (The pond was created when a glacier receded and left behind enormous salt blocks, which eventually melted, leaving kettle ponds such as this one in their wake. The ocean later broke through a land barrier to infiltrate Salt Pond.) The trail then turns away from the channel connecting pond to ocean and enters a forest of honeysuckle and cedar. It passes an open overlook above Nauset Marsh, which at one time was navigable. After entering a forest of red cedar and bayberry, the trail passes a side path leading nearly a mile to a good view of the marsh at a spot marked by the Doane Memorial, a plaque paying tribute to a family that once owned land here. The loop culminates near the visitors center parking lot.

User Groups: Hikers only. The Buttonbush Trail for the Blind is wheelchair accessible; instead of taking a right onto the Nauset Marsh Trail, wheelchair users can stay on the Buttonbush for a scenic loop back to the

MASSACHUSETTS

MASSACHUSETTS

visitors center. Bikes, dogs, and horses are prohibited.

Permits: Parking and access are free.

Maps: A trail guide is available in a box at the trailhead, and maps and information about the national seashore are available in the visitors center. The Cape Cod & North Shore Bicycle Map, a detailed map of roads and bike paths on Cape Cod and the Islands and Cape Ann and the North Shore, is available for $4.25 from Rubel BikeMaps (P.O. Box 401035, Cambridge, MA 02140, www.bikemaps.com) and from area stores listed at the website. Or get the waterproof Cape Cod National Seashore Map #250 for $11.95 from Trails Illustrated (800/962-1643, www.natgeomaps.com/ti_massachusetts.html). For a topographic area map, request Orleans from the USGS.

Directions: Drive U.S. 6 east to Eastham. Take the exit for Doane Road, following signs for national seashore information to the Salt Pond Visitor Center.

Trails are open to the public 6 A.M.–midnight. The Salt Pond Visitor Center is open daily 9 A.M.–4:30 P.M.

GPS Coordinates: 41.8404 N, 69.9616 W

Contact: Cape Cod National Seashore, 99 Marconi Station Site Rd., Wellfleet, MA 02667, 508/349-3785, www.nps.gov/caco/index.htm. Salt Pond Visitor Center (corner of Nauset Road and U.S. 6, Eastham), 508/255-3421. Province Lands Visitor Center, 508/487-1256.

28 CAPE COD RAIL TRAIL
25 mi one-way/12 hr

in Dennis, Harwich, Brewster, Orleans, East-ham, and Wellfleet

Following a former railroad bed, the paved Cape Cod Rail Trail extends for 25 miles from Route 134 in South Dennis to Lecount Hollow Road in South Wellfleet, near the Cape Cod National Seashore's Marconi Visitor Center, making for about a two-hour bike ride. The mostly flat, paved trail crosses cranberry bogs, forests, and several roads, providing numerous access and egress points, including at the entrance to Nickerson State Park on U.S. 6A in Brewster, and at Locust Road in Eastham, which is off U.S. 6 near the Cape Cod National Seashore's Salt Pond Visitor Center (Doane Road). The trail passes through Nickerson, which has its own hiking trail system and a bike path, and it connects with bike paths at the national seashore. The rail trail is very much a citizen's path—busy in the summer tourist months with cyclists, in-line skaters, walkers, wheelchair users, and adults and kids of all ages. You can do sections of varying length rather than the entire 25-mile distance, which is why this receives such an easy difficulty rating.

User Groups: Hikers, bikers, leashed dogs, horses, and wheelchair users.

Permits: Parking and access are free.

Maps: The Cape Cod & North Shore Bicycle Map, a detailed map of roads and bike paths on Cape Cod and the Islands and Cape Ann and the North Shore, is available for $4.25 from Rubel BikeMaps (P.O. Box 401035, Cambridge, MA 02140, www.bikemaps.com) and from area stores listed at the website. Or get the waterproof Cape Cod National Seashore Map #250 for $11.95 from Trails Illustrated (800/962-1643, www.natgeomaps.com/ti_massachusetts.html). For topographic area maps, request Dennis, Harwich, and Orleans from the USGS.

Directions: To reach the trail's western end, from U.S. 6 in Dennis, take Exit 9 onto Route 134 south. Proceed through two traffic signals to a large parking lot on the left for the Cape Cod Rail Trail. The eastern terminus is at Lecount Hollow Road in South Wellfleet, near the Cape Cod National Seashore's Marconi Visitor Center and off U.S. 6. The trail can be accessed at numerous points along its path. GPS Coordinates: 41.9176 N, 69.9864 W

Contact: Cape Cod Rail Trail/Nickerson State Park, P.O. Box 787, Brewster, MA 02631,

© MARIO GREEN

MASSACHUSETTS

the famous view of the lighthouse and cliffs at Aquinnah, Martha's Vineyard

508/896-3491, www.mass.gov/dcr/parks/
southeast/ccrt.htm. Massachusetts Division
of Forests and Parks, 100 Cambridge St., 19th
Floor, Boston, MA 02202, 800/831-0569 (in-
state only) or 617/626-1250 ext. 1451. Rails to
Trails Conservancy, 1100 17th St. NW, 10th
floor, Washington, DC 20036, 202/331-9696,
www.railtrails.org.

29 AQUINNAH
3 mi/1.5 hr   🚶2 ⛰9

in Aquinnah on Martha's Vineyard

BEST (

The vibrant pastels of the clay cliffs at Aquinnah, the westernmost point of Martha's Vineyard island, are an eye-catching attraction at
any time of day, but particularly striking at
sunset, when the sun's low, long rays bring out
the layered browns, yellows, reds, whites, and
deep grays. This hike is an easy walk along

Moshup Beach and is popular with tourists.
From the parking lot, follow the sandy trail,
sometimes crossing a boardwalk, which parallels Moshup Road. Within minutes you are on
the beach; turn right and follow the beach to
the cliffs. At high tide, you may have difficulty
walking to the far end of the cliffs. Head back
the way you came.

User Groups: Hikers only. No dogs or wheelchair facilities. This trail is not suitable for
bikes or horses.

Permits: A parking fee of $5 per hour or $15
maximum per day is charged Memorial Day
weekend–mid-October, although cyclists,
walkers, or anyone not parking a vehicle can
access the beach for free.

Maps: Although no map is needed for this
hike, for a topographic area map, request
Squibnocket from the USGS.

Directions: The cliffs at Aquinnah are on
Moshup Beach at the western tip of Martha's
Vineyard, in the town of Aquinnah, and at the

end of the State Road, which crosses the island from Vineyard Haven. Three seasonal ferry services make regular trips, May–October, to Vineyard Haven or Oak Bluffs from Falmouth (508/548-4800), and Hyannis on Cape Cod (508/778-2600), as well as from New Bedford, MA (508/997-1688). The Steamship Authority (508/477-8600) carries vehicles and passengers from Woods Hole on Cape Cod to Vineyard Haven year-round, and Woods Hole to Oak Bluffs May 15–October 15.

GPS Coordinates: 41.3877 N, 70.8348 W

Contact: Aquinnah Town Hall, 65 State Rd., Aquinnah, MA 02535, 508/645-2300. Martha's Vineyard Chamber of Commerce, P.O. Box 1698, Vineyard Haven, MA 02568, 508/693-0085, www.mvy.com/islandinfo/townAquinnah.html.

Rhode Island

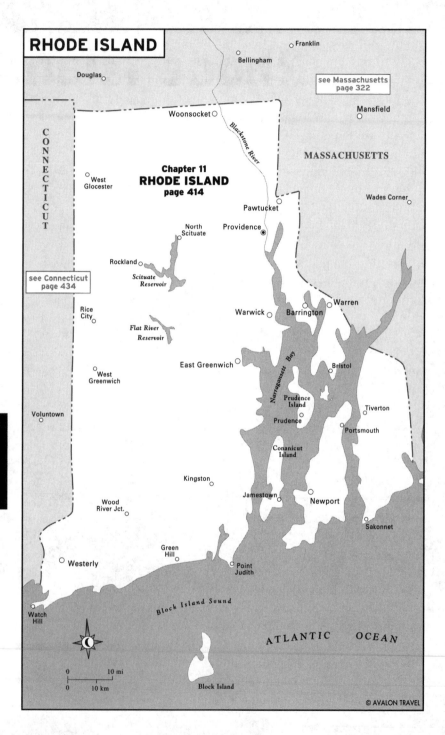

RHODE ISLAND

Franklin

Bellingham

Douglas

see Massachusetts
page 322

Woonsocket

Mansfield

C
O
N
N
E
C
T
I
C
U
T

West
Glocester

**Chapter 11
RHODE ISLAND
page 414**

Blackstone River

MASSACHUSETTS

Wades Corner

Pawtucket

North
Scituate

Providence

Rockland

*Scituate
Reservoir*

see Connecticut
page 434

Warren

Rice
City

Warwick   Barrington

*Flat River
Reservoir*

Bristol

East Greenwich

West
Greenwich

Narragansett Bay

Prudence
Island

Prudence

Tiverton

Voluntown

Portsmouth

*Conanicut
Island*

Kingston

Jamestown   Newport

Wood
River Jct.

Sakonnet

Green
Hill

Westerly

Point
Judith

Watch
Hill

Block Island Sound

ATLANTIC   OCEAN

0   10 mi

0   10 km

Block Island

© AVALON TRAVEL

RHODE ISLAND

RHODE ISLAND

© HEIDI J. BROWN

BEST HIKES

We all know good things come in small pack-

ages and tiny Rhode Island doesn't disappoint. The country's smallest state and one of its flattest, Rhode Island is home to multiple wildlife and bird preserves, countless state recreation areas, and great big ocean views. There are no soaring peaks in the Ocean State, but hikes here can take you to very different heights – from Newport's famed Cliff Walk and it's row of almost mountain-size Gilded Age mansions to the bluffs of Block Island, where hundreds of thousands of birds stop over during seasonal migrations. And like the rest of New England, hikes to waterfalls and hidden ponds, through lush forest and hilly terrain abound in Rhode Island, in numbers first-time visitors to the state might find surprising.

Most hiking trails in "Rhody" lie on either state park land or private preserves. Each state park's management creates regulations specific to its property, and many impose trail restrictions on bikes and require that dogs be leashed. The two premier public lands are the 3,489-acre George Washington Management Area, in the state's northwest corner, and the 14,000-acre Arcadia Management Area, in the southwest corner. Extensive forest, pond, and marsh habitats in both management areas provide for a rich mix of flora and fauna. Commonly spotted creatures include cottontail rabbits, wild turkey, ruffled grouse, woodcock, snowshoe hare, white-tailed deer and a variety of waterfowl, including wood duck, mallards, and black duck. Trees range from hemlock to hickory, with enough deciduous forest cover to make autumn color burn brightly.

Several hikes covered in this guide wind through Audubon-run bird sanctuaries or other preserves known to bird-watchers; the state's woods and waters around Narragansett Bay are a popular stop for migratory birds along the Atlantic Flyway. Private preserves are often open only to hikers (no pets of any kind), and some require a small fee for trail use. Though a visit to Block Island requires a ferry trip, trails on the island are free and open to the public.

Rhode Island's winters rarely see enough snow for cross-country skiing or snowshoeing and slushy, muddy winter trail conditions can make cold weather hiking a bit tricky. But many public lands, like the Arcadia Management Area, harbor a wealth of dirt roads perfect for mountain biking. Respect postings that prohibit bikes from certain trails. Hunting is generally allowed in season on any land that is not posted with signs specifically prohibiting it. The Arcadia Management Area requires trail users to wear fluorescent orange during the hunting season.

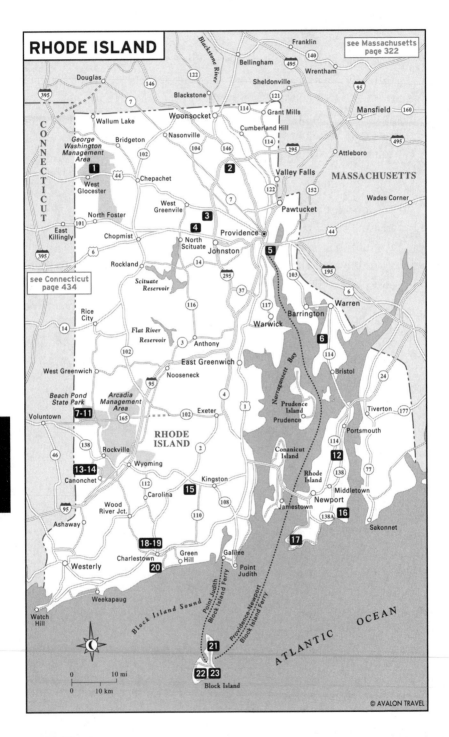

■ WALKABOUT TRAIL
2-8 mi/1-4 hr   🏃5 ⛰8

in the George Washington Management Area in Chepachet

Cut by Australian sailors holed up in the Ocean State waiting for their ship to be repaired, the Walkabout Trail is named for the Australian aborigine concept of "walkabout"— the sacred need to wander the landscape. The large, wooded loop really does wander as it winds along the shores of largely undeveloped ponds and through quiet woodlands punctuated by glacial-erratic boulders. Those ingenious Aussie trailblazers even gave hikers the ability to pick from three different loop lengths on this trail. Hikers can follow the entire orange-blazed trail for an eight-mile loop or take a red-blazed cut over to create a six-mile loop; for an even shorter hike, a blue-blazed cut through reduces the loop to a two-mile jaunt in the woods.

From the parking area, the orange, red, and blue blazes of the Walkabout Trail first lead you west to skirt the large Bowdish water reservoir. Turning north away from the reservoir, the trail reaches the shore of picturesque Willow Pond at one mile. Here, the blue-blazed trail leaves to the right and heads east (away from the pond) to complete its loop. Continuing on, the now orange- and red-blazed trail makes it way around the mountain laurel–ringed pond and then reenters the woods; in another mile, the red trail leaves to the right, cutting north to rejoin the main trail for the last four miles of the loop. The orange-blazed trail then passes several trail junctions on its meandering course and after two miles, is rejoined by the red blazes. The Walkabout heads next to a marsh (scenic, but often very buggy) and then back into the forest. Rambling along for the next three miles, the blue blazes rejoin the loop a little less than a mile before the trail returns to the parking area.

Special Note: The possibilities in this remote northwest corner of tiny Rhode Island begin with the Walkabout Trail, but the forest roads and trails that crisscross the George Washington Management Area open up countless other opportunities for easy hiking, skiing, and mountain biking.

User Groups: Hikers, leashed dogs, and horses; no wheelchair facilities. Bikes are prohibited on this trail.

Permits: Parking and access are free.

Maps: A trail map is available at the park headquarters on U.S. 44 in Glocester. For a topographic area map, request Thompson, CT, from the USGS.

Directions: From the intersection of U.S. 44 and Route 94 in Chepachet, follow U.S. 44 east 0.8 mile. Turn left at the sign and access road for the George Washington Management Area and proceed past the gatehouse. In another 0.3 mile, bear left into a parking area near the picnic area and boat launch. The trailhead is here, marked with orange, red, and blue blazes.

GPS Coordinates: 41.9237 N, 71.7568 W

Contact: George Washington Management Area, 2185 Putnam Pike, Chepachet, RI 02814, 401/568-2248. Rhode Island Division of Forest Environment, 1037 Hartford Pike, North Scituate, RI 02857, 401/647-1439, www.dem.ri.gov.

■ LIME ROCK PRESERVE
2 mi/1.5 hr   🏃1 ⛰6

in Lincoln

Only 10 minutes from downtown Providence, tranquil Lime Rock Preserve boasts a variety of distinctive regional habitats: rich woodlands, forested swamps, streams, and open water. Lime Rock also harbors 30 rare plant species, more than any other site in Rhode Island. (Dolomitic marble found here creates a unique blend of limey, calcerous soil.) This pleasant walk in the woods will take you past a long-abandoned electric railroad bed and around the shore of a duck-filled pond. Plant species you might spot on this trek include ferns, red and white baneberry, horse balm, violets, bellwort, nodding trillium, jack-in-the-pulpit, and trout lily.

From the dirt driveway, follow the railroad bed. Initially, it sits low and may be flooded—you can easily hike the higher ground to either side—but it gradually rises high above the surrounding terrain. Within about a half mile, just before you reach a point where the railroad bed passes above a little stream valley, turn onto a trail diverging right (the first you encounter on that side). It leads to the far end of the pond, which soon becomes visible through the trees, and across an earthen dam where you get a good view of the pond. Across the dam, ledges rise high up a hillside. Turn left with the trail, circling the pond and eventually reaching the railroad bed again, where turning left returns you to the parking area.

User Groups: Hikers, bikers, dogs, and horses. No wheelchair facilities.

Permits: Parking and access are free.

Maps: For a topographic area map, request Pawtucket from the USGS.

Directions: From Providence, take Route 146 to the Lincoln Woods exit (Twin River Road). Turn right at the end of the ramp and at the first light, turn right onto Route 246 (Louisquisset Pike). Follow Route 246 north to Wilbur Road (about 2.4 miles). Turn left onto Wilbur Road; roughly 0.5 mile on the right will be the entrance to the Lime Rock Preserve, a small pull-off from the road. The preserve is open to hikers year-round dawn–dusk.

GPS Coordinates: 41.9249 N, 71.4604 W

Contact: The Nature Conservancy Rhode Island Chapter, 159 Waterman St., Providence, RI 02906, 401/331-7110, www.nature.org/wherewework/northamerica/states/rhodeisland.

❸ POWDER MILL LEDGES
2 mi/1 hr   👫1 ⛰6

in Smithfield

The three well-marked loop trails through this bird sanctuary lead you past open meadows, a small pond and bog, and a thick pine forest. Although at times the traffic sounds from nearby U.S. 44 are audible, the birdsong is constant. This is an attractive local walk, not to mention a good place for birding. A lengthy list of the month's bird sightings is posted on an information board outside the visitors center. Some of the species known to frequent the preserve include the red-tailed hawk, downy woodpecker, black-capped chickadee, and white-breasted nuthatch. The center also conducts regular educational, guided walks and children's programs.

Pick up the trail behind the information board. This hike links all three loops around the refuge perimeter—the first blazed orange, the second blue, and the third yellow—but you can easily make a shorter loop. The yellow loop, the longest and outermost of the three, follows power lines for a time and can be very hot on a sunny summer day. The short orange loop (approximately one mile in length) offers a self-guided tour of its vegetation; pick up a pamphlet at the visitors center.

User Groups: Hikers only. No bikes, dogs, horses, or wheelchair facilities.

Permits: Parking and access are free.

Maps: A map is available in the Audubon Society Visitor Center. For a topographic area map, request North Scituate from the USGS.

Directions: From U.S. 44 in Smithfield, turn south on Route 5. Immediately on the left is the entrance to Powder Mill Ledges, at the Audubon Society of Rhode Island headquarters. From I-295, take exit 7B onto U.S. 44 West. At the fourth set of lights, turn left onto Route 5 (Sanderson Road). Turn left at the second driveway into the parking lot. Trails are open to the public dawn–dusk every day. Audubon Society Visitor Center is open Tuesday–Friday noon–5 P.M., and Saturday noon–4 P.M.

GPS Coordinates: 41.8690 N, 71.5310 W

Contact: The Audubon Society of Rhode Island, 12 Sanderson Rd., Smithfield, RI 02917, 401/949-5454, www.asri.org.

4 SNAKE DEN
0.5 mi/0.5 hr   👣1 △7

in Snake Den State Park in Johnston

The Snake Den is a narrow defile in the woods, barely more than 100 yards long, with broken rock ledges rising as much as 40 feet above the trail on one side of this tight gorge. A short, easy walk through scenic surroundings, you'll want to watch out for loose rock and slippery footing when out on the ledges.

From the pullout, follow the wide trail into the woods, bearing right where it forks. Within minutes, you drop down on a series of ledges into the Snake Den; the trail leads straight through and continues into the woods beyond. It is possible—exercising appropriate caution—to scramble up through natural breaks, or gullies, in the ledges and get atop these low cliffs; then take a trail that loops back to where you started hiking. Or, you can return the way you came.

User Groups: Hikers and dogs. This trail is not suitable for bikes or horses; no wheelchair facilities.

Permits: Parking and access are free.

Maps: For a topographic area map, request North Scituate from the USGS.

Directions: From U.S. 44 in Johnston, follow Route 5 southbound for 0.6 mile, turn right onto Brown Avenue, and drive 0.4 mile to a pullout on the right, across from a wide, unmarked trail blocked by large rocks. From U.S. 6, 2.6 miles west of I-295, turn north onto Brown Avenue and drive two miles to the pullout on the left.

GPS Coordinates: 41.8565 N, 71.5326 W

Contact: Rhode Island Division of Parks and Recreation, 2321 Hartford Ave., Johnston, RI 02919-1719, 401/222-2632, www.riparks. com.

5 EAST BAY BIKE PATH
14.5 mi/7 hr   👣1 △10

in Providence

BEST (

From Providence to Bristol, this 14.5-mile, 10-foot wide ribbon of repurposed railroad line provides a scenic thoroughfare suitable for cycling, walking, in-line skating, and is completely wheelchair accessible. Passing along or near the shore of Narragansett Bay, the path connects eight parks: India Point Park in Providence, Bold Point and Squantum Woods in East Providence, Haines and Veteran's Memorial Park in Barrington, Burr Hill Park in Warren, and Colt State and Independence Parks in Bristol. Multiple access points on the path provide for shorter or longer trips. The East Bay Bike Path's southern tip will soon link-up to the Blackstone Bikeway, another rail trail currently under construction.

User Groups: Hikers, dogs, bikes, horses, and wheelchair users.

Permits: Parking and access are free.

Maps: A map of the East Bay Bike Path, part of the Guide to Bicycling in the Ocean State, is available free of charge from the Rhode Island Department of Transportation. Copies can be ordered by calling 401/222-4203, ext. 4033 (or downloaded at www.dot.state. ri.us/bikeri).

Directions: To reach the bike path's Providence terminus, from Market Square in Providence, follow South Main Street north to the corner of College Street (the Rhode Island School of Design is here). Take a right, driving one block to the corner of Prospect Street. Turn left on Prospect and drive less than a block to a right turn on Waterman Street. Follow Waterman Street for several blocks, passing through the heart of the Brown University campus. Reaching an intersection with Gano Street, turn right and follow Gano Street for approximately 10 blocks. As it passes under the highway, Gano Street turns into India Street, the road leading to the park entrance and parking.

GPS Coordinates: 41.8175 N, 71.3907 W

Contact: East Coast Greenway Alliance, 27B North Rd., Wakefield, RI 02879, 401/789-4625, www.greenway.org.

6 MCINTOSH WILDLIFE REFUGE AND BOARDWALK
1 mi/0.5 hr   👭1 ⛰9

in Bristol

BEST (

Situated on the 28-acre McIntosh Wildlife Refuge, trails at the Audubon Society of Rhode Island's flagship Environmental Education Center wind through fields, woods, wetlands and along a boardwalk to unrivaled views of Narragansett Bay. A popular spot for birding, the refuge is home to a variety of winged creatures, including American robins, gray catbirds, starlings, eastern kingbirds, grackles, northern cardinals, herons, red-winged blackbirds, and song sparrows. This trail is excellent for wheelchair users; not only is the main access path (the hike described here) wheelchair accessible, but the trail bisects and serves as an entry point for the East Bay Bike Path, another wheelchair-accessible trail that travels for miles along Narragansett Bay.

From the education center, head back out the front doors to find the wide, even nature path, leaving to your left. Curving past the center, the trail leads first to a flower-filled butterfly garden and then edges its way along a lush meadow; interpretive panels explain more about the vegetation and wildlife in the area. Next, the trail comes to a cornfield, a reminder of the preserve's agricultural past as a centuries old Rhode Island family farm. The trail then reaches wetlands and eventually salt marsh; hikers ascend the boardwalk for this part of the journey, continuing on another 0.25 mile to a viewing area right on the bay. Return the way you came. Bike racks for those accessing the refuge from the East Bay Bike Path are located at the very beginning of the boardwalk.

User Groups: Hikers and wheelchair users. No bikes, dogs, or horses.

Permits: Parking and access to the trail are free. For admission to the Environmental Education Center (hands-on nature displays and learning activities), fees are $6 for adults and $4 for children, ages 4–12; children under 4 and Audubon Society of Rhode Island members, free.

Maps: No trail is needed for this hike, but an interpretative map is available at the education center.

Directions: From Providence, follow I-195 east 2.6 miles to Exit 7 in East Providence. Head south off the exit on Route 114, passing through East Providence, Barrington, and Warren, to the Bristol town line. Entrance is on the right, immediately after the Bristol/Warren town line (approximately 10 miles from leaving I-195).

GPS Coordinates: 41.71079 N, 71.2807 W

Contact: Environmental Education Center/Claire D. McIntosh Wildlife Refuge, 1401 Hope St. (Rte. 114), Bristol, RI 02809, 401/245-7500, www.asri.org/refuges/claire-d.-mcintosh-wildlife-refuge.html.

7 STEPSTONE FALLS
3.4 mi/2.5 hr   👭2 ⛰7

in the Arcadia Management Area in Exeter

One of the Arcadia Management Area's more scenic stretches is this short, out-and-back trek to the tumbling cascades of Stepstone Falls. Beginning on the yellow-blazed Ben Utter Trail, marked by a sign at the back of the parking area, the route runs parallel to the stone-littered brook known as Falls River. At one mile, the trail reaches the Stepstone Falls camping area and a trail junction. Instead of following the Ben Utter Trail to the left, stay straight ahead on the white blazes of the Falls River Trail, crossing a footbridge and then reaching a vantage point above the falls in another 0.7 mile. Return the way you came. For those who prefer a one-way hike, the trail actually ends at the dirt Falls River Road, just beyond the falls, which is reached via Escoheag Hill Road; by shuttling cars, you could make this a 1.7-mile walk and not have to double back.

User Groups: Hikers and dogs. Dogs must be leashed March 1–August 15. No bikes, horses, or wheelchair facilities. Hunting is allowed in season; all trail users are required to wear at least 200 square inches of fluorescent orange, as a cap and vest, during the hunting season (the second Saturday of October–the last day of February).

Permits: Parking and access are free.

Maps: A free trail map is available at the Arcadia headquarters and in various parking lots in the management area. For topographic area maps, request Hope Valley and Voluntown from the USGS.

Directions: From the junction of Routes 3 and 165 in Exeter, drive west on Route 165 for about 5.5 miles and turn right onto the paved Escoheag Hill Road. Continue another mile and turn right onto the dirt Austin Farm Road. Two roads diverge here; take the left one, drive past a former ranger station, and pull into a parking area on the left, immediately before the bridge over Falls River. Austin Farm Road is closed to motor vehicles at Escoheag Hill Road during the winter. Other roads open to traffic in summer but closed in winter include Brook Trail, Barber Trail, and Blitzkrieg Trail.

GPS Coordinates: 41.5978 N, 71.7463 W

Contact: Arcadia Management Area headquarters, 260 Arcadia Rd., Richmond, RI 02832, 401/539-1052. Rhode Island Division of Forest Environment, 1037 Hartford Pike, North Scituate, RI 02857, 401/647-1439, www.riparks.com/arcadia.htm.

🟦 PENNY HILL
1.6 mi/1 hr

in the Arcadia Management Area in Exeter

Although trees largely block any view from the 370-foot Penny Hill summit, this hike offers an appealing walk through the woods to hilltop ledges that young kids would enjoy scrambling around on. From the parking area, cross the bridge over Falls River and ignore the first yellow-blazed trail entering the woods on the right. About 75 feet past the bridge, turn right into the woods on the yellow-blazed Breakheart Trail. The trail crosses a brook in an area that is often muddy, emerges from the woods within a half mile of the start to cross Austin Farm Road again, and then ascends moderately to the craggy height of Penny Hill. From here, the Breakheart Trail descends to the east, but this hike returns the way you came.

User Groups: Hikers and dogs. Dogs must be leashed March 1–August 15. No bikes, horses, or wheelchair facilities. Hunting is allowed in season; all trail users are required to wear at least 200 square inches of fluorescent orange, as a cap and vest, during the hunting season (the second Saturday of October–the last day of February).

Permits: Parking and access are free.

Maps: A free trail map is available at the Arcadia headquarters and in various parking lots in the management area. For topographic area maps, request Hope Valley and Voluntown from the USGS Map.

Directions: From the junction of Routes 3 and 165 in Exeter, drive west on Route 165 for about 5.5 miles and turn right onto the paved Escoheag Hill Road. Continue another mile and turn right onto the dirt Austin Farm Road. Two roads diverge here; take the left one, drive past a former ranger station, and

© HEIDI J. BROWN

purple aster flowers near Penny Hill, Arcadia Management Area

RHODE ISLAND

pull into a parking area on the left about a mile from Escoheag Hill Road, immediately before the bridge over Falls River. Austin Farm Road is closed to motor vehicles at Escoheag Hill Road during the winter. Other roads open to traffic in summer but closed in winter include Brook Trail, Barber Trail, and Blitzkrieg Trail.

GPS Coordinates: 41.5978 N, 71.7463 W

Contact: Arcadia Management Area headquarters, 260 Arcadia Rd., Richmond, RI 02832, 401/539-1052. Rhode Island Division of Forest Environment, 1037 Hartford Pike, North Scituate, RI 02857, 401/647-1439, www.riparks.com/arcadia.htm.

⑨ BREAKHEART POND LOOP
1.5 mi/1 hr   👫1 ⛰7

in the Arcadia Management Area in Exeter

This relatively flat, 1.5-mile loop around Breakheart Pond provides a good introduction to hiking in Arcadia. The pond views are better from the trail on its west bank,

which you reach during the second half of this hike. From the parking area, pick up the Breakheart Trail—marked by a sign—and follow its yellow blazes counterclockwise around the pond. Water views are few here, though you could bushwhack off the trail to the shore. Reaching the pond's north end in about 0.7 mile, turn left with the blazed trail, cross a brook on a wooden footbridge beside a small beaver dam, and reach a junction of trails. Turn left and you soon come upon the pond's west shore, with decent views of Breakheart Pond. The loop finishes in the parking area.

User Groups: Hikers and dogs. Dogs must be leashed March 1–August 15. No bikes, horses, or wheelchairs. Hunting is allowed in season; all trail users are required to wear at least 200 square inches of fluorescent orange, as a cap and vest, during the hunting season (the second Saturday of October–the last day of February).

Permits: Parking and access are free.

Maps: A free map of trails and roads is available at the Arcadia headquarters and in various parking lots in the management area. For topographic area maps, request Hope Valley and Voluntown from the USGS.

Directions: From the junction of Routes 3 and 165 in Exeter, drive west on Route 165 for 2.9 miles and turn right at the sign for Camp E-Hun-Tee onto the dirt Frosty Hollow Road. Follow that road for 1.6 miles and turn right onto the dirt Austin Farm Road. Continue another half mile to the road's end at Breakheart Pond. Park in the lot to the right. Austin Farm Road is closed to motor vehicles at Escoheag Hill Road during the winter. Other roads open to traffic in summer but closed in winter include Brook Trail, Barber Trail, and Blitzkrieg Trail.

GPS Coordinates: 41.5993 N, 71.7443 W

Contact: Arcadia Management Area headquarters, 260 Arcadia Rd., Richmond, RI 02832, 401/539-1052. Rhode Island Division of Forest Environment, 1037 Hartford Pike, North Scituate, RI 02857, 401/647-1439, www.riparks.com/arcadia.htm.

10 FOREST ROADS LOOP
8 mi/4 hr   🏃5 ⛰7

in the Arcadia Management Area in Exeter

This eight-mile loop on dirt roads through Arcadia is less for hikers than it is for novice mountain bikers, including children, and cross-country skiers. You can also bike this loop to reach the trailheads for Breakheart Pond, Penny Hill, and Stepstone Falls (see listings for all three hikes in this chapter). And, the start of the trail to the Mount Tom Cliffs (see *Mount Tom Cliffs* listing in this chapter) lies just a half mile west of the parking area where this loop begins and ends. Be aware that some of these dirt roads are open to motor vehicles.

From the parking area, follow the dirt Brook Trail a short distance north and turn right on the first dirt road you encounter, passing a gate. Within a quarter mile, pass another gate and turn left on the dirt Frosty

Hollow Road. Continue about 1.5 miles to the dirt Austin Farm Road and turn right, reaching the foot of Breakheart Pond in a half mile, where you have a good view of the pond. Retrace that half mile and continue west on Austin Farm Road for another 2.2 miles, cross a bridge over the Falls River (where the Penny Hill and Stepstone Falls hikes begin), and go another half mile before turning left on the dirt Barber Road. Within two miles, the road leads to a T intersection; turn left, cross Falls River again, then turn right on the Brook Trail and follow it about a half mile back to the parking area.

User Groups: Hikers, bikers, dogs, and horses. There are no wheelchair facilities, but when the terrain is dry, this route could be suitable for some wheelchair hikers. Dogs must be leashed March 1–August 15. Hunting is allowed in season; all trail users are required to wear at least 200 square inches of fluorescent orange, as a cap and vest, during the hunting season (the second Saturday of October–the last day of February).

Permits: Parking and access are free.

Maps: A free trail map is available at the Arcadia headquarters and in various parking lots in the management area. For topographic area maps, request Hope Valley and Voluntown from the USGS.

Directions: From the junction of Routes 3 and 165 in Exeter, drive west on Route 165 for three miles and turn right onto the dirt road marked Brook Trail. Park in the large dirt lot immediately on the right. To reach the Arcadia Management Area headquarters from the junction of Routes 3 and 165, go west on Route 165 for 1.5 miles and turn left onto Arcadia Road. Drive 2.5 miles to a T intersection, turn left, and drive 0.6 mile to the headquarters on the right. Austin Farm Road is closed to motor vehicles at Escoheag Hill Road during the winter. Other roads open to traffic in summer but closed in winter include Brook Trail, Barber Trail, and Blitzkrieg Trail.

GPS Coordinates: 41.5772 N, 71.6963 W

Contact: Arcadia Management Area headquarters, 260 Arcadia Rd., Richmond, RI 02832, 401/539-1052. Rhode Island Division of Forest Environment, 1037 Hartford Pike, North Scituate, RI 02857, 401/647-1439, www.riparks.com/arcadia.htm.

🚹 MOUNT TOM CLIFFS
2.8 mi/1.5 hr   🚶2 ⛰8

in the Arcadia Management Area in Exeter

The cliffs that form the low ridge of Mount Tom offer what are probably Arcadia's most sweeping views of the surrounding forest landscape. From the back of the parking lot, follow the Mount Tom Trail's white blazes into the woods. The trail is flat and wide at first, passing several giant anthills, maybe a foot high and two feet across, best observed from a comfortable distance. In about a half mile, turn left onto the dirt road called Blitzkrieg Trail (watch closely for the white blazes), which reenters the woods on the right within 0.1 mile. The trail ascends easily for less than a mile until it reaches the open crest of the Mount Tom cliffs and a 270-degree view of gently rolling forest. Walk the trail over the ledges for about 0.1 mile, until the trail begins descending into the woods again, and then backtrack.

User Groups: Hikers and dogs. Dogs must be leashed March 1–August 15. No bikes, horses, or wheelchair facilities. Hunting is allowed in season; all trail users are required to wear at least 200 square inches of fluorescent orange, as a cap and vest, during the hunting season (the second Saturday of October–the last day of February).

Permits: Parking and access are free.

Maps: A free trail map is available at the Arcadia headquarters and in various parking lots in the management area. For topographic area maps, request Hope Valley and Voluntown from the USGS.

Directions: From the junction of Routes 3 and 165 in Exeter, drive west on Route 165 for 3.6 miles. Immediately after crossing the bridge over the Wood River, turn left at the sign for the hunter checking station into a large dirt parking lot beside a Quonset hut. Austin Farm Road is closed to motor vehicles at Escoheag Hill Road during the winter. Other roads open to traffic in summer but closed in winter include Brook Trail, Barber Trail, and Blitzkrieg Trail.

GPS Coordinates: 41.5738 N, 71.7212 W

Contact: Arcadia Management Area headquarters, 260 Arcadia Rd., Richmond, RI 02832, 401/539-1052. Rhode Island Division of Forest Environment, 1037 Hartford Pike, North Scituate, RI 02857, 401/647-1439, www.riparks.com/arcadia.htm.

🚺 NORMAN BIRD SANCTUARY
2 mi/1 hr   🚶1 ⛰8

in Middletown

BEST (

The Norman Bird Sanctuary lies along the major route of the Atlantic Flyway, and its advantage of being near the south end of Aquidneck Island in Narragansett Bay means returning migrants often stop in the vicinity of the sanctuary as a refueling and rest stop. The months of March, April, and early May are the best times to observe warblers, swallows, and such shore birds as black-crowned night heron. September, October, and November are also busy migration months as birds head south to their seasonal destinations. Elsewhere in the 450-acre sanctuary are eight miles of trails through forests, old fields, pastures, and swamps; other creatures spotted in the area range from pheasant to foxes. The most popular trail here is the Hanging Rock Trail, which traverses the narrow crest of a rock spine that seems wholly out of place rising 40–50 feet above the surrounding woods and marsh. Stunted trees, characteristic of high mountains, grow atop it. Although parts of the ridge are somewhat exposed, it's a fairly easy walk and offers an excellent vantage point for birding.

From the parking lot, walk past the visitors center (housed in a 125-year-old barn) onto the main path and follow it a short distance. Turn left onto the Quarry Trail, passing a field with bird feeders. Turn right on the Blue Dot Trail, skirting a former slate quarry on the left, now filled with water. Cross a boardwalk, climb a short hill past ledges, and turn left at a T junction. Beyond the views of Gardner Pond, the trail turns sharply uphill onto the Hanging Rock Trail. Go left, following the increasingly open ridge to its end, where it terminates abruptly at a short cliff with Narragansett Bay views. Double back, staying with the Hanging Rock Trail to its beginning, then turn right and follow signs back to the barn.

User Groups: Hikers only. No dogs, horses, bikes, or on-trail wheelchair facilities; the visitors center is wheelchair accessible.

Permits: There is a trail fee of $5 for adults and $2 for children ages 4–13. Sanctuary members and children under four are admitted free.

Maps: A map and trail guide is available at the visitors center. For a topographic area map, request Prudence Island from the USGS.

Directions: From Route 114, at the Middletown-Portsmouth town line, turn east onto Mitchell's Lane at a small sign for the Norman Bird Sanctuary. At 1.4 miles, turn left at a stop sign. Drive a half mile, then bear right at a fork and proceed another 0.3 mile to a four-way stop at a crossroads. Drive straight through the intersection and go another 0.8 mile to the sanctuary entrance on the right.

The sanctuary is open seven days a week, 9 A.M.–5 P.M., except Thanksgiving and Christmas.

GPS Coordinates: 41.4997 N, 71.2500 W

Contact: Norman Bird Sanctuary, 583 Third Beach Rd., Middletown, RI 02842, 401/846-2577, www.normanbirdsanctuary.org. Ask about guided group tours and workshops for adults and children.

13 GREEN FALLS POND
2 mi/1 hr

in Rockville

Here's a relatively easy two-mile walk through the woods which happens to include some interesting, if brief, scrambling over rock ledges on the way to a scenic little pond. From the trailhead at the parking turnout, the Narragansett Trail follows the Rhode Island–Connecticut state line for a short distance before turning west into Connecticut and reaching the shore of Green Falls Pond. Enjoy the view of ducks, geese, and other waterfowl at play. And although the blue-blazed trail continues west around the pond, this hike returns the way you hiked in.

User Groups: Hikers only. This trail is not suitable for bikes or horses; no wheelchair facilities. A portion of this hike lies on private land, and use restrictions can change. Dogs are not allowed unless otherwise posted.

Permits: Parking and access are free.

Maps: For a topographic area map, request Voluntown from the USGS.

Directions: From Route 138 in Rockville, turn onto Camp Yawgoog Road, drive 3.8 miles, passing Camp Yawgoog, and park in a turnout on the right.

GPS Coordinates: 41.5271 N, 71.7799 W

Contact: Connecticut Forest and Park Association Inc., 16 Meriden Rd., Rockfall, CT 06481-2961, 860/346-2372, www.ctwoodlands.org. Pachaug State Forest, RFD 1, Voluntown, CT 06384, 860/376-4075.

RHODE ISLAND

14 LONG POND
0.5 mi/0.5 hr

in Rockville

BEST (

This hike in the Long Pond Woods refuge packs a lot of scenery into a very short distance. From the parking area, the Narragansett Trail enters the woods, passing through thick stands of rhododendron and mountain laurel, which bloom in June, and over myriad rocks and boulders. Reaching the top of a small hill, yellow blazes lead right, but this hike turns left, following an unmarked but obvious path. A quarter mile from the road, skirt to the right around cliffs and emerge on ledges overlooking scenic Long Pond. Hike back along the same route.

User Groups: Hikers only. Bikes, dogs, and horses are prohibited; no wheelchair facilities.

Permits: Parking and access are free.

Maps: No map is needed for this short hike. For a topographic area map, request Voluntown from the USGS.

Directions: From Route 138 in Rockville, turn onto Winchek Road, follow it for 0.1 mile, and then turn onto Canonchet Road. Continue a half mile, bear right, and drive another mile to a small parking area on the left. There is also space for cars at the roadside just beyond the parking area. The refuge is open a half hour before sunrise–a half hour after sunset.

GPS Coordinates: 41.5055 N, 71.7579 W

Contact: The Long Pond Woods Refuge is jointly managed by two conservation organizations and a state agency: The Nature Conservancy Rhode Island Chapter, 159 Waterman St., Providence, RI 02906, 401/331-7110, www.nature.org; the Audubon Society of Rhode Island, 12 Sanderson Rd., Smithfield, RI 02917, 401/949-5454, www.asri.org; and the Rhode Island Department of Environmental Management, 235 Promenade St., Providence, RI 02908-5767, 401/222-6800, www.dem.ri.gov.

15 GREAT SWAMP MANAGEMENT AREA
5.5 mi/2.5 hr

in West Kingston

Popular with bird-watchers, the 3,349-acre Great Swamp, in the towns of South Kingston and Richmond, encompasses wildlife-friendly habitats ranging from freshwater wetlands to forest. Cottontail rabbit, white-tailed deer, fox, raccoon, coyote, mink, muskrat, wild turkey, grouse, and wood duck all call this vast preserve home. The best time for birding is during the spring migration in May when warblers, shore birds, and swallows pass through on their return flight north.

This loop through the preserve follows relatively flat, wide woods roads that make for easy hiking, biking, or skiing. From the parking area, go around the gate and follow the woods road straight (avoiding the side roads leading right) for a bit more than a mile until you reach the scenic Worden Pond shore. Double back on the woods road and take the second left onto another dirt road, which loops around the perimeter of the Great Swamp Impoundment, an artificially-made marsh of more than 130 acres and a good place for birding. Where that woods road ends beyond the swamp, turn left, and then left again at the next junction to return to the parking area.

User Groups: Hikers, bikers, leashed dogs, and horses. No wheelchair facilities.

Permits: Parking and access are free.

Maps: A trail map is available at the management area headquarters. For a topographic area map, request Kingston from the USGS.

Directions: From Route 138 in West Kingston, just west of the junction with Route 110, turn west onto Liberty Lane. Drive a mile to the road's end and then turn left onto the dirt Great Neck Road. Within a mile, you pass the headquarters on the right. The dirt road ends one mile from Liberty Lane, at a big parking area.

RHODE ISLAND

GPS Coordinates: 41.4773 N, 71.5754 W
Contact: Great Swamp Management Area, P.O. Box 218, West Kingston, RI, 401/789-0281. Rhode Island Division of Fish and Wildlife, Stedman Government Center, 4808 Tower Hill Rd., Wakefield, RI 02879, 401/789-3094, fax 401/783-4460, www.dem.ri.gov.

16 NEWPORT CLIFF WALK
6 mi/3 hr   🏃🏃5 △7

in Newport

BEST (

Come here during the height of the summer tourist season and the experience of your walk suffers from the crowds, which often form a conga line along the trail's length. But come here in the off-season—during the spring or fall—and you gain much more enjoyment from this scenic walk atop cliffs that fall away dramatically to the ocean. What is probably Rhode Island's most famous walk passes mansions built by some of the nation's wealthiest families in the late 19th and early 20th centuries—including Rosecliff, the house used in the filming of *The Great Gatsby*.

This hike brings you along the Cliff Walk and then down Bellevue Avenue for mansion views that are often better than the views from the Cliff Walk. From the Easton Beach parking, walk a short distance back up Memorial Boulevard to a large sign on the median strip indicating the start of the Cliff Walk (behind Cliff Walk Manor). Follow the wide walkway along the cliff tops; do not stray onto private property. Though the walk begins on flat and level ground, parts of it become rocky. After about three miles, you emerge at the end of a side street, Ledge Road. Turn right and follow Ledge Road straight onto Bellevue Avenue. Walk down Bellevue, past the mansions, back to Memorial Boulevard, and then turn right to return to Easton Beach.

User Groups: Hikers and leashed dogs. No bikes or horses. The northern section of the Cliff Walk is suitable for wheelchairs (up to Narragansett Avenue). If you chose to visit some of the mansions open for tours, the Breakers and Rosecliff are fully wheelchair accessible; Marble House and The Elms are partially wheelchair accessible.

Permits: Parking and Cliff Walk access are free.

Maps: No map is necessary for this walk, but for a topographic area map, request Newport from the USGS.

Directions: In Newport, follow Memorial Boulevard east to the Easton Beach parking area. The Cliff Walk is open to the public 6 A.M.–9 P.M.

GPS Coordinates: 41.4862 N, 71.2958 W

Contact: Newport County Convention and Visitor Bureau, 23 America's Cup Ave., Newport, RI 02840, 401/849-8098 or 800/976-5122, www.gonewport.com.

17 BRENTON POINT STATE PARK
2 mi/1 hr   🏃🏃1 △7

in Newport

This easy walk follows the rocky, wind-battered shoreline at Brenton Point. The land once belonged to the Budlong family, but before World War II the federal government took it over and built military facilities here. Later the land was turned over to the state for use as a park. Brenton Point is now one of Newport's most scenic public lands, with lots of room to roam and wide open views of Rhode Island Sound.

Driving to the farthest parking lot on the right, beside a field popular among kite flyers, leave your car, cross the road, and walk along the shore in the direction you came from in the car. Clamber up onto a crooked stone jetty jutting a short distance into the ocean. Continue along the shore, walking for about a mile, and then double back to your car.

User Groups: Hikers and dogs. A wheelchair-accessible paved sidewalk parallels the shoreline (also good for bikes). This trail is not suitable for horses.

Permits: Parking and access are free.

Maps: No map is necessary for this short walk, but for a topographic area map, request Newport from the USGS.

Directions: From the corner of Memorial Boulevard and Bellevue Avenue in Newport, follow Bellevue Avenue south for 1.1 miles to a right turn onto Ruggles Avenue. Follow 0.5 mile to a left turn on Carroll Avenue. Follow this street for 0.5 mile to a right turn onto Ocean Boulevard. Brenton Point State Park lies 1.3 miles ahead on the left, with several places to park.

GPS Coordinates: 41.4520 N, 71.3533 W

Contact: Rhode Island Division of Parks and Recreation, 2321 Hartford Ave., Johnston, RI 02919-1719, 401/222-2632, www.riparks.com.

18 VIN GORMLEY TRAIL
8 mi/4 hr   🏃5 △7

in Burlingame State Park in Charlestown

The Vin Gormley Trail makes a big loop around Watchaug Pond, the focal point of this very popular state park. The flat terrain around the pond is a nice walk along narrow footpaths, woods roads, and a short stretch of paved road. Watch for the yellow blazes of the Vin Gormley Trail, which crosses the parking lot. Cross several brooks and boardwalks through boggy areas. Near the loop's halfway point, a covered bridge with benches built across Perry Healy Brook makes a nice spot for a rest. The entire trail is well blazed and easy to follow. If off-road jogging is your cup of tea, the loop makes for good trail running, especially in the fall when the park is almost deserted and

the surrounding woods burn bright with autumn color. To keep some of the trail's more scenic features for the end of the loop, consider following the Vin Gormley in a counterclockwise direction.

User Groups: Hikers and bikes. Dogs and horses are prohibited; no wheelchair facilities.

Permits: Parking and access are free.

Maps: A map of the Vin Gormley Trail is available at the state park campground office off Klondike Road in Charlestown, which is open weekdays year-round, and at the picnic area off Prosser Trail, which is open Memorial Day–Labor Day. For a topographic area map, request Carolina from the USGS.

Directions: Take U.S. 1 to Charlestown and the exit for Burlingame State Park. Drive 0.6 mile to the park entrance on the left.

GPS Coordinates: 41.3606 N, 71.7021 W

Contact: Burlingame State Park, Sanctuary Rd., Charlestown, RI 02813, 401/322-8910. Rhode Island Division of Parks and Recreation, 2321 Hartford Ave., Johnston, RI 02919-1719, 401/222-2632, www.riparks.com.

19 KIMBALL WILDLIFE SANCTUARY
1.5 mi/0.75 hr   🏃1 △7

in Charlestown

Owned by the Audubon Society of Rhode Island, this 29-acre woodlands parcel on Watchaug Pond, abutting Burlingame State Park, has three well-marked loop trails through the woods. This hike makes a loop around the refuge, incorporating sections of all three trails. Begin behind the information kiosk, turning left onto the red trail and then left at each successive junction with the orange, green, and blue trails. Spring, when flowers bloom and the songbirds return, is the ideal time to visit this refuge.

User Groups: Hikers only. Bikes, dogs,

and horses are prohibited; no wheelchair facilities.

Permits: Parking and access are free.

Maps: A basic trail map is available at the information kiosk next to the parking area. For a topographic area map, request Carolina from the USGS.

Directions: Take U.S. 1 to Charlestown and the exit for Burlingame State Park. Take the first left at a small sign for the Kimball Wildlife Refuge. Drive to the end of the road, turn left again, and proceed to a dirt parking lot near an information kiosk.

GPS Coordinates: 41.3727 N, 71.6874 W

Contact: Kimball Wildlife Sanctuary, 180 Sanctuary Rd., Charlestown, RI 02813. The Audubon Society of Rhode Island, 12 Sanderson Rd., Smithfield, RI 02917, 401/949-5454, www.asri.org.

20 NINIGRET NATIONAL WILDLIFE REFUGE
1.4 mi/1 hr   🏃1 ⛰7

in Charlestown

BEST (

The Ninigret refuge occupies 407 acres of shrublands, grasslands, barrier beach, salt marshes, and Ninigret Pond, the largest saltwater pond in Rhode Island. The refuge is a popular stopover for migrating birds and a wintering spot for some northern bird species. This hike, following wide dirt roads through salt marsh and out to the shore of Ninigret Pond, is a good place to see herons, cormorants, geese, and migrating songbirds. The refuge was once a navy training site and runways and other remnants of this activity can still be seen here. Call the refuge headquarters (401/364-9124) for a list of bird species recently spotted at Rhode Island's national wildlife refuges, including Ninigret.

From the parking lot, walk on the runway to the left until you reach the kiosk at the start of the Grassy Point Nature Trail, which consists of two loops totaling 1.4 miles. Take the shorter loop first, beginning to the left of the kiosk and following the arrows, eventually returning to the kiosk. The second loop begins to the right. A wide spur road, not marked by arrows, diverges left from this trail out to Grassy Point, where an observation deck offers good views of Ninigret Pond and its birds. At the end of the loop, walk down a runway back to the kiosk.

User Groups: Hikers only. No bikes, dogs, or horses; no wheelchair facilities on this trail.

Permits: Parking and access are free.

Maps: A map is posted in an information kiosk at the trailhead, and a look at it is really all that's needed for this hike. For topographic area maps, request Carolina and Quonochontaug from the USGS.

Directions: Take U.S. 1 to Charlestown and the exit for Ninigret Park. Follow signs to the park, turn left into it, and then follow signs to the nature trails and a parking lot on an old runway.

GPS Coordinates: 41.3821 N, 71.6475 W

Contact: The U.S. Fish and Wildlife Service refuge headquarters is in Shoreline Plaza on Old Post Road/U.S. 1 in Charlestown, 401/364-9124. The office is open 8 A.M.–4:30 P.M. weekdays. Friends of the Rhode Island National Wildlife Refuges, P.O. Box 553, Charlestown, RI 02813, 401/364-9124, www.friendsnwr-ri.org.

21 BLOCK ISLAND: CLAY HEAD TRAIL AND THE MAZE
0.7 mi/0.75 hr   🏃1 ⛰8

in Clay Head Preserve, Block Island

BEST (

Block Island is a magnet for summer tourists, but in spring and fall, a different kind of visitor crowds the island's bluffs and beaches as hundreds of thousands of birds representing some 150 species descend on Block Island during their seasonal migrations. It's

© HEIDI J. BROWN

the bluffs at Clay Head, Block Island

an awesome sight and has led the Nature Conservancy to dub Block Island as one of the earth's "last best places" and the Clay Head Preserve as one of the best spots in the Northeast to see migratory songbirds in autumn.

From the trail post, the Clay Head Trail follows a sandy, grass-strewn bluff top, passing Clay Head Swamp, the edge of the Littlefield Farm, and numerous views of the bluffs, seashore, and birds. At first, several trails leading left into the dense scrub brush and forest are posted as private property. Once beyond these, however, you'll see many unmarked trails diverging off the Clay Head Trail and weaving through a cooked-spaghetti tangle of footpaths called the Maze. These trails are fun to explore, though they can get confusing. Retrace your steps and return the way you came.

Special Note: Bicycling from the ferry landing in Old Harbor to this and other Block Island trails in this chapter is recommended. Bikes can be brought over on the ferry or rented in Old Harbor when you get off the ferry.

User Groups: Hikers and leashed dogs. No horses, bikes (on the trail), or wheelchair facilities.

Permits: Access to hiking trails on the island is free.

Maps: Get a basic map of the island and its hiking trails at the Chamber of Commerce, which operates an information booth at the ferry landing in Old Harbor and a visitors center around the corner on Water Street. Bike shops within walking distance of the ferry landing have maps of island roads. For a topographic area map, request Block Island from the USGS.

Directions: The Interstate Navigation Co. operates ferries year-round from Point Judith and during the summer from Newport. The Block Island Express Ferry operates between New London, Connecticut, and Block Island May–October. From the island's ferry landing in Old Harbor, turn right on Water Street along the waterfront strip, left on Dodge Street, and then right at the post office onto Corn Neck Road. Continue about 3.5 miles to a dirt road on the right marked by a post indicating the Clay Head Trail. Follow the

RHODE ISLAND

dirt road about a half mile to the trailhead (there is a bike rack).

GPS Coordinates: 41.1890 N, 71.5684 W
Contact: Block Island Chamber of Commerce, P.O. Box D, Block Island, RI 02807, 401/466-2982 or 800/383-2474, www.blockislandchamber.com. Block Island Tourism Council, Dept. B, 23 Water St., P.O. Box 356, Block Island, RI 02807, 800/383-2474, www.blockislandinfo.com. Interstate Navigation Company, 401/783-4613, www.blockislandferry.com. Block Island Express Ferry, 860/444-4624, www.longislandferry.com/bif. For information about trails on conservation land, visit The Nature Conservancy's Block Island office on High Street near the harbor, 401/466-2129. The Nature Conservancy Rhode Island Chapter, 159 Waterman St., Providence, RI 02906, 401/331-7110, www.nature.org.

© HEIDI J. BROWN

near Rodman's Hollow, Block Island

22 BLOCK ISLAND: RODMAN'S HOLLOW

0.5 mi/0.75 hr

on Block Island

A depression left by a receding glacier, Rodman's Hollow is a wild little corner of the island overgrown with dense brush. A loop trail cuts through it, cresting one small hill with sweeping views of the homes and rolling hills at the southern end of the island. Rodman's Hollow was the inspiration for the 1970s conservation movement that helped protect a quarter of Block Island from development. It's also part of the Greenway, a network of interconnecting trail systems that includes the Enchanted Forest, Turnip Farm, and Fresh Swamp Preserve. The shadbush bloom in early to mid-May is a beautiful sight.

From just beyond the turnstile, follow the loop trail to the right; a sign indicates a "short loop" and a "long loop," but it's all one trail. The trail crests a hill at a wooden bench. From here, the path forks; following the right fork

brings you back to Black Rock Road (where you would turn right to return to the trailhead). Bear left instead, following the trail through the hollow and eventually back to the spot where the path first split. From here, return the way you came.

Special Note: Bicycling from the ferry landing in Old Harbor to this and other Block Island trails in this chapter is recommended. Bikes can be brought over on the ferry or rented in Old Harbor when you get off the ferry.

User Groups: Hikers and leashed dogs. No bikes (on the trail), horses, or wheelchair facilities.

Permits: Access to hiking trails on the island is free.

Maps: Get a basic map of the island and its hiking trails at the Chamber of Commerce, which operates an information booth at the ferry landing in Old Harbor and a visitors center around the corner on Water Street. Bike shops within walking distance of the ferry landing have maps of island roads. For a topographic area map, request Block Island from the USGS.

Directions: The Interstate Navigation Co. operates ferries year-round from Point Judith and during the summer from Newport. The Block Island Express Ferry operates between New London, Connecticut, and Block Island May–October. From the island's ferry landing in Old Harbor, turn left on Water Street and head straight through an intersection, passing the First Baptist Church on your left, onto Spring Street. It runs straight onto Southeast Light Road, passing two trails leading to the Mohegan Bluffs. The road becomes Mohegan Trail, then hooks right and becomes Lakeside Drive. About four miles from Old Harbor, turn left onto Cooneymus Road. The road doglegs left, then right, and then passes a stone wall and a sign on the left overlooking Rodman's Hollow. Just beyond that point, turn left onto the dirt Black Rock Road. A quarter mile farther is the trailhead, marked by a bike rack and a wooden turnstile. The road continues to a trail leading down to the beach.

GPS Coordinates: 41.1554 N, 71.5900 W

Contact: Block Island Chamber of Commerce, P.O. Box D, Block Island, RI 02807, 401/466-2982 or 800/383-2474, www.block-islandchamber.com. Block Island Tourism Council, Dept. B, 23 Water St., P.O. Box 356, Block Island, RI 02807, 800/383-2474, www.blockislandinfo.com. Interstate Navigation Company, 401/783-4613, www.block-islandferry.com. Block Island Express Ferry, 860/444-4624, www.longislandferry.com/bif. For information about trails on conservation land, visit The Nature Conservancy's Block Island office on High Street near the harbor, 401/466-2129. The Nature Conservancy Rhode Island Chapter, 159 Waterman St., Providence, RI 02906, 401/331-7110, www.nature.org.

23 BLOCK ISLAND: MOHEGAN BLUFFS

0.5 mi/0.75 hr 🏃2 ⛰8

on Block Island

BEST (

This hike is actually two short walks near one another. The first leads to Southeast Lighthouse and great views of the erod-hegan Bluffs (both island landmarks and can't miss destinations for visitors to Block Island). The lighthouse, built in 1873 on the eroding cliffs 150 feet above the sea, was moved back 200 feet in 1993 because the ocean had chewed away nearly all the land between it and the sea. Legend has it that in 1590 the island's first inhabitants, the Narragansett Indians—also known as the Manisses tribe—drove a party of invading Mohegan Indians over the cliffs here.

From the second trailhead, a trail leads to a wooden staircase that drops steeply down to the rocky beach, a nice place to walk below the bluffs. Don't try scrambling around on the cliffs themselves, though—the soil and rocks are as loose as they appear and dangerous rockslides occur frequently.

Special Note: The best way to explore Block Island's trails is to ride a bicycle from the ferry landing in Old Harbor to the trailheads. This way you see more trails and enjoy some scenic cycling on country roads through a landscape of rolling hills and open fields crisscrossed by an uncanny 2,042 miles of stone walls. Bikes can be brought over on the ferry or rented in Old Harbor when you get off the ferry.

User Groups: Hikers and leashed dogs. No bikes (on the trail), horses, or wheelchair facilities.

Permits: Access to hiking trails on the island is free.

Maps: Get a basic map of the island and its hiking trails at the Chamber of Commerce, which operates an information booth at the ferry landing in Old Harbor and a visitors center around the corner on Water Street. Bike shops within walking distance of the

© HEIDI J. BROWN

Southeast Lighthouse, Block Island

ferry landing have maps of island roads. For a topographic map, request Block Island from the USGS.

Directions: The Interstate Navigation Co. operates ferries year-round from Point Judith and during the summer from Newport. The Block Island Express Ferry operates between New London, Connecticut, and Block Island May–October. From the island's ferry landing in Old Harbor, turn left on Water Street and head straight through an intersection, passing the First Baptist Church on your left, onto Spring Street, which runs straight onto Southeast Light Road. About two miles from the ferry landing, a footpath on the left leads a short distance to Southeast Lighthouse, above the Mohegan Bluffs. A short distance up the road is a trailhead (with a rack for parking bicycles) leading to stairs that descend the bluffs to the beach.

GPS Coordinates: 41.0910 N, 71.3304 W

Contact: Block Island Chamber of Commerce, P.O. Box D, Block Island, RI 02807, 401/466-2982 or 800/383-2474, www.blockislandchamber.com. Block Island Tourism Council, Dept. B, 23 Water St., P.O. Box 356, Block Island, RI 02807, 800/383-2474, www.blockislandinfo.com. Interstate Navigation Company, 401/783-4613, www.blockislandferry.com. Block Island Express Ferry, 860/444-4624, www.longislandferry.com/bif. For information about trails on conservation land, visit The Nature Conservancy's Block Island office on High Street near the harbor, 401/466-2129. The Nature Conservancy Rhode Island Chapter, 159 Waterman St., Providence, RI 02906, 401/331-7110, www.nature.org.

RHODE ISLAND

Connecticut

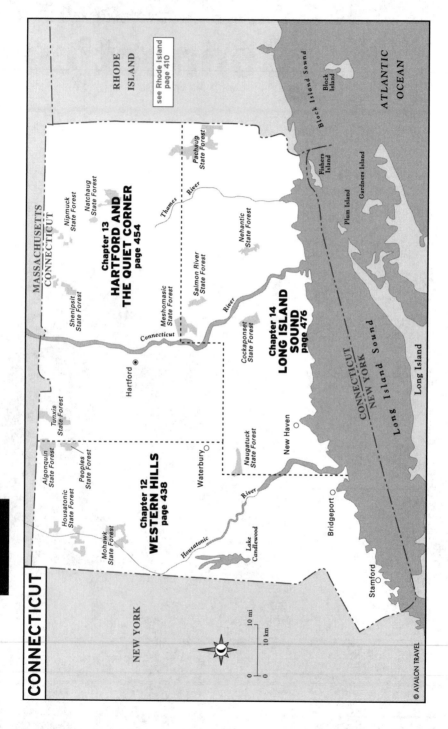

CONNECTICUT

CONNECTICUT

NEW YORK

RHODE ISLAND

MASSACHUSETTS
CONNECTICUT

ATLANTIC OCEAN

Block Island Sound

Block Island

Fishers Island

Gardners Island

Plum Island

Long Island Sound

Long Island

see Rhode Island page 410

Chapter 13
HARTFORD AND THE QUIET CORNER
page 454

Chapter 14
LONG ISLAND SOUND
page 476

Chapter 12
WESTERN HILLS
page 438

Nipmuck State Forest

Natchaug State Forest

Pachaug State Forest

Nehantic State Forest

Shenipsit State Forest

Meshomasic State Forest

Salmon River State Forest

Cockaponset State Forest

Naugatuck State Forest

Tunxis State Forest

Algonquin State Forest

Peoples State Forest

Housatonic State Forest

Mohawk State Forest

Thames River

Connecticut River

Hartford

Waterbury

New Haven

Bridgeport

Stamford

Lake Candlewood

Housatonic River

CONNECTICUT
NEW YORK

NEW YORK

10 mi

10 km

0

0

© AVALON TRAVEL

WESTERN HILLS

© JAROSLAW TRAPSZO

BEST HIKES

In Connecticut's rural northwestern corner, the

Appalachian Trail follows a chain of green hills above the beautiful Housatonic River valley for 52 miles, from the New York border to the Massachusetts line. In the eyes of many hikers, this part of Connecticut harbors the state's best hiking and certainly its biggest hills and best opportunities for longer day hikes and multi-day backpacking trips. The hikes up Bear Mountain and Lion's Head probably have no rivals in the state.

Off the Appalachian Trail, other trails in the region are worth a visit, including the hike to the summit Mount Tom and its distinctive stone tower overlook and the trek to Leatherman's Cave, a 40-foot long natural rock tunnel. The prime hiking season begins by April and extends into November. But winters are also milder than in northern New England; at certain times in winter you may find some of these trails with little or no snow on them.

Heavy deciduous forest cover marks the quaint landscape of rolling hills and makes northwestern Connecticut a leaf peeper's paradise during the first few weeks of October. (The step-back-in-time New England villages of Kent and Cornwall are good jumping off points for autumn excursions.) For bird-watchers, such winged favorites as golden-crowned kinglets, myrtle warblers, hermit thrushes, hawks, eagles, pileated woodpeckers, chickadees, titmice, and nuthatches await your binoculars. And for wildlife-spotters, the woods in this part of the state are home to the typical mix of northern forest inhabitants, including sightings of the reclusive black bear.

Blue-blazed hiking trails crisscrossing the region belong to the statewide Blue Trail system, established by the Connecticut Parks and Forest Association in 1929. The majority of blue-blazed trails are on private land and continue to be available for public use only through the good will of the landowner. As with any outing, make sure to carry out your trash and heed any no tresspassing or no parking signs. In just the past few years, excellent hiking terrain near Cornwall has been closed off to public use due to vandalism and arson.

Along the Appalachian Trail (AT), dogs must be kept under control, and horses, mountain bikes, hunting, and firearms are prohibited – although that rule does not preclude hunters inadvertently wandering near the AT. Cross-country skiing and snowshoeing are permitted on the AT, and much of the trail in Connecticut presents easy to moderate terrain for snowshoeing. In state parks, leashed dogs are allowed, as are mountain bikes on most trails. Along Blue Trails, although posted uses can vary, assume that dogs, horses, and mountain bikes are not allowed unless a trail is specifically marked for them. Most Blue Trails are open to cross-country skiing. Assume that hunting is permitted in season unless the land is posted with signs prohibiting it. Fires must not be lit except where officially designated fireplaces have been provided.

CONNECTICUT

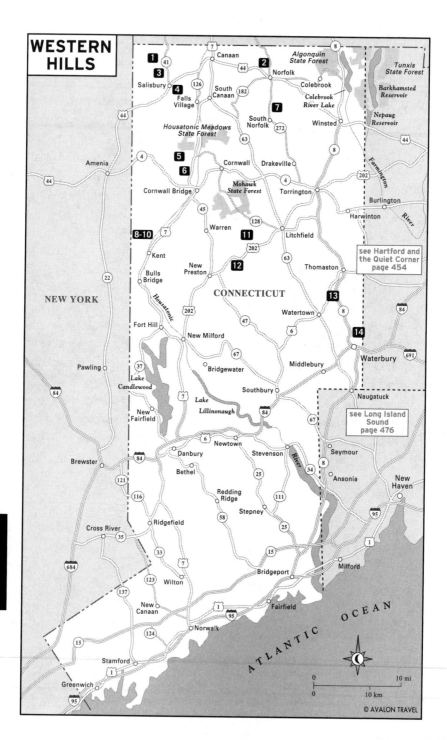

① BEAR MOUNTAIN
6.5 mi/4 hr   🏃5 ⛰10

in Salisbury

BEST (

This loop over the state's highest peak, 2,316-foot Bear Mountain, is one of Connecticut's most popular hikes and can be a busy place on nice weekends. Day hikers and fall leaf peepers flock here for the views and youth groups and backpackers make frequent use of the campsites along the Appalachian Trail just south of Bear's summit. Still, even here you can avoid the crowds with an early start—or a well-planned late one. For the adventurous, start this loop at dusk, just as the last few day hikers are returning to their cars. On a clear, moonlit night, the trail makes for a beautiful, and solitary, 2.4-mile walk to the Brassie Brook shelter camping area. Come morning, hit the trail early and have the summit all to yourself as you take in the sun rising over the peaceful rural landscape. This hike gains more than 1,600 feet in elevation. And one interesting footnote hikers making their way to Bear should know: The state's highest mountain peak is not the highest point in Connecticut; that's actually on the southern slope of Mount Frissell, whose summit lies just over the line into Massachusetts, northwest of Bear Mountain.

From the trailhead, follow the Undermountain Trail for an easy 1.9 miles to its junction with the white-blazed Appalachian Trail (AT), marked by a sign. To the left (south), three camping areas are spread out along the AT, from a half mile to 1.7 miles distant; the Brassie Brook camping area is the closest one to this junction. This hike turns right (north) on the AT for a quick climb to the Bear summit, breaking out of the trees for sweeping views of the hills, dense forest, and tiny towns that makes up this rural northwest corner of Connecticut; the views are also excellent from the enormous stone pile on the summit. To return to the parking area, stay on the AT as it descends the north side of Bear Mountain. It's steep and the rocky trail may be slippery with water or even ice in late fall or early spring. A half mile beyond the summit, turn right onto Paradise Lane Trail, walk two miles to the Undermountain Trail, and turn left for the parking area.

Camping is prohibited except in designated shelters and campsites along the Appalachian Trail. Campfires are prohibited; campers must cook with portable camp stoves.

User Groups: Hikers and dogs. Bikes, horses, and hunting are prohibited; no wheelchair facilities.

Permits: Parking and access are free.

Maps: For a trail map, refer to map 4 in the Map to the Appalachian Trail in Massachusetts and Connecticut, a five-map set available for $14.95 from the Appalachian Trail Conservancy. For topographic area maps, request Ashley Falls and Sharon from the USGS.

Directions: From the junction of U.S. 44 and Route 41 in Salisbury, drive north on Route 41 for three miles to a parking area on the left for the Undermountain Trail.

GPS Coordinates: 41.985309 N, 73.422518 W

Contact: Appalachian Trail Conservancy, 799 Washington St., P.O. Box 807, Harpers Ferry, WV 25425-0807, 304/535-6331, www.appalachiantrail.org. Connecticut Forest and Park Association Inc., 16 Meriden Rd., Rockfall, CT 06481-2961, 860/346-2372, www.ctwoodlands.org.

② HAYSTACK MOUNTAIN
3 mi/1.5 hr   🏃2 ⛰7

in Norfolk

Tucked away near the Massachusetts border, the unique, cylinder-shaped stone tower at the summit of Haystack Mountain (1,716 ft.) offers views as far away as Long Island Sound to the south, west to New York State, and north to the Berkshires. A climb of only a few hundred feet to the summit (though rugged

CONNECTICUT

in places), Haystack is a nice hike in late June when the mountain laurel blooms and in early fall as the spectacle of autumn foliage season unfolds across the surrounding landscape. Despite the lure of all this scenery, be prepared to see few other hikers on Haystack; popular day hikes on the nearby Appalachian Trail tend to attract most of the region's boot traffic.

The first mile of this trail takes place on the mountain's auto access road and can be either be hiked, biked, or driven. Twist and turn your way along the road, passing by a lovely pond. The road is lined on either side with mountain laurel (wild rhododendron) and mixed hardwood forest. From the small parking area on the mountain, the summit footpath first backtracks southeast as it skirts the mountain's steep southern flank. In 0.2 mile, the trail suddenly swings to the northwest as it makes a steep, 0.3 mile beeline for the Haystack summit. Climb the stone tower for the views and then head back the way you came.

User Groups: Hikers and leashed dogs. Bikes and horses only as far as the auto road. No wheelchair facilities.

Permits: Parking and access are free.

Maps: No map is available from Connecticut State Parks Division for this hike. For a topographic area map, request Tolland Center from the USGS.

Directions: From the intersection of Route 7 and U.S. 44 in Canaan, follow U.S. 44 east for 7.2 miles to a sharp left onto Route 272/North Street. Follow 0.9 mile to the Haystack Mountain State Park entrance. Follow signs to the mountain auto road. Park at the base of the road and walk or follow the twisting road almost a mile to the parking area and summit footpath trailhead.

GPS Coordinates: 41.9968 N, 73.2031 W

Contact: Haystack Mountain State Park, c/o Burr Pond State Park, 385 Burr Mountain Rd., Torrington, CT 06790, 860/482-1817. Connecticut State Parks Division, 79 Elm St., Hartford, CT 06106-5127, 860/424-3200, fax 860/424-4070, www.dep.state.ct.us/stateparks/index.htm.

🔢 LION'S HEAD
4.6 mi/2.5 hr

in Salisbury

BEST (

The ridge shared by Bear Mountain and Lion's Head in this wild northwestern corner of the state may harbor the most pleasant stretch of the Appalachian Trail through Connecticut—and the view from Lion's Head nearly rivals that from the enormously popular Bear Mountain just a few miles to the north (see *Bear Mountain* listing in this chapter). After a pleasant walk through the woods for 2.3 miles, you turn abruptly upward, scramble over exposed rock for the last 50 feet to the Lion's Head summit, and step up to wide views of hills, forest, and pastures that can only be described as quintessential New England. This hike climbs about 1,000 feet. Try this hike in fall for postcard-perfect autumn foliage views.

From the trailhead, follow the white blazes of the Appalachian Trail (AT) as it heads west, then swings northward. After you've gone about two miles, you will see the blue-blazed Lion's Head Trail entering from the left; stay on the AT as it swings right and climbs steeply but briefly to the 1,738-foot Lion's Head summit. A ledge about 30 feet south of the actual summit offers the best view, encompassing the Twin Lakes, Prospect Mountain, and the rural beauty of the Housatonic Valley. Return the way you came.

Camping is prohibited except in designated shelters and campsites along the Appalachian Trail. Campfires are prohibited; campers must cook with portable camp stoves.

User Groups: Hikers and dogs. Bikes and horses are prohibited; no wheelchair facilities.

Permits: Parking and access are free.

Maps: For a trail map, refer to map 4 in the Map to the Appalachian Trail in Massachusetts and Connecticut, a five-map set available for $14.95 from the Appalachian Trail Conservancy. For topographic area maps, request Ashley Falls and Sharon from the USGS.

© BRIAN E. WHITE

cascades along the Appalachian Trail on the way to Lion's Head

Directions: From the junction of U.S. 44 and Route 41 in Salisbury, drive north on Route 41 for 0.8 mile to a somewhat hidden parking area on the left for the Appalachian Trail. GPS Coordinates: 41.9853 N, 73.4225 W **Contact:** Appalachian Trail Conservancy, 799 Washington St., P.O. Box 807, Harpers Ferry, WV 25425-0807, 304/535-6331, www.appalachiantrail.org. Connecticut Forest and Park Association Inc., 16 Meriden Rd., Rockfall, CT 06481-2961, 860/346-2372, www.ctwoodlands.org.

4 PROSPECT MOUNTAIN AND RAND'S VIEW
5.2 mi/2.5 hr 🏃3 ⛰9

in Salisbury

Like a glimpse into New England's past, the scenic tableau that makes up Rand's View has been praised by many as the highlight of the Appalachian Trail's trek through the Nutmeg State. That's a big claim, but as you gaze north across a classic New England countryside of broad pastures and hills, it's also a difficult one to dispute. In the left foreground rises the low ridge of Wetauwanchu Mountain and in the distance, from left to right, are Bear Mountain (see *Bear Mountain* listing in this chapter), Mount Everett in Massachusetts, and the abrupt end of the ridge at Jug End, Massachusetts. On a clear day, you can see Mount Greylock, 50 miles away, on the center-right horizon. The cumulative elevation gained on this hike is about 2,000 feet.

From the parking area, cross Housatonic River Road to the left and pick up the white-blazed Appalachian Trail (AT). The trail is gentle here and most hikers will be able to quickly walk (or even trail run in places) the two miles to Prospect Mountain's 2,690-foot summit, with its view of the Housatonic Valley and nearby Canaan Mountain. Continue to follow the white blazes over Prospect Mountain another half mile to where the AT turns sharply right to reach a trail junction. A blue-blazed trail (marked by a sign) leads left a half mile to Limestone shelter, but you need to look for a second sign pointing to the right toward Rand's View, just 500 feet farther

CONNECTICUT

down the Appalachian Trail. Hike back along the same route.

Camping is prohibited except in designated shelters and campsites along the Appalachian Trail. Campfires are prohibited; campers must cook with portable camp stoves.

User Groups: Hikers and dogs. Bikes and horses are prohibited; no wheelchair facilities.

Permits: Parking and access are free.

Maps: For a map of hiking trails, refer to map 4 in the Map to the Appalachian Trail in Massachusetts and Connecticut, a five-map set available for $14.95 from the Appalachian Trail Conservancy. For topographic area maps, request South Canaan and Sharon from the USGS.

Directions: From the junction of U.S. 7 and Route 126 in Falls Village, take Route 126 north for 0.6 mile and turn left on Point of Rocks Road. Drive 0.1 mile and turn right on Water Street. Drive another 0.3 mile, cross the famous Iron Bridge (look for the white blazes of the Appalachian Trail, which crosses this bridge and enters the woods on the right), bear right after the bridge, and then take an immediate right onto Housatonic River Road. Continue 0.4 mile to a parking area on the right marked by a sign reading Cartop boat launch/Historic Trail. Park on the left, away from the boat launch area.

GPS Coordinates: 41.958224 N, 73.370724 W

Contact: Appalachian Trail Conservancy, 799 Washington St., P.O. Box 807, Harpers Ferry, WV 25425-0807, 304/535-6331, www.appalachiantrail.org. Connecticut Forest and Park Association Inc., 16 Meriden Rd., Rockfall, CT 06481-2961, 860/346-2372, www.ctwoodlands.org.

5 PINE KNOB LOOP
2.5 mi/1.5 hr

in Housatonic Meadows State Park in Sharon

This loop hike leads to a pair of scenic views of the hills lining the Housatonic River Valley. The vertical ascent is about 500 feet. From the parking area, follow the blue-blazed Pine Knob Loop Trail. The trail ascends gradually over Pine Knob, arriving at the first view, among low pine trees, about one mile from the trailhead. Another 0.2 mile past that view, the trail turns left (south) to coincide with the white-blazed Appalachian Trail (marked by a sign). The next view lies about a half mile beyond the trail junction, and it also looks southeast over the Housatonic Valley. Continuing south on the Appalachian Trail (AT), you reach a junction (marked by a sign) in 0.3 mile. The AT leads straight ahead, but this hike turns left, descending the blue-blazed Pine Knob Loop Trail 0.5 mile to the parking area.

Camping is prohibited except in designated shelters and campsites along the Appalachian Trail. Campfires are prohibited; campers must cook with portable camp stoves.

User Groups: Hikers and leashed dogs. Bikes and horses are prohibited; no wheelchair facilities.

Permits: Parking and access are free.

Maps: For a map of hiking trails, refer to map 4 in the Map to the Appalachian Trail in Massachusetts and Connecticut, a five-map set available for $14.95 from the Appalachian Trail Conservancy. For topographic area maps, request Ellsworth and Cornwall from the USGS.

Directions: The trail begins at a parking area marked by a sign on U.S. 7 in Housatonic Meadows State Park, between the towns of Cornwall Bridge and West Cornwall, one mile north of the junction with Route 4 and 0.4 mile south of the state park campground entrance.

GPS Coordinates: 41.8326 N, 73.3826 W

Contact: Appalachian Trail Conservancy,

799 Washington St., P.O. Box 807, Harpers Ferry, WV 25425-0807, 304/535-6331, www.appalachiantrail.org. Connecticut Forest and Park Association Inc., 16 Meriden Rd., Rockfall, CT 06481-2961, 860/346-2372, www.ctwoodlands.org. Housatonic Meadows State Park, c/o Macedonia Brook State Park, 159 Macedonia Brook Rd., Kent, CT 06757, 860/927-3238. Connecticut State Parks Division, 79 Elm St., Hartford, CT 06106-5127, 860/424-3200, fax 860/424-4070, www.dep.state.ct.us/stateparks/index.htm.

6 BREADLOAF MOUNTAIN
1 mi/0.75 hr   👫3 ⛰7

in Housatonic Meadows State Park in Sharon

Rising up from the rock-strewn valley of the Housatonic River, views from the top of rugged Breadloaf Mountain offer that classic northern Connecticut landscape of rolling hills, quaint villages, and just below, the river, a meandering stream dotted with anglers and other outdoor enthusiasts in summer. You will have to pay a little to get these views: The summit is reached by a short, steep stretch through the woods, a total elevation gain of 500 feet spread out over only a half-mile ascent.

From the trailhead, follow the blue-blazed Breadloaf Mountain Trail as it dips into the woods and then begins its relentless uphill climb. Making up for what can be a grueling effort is the majestic mixed hardwood forest all around you. Finally reaching the 1,050-foot Breadloaf summit, check out the ledge on the northern end for the best scenery. The Appalachian Trail is located just 0.1 mile beyond the summit, but this hike returns down the Breadloaf Mountain Trail to the parking area.

Camping is prohibited except in designated shelters and campsites along the Appalachian Trail. Campfires are prohibited; campers must cook with portable camp stoves.

User Groups: Hikers, snowshoers, and leashed dogs. No wheelchair facilities. This trail is not suitable for skis. Bikes, horses, and hunting are prohibited.

Permits: Parking and access are free.

Maps: For a map of hiking trails, refer to map 4 in the Map to the Appalachian Trail in Massachusetts and Connecticut, a five-map set available for $14.95 from the Appalachian Trail Conservancy. For topographic area maps, request Ellsworth and Cornwall from the USGS.

Directions: The trail begins at a parking area marked by a sign for the Mohawk Trail, on U.S. 7 in Housatonic Meadows State Park, between the towns of Cornwall Bridge and West Cornwall, 0.1 mile north of the junction with Route 4 and 1.4 miles south of the state park campground entrance.

GPS Coordinates: 41.823289 N, 73.377442 W

Contact: Connecticut Forest and Park Association Inc., 16 Meriden Rd., Rockfall, CT 06481-2961, 860/346-2372, www.ctwoodlands.org. Housatonic Meadows State Park, c/o Macedonia Brook State Park, 159 Macedonia Brook Rd., Kent, CT 06757, 860/927-3238. Connecticut State Parks Division, 79 Elm St., Hartford, CT 06106-5127, 860/424-3200, www.dep.state.ct.us/stateparks/index.htm. Appalachian Trail Conservancy, 799 Washington St., P.O. Box 807, Harpers Ferry, WV 25425-0807, 304/535-6331, www.appalachiantrail.org.

7 DENNIS HILL
1.5 mi/1 hr   👫2 ⛰8

in Dennis Hill State Park in Norfolk

Dennis Hill (1,627 ft.) was once the private mountain escape of noted New York surgeon, Dr. Frederick Shepard Dennis. After his death in 1935, the land was donated to the state for public use. The doctor's private residence, now a unique mountaintop rest area and pavilion, still stands at the summit of Dennis Hill.

CONNECTICUT

From the mountain's cleared summit, extensive views reach north to Haystack Mountain, Mount Greylock, and the Green Mountains of Vermont. This is a very popular place to be during peak fall foliage season when the summit auto road is opened to cars on weekends in October. Otherwise, this is a walk-in only state park that's a great getaway for peace and solitude. The climb to the summit is steep in sections, with a net elevation gain of under 400 feet.

From the parking area at the state park entrance, follow the auto summit road past the picnic area to a yellow-blazed trail departing to the left. Follow the yellow blazes a bit more than 0.1 mile to a trail junction. Here, turn right on the white-blazed trail. In another quarter mile, after a somewhat steep ascent through hardwood forest, the trail meets back up with the summit auto road. Turn right and it's a quarter-mile walk up the curving road to reach the summit. Explore the summit house, enjoy the views, and then retrace your steps back to the parking area.

Special Note: In fall, when leaf peepers are allowed to access the road in moving vehicles, the upper auto road portion of this hike can be unnerving for those on foot (especially when drivers are busy oohing and ahhing over the color). Remember, this is essentially someone's old driveway and sharing the road can be hazardous; during fall foliage season, consider hiking Dennis Hill on a weekday when the auto road is closed to cars.

User Groups: Hikers, leashed dogs, bikes, and horses. The trail is accessible for wheelchairs as far as the picnic area at the base of the hill.

Permits: Parking and access are free.

Maps: A free trail map is available at the park entrance and online from the Connecticut State Parks Division. For a topographic area map, request Norfolk from the USGS.

Directions: From the Norfolk Village Green, drive south on Route 272. At approximately 2.5 miles past the green, find the entrance to Dennis Hill State Park on the left. Park at the entrance.

GPS Coordinates: 41.9521 N, 73.2060 W

Contact: Dennis Hill State Park, c/o Burr Pond State Park, 385 Burr Mountain Rd., Torrington, CT 06790, 860/482-1817. Connecticut State Parks Division, 79 Elm St., Hartford, CT 06106-5127, 860/424-3200, fax 860/424-4070, www.dep.state.ct.us/stateparks/index.htm.

8 KENT FALLS
0.8 mi/0.75 hr

in Kent State Park in Kent

In its spectacular quarter-mile long finish before joining the Housatonic River, the mountain stream of Falls Brook first drops a roaring 70 feet at Kent Falls and then races to the bottom of the valley along a series of crashing cascades and smaller falls. One of the area's most popular tourist attractions, the Kent Falls Trail winds its way past all this wet splendor, offering many scenic vantage points. Although not difficult to walk, it is steep and may be difficult for those with knee problems.

From the parking area, a paved trail first takes you past the picnic area and the brook's lower falls. After a brief 0.1 mile, the trail turns into a series of terraced steps running right next to the brook, with frequent, wide stopping points. Continue up the steps for the next 0.3 mile until finally reaching foaming white Kent Falls. The towering cascade's flow is normally heaviest in the spring when the winter snow is melting. However, the falls can be dramatic at any time of the year, particularly after a heavy bout of summer rain. Return the way you came.

User Groups: Hikers and leashed dogs. No bikes or horses. The trail is accessible for wheelchairs as far as the picnic area (with views of the lower falls).

Permits: On weekends Memorial Day–Labor Day, a $7 parking fee is charged for Connecticut vehicles, $10 to nonresidents; on weekdays, parking and access are free.

Kent Falls

Maps: A free trail map is available at the state park entrance and online from the Connecticut State Parks Division. For a topographic area map, request Ellsworth from the USGS.

Directions: From the corner of North Main Street and Maple Street in Kent's village center, drive north on North Main Street 5.1 miles to the entrance for Kent Falls State Park (on the right).

GPS Coordinates: 41.775925 N, 73.418974 W

Contact: Kent Falls State Park, c/o Macedonia Brook State Park, 159 Macedonia Brook Rd., Kent, CT 06757, 860/927-3238. Connecticut State Parks Division, 79 Elm St., Hartford, CT 06106-5127, 860/424-3200, fax 860/424-4070, www.dep.state.ct.us/stateparks/index.htm.

⑨ COBBLE MOUNTAIN AND PINE HILL
2.5 mi/2 hr

in Macedonia Brook State Park in Kent

This loop in Macedonia Brook State Park offers a range of hiking, from easy walking down a flat forest road to steep, rocky stretches and summit views of hills unblemished by signs of development. It's a good hike for young children, ascending only about 500 feet in elevation.

From the parking area, cross the road and pick up the white-blazed Cobble Mountain Trail (marked by a sign). Follow the trail a quarter mile and turn right onto the wide CCC Road (a grassy woods road). Watch for the white blazes turning left into the woods again in another quarter mile. The trail then ascends Cobble Mountain, taking you over rock slabs as you near the top. About a half mile from the CCC Road, turn right (north) on the blue-blazed Macedonia Ridge Trail and walk 0.1 mile to the Cobble Mountain summit, where open ledges offer views west all the way to the Catskills in New York. The trail follows these ledges for about 100 yards, then enters the woods again and descends steeply over rocky ground to a junction with the Pine Hill Trail (entering from the right) within a half mile. Bear left, staying on the Ridge Trail; you soon reach the top of Pine Hill, where ledges offer a view eastward. A quarter mile past Pine Hill, turn right onto the Old CCC Road and follow it straight for about a mile. Turn left on the white-blazed Cobble Mountain Trail to return to the pavilion parking area.

User Groups: Hikers and leashed dogs. Bikes and horses are prohibited; no wheelchair facilities.

Permits: Parking and access are free.

Maps: A basic map of hiking trails with park information is available at the park office. For topographic area maps, request Amenia,

Ellsworth, Dover Plains, and Kent from the USGS.

Directions: From the junction of U.S. 7 and Route 341 in Kent, drive west on Route 341 for 1.8 miles. Turn right at the sign for Macedonia Brook State Park and then follow the signs to the park office, which is two miles from Route 341. Park in the pavilion lot on the right, 0.1 mile beyond the office. Macedonia Brook State Park is open 8 A.M.–sunset year-round.

GPS Coordinates: 41.7478 N, 73.4943 W

Contact: Macedonia Brook State Park, 159 Macedonia Brook Rd., Kent, CT 06757, 860/927-3238. Connecticut State Parks Division, 79 Elm St., Hartford, CT 06106-5127, 860/424-3200, www.dep.state.ct.us/stateparks/index.htm. Connecticut Forest and Park Association Inc., 16 Meriden Rd., Rockfall, CT 06481-2961, 860/346-2372, www.ctwoodlands.org.

🔟 ST. JOHNS LEDGES AND CALEB'S PEAK
2.4 mi/2 hr   🏃4 ▲7

in Kent

This pleasant stretch of the Appalachian Trail (AT), leaving from the quaint village of Kent, atop St. Johns Ledges and nearby Caleb's Peak, offers broad views of the splendid Housatonic Valley in all its pastoral glory. The AT here includes a very steep 0.1-mile stretch up large rocks laid out as steps by trail crews, but it's easy walking along the ridge from St. Johns Ledges to Caleb's Peak. This hike's vertical ascent is about 750 feet.

From the turnout, head west into the woods. Within about 0.1 mile, an unmarked side path diverges left to low cliffs frequented by rock climbers. Stay on the white-blazed AT as it continues straight ahead. Turn left (southwest) with the trail, ascend below slab cliffs, and then turn steeply upward, reaching St. Johns Ledges 0.6 mile from the road. Continue

another 0.6 mile south on the AT to Caleb's Peak. Hike back along the same route.

Camping is prohibited except in designated shelters and campsites along the Appalachian Trail. Campfires are prohibited; campers must cook with portable camp stoves.

User Groups: Hikers and dogs. No bikes, horses, or wheelchair facilities.

Permits: Parking and access are free.

Maps: For a map of hiking trails, refer to map 5 in the Map to the Appalachian Trail in Massachusetts and Connecticut, a five-map set available for $14.95 from the Appalachian Trail Conservancy. For topographic area maps, request Ellsworth and Kent from the USGS.

Directions: From Route 341 on the west side of the Housatonic River in Kent, turn north onto Skiff Mountain Road. Drive 1.1 miles and bear right onto a dirt road marked by a sign for the Appalachian National Scenic Trail. Continue another 1.6 miles to a turnout on the left where the Appalachian Trail's white blazes enter the woods. The dirt access road to the Appalachian Trail closes at sunset.

GPS Coordinates: 41.741319 N, 73.470708 W

Contact: Appalachian Trail Conservancy, 799 Washington St., P.O. Box 807, Harpers Ferry, WV 25425-0807, 304/535-6331, www.appalachiantrail.org. Connecticut Forest and Park Association Inc., 16 Meriden Rd., Rockfall, CT 06481-2961, 860/346-2372, www.ctwoodlands.org.

🔢 PROSPECT MOUNTAIN
2.5 mi/1.5 hr   🏃2 ▲7

in the Bantam section of Litchfield

Although the start of this hike to Connecticut's other Prospect Mountain lacks much scenic appeal, ledges in two spots offer decent views of western Connecticut's forested hills, including Mount Tom, with its distinctly visible observation tower. The trail also passes between interesting rock ledges just below the

Appalachian Trail stream crossing atop railroad ties

summit, which is only about 400 feet higher than the trailhead.

From the rock with the blue blaze, follow the Mattatuck Trail, ascending steadily. The trail reaches a ridge crest near the one-mile mark, dips briefly through the ledges, and then emerges from the woods onto a broad, open ledge with good views west to Mount Tom. Continue another 0.1 mile; where the trail turns sharply left, a footpath leads to the right up onto the summit ledges with some views of the surrounding hills. Return the way you came.

User Groups: Hikers only. No wheelchair facilities. Portions of this trail lie on private land, and use restrictions can change. Assume that bikes, dogs, and horses are not allowed unless a trail is specifically marked for them (although many landowners do not object to dogs).

Permits: Parking and access are free.

Maps: For topographic area maps, request New Preston and Litchfield from the USGS.

Directions: From the junction of U.S. 202 and Route 209 in Bantam (west of Litchfield), drive west on U.S. 202 for 0.6 mile and turn right onto Cathole Road. Drive 1.6 miles to a turnout on the left. There is no trail sign, but look for a rock with a blue blaze (difficult to see from the road) marking the trail.

GPS Coordinates: 41.7275 N, 73.2496 W

Contact: Connecticut Forest and Park Association Inc., 16 Meriden Rd., Rockfall, CT 06481-2961, 860/346-2372, www.ctwoodlands.org.

12 MOUNT TOM STATE PARK TOWER

1 mi/0.75 hr   🏃2 ⛰8

in Mount Tom State Park in Litchfield and Washington

BEST (

This very short hike—a good one for young children—climbs easily to a stone tower on Mount Tom's summit that you can climb to enjoy a panorama of the western Connecticut countryside. Early-bird hikers often come here just to watch the sunrise, and in fall, Mount Tom is popular among leaf peepers as a prime

CONNECTICUT

place to take in the colorful autumn landscape. From the parking lot, head up a dirt road. Where it forks, bear right at a sign directing you to the Tower Trail. At the next fork, bear right, following yellow blazes through a few more turns. The trail skirts a wet area, then turns right, and climbs to the summit. Return the way you came.

User Groups: Hikers only. No bikes, dogs, horses, or wheelchair facilities.

Permits: On weekends Memorial Day–Labor Day, a $7 parking fee is charged for Connecticut vehicles, $10 to nonresidents; on weekdays during this period, residents pay $6 and nonresidents $7.

Maps: A trail map is available free at the park entrance and from the Connecticut State Parks Division. For a topographic area map, request New Preston from the USGS.

Directions: From I-84, take Exit 39 (Route 4). Follow Route 4 to Route 118. Continue on Route 118 into Litchfield, then pick up Route 202. Mount Tom is on Route 202. When you see a lake on the left, look for park signs. Inside the park entrance, turn right into a parking lot marked by a sign for the picnic area and Tower Trail.

GPS Coordinates: 41.6971 N, 73.2825 W

Contact: Mount Tom State Park, c/o Lake Waramaug State Park, 30 Lake Waramaug Rd., New Preston, CT 06777, 860/868-2592. Connecticut State Parks Division, 79 Elm St., Hartford, CT 06106-5127, 860/424-3200, fax 860/424-4070, www.dep.state.ct.us/stateparks/index.htm.

13 LEATHERMAN'S CAVE/ CRANE LOOKOUT
2 mi/1 hr 👫2 ⛰7

in Watertown

Leatherman's Cave is the sort of place that excites both children and adults: a dark, cool 50-foot passageway formed by dozens of giant boulders that have fallen, over the centuries, from the cliff above. On the way, take in fine views from Crane Overlook and enjoy a peaceful walk in the birch-filled woods. Though there are a few small hills on this hike, the elevation gain is negligible.

From the turnout, cross the highway and follow Mattatuck Trail's blue blazes into the woods. You soon scramble up exposed rock and traverse a classic Connecticut traprock ridge with views of rolling, wooded hills. Descending the other end, you soon reach a woods road. Turn left with the blazes onto the road, following it a short distance through a sometimes-wet area. Bear right and then reach the junction of three trails; take the far left trail to continue on the Mattatuck Trail, now an eroded gully that ascends through a birch forest. At the next trail junction, turn left on an unmarked spur and walk out onto Crane Lookout, which offers views of the craggy hills to the north and of the industrial areas to the east. Leatherman's Cave is below you, out of sight. Double back to the main trail and veer down and left with the blue blazes. Reaching a large boulder with arrows on it, take a left, descending quickly to Leatherman's Cave. Be careful here with footing, especially after a recent rain or in early spring when icy conditions may persist. To return to U.S. 6, retrace your steps the same way you came.

User Groups: Hikers only. No wheelchair facilities. Portions of this trail lie on private land, and use restrictions can change. Assume that bikes, dogs, and horses are not allowed unless a trail is specifically marked for them.

Permits: Parking and access are free.

Maps: For a topographic area map, request Thomaston from the USGS.

Directions: From the traffic lights at the junction of U.S. 6 and Route 109 in Watertown, drive 0.9 mile west on U.S. 6 to a turnout on the right at a small sign for the Mattatuck Trail.

GPS Coordinates: 41.6471 N, 73.0947 W

Contact: Connecticut Forest and Park

Association Inc., 16 Meriden Rd., Rockfall, CT 06481-2961, 860/346-2372, www.ct-woodlands.org.

🔳 HANCOCK BROOK/LION'S HEAD LOOP

2.5 mi/1.5 hr   🏃2 ⛰7

in the Waterville section of Waterbury

Okay, so after driving through industrial Waterville and parking next to a gravel pit, your expectations for this hike may be a bit modest. But after leaving the gravel pit behind, this actually becomes a decent little hike to the pleasantly scenic Lion's Head ledge. The highlight is cascading Hancock Brook, best visited in spring when meltwaters create a raucous flow.

The trail begins next to the parking area at a post marked with a blue blaze. Walk the right edge of the gravel pit's property. At a rock where a blue arrow directs you into the woods, stop and look left; the gravel road leading uphill is where this loop finishes. Soon after entering the woods, the sound of heavy machinery is replaced by the sound of running water—or rather, falling water—as Hancock Brook drops steeply through a narrow ravine. Follow the wide and flat path of what resembles an old rail bed (watch on the right for a cascade tumbling into the brook on its opposite bank). Abundant hardwoods create a shady, cool corridor along the brook. Although it lies well down a steep embankment at the outset, the brook gradually rises nearly to trail level. After the brook becomes more placid (around the hike's one-mile mark), the well-blazed trail turns left and ascends steeply up a small hill onto the open Lion's Head ledge, with decent views in all directions of central Connecticut's rolling hills and the surrounding communities. Backtrack the way you came, following the blazes to the gravel pit.

User Groups: Hikers and snowshoers. No wheelchair facilities. Portions of this trail lie on private land, and use restrictions can change. Assume that bikes, dogs, and horses are not allowed unless a trail is specifically marked for them (although many landowners do not object to dogs). Most trails are open to cross-country skiing. Assume that hunting is allowed in season unless otherwise posted.

Permits: Parking and access are free.

Maps: For a topographic area map, request Waterbury from the USGS.

Directions: Take Exit 37 off Route 8 and head east a short distance to Thomaston Avenue (old Route 8). Turn right and drive 1.9 miles into Waterville, then turn left onto Sheffield Street. Follow it to the end and park at the roadside on the right just before the sand and gravel pit.

GPS Coordinates: 41.5970 N, 73.0472 W

Contact: Connecticut Forest and Park Association Inc., 16 Meriden Rd., Rockfall, CT 06481-2961, 860/346-2372, www.ctwoodlands.org.

HARTFORD AND
THE QUIET CORNER

© HEIDI J. BROWN

BEST HIKES

There's a good reason northeastern Connecticut

is known as "The Quiet Corner": It's off the beaten tourist path of western Connecticut and far away from all but a few urban centers. Hilly and rugged or flat and wooded, hikes in this region present the irresistible opportunity to simply get away from it all. From Mashamoquet Brook State Park to Nipmuck and Peoples State Forests, a wealth of uncrowded trails lead you to such places as Breakneck Pond, a backwoods pond tucked away in a big patch of serene forest, and Chaugham Lookout, a timeless view of the still-pastoral Farmington River Valley.

Much of the region's mountain trails are along the Connecticut River Valley's distinctive traprock ridges. Created by volcanic eruptions some 170 million years ago, the columnar patterns of basaltic rock fracture at near 90 degree angles, giving the rock a step-like appearance (trap means step or stair in Swedish).

Though rarely more than a few hundred feet high, ridges like those at Talcott Mountain, Tariffville Gorge, Ragged Mountain, Lamentation Mountain, and others jut abruptly above the valley, often in cliffs with open ledges offering long views of the river valley. Although the trails leading up onto them can be very steep, the climbs are relatively short; many of these hikes are at most a half-day outing, often shorter. Some hikes are on state lands, some in private reserves, and many on the state's Blue Trail system where access is granted by the landowner and can be revoked at any time.

CONNECTICUT

The long distance Metacomet and Mattabesett Trails run up the spine of the north-south steprock ridges and have been recently designated as part the new New England National Scenic Trail, a set of connected footpaths that will eventually run all the way from southern Connecticut to New Hampshire. Despite being easily accessible and close to Hartford and other large towns and cities in the area, the Metacomet and Mattabesset Trails still retain a remarkably rugged and wild feel.

Prime hiking season in central Connecticut runs April–November. The area typically sees heavy, nor'easter-type snowstorms each winter, but temperatures tend to be milder than in northern New England and it's often possible to hike well beyond the prime April–November season (although you could be on snowshoes December–March).

In Connecticut state parks and forests, dogs must be leashed and bikes and horses are allowed on some trails and forest roads. Hunting is allowed in season in state forests, but not in state parks, and is prohibited on Sundays. Access fees are levied at some state lands, but most allow free entrance year-round. Along Blue Trails, although posted uses can vary, assume that dogs, horses, and mountain bikes are not allowed unless a trail is specifically marked for them. Most Blue Trails are open to cross-country skiing. Assume that hunting is permitted in season unless the land is posted with signs prohibiting it. Fires must not be lit except where officially designated fireplaces have been provided.

CONNECTICUT

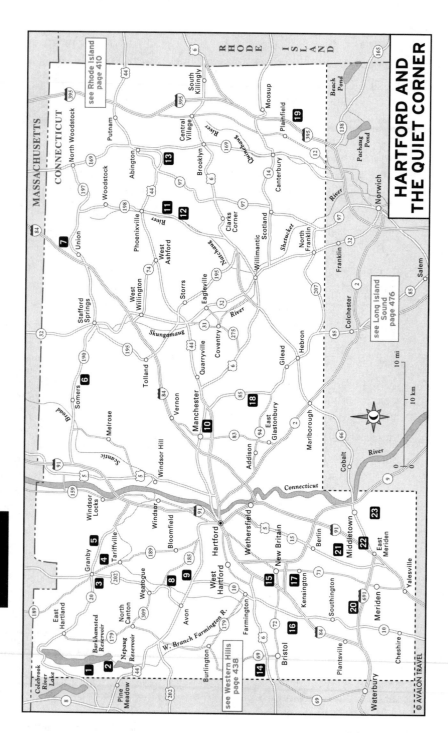

HARTFORD AND
THE QUIET CORNER

◻ JESSIE GERARD TRAIL

3 mi/2 hr   🚶🚶3 △9

in Peoples State Forest in Barkhamsted

BEST (

With its breathtaking views of the largely undeveloped landscape of the Farmington River Valley (an especially lovely sight in fall), this hike to open ledges at the Overlook and Chaugham Lookout is the 2,000-acre People State Forest's can't-miss trail. Starting out on an old Native American settlement called Barkhamsted Lighthouse, the Jessie Gerard Trail is a short, sharp ascent offering a net elevation gain of 700 feet.

From the turnout, cross the road and follow the yellow-blazed trail on a steep and strenuous climb of the famous stone stairway known as the 299 Steps, paralleling the cascades of a brook. Shortly after a brook crossing, where the trail hooks right, look to trees on the right; the holes you see all over the bark were created by the woodpeckers, a common site (and sound) in the forest. Next, pass a waterfall and then follow the trail as it ascends more moderately. A little more than a mile from the trailhead lies the Overlook, with this hike's best views. Another 0.3 mile ahead is Chaugham Lookout; shortly beyond that, the trail passes between enormous, twin glacial erratics called the Veeder Boulders. This hike doubles back from the boulders, though Greenswoods Road lies just 0.3 mile beyond that.

User Groups: Hikers and leashed dogs. This trail is not suitable for bikes or horses; no wheelchair facilities.

Permits: Peoples State Forest has a weekend and holiday entrance fee of $7 per vehicle with a Connecticut registration and $10 per out-of-state vehicle. Weekdays are free.

Maps: A free, noncontour map of hiking trails in the Peoples and American Legion State Forests is available at several locations, including boxes at the Peoples State Forest office and museum, the Austin F. Hawes Campground on West River Road (which runs north from the junction of Routes 318 and 181 in Barkhamsted), and the field office on West River Road. You can also try the Pleasant Valley Store or the Riverton Store (both located in the center of those towns). For topographic area maps, request Winsted and New Hartford from the USGS.

Directions: From the junction of Routes 318 and 181 in Pleasant Valley/Barkhamsted, drive east over the Farmington River bridge and take an immediate left onto East River Road. Proceed another 2.4 miles (passing a road on the right, marked by a sign, which leads to the state forest office) and park in the turnout on the left, across from a sign marking the Jessie Gerard Trail.

GPS Coordinates: 41.9279 N, 72.9983 W

Contact: Peoples State Forest, P.O. Box 1, Pleasant Valley State Park, CT 06063, 860/379-2469. Connecticut State Parks Division, 79 Elm St., Hartford, CT 06106-5127, 860/424-3200, www.dep.state.ct.us/stateparks/index.htm.

◻ BRAILLE TRAIL

0.6 mi/0.5 hr   🚶🚶1 △8

in the Goosegreen Recreation Area in Barkhamsted

BEST (

On the scenic Lake McDonough shores, this short, paved loop is designed for people with visual and other physical impairments and walkers who prefer a gentle grade. Managed by the Metropolitan District Commission, it has information signs in English and Braille, a guide rope for visitors to follow to each station, and signs that point out various features of geology, vegetation, and wildlife. The blacktop trail is in full compliance with Americans with Disabilities Act regulations, features more than 30 natural landmarks where visitors can read about and touch many of the trees and rocks that are indigenous to southern New England. And it's right on the water, with the pleasant sound of lapping water and views of the lake and hills for all to enjoy.

CONNECTICUT

User Groups: Hikers, dogs, and wheelchair users. No bikes or horses. This trail is closed in the winter.

Permits: Parking and admission are free, however reservations are required.

Maps: No map is needed for this short walk, but for a topographic area map, request New Hartford from the USGS.

Directions: From the junction of Routes 318 and 181 in Pleasant Valley/Barkhamsted, drive east over the Farmington River bridge and follow Route 181 past the Pleasant Valley firehouse. Turn right onto Goosegreen Road, which is the first paved road on the right. Drive about 0.1 mile and turn left into the Metropolitan District Commission's Goosegreen Recreation Area. Follow signs to the Braille Trail.

The recreation area is open daily 8 A.M.–8 P.M., beginning April 1 until the first snowfall.

GPS Coordinates: 41.9114 N, 72.9790 W

Contact: For trail reservations, contact the Metropolitan District Commission (MDC), Supply Division, 39 Beachrock Rd., Pleasant Valley, CT 06063, 860/379-0938; or the MDC's main office in Hartford, 860/278-7850, www.themdc.com/lakemcdonough. htm.

❸ MCLEAN GAME REFUGE SUMMIT HIKE LOOP
2.6 mi/1.5 hr 🏃2 ⛰7

in Granby

Former U.S. Senator George P. McLean created the 3,480-acre refuge that bears his name in an act of his will when he died in 1932. A methodically collected set of old farms and wild acres, McLean hunted and fished the land, sharing it with his friend Gifford Pinchot, first Chief of the U.S. Forest Service, and with Presidents Coolidge, Taft, and Hoover. Hunting and trapping are now

Bissell Brook in McLean Game Refuge

HEIDI J. BROWN

prohibited at the refuge, and the land has become a pleasant set of woods roads and foot trails meandering through the gently rolling, forested terrain. Several loops are possible through the refuge, with the opportunity to spot red fox, fisher cats, white-tailed deer, beaver, otter, muskrats, and wild turkeys wandering along with you through the lush woodlands.

This hike takes you to an overlook atop the Barndoor Hills with a view of a bucolic valley and surrounding wooded hills. From the parking lot, walk past the wooden gate and follow the woods road across a wooden bridge over Bissell Brook. Just beyond the bridge, turn right onto the Blue Loop. Follow the blue blazes through a mixed forest with slight ups and downs. At an intersection with a woods road, the Blue Loop turns left to return to the start, but you turn right, following the road through a dark hemlock grove. At a junction of woods roads, with a hillside of shattered rock on your left, a sign directs you to turn left for the Barndoor Hills summit. Do not go straight onto Barndoor Hill Road. Go left and follow the road steadily uphill and then turn right onto the blue-blazed summit trail, which soon leads to the open ledge with unobstructed views. Backtrack down the summit trail and turn left on the woods road, returning the way you came. But at the next road's junction, bear right into the woods onto a trail marked by faded blue blazes. Within minutes, turn left onto another trail, which deposits you onto the same woods road where the Blue Loop emerged earlier. Turn right to return to the parking lot, passing scenic Trout Pond on the way.

User Groups: Hikers and leashed dogs. No bikes, horses, or wheelchair facilities.

Permits: Parking and access are free.

Maps: A map of hiking trails is posted with refuge regulations on an information board in the parking lot. For a topographic area map, request Tariffville from the USGS.

Directions: From the junction in Granby of Routes 20, 10, and 189 and U.S. 202, drive south on Route 10/U.S. 202 for one mile and turn right onto the entrance road (which is 1.6 miles north of the Simsbury town line). Park in the lot at the end of the road. The refuge trails are open daily 8 A.M.–dusk.

GPS Coordinates: 41.9417 N, 72.7926 W

Contact: Trustees of the McLean Fund, 75 Great Pond Rd., Simsbury, CT 06070, 860/653-7869.

◢ TARIFFVILLE GORGE
0.4 mi/0.5 hr

near East Granby, Bloomfield, and Simsbury

This short hike climbs a steep hillside to one of the Metacomet Trail's finest views: looking out over the village of Tariffville, the Farmington River, and the surrounding hills from an open ledge hundreds of feet above the river. Because this hike is so short and ascends only a couple hundred feet in elevation, you can do it at odd times of day—perhaps early morning, with a fog over the river, or toward evening if a nice sunset is starting to take shape. Enter the woods on the east side of the road and follow the blue blazes. Once you gain the ridge top, it's a short walk to the open ledge overlooking the river. Return the same way.

User Groups: Hikers only. This trail is not suitable for bikes, dogs, or horses; no wheelchair facilities.

Permits: Parking and access are free.

Maps: For topographic area maps, request Tariffville and Windsor Locks from the USGS.

Directions: Take Route 189 north into Tariffville. Pass the town center, cross the Farmington River, and park on the other side of the bridge. The Metacomet Trail's blue blazes enter the woods on the east side of the road.

GPS Coordinates: 41.9121 N, 72.7619 W

Contact: Connecticut Forest and Park Association Inc., 16 Meriden Rd., Rockfall, CT 06481-2961, 860/346-2372, www.ctwoodlands.org.

5 PEAK MOUNTAIN

2 mi/1 hr

in East Granby

BEST (

Some might say that Peak Mountain, at 672 feet, is neither a peak nor a mountain. But the open ledges at its summit offer long views to the west and make an attractive local spot to catch the sunset. The ledges are easily reached on a one-mile uphill climb that gains only 300 feet.

From the turnout, follow the blue-blazed Metacomet Trail as it ascends a steep hillside, quickly reaching the ridge. Then turn left (north), following the blue blazes to the broad rock outcropping a mile from the trailhead. Either double back from here or continue north along the ridge for nearly another mile to enjoy two more long views of the Granby area and the hills farther west, one from an open area and another from an outcropping. Retrace your steps back to the trailhead.

User Groups: Hikers only. No wheelchair facilities. Portions of this trail lie on private land, and use restrictions can change. Assume that bikes, dogs, and horses are not allowed unless a trail is specifically marked for them (although many landowners do not object to dogs).

Permits: Parking and access are free.

Maps: For topographic area maps, request Tariffville and Windsor Locks from the USGS.

Directions: On Route 20 in East Granby, 0.7 mile west of the junction with Route 187 and 2.6 miles east of the junction in Granby of Routes 20, 10, and 189 and U.S. 202, turn north onto Newgate Road (there is a sign for the Old Newgate Prison, which is open to visitors). Pull into the turnout on the right; the blue-blazed Metacomet Trail enters the woods there.

GPS Coordinates: 41.9482 N, 72.7408 W

Contact: Connecticut Forest and Park Association Inc., 16 Meriden Rd., Rockfall, CT 06481-2961, 860/346-2372, www.ctwoodlands.org.

6 SOAPSTONE MOUNTAIN

1 mi/0.5 hr

in Shenipsit State Forest in Somers and Stafford Springs

BEST (

The first thing most hikers notice on a climb up Soapstone Mountain (1,075 ft.) are the trees. As a result of repeated clear cutting and a forest fire, Soapstone's woods have become dominated by nearly pure stands of oak, particularly red oak. The soaring trees produce a beautiful deep red foliage in fall, but more importantly, their acorns provide ample nutrition for the state forest's abundant populations of deer, wild turkey, squirrels, and other northern wildlife. Following the Shenipsit Trail, this short trek to the Soapstone summit brings you to an observation deck with long views in all directions. The climb offers a modest elevation gain of a few hundred feet and has earned a reputation as a favorite Quiet Corner hike for families.

From the parking area, leave on the blue-blazed Shenipsit Trail, walking a relatively flat quarter mile through the woods to a junction. Bear left with the blue blazes (on the way to the summit, the trail here is also blazed with green dots) and start the summit ascent. Steep in only a few spots, but nothing a kid or beginner couldn't handle, in another quarter mile, the trail reaches the Soapstone Summit and observation tower. From the rolling green horse pastures and woods of the surrounding landscape to the Connecticut River Valley and the Springfield, Massachusetts, skyline, the vistas afforded from this vantage point are simply spectacular. Return the way you came.

User Groups: Hikers and leashed dogs. No bikes, horses, or wheelchair facilities.

Permits: Parking and access are free.

Maps: Trail maps are available at the information board beside the parking lot or online from the Connecticut State Parks Division. For a topographic area map, request Marlborough from the USGS.

CONNECTICUT

Directions: From the junction of Routes 190 and 83 in Somers, head east for 1.2 miles on Route 190/Main Street to a right turn on Gulf Road. Follow Gulf Road a short distance to the entrance gate and parking for Shenipsit State Forest/Soapstone Mountain.

GPS Coordinates: 41.9775 N, 72.4198 W

Contact: Shenipsit State Forest, 166 Chestnut Hill Rd. (Rte. 190), Stafford Springs, CT 06067, 860/684-6430. Connecticut State Parks Division, 79 Elm St., Hartford, CT 06106-5127, 860/424-3200, www.dep.state.ct.us/stateparks/index.htm.

7 BREAKNECK POND
6.5 mi/4.5 hr   🏃3 ⛰9

in Bigelow Hollow State Park and Nipmuck State Forest in Union

Located in one of the more rural parts of Connecticut, this relatively flat, 6.5-mile loop through Bigelow Hollow State Park and Nipmuck State Forest circles around picturesque Breakneck Pond, a long, narrow, and—notable in the Constitution State—undeveloped finger of fresh water hidden away in quiet woods. For its relative sense of remoteness, scenic qualities, and even a bit of rugged trail along the pond's west shore, this could quickly become your favorite low-terrain hike in the state.

This hike begins in Bigelow Hollow State Park, but most of it is within Nipmuck State Forest. From the parking area, cross the road to the information board at the trailhead, where maps are available. The trail immediately splits; bear right onto the white-blazed East Ridge Trail. Within 0.1 mile, it reaches and turns left onto an old logging road, following it 1.1 miles to a trail junction near the south end of Breakneck Pond. Turn left onto the Breakneck Pond View Trail, marked by blue blazes with white dots. The trail crosses a wet area and emerges at the pond's southern end, where you get your first almost complete view

of the 1.5-mile-long pond. The trail then bears right, still following the blue-white blazes.

For the next two miles, the footpath hugs the pond's western shore, traversing rocky ground in a thick forest with almost constant pond views. This is the most difficult stretch of this hike. Near the pond's north end (where beaver activity may necessitate bushwhacking or eventual trail rerouting), turn right at a trail junction, following the View Trail across an outlet stream (on rocks and a log), and turn right (south) again onto the blue-blazed Nipmuck Trail. The Nipmuck soon bears right off a logging road and becomes a footpath for two miles along the pond's eastern shore. Now you have nearly constant views in the other direction, looking west across the pond, giving you a whole new perspective. At the next trail junction, turn right with the East Ridge Trail's white blazes, walk about 0.1 mile to the first trail junction you reached on this hike, then turn left, and follow the East Ridge Trail along the logging road for the 1.1 miles back to the trailhead.

User Groups: Hikers and leashed dogs. Horses can access the woods road on this hike; no bikes or wheelchair facilities.

Permits: There's a weekend and holiday entrance fee Memorial Day–Labor Day of $7 per vehicle with a Connecticut registration and $10 per out-of-state vehicle. Weekdays are free.

Maps: A basic trail map is available free at the trailhead and from the Connecticut State Parks Division. For topographic area maps, request Eastford, Westford, and Southbridge from the USGS.

Directions: From the north, take I-84 to Exit 74. Follow Route 171 east into Union for 2.4 miles to the junction with Route 190. Turn left, staying on Route 171; proceed 1.4 miles and then turn left into Bigelow Hollow State Park. Continue 0.7 mile to the picnic area parking lot and trailhead. From the south, take I-84 to Exit 73. Turn right onto Route 190 east, follow it for two miles into Union, turn right onto Route 171, and continue 1.4

miles to the state park entrance. Bigelow Hollow State Park closes at sunset.

GPS Coordinates: 41.9910 N, 72.1300 W

Contact: Bigelow Hollow State Park, c/o Shenipsit State Forest, 166 Chestnut Hill Rd., Stafford Springs, CT 06076, 860/684-3430. Connecticut State Parks Division, 79 Elm St., Hartford, CT 06106-5127, 860/424-3200, fax 860/424-4070, www.dep.state.ct.us/stateparks/index.htm. Connecticut Forest and Park Association Inc., 16 Meriden Rd., Rockfall, CT 06481-2961, 860/346-2372, www.ctwoodlands.org.

8 TALCOTT MOUNTAIN
5 mi/3 hr   🥾3 ⛰8

in Talcott Mountain State Park in Bloomfield

This five-mile round-trip hike takes in the quarter mile of the Metacomet Trail along the exposed ridge in Talcott Mountain State Park—the most scenic stretch of what may be the state's premier trail—and the Heublein Tower, which offers a panorama of the surrounding countryside. The vertical ascent is about 400 feet.

From the parking lot, follow the blue-blazed Metacomet Trail south across Route 185 and into the woods. Within 0.2 mile, the trail crosses power lines; don't cross straight onto a woods road, but bear right across the power lines, looking for a footpath and a blue blaze at the forest's edge. The Metacomet Trail then zigs and zags along various woods roads for nearly a mile, ascending gently to the ridge and to more interesting hiking along a footpath through eastern hemlock trees. At 2.3 miles from the parking lot, the trail emerges onto an open ledge with a view stretching for miles out to the western Connecticut hills. Just 0.1 mile farther south, the trail passes by the impressive 165-foot tower built in 1914 by Gilbert Heublein and used as his summer home until 1937. Continue 0.1 mile past the tower to a traprock ledge to the left of the

© HEIDI J. BROWN

view from Talcott Mountain

picnic area for Farmington River Valley views. Hike back the way you came.

User Groups: Hikers and leashed dogs. The trail is not suitable for bikes or horses; no wheelchair facilities.

Permits: Parking and access are free.

Maps: For a topographic area map, request Avon from the USGS.

Directions: From the junction of Routes 178 and 185 in Bloomfield, drive west on Route 185 for 1.2 miles to the entrance of Penwood State Park. This hike begins from the parking lot 0.1 mile inside the park entrance. From Simsbury, the park entrance is 1.7 miles east of the junction of Route 185 and Route 10/U.S. 202. The Heublein Tower and the small museum at the summit are open daily June 1–November 1 and on weekends in May.

GPS Coordinates: 41.8384 N, 72.7861 W

Contact: Talcott Mountain State Park, c/o Penwood State Park, 57 Gun Mill Rd., Bloomfield, CT 06002, 860/242-1158. Connecticut State Parks Division, 79 Elm St., Hartford,

CT 06106-5127, 860/424-3200, www.dep. state.ct.us/stateparks/index.htm. Connecticut Forest and Park Association Inc., 16 Meriden Rd., Rockfall, CT 06481-2961, 860/346-2372, www.ctwoodlands.org.

9 WEST HARTFORD RESERVOIR

8 mi/4 hr

in West Hartford

With an extensive network of trails and old woods roads weaving through the forest and around a chain of reservoir ponds, the West Hartford Reservoir area is a popular local recreation spot. Roughly encircling the southern half of the water district land, this approximately eight-mile loop is great for hiking, mountain biking, cross-country skiing, or trail running. Trail maps are posted at several strategic junctions, but it's a good idea to carry one. This route climbs some small hills, but has relatively little elevation gain and loss.

The hike's first half is on the blue-blazed Metacomet Trail. From the turnout on U.S. 44, follow the blue blazes up onto the earthen dike and turn right (west), following the dike about 200 yards to a gate beside the highway on your right. Turn left with the Metacomet Trail, continuing along an old woods road until the trail hooks left, crossing a brook onto a footpath. The trail then passes through fairly open woods and over occasional rock ledges for more than two miles before emerging on the rough Finger Rock Road. Turn right on the road, still following the Metacomet Trail, and descend a steep slope of broken rock. Within a half mile, bear left with the blue blazes, off the woods road and onto a path. About half a mile farther, turn left onto a paved section of Finger Rock Road and then right onto the paved Red Road. In about 0.3 mile, turn left onto a wide woods road and then take the

next left, near a map board, onto the dirt Overlook Road.

Stay on Overlook Road for about 1.2 miles and cross Reservoir Number 5 on a bridge, where you enjoy the nicest views along this route of forest tightly embracing the reservoir waters on both sides of the bridge. Then take two lefts in rapid succession. You are on the paved Reservoir Road Extension; follow it to the left around the end of the reservoir, through quiet woods, and then turn right onto the paved Northwest Road, which becomes dirt within about 0.3 mile. Continue about another 0.3 mile and take the first trail on the right. Stay left through the next two trail intersections and then bear right twice, the second time at the edge of an open meadow. Follow the obvious path, which leads onto the earthen dike, about 1.2 miles back to the U.S. 44 turnout.

User Groups: Hikers, bikers, leashed dogs, and horses. No wheelchair facilities.

Permits: Parking and access are free.

Maps: A good map of the West Hartford Reservoir Area (also called the Talcott Mountain Reservoir Area) can be ordered for $2 from the Metropolitan District Commission; call 860/278-7850 and ask for West Hartford Filters. Maps are also available at the West Hartford Reservoir Administration Building, weekdays 7:30 A.M.–4 P.M. For a topographic area map, request Avon from the USGS.

Directions: This loop begins from a dirt turnout on the south side of U.S. 44 in West Hartford, 2.1 miles east of the easternmost junction of U.S. 44 and Route 10 in Avon and 0.1 mile west of a large paved parking lot and entrance to the reservoir area. You could also park in the paved lot and walk (or bike) up U.S. 44 to access this loop.

The reservoir is open 8 A.M.–8 P.M. mid-April–late October, and 8 A.M.–6 P.M. during the rest of the year.

GPS Coordinates: 41.7934 N, 72.7949 W

Contact: Metropolitan District Commission, Supply Division, 39 Beachrock Rd., Pleasant

CONNECTICUT

Valley, CT 06063, 860/379-0938, www.themdc.com/talcottmountain.htm.

10 CASE MOUNTAIN
2 mi/1 hr 　　　　　🏃2 ⛰6

in the Highland Park section of Manchester

This fairly easy two-mile hike incorporates the Shenipsit and other trails through the Case Mountain Open Space to loop over the Lookout, a cleared area with nice views west toward Hartford. For the most part, this hike remains in the woods, but it's a nice refuge for a short hike on the fringes of a fairly populous urban area. Wildlife commonly spotted on or near the trail include salamanders, chickadees and warblers, wild turkey, white-tailed deer, grey squirrel, and, near the summit, circling hawks. Trails are well blazed and generally easy to follow, and distances between junctions described here are rarely more than 0.3 mile.

From the parking area, walk past the gate, following the wide path of the white-blazed Carriage Road Trail about 150 yards, and then turn right onto the red-blazed Highland Park Trail at a sign that reads Trail to Lookout. Follow the red trail past a junction where the orange-blazed Boulder Trail diverges left and then turn right, following the white trail uphill 0.1 mile to the Lookout. Turn left on the yellow-blazed Lookout Trail, which coincides briefly with the blue-blazed Shenipsit Trail; bear right on the yellow trail after the two split again. After crossing the white trail, turn left onto a newer trail blazed blue and yellow (watch closely for it). Turn left on the blue and yellow trail, walk 100 yards, and then turn right on the white trail, which soon bears left off the woods road onto a footpath leading straight onto the red trail. Upon rejoining the white trail, turn right and follow it back to the parking area.

User Groups: Hikers, bikers, and leashed dogs; no wheelchair facilities. Horses and hunting are prohibited.

© HEIDI J. BROWN

Case Pond Dam, near the base of Case Mountain

Permits: Parking and access are free.

Maps: A trail map is posted at several major trail junctions and a free copy of the map is available through the Manchester Parks and Recreation Department. For topographic area maps, request Manchester and Rockville from the USGS.

Directions: From I-384 westbound, take Exit 4 in Manchester. Turn right onto Highland Street, drive 0.3 mile, and then turn right again onto Spring Street. Continue another 0.3 mile to a parking turnout on the left just over a bridge. From I-384 eastbound, take Exit 4 in Manchester and turn right onto Spring Street. Continue 0.2 mile to the same parking turnout on the left.

GPS Coordinates: 41.7602 N, 72.4918 W

Contact: Manchester Parks and Recreation Department, P.O. Box 191, Manchester, CT 06045-0191, 860/647-3084, fax 860/647-3083. Connecticut Forest and Park Association Inc., 16 Meriden Rd., Rockfall, CT 06481-2961, 860/346-2372, www.ctwoodlands.org.

11 NATCHAUG STATE FOREST ROAD LOOP
4 mi/2 hr   𝑿𝑿2 ◢7

in Eastford

This loop, ideal for mountain bikers and hikers looking for an easy woods walk, introduces you to a 12,500-acre expanse of state forest cut by several trails and forest roads, including the Natchaug Trail. Get a map and explore. Some major trail junctions are marked by numbered signs. There is very little elevation gain.

From the parking area, double back on the park road a short distance to where it hooks right. Here, continue straight onto the gravel Kingsbury Road. Go past trail junction 5, where a gas line right-of-way leads left, to junction 6, where you turn left. Bear right around a horse camp and then bear left at the next fork. The trail descends, and just before crossing a brook, you turn left. You're now on the gas line right-of-way, which leads back to junction 5 on Kingsbury Road. Bear in mind that snowmobilers use these trails in winter, as do hunters in late fall.

User Groups: Hikers, bikers, leashed dogs, and horses; no wheelchair facilities.

Permits: Parking and access are free.

Maps: A free trail map is available at the park, outside the maintenance building across from the parking area, or from the Connecticut State Parks Division. For a topographic area map, request Hampton from the USGS.

Directions: From I-395, take Exit 93 for Dayville onto Route 101 west. In Phoenixville, turn right (south) onto Route 198. Watch for a sign and the park entrance on the left. Follow the main park road to the headquarters building and park at a roadside pullout across from the large maintenance building.

GPS Coordinates: 41.8675 N, 72.0899 W

Contact: Natchaug State Forest, c/o Mashamoquet Brook State Park, 147 Wolf Den Dr., Pomfret Center, CT 06259, 860/928-6121. Connecticut State Parks Division, 79 Elm St., Hartford, CT 06106-5127, 860/424-3200, fax 860/424-4070, www.dep.state.ct.us/stateparks/index.htm.

12 ORCHARD HILL LOOKOUT
2 mi/1 hr   𝑿𝑿1 ◢5

in Chaplin

This hike does not lead to any spectacular views, or to orchards for that matter. It's simply a pleasant little stroll through the woods to a lookout where, when the leaves are down, the view of the valley to the west is only partly obscured by trees. The trail is well blazed, so you're not likely to even need a map. Orchard Hill is a nice choice for a late fall walk when the fading afternoon sun bathes the bare tree branches and remaining foliage in an almost fluorescent yellow light.

From the trailhead, follow the blue blazes of the Natchaug Trail into the woods. Birch, elm, and hickory trees line the path, the sound of tapping woodpeckers often fills the air, and the walking is easy as the trail winds along, crossing a brook and over a stone wall, before reaching the lookout at one mile out. Return the way you came.

User Groups: Hikers and dogs. No wheelchair facilities. This trail is not suitable for horses or mountain bikes.

Permits: Parking and access are free.

Maps: For topographic area maps, request Hampton and Spring Hill from the USGS.

Directions: From the junction of U.S. 44 and Route 198 in Eastford, drive south on Route 198, past the entrance to Natchaug State Forest, into Chaplin. Turn left onto Morey Road, cross a bridge over a stream, and turn right onto Marcy Road. About 0.2 mile farther, the blue-blazed Natchaug Trail crosses Marcy Road. Park here along the roadside.

GPS Coordinates: 41.8186 N, 72.0972 W

Contact: Connecticut Forest and Park Association Inc., 16 Meriden Rd., Rockfall, CT 06481-2961, 860/346-2372, www.ctwoodlands.org.

CONNECTICUT

13 MASHAMOQUET BROOK STATE PARK LOOP

3.5 mi/2 hr   🏃3 ▲8

in Mashamoquet

Mashamoquet dispels any suggestion that Connecticut's northeast corner is flat. This hike almost immediately ascends a hillside, then winds through forested hills and a classic, glacier-scoured landscape of rocky ledges and boulders. This is a great hike for young children. All trails are well marked.

From the first picnic area, head a short distance up the road and cross Mashamoquet Brook on a wooden bridge. Follow the trail to the right and uphill. The blue-blazed trail branches to the right; stay on the red-blazed trail. Shortly after crossing Wolf Den Drive, you see Table Rock on the left, two flat boulders stacked like a table. Beyond it, the blue and red trails converge and enter an area of rocky ledges. Approximately 1.7 miles into the hike, a rock-mounted plaque on the right marks the Wolf Den site, where in 1742 Israel Putnam crept into the cavelike channel in the boulders and shot what was reputedly the last wolf in Connecticut, an animal suspected of killing numerous sheep in the area. Continue following the blue blazes to the Indian Chair—another unique rock formation—through more ledges, across an open field, and finally to the first junction with the red-blazed trail.

User Groups: Hikers, bikers, and leashed dogs. No horses or wheelchair facilities. Bikes are not allowed during the spring mud season, April–mid-May.

Permits: There's a parking fee of $7 for Connecticut vehicles, $10 for out-of-state vehicles, on weekends and holidays Memorial Day–Labor Day; weekdays are free. Parking is free at the state park office on Wolf Den Road, more than a mile east of the park main entrance and picnic area; from the office, you can pick up a blue-blazed trail leading a mile to the red-blazed trail described here.

Maps: A free trail map is available from the park office or the Connecticut State Parks Division. For a topographic area map, request Danielson from the USGS.

Directions: From I-395, take Exit 93 for Dayville onto Route 101 west. In Pomfret, beyond the junction with Route 169 and U.S. 44, watch for a sign and the park main entrance and picnic area on the left.

GPS Coordinates: 41.9028 N, 71.9416 W

Contact: Mashamoquet Brook State Park, 147 Wolf Den Dr., Pomfret Center, CT 06259, 860/928-6121. Connecticut State Parks Division, 79 Elm St., Hartford, CT 06106-5127, 860/424-3200, fax 860/424-4070, www.dep.state.ct.us/stateparks/index.htm.

14 BUTTERMILK FALLS

0.2 mi/0.25 hr   🏃1 ▲7

in Plymouth

As soon as you step out of your car, the sound of Buttermilk Falls reaches your ears. It's a short, relatively flat walk to the waterfall, which plummets about 100 feet through several drops. A popular place to bring young children, Buttermilk sees lots of visitors, especially on weekends in summer, so parking here can be difficult at times. The preserve also, unfortunately, attracts illegal after-hours activity. Lend a hand by picking up trailside litter on your visit here.

From the roadside parking area, the trail leads into the woods, traversing fairly level terrain a short distance to the falls, where you can easily walk up or downhill for various waterfall views.

User Groups: Hikers only. No wheelchair facilities. Bikes, dogs, horses, and hunting are prohibited.

Permits: Parking and access are free.

Maps: No map is needed for this short walk, but for a topographic area map, request Thomaston from the USGS.

Directions: Take U.S. 6 into Terryville/Plymouth. Turn south onto South Main Street, which makes a right turn in 0.2 mile and again in another 1.2 miles. After the second right, drive 1.3 miles and turn left onto Lane Hill Road. Drive 0.2 mile to a small turnout on the right marked by a sign for the Nature Conservancy, where the Mattatuck Trail's blue blazes enter the woods. There are also turnouts along the road just before and beyond the trailhead.

GPS Coordinates: 41.6451 N, 73.0072 W

Contact: The Nature Conservancy Connecticut Chapter, 55 High St., Middletown, CT 06457-3788, 860/344-0716, www.nature.org. Connecticut Forest and Park Association Inc., 16 Meriden Rd., Rockfall, CT 06481-2961, 860/346-2372, www.ctwoodlands.org.

15 RATTLESNAKE MOUNTAIN
5.4 mi/3 hr   ᛣᛣ3 ◭7

in Plainville

Here's another relatively easy ridge walk that begins in a heavily industrialized area, yet leads to some pretty good views from a series of cliff tops. A few of the cliff faces, including Pinnacle Rock, are popular destinations for technical rock climbers. The cumulative elevation gain is less than 1,000 feet.

Follow the blue-blazed Metacomet Trail along a fence and then up a hillside into the woods. The trail makes numerous turns, finally reaching and following the western side of the low ridge past rock outcroppings. At 1.7 miles, you reach Pinnacle Rock's bare top, with views in all directions. You may see or hear rock climbers below; be careful not to dislodge any loose stones, and certainly do not walk toward the cliff edge. Continue north, descending past an old stone foundation and crossing a dirt road. The trail turns left and reenters the woods. It eventually reaches Rattlesnake Mountain, ascending a slope of loose rocks and traversing below its vertical cliffs (another popular spot for climbers), passing through a tunnel-like passage in rocks.

The trail ascends the end of the cliffs to the open ledges atop them, with good views to the north, east, and south (including Hartford's skyline to the northeast). A short distance farther along the Metacomet Trail lies Will Warren's Den, an area of huge boulders worth checking out before you retrace your steps on the return hike. (A local legend, which dates back to colonial times, has it that a man named Will Warren was flogged for not going to church, and in a fit of vengeance, he tried to burn down the entire Farmington village. As a result, he was chased by the villagers into the nearby hills, where a Mohegan woman hid him in this cave.)

User Groups: Hikers only. No wheelchair facilities. Portions of this trail lie on private land, and use restrictions can change. Assume that bikes, dogs, and horses are not allowed unless a trail is specifically marked for them (although many landowners do not object to dogs).

Permits: Parking and access are free.

Maps: For a topographic area map, request New Britain from the USGS.

Directions: This hike begins along Route 372 in Plainville at a sign for the Metacomet Trail, 1.5 miles east of the junction with Route 10 and two miles west of Exit 7 off Route 72. Parking here is difficult. Heed the No Trespassing signs. You might ask permission to park at one of the gas stations just east of the trailhead on Route 372.

GPS Coordinates: 41.6734 N, 72.8339 W

Contact: Connecticut Forest and Park Association Inc., 16 Meriden Rd., Rockfall, CT 06481-2961, 860/346-2372, www.ctwoodlands.org.

16 COMPOUNCE RIDGE
2 mi/1 hr   ᛣᛣ3 ◭7

in Southington

This popular ridge walk brings you to the Norton Outlook, a fine, open ledge with long distance views reaching north in to

CONNECTICUT

Massachusetts and south to Long Island sound. Steep in sections, this hike climbs just under 500 feet.

From Panthorn Trail, the blue-blazed Steep Climb Trail does indeed ascend steeply, climbing relentlessly uphill and managing to cross two brooks along the way. (The physical demand is so immediate, it's best to stretch and do a few warmup exercises before starting out.) At a half mile, turn right onto the Compounce Ridge Trail (CRT)—a part of the Tunxis Trail—and watch for a side path that leads right to an overlook; visit the overlook is you like, it adds only a few feet of extra trail mileage. Continue uphill on the CRT to the bald cap of Norton Outlook, at 931 feet, the ridge's actual high point. On a clear day, take in Long Island to the south and Mount Tom in Massachusetts to the north. Return the way you came, taking care on the very steep descent back to Panthorn Trail.

User Groups: Hikers only. No wheelchair facilities. Portions of this trail lie on private land, and use restrictions can change. Assume that bikes, dogs, and horses are not allowed unless a trail is specifically marked for them (although many landowners do not object to dogs). Most trails are open to cross-country skiing. Assume that hunting is allowed in season unless otherwise posted.

Permits: Parking and access are free.

Maps: For a topographic area map, request Bristol from the USGS.

Directions: From the junction of Routes 72 and 229 in Bristol, drive south on Route 229 1.7 miles to a right turn onto Panthorn Trail, a paved residential street; park roadside. The blue blazes of the Steep Climb Trail enter the woods at the end of the street.

GPS Coordinates: 41.6320 N, 72.9248 W

Contact: Connecticut Forest and Park Association Inc., 16 Meriden Rd., Rockfall, CT 06481-2961, 860/346-2372, www.ctwoodlands.org.

17 RAGGED MOUNTAIN PRESERVE TRAIL LOOP

6 mi/3 hr   🏃3 ⛰9

in Southington

BEST (

Traversed by the long distance Metacomet Trail, Ragged Mountain is a classic example of Connecticut's distinctive traprock ridges. At 761 feet, this tall hill is known for its expansive vistas, vertical cliff faces, mountain ridge reservoirs, and rare plant communities. Ragged Mountain is also an important raptor migration path, and each year hawks, eagles, and vultures can be seen passing through on their seasonal journeys. Try this hike in early fall for great hawk-watching and beautiful views of autumn foliage.

From the turnout, walk the woods road 0.1 mile to the Ragged Mountain Preserve Trail loop. Follow its blue blazes with red dots to the left. Within half a mile you reach the tall cliff tops high above Hart Ponds, with wide views to the southeast. The trail follows the cliff tops along the southern edge of Ragged Mountain for the next mile or so, passing one cliff, at about 1.5 miles out, where a wall stands completely detached from the main cliff. Turn right onto the blue-blazed Metacomet Trail, which follows the west ridge of Ragged Mountain, high above Shuttle Meadow Reservoir, with excellent views to the south, west, and northwest. After dropping off the ridge, the Metacomet heads north; bear to the right (east) on the blue- and red dot-blazed Ragged Mountain Preserve Trail, which eventually turns south through the woods, at one point climbing a slope of loose stones. The loop trail ends where you started; turn left and walk 0.1 mile back to your vehicle.

User Groups: Hikers and leashed dogs. No wheelchair facilities. This trail is not suitable for bikes or horses.

Permits: Parking and access are free.

Maps: For topographic area maps, request New Britain and Meriden from the USGS.

Directions: From Route 71A in Berlin, 1.2

miles south of the junction of Routes 71A and 372 and 1.2 miles north of the junction of Routes 71A and 71, turn west onto West Lane. Proceed 0.6 mile to a turnout on the right at Ragged Mountain Preserve's gated entrance. Ragged Mountain Preserve closes at dusk. GPS Coordinates: 41.6289 N, 72.7967 W

Contact: Ragged Mountain Foundation, P.O. Box 948, Southington, CT 06489, www. raggedmtn.org. Connecticut Forest and Park Association Inc., 16 Meriden Rd., Rockfall, CT 06481-2961, 860/346-2372, www.ct-woodlands.org.

🔟 GAY CITY GHOST TOWN

2.8 mi/1.5 hr

in Gay City State Park in Bolton, Hebron, and Glastonbury

Named after one of the families who settled the area, Gay City was once the home of an 18th century isolationist religious sect and is now a 1,569-acre tract of parkland offering swimming, picnicking, and an almost endless opportunity for exploration. The most intriguing trails in the park wander through the woods past tumbling stone walls, grass-filled cellar holes, and an old mill foundation that hint at the mysterious past of the land's former residents. This loop hike to a real New England ghost town is a flat, pleasant walk in the woods that also takes you to the Blackledge River and the shores of an old mill pond.

From the parking area just beyond the park entrance, pick up the white trail, heading almost due north through the woods. At 0.6 mile, the trail abruptly turns left and in another 0.4 mile arrives at the old mill pond's swimming beach. The trail explores the shore a bit before turning right to cross a bridge over the Blackledge River. In the next half mile, the trail follows the boundary of an old stone wall and then coincides briefly with French Road (the park's perimeter road),

before turning back into the woods. Quickly reached is the foundation remains of an early 19th century sawmill; other cellar holes are further out in the woods. Continuing on for another 0.3 mile, the white trail reaches a junction with the blue-blazed Shenipsit Trail. Bear left on the Shenipsit, and follow for 0.2 mile back to the access road and parking area.

Special Note: To visit the gravestones of the area's former residents, backtrack to the park entrance and turn left (north) on French Road. The small cemetery is located a short walk up the road on the left.

User Groups: Hikers and leashed dogs. No wheelchair facilities. Mountain bikes and horses are allowed on the white trail only.

Permits: There's a parking fee of $7 for Connecticut vehicles, $10 for out-of-state vehicles, on weekends and holidays the third weekend of April–Columbus Day. On weekdays, parking and access are free.

Maps: Trail maps are available at the information board beside the parking lot or online from the Connecticut State Parks Division. For a topographic area map, request Marlborough from the USGS.

Directions: From the intersection of Main Street and Gilead Street in downtown Hebron, turn right to head northwest on Route 85/Gilead Street. Follow for 4.6 miles to a right turn onto North Street (Route 85 also turns right here). Follow Route 85/North Street for approximately 2.5 miles to the entrance of Gay City State Park. The state park is open 8 A.M.–sunset.

GPS Coordinates: 41.7247 N, 72.4366 W

Contact: Gay City State Park, c/o Eastern District HQ, 209 Hebron Rd., Marlborough, CT 06447, 860/295-9523. Connecticut State Parks Division, 79 Elm St., Hartford, CT 06106-5127, 860/424-3200, www.dep.state.ct.us/stateparks/index.htm.

CONNECTICUT

19 DEVIL'S DEN

1 mi/0.5 hr   🏃🏃₁ ⛰₅

in Plainfield

This relatively flat hike follows a rough woods road for a half mile to a faint side path on the right. The path—easily overlooked—leads 30 feet downhill to ledges in the woods that feature cavelike cavities and a narrow passageway known as Devil's Den.

From the parking area, walk out via the road (closed to cars beyond the parking area), following the blue-blazed Quinebaug Trail. Watch for a faint path on the right, just after walking a slight downhill over a slab in the road and before the road levels out—this is the short path that will lead you to Devil's Den. (If you reach the yellow-blazed Pachaug-Quinebaug Trail, you have gone about 0.1 mile past the turnoff for Devil's Den.) It's only a short distance through the woods before the path ends at the ledges. Return the way you came.

User Groups: Hikers only. No wheelchair facilities. Portions of this trail lie on private land, and use restrictions can change. Assume that bikes, dogs, and horses are not allowed unless a trail is specifically marked for them (although many landowners do not object to dogs).

Permits: Parking and access are free.

Maps: Although a map is not necessary for this hike, for topographic area maps, request Plainfield and Oneco from the USGS.

Directions: From I-395, take Exit 88 in Plainfield and follow Route 14A east for 1.6 miles. Turn right on Spaulding Road and drive two miles to its end. Turn left on Flat Rock Road and continue another 0.7 mile; just beyond where the road becomes pavement, park in a turnout on the left.

GPS Coordinates: 41.6505 N, 71.8748 W

Contact: Connecticut Forest and Park Association Inc., 16 Meriden Rd., Rockfall, CT 06481-2961, 860/346-2372, www.ctwoodlands.org.

20 CASTLE CRAG AND WEST PEAK

6 mi/3 hr   🏃🏃₃ ⛰₈

in Hubbard Park in Meriden

BEST (

This popular six-mile hike to a small, castle-like stone tower is one of the area's nicest and a great adventure for children because it follows the crest of high cliffs for much of its distance. You can cut this hike in half by just going to Castle Crag. Out-and-back, the entire hike involves about 600 feet of uphill walking.

From the parking area, walk across the dam bridge. At its far end, pick up the blue-blazed Metacomet Trail, which turns left into a rock-strewn gully, then immediately left again, climbing a hillside out of the gully. An easy hike, with a few short, steep sections, brings you to the crest of the ridge high above Merimere Reservoir, with sweeping views of the surrounding hills and the city of Meriden. Follow the trail along the ridge, passing several viewpoints. At 1.5 miles, you will reach Castle Crag lookout tower, where the castle stands atop cliffs; you can climb its stairs for a 360-degree panorama. To make this a three-mile round-trip, return the way you came.

To continue on to West Peak for the full hike, cross the parking lot at Castle Crag to a blue arrow marking the Metacomet Trail, which leaves the castle and follows along the tops of cliffs with almost constant views. The trail parallels the road to Castle Crag for about 0.3 mile, then turns left and descends fairly steeply for 0.2 mile. At the bottom of the hill, turn right onto an old woods road for about 50 feet, then right onto a footpath (watch for the blue blazes), slabbing uphill. Within 0.1 mile, you pass below cliffs, then ascend a short hillside to a woods road. Turn left and walk the road about 75 yards to where it terminates atop high cliffs of West Peak. From this perch, commanding views to the south offer the profile of the Sleeping Giant, a chain of low hills just north of New Haven that resembles a man lying on his back. To return to this hike's start,

© HEIDI J. BROWN

view of the Merimere Reservoir in Hubbard Park, Meriden

you can backtrack the way you came by following the woods road, past the trail to the end of the paved road (there are transmission towers to the left). Follow the woods road downhill, passing the right turn that leads to Castle Crag, all the way back to the reservoir dam, a walk of roughly three miles.

User Groups: Hikers only. No wheelchair facilities. Portions of this trail lie on private land, and use restrictions can change. Assume that bikes, dogs, and horses are not allowed unless a trail is specifically marked for them (although many landowners do not object to dogs).

Permits: Parking and access are free.

Maps: For a topographic area map, request Meriden from the USGS Map Sales.

Directions: Take I-691 to Exit 4 in Meriden. Turn east, continue 0.8 mile, and take a left into Hubbard Park. Continue 0.2 mile and bear right, then go another 0.1 mile to a stop sign and turn left. Follow that road 0.3 mile to its end, passing under the highway. Turn left and drive another 1.1 miles, along the

Merimere Reservoir, and park at a barricade at the end of the reservoir.

GPS Coordinates: 41.5526 N, 72.8273 W

Contact: Connecticut Forest and Park Association Inc., 16 Meriden Rd., Rockfall, CT 06481-2961, 860/346-2372, www.ctwoodlands.org.

21 CHAUNCEY PEAK/ LAMENTATION MOUNTAIN
4.2 mi/3 hr   👥4 ⛰8

in Giuffrida Park and Lamentation Mountain State Park in Middletown

Chauncey Peak and Lamentation Mountain comprise one of the finest hikes along the Mattabesett Trail, if not among all the traprock ridge walks of the Connecticut River Valley. Although it entails some steep hiking for brief periods, and involves some 750 feet of uphill hiking, this 4.2-mile trip amply rewards you for the modest effort. The constant views from atop the ridge are especially compelling in autumn, during peak fall foliage season.

From the parking lot, cross the field below the dam and bear right onto a flat trail, following it 0.1 mile to the blue-blazed Mattabesett Trail. Turn left, soon climbing steeply to the summit of Chauncey at 0.4 mile, where you walk along the brink of a sheer cliff overlooking a pastoral countryside of fields and woods. Continue along the Mattabesett around the upper edge of a quarry to the open ridge and a view at 0.8 mile from high above Crescent Lake. Walk the open ridge with long views, mostly to the west, for about 0.2 mile, then descend a steep hillside of loose rocks. At 1.2 miles, cross a small brook, then begin climbing Lamentation, reaching the first view at 1.7 miles. From here, walk the ridge for 0.4 mile—with nearly constant views south, west, and north—to the summit, or high point on the ridge, at 2.1 miles. Visible are the Sleeping Giant to the south and Castle Crag to the west. Hike back along the same route.

CONNECTICUT

User Groups: Hikers only. No wheelchair facilities. Portions of this trail lie on private land, and use restrictions can change. Assume that bikes, dogs, and horses are not allowed unless a trail is specifically marked for them (although many landowners do not object to dogs).

Permits: Parking and access are free.

Maps: A map of Giuffrida Park trails is available at the caretaker's house across the road from the parking lot. For a topographic area map, request Meriden from the USGS.

Directions: Take I-91 to Exit 20 in Middletown. Head west on Country Club Road, which becomes Westfield Road; 2.5 miles from the highway—where the Mattabesett Trail enters the woods on the right—bear right and continue 0.1 mile to the parking area on the right at Giuffrida Park.

GPS Coordinates: 41.5559 N, 72.7632 W

Contact: Connecticut Forest and Park Association Inc., 16 Meriden Rd., Rockfall, CT 06481-2961, 860/346-2372, www.ctwoodlands.org. Connecticut State Parks Division, 79 Elm St., Hartford, CT 06106-5127, 860/424-3200, www.dep.state.ct.us/stateparks/index.htm.

22 HIGBY MOUNTAIN
2.4 mi/1.5 hr 👟2 ⛰6

in Middlefield

Unfortunately, you never escape the traffic sounds on this fairly easy, 2.4-mile walk, but it leads through a forest to a good spot to catch the sunset over the Meriden cityscape. The hike goes up about 250 feet.

From the parking lot, pick up the trail marked by blue blazes with purple dots, which begins beside the restaurant. (Don't take the trail from the rear of the lot marked only with a sign reading No Snowmobiles.) This connector trail follows flat ground for nearly 0.4 mile to the blue-blazed Mattabesett Trail (by turning left here, you could reach Route 66 in 0.1 mile). Bear right onto the Mattabesett

and continue 0.3 mile to where it turns sharply right and climbs steeply onto the ridge, an ascent that is brief but can leave you short of breath. About 1.2 miles from the parking lot, you reach the Pinnacle, a tall rock outcropping offering long views in nearly every direction, especially to the west. Return the way you came.

User Groups: Hikers only. No wheelchair facilities. Portions of this trail lie on private land, and use restrictions can change. Assume that bikes, dogs, and horses are not allowed unless a trail is specifically marked for them (although many landowners do not object to dogs).

Permits: Parking and access are free.

Maps: For a topographic area map, request Middletown from the USGS.

Directions: From the intersection of Broad Street and E. Main Street in Meriden, head north on Broad Street for 0.6 mile to a right turn onto the ramp to Route 66 eastbound (also I-691 for the first mile). Continue on Route 66 east for 4.2 miles. At the intersection with Meriden Road (Route 147), make a U-turn (legal) at the lights, now on Route 66 westbound. Trailhead parking is on Route 66 west, just past Guida's Restaurant in a small turnout on the right-hand side of the road.

GPS Coordinates: 41.5441 N, 72.7481 W

Contact: The Nature Conservancy Connecticut Chapter, 55 High St., Middletown, CT 06457-3788, 860/344-0716, www.nature.org. Connecticut Forest and Park Association Inc., 16 Meriden Rd., Rockfall, CT 06481-2961, 860/346-2372, www.ctwoodlands.org.

23 WADSWORTH FALLS STATE PARK
3.2 mi/1.5 hr 👟3 ⛰8

in the Rockfall section of Middlefield

BEST (

The highlights of this fairly flat, easy, 3.2-mile jaunt through the woods are the two waterfalls along the way—the first a tall cascade, the second a thundering column of water. The park is a great spot for an after-work or weekend walk or run, with several other trails to access besides this route.

Behind the restrooms off the parking lot, pick up the orange-blazed Main Trail, a wide, mostly flat path. In a half mile, opposite a park map board, look for the giant mountain laurel (also known as wild rhododendron). Continue on the Main Trail for 0.2 mile and then bear right at a sign for Little Falls, following a blue trail 0.2 mile to where the Coginchaug River tumbles 40 feet through a series of ledges. Rejoining the Main Trail above Little Falls, turn right. At 1.5 miles from the start, the Main Trail ends at a paved road. Turn right and follow the road 0.1 mile to a parking area on the right, then follow the sound of crashing water about 100 yards to the Big Falls. Retrace your steps back to the parking lot.

User Groups: Hikers and leashed dogs. No wheelchair facilities. The blue side trail is not suitable for bikes or horses.

Permits: There's a parking fee of $7 for Connecticut vehicles, $10 for out-of-state vehicles, on weekends and holidays Memorial Day–mid-September. On weekdays the fee is $6 for residents and $7 for nonresidents. Access is free the rest of the year.

Maps: Trail maps are available at the information board beside the parking lot. For a topographic area map, request Middletown from the USGS.

Directions: From the junction of Routes 66 and 157 in Middletown, drive south on Route 157 for 1.5 miles and turn left into the state park entrance and parking lot. The state park is open 8 A.M.–sunset.

GPS Coordinates: 41.531474 N, 72.684274 W

Contact: Wadsworth Falls State Park, c/o Chatfield Hollow State Park, 381 Rte. 80, Killingworth, CT 06419, 860/663-2030. Connecticut State Parks Division, 79 Elm St., Hartford, CT 06106-5127, 860/424-3200, www.dep.state.ct.us/stateparks/index.htm.

LONG ISLAND SOUND

The southernmost swath of Connecticut may

feel in some places like an eastern extension of New York City, but hikes in the region are a resounding testimony to the land's still very distinct New Englandness. Rugged hills lead to views of a rolling countryside that seems almost untouched by time. And forest trails to gorges, ponds, and waterfalls abound – as do lots of places where the only traffic noise heard is the rustling of a deer.

Numerous state parks and forests provide for an almost endless supply of quality hikes: Devil's Hopyard and Patchaug State Forest are state land gems; as are Rocky Neck and Bluff Point, two state parks that bring you directly to the sandy shore and marshy inlets of Long Island Sound. But if you have to pick just one to visit, make it Sleeping Giant. Not far from New Haven, this classic steprock ridge runs east-west and trails on the Sleeping Giant lead to challenging ledges and long views from the historic stone tower lookout. It's beautiful here during peak fall foliage season (the last few weeks of October). And yes, the ridge crest really does look like the profile of a recumbent giant, especially when viewed from the south.

The land's diverse geography also provides for an eclectic mix of flora and fauna. Wild rhododendron and sassafras (a native tree species) flourish in the inland forest, while the Sound's salt marshes and tidal flats harbor a mix of bayberry, marsh elder, and sea lavender. Commonly spotted wildlife include barn owls, horned owls, golden eagles, gulls, marsh hawks, hummingbirds, wild turkeys, Canada geese, mallards, herons, beavers, lynx, red fox, coyotes, deer, raccoons, and opossums.

Several hikes in this chapter use Connecticut's Blue Trails System. Crossing through private land, the Connecticut Forest and Park Association has secured landowner permission only for hiker access. Changes in everything from land use to ownership constantly threaten the Blue Trail System, making it imperative that hikers respect any closures of trails, whether temporary or permanent. Although uses can vary, assume that dogs, horses, and mountain bikes are not allowed unless a trail is specifically marked for them. Most Blue Trails are open to cross-country skiing. Assume that hunting is permitted in season unless the land is posted with signs prohibiting it. Fires must not be lit except where officially designated fireplaces have been provided.

The prime hiking season this far south begins by April and extends into November, but winters are also milder near the coast; at certain times in winter you may find some of these trails with little or no snow on them.

In Connecticut state parks and forests, dogs must be leashed and bikes and horses are allowed on some trails and forest roads. Hunting is allowed in season in state forests, but not in state parks, and is prohibited on Sundays. Access fees are levied at some state lands, but most allow free entrance year-round.

CONNECTICUT

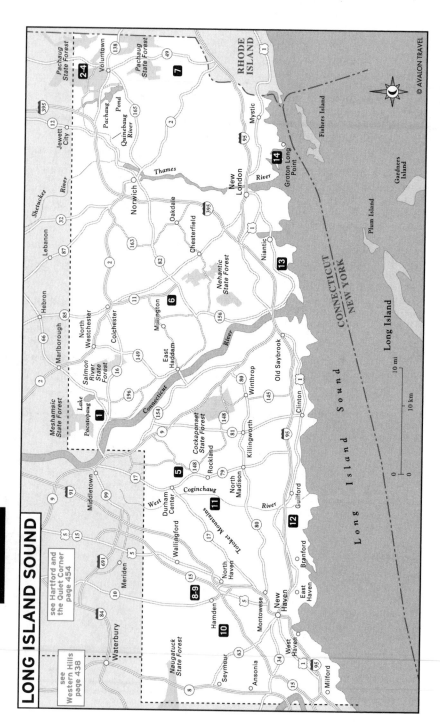

LONG ISLAND SOUND

see Hartford and the Quiet Corner page 454

see Western Hills page 438

© AVALON TRAVEL

1 GREAT HILL
1 mi/0.75 hr   🏃2 ▲7

in Meshomesic Forest in East Hampton

This fairly easy hike of just one mile round-trip and a few hundred feet uphill leads to interesting quartz ledges with a good view over Great Hill Pond and the Connecticut River Valley, framed by the town of Middletown in the distance. On the way to the ledges, the trail passes below low, rugged cliffs, and through a forest marked by birch, yellow poplar, and sassafras, one of the Nutmeg State's more unique native tree species. Sassafras is easiest to identify in early autumn when the trees produce a small blue fruit, a favorite fall snack for white-tailed deer, squirrels, wild turkey, and several species of woodland birds. But don't bushwhack off-trail in search of sassafras: Poison ivy abounds here and rattlesnakes are frequently spotted in the vicinity of Great Hill.

From the parking area, cross the road and follow the blue-blazed Shenipsit Trail into the woods. The trail is easy at first, then begins slabbing up Great Hill, traversing ledges. Atop the hill, the Shenipsit Trail makes a hairpin turn with two quick, sharp right turns; at the second of those, a white-blazed side trail leads to the left about 0.1 mile to the quartz ledges. Return the way you came.

User Groups: Hikers only. No wheelchair facilities. Portions of this trail lie on private land, and use restrictions can change. Assume that bikes, dogs, and horses are not allowed unless a trail is specifically marked for them (although many landowners do not object to dogs).

Permits: Parking and access are free.

Maps: For a topographic area map, request Middle Haddam from the USGS.

Directions: From the junction of Routes 66 and 151 in Cobalt/East Hampton, turn north onto Depot Hill Road, drive 0.1 mile, then bear right, uphill, following the road another 0.1 mile. Turn right onto Gadpouch Road and proceed a half mile (the road becomes dirt) to a small dirt parking area on the right.

GPS Coordinates: 41.5772 N, 72.5505 W

Contact: Connecticut Forest and Park Association Inc., 16 Meriden Rd., Rockfall, CT 06481-2961, 860/346-2372, www.ctwoodlands.org.

2 PACHAUG STATE FOREST RHODODENDRON SANCTUARY
0.5 mi/0.25 hr   🏃1 ▲7

in Pachaug State Forest in Voluntown

Pachaug State Forest is the largest state forest in Connecticut encompassing over 24,000 acres of ponds, rivers, hills, and woods. Among Pachaug's patchwork of unique offerings is its 26-acre wild rhododendron sanctuary, designated a Natural Area Preserve by the state. This short, wheelchair-accessible hike begins to the right of the field parking area, at the Rhododendron Sanctuary sign. The level trail leads through the shady forest, lined on both sides with vast stands of massive rhododendrons. The best time to visit is in late June and July when the pinkish purple blossoms are in full bloom. Return the way you came. Just down the road is the start of the blue-blazed Pachaug Trail hike up Mount Misery (see *Mount Misery* listing in this chapter).

User Groups: Hikers, wheelchair users, and leashed dogs. This trail is not suitable for bikes or horses.

Permits: Parking and access are free.

Maps: A free map of Pachaug State Forest is available at the state forest headquarters or from the Connecticut State Parks Division. For topographic area maps, request Voluntown, Jewett City, Oneco, and Plainfield from the USGS.

Directions: From the intersection of Routes 49 and 14A in Voluntown, drive 7.9 miles south on Route 49 to reach a left turn for Headquarters Road (Pachaug State Forest's main entrance). Follow Headquarters Road 0.8 mile, bear left at a fork, and drive another

CONNECTICUT

0.1 mile to a field and parking; to the right is a sign at the Rhododendron Sanctuary entrance. To reach the state forest headquarters, follow Headquarters Road for 0.3 mile from Route 49, turn right, and continue another 0.1 mile to the office on the left.

GPS Coordinates: 41.5921 N, 71.8649 W
Contact: Pachaug State Forest, Rte. 49, P.O. Box 5, Voluntown, CT 06384, 860/376-4075. Connecticut State Parks Division, 79 Elm St., Hartford, CT 06106-5127, 860/424-3200, www.dep.state.ct.us/stateparks/index.htm. Connecticut Forest and Park Association Inc., 16 Meriden Rd., Rockfall, CT 06481-2961, 860/346-2372, www.ctwoodlands.org.

3 MOUNT MISERY
1 mi/0.75 hr   ▩2 ◮7

in Pachaug State Forest in Voluntown

You might not expect to find any real views from a 441-foot hill in eastern Connecticut, but scramble over rocks to the Mount Misery summit and you are in for a surprise: a sweeping panorama of forest carpeted countryside. Perfect for a quick, colorful outing in early fall when the birch- and elm-filled woods turn golden, this one-mile round-trip hike is fairly flat for much of its length and a good one for young children.

To reach the trailhead from the parking turnout, cross Cutoff Road and walk about 50 yards back in the direction of the campground. At the trail sign marker, follow the blue blazes a short distance to the top of Mount Misery. Explore the views from atop Misery and then return the way you came. This hike is very near the Rhododendron Sanctuary (see *Pachaug State Forest Rhododendron Sanctuary* listing in this chapter); in fact, you can park at the Rhododendron Sanctuary trailhead and walk a short distance down the road (which the Pachaug Trail follows) to this hike.

User Groups: Hikers and leashed dogs. No

© HEIDI J. BROWN

the low-lying cliffs of Mount Misery

wheelchair facilities. The trail is not suitable for bikes or horses.

Permits: Parking and access are free.

Maps: A free map of Pachaug State Forest is available at the state forest headquarters or from the Connecticut State Parks Division. For topographic area maps, request Voluntown, Jewett City, Oneco, and Plainfield from the USGS.

Directions: From the intersection of Routes 49 and 14A in Voluntown, drive 7.9 miles south on Route 49 to reach a left turn for Headquarters Road (Patchaug State Forest's main entrance). Follow Headquarters Road 0.8 mile, bear left at a fork, and drive another 0.1 mile to a field. Bear right on the dirt Cutoff Road and drive another 0.2 mile to a turnout on the right, about 125 feet beyond a left turn for the campground. To reach the state forest headquarters, follow Headquarters Road for 0.3

mile from Route 49, turn right, and continue another 0.1 mile to the office on the left. GPS Coordinates: 41.5948 N, 71.8675 W

Contact: Pachaug State Forest, Rte. 49, Box 5, Voluntown, CT 06384, 860/376-4075. Connecticut State Parks Division, 79 Elm St., Hartford, CT 06106-5127, 860/424-3200, www.dep.state.ct.us/stateparks/index.htm. Connecticut Forest and Park Association Inc., 16 Meriden Rd., Rockfall, CT 06481-2961, 860/346-2372, www.ctwoodlands.org.

❹ PACHAUG STATE FOREST ROADS LOOP
9 mi/4.5 hr   🏃3 ⛰7

in Pachaug State Forest in Voluntown

With miles of dirt roads laced throughout the sprawling Pachaug State Forest, the area is fertile ground for a long, flat hike or a loop ride on a mountain bike. The loop described here covers about nine miles and much of the state forest, including, somewhat surprisingly, a few pretty good hills and a 20-minute side hike over 441-foot Mount Misery, which offers a sweeping view of forested countryside from atop low cliffs. This loop would make a good outing on cross-country skis as well.

From the picnic area, head out Trail 1 Road, which becomes dirt within about 150 feet. Pass a dirt road entering from the right and cross Gardner Road within the first mile. Follow Trail 1 Road another mile or more to a paved road and turn left. In about a half mile, turn left at a four-way intersection onto the dirt Breakneck Hill Road. Within a mile, turn left onto the first major dirt road, Lawrence Road, and begin a long descent. Reaching a T intersection, turn right on Forest Road, climb a hill, and then turn left on Cutoff Road, descending again. Turn onto the first dirt road on the right (watch for it), Firetower Road, and follow it a half mile to a gate. Before passing the gate, turn left

down the side dirt road, which ends within a few hundred feet at a pair of trails leading up Mount Misery.

Hike the trail on the right, which traverses below low cliffs, circles around Mount Misery, and then turns left (uphill) on the blue-blazed Pachaug Trail heading toward the summit. After checking out the view, continue over the top of Mount Misery, following the blue blazes back. Go back to the gate and turn left past it, following Firetower Road another half mile or more to another gate. Continue around the gate and turn left; this is Trail 1 Road. Follow it more than a mile back to the picnic area.

User Groups: Hikers, bikers, leashed dogs, and horses. No wheelchair facilities, though some wheelchair hikers would be able to use the dirt roads contained in this hike (in dry weather).

Permits: Parking and access are free.

Maps: A free map of Pachaug State Forest is available at the state forest headquarters or from the Connecticut State Parks Division. For topographic area maps, request Voluntown, Jewett City, Oneco, and Plainfield from the USGS.

Directions: From the intersection of Routes 49 and 14A in Voluntown, drive 7.9 miles south on Route 49 to reach a left turn for Headquarters Road (Patchaug State Forest's main entrance). Follow Headquarters Road 0.8 mile, bear right at a fork onto Trail 1 Road, and drive another 0.1 mile to parking on the right at a picnic area. To reach the state forest headquarters, follow Headquarters Road for 0.3 mile from Route 49, turn right, and continue another 0.1 mile to the office on the left. GPS Coordinates: 41.5921 N, 71.8649 W

Contact: Pachaug State Forest, Rte. 49, Box 5, Voluntown, CT 06384, 860/376-4075. Connecticut State Parks Division, 79 Elm St., Hartford, CT 06106-5127, 860/424-3200, www.dep.state.ct.us/stateparks/index.htm. Connecticut Forest and Park Association Inc., 16 Meriden Rd., Rockfall, CT 06481-2961, 860/346-2372, www.ctwoodlands.org.

CONNECTICUT

5 COGINCHAUG CAVE

1.4 mi/1 hr   👥2 ⛰7

in Durham

An easy round-trip of 1.4 miles with minimal uphill walking, this quiet Mattabesett Trail stretch leads to a huge overhanging rock wall known as Coginchaug Cave. Tools and other artifacts discovered here have lead archaeologists to believe Coginchaug Cave was once used as a shelter by local Native American tribes.

From the parking area, follow the rough jeep road 100 feet and turn right with the blue blazes onto a footpath into the woods. The trail crosses one small brook, makes a very short but steep hillock climb, and circles around exposed ledges in the forest to the cave, 0.7 mile from the hike's start. Return the way you came.

User Groups: Hikers only. No wheelchair facilities. Portions of this trail lie on private land, and use restrictions can change. Assume that bikes, dogs, and horses are not allowed unless a trail is specifically marked for them (although many landowners do not object to dogs).

Permits: Parking and access are free.

Maps: For a topographic area map, request Durham from the USGS.

Directions: From the junction of Routes 17 and 79 in Durham, drive south on Route 79 for 0.8 mile and turn left onto Old Blue Hills Road. Bear right immediately, following blue blazes on the utility poles for 0.7 mile to the end of the road, where there is limited parking.

GPS Coordinates: 41.4575 N, 72.6511 W

Contact: Connecticut Forest and Park Association Inc., 16 Meriden Rd., Rockfall, CT 06481-2961, 860/346-2372, www.ctwoodlands.org.

6 DEVIL'S HOPYARD STATE PARK VISTA TRAIL LOOP

2.5 mi/1.5 hr   👥2 ⛰7

in East Haddam

To Connecticut's early colonists, the curiously round potholes found at the base of Chapman Falls looked like something only a supernatural being could create. Add to that the fact that an old brewery once stood at this site, and there you have the background for one of New England's more unusual place names. This mostly wooded 2.5-mile loop hike through Devil's Hopyard State Park begins with spectacular Chapman Falls, a frothing, 40-foot tall white tower. Just downstream are the potholes, ranging in size from a few inches to a few feet in diameter. The trail then passes a beautiful view from an open ledge—be sure to take the time to enjoy the vistas, including a dark gorge along the Eight Mile River. The hills here are small, with just a few hundred feet of elevation gain.

From the parking lot, cross the road to the map board beside Chapman Falls. Follow the footpath past the falls and potholes for 0.1 mile to the picnic area and the covered bridge. Once over the bridge, turn left, following the orange blazes of the Vista Trail. Within the first half mile you cross a brook on stones, which could be tricky in high water. The trail passes through a hemlock grove and some wet areas, and at 1.3 miles reaches an open ledge with a pastoral view to the south. The trail, which can be tricky to follow from here, descends to the right through mountain laurel and then mixed forest, reaching the Eight Mile River just downstream from a gorge. Before the gorge, the trail turns right, climbing a hillside and eventually reaching an old woods road that leads back to the covered bridge. Backtrack from here to the parking lot.

User Groups: Hikers and leashed dogs. This trail is not suitable for bikes or horses; no wheelchair facilities.

Permits: Parking and access are free.

Maps: A map of the state park is posted at an information board across the street from the parking lot. For topographic area maps, request Colchester and Hamburg from the USGS.

Directions: From the center of Millington, north of the state park, drive east on Haywardville Road for 0.7 mile and turn right onto Hopyard Road at a sign for Devil's Hopyard State Park. Continue 0.8 mile and turn left at a sign for Chapman Falls (0.1 mile beyond the park headquarters). Turn immediately left into the parking lot. Or from the junction of Routes 82 and 158 in East Haddam, south of the park, drive 0.2 mile east on Route 82 and turn left onto Hopyard Road. Continue 3.5 miles, turn right at the sign for Chapman Falls, and left into the parking lot. The park closes at sunset.

GPS Coordinates: 41.4851 N, 72.3421 W
Contact: Devil's Hopyard State Park, 366 Hopyard Rd., East Haddam, CT 06423, 860/873-8566. Connecticut State Parks Division, 79 Elm St., Hartford, CT 06106-5127, 860/424-3200, www.dep.state.ct.us/stateparks/index.htm.

🐾 HIGH AND BULLET LEDGES
4.4 mi/2 hr 👥2 ⛰6

in North Stonington

This relatively easy hike—with just a couple of steep, if short, climbs—on a 2.2-mile stretch of the blue-blazed Narragansett Trail brings you to two very different ledges hidden away in the woods. Neither offers any views; the appeal here lies in a quiet walk through the forest and a pair of interesting rock formations.

From the parking lot, continue 0.1 mile farther down the road to where blue blazes turn left onto a woods road. Follow it a quarter mile and then continue straight ahead with the blue blazes, while the woods road bears left. The trail ascends a steep hillside, turns right, and reaches High Ledge just 0.8 mile from the

parking area. The trail circles the small ledge and follows another woods road, descending somewhat and passing below the base of a cliff some 40 feet high. At the cliff's far side, the trail turns right, ascends left of the cliff, and reaches its top—Bullet Ledge, 2.2 miles from the parking area. Head back to the parking lot the same way you came.

User Groups: Hikers only. No wheelchair facilities. Portions of this trail lie on private land, and use restrictions can change. Assume that bikes, dogs, and horses are not allowed unless a trail is specifically marked for them (although many landowners do not object to dogs).

Permits: Parking and access are free.

Maps: Although a map is not necessary for this hike, for topographic area maps, request Old Mystic and Ashaway from the USGS.

Directions: Drive Route 2 to North Stonington and turn off the highway onto Main Street at the village sign. Drive 0.4 mile and turn onto Wyassup Road. Continue 3.1 miles, turn left onto Wyassup Lake Road, and follow it 0.7 mile to parking at a boat launch area on the right.

GPS Coordinates: 41.4929 N, 71.8732 W
Contact: Connecticut Forest and Park Association Inc., 16 Meriden Rd., Rockfall, CT 06481-2961, 860/346-2372, www.ctwoodlands.org.

🟦 SLEEPING GIANT STATE PARK BLUE-WHITE LOOP
5.6 mi/3 hr 👥3 ⛰9

in Hamden

The Sleeping Giant is a chain of low hills which, from a distance, resemble a giant lying on his back. This fairly rugged, 5.6-mile loop in Sleeping Giant State Park on the blue and white trails passes over all of the major features of the giant—including the towering cliffs at his chin—and numerous ledges with excellent views. Although the loop could be done in either direction, consider hiking it counterclockwise, starting on the white trail. The only drawback of going in this direction is that you have to descend—rather than climb, which is easier—the steep, exposed slabs on the Head's south slope. (To avoid the slabs descent, backtrack north on the blue trail from the chin's cliff tops to the wide Tower Trail, which provides an easy descent to the parking area.) On the other hand, hiking this loop counterclockwise allows you to finish this hike with the cliff walks over the Head, which boasts the most striking and precipitous cliffs in the park. All trails are well blazed and the state park trail map is suitable for navigation. This hike's cumulative elevation gain is no more than 500 feet.

From the parking lot, follow the paved road about 0.1 mile to the picnic grounds and watch for the white-blazed trail branching to the right. Follow the white trail eastward across the park for nearly three miles to where it crosses the blue-blazed trail near Hezekiah's Knob. Turn left onto the blue trail and follow it back, passing by the stone tower and finishing over the Head. After descending steeply to the south off the Head, watch for a connector trail leading to the left (east) back to the picnic area. If you miss the first connector trail and start seeing Mount Carmel Avenue through the woods, take the violet-blazed trail, which also leads you back to the picnic area.

User Groups: Hikers and leashed dogs. No bikes, horses, or wheelchair facilities.

Permits: There's a parking fee of $7 for Connecticut vehicles, $10 for out-of-state vehicles, on weekends and holidays April 1–November 1; weekdays are free.

Maps: A basic trail map is available at the state park and from the Connecticut State Parks Division. For topographic area maps, request Mount Carmel and Wallingford from the USGS.

Directions: From Route 10 in Hamden, about 1.4 miles north of the junction of Routes 10 and 40, turn east onto Mount Carmel Avenue. Continue 0.2 mile to the state park entrance and parking on the left, across from Quinnipiac College. The park closes at sunset.

GPS Coordinates: 41.4208 N, 72.8988 W

Contact: Sleeping Giant State Park, 200 Mount Carmel Ave., Hamden, CT 06518, 203/789-7498. Connecticut State Parks Division, 79 Elm St., Hartford, CT 06106-5127, 860/424-3200, www.dep.state.ct.us/stateparks/index.htm. Connecticut Forest and Park Association Inc., 16 Meriden Rd., Rockfall, CT 06481-2961, 860/346-2372, www.ctwoodlands.org.

⑨ SLEEPING GIANT STATE PARK TOWER TRAIL

3.2 mi/1.5 hr   🏃3 ⛰8

in Hamden

This relatively easy, 3.2-mile round-trip climbs about 500 feet and leads to Sleeping Giant State Park's stone tower, which has stairs leading to its top and panoramic views of the countryside and, to the south, New Haven Harbor. The almost medieval looking stone tower was actually built in 1936 by the Works Progress Administration and is now listed on the National Register of Historic Places.

From the parking area, walk the paved road about 100 feet and turn right at a large sign for the Tower Trail. It rises gently, following the carriage road 1.6 miles to the stone tower. Climb the steps in the tower to its top, where you may find yourself standing in a strong breeze, looking out over the New Haven skyline and the long ridge of the Sleeping Giant stretching off to the east and west. Retrace your steps to return to the parking area.

User Groups: Hikers and leashed dogs. No bikes, horses, or wheelchair facilities.

Permits: There's a parking fee of $7 for Connecticut vehicles, $10 for out-of-state vehicles, on weekends and holidays April 1–November 1; weekdays are free.

Maps: A basic trail map is available at the state park and from the Connecticut State

the stone summit tower at Sleeping Giant State Park, Hamden

Parks Division. For topographic area maps, request Mount Carmel and Wallingford from the USGS.

Directions: From Route 10 in Hamden, about 1.4 miles north of the junction of Routes 10 and 40, turn east onto Mount Carmel Avenue. Continue 0.2 mile to the state park entrance and parking on the left, across from Quinnipiac College. The park closes at sunset. GPS Coordinates: 41.4208 N, 72.8988 W

Contact: Sleeping Giant State Park, 200 Mount Carmel Ave., Hamden, CT 06518, 203/789-7498. Connecticut State Parks Division, 79 Elm St., Hartford, CT 06106-5127, 860/424-3200, www.dep.state.ct.us/stateparks/index.htm. Connecticut Forest and Park Association Inc., 16 Meriden Rd., Rockfall, CT 06481-2961, 860/346-2372, www.ctwoodlands.org.

🔟 WEST ROCK RIDGE STATE PARK
10 mi/5 hr

in Hamden, Bethany, and Woodbridge

This is an out-and-back hike along West Rock Ridge, the seven-mile-long traprock mountain ridge located on the west side of New Haven. On this walk along a continuous line of exposed cliffs, the first views of houses and other buildings in Hamden and the New Haven skyline in the distance are reached after 1.8 miles. There is very little elevation gain on this hike.

From the parking area, follow Sanford Feeder Trail, marked by blue blazes with red dots, along various woods roads for 0.6 mile. Reaching a junction, turn right (uphill) onto the blue-blazed Regicides Trail. Within 0.2 mile, the trail reaches and parallels paved Baldwin Road, which runs through West Rock Ridge State Park and is only open during the warmer months. The trail crosses the road 0.6 mile after first reaching it; continue 0.4 mile along the Regicides Trail to the first view. The trail reenters the woods and then crosses Baldwin Road again 0.1 mile beyond that first viewpoint. Over the next roughly 3.5 miles, the Regicides Trail passes several more outlooks. Return along the same route.

User Groups: Hikers and leashed dogs. The trail is not suitable for bikes or horses; no wheelchair facilities.

Permits: Parking and access are free.

Maps: For topographic area maps, request New Haven and Mount Carmel from the USGS.

Directions: From the Wilbur Cross Parkway (Route 15) in New Haven, take Exit 60. Turn right off the exit ramp onto Dixwell Avenue/Route 10 South. Take a right at the next light onto Benham Street. Follow Benham Street to the end. Turn left onto Main Street and continue to the end and then take a right onto Wintergreen Avenue. Go under the parkway. The main park entrance will be on the right.

the long traprock outcropping at West Rock Ridge State Park in Hamden

If the gate is closed, park at West Rock Nature Center across the street.

GPS Coordinates: 41.3455 N, 72.9672 W

Contact: Connecticut Forest and Park Association Inc., 16 Meriden Rd., Rockfall, CT 06481-2961, 860/346-2372, www.ctwoodlands.org. West Rock Ridge State Park, c/o Sleeping Giant State Park, 200 Mount Carmel Ave., Hamden, CT 06518, 203/789-7498. Connecticut State Parks Division, 79 Elm St., Hartford, CT 06106-5127, 860/424-3200, fax 860/424-4070, www.dep.state.ct.us/stateparks/index.htm.

11 BLUFF HEAD/ TOTOKET MOUNTAIN
2.5 mi/1.5 hr   🚶2 ⛰8

in North Guilford

After a brief, steep climb, the trail follows the edge of high cliffs all the way to the rocky outcropping known as Bluff Head. There's an almost continuous, 180-degree vista of the forest and low hills in this rural corner of southern Connecticut, taking in the distant Long Island Sound and the tip of Long Island, as well as the Hartford skyline.

From the parking area, follow the Mattabesett Trail's blue blazes to the left (south) for about 50 feet, where the trail turns right and ascends steeply. After about 0.2 mile, it levels out and follows a low ridge to an overlook at 0.4 mile. From here, a trail leaves to the left (west); you will return to it, but this hike continues north on the Mattabesett Trail another 0.8 mile to Bluff Head, a high outcrop atop cliffs with wide and long views to the north, east, and south. Double back on the Mattabesett Trail to the trail junction at the first overlook and turn right (west). Descend about 0.3 mile, turn left, and follow a woods road 0.2 mile back to your vehicle.

User Groups: Hikers only. No wheelchair facilities. Portions of this trail lie on private land, and use restrictions can change. Assume that bikes, dogs, and horses are not allowed unless a trail is specifically marked for them (although many landowners do not object to dogs).

Permits: Parking and access are free.

Maps: For a topographic area map, request Durham from the USGS.

Directions: From the junction of Routes 77 and 80 in Guilford, drive north on Route 77 for 4.3 miles and turn left into an unmarked dirt parking area.

GPS Coordinates: 41.3767 N, 72.7107 W

Contact: Connecticut Forest and Park Association Inc., 16 Meriden Rd., Rockfall, CT 06481-2961, 860/346-2372, www.ctwoodlands.org.

12 WESTWOODS PRESERVE
2 mi/1 hr   🏃1 ⛰6

in Guilford

With 1,000 acres, Westwoods is a popular local place for hiking, cross-country skiing, and mountain biking because of its trail network and the remote feeling it inspires just a few miles from busy I-95 and a short drive from New Haven. From the parking area, follow the obvious trail 0.1 mile and then turn left onto the white-blazed trail. You soon pass a side path leading left to large stone blocks; this detour rejoins the white trail within 0.1 mile. The white trail continues past marshes on the left and past Lost Lake, a protected little body of water ringed by woods and bordering on a wildlife refuge. Expect to see lots of birds, such as egrets, ducks, and osprey. The trail turns back into the woods, passing numerous glacial erratics, including one boulder split into halves, between which grows a stout cedar tree. At a trail junction at a nice overlook of Lost Lake, turn right onto the orange trail, following it back to the parking area.

User Groups: Hikers and leashed dogs. No wheelchair facilities. Only a portion of this trail is suitable for bikes and horses.

Permits: Parking and access are free.

Maps: A map board is posted at the trailhead, and maps of Westwoods Preserve are sold in several local stores. For a topographic area map, request Guilford from the USGS.

Directions: Take I-95 to Exit 58 in Guilford. Drive south on Route 77 for half a mile and turn right onto U.S. 1 heading south. Continue 0.2 mile, turn left onto River Road, go another 0.6 mile, and turn right onto Water Street/Route 146. Follow it 0.8 mile, turn right onto Sam Hill Road, and park in the turnout immediately on the left.

GPS Coordinates: 41.2696 N, 72.6960 W

Contact: Guilford Land Conservation Trust, P.O. Box 200, Guilford, CT 06437, 203/457-9253, www.guilfordlandtrust.org.

13 ROCKY NECK STATE PARK
2 mi/1 hr   🏃1 ⛰9

in Niantic

Bounded on the west by a tidal river and to the east by a broad salt marsh, local Native American tribes and colonists valued Rocky Neck for its abundance of fish and wildlife. Today, high tides in spring still bring schools of alewives (herring) to swim into Bride Brook toward inland spawning grounds. This loop takes you along Bride Brook, through dunes and tall grasses, salt marshes, and finally to a sandy beach right on Long Island Sound. If it's a hot summer day, don't forget to pack your bathing suit. Rocky Neck is a popular spot to swim.

Leaving from the east side of the parking lot, a wheelchair accessible trail leads just a few feet to a wildlife viewing platform overlooking the salt marsh ecosystem of Bride Brook. In early summer, the osprey, or fish hawk, is a frequent visitor to the marsh; in the fall, cranes, herons and mute swans wade among the cattails and rose mallow. Leaving the platform, backtrack to the parking lot and this time head to its western edge to pick up the red-blazed trail. With the Bride Brook to the right (east), the trail edges the marsh and brook heading north. At 0.7 mile from the parking lot, the trail veers left away from the brook. In another 0.2 mile, reach a trail junction. Here, pick up the blue trail, following it for one mile as it heads back towards the Sound, passing an old shipyard (at 1.2 miles from the parking lot) and the Tony's Nose Overlook (at 1.9 miles), with views towards Four Mile River. The blue trail ends at the paved park road. Take a left and follow the road as it loops around to the boardwalk and sandy beach (passing the parking lot you left from on the way). Enjoy the beach and then backtrack to the paved road, following it to the parking lot.

User Groups: Hikers, leashed dogs, bikes, and horses. Wheelchair users can follow this route to the wildlife viewing area and then, instead of heading back to the parking area, may continue on the accessible trail as it quickly advances to the eastern edge of the beach's quarter-mile-long boardwalk.

Permits: On weekends and holidays Memorial Day weekend–Labor Day, a parking fee of $10 is charged for Connecticut vehicles, $15 for out-of-state vehicles, and $5 for any vehicle entering after 5 P.M. On weekdays Memorial Day–Labor Day, a parking fee of $7 is charged for Connecticut vehicles, $10 for out-of-state vehicles, and $5 for any vehicle entering after 5 P.M. Off-season access to Rocky Neck is free.

Maps: A free map of the park (with hiking trails) is available at the park entrance (download from state park website). For topographic area maps, request Niantic from the USGS.

Directions: From Exit 72 off I-95, follow the turnpike connector south to Route 156. Turn left and follow Route 156 east through Niantic for 0.25 mile to the park entrance. Follow the road past the campground to reach the parking area.

GPS Coordinates: 41.3164 N, 72.2413 W

Contact: Rocky Neck State Park, 244 West Main St., Niantic, CT 06357, 860/739-5471. Connecticut State Parks Division, 79 Elm St., Hartford, CT 06106-5127, 860/424-3200, fax 860/424-4070, www.dep.state.ct.us/stateparks/index.htm.

14 BLUFF POINT
4.2 mi/2 hr

in Groton

A truly unique find in a state that's home to over three million people, Bluff Point is recognized as the last remaining significant piece of undeveloped land along the Connecticut coastline. Jutting out into the waters of Long Island Sound, the wooded peninsula is a designated natural area and coastal preserve. This loop hike leads you all the way out to the tip of Bluff Point and back, exploring both sides of the peninsula along the way. Winds can be heavy at times on Bluff Point, evidenced by the sparse and diminutive vegetation here; bring along a jacket even on what can seem as a warm, breezeless day farther inland.

From the parking area, head almost due east along the gravel road. At 0.4 mile, a fork is reached. Bear right, soon coming in sight of Mumford Cove. As the road gives way to a footpath, the trail edges along the shore, bringing you down to the water's edge approximately one mile into this hike. The trail eventually heads away from the water and hooks right, cutting across the wooded center of the peninsula. At 1.5 miles, turn left onto another gravel road. Follow south approximately one mile to reach Bluff Point's end of land at Long Island Sound. The road edges west along the bluff for 0.2 mile to reach a scenic viewing area at the very tip. From here, the road turns and heads almost due north for the next 1.5 miles back to the parking area, passing views of the Poquonnock River (and Groton Airport) on the return.

User Groups: Hikers, leashed dogs, bikes, and horses. No wheelchair facilities, though some wheelchair hikers may feel comfortable using the wide gravel paths. It would be possible to leave the parking lot heading south on the gravel path for 1.5 miles to reach the Bluff Point scenic viewing area (the return leg of the loop hike), a round-trip of three miles.

Permits: There are no parking fees at Bluff

Point State Park. However, a local permit is required for shell fishing. Permits are issued at Groton's Town Hall during business hours. **Maps:** A free trail map is available from the state park website. For topographic area maps, request New London from the USGS.

Directions: From the corner of Route 117 and U.S. 1 in Groton, take a right on U.S. 1. Follow 0.3 mile to a left turn onto Depot Road. Follow Depot Road 0.7 mile to its end in the Bluff Point State Park parking area.

GPS Coordinates: 41.3356 N, 72.0333 W

Contact: Bluff Point State Park, c/o Fort Trumbull State Park, 90 Walbach St., New London, CT 06320, 860/444-7591. Groton Town Hall, 45 Fort Hill Rd., Groton, CT 06340, 860/441-6640. Connecticut State Parks Division, 79 Elm St., Hartford, CT 06106-5127, 860/424-3200, fax 860/424-4070, www.dep.state.ct.us/stateparks/index.htm.

RESOURCES

© DAMIEN PINAULT

STATE PARKS

Baxter State Park
64 Balsam Dr.
Millinocket, ME 04462-2190
207/723-5140
www.baxterstateparkauthority.com

Blue Hills Reservation Headquarters
695 Hillside St.
Milton, MA 02186
617/698-1802
www.mass.gov/dcr/parks/metroboston/blue.htm

Connecticut State Parks Division
79 Elm St.
Hartford, CT 06106-5127
860/424-3200, fax 860/424-4070
www.ct.gov/dep
dep.stateparks@ct.gov

Maine Bureau of Parks and Lands
Department of Conservation
mailing address: 22 State House Station
18 Elkins Lane (AMHI Campus)
Augusta, ME 04333-0022
207/287-3821, fax 207/287-8111
www.maine.gov/doc/parks

Massachusetts Division of State Parks and Recreation
251 Causeway St., Suite 600
Boston, MA 02114-2104
617/626-1250, fax 617/626-1351
www.state.ma.us/dem/forparks.htm
mass.parks@state.ma.us

New Hampshire Division of Parks and Recreation
P.O. Box 1856
172 Pembroke Rd.
Concord, NH 03302
603/271-3556, fax 603/271-2629
camping reservations: 603/271-3628
www.nhstateparks.org
nhparks@dred.state.nh.us

Rhode Island Department of Environmental Management
Note: This department oversees the Division of Parks and Recreation and the Division of Forest Environment.
235 Promenade St.
Providence, RI 02908-5767
401/222-6800
www.dem.ri.gov

Rhode Island Division of Forest Environment
1037 Hartford Pike
North Scituate, RI 02857
401/647-4389 or 401/647-3367, fax 401/647-3590
www.dem.ri.gov/programs/bnatres/forest

Rhode Island Division of Parks and Recreation
2321 Hartford Ave.
Johnston, RI 02919-1719
401/222-2635
www.riparks.com

Vermont Department of Forests
Parks and Recreation Commissioner's Office
103 South Main St.
Waterbury, VT 05671-0601
802/241-3655, fax 802/244-1481
www.vtfpr.org
ed.leary@state.vt.us

NATIONAL PARKS

Acadia National Park
P.O. Box 177
Eagle Lake Rd.
Bar Harbor, ME 04609-0177
207/288-3338, fax 207/288-5507

www.nps.gov/acad
Acadia_Information@nps.gov

Boston Harbor Islands Partnership

408 Atlantic Ave., Suite 228
Boston, MA 02110
617/223-8666
www.nps.gov/boha

Cape Cod National Seashore

99 Marconi Site Rd.
Wellfleet, MA 02667
508/771-2144, fax 508/349-9052
www.nps.gov/caco/index.htm
CACO_Superintendent@nps.gov
also: Salt Pond Visitor Center
508/255-3421
also: Province Lands Visitor Center
508/487-1256

Marsh-Billings-Rockefeller National Historical Park

54 Elm St.
Woodstock, VT 05091
802/457-3368
www.nps.gov/mabi

Minute Man National Historical Park

250 North Great Rd.
Lincoln MA, 01773
978/369-6993
www.nps.gov/mima/index.htm

NATIONAL FOREST AND WILDLIFE REFUGES

Great Meadows National Wildlife Refuge

73 Weir Hill Rd.
Sudbury, MA 01776
978/443-4661, fax 978/443-2898
www.fws.gov/northeast/greatmeadows
fw5rw_emnwr@fws.gov

Green Mountain National Forest Supervisor

231 North Main St.
Rutland, VT 05701
802/747-6700, fax 802/747-6766
www.fs.fed.us/r9/gmfl

Parker River National Wildlife Refuge

6 Plum Island Turnpike
Newburyport, MA 01950
978/465-5753 or 800/877-8339 for the
hearing impaired, fax 978/465-2807
parkerriver.fws.gov
fw5rw_prnwr@fws.gov

White Mountain National Forest Supervisor

719 North Main St.
Laconia, NH 03246
603/528-8721 or TDD 603/528-8722
www.fs.fed.us/r9/white

MAP SOURCES

New England Cartographics

413/549-4124 or toll-free 888/995-6277
www.necartographics.com
info@necartographics.com

Rubel BikeMaps

P.O. Box 401035
Cambridge, MA 02140
www.bikemaps.com
info@bikemaps.com

Trails Illustrated

800/962-1643
http://maps.nationalgeographic.com/trails

United States Geological Survey

Information Services
Box 25286
Denver, CO 80225
888/275-8747, fax 303/202-4693
www.usgs.gov/pubprod

HIKING GEAR RETAILERS

Climb High
191 Bank St.
Burlington, VT 05401
802/865-0900
www.climbhigh.com
email@climbhigh.com

Gulliver's Travel Books and Maps
7 Commercial Alley
Portsmouth, NH 03801
603/431-5556
gulliversbooks.biz
www.gulliversbooks.biz

Housatonic River Outfitters
24 Kent Rd.
Cornwall Bridge, CT 06754
860/672-1010
www.dryflies.com
hflyshop@aol.com

International Mountain Equipment
2733 White Mountain Hwy.
North Conway, NH 03860
603/356-7013
www.ime-usa.com
info@ime-usa.com

Kittery Trading Post
301 U.S. 1
Kittery, ME 03904-5619
207/439-2700
www.kitterytradingpost.com
Orders@ktp.com

L.L.Bean
95 Main St.
Freeport, ME 04033
877/755-2326
www.llbean.com

Mountain Wanderer Map & Book Store
Rte. 112
Lincoln, NH 03251
800/745-2707
www.mountainwanderer.com
info@mountainwanderer.com

TRAIL CLUBS AND ORGANIZATIONS

Appalachian Mountain Club
5 Joy St.
Boston, MA 02108
617/523-0636, fax 617/523-0722
www.outdoors.org
information@outdoors.org

Appalachian Mountain Club Pinkham Notch Visitor Center
P.O. Box 298
Gorham, NH 03581
603/466-2721
www.outdoors.org
information@outdoors.org

Appalachian Trail Conservancy
799 Washington St.
P.O. Box 807
Harpers Ferry, WV 25425-0807
304/535-6331, fax 304/535-2667
www.appalachiantrail.org
info@appalachiantrail.org

Ascutney Trails Association
P.O. Box 147
Windsor, VT 05089
www.ascutneytrails.org
info@ascutneytrails.org

Cardigan Highlanders Club
Craig Sanborn
P.O. Box 104

Enfield Center, NH 03749-0104
603/632-5640

Connecticut Forest and Park Association Inc.
16 Meriden Rd.
Rockfall, CT 06481-2961
860/346-2372, fax 860/347-7463
www.ctwoodlands.org
info@ctwoodlands.org

Friends of the Blue Hills
P.O. Box 416
Milton, MA 02186
781/828-1805
www.friendsofthebluehills.org

The Friends of the Middlesex Fells Reservation
4 Woodland Rd.
Stoneham, MA 02180
781/662-2340
www.fells.org

Friends of the Wapack
P.O. Box 115
West Peterborough, NH 03468
www.wapack.org

Green Mountain Club Inc.
4711 Waterbury-Stowe Rd.
Waterbury Center, VT 05677
802/244-7037, fax 802/244-5867
www.greenmountainclub.org
gmc@greenmountainclub.org

Guilford Land Conservation Trust
P.O. Box 200
Guilford, CT 06437
203/457-9253
www.guilfordlandtrust.org

Maine Appalachian Trail Club
P.O. Box 283
Augusta, ME 04332-0283
www.matc.org

Monadnock-Sunapee Greenway Trail Club (MSGTC)
P.O. Box 164
Marlow, NH 03456
www.msgtc.org

Ragged Mountain Foundation
P.O. Box 948
Southington, CT 06489
www.raggedmtn.org

Randolph Mountain Club
P.O. Box 279
Gorham, NH 03581
www.randolphmountainclub.org

Squam Lakes Association
P.O. Box 204
Holderness, NH 03245
603/968-7336
www.squamlakes.org

Wonalancet Out Door Club (WODC)
HCR 64 Box 248
Wonalancet, NH 03897
www.wodc.org

OTHER LAND MANAGERS

The Trustees of Reservations
Long Hill
572 Essex St.
Beverly, MA 01915-1530
978/921-1944
www.thetrustees.org
information@ttor.org

Index

www.moon.com

DESTINATIONS | ACTIVITIES | BLOGS | MAPS | BOOKS

MOON.COM is ready to help plan your next trip! Filled with fresh trip ideas and strategies, author interviews, informative travel blogs, a detailed map library, and descriptions of all the Moon guidebooks, Moon.com is all you need to get out and explore the world—or even places in your own backyard. While at Moon.com, sign up for our monthly e-newsletter for updates on new releases, travel tips, and expert advice from our on-the-go Moon authors. As always, when you travel with Moon, expect an experience that is uncommon and truly unique.

MOON IS ON FACEBOOK—BECOME A FAN!
JOIN THE MOON PHOTO GROUP ON FLICKR